*Murder Cases
of the Twentieth Century*

Murder Cases of the Twentieth Century

Biographies and Bibliographies of 280 Convicted or Accused Killers

by
David K. Frasier

with a foreword by Michael Newton

McFarland & Company, Inc., Publishers
Jefferson, North Carolina, and London

British Library Cataloguing-in-Publication data are available

Library of Congress Cataloguing-in-Publication Data

Frasier, David K., 1951–
    Murder cases of the twentieth century : biographies and bibliographies
of 280 convicted or accused killers / by David K. Frasier.
      p. cm.
    Includes bibliographical references and indexes.
    ISBN 0-7864-0184-2 (library binding. : 50# alk. paper) ∞
    1. Murderers—Biography—Encyclopedias. 2. Murder—History—
20th century—Encyclopedias. I. Title.
HV6245.F74 1996
364.1'523'0922—dc20
[B]   96-14984
                                                                                    CIP

Manufactured in the United States of America

McFarland & Company, Inc., Publishers
  Box 611, Jefferson, North Carolina 28640

To Kenneth Anger,
filmmaker, cinema historian,
and loyal friend,
with affection and respect

Contents

Acknowledgments

I wish to acknowledge and thank the following individuals without whose kind and generous support this book could not have been written:

Michael Newton, author of *Hunting Humans: An Encyclopedia of Modern Serial Killers* and *Raising Hell: An Encyclopedia of Devil Worship and Satanic Crime*, a dear friend who makes living on this planet a bit easier to do. This book owes much to the hundreds of hours we spent discussing serial killers whilst downing meaningful measures of grog in the dark and smokey environs of Nashville, Indiana's premier tavern, The Pine Room. James Dryden, a skilled librarian who conducted extensive research into the majority of the cases to be found in this collection. I value his friendship and humor. Kenneth Anger, filmmaker and cinema historian, to whom I respectfully and affectionately dedicate this book. For over a decade now you have faithfully sent me newspaper and magazine clippings on hundreds of murder cases. Your friendship, talent, integrity, and goodness have immeasurably enriched my life. My father, Eliegey T. Frasier, who first told me of the remarkable Carl Panzram and, to my brother Joe and his wife Debbie, who always showed an interest in the work. Dr. Samuel Stetson, one of nature's noblemen, a valued crony and confidant. I would also like to individually thank the reference department staff of the main library, research collections at Indiana University. Ann Bristow, the department head and my boss, tolerated and supported this project although she found its subject matter (and my fascination with it) to be personally distasteful. I harbor many fond memories of being "ushered" out of her office in mid-sentence while attempting to discuss my research. Frank Quinn, associate librarian, one of my few "normal" companions whose friendship and professionalism have meant so very much to me. Jeff Graf, reference computing coordinator, a consummate professional and friend without whose advice and counsel I would never begin or, more importantly, complete any project. Pat Riesenman, librarian and assistant department head, who uncomplainingly worked around my rather eccentric schedule. Tom Glastras, associate librarian emeritus, perhaps the finest man I know. Mark Day, associate librarian, a respected colleague and Clay Housholder and Mary Buechley. Jian Liu, assistant librarian, a new department member whose computer expertise has dragged me into the slow lane of the information superhighway. Celestina Wroth, senior reference assistant, a budding librarian in the Ann Bristow mold who shares that individual's revulsion for the subject of my research. The corps of student reference assistants both past and present: Tim Good, Marguerite Duffy, Cindy Pierard, Sarah Prown, Beau Case, Tom Greives, Anne Graham, Karin Sedestrom, Scott Silet, Jennifer Stumpo, Jennifer Heffron, Dan Thomas, Lisa K. Williams, and Sharon Verba. Special thanks to the Indiana University interlibrary loan department which supplied me with literally hundreds of books from libraries throughout the world. Longtime colleagues and friends Rhonda Long and Ron Luedemann were tireless in their efforts to obtain obscure books for me as were their coworkers Marilyn Wood, Jay Wilkerson, Gail McKenzie, Jeffrey Matlak, and Cheryl Smith. Diana Hanson and Marty Sorury of the microforms department and Jim Onken and Hugh Barbry of the mail room also added more to this project than they will ever know. A special thanks as well to Eddie Dean of the I.U. photocopy office, a man whose hiring practices I respect. Also deserving of note is the access services department capably staffed by Suzanne Trisler, Randy Lent, Vivian Whaley, Cathy Gilbert, Tammy Peregrine, Marianna Brough, Linda Stewart, and Hillary Byrn. Robert U. Goehlert, librarian for economics, political science, and criminal justice, served as the "midwife" for this book when years ago he commented on the public's ongoing fascination with murder. He has since built an excellent true crime collection at Indiana University. Michael Cavanagh, photographer at the Indiana University art museum, a longtime friend who uncomplainingly works long hours on short deadlines. Murray Sperber, associate professor of English and American studies, former teacher of Steven Judy and a restless voice of sanity within the university.

I would also like to thank the following individuals and institutions, most notably for the information they supplied and their support. Geographically, they include:

Australia: Peter Wagner, New South Wales Police Headquarters librarian, Sydney.

Arizona: Michael A. Arra, public information officer, Arizona Department of Corrections.

California: Ron Blakely, public information officer, California Institution for Men, Chino. Dean Crenshaw, administrative assistant and public information officer, Department of Corrections, California State Prison, Los Angeles County. Dave Heinz, public information officer, Department of Corrections, Folsom State Prison. Russ Meyer, president, R.M. Films International, Hollywood. Jim Holliday, adult film director and senior columnist for *Adult Video News*.

Colorado: Focus on the Family.

District of Columbia: Susan R. Falb, historian, Public Affairs Office, Federal Bureau of Investigation. Cathy Zeljak, George Washington University.

Florida: Eugene Morris, information services administrator, Florida Department of Corrections.

Illinois: Nic Howell, chief public information officer, Illinois Department of Corrections. James Turanto, literary and artistic executor of the John Wayne Gacy estate. Elmer Gertz, attorney-at-law, for his insights into Nathan Freudenthal Leopold, Jr.

Indiana: This project was supported by an Indiana University Librarians Support Grant (1991), an I.U. Research Leave (1992), as well as a sabbatical leave (September 1994–January 1995). James G. Neal, former Dean of Indiana University Libraries, was a champion and defender of this work against those in the system whose narrow definition of what constitutes so-called "library-related" research would condemn us all to writing dust dry studies to be read by only a handful of "information specialists." I am happy to report that under Dean Neal's leadership intellectual freedom flourished in the I.U. library system. *Martinsville Daily Reporter*, Bette Nunn, reporter.

Louisiana: Martha H. Jumonville, public information, Department of Public Safety and Corrections.

Maryland: Lt. Michael H. Waudby, central records division, Baltimore Police Department.

Michigan: Karen S. Braun, public information officer, State of Michigan, Department of Corrections. D/Sgt. Donald A. Brooks, State of Michigan, Department of State Police.

Minnesota: Penny H. Karasch, facility information center supervisor, Minnesota Correctional Facility, Oak Park Heights.

Missouri: Sergeant Troy Cole, Kansas City Police Department. Tim Kniest, public information officer, Missouri Department of Corrections. Steve Dryden, photographer and seeker after the bizarre.

New Jersey: Patterson Smith, bookseller and staff (Montclair).

North Carolina: Bill Poston, North Carolina Department of Corrections.

Oklahoma: Fred C. Cook, unit manager, Death Row Unit, Oklahoma State Penitentiary.

Oregon: State of Oregon, Department of Corrections, Oregon State Penitentiary.

Texas: Texas Department of Criminal Justice, institutional division, Public Information Office.

Lastly, I would like to especially thank my wife, Mary, and son, Hayden, for their love, patience, and understanding. Hayden, in particular, has never known a time when his father has not been immersed in the chilly psychic waters of some tormented human predator. Mary, I remember you once commenting that I spent more time in the basement than John Wayne Gacy. Now you know what I was doing down there.

David K. Frasier   *Bloomington, Indiana*   January 1996

Foreword

"I am still of the opinion," poet William Butler Yeats wrote to a friend, in 1927, "that only two topics can be of the least interest to a serious and studious mind—sex and the dead." It may have seemed a startling viewpoint at the time, but history has largely validated Yeats' judgment. Sex and death still fascinate us, come what may, and if the two go hand in hand, as in a kinky murder case, so much the better.

Our historic love affair with crime—or, rather, let us say *reports* of crime— is traceable to the Old Testament, as surely as Judaeo-Christian values are depicted in the Book of Genesis. Cain murdered Abel out of spite … and thereby hangs the tale. His motive, and the consequence that flowed from the unseemly act, is still discussed among believers of the Word, as if the crime had happened yesterday. Small wonder, then, that the descendants of a famous murderer are daily captivated by the exploits of his spiritual heirs.

One problem with enjoying crime—or murder, more specifically—is knowing where to look. We have no dearth of homicides to choose from, granted, but the vast majority are perfectly mundane. They are the sort of crimes, devoid of all imagination, that made Sherlock Holmes lament the sorry state of "modern" criminals a hundred years ago. We long for something more original, more titillating. Something we can sink our teeth into, with relish. From that guilty craving springs an industry—not journalism, strictly speaking; rather, add a dash of sociology, a tablespoon of voyeurism, wrapped up in "the public's right to know"—that we are pleased to call True Crime.

Of course, it isn't *always* true, and therein lies a problem for the reader. When confronted with a flood of books on Jeffrey Dahmer, or a John Wayne Gacy, whose word should we accept as final? What can we believe?

Inquiring minds want to know.

There has, in recent years, been something of a glut in "crime encyclopedias," some fairly specialized, while others take a fling at printing "all there is to know" about felonious behavior from the dawn of man to yesterday's edition of *Geraldo*. Most fall short on scholarship, and some depart so widely from objective truth that they are better viewed as rambling novels than as history. For ages now, the field of murder has cried out for an authoritative reference work that would combine the elements of scholarship and entertainment, serv-ing "buffs," professionals, and students equally.

You hold that long-awaited volume in your hands.

Murder Cases of the Twentieth Century is a priceless and unique addition to the list of volumes currently available on the intriguing subject of man's ten-dency to massacre his fellow man. Unwilling to be sidetracked in the well-worn footsteps of the herd, Dave Frasier has compiled a true all-purpose reference work, of equal value to the casual reader, would-be writer, and devoted crim-inologist alike. His choice of vintage murders, plus inclusion of obscure and foreign cases with the headline-grabbers of our own day, make the text par-ticularly valuable for comparison of murders on a global scale, throughout the present century. Librarians, booksellers, and collectors will find the annotated bibliography appended to each case a godsend in selecting works for purchase or review. And, when imagination flags, a struggling novelist could do far worse than to consult these pages for a dazzling potpourri of motives, mad-men, and sadistic *modus operandi.*

Versatility aside, the best thing about Frasier's work is his meticulous attention to detail. For any working writer, like myself, who has been publicly embarrassed on occasion after trusting the "definitive accounts" of certain name-brand authors in the true crime genre, Frasier's book offers a concise, straightforward recitation of the facts, accompanied by referrals for more detailed research that include, quite literally, every book-length publication in the English language for a given case. There simply is no better, more acces-sible or user-friendly source available to students of contemporary homicide. Case closed.

In 1983, when Britain's premier butcher, Dennis Nilsen, was interrogated as to motive in his 15 murders, he informed the London bobbies, "Well, enjoy-ing it is as good a reason as any." The same can easily be said for reading this book—and, I privately suspect, for writing it, as well. We study homicide for reasons as diverse as those that motivate the act itself; a fascination with detec-tive work, sheer morbid curiosity, a touch of latent cruelty, as a form of psy-chic self-defense, or from sincere commiseration with the victims of a human tragedy—there, but for Someone's grace, go you and I. Whatever draws us to the crime scene, we all stand on level ground before the Reaper. No one here gets out alive.

But in the meantime, we can take a stroll with monsters, eavesdrop on their dreams and nightmares, keeping them at arm's length all the while. It is safer—not to mention cheaper—than a cab ride in New York, and while you may not always know your final destination in advance, the trip will almost certainly be more rewarding in the end.

Come on, they're waiting. Just around that corner. In the dark.

Michael Newton (author, *Hunting Humans*)

Preface

Murder Cases of the Twentieth Century is an attempt to impose some sort of bibliographic order on the vast genre of twentieth century "true crime" literature, or, perhaps more accurately, the case histories of those both accused and convicted of murder. In this book, I have limited myself to some 280 of this century's most infamous and intriguing murder cases, chronicled the crimes in detailed essays, and in the bibliographic section concluding each entry provided an exhaustive list of those English language monographs written *specifically* on that case. In most instances, fictional accounts of the case have also been included. Other anthologies of murderers (Gaute and Odell's *The New Murderers' Who's Who* and Newton's *Mass Murder: An Annotated Bibliography*) already provide access to discussions on killers contained in other collections. The structure of this book owes more to Thomas M. McDade's excellent study *The Annals of Murder: A Bibliography of Books and Pamphlets on American Murders from Colonial Times to 1900* with its narrowly defined focus on monographs devoted primarily to a single murder case. Like McDade, I have endeavored to provide a detailed bibliographic description of the title, and, because so many readers of true crime literature are inveterate collectors, I have also supplied as complete an edition history for each title as possible (omitting book club editions) based upon exhaustive searches of numerous bibliographic databases and catalogs.

Any discerning reader of true crime literature, especially of those titles written in the last twenty years, quickly becomes aware of one disturbing fact: because so many of the books are hurriedly written to cash in on the sensational publicity generated by the case, they are filled with factual errors and misinformation. As a reference librarian at a major university library, I have enjoyed access to a wide variety of research tools not generally available to true crime writers feverishly working to meet a publisher's deadline. I have not blindly accepted what they have written as fact, but rather have meticulously researched each case contained in this book, often contacting penal institutions and individuals directly involved with the case. The entries, therefore, are not limited to the information contained within the books cited in a particular killer's bibliography. In every applicable case, I have updated the entries to reflect the subject's current legal status or to provide some interesting current biographical information.

The public's fascination with murder and those connected with it has generated an incredibly rich bibliography, particularly in a century defined by its lust for the sensational. As such, the true crime bibliographer is confronted at the outset with some editorial decisions which can make such a daunting undertaking at least technically feasible. I have chosen to exclude certain groups like so-called "political killers" (Lee Harvey Oswald, James Earl Ray, Leonard Peltier) and gangsters (John Dillinger, Bonnie and Clyde) which I feel warrant a separate study. In this volume, I have included those murderers or accused murderers throughout the world whose cases have proven to be of historical significance, have set some legal precedent, have not been previously anthologized, or have simply shocked and amazed with their sheer audacity or brutality. The murder cases selected for this book are limited to those which occurred prior to the end of 1992. All bibliographies, however, are current through 1995.

Murder Cases of the Twentieth Century is alphabetically arranged by the murderer's or the accused's last name with cross references provided if there was an accomplice. For example, the entry on Myra Hindley, the female component of the "Moors Murders," refers to the expanded entry on Ian Brady. Each entry, when applicable, contains the subject's alias(es), birth and death dates, occupation, location(s) where the murder(s) occurred, number of victims, weapon(s) used, and the time period when the killing(s) occurred. Films, theatre pieces, television, video, and audio programs based on or inspired by the case are cited under the heading "Media." In this section, the following codes are used to identify the production's country of origin: US (United States), GB (Great Britain), GER (Germany), FR (France), IT (Italy), NZ (New Zealand), SP (Spain), PN (Panama), and MEX (Mexico). Quotes are often included, followed by a detailed entry, and a bibliography of English language works (with edition histories). In addition to a General Index (citing page numbers), I have included two other elements tailored to the researcher, the bibliographer and the general reader: an Author and Title Index to the Bibliographic Entries (citing serial numbers of the books listed at the ends of the entries), and an Appendix: A Classification of the Cases (citing names and inclusive page numbers), which should be particularly useful; it is based on Colin Wilson and Patricia Pitman's classic study, *Encyclopaedia of Murder*, and Gaute and Odell's previously cited volume.

The Cases

Abbott, Jack Henry
(a.k.a. "Jack Eastman")

Born January 21, 1944, in Oscoda, Michigan. Career criminal. Provo, Utah, and New York City, New York; 2 murders; knife; December 1966 and July 18, 1981.

Theatre: *In the Belly of the Beast* (1985), a play based on Abbott's book of the same title adapted and updated by Adrian Hall and the director, Robert Woodruff, opened at New York's Joyce Theater on August 8, 1985.

"It is a little excessive, your honor, I would say."—Abbott's reaction to a Manhattan jury's award of $7.7 million in damages to Adan's widow in June 1990.

Career criminal freed to kill again by the New York literary establishment. Born to a prostitute on an Army base in Michigan in 1944, Abbott's childhood was spent in and out of foster homes. Within six months of being released at 18 from a juvenile detention center, Abbott was convicted of "issuing a check against insufficient funds" and imprisoned. Three years later in December 1966 he killed another inmate. Abbott escaped for six weeks in 1971, robbed a bank, and was quickly recaptured. Abbott had already spent 20 years in maximum security prisons (14 in solitary confinement) when he

read a news report concerning Norman Mailer's upcoming book on Utah killer Mark Gary Gilmore, *The Executioner's Song*. Abbott wrote a series of long letters to the famed author offering as a "state-raised convict" to describe what life was like in an American prison. Mailer was so impressed by Abbott's writing ("as good as any convict's prose that I had read since Eldridge Cleaver") that he arranged a book contract for the prison author. *In the Belly of the Beast*, a collection of Abbott's letters to Mailer, was published in 1981 to near universal critical acclaim. Based largely on the support of Mailer and the literati, Abbott was conditionally released in June 1981 with a parole date set for August 25, 1981. While working as Mailer's research assistant, the 37-year-old ex-con lived in a Salvation Army halfway house on Manhattan's Lower East Side. Shortly after 5:00 a.m. on July 18, 1981, Abbott and two female friends dropped into the BiniBon restaurant about three blocks from where he was staying. When informed by part-time waiter Richard Adan, a 22-year-old Cuban-born actor, that the restaurant's toilet was reserved for employees Abbott angrily asked him to step outside. On the street, Abbott stabbed Adan once through the heart with a paring knife. Two months later on September 23, 1981, Abbott was arrested at an oil workers' camp outside Morgan City, Louisiana. Commenting at the time on the risk career criminals like Abbott posed to society, Mailer was quoted as saying, "Sometimes culture is worth the risk." At his January 1982 trial before the state supreme court in Manhattan, Abbott tearfully explained the killing as a "tragic accident" that occurred while he was trying to defend himself. On January 21, 1982, Abbott's 38th birthday, the "state-raised convict" was found guilty of first degree manslaughter. Abbott was subsequently sentenced to a minimum 15 years to life to be served after serving the remaining eight years for his previous federal convictions. In 1983 a play adapted from *In the Belly of the Beast* was presented in Chicago. On July 15, 1990, a Manhattan jury awarded Adan's widow $7.7 million in damages against Abbott to be paid from any of his future earnings.

1. Abbott, Jack Henry. *In the Belly of the Beast: Letters from Prison.* Introduction by Norman Mailer. 1st ed. New York: Random House, 1981. xvi, 166 pp.; 22 cm.

_____. [Same as 1.] Introduction by Norman Mailer. 1st Vintage Books ed. New York: Vintage Books, 1982. xxii, 198 pp.; 18 cm.; paperback.

_____. [Same as 1.] Introduction by Norman Mailer. London: Hutchinson, 1982. xvi, 166 pp.; 23 cm.

_____. [Same as 1.] Introduction by Norman Mailer. London: Arrow, 1982. xvi, 166 pp.; 18 cm.; paperback.

_____. [Same as 1.] Introduction by Norman Mailer. Vintage Books ed. New York: Vintage Books, 1991. xvi, 166 pp.; 21 cm.

Abbott's brilliant depiction of prison life is perhaps the finest book ever written on the effects of long-term incarceration on the human psyche. Highly recommended.

"Acid Bath Murders" *see* **Haigh, Jo hn George**

Adams, John Bodkin
(acquitted)

Born January 21, 1899, in Randalstown, Antrim, England. Died July 5, 1983. Eastbourne, England; 3 murders (acquitted) (suspected of as many as 17); drugs; 1935–July 1956.

Eastbourne doctor acquitted after a sensational Old Bailey trial of poisoning wealthy patients who named him in their wills. Born in 1899, Adams earned his medical degree from Queen's College, Belfast, in 1921. Answering an ad for a "Christian doctor assistant," Adams relocated to Eastbourne, an affluent resort town on the southeast coast of England, where he impressed his future partners with his willingness to perform night calls. Deeply religious and soft-spoken, the teetotaling bachelor became the doctor of choice among the town's well-to-do. Dr. Adams first came to public attention in 1935 after Mrs. Matilda Whitton, a 72-year-old patient, died and left him £2,000 in her will. Over the years, Adams was named as beneficiary in an additional 132 wills. Between 1944 and 1955, 14 elderly patients bequeathed him £21,600. In July 1956 Adams inherited a Rolls Royce and a check for £1,000 after his patient, 56-year-old Gertrude Hullett, committed suicide with barbiturates. An autopsy confirmed death by overdose, but the chief constable enlisted the aid of Scotland Yard to "investigate certain deaths in the neighborhood." As a result of their investigation, Adams was arrested on November 24, 1956, and charged with the November 1950 murder of Edith Alice Morrell, 82, a chronic arthritis sufferer. Adams had prescribed regular doses of heroin and morphine to control the woman's pain. After her death, Adams produced a will in which Morrell had promised him a car and a case of silver. Tried in the Old Bailey in March 1957, Adams did not testify in his own defense, a legal tactic which barred the prosecution from introducing evidence relating to the doctor's involvement in eight other suspected murders. Four nurses, who gave their account from memory of Morrell's treatment six years earlier, were refuted by Adams' counsel who produced their actual notebooks written at the time. The notebooks showed that the amount of drugs administered to Morrell were actually far less than that prescribed by Adams. A jury needed only 44 minutes on April 10, 1957, to acquit the doctor. Adams was subsequently banned from practicing medicine for four years and fined £2,400 by a Magistrates' Court for various offenses over cremation certificates, forgery of prescriptions, and not keeping proper records of dangerous drugs. After the suspension, Dr. Adams continued practicing medicine among his loyal legion of patients in Eastbourne. The general practitioner died in Eastbourne General Hospital on July 5, 1983, after breaking a leg.

2. Bedford, Sybille. *The Best We Can Do: An Account of the Trial of John Bodkin Adams.* London: Collins, 1958. 254 pp.: ill.; 21 cm.

_____. [Same as 2, but U.S. ed. retitled: *The Trial of Dr. Adams.*] New York: Simon and Schuster, 1959. 245 pp.; 22 cm.

_____. [Same as 2 minus subtitle.] Harmondsworth, Middlesex: Penguin, 1961. 221 pp.; 18 cm.; paperback.

_____. [Same as 2, but U.S. ed. retitled: *The Trial of Dr. Adams.*] 1st Black Cat ed.

New York: Grove Press, 1962. 245 pp.; 18 cm. ("A Black Cat book; BA-21"); paperback.

3. Devlin, Patrick. *Easing the Passing: The Trial of Dr. John Bodkin Adams.* London: Bodley Head, 1985. 228 pp., [8]pp. of plates: ill.; 23 cm.

_____. [Same as 3.] London; Boston: Faber and Faber, 1986. 236 pp., [8]pp. of plates: ill., ports.; 20 cm.; paperback.

Mr. Justice Devlin, who presided over Adams' case at the Old Bailey, agreed with the not guilty verdict, but believed the doctor was probably a "greedy mercy killer." Devlin, 86, died at his home in Wiltshire, England, on August 9, 1992.

4. Hallworth, Rodney, and Williams, Mark. *Where There's a Will—: The Sensational Life of Dr. John Bodkin Adams.* Jersey [Eng.]: The Capstans Press, 1983. 246 pp.: ill.; 21 cm.

Former Detective Chief Superintendent Charles Hewitt, an investigator on the case, is quoted by former crime reporter Hallworth as saying that Adams was "without a doubt a mass murderer who deserved to hang twenty times over.... The doctor was beneficiary in 132 wills and I think he helped many of those people on their way. He eased them out of this life often for gain."

5. Hoskins, Percy. *Two Men Were Acquitted: The Trial and Acquittal of Doctor John Bodkin Adams.* London: Secker & Warburg, 1984. ix, 220 pp., [8]pp. of plates: ill.; 24 cm. (Errata slip inserted.)

The former chief crime reporter of the *Daily Express* who covered the trial and spent three weeks with Adams after the verdict working on a newspaper piece remains convinced of the doctor's innocence.

"Agra Double Murder" *see* **Fullam, Augusta Fairfield (and) Clark, Henry Lovell William**

Allaway, Thomas Henry (a.k.a. "T. Wood")

Born circa 1886 in Kilburn, England. Executed August 19, 1922. Chauffeur, ex-soldier. Tuckton, England; 1 murder; bludgeon; December 22, 1921.

"I am innocent of this crime, absolutely."

British chauffeur convicted of and executed for murder based upon a study of his handwriting. On December 20, 1921, 31-year-old Irene May Wilkins of Streatham placed an ad in the London *Morning Post* for a position as a school cook. Two days later she received a telegram from a prospective employer, "T. Wood," instructing her to travel by train to Bournemouth where she would be met by a car. One hour after departing for the station her confirmation telegram was returned as undeliverable. No such street address existed. Wilkins' body, her head crushed by numerous blows from a heavy object, was found at dawn on December 23, 1921, in a field at Tuckton between the towns of Bournemouth and Christchurch. Fresh tracks found at the scene from a car outfitted with Dunlop-Magnum tires prompted police to contact all chauffeurs and drivers in the area. Three bogus handwritten telegrams to Wilkins from her "employer" were examined and found to contain numerous misspellings. Nine days later, an attache case and a purse belonging to the victim were found eight miles from the murder scene in Branksome Park. The murder remained unsolved for months as public pressure for an arrest mounted. A re-review of the 22,000 documents amassed in the case led authorities to reconsider Thomas Allaway, a chauffeur in Bournemouth and a former army deserter. On a prior interview, Allaway

had provided detectives with a handwriting sample which they were now anxious to compare with a sample he wrote *before* the date of the murder. Their search of his rooms in Boscombe revealed that the chauffeur had disposed of any such documents.

On April 20, 1922, Allaway stole his employer's checkbook and forged his name to checks totalling almost £20. When arrested in Reading eight days later he was carrying betting slips which appeared to be written in the same hand as the telegrams to Wilkins. While he was on remand at Winchester Prison on forgery charges, authorities questioned his wife and secured postcards and a letter written by Allaway to her dated before Wilkins' murder. Allaway later denied writing the letter, insisting that after he injured his hand a friend wrote it for him. The friend was located and denied writing the letter. In rewriting the bogus telegrams from police dictation Allaway attempted to conceal his handwriting, but made several of the same spelling errors found in the originals. Various witnesses placed Allaway at the Bournemouth Central Railway Station at the time Wilkins' train arrived and noted that a man fitting his description was seen driving away with a woman in a large Mercedes (his employer's car.) More damningly, the day after the discovery of the murder Allaway was observed replacing one of the car's Dunlop-Magnum tires with a Michelin. The trial opened at the Hampshire Summer Assizes in the Castle of Winchester on July 3, 1922, and lasted five days. The mass of circumstantial evidence combined with expert testimony matching Allaway's handwriting with that on the telegrams led an all-male jury to find the chauffeur guilty on July 7, 1922, after deliberating only one hour. Allaway was sentenced to death, but continued to maintain his innocence until the eve of his execution when he finally confessed. Hanged at Winchester Prison on August 19, 1922, Allaway died slowly from strangulation rather than instantaneously by dislocated vertebra when the noose shifted during the execution.

6. Woodland, W. Lloyd. *The Trial of Thomas Henry Allaway.* Famous Trials Series. General editor: George Dilnot. London: Geoffrey Bles, 1929. vii, 262 pp., [10] leaves of plates: port., facsims.; 23 cm.

Entry in the Famous Trials Series covering Allaway's trial at the Hampshire Summer Assizes, July 1922, for the murder of Irene May Wilkins (1890?–1921). Woodland's introduction to the case notes that despite Allaway's last minute confession many believe "that he was the tool of another." Appendix: "The Case Before the Court of Criminal Appeals."

Allen, Peter Anthony

Born April 4, 1943, in Wallasey, Cheshire, England. Executed August 13, 1964. Dairyman, truck driver, sheet metal worker. Workington, Cumberland, England; 1 murder; bludgeon, knife; April 7, 1964.

"I would like to say I am very sorry for what I took part in and to say I am glad I was caught as I could not have lived noing [sic] I had helped in taking a human life, for who am I to take a man [sic] life and destroy it."— Allen in a written statement to police; *see also* Evans, Gwynne Owen.

"Alpine Manor Murders" *see* Wood, Catherine May (and) Graham, Gwendolyn Gail

Anderson, Craig Alan

Born circa 1956. Paint supply store owner. Burlingame, California, area; 1 murder; unknown weapon; November 11, 1985.

"I did not know that a murder conviction was possible without a corpse (proof of a murder)."—From a letter by Anderson to *The San Mateo Times* published June 6, 1986

Thirty-year-old San Carlos, California, paint store owner who murdered his ex-fiancée in a jealous rage after she refused to reconcile with him. On November 11, 1985, 23-year-old Denise Susan Redlick disappeared from a parking lot in Burlingame, California. Redlick had broken off her engagement with Craig Anderson on September 28, 1985, after he had slapped her in the face at a friend's wedding reception. The unexpected blow capped a relationship which had begun as idyllic but had slowly deteriorated due to Anderson's possessiveness and mercurial temper. Anderson was arrested after circumstantial evidence against him began to accumulate. Authorities learned that Anderson had attempted to bribe several people to produce an alibi for him on the day of Redlick's murder. Bloodstains found in a van rented by Anderson matched Redlick's type. Several individuals also noted that immediately after Redlick's disappearance Anderson's hands and arms were covered with scratches. Despite the absence of the victim's body or a murder weapon, Anderson was convicted of first degree murder in San Mateo County Superior Court on May 29, 1986. He sat impassively through his sentencing hearing as Redlick's mother pleaded with him to disclose the location of her daughter's body. Afterwards, he was sentenced to 25 years to life in prison. In a separate trial bearing no connection with the Redlick case, Anderson was acquitted on December 12, 1986, of soliciting the death of a former live-in girlfriend's ex-husband after the woman reconciled with him. Denise Redlick's remains were subsequently found on August 12, 1987, by workers grading the dry Cupertino Creek near Santa Clara, California.

7. Beck, Janet Parker. *Too Good to Be True: The Story of Denise Redlick's Murder.* Far Hills, N.J.: New Horizon Press, 1991. vi, 360 pp.: ill.; 24 cm.

_____. [Same as 7.] New York: Penguin Group, 1992. 380 pp.; 18 cm.; paperback.

Andre, Carl *(acquitted)*

Born September 16, 1935, in Quincy, Massachusetts. Sculptor. New York, New York. 1 murder (acquitted); defenestration; September 8, 1985.

"Justice has been done."—Andre commenting on his acquittal

A world renowned sculptor three times indicted for, and ultimately acquitted of, pushing his wife to her death from an upper story window. On the morning of September 8, 1985, police were summoned to the Greenwich Village apartment shared by 49-year-old Carl Andre, the internationally famed founder of the Minimalist school of sculpture, and his wife, Cuban-born artist Ana Mendieta, 36. Her body, clad only in bikini underwear, lay on the roof of a delicatessen located directly below the bedroom window of their 34th floor apartment. Andre, bearing a fresh scratch on his nose, told police that they had argued and Mendieta had retired to their bedroom where she jumped from a window. Andre was arrested on a charge of second degree

murder when a doorman across from their apartment house reported hearing a woman scream, "No, no, no, no," just before Mendieta's body struck the roof at 120 miles per hour. Twice, in 1985 and 1986, grand jury indictments against Andre were voided due to procedural errors committed by the New York City district attorney's office. On March 18, 1987, Andre was re-indicted for an almost unprecedented third time. Andre waived a trial by jury and Supreme Court Justice Alvin Schlesinger began hearing testimony in the case on January 29, 1988. The prosecution maintained that Andre pushed Mendieta from the window following a heated argument in which she accused him of having an affair. Under defense cross-examination the doorman that allegedly heard Mendieta's screams admitted having been hospitalized three times in the past for psychological problems which included auditory hallucinations. The defense contended that Mendieta either committed suicide or drunkenly fell trying to open a window, contentions discounted by the prosecutor who pointed to Mendieta's fear of heights, her optimistic mood before her death, and the high placement of the bedroom window which would almost preclude such an accident. Citing that "the evidence does not satisfy me beyond a reasonable doubt," Judge Schlesinger acquitted Andre on February 11, 1988.

8. Katz, Robert. *Naked by the Window: The Fatal Marriage of Carl Andre and Ana Mendieta.* 1st ed. New York: Atlantic Monthly Press, 1990. xii, 428 pp., [8] pp. of plates : ill. ; 24 cm.

Katz, a visiting lecturer in investigative journalism at the University of California at Santa Cruz, attended the preliminary hearings prior to the trial, the trial, and interviewed over 200 people connected with the case. Though richly documented, Katz's efforts were hampered by the sealing of the court records following the not guilty verdict and by the refusal of Andre and many close to him to be interviewed. Informed that a book was being written on the case, Andre replied, "A pity."

Andrews, William A.
(a.k.a. "Hi-Fi Killer")

Born circa 1955 in Jonesboro, Louisiana. Executed July 30, 1992. United States Air Force airman. Ogden, Utah; 3 murders (accomplice); .25 caliber pistol, .38 caliber pistol; April 22, 1974.

"Thank those who tried so hard to keep me alive. Tell my family goodbye, and that I love them." —Andrews' last words; see also Pierre, Dale Selby.

Armstrong, Herbert Rowse
(a.k.a. "The Hay Poisoner")

Born May 13, 1869, in Plymouth, England. Executed May 31, 1922. Hay-on-Wye, Wales; 1 murder; poison (arsenic); February 22, 1921.

Television: "Dandelion Dead," a two-part ITV production shot in Hay-on-Wye, Wales, aired in Britain on February 6 and 13, 1994. Cast includes Michael Kitchen (Herbert Armstrong), Sarah Miles (Mrs. Armstrong), and David Thewlis (Martin).

"Yes, I am sure it must be most unpleasant for you." —Armstrong's reply to the governor of Gloucester Prison who told the condemned solicitor that he did not like this "hanging business"

Henpecked wife poisoner who was the first solicitor to be hanged in Britain. Armstrong, a major in the Royal Engineers engaged in depot work throughout England during World War I, somewhat officiously retained his mil-

itary title after the war. He married Katharine Mary Friend in 1907 and with their three children lived in a house called "Mayfield" in Cusop Dingle, a valley on the Welsh-English border one half mile from the town of Hay where Major Armstrong maintained a modest law practice. Despite his military mien, the diminutive 98-pound solicitor was dominated by his wife who refused to let him drink except on rare occasions, confined his smoking to a single room in the house, and once called him from a public meeting because it was his "bath night." Armstrong seemed not to mind these domestic humiliations and found tranquility in gardening. On August 22, 1920, one month after signing a will drafted by Armstrong which made him the sole beneficiary of her £2000 estate, Mrs. Armstrong became violently ill and was taken to an asylum in Gloucester. Her claims of being poisoned were dismissed as delusional by doctors familiar with her long history of depression and nervous afflictions. Mrs. Armstrong's symptoms improved sufficiently to be released, but upon returning home to Mayfield in January 1921 her condition rapidly worsened. Her death on February 22, 1921, was attributed to gastritis with heart disease and nephritis mentioned as contributory factors.

Major Armstrong enjoyed his newfound freedom by hosting a number of dinner parties in which he now served alcohol. Oswald Norman Martin, a rival solicitor whose office on Broad Street in Hay stood directly opposite Armstrong's, consistently refused the major's regular invitations to tea. Relations between the pair were strained owing to a business transaction in which Martin had threatened legal action against his colleague. On

September 20, 1921, Martin received a one pound box of chocolates in the post from an anonymous sender. Though not eating any himself, he served some to a dinner guest who became ill shortly afterwards. Police later examined the uneaten chocolate and found some contained small holes drilled into the base through which arsenic had been inserted. Armstrong continued to deluge Martin with daily invitations to tea and the harried solicitor finally acquiesced to meet the major at Mayfield on October 26, 1921. During tea Armstrong handed Martin a buttered scone with the apology, "Excuse my fingers." Martin returned home and was immediately racked with diarrhea, gastric pain, and vomiting. A local doctor, suspicious that these symptoms were reminiscent of Mrs. Armstrong's condition, collected a liquid sample from Martin and sent it to a lab for analysis. When 1/33 of a grain of arsenic was found in the specimen authorities conducted an exhaustive behind the scenes investigation of Armstrong.

When Major Armstrong was arrested for the attempted murder of Martin on December 31, 1921, detectives found a packet of arsenic on his person. Armstrong explained that the poison was 1/20 of one ounce of arsenic he purchased for eradicating 20 dandelions. The device used by the avid gardener to inject the arsenic into the roots of the dandelions, a small syringe with a fine nozzle, fit perfectly the holes found in the bases of the poisoned chocolates. A larger packet of arsenic, the remainder of his purchase according to Armstrong, was found in his bureau drawer. Mrs. Armstrong's body was exhumed from the Cusop Churchyard on January 2, 1922, and found to contain one of the largest amounts of arsenic ever seen in a mur-

der victim. Tried for the murder of his wife at the Hereford Assizes beginning on April 3, 1922, Armstrong's counsel maintained that the woman had taken her own life during a period of mental instability. Testifying in his own defense, the major was unable to give a satisfactory answer as to why he went to the trouble of dividing the arsenic into separate packets to poison 20 individual dandelions. On April 13, 1922, a jury needed only 48 minutes to find Armstrong guilty on largely circumstantial evidence and he was sentenced to death. Following a failed appeal, Major Armstrong (still professing his innocence) was hanged at Gloucester Prison on May 31, 1922, at 8:00 a.m.

9. Odell, Robin; Gaute, J.H.H.; Trumper, H.B. *Exhumation of a Murder: The Life and Trial of Major Armstrong.* Foreword by Edgar Lustgarten. London: Harrap, 1975. 250 pp., [8] leaves of plates: ill.; 23 cm.

_____. [Same as 9.] London: Prize Paperbacks, 1978. 250 pp., [16]pp. of plates: ill., facsims., ports.; 22 cm.; paperback.

_____. [Same as 9.] London; New York: Proteus, 1978. 250 pp., [8] leaves of plates: ill.; 23 cm.; paperback.

_____. [Same as 9.] Foreword by Richard Whittington-Egan. Classic Crime Series. London: Souvenir Press, 1988. 250 pp., [8] leaves of plates: ill.; 23 cm. (Also a paperback edition.)

_____. [Same as 9.] 1st U.S. ed. New York: St. Martin's Press, 1988. 250 pp., [16]pp. of plates: ill.; 22 cm. ("A Thomas Dunne book.")

Definitive study of the Armstrong case, exhaustively researched, wonderfully illustrated, and beautifully written. Includes a bibliography, index, and an appendix containing the statement made by Armstrong to the police on December 31, 1921.

10. Young, Filson, ed. *Trial of Herbert Rowse Armstrong.* Notable British Trials.

Edinburgh; London: W. Hodge, 1927. x, 396 pp.: ill., ports.; 23 cm.

_____. [Same as 10.] Notable British Trials. Toronto: Canada Law Book Co., 1927. x, 396 pp.: ill., ports.; 23 cm.

_____. [Same as 10.] Notable British Trials. New York: J. Day, 1927. x, 396 pp.: ill., ports.; 23 cm.

Entry in the important Notable British Trials Series which in addition to Young's brief introduction and the trial transcript also includes acquitted wife poisoner and trial observer Harold Greenwood's article "Armstrong's Fight for Life" published in *John Bull* on April 22, 1922.

Atkins, Susan Denise
(a.k.a. "Sadie Mae Glutz," "Sexy Sadie," "Sharon King," "Donna Kay Powell")

Born circa May 1948 in California. Cult member. Los Angeles, California; 6 murders; gun, knife, bludgeon; July 30, 1969, and August 9, 1969.

"He represented a God to me that was so beautiful that I'd do anything for him."—Atkins speaking of Manson; *see also* Manson, Charles Milles.

"Atlanta Child Killings [or] Murders" *see* Williams, Wayne Bertram

Baniszewski, Gertrude

Born circa 1923. Housewife. Indianapolis, Indiana; 1 murder; bludgeon; October 26, 1965.

Indiana woman who led her children and 15 neighborhood children in the torture murder of a 16-year-old girl left in her care. Described as "the most heinous crime in Indiana history," the body of 16-year-old Sylvia Marie Likens was found on October 26, 1965, after she had been beaten, burned, and tattooed by Gertrude Baniszewki, 37, and others. An autopsy revealed that Likens suffered from severe malnutrition and shock before death had resulted from brain swelling and hemorrhaging caused by a sharp blow to the head. Prior to the girl's death, someone had burned "prostitute" on her chest. Baniszewski, who maintained she was on drugs during the days Likens was tortured, was convicted of first degree murder on May 19, 1966, a verdict upheld in August 1971 after the Supreme Court ordered a new trial. Citing "her success in overcoming the serious problems that contributed to her involvement in this crime," the Indiana parole board in a 3–2 vote granted Baniszewski parole in 1985. On December 4, 1985, the 57-year-old Baniszewski was released from the Indiana Woman's Prison after serving 20 years. On the day of her parole she told reporters, "I just wish, you know, people would please forgive me. I can't undo anything. I know that the Lord has forgiven me. I have my peace inside. And I still have to live with this every day, and it's terrible."

11. Dean, John. *The Indiana Torture Slaying.* New York: Bee-Line Books, 1966. 186 pp.; 18 cm.; paperback.

12. Millett, Kate. *The Basement: Meditations on Human Sacrifice.* New York: Simon and Schuster, 1979. 341 pp., [5] leaves of plates: ill., ports. ; 22 cm.

_____. [Same as 12 with added subtitle: *With a New Introduction.*] 1st Touchstone ed. New York: Simon and Schuster, 1991. 341 pp.: ill.; 22 cm. ("A Touchstone book.") (Paperback ed. also available.)

Barfield, Margie Velma (a.k.a. "Margie Velma Bullard" [maiden name], "Lillie Bullard")

Born October 29, 1932, in Cumberland County, North Carolina. Executed November 2, 1984. Nurse's aide. North Carolina; 5 murders; ant and roach poison; March 1971—February 1978.

Audio: Woman on Death Row, a six-cassette, six-hour unabridged recording of Barfield's book read by Rob Gregory, was published in 1987 by Christians Listening (Van Wyck, South Carolina).

"I want to say that I am sorry for all the hurt that I have caused. I know that everybody has gone through a lot of pain, all the families connected, and I am sorry and I want to thank everybody who has supported me all these six years."—Barfield's last words

Poisoner, "born again" Christian, political issue, grandmother, drug addict … Velma Barfield managed to assume each of these roles before her controversial execution at Central Prison in Raleigh, North Carolina, on November 2, 1984. Thousands of supporters nationwide, including the wife of evangelist Billy Graham, had rallied to block the execution of the 52-year-old grandmother and self-confessed killer of five. Sister Mary Teresa Floyd, a Roman Catholic nun and coordinator of the Velma Barfield Support Committee, spoke for many when she argued that Barfield had rehabilitated herself in prison, helped several inmates, and deserved to have her death sentence commuted to life imprisonment. Robeson County prosecutor Joe Freeman Britt was skeptical: "She may look like a sweet little old grandmother, but she is a cold-blooded murderess." North

Carolina Governor James B. Hunt, Jr., then embroiled in a hotly contested Senate race with Republican Jesse Helms, agreed. In a statement denying her clemency issued September 27, 1984, Hunt noted the extreme cruelty of Barfield's crimes: "Death by arsenic poisoning is slow and agonizing. Victims are literally tortured to death."

Born in North Carolina's Cumberland County on October 29, 1932, Margie Velma Bullard was one of nine children in a family dominated by father Murray Bullard, a loom repairman and alcoholic. Barfield's mother, unable to prevent her drunken husband's beatings of her or the children, stayed in the marriage out of economic necessity. According to Barfield's autobiography, *Woman on Death Row*, her father raped her when she was 13 and to escape him she eloped at 17 with schoolmate Thomas Burke on December 1, 1949. The marriage produced two children, son Ronald and daughter Kim, before it began to sour in 1965. In a replay of Barfield's pre-married life, husband Burke began drinking and physically abusing her. When he lost his job, Barfield compensated by taking two—working by day as a clerk in a department store in Fayetteville and at night as a machine operator in a cotton mill in Hope Mills, North Carolina. In 1968 Barfield cracked under the pressure and suffered a nervous breakdown. Doctor-prescribed tranquilizers like Butisol, Librium, and Valium brought Barfield relief, but over time led to a ten year drug addiction that she maintained was instrumental in prompting the murders.

On April 19, 1969, Thomas Burke died from smoke inhalation after allegedly falling asleep with a lighted cigarette. Depressed over his death, Barfield turned to pills and by 1970 was a full-blown drug addict who supported her habit by visiting several doctors in the area for prescriptions. On August 23, 1970, the widow remarried Jennings Barfield, a recently widowed retiree suffering from emphysema and diabetes. Although she had married for companionship, she soon tired of her role as a live-in nurse. In March 1971, six months after the marriage, Velma Barfield purchased a bottle of ant and roach poison and sprinkled some in her husband's food. He died the next day from what doctors at the time assumed to be natural causes. An exhumation and autopsy in 1978 revealed his body to contain a lethal level of arsenic. Barfield overdosed twice in 1970 and attempted to end her life with pills. Strung out on Valium and barely functional, she was fired from the department store in late 1971 and moved in with her parents in Parkton, North Carolina. During this period, Barfield turned to religion, becoming an active member of the First Pentecostal Holiness Church and a Sunday school teacher. Tension between Barfield and her 74-year-old mother, however, was running high when her father died of lung cancer in April 1972. The elderly woman warned house guests to hide any medicine they might have in their purses "because Velma will take any kind of pill she can find." By fall 1974 Barfield was desperate for money to support her drug habit. She forged her mother's name, Lillie Bullard, on a $1,000 check from a loan company in Lumberton. Fearful of discovery, Barfield purchased a bottle of ant and roach poison and placed it in her mother's soft drink. Bullard died of a "massive heart attack" on December 30, 1974 following days of intense diarrhea, cramping, and vomiting. The autopsy failed to turn up arsenic poisoning and

Barfield paid off the $1,000 loan with her mother's insurance money.

In November 1975 Barfield became a live-in nurse for an elderly Lumberton couple, Montgomery Edwards, 93, and his wife Dollie Taylor, 85. Barfield met their nephew, Stuart Taylor, a thrice divorced tobacco farmer from St. Pauls, North Carolina, in September 1976 and began dating him intermittently. Following Montgomery Edwards' death by natural causes in January 1977, Barfield agreed to stay on as Dollie's maid. The old woman reminded Barfield of her mother so in February 1977 she laced Edwards' cereal with ant and roach poison. Barfield remained at the woman's bedside for three days as she writhed in agony before finally dying on February 28, 1977, from "acute gastroenteritis," an inflammation of the stomach and intestinal lining. In April 1977 Barfield was employed as a live-in nurse at the home of John Henry Lee, 80, and his 76-year-old wife Record. Not long afterwards, she discovered one of the man's blank checks and, filling in the amount for $50, forged his name on it. According to Barfield, she had no intention of killing Lee when she laced his tea and beer with arsenic-based insecticide. She just meant to "make him sick" enough to buy time so she could replace the missing $50 in his account. Lee died from "acute gastroenteritis" on June 4, 1977, after losing 65 pounds during the several days he spent racked with diarrhea, vomiting, and convulsions. Before leaving his widow's employ, Barfield placed just enough insecticide in Record Lee's tea to make her violently ill.

Barfield was living alone in a trailer in Lumberton and working as a nurse's aide in a nearby nursing home when Stuart Taylor, 56, re-entered her life after nearly a year-long absence. He informed her that they could be married when his divorce (his third) became final. Chinks began to form in the relationship, however, when Taylor learned that in 1974 his fiancée had served four months at the Correctional Center for Women in Raleigh for check fraud. This could perhaps be forgiven, but when Taylor discovered in November 1977 that she had forged his name on a blank check for $195 he threatened to prosecute. In January 1978, Barfield used the next check she forged Taylor's name on to buy a bottle of ant and roach poison. On January 31, 1978, she spiked Taylor's beer before accompanying him to a Rex Humbard gospel meeting. She listened attentively to the evangelist as Taylor spent the evening vomiting in the parking lot. When Taylor died on February 4, 1978, his family rejected the cause of death as "gastroenteritis" and insisted on other tests which revealed the man had died from arsenic poisoning. Questioned by police on March 10, 1978, Barfield initially denied any involvement in the murder, but confessed the next day to poisoning Taylor as well as her mother, Dollie Taylor Edwards, and John Henry Lee. Their bodies along with that of Jennings Barfield were exhumed and found to contain high levels of arsenic.

Charged with the first degree murder of Taylor, Barfield underwent a religious conversion while in jail listening to a radio program by evangelist J. K. Kinkle. Barfield pleaded not guilty by reason of insanity at her trial in Elizabethtown, although not one psychiatrist diagnosed her as suffering from any mental illness. On the stand, Barfield maintained that she never intended to murder Taylor or any other of her victims. She merely wanted to make them sick long enough for her to repay the money she had stolen. Re-markably, her court-appointed attorney made little of her well-documented history of drug addiction, a point which might have mitigated the possible death penalty she faced for first degree murder. A jury needed less than three hours in December 1978 to find Barfield guilty and sentence her to death.

Barfield's conviction set off a six year round of litigation during which time the United States Supreme Court rejected three of her appeals. As several of her execution dates were set then stayed, Barfield filled her time at Central Prison's death row by counseling young female prisoners in the tenets of her Christian faith. Ruth Graham, wife of internationally renowned evangelist Billy Graham, became one of her staunchest supporters and lent her voice to the thousands who called for Governor Hunt to commute her death sentence to life imprisonment. When he refused to do so, Barfield accepted her fate, instructed her attorney not to file any more appeals, and chose as her "gateway to heaven" lethal injection over the gas chamber. November 1, 1984, the day before her execution, Barfield spent listening to religious recordings and saying farewell to family and friends. She chose to be executed in a pair of pink pajamas and blue house slippers and forewent the usual specially prepared last meal in favor of Cheez Doodles and Coca-Cola. At 2:15 a.m. on November 2, 1984, Velma Barfield was pronounced dead after being injected minutes before with the drug procuronium bromide, a muscle relaxant that stops the heart. She had pre-donated her organs to science and was buried in accordance with her wishes in a rural cemetery in Parkton, North Carolina, near her childhood home. Barfield's execution marked the first time in 22 years a woman had been put to death in the United States.

13. Barfield, Velma. *Woman on Death Row*. Nashville: Oliver-Nelson, 1985. ix, 175 pp.; 21 cm.; trade paperback.

_____. [Same as 13.] Minneapolis, Minn.: World Wide Publications, 1985. ix, 175 pp.; 21 cm.

_____. [Same as 13, but U.K. ed. retitled: *On Death Row: Condemned to Die Yet She Served Christ*.] Basingstoke: Marshall Pickering, 1986. ix, 175 pp.; 18 cm.; paperback.

Written in prison after her conversion to Christianity, Barfield's "spiritual autobiography" lays partial blame for the murders on her ten year addiction to drugs.

Barney, Elvira Dolores
(acquitted; a.k.a. "Elvira Dolores Mullen" [maiden name], "Dolores Ashley" [stage name])

Born circa 1905 in England. Died December 25, 1936. Knightsbridge, London, England; 1 murder (acquitted); .32 caliber revolver; May 31, 1932.

Television: A dramatic recreation of the case entitled "Laugh Baby Laugh" appeared on the Granada produced British television program "In Suspicious Circumstances" on March 16, 1993. Narrated by Edward Woodward, the cast includes Nicola Duffett (Elvira Barney) and Paul Freeman (Sir Patrick Hastings).

"I am the one who shot her lover—so take a good look!"—Statement allegedly shouted by Barney on the dance floor of the Cafe de Paris some time after being acquitted of Stephen's murder

Twenty-seven-year-old former actress and member of London's Bohemian set acquitted of murdering her lover in a sensational Old Bailey trial in 1932. Born to titled parents, Elvira Barney preferred the wild nightlife of Knightsbridge to the more staid surroundings of their Belgrave Square home. Shortly after appearing in a West End production under the stage name "Dolores Ashley," the young socialite met American cabaret singer John Sterling Barney. She married him on a lark on August 2, 1928, but the marriage quickly failed after the singer showed a penchant for burning his wife with lighted cigarettes. Following the breakup, Elvira Barney launched herself into a dizzying round of cocaine, wild parties, and love affairs among London's dissolute upper class. In early 1932, Barney took Michael Scott Stephen (real name William Scott Stephen) as her lover. Stephen, a 25-year-old self-described "dress designer," was a heavy user of cocaine and reportedly sold drugs. Cut off from a private allowance by a banker father disgusted by his lifestyle, Stephen was kept by Barney in what was described as an "exotically furnished little house" at 21 Williams Mews, Lowndes Square, Knightsbridge. Furnished with erotic paintings, sexual paraphernalia, and a large pornography library, the house was the frequent scene of parties and loud fights between the lovers.

On May 30, 1932, the pair hosted a party at their home, dined afterwards at the Cafe de Paris, and stopped for drinks at the Blue Angel Club in Soho before returning to 21 Williams Mews after midnight. Neighbors reported hearing a spirited argument between Barney and Stephens begin around 3:00 a.m. which steadily increased in intensity before ending with a loud noise. Police arrived to find Barney hysterical and Stephens dead from one gunshot wound to the left lung. According to Barney, the quarrel started over Stephen's interest in another woman and escalated to the point where she threatened to kill herself with a .32 caliber revolver after he announced he was leaving her. The gun accidentally went off during Stephen's struggle to disarm the distraught woman. Barney was arrested at her parents' home on June 3, 1932, after her story of the accident proved untenable. One neighbor reported hearing Barney shout "I'll shoot you" just before the shot while another testified that more than one shot was fired (seemingly verified by the discovery of a bullet mark on the bedroom wall.) Both neighbors reported an earlier incident in which Barney had shot at Stephen from the window of the house as he was walking in the mews.

The "murder in the high life" brought unprecedented crowds to the Old Bailey as Barney's trial began on July 4, 1932, before Mr. Justice Humphreys. Brilliantly defended by Sir Patrick Hastings, Barney pleaded not guilty in the face of seemingly overwhelming evidence against her. Hastings neutralized noted pathologist Sir Bernard Spilsbury's testimony that Stephen's death could not have been suicide by forcing him to admit that his findings did not preclude an accidental shooting. Expert gunsmith Robert Churchill reported that the murder weapon, a five shot .32 caliber revolver, was among the safest guns made and needed a considerable amount of pressure to pull the trigger. Hastings pointed out that the gun lacked a safety and easily pulled the trigger several times. Hastings, however, saved his most dramatic bit of courtroom theatrics for his questioning of Barney. Placing the gun directly

in front of her on the ledge of the witness box, Hastings unexpectedly shouted, "Pick up that revolver, Mrs. Barney." The startled woman did so with her right hand casting doubt on a neighbor's claim that she had fired the weapon at Stephen with her left hand during the earlier shooting incident. News of Barney's acquittal on July 6, 1932, was greeted with choruses of "Three Cheers for Mrs. Barney" and "For She's a Jolly Good Fellow" from hundreds of people jamming the street outside the courtroom. She was later fined £50 and £10 in costs for being in possession of a gun without a license. Days after her acquittal, Barney signed a contract with the *Sunday Dispatch* to write a series of articles entitled "My Life." The series was canceled by mutual agreement after the first installment was published on July 10, 1932. Barney subsequently changed her name and moved to Paris where she continued her flamboyant lifestyle unabated. On Christmas Day 1936, Barney was found dead from an apparent hemorrhage in the bedroom of her Paris hotel after spending the night before in what the *Daily Mirror* called a "tour of the gay cafes and restaurants of Montmartre, Montparnasse and the Latin Quarter."

14. Cotes, Peter, ed. *Trial of Elvira Barney*. Celebrated Trials Series. Newton Abbot; North Pomfret, Vt.: David and Charles, 1976. 127 pp.: ill., facsims., ports.; 23 cm.

A brief recounting of the Barney case introduces excerpts from the sensational trial. This entry in the Celebrated Trials Series includes a table of leading dates in the case and reprints from the press.

Beck, Martha Jule (Seabrook)
(a.k.a. "The Lonely Hearts Murderer [or] Killer," "The Overweight Juliet," "Martha Jule Carmen," "Martha Martin," "Martha Fernandez")

Born May 6, 1920, in Florida. Executed March 8, 1951. Nurse, confidence woman. Illinois, Long Island, New York, Michigan; 4 murders (1 conviction); drugs, ligature strangulation; gun, drowning, bludgeon (hammer); August 1948–March 1949.

"The prison and the death house have only strengthened my feelings for Raymond and in the history of the world how many crimes can be attributed to love. My last words and my last thoughts are 'He who is without sin cast the first stone.'"—Beck in a statement issued shortly before her execution; see also Fernandez, Raymond Martinez.

Bembenek, Lawrencia
(a.k.a. "Bambi," "Jennifer Lee Gazzana")

Born circa 1951. Ex–police officer, aerobics instructor, Playboy Club bunny. Milwaukee, Wisconsin; 1 murder; .38 caliber pistol; May 28, 1981.

Film: Used Innocence (US, 1988), a 95-minute 16mm, color documentary directed by James Benning and distributed by First Run Features, was shown at the Berlin Film Festival on February 10–21, 1989, and opened in New York City on February 22, 1989. Cast includes Jean Milner (Laurie Bembenek), Dick Blau (Narrator), and the voices of James Benning and Lawrencia Bembenek.

Television: Calendar Girl, Cop, Killer? The Bambi Bembenek Story (1992), a two-hour made-for-television movie, originally aired on ABC on May 18, 1992. Cast includes Lindsay Frost (Lawrencia "Bambi" Bembenek) and Timothy Busfield (Elfred Schultz).

Ex-cop and *Playboy* bunny convicted of the murder of her husband's ex-wife who won folk hero stature and freedom following a highly publicized prison break. Lawrencia Bembenek, a 22-year-old probationary officer on the Milwaukee Police Department, was fired in August 1980 on suspicion of smoking dope. While working as an aerobics instructor and *Playboy* bunny, Bembenek met Elfred Schultz, Jr., a 33-year-old police detective recently divorced from his wife, Christine Jean. The financially strapped Schultz, in addition to paying the monthly mortgage payment on the house occupied by his ex-wife, also paid child support for his two sons, aged eleven and seven. After the detective married Bembenek, money became so tight that they considered moving to a cheaper apartment. In the early hours of May 28, 1981, an intruder entered Jean Schultz's southside Milwaukee home, bound and gagged the woman, and fired a fatal .38 caliber shot into her back which pierced her heart. The children later told police that the intruder had worn a green jogging suit. Bembenek was arrested on June 24, 1981, after several incriminating items were located in her apartment building including a green jogging suit and a wig found flushed down a toilet. Hairs in the wig were subsequently found to be similar to synthetic hairs collected at the murder scene. At trial, ballistics tied the fatal bullet to Elfred Schultz's off-duty revolver. He had an alibi; Bembenek did not. Arguing that Bembenek had killed the woman in order to terminate the monthly financial drain on her husband, the prosecution won a first degree murder conviction against her on March 9, 1982. Bembenek was sentenced to life imprisonment at Taycheeda Correctional Institution near Fond du Lac, Wisconsin. Schultz and Bembenek divorced in June 1984.

Bembenek continued to maintain her innocence and found several supporters who felt the state had convicted her on highly suspect circumstantial evidence. Two appeals had failed when Bembenek, aided by her fiancé Dominic Gugliatto, escaped from Taycheeda on July 15, 1990. The beauty's prison break captured the public's imagination. In Milwaukee, rallies were held celebrating the escape. Restaurants featured "Bembenek Burgers" while street vendors hawked "Run, Bambi, Run" tee-shirts. "Bambi" Bembenek and Gugliatto remained at large for three months until a segment on the television program "America's Most Wanted" led to their capture on October 17, 1990, in Thunder Bay, Ontario, Canada, where she was working as a waitress under the name "Jennifer Lee Gazzana." Bembenek's application for refugee status based on the claim that she was a victim of persecution was sympathetically received by the Canadian government. A tribunal convened and heard testimony from a Canadian forensic expert who insisted that the handgun used to convict Bembenek could not have been the murder weapon. A top polygraph expert further testified that based on two days of lie detector tests with the fugitive he was convinced of Bembenek's innocence. Sensing that public opinion was now on her side, Bembenek gave up her claim of refugee status on February 29, 1992. She returned to Milwaukee and cooperated in a "John Doe" investigation, a formal inquiry conducted by a judge to determine whether a crime has been committed. Based on compelling new evidence, an agreement was reached between Bembenek's counsel and the Milwaukee County prosecutor's office. The first degree murder conviction was thrown out and replaced by a charge of second degree murder. Bembenek pleaded *nolo contendere*, a plea which allowed her to maintain her innocence. On December 9, 1992, a Chicago judge sentenced Bembenek to 20 years in prison, but because she had already served nearly 11 years, the 34-year-old was immediately released on parole.

15. Bembenek, Lawrencia. *Born Under Saturn: The Art of Lawrencia Bembenek.* Milwaukee, Wis.: UWM Art Museum, 1992. 1 v. (unpaged): ill.; 22 × 28 cm.

Catalog of an exhibition held at the Art History Gallery, University of Wisconsin–Milwaukee, May 6–22, 1992.

16. _____. *Woman on Trial.* 1st ed. Toronto: HarperCollins, 1992. 351 pp., [8]pp. of plates: ill.; 25 cm.

_____. [Same as 16.] 1st pbk. ed. Toronto: HarperCollins, 1992. 360 pp., [8]pp. of plates: ill., ports.; 18 cm.; paperback.

_____. [Same as 16.] New York: Harper-Paperbacks, 1992. 360 pp., [8]pp. of plates: ill.; 18 cm.; paperback.

Bembenek maintains her innocence in a frank account of the case published before her parole.

17. Radish, Kris. *Run, Bambi, Run: The Beautiful Ex-Cop and Convicted Murderer Who Escaped to Freedom and Won America's Heart.* New York: Carol, 1992. xi, 291 pp.: ill.; 24 cm. ("A Birch Lane Press book.")

A Wisconsin journalist's account based on court transcripts, police reports, and interviews with the main participants including Bembenek.

18. Roddick, Bill. *The Thirteenth Juror: At the Lawrencia Bembenek Trial; Questions Left Unanswered.* Milwaukee, Wis.: Tech/Data Publications, 1982. 96 pp.: ill.; 23 cm.

19. _____, and Korotko, Robin. *After the Verdict: A History of the Lawrencia Bembenek Case.* Milwaukee, Wis.: Composition House, 1990. 224 pp., [16]pp. of plates: ill.; 21 cm.

Bennett, Herbert John
(a.k.a. "Yarmouth Beach Murderer," "W.A. Phillips," "H.J. Bartlett")

Born circa 1880 in Gravesend, Kent, England. Executed March 21, 1901. Former greengrocer, salesman. Yarmouth, England; 1 murder; ligature strangulation (bootlace); September 22, 1900.

"No confession."—Bennett's reply to prison officials when asked on the day of his execution if he had any statement to make

Twenty-year-old opportunist who strangled his wife to death on Yarmouth Beach in 1900. Herbert John Bennett was nearly 17 years old when he married his 20-year-old music teacher Mary Jane Clarke in 1897. The pair supported themselves by selling fake violins and later sewing machines on commission. By the beginning of 1900 when Bennett met Alice Meadows, an attractive parlormaid in Bayswater, his relationship with Mrs. Bennett had soured to the point that they were living separate lives in separate dwellings. Hiding the fact that he was already the married father of an infant, Bennett began a relationship with Meadows that he promised would end in marriage. On her husband's suggestion, Mrs. Bennett with her child travelled to Yarmouth on a vacation in mid–September 1900. The woman checked into a roominghouse there under the alias "Mrs. Hood" where the landlady noted that she was wearing an impressive gold chain. Bennett joined his wife on September 22, 1900, and strangled her to death with a mohair bootlace as they walked together along an isolated stretch of beach. Her body was found the next day, her clothes disarranged to suggest a sex crime, the gold chain missing, and the bootlace still knotted tightly around her neck. By this time "Mrs. Hood" had been reported missing by the landlady who also produced a photograph of the dead woman taken days earlier by a beach photographer in which she was wearing the gold chain. Further clues were provided by an examination of the victim's clothing which revealed the laundry mark "599" on some of the items.

Bennett wasted little time in "courting" Meadows, giving the parlormaid some of his wife's jewelry and clothes. Scotland Yard was called in and traced the "599" mark to a laundry in Bexley Heath frequented by Mrs. Bennett. Soon after the discovery, authorities made the connection between "Mrs. Hood" and Mrs. Bennett. Herbert John Bennett was arrested in Woolwich on November 6, 1900. A search of his lodgings revealed the gold chain worn by his wife on the day of her murder and other clothes bearing the telltale "599" laundry mark. The trial, moved from Yarmouth to London's Old Bailey because of local outrage against Bennett, began on February 25, 1901. Four days later a jury convicted Bennett of murder after a 35-minute deliberation. Protesting his innocence, the "Yarmouth Beach Murderer" was sentenced to death and hanged at Norwich Gaol on March 21,

1901. Ironically, on July 14, 1912, the body of another young woman (Dora May Gray) was found strangled with a bootlace in the exact location on Yarmouth Beach where Mrs. Bennett had been murdered almost 12 years before.

20. Wallace, Edgar, ed. *The Trial of Herbert John Bennett (The Yarmouth Beach Murder).* Famous Trials Series. London: G. Bles, 1929. 216 pp., [5] leaves of plates: ill., ports.; 22 cm.
 Entry in the Famous Trial Series edited and with an introduction by Wallace.

Benson, Steven Wayne

 Born July 26, 1951, in Baltimore, Maryland. Businessman, entrepreneur. Naples, Florida; 2 murders; pipe bomb; July 9, 1985.
 "This is a terrible ordeal for my family and me, but I am confident I have the strength to make it through. I feel overwhelming grief over the loss of my mother and my brother and for the suffering of my sister. I am frustrated and angry over the fact that I am under arrest for a crime I did not commit."—Benson's statement to the press read by his attorney on August 30, 1985
 Tobacco heir convicted of the pipe bomb deaths of two family members in order to claim a larger portion of the inheritance. On the morning of July 9, 1985, the exclusive Quail Creek subdivision of Naples, Florida, was rocked by an explosion in the driveway of 13002 White Violet Drive, the $300,000 residence of 63-year-old tobacco heiress Margaret H. Benson. Next in line for the $400 million fortune amassed by her father Harry Hitchcock, founder of the Lancaster Leaf Tobacco Company, the widowed Benson commanded

a personal estate valued at $10 million. Accompanied by her two children, 21-year-old adopted son Scott Roland Benson and visiting 40-year-old daughter Carol Lynn Benson Kendall, the heiress planned to visit some nearby family real estate at the urging of her other son, 34-year-old Steven Wayne Benson. As his family prepared to leave in a 1978 Chevrolet Suburban passenger wagon, Steven Benson ran back to the house to get a tape measure. Scott turned the key in the car's ignition detonating two bombs which threw debris 200 feet into the air. He was killed instantly as was Margaret Benson. Carol Kendall, just getting into the back seat, was thrown clear from the flaming wreckage by the first blast, but suffered severe burns over 30 percent of her body including her face. Investigators determined that the deadly explosions had been caused by two 27-pound pipe bombs filled with black gunpowder hidden in the car's console and under the back seat.
 The spectacular murder of two members of the prestigious Benson clan revealed the darkest secrets of the troubled family in a blaze of sensationalized media coverage bordering on soap opera. One local Naples television station carried an hour-long show entitled "The Benson Chronicles" each day of the proceedings. It was reported that Scott Benson, an aspiring tennis pro, had a history of violent behavior against his mother and chronic drug use involving cocaine and nitrous oxide (laughing gas). Carol Kendall, in a startling revelation, confessed that "brother" Scott was in reality her illegitimate son born when she was an unmarried 19-year-old. The young man was never told. To spare the family name, Margaret Benson adopted

the child and raised it as her own. Like his half-brother, Steven Wayne Benson also enjoyed the material advantages provided by great wealth. A pampered, but emotionally deprived child, Benson excelled in electronics and by age ten had built a television set and an elevator to his tree house. He later installed security systems in the houses owned by his family. In 1969, Benson enrolled in Franklin and Marshall College, but dropped out three times before quitting in his sophomore year. For the next 16 years, Benson drifted aimlessly through a variety of jobs either connected with the family business or bankrolled by his mother. Between 1981 and 1985 she financed at least a dozen businesses in the Naples-Fort Myers, Florida, area that her son started, then abandoned.

On August 22, 1985, Benson was arrested and charged with two counts of first degree murder and one count of attempted murder after police found his finger and palm print on a receipt from a Naples plumbing supply company for two foot-long sections of galvanized steel pipe and caps. Benson pleaded innocent to all charges and stood trial in Fort Myers in July 1986. Carol Benson Kendall, the lone survivor of the blast, testified that on the day of the bombing Steven had used the Chevy Suburban, rather than his own car, to pick up doughnuts from a nearby bakery. While the trip should have taken a few minutes, he did not return for an hour. After the explosion, Kendall stated that Benson did nothing to help her. The prosecution presented Margaret Benson's attorney-business consultant to establish that Steven Benson's motive for murder was his fear of being dropped from his mother's will. He testified that the day before the bombing, mother and son had engaged in "heated discussions" over Benson's possible misappropriation of funds from the companies he managed using her money. Earlier in the year, Margaret Benson had given her son two blank checks to meet a business payroll. He filled in the checks for a total of $60,000 and used the money as a down payment on a house in Fort Myers. According to the prosecution, Benson stood only to gain from the deaths of his family. Rather than sharing a third of the $10 million estate with co-heirs Scott Benson and Carol Kendall, Benson would now halve the inheritance with his surviving sister. As a defense, Benson's attorney argued that one of Scott Benson's drug connections had committed the crime.

Benson was found guilty of all counts on August 7, 1986, and, following the jury's recommendation, a judge sentenced Benson on September 2, 1986, to two consecutive life terms. According to the terms of the sentence, Benson must serve 25 years on each conviction, a total of 50 years, before being considered eligible for parole. The ex-heir also received an additional 22 years for attempted murder and explosives charges. With credit for 377 days already served in jail, Benson will be 84 when first eligible for parole. His request for a new trial was denied on September 23, 1986, and on May 20, 1988, a Florida court of appeals upheld all convictions against him. Benson scored his only legal victory in September 1989 when an appeals court upheld a lower court's ruling that his three children were entitled to their part of their grandmother's $10 million estate. After taxes and legal fees his children will share almost $2 million.

21. Andersen, Christopher P. *The Serpent's Tooth*. 1st ed. New York: Harper & Row, 1987. 246 pp., [16]pp. of plates: ill.; 24 cm.

_____. [Same as 21.] 1st St. Martin's mass market ed. New York: St. Martin's Press, 1988. 246 pp., [16]pp. of plates: ill.; 18 cm.; paperback.

Minor account of the sensational case written by a senior editor of *People Weekly*.

22. Greenya, John. *Blood Relations*. 1st ed. San Diego: Harcourt Brace Jovanovich, 1987. xx, 358 pp., [32]pp. of plates: ill.; 24 cm.

Greenya, who covered the trial for the *Washington Post*, cut a deal with blast survivor and the state's star witness Carol Lynn Kendall who agreed to cooperate in exchange for an unspecified share of the royalties.

23. Mewshaw, Michael. *Money to Burn: The True Story of the Benson Family Murders*. New York: Atheneum, 1987. 406 pp., [8]pp. of plates: ill., ports.; 24 cm.

_____. [Same as 23.] New York: Pinnacle Books, 1988. 475 pp., [8]pp. of plates: ill., ports.; 18 cm.; paperback.

Superior account which takes issue with Carol Lynn Kendall's observations on the case which Mewshaw, unlike John Greenya, refused to purchase. Effectively shows how inaccurate media reporting was accepted in the trial transcript as fact.

24. Walton, Mary. *For Love of Money*. New York: Pocket Books, 1987. ix, 271 pp.: ports.; 17 cm.; paperback.

Bentley, Derek William

Born June 30, 1933, in Blackfriars, England. Executed January 28, 1953. Unemployed at time of arrest. Croydon, England; 1 murder; .45 caliber Colt revolver; November 2, 1952.

"Dad, I'm not afraid to die because I am innocent... Everybody knows I didn't kill Mr. Miles, so I've got nothing on my conscience."

A landmark case in the history of British law that marked the first time an accomplice in a murder (Bentley) was executed while the actual killer (Christopher Craig) was not. The 16-year-old Craig, in the company of Bentley, shot Police Constable Sidney George Miles to death during a foiled burglary attempt in Croydon on November 2, 1952. Bentley, a 19-year-old illiterate judged "mentally substandard" for national service, and Craig, also illiterate but with a gun fixation, were found guilty of first degree murder at London's Old Bailey on December 11, 1952. Though the jury recommended mercy for Bentley, the Lord Chief Justice sentenced him to death. Before sentencing the under-aged Craig to an indefinite period of detainment "at Her Majesty's pleasure," the judge pronounced him to be "the more guilty of the two." Bentley was hanged at Wandsworth Prison on January 28, 1953, amid outraged public protest. Craig is still imprisoned.

25. Bentley, William George. *My Son's Execution*. London: W.H. Allen, 1957. 175 pp.: ill.; 23 cm.

Bentley's father passionately maintains his son's innocence and protests his execution.

26. Hyde, H. Montgomery, ed. *Trial of Christopher Craig and Derek William Bentley*. Notable British Trials. London: William Hodge and Company Limited, 1954. xi, 263 pp.: ill., ports.; 22 cm.

Trial for the murder of Sidney George Miles, held at the Central Criminal Court, Old Bailey, London, Dec. 9–11, 1952.

Berdella, Robert Andrew, Jr.

Born January 31, 1949, in Canton, Ohio. Died October 8, 1992. Flea market operator. Kansas City, Missouri; 6 murders; asphyxiation (plastic trash bag), torture, poison; July 1984–August 1987.

"I treated them as something less than human ... nothing more than a play toy or a play object."—Berdella in a 1989 television interview describing his attitude toward his victims

Homosexual sadist and serial killer apprehended when one of his intended victims escaped. On April 2, 1988, a meter reader working the Hyde Park section of midtown Kansas City, Missouri, encountered a frightened 22-year-old man wearing nothing but a dog collar. The victim, Christopher Bryson, told police that he had been picked up hitchhiking by Robert A. Berdella, a 39-year-old flea market operator, and taken to the man's home at 4315 Charlotte Street. There, he was drugged, stripped, tied to a bed, threatened by Berdella with death, and physically abused, sodomized, and tortured with electrical shocks for five days. After Berdella left the house for work on April 2, Bryson freed himself and escaped by jumping from a second floor window. Later that day, Berdella was arrested at his curio shop, Bob's Bazaar Bizarre, in the Westport area of Kansas City. A search of his Charlotte Street home yielded more than 200 photos of men being tortured (including Bryson), a diary in which he minutely chronicled the abuse of his victims, an electrical transformer, pornographic magazines, a recording of the Black Mass, and two skulls. Police expanded their search to the backyard where they unearthed a human head with skin, hair, teeth, and brain matter still attached. Pending murder charges, police held Berdella in the Bryson case on seven counts of sodomy and one count each of felonious restraint and first degree assault. Bond was set at $750,000.

Neighbors and friends of the quiet, genial shopkeeper were stunned. Berdella had lived in the area for 15 years and was an active member of the neighborhood crime watch association. Graduating from Cuyahoga Falls High School in northeastern Ohio in 1967, Berdella came to Kansas City the same year to study at the prestigious Kansas City Art Institute. Although a talented student, he dropped out after two years. An excellent cook, Berdella worked in several restaurants including the renowned University Club and Carriage Club, before opening his own flea market, Bob's Bazaar Bizarre. In his shop, located in the Old Westport Flea Market, Berdella carried a wide range of ancient and ethnic artifacts that included Roman glass and tear vials, terra cotta bowls, and other antiquities from Egypt, India, and southeast Asia. Berdella, however, was not unknown to Kansas City authorities who twice arrested him in 1969 on drug charges. One case was dropped for lack of evidence, but Berdella received a 5-year suspended sentence on the other. Berdella again became the object of police surveillance in 1984 when they responded to the complaint of the father of missing 19-year-old Gerald Howell. The father told police his son was last seen with Berdella, but investigators dropped the case when it turned up no leads. Howell was subsequently identified in one of the photos found in Berdella's home as the apparently dead man hanging by his ankles in the basement of 4315 Charlotte Street. In August 1987 Berdella received emergency treatment for a penile injury received during oral sex. In the police report he identified his sex partner as "Larry W. Person," a slight variation on the spelling of Larry W. Pearson, a 21-year-old Wichita, Kansas, man reported missing for over a year.

While Berdella languished in jail on a $750,000 bond and proclaimed his innocence on the sodomy and assault charges, police meticulously built a murder case against the shopkeeper. On May 10, 1988, X rays and dental records confirmed the skull retrieved from one of Berdella's bedroom closets was that of missing California man Robert A. Sheldon, 23. Sheldon was one of 22 men pictured in photos found in Berdella's house. Two days later, dental records identified the decomposed head found in Berdella's backyard as that of Larry W. Pearson, 21. Like fellow-victim Sheldon, Pearson too had lived in Berdella's house during his stay in Kansas City. On July 22, 1988, Berdella was indicted on a charge of first degree murder in the killing of Pearson sometime between June 7, 1987, and April 3, 1988. As the result of a plea bargain agreement reached between him and the state on August 3, 1988, Berdella pleaded guilty to Pearson's murder in exchange for a sentence of life in prison without the possibility of parole. Having escaped a possible death sentence, Berdella confessed that around August 5, 1987, he asphyxiated the bound Pearson by placing a plastic bag over his head and tying it off with a rope. On August 24, 1988, Berdella changed his plea in the Bryson sodomy and assault case and received sentences of life imprisonment and seven years, respectively.

Berdella was indicted for the murder of Robert Sheldon on September 2, 1988, and formally entered a plea of not guilty to the charge 11 days later. That November, Berdella's massive collection of over 2,000 ethnic and ancient artifacts which he amassed over a 20-year period of careful buying was auctioned off in a warehouse in Kansas City to help pay his legal fees. The second day of the auction, featuring items from the Berdella house, aroused the most public interest. The beds upon which the sadistic shopkeeper tortured and killed his victims were purchased by Del Dunmire, an eccentric Kansas City millionaire once convicted of robbing a bank in Abilene, Kansas. The two-day auction raised over $67,000 for Berdella's legal defense. On December 17, 1988, Berdella reached another agreement with the state. In exchange for their waiving the death penalty in favor of life imprisonment without the possibility of parole, Berdella agreed to confess to five other murders. Two days later in a packed Kansas City courtroom under tight security, Berdella provided chilling details surrounding the series of murders he committed from 1984 through 1986 which claimed the lives of Robert Sheldon, Gerald Howell, Todd Stoops, Mark Wallace, and Walter Ferris, 24. All the victims were under the age of 30 and voluntarily came to his house. Four (excluding Sheldon) were injected with animal tranquilizers, stripped, gagged, tied to a bed, then sodomized and tortured with an electrical device. Those that failed to die as a result of the chemical injections and gagging, were asphyxiated with a plastic bag secured around their necks with a rope. All the victims were dismembered, their body parts (with the exception of the two heads recovered from his property) wrapped in plastic bags, and put out for garbage collection. The first of the group to die was Jerry Howell on July 6, 1984, followed by Robert Sheldon on April 15, 1985, Mark Wallace on June 23, 1985, Walter Ferris on

September 27, 1985, and Todd Stoops on July 1, 1986. Stoops, held captive longer than any other victim (from June 17 through July 1, 1986), sustained a daily round of torture and rape from the sadist before dying from a combination of the injections, infection, and blood loss due to the continual insertion of Berdella's fist into his anus. Berdella offered no motives for his crimes other than hinting at "certain dark fantasies" that sometimes came to life and a nebulous feeling that he wanted revenge for abuses and mistreatment he had suffered from unnamed people.

In a January 2, 1989, television interview aired eight days later in Kansas City, Berdella criticized the press coverage of his case complaining that the media treated him as badly as he treated his victims. While he could not reduce his murderous actions to any single event in his life, the killer blamed police for failing to control crime in areas where prostitution flourished. If they had done their job, he reasoned, they could have "scared me off" and prevented some of the murders. In the same vein, Berdella berated the police description of his so-called "torture journal" as "meticulous, methodical diaries." According to him, they were just sheets of paper on which he noted the amount and times of the chemical injections he gave his victims as well as their reactions to the drugs and his sexual abuse. As an inmate of the Missouri Corrections Department, Berdella distinguished himself as a chronic complainer. In 1989 during one four-hour period at the state's Potosi facility, he filed 36 grievances prompting the assistant superintendent to write back, "You are a true bellyacher." On January 8, 1992, a Missouri court awarded the mother of Berdella victim

Todd Stoops $5 billion in one of the largest wrongful death suits ever litigated in the United States. The amount is to be paid from any monies received through the sale of the publication or film rights to the serial killer's story. Berdella, 43, was found dead from an apparent heart attack in his cell in the Missouri State Penitentiary on October 8, 1992.

27. Jackman, Tom, and Cole, Troy. *Rites of Burial.* New York: Windsor, 1992. 368 pp., [16]pp. of plates: ill.; 18 cm.; paperback.

A solid collaboration between Jackman, a local investigative journalist, and Cole, a sergeant in the Kansas City Police Department's homicide unit and the chief investigating officer on the Berdella case. Contains lengthy excerpts from Berdella's detailed confessions and 16 pages of some of the most graphic photos ever published in a case history.

Berkowitz, David
(a.k.a. "Son of Sam," ".44-Caliber Killer," "Mr. Monster," "Richard David Falco" [birth name], "Wolf" [army nickname])

Born June 1, 1953, in Brooklyn, New York. Post office letter sorter. New York City area; 6 murders; .44 caliber pistol; July 1976–August 1977.

Television: "Out of the Darkness" (1985), a two-hour, made-for-television movie, first aired on CBS on October 12, 1985. Cast includes Martin Sheen (Ed Zigo) and Robert Trebor (David Berkowitz).

"Sam's a thirsty lad. He won't let me stop killing until he gets his fill of blood."—The "Son of Sam," in a letter to newspaper columnist Jimmy Breslin

Infamous "Son of Sam" killer who

stalked the New York metropolitan area for one year and twelve days during 1976 and 1977. The illegitimate son of a woman who gave him up at birth, Berkowitz was a withdrawn child whose behavior became more aberrant as he matured. As a youth the pudgy child tortured animals, feeding bits of cleaning powder to his adoptive mother's parakeet until it died. From his teen years on Berkowitz channeled his aggression through pyromania. When authorities finally arrested Berkowitz they found notebooks in his cluttered apartment in which he minutely detailed some 1,411 fires he set in the New York City area. By November 1975 Berkowitz was experiencing auditory hallucinations in which the disembodied voices in his head took on the form of screaming dogs. Holed up for weeks in his apartment in Yonkers, Berkowitz fixated on a black Labrador retriever owned by a neighbor in the next block. In his full blown paranoia, Berkowitz now believed the dog was the agent of a 6,000-year-old demon named Sam who issued his murderous instructions to him through the animal's continual barking. In the early morning of July 29, 1976, Berkowitz placed his five shot .44 caliber Charter Arms Bulldog revolver into a paper bag and drove to the Bronx. Donna Lauria, 18, and Jody Valenti, 19, were parked in front of Lauria's house when Berkowitz walked up, crouched into a firing position, and emptied his revolver into the car. Valenti sustained a thigh wound, but Lauria was killed instantly.

On October 23, 1976, Rosemary Keenan, the 18-year-old daughter of a New York City police detective, and her friend Carl Denaro, 20, were parked outside of Keenan's house in Queens. Berkowitz quietly approached the pair and fired five rounds. Denaro, struck once in the head, survived. Keenan was uninjured. Berkowitz next struck in Queens on November 27, 1976. Donna DeMasi, 16, and Joanne Lomino, 18, were walking up the front steps of Lomino's house shortly after midnight when two shots rang out. DeMasi sustained a flesh wound, but the other shot shattered Lomino's spine, paralyzing her for life. Berkowitz welcomed in the New Year by driving to the Forest Hills section of Queens in the early morning of January 30, 1977. Thirty-year-old John Diel and his 26-year-old fiancée Christine Freund were parked when Berkowitz walked up and shot the woman twice in the head and neck. Freund died ten minutes later at the hospital. Diel was unharmed. Authorities, recognizing that they were dealing with a serial killer, established a task force on February 2, 1977. Ballistics tied the cases together as did the killer's victim of choice: beautiful young women with long dark hair. Still the killings continued. On March 8, 1977, Virginia Voskerichian, a 21-year-old student at Columbia, was walking down a street in the Forest Hills section of Queens when Berkowitz shot her in the mouth, killing her instantly. Berkowitz moved to the Bronx for a double murder on April 17, 1977. Alexander Esau, 20, and Valentina Suriani, 18, were parked when Berkowitz walked up and shot them both to death. Berkowitz left a scribbled letter at the scene addressed to the head of the task force. In it, he identified himself as the "Son of Sam" and signalled his intention to continue prowling the streets in search of "fair game." In June 1977 Berkowitz also wrote to *Daily News* columnist Jimmy Breslin intimating that the killings would continue.

On June 25, 1977, Judy Placido, 17, and Salvatore Lupo were parked in Queens when four shots exploded the windshield of their car. Both were wounded, but survived. On July 30, 1977, Robert Violante, 20, and his date Stacy Moskowitz, 20, were parked in Brooklyn when Berkowitz approached and squeezed off three rounds. Moskowitz, struck once in the head, died 38 hours later in a hospital. Violante, shot twice in the face, lost his right eye, but survived with permanent partial blindness in the other. On this murder, however, the "Son of Sam" was careless. A woman walking her dog near the scene saw Berkowitz get into his 1970 Ford Galaxie and drive off. She notified police three days later and when pressed remembered that officers had ticketed several cars in the area that day for parking violations. When a record check revealed that Berkowitz's car had been ticketed, police staked out his apartment on Pine Street in Yonkers. In Berkowitz's car parked outside the building police saw a bag of weapons in plain view on the backseat. The "Son of Sam" was arrested at 10:00 p.m. on August 10, 1977, as he opened the door of his car. "Well, you got me!" was his only reaction.

Berkowitz's bizarre pathology made him an outstanding candidate for a legal defense based on insanity. Initially examined by a team of three psychiatrists, Berkowitz was declared to be legally insane and unfit to stand trial. The district attorney, however, had the judgment set aside and engaged psychiatrist Dr. David Abrahamsen to examine Berkowitz. While Abrahamsen found that Berkowitz possessed paranoid traits, he declared they would not interfere with his ability to stand trial. Berkowitz was subsequently declared legally sane prompt-

ing his attorneys to change his not guilty by reason of insanity plea to guilty. On June 12, 1978, Berkowitz was sentenced to six consecutive 25-year-to-life sentences (one for each murder). In February 1979, Berkowitz called a press conference in Attica and announced that his stories about demons were fabrications that he invented to condone the murders, a claim discounted by many psychiatrists who believe that he did suffer from pronounced delusions. On July 10, 1979, Berkowitz had his throat slashed by an unidentified inmate while delivering water in Attica to segregated prisoners. The near fatal wound required 60 stitches to close. Berkowitz refused to identify his attacker. In his first interview in 16 years, Berkowitz told journalist Maury Terry in November 1993 that a satanic cult pushed him into the murders and even helped him commit some. "Our goal was to create havoc, lawlessness, create fear, to bring chaos to the city. We did succeed, tragically, in bringing the City of New York to its knees," Berkowitz said.

28. Abrahamsen, David. *Confessions of Son of Sam*. New York: Columbia University Press, 1985. xiv, 245 pp.; 24 cm.

Abrahamsen, the psychiatrist engaged by the prosecution who determined Berkowitz was mentally fit for trial, was contacted by the killer one month after his February 1979 news conference in which he admitted inventing the story about the demons. At Berkowitz's request, Abrahamsen made several trips to Attica to interview the "Son of Sam."

29. Breslin, Jimmy, and Schaap, Dick. *.44*. New York: Viking Press, 1978. vii, 323 pp.; 24 cm.

Fictionalized account of the case.

30. Carpozi, George. *Son of Sam: The .44-Caliber Killer*. New York: Manor Books, 1977. 320 pp.: ill.; 18 cm.; paperback.

The earliest and most sensational account of "Son of Sam" by a reporter for the *New York Post*.

31. Klausner, Lawrence D. *Son of Sam: Based on the Authorized Transcription of the Tapes, Official Documents and Diaries of David Berkowitz*. New York: McGraw-Hill, 1981. xi, 430 pp., [30] leaves of plates: ill.; 24 cm.

Meticulous account which reproduces facsimiles of Berkowitz's diaries, notes, and letters written after his capture. Includes index.

32. Terry, Maury. *The Ultimate Evil: An Investigation into America's Most Dangerous Satanic Cult*. 1st ed. Garden City, N.Y.: Doubleday, 1987. xiii, 512 pp., [8]pp. of plates: ill., ports.; 24 cm. ("A Dolphin book.")

_____. [Same as 32 with variant subtitle: *An Investigation into a Dangerous Satanic Cult*.] Bantam ed. New York: Bantam, 1989. xiii, 640 pp., [16]pp. of plates: ill., ports.; 18 cm.; paperback.

Terry's provocative book maintains that Berkowitz was a triggerman for a satanic cult called the Process. Fascinating, essential study based on extensive research.

33. Thompson, Doris V. *Horoscope of Murder: A Study of David Berkowitz "Son of Sam."* Tempe, Ariz.: American Federation of Astrologers, 1980. 187 pp.: ill., charts; 23 cm.

Astrologist Thompson, author of *Chart Your Own Stars*, charts Berkowitz's horoscope and links his various attacks to the movement of the planets.

34. Willeford, Charles. *Off the Wall: A True Life Novel*. Montclair, N.J.: Pegasus Rex Press, 1980. x, 277 pp.: ill.; 23 cm.

Fictionalized account of the case.

Bianchi, Kenneth Alessio
(a.k.a. "Hillside Strangler,"
"Steve Walker," "Billy," "Ish,"
"Anthony A. D'Amato,"
"Nicholas Fontana")

Born circa May 1951 in Rochester, New York. Security guard. Glendale, California, and Bellingham, Washington; ligature strangulation, asphyxiation; 7 murders (convictions, suspected of an additional 5); October 17, 1977–January 11, 1979.

Television: "The Case of the Hillside Stranglers" (1989), a two-hour, made-for-television movie based on Darcy O'Brien's book *Two of a Kind: The Hillside Stranglers*, originally aired on NBC on April 2, 1989. Cast includes Billy Zane (Kenneth Bianchi), Dennis Farina (Angelo Buono), and Richard Crenna (Det. Bob Grogan). "The Mind of a Murderer," a two-hour segment of the PBS television program "Frontline" produced and directed by Michael Barnes, originally aired on March 19, 1984. The program is also available on videocassette from PBS Video.

Audio: Two of a Kind: The Hillside Stranglers, a two-sound cassette, three-hour abridgement of Darcy O'Brien's book of the same title, was published in 1990 by Audio Renaissance Tapes (Los Angeles).

"When the Lord is ready to release me to the streets, He'll open the doors. I have absolute faith in Him."—Bianchi, shortly after his 1989 conversion to Christianity, commenting on his parole chances

On January 11, 1979, the bodies of two Western Washington University coeds, Karen Mandic and Diane Wilder, were found stuffed in the trunk of Mandic's car in Bellingham, Washington. Police, reconstructing the victims' last hours, found that Mandic was last seen alive on the way to check out an overnight housesitting job recommended to her by Kenneth Alessio Bianchi, a 27-year-old security guard whose company was employed to watch the house. Police followed up the connection and their search of Bianchi's home yielded numerous items stolen from houses he was paid to watch. A forensic team scoured the Bellingham house Mandic was planning to housesit and recovered pubic hairs from the front stairs later identified as Bianchi's. In custody, Bianchi initially denied any involvement in the killings, but later under hypnosis confessed to the raping and strangling both of the women in the empty house. More importantly, Bianchi's confession implicated him and his adoptive cousin Angelo Buono, Jr., a 45-year-old car upholsterer living in Glendale, California, in the so-called "Hillside Stranglings," a string of ten murders committed in Southern California between October 1977 and February 1978. During that period, ten women (some prostitutes and runaways) between the ages of 12 and 28 had been abducted, raped, strangled, and their naked bodies dumped on hillsides and along roads in the Los Angeles area. In each instance, the victims bore ligature marks on their necks, wrists, and ankles. Under hypnosis, Bianchi attempted to feign multiple personalities revealing a bad personality named "Steve Walker" who claimed credit for the murders. After psychiatrists determined that Bianchi was faking, the killer cut a deal with Washington authorities and the Los Angeles district attorney's office on October 19, 1978. Under the terms of the plea bargain arrangement, Bianchi agreed to admit to killing the two Bellingham women and five of the ten "Hillside Strangler" murders and to testify against his cousin Angelo Buono. In return, prosecutors agreed not to seek the death penalty against him. Bianchi was subsequently con-

victed on seven counts of first degree murder.

Transported to California, Bianchi provided details to his association with Angelo Buono and their deadly partnership. Failing to become a police officer in his native town of Rochester, New York, Bianchi moved to Los Angeles in 1976 and roomed with Buono in the car upholsterer's suburban Glendale home at 703 E. Colorado Street. A violent sexual sadist, Buono ran a small time prostitution ring and was well known for roughing up his prostitutes. During 1977, one of Buono's prostitutes burned him on a business deal. Vowing revenge, Buono and Bianchi tried to track down the woman. Failing, they abducted her friend, 20-year-old prostitute Yolanda Washington, on October 17, 1977. The pair drove Washington back to Buono's house in Glendale where they took turns raping her before strangling her to death with a towel. Afterwards, they dumped her naked body in an empty lot near Forest Lawn Cemetery where it was found the next day. In the ensuing four month period, the pair refined their murderous technique, often posing as police officers and flashing badges to lure women into their car. In each instance, the victim was then taken to Buono's house, raped, tortured, then strangled to death. The last victim, 20-year-old student Cindy Lee Hudspeth, was murdered on February 17, 1978. Her body was found in the trunk of her car at the bottom of a cliff in the Angeles National Forest.

While waiting in the Los Angeles County Jail to testify against Buono, Bianchi struck up a correspondence with Veronica Lyn Compton, a 24-year-old aspiring playwright with a taste for the bizarre. At Bianchi's urging, Compton attempted to commit a "copy cat" murder that would show authorities that the real "Hillside Strangler" was still at large. On September 19, 1980, Compton posed as a pregnant woman and lured Kim Breed, a cocktail waitress, into a motel room in Bellingham, Washington. Compton attempted to strangle Breed to death with a rope, but the woman broke free and notified authorities. Convicted of attempted murder on March 20, 1981, Compton was sentenced to life in prison. On July 27, 1988, Compton escaped from the Correctional Center for Women in Purdy, Washington, but was recaptured on August 5 as she was leaving an apartment complex in Tucson, Arizona.

In pre-trial hearings conducted in July 1981, Bianchi disavowed his confession, then later described in detail how the killings were done. Convinced that Bianchi had destroyed his credibility as a witness against Buono, the Los Angeles district attorney's office tried to drop the ten murder counts against the car upholsterer. Superior Court Judge Ronald George refused to let the prosecution dismiss the charges stating that the evidence against Buono was strong enough to go to a jury. The L.A. district attorney subsequently turned the case over to the office of the state attorney general for prosecution. In what would be the longest and costliest trial (estimated at $1.5 million) in California history up to that time, jury selection began in Los Angeles on November 16, 1981, and took three months to complete. Bianchi testified for 80 straight court days and admitted that he faked a multiple personality in 1979 to help establish an insanity defense on the murder charges. In bloodcurdling detail, Bianchi told of helping Buono abduct 20-year-old art student Kristina Weck-

ler on November 19, 1977. Weckler was taken to Buono's house where she was raped, then gassed to death by having a plastic bag placed over her head and a gas pipe inserted into it. Physical evidence and witnesses also tied Buono to the murders. Carpet fibers found on two of the victims matched those taken from Buono's house. Catharine Lorre, daughter of the late actor Peter Lorre, testified that she had been approached by the pair posing as police officers in North Hollywood. One witness told of seeing the pair trying to force a woman into a car. Two years after the start of the trial which produced 56,000 transcript pages, over 400 witnesses, and 2,000 exhibits, a jury in November 1982 found Buono guilty on nine of the ten counts of murder (excluding Yolanda Washington). Buono was subsequently sentenced to nine concurrent life terms without the possibility of parole. Bianchi received five concurrent life sentences.

Noting that Bianchi had failed to testify truthfully and completely against Buono as per his plea agreement, Judge Ronald George sent the killer back to the state of Washington to serve his sentences. In protective custody at the Washington State Penitentiary in Walla Walla, Bianchi has continued to make news. In 1985, he changed his name first to "Anthony A. D'Amato" then to "Nicholas Fontana" in order to "protect his life in prison." On November 5, 1987, Bianchi filed a multi-million dollar suit in federal court against Darcy O'Brien charging that the author's book on the case, *Two of a Kind: The Hillside Stranglers*, contained gross inaccuracies. The case was dismissed in September 1988 following a judge's ruling that Bianchi already had a "tarnished reputation" and was therefore "libel proof." In March 1989,

Bianchi announced that he was a "born again" Christian and six months later married his pen pal, 36-year-old Shirlee Joyce Book, in a September 21 ceremony conducted in the prison chapel. According to prison policy, he can apply for conjugal visitation rights. In December 1992, Bianchi filed a $2 million suit against Eclipse Comics, the creator of "True Crime" trading cards, arguing that a caricature of him on card number 106 represented an unfair commercial use of his name. The case had not been settled at the time of this writing.

35. *Mind of a Murderer.* "Frontline"; vol. 206. Boston: WGBH Transcripts, 1984. 2 pts.; 22 cm.; paper covers.

Transcript of the "Frontline" television program of March 19, 1984.

36. O'Brien, Darcy. *Two of a Kind: The Hillside Stranglers.* New York: New American Library, 1985. xxiv, 418 pp.; 24 cm.

_____. [Same as 36.] New York: New American Library, 1987. xxiv, 423 pp., [8]pp. of plates: ill., ports.; 18 cm.; paperback.

_____. [Same as 36.] Updated ed. New York: New American Library, 1989. xxiv, 435 pp., [8]pp. of plates: ill.; 18 cm. ("A Signet book"); paperback.

Definitive treatment of the case.

37. Schwarz, Ted. *The Hillside Strangler: A Murderer's Mind.* 1st ed. Garden City, N.Y.: Doubleday, 1981. 255 pp.; 22 cm.

_____. [Same as 37.] New York: New American Library, 1982. 274 pp.; 18 cm. ("A Signet book"); paperback.

Schwarz was duped by Bianchi's "multiple personality" hoax.

"Bible John"

Unknown. Glasgow, Scotland; 3 murders; manual and ligature strangu-

lation (victims' underwear); August 16, 1969–October 31, 1969.

Television: "Dancing with Death," part of an episode of the Granada-produced true-crime television series "In Suspicious Circumstances," aired March 16, 1993, on BBC2. It was narrated by Edward Woodward. In early March 1966, a television documentary entitled "Calling Bible John: Portrait of a Serial Killer," which was directed by Sarah Barclay, was broadcast on Channel 4 in Glasgow, Scotland. The documentary was based on a chapter in Scottish writer Andrew O'Hagan's book, *Missing Persons*, published in 1995.

Unknown and unapprehended serial killer of three women in Glasgow, Scotland, over a 20-month period in the late 1960s. Nicknamed "Bible John" because he made biblical references while in the company of a victim's friend, the killer followed a rigid *modus operandi.* The nicely dressed, clean cut man selected all three of his victims from Glasgow's Barrowland Ballroom, won their confidence over an evening of dancing, then later strangled each either manually or with their underwear. None of the victims were sexually assaulted although each was menstruating at the time of her death. The largest manhunt in the history of Glasgow featured over 300 identification parades, undercover police officers posted in the dance hall, and even the cooperation of famed Dutch clairvoyant Gerard Croiset. Every investigative approach to date has proved unsuccessful and the case remains open. In March 1993 BBC2 presented a reconstruction of the murders in an episode of the Granada produced true-crime television series "In Suspicious Circumstances." George Puttock, the husband of Bible John victim Helen Puttock, lodged a protest with the Broadcasting Complaints Commission contending that the program was "an unwarranted infringement of privacy." The BCC agreed and Granada issued a statement apologizing to Mr. Puttock for causing him any distress.

38. Stoddardt, Charles N. *Bible John: Search for a Sadist.* Edinburgh: Paul Harris, 1980. ix, 153 pp., [8]pp. of plates: ill., ports.; 23 cm.

Documents well the intensive police manhunt for Bible John and concludes with the essay, "The Sadistic Murderer," by the late forensic psychiatrist Robert P. Brittain.

"Blackburn Baby Murder" *see* **Griffiths, Peter**

Blaikie, James Francis, Jr.

Born August 16, 1945, in Waltham, Massachusetts. Insurance agent. Brookline, Massachusetts; 1 murder (suspected in 2 others); .38 caliber revolver; January 14, 1975.

High living insurance agent (suspected in the "suicide" deaths of his mother and a business associate) subsequently convicted of first degree murder after authorities uncovered the mummified remains of a friend in the basement of his home. On August 14, 1973, the body of 64-year-old Alma Blaikie was found in the basement of her Waltham, Massachusetts, home by 27-year-old son James. Dead from an apparent self-inflicted .38 caliber gunshot wound to the back of the head, the woman left a suicide note which read, "I can't stand how I am anymore." James Blaikie, in an upstairs room at the time of the incident, reported not hearing the shot. Her death was ruled

a suicide and Blaikie used a portion of his $33,000 inheritance to purchase a luxurious home in the Fisher Hill area of Brookline, Massachusetts. On July 29, 1974, history seemed to repeat itself when 44-year-old insurance company executive Edwin Conant Bacon, a business associate of Blaikie's who shared offices with him, was found dead on the floor of his office in Boston. Under his body investigators found a suicide note which read, "I can't stand it anymore." An autopsy determined cyanide poisoning and Bacon's death was formally declared a suicide. The coincidental suicides of two individuals who knew Blaikie caused the Bacon family to suspect foul play. Their suspicions were confirmed several weeks later with the revelation that a short time before his death Edwin Bacon had replaced his family as the sole beneficiary on a $50,000 life insurance policy with James Blaikie. The FBI later determined that Bacon's signature had been forged on the document, but stopped short of identifying Blaikie (the sole co-signing witness) as the forger.

At the request of the Bacon family, Boston police began a background check on Blaikie. They quickly determined that the former volunteer treasurer of McGovern's Massachusetts Presidential Campaign Committee was living well beyond his means and was nearly $100,000 in debt. Unknown to authorities, Blaikie had borrowed close to $12,000 from Caesar David Dealt, a friend of his wife's who owned a successful auto repair shop. The men were friendly, but Dealt was concerned that Blaikie would be unable to repay him. On January 14, 1975, Dealt disappeared after meeting with Blaikie to discuss the loan. Questioned by detectives, Blaikie told them conflicting stories about his business relationship with the missing man. Financially destitute, Blaikie and his wife put their house up for sale and skipped town. On May 30, 1975, Blaikie was picked up in Phoenix, Arizona, and charged with two counts of armed robbery. Sentenced to 45 days in prison and a ten year probation after his release, Blaikie was out and living in Phoenix when arrested on September 20, 1975, on forgery and embezzlement charges stemming from the Bacon case. Blaikie was incarcerated in a Boston jail awaiting trial when the new owner of his house noticed a slight depression in the concrete floor of the basement. On November 24, 1975, authorities dug up the floor and found Dealt's mummified remains stuffed in a garbage bag filled with cement lime buried under a layer of coal to mask the smell of decomposition. The killer had mistakenly used concrete lime (a preservative) rather than quick lime which would have destroyed the body. Dealt had been shot once in the back of the head with a .38 caliber revolver.

Jury selection began in Dedham, Massachusetts, on August 10, 1975. Blaikie maintained that he killed Dealt in self defense after the garage owner threatened him over repayment of the loan. Afterwards, he panicked and hid the body. A procedural error resulted in a mistrial days later and Blaikie was retried in Fall River, Massachusetts, during the first week of November 1976. Blaikie's claim that he shot Dealt during a struggle on the floor of his home was refuted by a forensic expert who testified that the line of fire suggested the victim was standing upright at the time of the shot. Blaikie was convicted of first degree murder without the possibility of parole on November 20, 1976. A subsequent reinvesti-gation of his mother's death uncovered no new evidence to change the original ruling of suicide. In a civil court case brought by Bacon's family against the insurance company, the court ruled that "there was sufficient evidence to warrant a finding that Blaikie murdered Bacon." Blaikie's first wife subsequently divorced him and the convicted killer married a social worker in 1985. After serving 15 years, Blaikie can request a commutation of his sentence to second degree murder and, with good behavior, become eligible for parole (no further information on his case at the time of this writing).

39. Sonzski, William. *Fatal Ambition: Greed and Murder in New England.* New York: Penguin, 1991. 381 pp., [8]pp. of plates: ill.; 18 cm. ("An Onyx book"); paperback.

Freelance journalist Sonzski's ponderous account is marred by annoying melodrama and a lack of insight.

"Blazing Car Mystery [or] Murder" *see* Rouse, Alfred Arthur

Bonney, Thomas Lee (a.k.a. "Hitman," "Preacher," "Demian," "Viking," "Tom," "Tommy," "Dad," "Kathy," "Satan," "Mammy," "Bones")

Born June 12, 1943, in Virginia. Auto salvage dealer. Camden County, North Carolina; 1 murder; .22 caliber pistol; November 21, 1987.

Television: "Deadly Whispers" (1995), a two-hour, made-for television movie based on Ted Schwarz's book of the same title, originally aired on CBS on May 10, 1995. Cast includes Tony Danza (Tom Acton/Thomas Lee Bonney), Heather Tom (Kathy Acton), and Pamela Reed (Mrs. Acton).

"You're just a mortal. You don't know anything."—A statement uttered to a psychiatrist by one of Bonney's purported ten personalities during a session of hypnosis to determine if the alleged killer had a multiple personality disorder

"Demonically possessed" father who brutally murdered his teenaged daughter when he learned of her affair with a married man. The troubled relationship between Tom Bonney and his 19-year-old daughter Kathy reached its crisis in November 1987 with his discovery of a torrid letter she had written to a married lover. Kathy Carol Bonney disappeared on November 21, 1987. The next day her nude body was found on the bank of the Great Dismal Swamp Canal in Camden County, North Carolina. Shot 27 times in the face, neck, chest and legs with a .22 caliber pistol, her sweater and underwear were found nearby. While the position of the body suggested a sex crime, there was no evidence of intercourse. The extreme violence of the murder, however, suggested to police either the work of a lunatic or a jealous lover.

Bonney told investigators that on the day of Kathy's disappearance a man named "John" called his auto salvage business in Chesapeake, Virginia, wishing to sell a Chevy Blazer. Bonney, who wanted the car for his daughter, agreed to meet the man with Kathy at a nearby 7-Eleven. The last Bonney saw of Kathy she was leaving with "John" for a test drive. Unable to locate the man, authorities questioned Bonney more closely and were not satisfied by his answers. At their request, he was unable to produce either the Chevy Impala he drove to the 7-Eleven meeting or the .22 caliber pistol he admitted owning. Both, he claimed, had

been recently sold. On December 10, 1987, Bonney fled the area in a 30-foot mobile home bound for Florida. The same day, police located the bloodstained Impala and questioned Bonney's wife who related being handcuffed and violently raped by her husband shortly after he learned of Kathy's death. On December 15, 1987, Camden County issued a first degree murder warrant on the fugitive. Bonney's travels took him to New Jersey, Ohio, Florida, and Georgia before he was arrested in Indianapolis, Indiana, on January 31, 1988.

Bonney told North Carolina authorities that he "cracked" during an argument with Kathy over her married lover and the gun "just went off" during a moment of "temporary insanity." Shell casings for the 27 rounds were subsequently recovered from the gas tank of a wrecker formerly owned by Bonney. Prior to trial, a judge ordered that a psychiatric evaluation be conducted on Bonney to determine his competency to participate in his own defense. Under hypnosis, a defense psychiatrist uncovered ten separate personalities warring for control within Bonney. Constructed as a defense mechanism against his abusive father, Bonney's violent personalities ("Demian" and "Satan") were allegedly triggered by extreme stress and trauma. In hours of videotaped sessions with the psychiatrist, various alter-egos emerged from the hypnotized Bonney including "Satan" who boasted "I can do what I want to, when I want to. I control Tom."

Bonney pleaded not guilty by reason of insanity contending that he was "possessed" at the time of the murder by a personality which he could not control. In their opening statement on October 31, 1988, the prosecution claimed the diagnosis of multiple personality disorder was unreliable because Bonney had threatened to kill his family on several occasions. He was simply a jealously possessive father made homicidal by his daughter's affair with a married man. The jury viewed nearly 20 hours of Bonney's videotaped psychiatric sessions. In one, under hypnosis he claimed that his daughter was still alive and visiting him nightly in his cell. A state psychiatrist agreed that while Bonney may exhibit multiple personality disorder, he knew right from wrong at the time of the murder. Bonney was found guilty on November 25, 1988, and sentenced to death. The North Carolina Supreme Court overturned that sentence in 1991 when psychiatrists testified that Bonney suffered from multiple personality disorder. While awaiting resentencing at Raleigh's Central Prison, Bonney and convicted rapist James Stromer escaped on June 29, 1994. Bonney was recaptured on August 2, 1994, in Norfolk, Virginia, where he had gone to visit the graves of his mother and daughter.

40. Schwarz, Ted. *Deadly Whispers*. New York: St. Martin's Paperbacks, 1992. vi, 298 pp., [8]pp. of plates: ill., ports.; 18 cm.; paperback.

Brady, Ian Duncan
(a.k.a. "Ian Duncan Stewart" [real name], "Neddy," "Moors Murderer")

Born January 2, 1938, in Glasgow, Scotland. Stock clerk. Manchester, England, area; 5 murders (3 convictions); strangulation, gun, knife, hatchet; July 1963–October 1965.

"I've also given Mr. Topping details of 'happenings' but he doesn't seem interested in them, i.e. a man on a piece of wasteground near Picadilly (Manchester); a woman in a canal; a man in Glasgow, and another on the slopes of Loch Long, etc. (the latter two were shot at close range)."—Brady in an August 1987 letter to the BBC claiming that he had notified Senior Detective Peter Topping of the Greater Manchester Police of five additional murders he allegedly committed

Architect, along with accomplice Myra Hindley, of the infamous "Moors Murders" which continue to exert a profound effect on the British consciousness. The son of a waitress and a man he never met, Ian Brady (birth name Ian Stewart) was raised by foster parents in the economically depressed Gorbals district of Glasgow. By nine, Brady's natural bent for cruelty was already beginning to show itself through his torture of animals, insects, and his bullying of weaker schoolchildren. Arrested on charges of housebreaking and attempted theft in 1951, Brady was put on probation for two years, but rearrested on similar charges in July 1952. Dropping out of school in 1953, the 15-year-old held jobs as a butcher's assistant and teaboy in a shipyard, before his 1954 appearance before the Glasgow sheriff court on nine charges of housebreaking and theft. Brady was given two years probation on condition that he return to his mother who was married and living in the poor Moss Side suburb of Manchester. Brady's stepfather, Patrick Brady, got his stepson a job in a fruit market, but the youth's theft of lead seals from boxes of bananas landed him in city magistrate's court in November 1955. Convicted, Brady received two years of Borstal training at Hull and Hatfield. Upon his release in November 1957, Brady returned to his parents who were now living in Longsight, another suburb of Manchester. Brady refined his already excessive drinking habits during a seven month stint as a laborer in a brewery close to Strangeways Prison. In February 1959, Brady secured a £12 a week stock clerk's position at Millward's Merchandise Ltd., a chemical distributing firm in the Gorton district of Manchester. A good employee, Brady had little to do with his coworkers and spent his lunch breaks alone indulging his obsession with Naziism. A voracious reader on anything to do with Hitler and the Third Reich, Brady often ordered tapes of German marching songs and the speeches of his beloved Nazi leaders. At home, Brady's bookshelf filled with titles like *The Life and Ideas of the Marquis De Sade* and *The History of Torture Through the Ages,* which reflected the other consuming passion of his life.

Brady had been at Millwards almost two years when Myra Hindley, a tall, chain-smoking, working class 19-year-old from Gorton, was hired in January 1961 as a shorthand typist at £8.50 a week. Raised by her grandmother, Hindley was well-liked by classmates although she was assessed on her first high school report card as "not very sociable." Soon after starting at the firm, Hindley became infatuated with Brady. During the next 12 months, the *Mein Kampf*-reading invoice clerk ignored Hindley's overt advances. However, not to be dissuaded, Hindley chronicled his every move in her diary logging such entries as "Ian looked at me today" and "Ian wore a black shirt and looked smashing." Just before Christmas 1961, Brady took the smitten typist to the movies to see *Trial at Nuremburg,* a film documenting Nazi war atrocities. That night, Hindley lost her virginity to Ian

Brady at her aged grandmother's house. Afterwards, the lovers became inseparable and soon Brady's influence on Hindley became apparent. At her lover's request, Hindley bleached her hair blonde, wore Nazi-style black leather boots, and was rewarded by Brady with the affectionate nickname "Myra Hess." An amateur photographer, Brady took snaps of Hindley in obscene poses complete with sexual paraphernalia and took shots of them having sex. Failing to sell them locally, Brady turned from pornography to planning bank robberies with David Smith, the husband of Hindley's sister, Maureen. According to Smith's later testimony, Brady confided to him during drunken late night strategy sessions that he had killed young people, photographed them, then buried the bodies on the moors.

Brady and Hindley had been living together for less than a month near the Smiths in Gorton when 16-year-old Pauline Reade disappeared on her way to a dance at the Railway Social Club on July 12, 1963. On November 23, 1963, 12-year-old John Kilbride vanished in Ashton-under-Lyne after attending a movie with a friend. The killers next struck on June 16, 1964, when they picked up 12-year-old Keith Bennett in the Longsight district of Manchester near where Brady had at one time lived with his mother. On December 26, 1964, Brady and Hindley abducted ten-year-old Lesley Ann Downey off a Manchester street. They transported Downey to Hindley's bedroom where she was photographed having sex with Brady and her final moments of torture were forever captured on audiotape. Throughout the carefully planned and executed reign of murders, Brady was patiently at work on a subtle campaign to corrupt David

Smith by loaning him books on sadism and discussing his "philosophy" of murder.

On October 6, 1965, Brady gave Smith his final "lesson." Picking up Edward Evans, a 17-year-old homosexual engineering apprentice in a bar in Manchester, Hindley and Brady drove the inebriated youth to their home in Hattersley. On the pretext of showing Smith some miniature wine bottles, Brady called the man over to his house. Smith was in the kitchen examining them when he heard a bloodcurdling scream. He ran into the living room just in time to see Brady slaughtering Evans with a hatchet. Afterwards, Brady accelerated death by strangling him with a cord. Terrified and sickened, Smith returned home and called the police. The next day, Brady and Hindley were arrested at their home. In an upstairs bedroom Evans' body was found wrapped in a blanket, the bloody hatchet was nearby in a carrier bag.

House-to-house inquiries led police to a 12-year-old girl who stated that she had often accompanied the couple on their frequent jaunts to Saddleworth Moor, northeast of Manchester, near the Pennine Way. She led authorities to the spot where she had been taken and on October 16, 1965, authorities recovered the naked body of Lesley Ann Downey. The body was too decomposed to determine a cause of death. Two luggage tickets found in Hindley's white prayer book led police to the Manchester Central Station. Inside the retrieved suitcases, they found coshes, wigs, masks, pornographic photos of Downey and the audiotape recording her torture in which both Brady and Hindley are heard threatening the child. Twenty-two photographs of the Saddleworth

Moor prompted another round of excavation and on October 21, 1965, the body of John Kilbride was unearthed. The search for more victims continued until November and the advent of winter. Tried in Chester before Mr. Justice Fenton Atkinson on April 19, 1966, the pair pleaded not guilty to the murders of Edward Evans, Lesley Ann Downey, and John Kilbride. The Downey tape combined with David Smith's testimony ultimately damned the lovers who by now achieved the distinction of being the most hated criminals in Britain. Brady openly lied on the stand while Hindley expressed shock over Evans' murder and termed "indefensible" her treatment of Downey recorded on the 16-minute tape. On May 6, 1966, the all-male jury retired for slightly over two hours before finding Brady guilty of all three murders and Hindley guilty of the killings of Evans and Downey. Both were sentenced to concurrent life sentences for each of the murder charges with Hindley given an additional seven years for being an accessory after the fact in the Kilbride killing. At his own request, Brady is serving his sentence under a rule which restricts his contact with other prisoners.

In September 1972, the convicted "Moors Murderess" was allowed to visit the Hampstead Heath in the company of the female governor of Holloway Prison. The outing elicited such public outrage that Hindley was never again allowed on such day trips. Hindley ultimately broke with Brady, changed her name to Myra Spencer, and became romantically involved with a female prison guard, Pat Cairns, at Holloway Prison. An unsuccessful prison break engineered by the pair in 1973 resulted in Hindley receiving a token one year sentence for conspiracy. Hindley was incarcerated in Durham Prison in spring 1980 when she earned her bachelor's degree in the humanities from the Open University after taking six years of correspondence classes. In November 1986, Brady, in an apparent bid to be moved from prison into a maximum security medical facility, confessed to the murders of Pauline Reade and Keith Bennett. Hindley subsequently aided Manchester police in a search of Saddleworth Moor which failed to turn up any bodies. However, Pauline Reade's body was found on July 1, 1987, not far from where Lesley Ann Downey was recovered some 22 years before. In August 1987 Brady claimed in a letter to a BBC reporter that he had killed five other victims in Manchester and Glasgow. To date, these murders have not been verified. Hindley, now a fervent Roman Catholic, continues to seek parole with the support of prison reformer Lord Longford, but is actively opposed by Brady and the victims' families. At one point, Brady told the *Sunday People* that "if I revealed what really happened Myra would not get out in one hundred years." For his part, Brady has consistently maintained that he will never seek release from prison. In a 1994 bid for possible parole, Hindley offered to take a "truth drug" to aid her in remembering where they buried the body of 12-year-old Keith Bennett. A phone poll conducted in July 1994 by the British newspaper *The People* revealed that 98 percent of nearly 40,000 respondents believed strongly that Hindley should never be freed. On December 16, 1994, Hindley received papers from the home office informing her that she would serve the rest of her natural life in prison. In a letter to a Liverpool news agency published in late December 1994, Ian Brady revealed that he had spent 15 years writing the true account of the Moors Murders in order "to set the record straight." In accordance with his wishes, the American publisher will not release the book until after Brady's death and then all royalties will be donated to charity.

41. Goodman, Jonathan. *Trial of Ian Brady and Myra Hindley: The Moors Case.* Celebrated Trials Series. Newton Abbot: David and Charles, 1973. 256 pp.: facsims., maps, plans; 23 cm.

Excellent day-by-day summary of the trial taken from the official transcript of the shorthand notes, depositions taken at the committal proceedings, and press reports.

42. Harrison, Fred. *Brady and Hindley: Genesis of the Moors Murders.* Bath, Avon: Ashgrove Press, 1986. 189 pp., [16]pp. of plates: ill.; 23 cm.

_____. [Same as 42.] Specially updated ed. London: Grafton, 1987. 197 pp., [16]pp. of plates: ill.; 18 cm.; paperback.

43. Hart, Christine. *The Devil's Daughter.* Foreword by Colin Wilson. South Woodham Ferrers: New Author, 1993. 281 pp.; 22 cm.; trade paperback.

Hart, 29, claims to be Brady's illegitimate, orphaned daughter although the killer has refused to take a blood test to determine the issue. Correspondence with Brady ultimately led Hart to a meeting with him in Park Lane Hospital for the criminally insane.

44. Johnson, Pamela Hansford. *On Iniquity: Some Personal Reflections Arising Out of the Moors Murder Trial.* London: Macmillan, 1967. 144 pp.; 23 cm.

_____. [Same as 44.] New York: Scribner, 1967. 142 pp.; 22 cm. (Paperback ed. is also available.)

45. Jones, Janie, and Clerk, Carol. *The Devil and Miss Jones: The Twisted Mind of*

Myra Hindley. London: Smith Gryphon, 1993. ix, 245 pp., [16]pp. of plates: ill.; 23 cm. (Paperback edition is also available.)

46. Marchbanks, David Affleck. *The Moor Murders.* London: Frewin, 1966. 176 pp., [8]pp. of plates: ill., ports., facsims.; 22 cm.

Succinct summary of the case. Marchbanks concludes that a study of Brady and Hindley could profit medical science: "The primary object would be a cure; the result would be valuable information of practical use. In the meantime, the psychiatrists can observe their mental state and plot their behaviour so that we might better understand what it is that turns individuals into cruel, remorseless killers."

47. Potter, John Deane. *The Monsters of the Moors: The Full Account of the Brady-Hindley Case.* London: Elek, 1966. 255 pp.: ill.; 20 cm.

_____. [Same as 47.] 1st American print. New York: Ballantine, 1968. 285 pp., [4] leaves of plates: ill., ports.; 18 cm.; paperback.

Early paperback account of the case by a former crime reporter for the London *Daily Express.* On cover of the American edition: "The first factual treatment of the story told in Emlyn Williams' $5.95 bestseller *Beyond Belief.*"

48. Ritchie, Jean. *Myra Hindley: Inside the Mind of a Murderess.* London: Angus & Robertson, 1988. 290 pp., [14]pp. of plates: ill., ports.; 18 cm.; paperback.

_____. [Same as 48.] Sydney: Bay Books, 1988. ix, 290 pp., [14]pp. of plates; 18 cm.; paperback.

_____. [Same as 48.] London: Harper/Collins, 1993. ix, 290 pp., [16]pp. of plates: ill.; 18 cm.; paperback.

Excellent, gripping account of Myra Hindley which is of particular interest because it reports on the killer's adjustment to prison life including her numerous lesbian lovers. Ritchie on Hindley: "At the end of my research I conclude

that she has cynically exploited every situation to her own ends, and her belated confession was prompted not by remorse but by the eventual realisation that any hope of release hinged on wiping her slate clean, assuaging the grief of the relatives of her victims as best she can, and hoping that, with patience, she will have worked her ticket to freedom.... She can never atone for what she has done but she can be—and is being—punished. It is right and fitting that her punishment should be lifelong."

49. Sparrow, Gerald. *Satan's Children.* Foreword by R.C. Mortimer. London: Odhams, 1966. 191 pp., [4]pp. of plates: ill., ports.; 22 cm.

Philosophical discussion of the case which examines the criminals' mental state and argues for a more liberal rewriting of Britain's law on insanity and murder. Of the killers, Sparrow writes: "I was certain the terrible deeds that these two young people committed were due more to their psycho-sexual development than to their environment. I was convinced that both of them, and in particular Myra Hindley, could be made the subject of successful psycho-therapy."

50. Syme, Anthony V. *Murder on the Moors.* 1st ed. London: Horwitz, 1966. 130 pp.: ill., ports.; 18 cm.; paperback.

Earliest paperback account of the case.

51. Topping, Peter, and Ritchie, Jean. *Topping: The Autobiography of the Police Chief in the Moors Murder Case.* London: Angus & Robertson, 1989. 303 pp., [16]pp. of plates: ill., ports.; 24 cm.

Topping, a senior detective with the Greater Manchester Police, reopened the search for additional Moors Murders victims after Hindley's confession in 1986. The search resulted in the discovery of Pauline Reade's body on July 1, 1987. Topping was subsequently sued by the Manchester Police Authority for alleged breach of copyright and confidentiality stemming from the publishing of Hindley's confession. The suit was settled out of court in June 1993 after Topping agreed to pay an undisclosed sum. The action is believed to have established the principle that it is improper for serving or former police officers to publish confidential material they gained access to in the course of their professional duties.

52. West, Ann. *For the Love of Lesley: The "Moors Murders" Remembered by a Victim's Mother.* Foreword by John Stalker. London: W.H. Allen, 1989. ix, 196 pp.: ill.; 21 cm.

_____. [Same as 52.] Foreword by John Stalker. London: Warner, 1993. xi, 209 pp.: ill., ports.; 18 cm.; paperback.

Emotionally moving account written by the mother of victim Lesley Ann Downey. Foreword by John Stalker, the deputy chief constable of Greater Manchester Police who conducted the initial investigation. Includes a facsimile of a letter sent by Ian Brady to Ann West. Of the correspondence, she writes: "Who can say why my daughter's killer feels the need to write the mother whose life he destroyed as surely as he destroyed her child's? Who can say why *I* need to continue this traumatic communication with the last person to see Lesley alive? I suspect that we will go on with our letters till one or other of us dies. How strange and how pathetic—two people with so little, yet so much, in common, forever linked by this succession of letters."

53. Williams, Emlyn. *Beyond Belief: A Chronicle of Murder and Its Detection.* London: H. Hamilton, 1967. xiv, 370 pp.; 21 cm.

_____. [Same as 53.] 1st American ed. New York: Random House, 1968. xii, 354 pp.; 22 cm.

_____. [Same as 53.] London: Pan Books, 1969. 380 pp.; 18 cm.; paperback.

Superb novelization of the case by the author of *Night Must Fall.* Includes detailed index.

54. Wilson, Robert. *Devil's Disciples.* London: Express Newspapers, 1986. 208 pp.: ill., 1 map, ports.; 20 cm.

_____. [Same as 54.] Poole: Javelin, 1986. 208 pp.: ill., 1 map, ports.; 18 cm.; paperback.

Sensational account by a veteran British tabloid journalist.

55. _____. *Return to Hell: The Continuing Story of the Moors Murderers Brady and Hindley.* London: Javelin, 1988. 189 pp.: ill., 1 map, ports.; 18 cm.; paperback.

At head of title: "The chilling sequel to *Devil's Disciples.*"

Branion, John Marshall, Jr. (a.k.a. "Arthur McCoo")

Born circa January 1926. Died September 8, 1990. Medical doctor. Chicago, Illinois; 1 murder; revolver; December 22, 1967.

Television: The Branion case was featured in a segment of the NBC series "Unsolved Mysteries" which aired on December 19, 1989. A Michael Neiderman documentary, "Presumed Guilty," aired on the Chicago public television station, WTTW/Channel 11, on July 25, 1990.

"But I didn't really think it would come to trial. I was convinced they'd drop the charges before that, for lack of evidence. I was *sure* of it."—Branion in retrospect

Prominent African-American doctor convicted of murdering his wife on largely circumstantial evidence who then fled the country. Police speculate that on December 22, 1967, affluent physician John Branion left his clinic, drove to the luxurious Hyde Park apartment he shared with wife Donna, choked and shot the woman 13 times following an argument over his extramarital affair, picked up his four-year-old son from nursery school, visited a friend, then returned home to find his wife dead—all in a span of 27 minutes. Medical testimony determined that the murder took 15 minutes to commit, a point Branion's counsel argued made it impossible timewise for him to have committed the murder. They alleged that intruders choked then shot Mrs. Branion to death with a 9mm, .38 caliber Walther PPK taken from her husband's gun collection. The weapon was never found. A jury agreed with the prosecution's version of Branion's timetable and found him guilty on May 28, 1968. Branion was subsequently sentenced to 20–30 years. A case already resembling an Alfred Hitchcock murder script became even more complicated when charges were subsequently made that the judge in the trial, since convicted of extorting bribes, solicited $20,000 from Branion supporters to set aside the jury verdict and free the doctor. Branion, free on $5,000 bond pending an appeal to the U.S. Supreme Court, fled the country in June 1971 when that body upheld his conviction. When he was arrested in Uganda on October 12, 1983, he had served as dictator Idi Amin's personal physician for seven years. Branion was sentenced to 20–30 years and given 1–3 years on bail jumping charges. On August 7, 1990, Illinois Governor James Thompson commuted Branion's sentence to time served when it was learned he was suffering from a terminal heart ailment and brain tumor. The 64-year-old doctor died at the University of Illinois Hospital on September 8, 1990.

56. D'Amato, Barbara. *The Doctor, the Murder, the Mystery: The True Story Behind the Dr. John Branion Murder Case.* Chicago: Noble Press, 1992. xii, 319 pp., [4]pp. of plates: ill.; 24 cm.

D'Amato, a mystery novelist and wife of the Northwestern University School of Law professor who handled some of Branion's appeals, offers compelling evidence of the doctor's innocence. The appendix contains a detailed timetable of Branion's disputed movements on the morning of the murder. Winner of the 1992 Anthony Award as best true crime book.

"Brides in the Bath Murders" *see* **Smith, George Joseph**

Broderick, Elisabeth Anne (Betty)
(a.k.a. "Betty Bisceglia" [maiden name], "Bets")

Born circa 1947 in Eastchester, New York. Housewife. San Diego, California; 2 murders; .38 caliber, five-shot revolver; November 5, 1989.

Television: "A Woman Scorned: The Betty Broderick Story" (1992), a two-hour, made-for-television movie, originally aired on CBS on March 1, 1992. Cast includes Meredith Baxter (Betty Broderick), Stephen Collins (Dan Broderick), and Michelle Johnson (Linda Kolkena.) A two-hour, made-for-television movie, "Her Final Fury: Betty Broderick, the Last Chapter" (1992), originally aired on CBS on November 1, 1992. Cast includes Meredith Baxter (Betty Broderick), Judith Ivey (District Attorney Kerry Wells), and Ray Baker (Jack Earley.) This sequel to "A Woman Scorned" focuses on Broderick's two murder trials.

Video: Betty Broderick on Trial: Victim or Criminal?, a 115-minute videocassette, was released in 1993 by the Courtroom Television Network (New York, N.Y.). Also known as *CA v. Broderick.*

"It's true—they do shit their pants. I could hear him gurgling in his own blood."—Broderick in a phone call to a friend immediately after the double homicide

Murderess who, in killing her ex-husband and his young wife, has become to many a national symbol of the divorced woman's rage and desire for revenge. In the pre-dawn hours of November 5, 1989, Betty Broderick, 42, entered the San Diego home of her ex-husband Daniel T. Broderick, III, a successful malpractice attorney, and his wife of seven months, 28-year-old Linda Kolkena Broderick, his former assistant. As the pair slept, she fired two rounds from a five-shot .38 caliber pistol into the young wife's neck and chest killing her instantly. She then emptied the gun at her 44-year-old former husband of 16 years striking him once in the back. As he lay dying on the floor, Broderick yanked the phone out of the wall before leaving the scene. Shortly afterwards she turned herself in to authorities. The murders were a culmination of the most bitter divorce action in the history of San Diego jurisprudence. In many respects the classic scorned wife, Broderick helped put her husband through Harvard Law School and later Cornell University Medical College while bearing him four children. She was enjoying her socialite status in La Jolla when Daniel Broderick hired · attractive ex-stewardess Linda Kolkena as a paralegal in September 1983. The resultant affair sparked a three-year long emotional and legal battle between the estranged couple punctuated by a series of bizarre and increasingly violent outbursts from the rejected wife. On one occasion, she drove her car through the front door of his new home. Daniel Broderick was awarded sole custody of their children at their divorce on July 16, 1986, and ordered to pay $16,100 a month in alimony (significantly less than the $30,000 she demanded). He married Kolkena in April 1989.

Broderick pleaded innocent to murder charges at her trial in October 1990. In pre-trial interviews she had claimed the killings were a "desperate act of self defense" against a man who had taken everything away from her and then planned to control her financially. In her testimony, she claimed that she never intended to kill the pair, but rather planned to commit suicide in front of them. She had no memory of firing the fatal shots. A mistrial was declared on November 20, 1990, when jurors deadlocked over whether to find her guilty of first degree murder or manslaughter. At the second trial in October 1991, Broderick's counsel argued for a verdict of voluntary manslaughter maintaining that she was driven to the slayings by years of psychological abuse and by what she characterized as "overt emotional terrorism." After deliberating four days, a jury convicted Broderick on two counts of second degree murder and she was subsequently sentenced to 32 years to life in prison. She is ineligible for parole for at least 18 years. In 1993, three of her four children filed a $20 million wrongful death suit against her to be paid out of any future book or movie profits.

57. Schwartz-Nobel, Loretta. *Forsaking All Others: The Real Betty Broderick Story: Including Prison Interviews.* 1st ed. New York: Villard, 1993. xvii, 237 pp.: ill.; 24 cm.

Broderick tells her side of the story in a series of prison interviews presented under chapter headings like "Betty Broderick on Dan and Linda's Emotional Tactics." Provides interesting insights into Broderick's belief that she, not the people she murdered, is the true victim in the case.

58. Stumbo, Bella. *Until the Twelfth of Never: The Deadly Divorce of Dan & Betty Broderick.* New York: Pocket Books, 1993. xiv, 546 pp., [32]pp. of ill.; 24 cm.

The former *Los Angeles Times* reporter portrays Broderick as a victim of her own traditional notions of wife and motherhood. Once her identity was shattered by the divorce, Broderick had but two options: suicide or murder. The title refers to the song played at the couple's wedding on April 12, 1969. The best book to date on the case.

59. Taubman, Bryna. *Hell Hath No Fury.* St. Martin's True Crime Library. New York: SMP, St. Martin's, 1992. 214 pp., [8]pp. of plates: ill.; 22 cm.

_____. [Same as 59.] St. Martin's Paperback ed. St. Martin's True Crime Library. New York: SMP, St. Martin's Paperbacks, 1992. 278 pp., [8]pp. of plates: ill.; 18 cm.; paperback.

Taubman, who chronicled the Robert Chambers case in her book *The Preppy Murder Trial* (see 82), here rehashes newspaper accounts of the crime.

Brooks, David Owen *see* Corll, Dean Arnold

"Brownout Murders" *see* Leonski, Edward Joseph

Browne, Frederick Guy
(a.k.a. "Leo Brown" [probably real name])

Born circa 1881 in Catford, England. Executed May 31, 1928. Motor engineer. Stapleford Abbotts, Essex, England; 1 murder; Webley revolver; September 26, 1927.

"I am not guilty according to the One above that knows. I am not guilty, but the Court says I am. I am quite

content, my conscience is clear."—Browne's statement to Mr. Justice Avory prior to having the sentence of death passed upon him

British petty criminal who in tandem with his accomplice, William Henry Kennedy, was convicted of murdering a police constable in an early case in which ballistic evidence prominently figured. On September 27, 1927, the body of P.C. George William Gutteridge was found by the side of a road near Stapleford Abbotts. The policeman had been shot twice in the left cheek and once through each eye. The pencil grasped in his right hand and his notebook nearby suggested that Gutteridge was about to make an entry when he was shot by surprise. A spent cartridge was found at the scene. An hour before the murder (estimated to have been four or five hours before the discovery of the body), a Morris-Cowley car had been stolen from the garage of Dr. Edward Lovell's home some ten miles away in Billericay. It was later found damaged in Brixton. A search of the vehicle yielded no fingerprints. However, bloodstains (assumed to be from Gutteridge) were found on the running board and an empty cartridge case scarred by the breech lock of the gun that fired it was discovered under the front seat. Ballistics established the murder weapon had been a Webley revolver. The investigation stalled for months although authorities kept a weather eye out for known car thieves and those with similar records operating in South London. Their persistence paid off with the arrest of Frederick Guy Browne, a 46-year-old mechanic, on a charge of auto theft at his garage in Clapham Junction on January 20, 1928. A search of the garage uncovered the Webley which ballistics later identified as the murder weapon. Browne's accomplice in the auto theft, William Henry Kennedy, was arrested five days later.

Browne and Kennedy each sported a long criminal history of petty theft with Browne, who also had a record for carrying firearms, perhaps the more aggressive of the pair. While serving time in Parkhurst Convict Prison for car theft and insurance fraud, Browne had become so violent that he was transferred to Dartmoor Convict Prison "to be tamed." It was at Dartmoor that Browne probably met Kennedy sometime in 1927. Kennedy, a former soldier in the Loyal North Lancashire Regiment in 1911, served time for indecent exposure but was primarily known to the police for housebreaking, theft, and larceny. Released before Kennedy, Browne offered his fellow-inmate a job as manager of his garage at Clapham Junction. In custody and charged with Gutteridge's murder, Browne told detectives that he knew nothing of the incident. Kennedy cooperated with authorities and in what amounted to a confession told of helping Browne steal Dr. Lovell's car in Billericay. P.C. Gutteridge later flagged them down and Browne shot him twice in the cheek before standing over the fallen policeman and shooting out his eyes. Tried before Mr. Justice Avory at the Old Bailey on April 23, 1928, the codefendants presented a study in contrasts. Browne ranted at the prosecution while Kennedy in a statement from the dock apologized to the constable's widow for having been in the stolen car on the night of the murder. Ballistics evidence, however, convicted the pair when it scientifically proved that the gun found in Browne's garage was the weapon used to murder Gutteridge. Both men were found guilty on April 27, 1928, and sentenced to

death. Following their failed appeals, Browne was hanged at Pentonville at 9:00 a.m. on May 31, 1928, with Kennedy simultaneously put to death at Wandsworth Prison.

60. Berry-Dee, Christopher, and Odell, Robin. *The Long Drop: Two Were Hanged, One Was Innocent.* London: True Crime, 1993. xix, 232 pp., [8]pp. of plates: ill., ports.; 18 cm.; paperback.

61. Shore, W. Teignmouth, ed. *Trial of Frederick Guy Browne and William Henry Kennedy.* Notable British Trials. Edinburgh; London: W. Hodge, 1930. x, 218 pp., [14] leaves of plates: ill., ports., plan, facsim.; 22 cm.

_____. [Same as 61.] Notable British Trials. Toronto: Canada Law Book Co. x, 218 pp., [14] leaves of plates: ill., ports., plan, facsim.; 22 cm.

Transcript from their trial at the Central Criminal Court, London, April 1928, for the murder of George William Gutteridge. Appendices include the May 22, 1928, appeal before the Lord Chief Justice's Court and Kennedy's last letter to his wife.

Brudos, Jerome Henry
(a.k.a. "The Lust Killer")

Born January 31, 1939, in Webster, South Dakota. Electrician. Oregon; 4 murders (3 convictions); bludgeon, manual strangulation; January 1968–April 1969.

Violent sexual criminal whose foot fetishism led to numerous assaults and four murders. Serial killer Jerry Brudos was an unwanted child and knew it. As the son of a verbally abusive father and a mother who wanted a daughter, Brudos grew to hate her and, later, all women. Already a blossoming high heeled shoe fetishist by age five, an adolescent Brudos expanded his masturbatory fantasies to include women's undergarments stolen from clotheslines and houses. At 16, he dug a hillside tunnel where he fantasized keeping captive women. Less than a year later, Brudos enticed an 18-year-old girl to his house, where masked, he forced her at knifepoint to pose naked for photographs. An abortive rape attempt brought the high school sophomore to the attention of the Oregon State Police who found hidden in his room a "collection" of women's shoes, lingerie, and homemade photos. He was committed to the Oregon State Hospital in 1956 when the girl he photographed at knifepoint stepped forward. Diagnosed as a "borderline schizophrenic," he was discharged in less than a year and advised to "grow up." A brief stint in the Army ended on October 15, 1959, when he was discharged for manifesting bizarre sexual obsessions.

Still a virgin at 23, he married 17-year-old Darcie Metzler in 1962. As a dutiful wife, she submitted to being photographed nude in bizarre poses and to wearing painful high heeled shoes. Often depressed, Brudos continued to seek relief by stealing underwear and shoes. Although a skilled electrician, an uneven temperament prevented him from staying too long at any job. In their first seven years together, Brudos, his wife and two children would live in 20 different houses. The birth of his son in 1967 plunged Brudos into despair. A long-time sufferer of migraine headaches and blackouts, Brudos went trolling in Portland for a woman to lift his spirits. After selecting a victim in high heels, he broke into her apartment, raped her, and stole her shoes. In 1968, an unemployed Brudos moved to Salem, Oregon, and quickly declared the home's padlocked garage and base-ment-workshop off-limits to his wife. Their marriage was already disintegrating when Brudos appeared before the shocked woman wearing only a bra stuffed with paper, a girdle, stockings, garters and high heeled shoes.

Brudos' fantasy of setting up an "underground butcher shop" where he could murder, keep, and photograph women was partially fulfilled on January 26, 1968. On that day, encyclopedia salesperson Linda K. Slawson, 19, was lured into his workshop and bludgeoned to death with a two-by-four. Upstairs, his unsuspecting family was preparing for supper. Sending them out for food, Brudos amused himself for hours by dressing Slawson's corpse in his "collection" of bras, panties, and shoes. That night, after severing her left foot for a memento, Brudos tied an engine head to the body and dumped it in the Willamette River. Ten months later to the day on November 26, 1968, 23-year-old University of Oregon coed Jan Susan Whitney disappeared while driving along the I-5 corridor between McMinnville and Portland. Her disabled car was found in a rest area north of Albany, Oregon. Brudos later confessed to abducting Whitney and strangling her to death in a car parked in his driveway. In his workshop, Brudos alternately had sex with the corpse while photographing her in his "collection" of lingerie. As a trophy, he cut off one of her breasts to make a paperweight. Her body was not recovered from the Willamette River until the summer of 1970.

On March 27, 1969, Karen Elena Sprinker, a 19-year-old freshman at Oregon State University-Corvallis, was kidnapped from a department store in Salem. Police found her car in the mall's rooftop parking garage and witnesses testified to seeing a man dressed as a woman loitering in the area. In his confession, Brudos described forcing the girl at gunpoint into a car and raping her on the floor of his workshop. After photographing her in his "collection," he hanged, and then violated the corpse. Cutting off both breasts to make molds, he tied the head of a six cylinder engine to the body and dumped it in the Long Tom River. When recovered in mid–May of 1969, police were shocked to find the corpse outfitted in a 38D bra stuffed with brown paper. The next month, Brudos bungled two attempted abductions. On April 21, 1969, he attacked 24-year-old Sharon Wood in broad daylight as she walked to her car in the parking garage at Portland State University. Refusing to be intimidated by the gun he brandished, she screamed and bit Brudos as he strangled and beat her. He fled when a car appeared. The next day in Salem, Brudos failed to abduct a teenaged girl who was lucky enough to break his grip and escape. Brudos began calling dormitories at Portland State University and asking coeds to go out with him. Remarkably, one did. She agreed to notify police if he called again.

Brudos was more successful on April 23, 1969, in Portland. Posing as mall security, he "arrested" 22-year-old Linda Salee for "shoplifting" and drove the woman 47 miles to his home in Salem. Inconvenienced by the presence there of his wife, he tied Salee up in his workshop, ate dinner with his wife, and afterwards, simultaneously raped and strangled his captive to death. Brudos further violated the corpse with electric prods. On May 10, 1969, her body, tied to a car transmission, was pulled from the Long Tom River 12 miles south of Corvallis. The case broke on May 25, 1969, when Brudos contacted the Port-

land State University coed for another date. Met by police at the dorm, he was questioned closely concerning statements made to the girl about the dead women. A search of his workshop turned up knots similar to those found tied to the recovered bodies. Brudos was arrested for assault on May 30 after the teenaged girl he tried to abduct picked his photo out of several mugshots. In custody, he confessed to the murders and police found boxes of women's clothes, breast molds, and photos of the victims in his workshop. In one, Brudos was clearly visible photographing a corpse.

Arraigned for the Sprinker murder on June 4, 1969, Brudos pleaded "not guilty by reason of insanity," but later changed his plea when seven examining psychiatrists agreed he was not psychotic. On June 27, 1969, he was sentenced to three consecutive life sentences for the Sprinker, Whitney, and Salee murders. With "good behavior" time, he could be out in 36 years. His wife was subsequently tried as an accomplice in the Sprinker case, but acquitted. They divorced in 1970. Incarcerated in the Oregon State Penitentiary, Brudos is a model prisoner who makes leather key fobs and helps out with the prison's computer system. Parole board members voted in June 1995 to keep Brudos jailed for the rest of his life.

62. Rule, Ann [Stack, Andy]. *Lust Killer.* Andy Stack's True Crime Annals, vol. 1. New York: New American Library, 1983. 224 pp.; 18 cm. ("A Signet book"); paperback.

_____. [Same as 62.] Updated ed. New York: New American Library, 1988. 238 pp., [8]pp. of plates: ill.; 18 cm. ("A Signet book"); paperback.

Ann Rule originally wrote this book in 1983 under her pseudonym "Andy

Stack." Updated edition (1988) notes "Ann Rule writing as Andy Stack."

Buckfield, Reginald Sidney (a.k.a. "Smiler," "Gunner X")

Soldier. Strood, England; 1 murder; knife; October 9, 1942.

"It's funny, every time I break out, something always happens, either a break or a murder."—Statement made by Buckfield during a police interrogation

Deserter from the British army whose fictional account of a murder written to prove his innocence ultimately convicted him. On the night of October 9, 1942, Ellen Ann Symes was pushing her four-year-old child in a baby carriage on the Brompton Road near the town of Strood when she was fatally knifed by a man described as a soldier by her unharmed child. The next day Reginald Sidney Buckfield, a deserter from a local army base known as "Smiler" for his perpetual idiot grin, admitted to police that although he was in the area at the time of the murder, he was not the killer. Two hours after his arrest for desertion a bone-handled table knife with its blade sharpened to a point was found in an orchard near the murder scene. Buckfield denied owning such a knife, but two witnesses testified at the trial that he used a similar one while working on farms in the area. In custody, Buckfield wrote a short story entitled "The Mystery of Brompton Road" by "Gunner X" designed to exonerate him. Instead, authorities maintained the story mentioned details of Symes' killing which could only be known to the killer. The manuscript was subsequently read by the clerk of the court at Buckfield's trial at the Old Bailey in January 1943.

Refusing to believe the deserter's contention that he had gleaned the self-incriminating facts contained in the manuscript from conversations with the police, a jury found Buckfield guilty on January 26, 1943, after deliberating only 63 minutes. Mr. Justice Hallett sentenced Buckfield to death with the proviso that an investigation be conducted to determine if there was "a medical explanation" for the act. Weeks later the home office determined Buckfield to be insane and sentenced him to Broadmoor.

63. Roberts, C.E. Bechhofer, ed. *The Trial of Reginald Sidney Buckfield*. Old Bailey Trial Series. London; New York: Jarrolds, 1944. 192 pp.: ill.; 23 cm.

Entry in the Old Bailey Trial Series edited by barrister Roberts of Gray's Inn and the South-Eastern Circuit. A brief recap of the case featuring Buckfield's short story "The Mystery of Brompton Road" (in its entirety) introduces excerpts from the trial transcript (Central Criminal Court, London, January 20–26, 1943). Concludes with Roberts' essay "A Note on Crime and Insanity."

Buenoano, Judias (a.k.a. "The Black Widow," "The Panhandle Black Widow," "Judy Ann Goodyear," "Judias Anna Lou Welty," "Ann Schulz" [Changed name from "Goodyear" to "Buenoano," Spanish for "good year" in 1978])

Born April 4, 1943, in Quanah, Texas. Licensed practical nurse, manicure salon owner. Florida, Colorado; 3 murders; arsenic, thorazine, drowning; September 1971–May 1980.

"I look forward not only to being

with Christ, but to being like Him. All glory and praise and honor be to God who chose me from Death Row to be a vessel of His mercy and grace."— Buenoano writing in *The Son*, a Las Vegas–based bimonthly publication featuring poetry, articles, and testimonials from condemned murderers who have been "born-again"

Characterized by a prosecutor as "a black widow" who fed off the men in her life, "Judi" Buenoano left a trail of two dead husbands and a drowned son en route to collecting thousands of dollars in life insurance. The daughter of a Texas farm worker and a full-blooded Apache mother, Buenoano (Spanish for "good year") claimed Geronimo as her great-great grandfather. Buenoano was two when her mother died and her father sent her to live with a grandmother. Ten years later, following one of her father's many remarriages, the family was reunited in Roswell, New Mexico. Buenoano endured two years of beatings and starvation before attacking her stepmother. The 14-year-old spent 60 days in jail, finally deciding that reform school was preferable to returning home. The teen was placed in a juvenile detention center in Albuquerque and graduated high school in May 1959 at the age of 16.

Buenoano, living and working as a nurse's aide in Roswell under the name "Ann Schulz," bore (as "Ann Lou Welty") an illegitimate child named Michael on March 30, 1961. His father, Air Force sergeant Arthur Schulz, would adopt the boy in 1965. Months later Buenoano met another career Air Force sergeant, James Edgar Goodyear, whom she married on January 21, 1962. In 1966, Buenoano's second and favorite son, James A. Goodyear, was born. A daughter was born in Orlando, Florida, in 1967. Back from a tour of duty in Vietnam in 1971, Goodyear was stricken with severe stomach pains. During the months he suffered, Buenoano intimated to friends that her husband had contracted a plague in Vietnam. His death on September 16, 1971, baffled doctors who failed to perform an autopsy. The official cause of death was listed as pneumonia and heart failure. Buenoano collected $92,000 in insurance and veteran's benefits. Later that year she would collect another $90,000 when her Orlando home mysteriously burned. When Goodyear's body was exhumed almost 13 years later it contained an arsenic level more than 1,000 times that of a lethal dose.

In 1973, Buenoano and her children relocated to Pensacola, Florida, where she met and lived with construction worker Bobby Joe Morris until he moved to Trinidad, Colorado, in 1977 to work in a water purification plant. Buenoano and the children joined him six months later, but not before she collected fire insurance for the loss of her home in Pensacola. On January 4, 1978, Morris was admitted to a Trinidad hospital with abdominal pains. He recovered sufficiently in a couple of weeks to return home under Buenoano's care. In two days Morris was rushed to the emergency room with vomiting and diarrhea. The formerly healthy 35-year-old died inexplicably of cardiac arrythmia on January 28, 1978. A hastily performed autopsy conducted while Morris lay in his coffin revealed some levels of Thorazine, but not enough to arouse suspicion. His widow collected over $80,000 on three life insurance policies. It was later determined that she had forged Morris' signature on the documents.

Buenoano had always been

ashamed of first son Michael, a hyper-active child with physical, emotional, and behavioral problems. A former babysitter testified that Buenoano routinely hid the child when company was expected because his slobbering embarrassed her. Shuffled to various institutions for most of his life, Michael joined the Army in June 1979 and was trained as a water purification specialist like his dead "stepfather." Upon completion of basic training, he visited his mother in Gulf Breeze, Florida, for ten days prior to reporting to Fort Benning on November 6, 1979. Upon his return to the base, Michael exhibited the classic symptoms of paralysis associated with metal-base poisoning. Subsequent tests revealed arsenic levels in his body seven times the norm. Six weeks after being hospitalized, Goodyear could neither walk nor use his hands. Discharged, he made the fatal mistake of returning home to live with his mother. On May 13, 1980, Buenoano took Michael and his 14-year-old brother James for a canoe ride on the East River near Milton, Florida. Paralyzed from knees to toes and from elbows to fingers, Michael's leg braces and his arm pros-thesis weighed twelve pounds apiece. Buenoano placed her paralyzed son without a life vest in a lawn chair in the middle of the canoe. According to her testimony, the canoe capsized when a fishing line, becoming entangled in an overhanging tree, caused a branch with a snake on it to fall in the boat. In the ensuing confusion, Buenoano and James (both wearing life vests) man-aged to swim to safety. Michael drowned. Buenoano collected $108,000 from various life insurance policies on her dead son. Later investigations revealed that she had forged Michael's signature on the policies.

Businessman John Wesley Gen-try, 37, met Buenoano in February 1982 at an Orlando, Florida, road-house. Within six months, he had moved in with her and was planning marriage. Just after Christmas in 1983, however, Gentry began experiencing stomach pains. The vitamin pills sup-plied by Buenoano only aggravated his condition, which improved after he was hospitalized and discontinued their use. The capsules were later dis-covered to contain paraformaldehyde, a slow acting poison. On June 25, 1983, Gentry drove to a Pensacola restaurant to attend a party thrown by Buenoano for an employee of her Fingers N Faces manicure boutique. As he was prepar-ing to drive away in his car after the meal, Gentry started the engine and detonated two sticks of dynamite hid-den in the trunk. The Vietnam vet was severely injured, but miraculously sur-vived the blast. A police background check of Gentry's associates revealed his fiancée's pattern of profiting from the deaths of the men in her life. Ques-tioned in the hospital, Gentry was unaware of the $500,000 insurance policy Buenoano had taken out on him in 1982. A search of her house uncov-ered strands of wire in James Bueno-ano's bedroom similar to those used in the car bomb. On July 27, 1983, Judi Buenoano was arrested for the at-tempted murder by poisoning of Gen-try, but remained free on $50,000 bond while police continued to probe her past.

On January 11, 1984, Buenoano was arrested on charges of poisoning and drowning her son Michael in order to fraudulently collect insurance. The trial opened in Milton, Florida, on March 21, 1984, with Buenoano's attor-ney maintaining that Michael's drown-ing was accidental and that the high arsenic level in his body was caused by his exposure to the poison during military training. More difficult to explain was the fact that for three years Buenoano had told Michael's relatives that he had died during Army maneuvers. Motive was provided by a graphologist who testified that the signatures on Michael's life insurance policies benefitting Buenoano were forged. Six hours after receiving the case on March 31, 1984, a jury found her guilty of first degree murder and grand theft. Buenoano was sentenced to life imprisonment on April 2, 1984.

Buenoano's legal troubles were only beginning. While awaiting the verdict in Michael's murder, she and son James were arrested on March 30, 1984, for the attempted murder of John Gentry. In a separate trial, James Buenoano was acquitted on August 10, 1984. Judi Buenoano was found guilty in an Orlando, Florida, courtroom on October 18, 1984, after a jury deliberated only 30 minutes. She received a 12-year sentence. Authorities exhumed the body of Buenoano's first husband, James Edgar Goodyear, and found it riddled with arsenic. Buenoano was convicted of his first degree murder on November 2, 1985, and sentenced to death. A "born again" Christian, Buenoano was working on an associate degree in ministry and has earned a teaching certificate. She has twice received indefinite stays of execution and in August 1992 won a major U.S. circuit court of appeals victory that vacated and remanded her death conviction based upon her counsel's conflict of interest (he held book and movie rights to her case) and his failure to present her abused and deprived childhood as mitigating factors in her defense. A new trial could be imminent.

64. Anderson, Chris. *Bodies of Evidence: The True Story of Judias Buenoano, Florida's Serial Murderess.* Secaucus, N.J.: Carol Pub. Group, 1991. ix, 319 pp.: ill; 24 cm. ("A Lyle Stuart book").

_____. [Same as 64.] New York: St. Martin's Paperbacks, 1992. 371 pp., [8]pp. of plates: ill.; 18 cm.; paperback.
Well researched and written account.

Bulloch, Dennis Neal
(a.k.a. "John Mason," "Dennis Block," "John Block," "Dennis Toksvig," "Jonathan Dennis," "Dennis Bender," "David Johnson," "John Masterson")

Born November 29, 1953, in Hollywood, California. Senior management consultant at Price Waterhouse. Ballwin, Missouri; 1 murder; strangulation; May 6, 1966.

In mid–1985 Julia (Julie) Alice Miller, a 31-year-old manager in the St. Louis office of Southwestern Bell, took her first step into the ofttimes murky singles world by calling in to a late-night radio dating show. Unimpressed by the men she met, Miller placed an ad in the "Eligibles" column of a weekly newspaper asking for a "Really Nice Guy" to respond to a "Nice Girl." When a concerned friend questioned the potential danger in placing such an ad, Miller offered assurances that she intended to check out each guy before dating them. Among those responding to Miller's ad was Dennis Neal Bulloch, a good-looking, 32-year-old senior management consultant at the prestigious accounting firm of Price Waterhouse. Miller told her friend that Bulloch "look[ed] good on paper." Their first date on August 14, 1985, ultimately led to Miller's grisly death and marked her with the dubious distinction of being the first woman in America to die during partner sexual bondage. The subsequent legalities of the Bulloch case introduced the controversial "sex-death defense," often mockingly referred to as the "oops! defense," and represented what many in the law enforcement community consider to be among the most serious miscarriages of justice in the annals of twentieth century American jurisprudence.

"On paper" Dennis Bulloch looked like ideal husband material. Born into a working class family, he applied himself in school, became a member of the national honor society, won a full scholarship to college, and earned an M.B.A. Ironically, Bulloch married a young woman in the early 1980s who, like Miller, also worked for Southwestern Bell. Initially the marriage thrived, but the woman resisted Bulloch's attempt to totally control the relationship. She refused to indulge his unusual tastes for sexual bondage and golden showers and divorced him on December 20, 1985, after he had earlier beat her in a jealous fit. Obsessed with success and eager to make a good appearance, Bulloch applied himself with equal intensity in an effort to fit in with the *crème de la crème* of St. Louis society. He became a Young Republican and a member of the Classical Guitar Society and Friends of the Art Museum. Bulloch's lucrative salary, however, was not enough to finance his dating of the daughters of "old money" St. Louis and he was soon in debt.

In September 1985 Julie Miller suffered an emotional breakdown and was admitted to the psychiatric ward of a local hospital for acute depression. During her seven-and-a-half week stay, she manifested what doctors termed "bizarre preoccupations with religious, sexual, lesbian, and grandiose thoughts." At one point, she believed sublime messages were being transmitted to her in the static from cable television. Diagnosed with borderline personality disorder, Miller was placed on anti-psychotic medicine and discharged almost two months later. Bulloch, solicitous throughout her hospital stay but still sleeping with other women, began proposing marriage to Miller around the time his divorce from his first wife was being finalized. Slavishly devoted to Bulloch from their first meeting, Miller was initially reluctant to accept his offer especially after finding the "little black book" in which he had listed her name along with the numbers of her investment accounts and credit cards. Nevertheless, Miller became Mrs. Bulloch in a private ceremony on February 22, 1986. Days later, she added his name to all her assets although he never reciprocated. Her last vestige of independence disappeared on March 12, 1986, when she signed over her power of attorney to her new husband.

Bulloch failed to live up to his "on paper" image. Refusing to wear a wedding band out of fear that it might get caught and hurt his hand, Bulloch moved into his own room in Julia's lavish home at 251 White Tree Lane in Ballwin, an upscale suburb in St. Louis County. He kept his house in nearby University City and often slept there, he told her, to guard it against break-ins. When traveling, Bulloch refused to give her a number where he could be reached and continued a long-term sadomasochistic bondage relationship with another woman. Bulloch used his wife's money to date socialites and even accompanied one to a ski resort in Jackson Hole, Wyoming. Though he never informed Price Waterhouse of his marriage, he told one of the women he was seeing that he did not love Julia and married her only after she threatened suicide. He planned to have the marriage annulled. Julia chronicled her frustration in copiously detailed diaries and six weeks after the wedding presented Bulloch with a 55-minute audiotape in which she tearfully begged him to love and pay attention to her. In mid–April 1986 Julia confided to a friend that she was considering a divorce. On April 22, 1986, their two month anniversary, Bulloch sold his house and permanently moved into their home on White Tree Lane. Days later he informed Julia that he would be leaving May 3 on a business trip to St. Paul, Minnesota.

Acting on a police dispatcher's call, firefighters sped to 251 White Tree Lane at 5:45 a.m. on May 6, 1986. Inside the blazing garage, horrified firemen discovered a bizarre tableau between two burned out cars. Julia Bulloch's nude and badly charred body had been bound to an oak rocker with more than 70 feet of duct tape and left to incinerate in what was obviously a case of arson. The excessive amount of tape and its placement around her face, hair, and crisscrossing her breasts strongly suggested a sexual bondage ritual. Death resulted from asphyxiation caused by two terrycloth gags found jammed in her mouth. With her airway obstructed, she could not have survived for more than eight minutes. Hand swelling indicated that Julia was bound between 5–10 minutes before she died and no attempt had been made pre-mortem to remove her bindings. The fire had burned away any bruises or fingerprints on the body. Her death was ruled a homicide.

Dennis Bulloch became the prime suspect after investigators learned that he was the sole beneficiary of her estate. His story of being in St. Paul during the time of the murder quickly crumbled after a business colleague on the same trip informed police Bulloch had asked him to serve as an alibi. Police suspicions were further aroused by Bulloch's failure to attend Julia's funeral and the discovery of nude photographs of past lovers among his possessions.

Bulloch disappeared on May 9, 1986, and two days later his mother's car was found abandoned by the Martin Luther King Bridge near the Mississippi River. It contained a suicide note written by Bulloch and dated May 8 which insinuated that Julia's need for "tender roughness" had caused her own death. One line, "I am taking my final baptism," failed to convince police that he had jumped from the bridge and an all points bulletin was immediately issued. FBI wiretaps on the phones of Bulloch's friends and family led to his arrest in Santa Cruz, California, on July 3, 1986, where he was using the alias "Jonathan Dennis."

Jury selection in Bulloch's first degree murder trial began in Clayton, Missouri, on May 26, 1987, more than ten months after his arrest. In opening arguments, the prosecution portrayed Bulloch as a social climbing sadist who married Julia for her money and then tied her up and watched her suffocate when he could no longer control her. Bulloch's counsel countered with the controversial "sex-death" defense that essentially blamed the young woman for her own death. The defense argued that Julia was not the victim in bondage, but rather the "sexually promiscuous" initiator and instructress. Bulloch had never before engaged in bondage until his "femme fatale" wife demanded it. Her death was just an "accident." As Julia's pathetic audiotape was barred as hearsay evidence, a former lover of Bulloch's testified that she had engaged in a bondage relationship with him well before he met Julia. The defense's star witness, a highly paid forensic psychiatrist, testified that Bulloch knew nothing of bondage until he met Julia and that her death *could* have been accidental.

On June 2, 1987, a packed courtroom listened as Dennis Bulloch attempted to recount the confused events leading to his wife's death. As part of their lovemaking ritual, he bound her to the chair as she instructed and watched as she placed the strips of cloth in her own mouth before he taped her mouth shut with over 30 feet of duct tape. Drunk and nauseous from alcohol, Bulloch went to the bathroom and fell asleep. Sometime later he awoke to discover his wife had fallen over in her chair. She did not respond to resuscitation. No longer wanting to live, he carried her to the garage intending to commit suicide by carbon monoxide poisoning, but the car would not run. Confused, Bulloch decided to immolate himself with Julia, but first wanted to read her diaries so as to become "closer to her." What he read there so enraged him that he used the diary to start the fire. Unable to withstand the intense heat, Bulloch fled the scene and flew back to St. Paul under an assumed name. When he later felt that Julia may have been burned alive, Bulloch testified that the only thing which prevented him from jumping from the Martin Luther King Bridge was "my fear that I could burn in hell forever."

The prosecution was confident that Bulloch would be convicted of first degree murder and face the death penalty when the case went to the jury on June 3, 1987. Six hours later, they returned with a verdict of "involuntary manslaughter" for which Bulloch was sentenced to the maximum of 7 years and fined $5,000 on July 10, 1987. Public outrage was so great over the verdict that the jury received hate mail. Declaring the verdict to be "a terrible mistake," the prosecution filed charges of arson and tampering with evidence (burning Julia's diary) against Bulloch 15 days after the verdict. Opening arguments began in Cape Girardeau on July 12, 1988, and the next day Bulloch was found guilty and subsequently sentenced on November 4, 1988, to an 11-year prison sentence (6 for arson, 5 for tampering). The state appeals court overturned these convictions on February 13, 1990, citing prosecutorial error in referring to Bulloch's failure to testify in his second trial. Bulloch was released seven months early on June 18, 1990, after having served 4 years and 7 months on his manslaughter conviction. He remained free on $150,000 bond awaiting his retrial on arson and evidence tampering. In less than 90 minutes of deliberation, a Columbia, Missouri, jury reconvicted Bulloch of the charges on August 29, 1990. On October 9, 1990, Bulloch was given the maximum sentences of 7 years for arson and 5 years for evidence tampering to run consecutively. In November 1992 the Missouri court of appeals ruled that both sentences be served concurrently. On January 26, 1993, Bulloch was paroled from the Central Missouri Correctional Center where he lived in a minimum security dormitory and worked in the food service area. Seven years after her murder, Julia Bulloch's estate was settled on March 2, 1993. Dennis Bulloch received nothing.

65. Harris, Ellen Francis. *Dying to Get Married: The Courtship and Murder of Julie Miller Bulloch*. Secaucus, N.J.: Carol Pub. Group, 1991. xiii, 267 pp., [8]pp. of plates: ill.; 24 cm. ("A Birch Lane Press book.")

_____. [Same as 65.] New York: Harper-Paperbacks, 1992. xv, 329 pp.: ill.; 17 cm.; paperback.

_____. [Same as 65.] London: True Crime, 1993. xiii, 267 pp., [8]pp. of plates: ill., ports.; 18 cm.; paperback.

Former *St. Louis Globe* reporter Harris was so outraged by the Bulloch verdict that she immediately began writing this book based in large part on interviews with his friends and associates who nearly all requested anonymity out of fear that he would "violently revenge himself on their children or themselves." According to Harris, Bulloch is not on death row today because he is good looking, had excellent legal representation, and the "jurors chose to believe the unbelievable."

Bundy, Carol Mary
(a.k.a. "Carol Mary Peters" [maiden name], "Carol Ann Bundy," "Petunia," "Blind Bat," "Motor Mouth," "Claudia")

Born circa 1942. Licensed practical nurse. Los Angeles, California (Hollywood area); 2 murders; .25 caliber pistol, knife; June 20, 1980–August 3, 1980.

"The honest truth is, it's fun to kill people and if I was allowed to run loose I'd probably do it again."—Bundy talking to police in August 1980; *see also* Clark, Douglas Daniel.

Bundy, Theodore Robert
(a.k.a. "Theodore Robert Cowell" [birth name], "Theo-dore Robert Nelson," "Rex Bundy," "Chris Hagen," "Kenneth R. Misner," "Officer Roseland," "The Ted Killer," "The Chi Omega Killer," "The Love Bite Killer")

Born November 24, 1946, in Burlington, Vermont. Executed January 24, 1989. Psychiatric counselor, law student. Washington, Utah, Idaho, Colorado, Florida, Oregon, California; 30 murders (confessed to; estimated total of between 36 and 50); ligature strangulation, bludgeon; February 1974–February 1978.

Television: "The Deliberate Stranger" (1986), a two-part, four-hour, made-for-television miniseries based on Richard W. Larsen's book *Bundy: The Deliberate Stranger*, originally aired on NBC on May 4 and 5, 1986. Cast includes Mark Harmon (Ted Bundy), Frederic Forrest (Det. Bob Keppel), and George Grizzard (Richard Larsen).

Video: Fatal Addiction (US, 1989), a 56-minute videotaped interview with Bundy conducted the day before his execution by Dr. James C. Dobson, was published in 1989 by Focus on the Family (Pomona, California).

Audio: The Stranger Beside Me, a two–sound cassette, three-hour abridgement of Ann Rule's book of the same title read by the author, was published in 1992 by Simon & Schuster Audio (New York).

"I'm so sorry I've given you all such grief ... but a part of me was hidden all the time."—Bundy in a phone call to his mother made five hours before his execution. Her reply, "You'll always be my precious son."

University educated serial sex killer whose good looks and charm enabled him to lure at least 30 young women to their deaths. Called by U.S. District Judge G. Kendall Sharp "the most competent serial killer in the country ... a diabolical genius," Ted Bundy was the all–American boy gone terribly wrong. Handsome, intelligent, and socially facile, the patrician looking former law student had been a Boy Scout, a college graduate with a degree in psychology, a rising Young Republican in Washington State party politics, and had even served as a suicide telephone hotline counselor at the Seattle Crisis Clinic. Bundy's carefully constructed and studied social persona, however, masked an efficient killing machine whose perverted sexual compulsions drove him to slaughter an estimated 50 or more young women and girls in a five-year, seven-state rampage of rape, murder, dismemberment, and necrophilia. Selecting as his victims of choice attractive females who parted their dark shoulder length or longer hair down the middle, Bundy trolled shopping malls, college campuses, and parks posing as a police officer or fire examiner to lure victims into his car. Often, Bundy affected the role of a disabled man sporting crutches or an arm cast and used his victim's unselfish willingness to help as a means to ensnare her. Once the victim was alone with Bundy, he often quickly rendered her unconscious or dead with a blow to the head delivered by an iron bar or tire tool, drove hundreds of miles to a remote wilderness location, raped then strangled and mutilated his victim (many experts argue which occurred first), then left the body to be devoured by animals. He often returned to the scene to commit necrophilic acts until the stench from the rotting body became unbearable.

The illegitimate son of Louise Cowell and a man she described only as "a sailor," Bundy was born Theodore Robert Cowell on November 24, 1946, in the Elizabeth Lund Home for Unwed Mothers in Burlington, Vermont. To avoid embarrassing questions about his lineage, Cowell's parents passed the boy off as their own adopted son. The young Bundy worshipped his grandfather, Sam Cowell, and later described in idyllic terms his early childhood at their home in Philadelphia. In reality, Sam Cowell was a verbally and physically abusive tyrant who vented his mercurial temper on anything or anybody within reach. At such times, dogs unfortunate to wander near him were kicked and cats swung by the tail over his head. Bundy's grandmother was repeatedly hospitalized and underwent electroshock therapy for depression before developing into a full-blown agoraphobic. While no hard evidence exists that the grandfather ever physically or sexually abused his grandson, Bundy was already beginning to manifest bizarre behavior while still a child. An aunt later recalled that when she was 15 she awoke to find the three-year-old grinning youngster gently lifting up the bed covers and placing three butcher knives beside her. The child was devastated when his mother, hoping to present herself as a divorcée or widow, moved from the family home to Tacoma, Washington, to live with relatives. In a further attempt to obscure his paternity, Louise Cowell had the boy's official surname changed to "Nelson." Though still a matter of sharp debate, some writers believe that the charade to mask Bundy's bastardy was carried to such an extreme that for years Louise passed herself off as the child's sister. Shortly after arriving in Tacoma, she married Johnnie Culpepper Bundy, a working class hospital cook recently discharged from the Navy. Bundy officially adopted the child whose new name, Theodore Robert Bundy, was his third by age five.

By most accounts, Bundy's childhood was outwardly normal except for his flashes of violent temper. Though shy and somewhat insecure, Bundy maintained a "B" average in school and was a Boy Scout. At age ten or twelve Bundy learned that he was illegitimate when a cousin cruelly taunted him about being a "bastard." The incident deeply humiliated Bundy who blamed his mother for subjecting him to such ridicule. Many psychiatrists consider this moment of self-revelation to have been of crucial import in the development of Bundy's psyche. By adolescence, Bundy was manifesting the classic signs of sexual maladjustment. By day he was the vice president of the Methodist Youth Fellowship; at night the teenager wandered his neighborhood peeping in windows to watch women undress. A compulsive masturbator, Bundy once told a psychiatrist that classmates taunted and tossed ice water on him after they caught him masturbating in a closet at school. Bundy also turned to soft core pornography and detective magazines which featured violent images of sex and violence to fuel and sate his rapidly evolving sadistic fantasies. Also at this time, Bundy began shoplifting status items like ski equipment and expensive clothes in an effort to fashion a public persona antithetical to his humble beginnings. He was caught stealing a car but let off with a stern warning. Carefully crafting a mask of normalcy, Bundy earned a scholarship to the University of Puget Sound, but quickly transferred to the University of Washington to study Chinese. There, the

20-year-old met a beautiful coed from an affluent San Francisco family who many psychiatrists feel represented to Bundy everything for which he was striving: money, position, social status. Prophetically, the young woman had long dark hair which she parted in the middle. Hoping to marry her, Bundy followed the woman to Stanford University where she broke off with him in the summer of 1967.

Bundy returned to the University of Washington to study psychology and with cold calculation began the construction of a social persona that would attract and beguile both women and men alike. He became active in the Washington State Republican party and when not campaigning worked on a suicide hotline. Graduating in 1972 with a degree in psychology, Bundy was initially rejected by several law schools until one of his political contacts, Republican Governor Dan Evans, wrote a glowing letter of recommendation that secured him a place at the law school of the University of Utah. Bundy remained in Washington awaiting the start of the fall 1974 semester. Although romantically involved with another woman, Bundy once again resolved to meet the wealthy California coed who had rejected him. Self-assured, attractive, witty, and urbane, the Bundy she now met was totally changed from the man she dumped. Bundy dazzled the woman into thinking they were engaged, then unceremoniously dumped her as an act of sweet revenge. The pre-law student was involved with his long-time girlfriend "Liz Kendall" (a pseudonym) when he committed the first of what police in the Pacific Northwest would officially call "the Ted Killings." On February 1, 1974, Lynda Ann Healy, a 21-year-old University of Washington psychology student, was reported missing from her basement apartment near the school. Investigators found caked blood on the pillow, mattress, and the woman's night gown carelessly jammed into the back of a closet. Over the next seven months, eight more women between the ages of 18 and 23, all similar in appearance with long dark hair parted in the middle, disappeared from Seattle and Corvallis, Oregon. In each instance, no one saw any of the women kidnapped.

Police dubbed the slayings "the Ted Killings" after Janice Ott, a 23-year-old married probation officer, and 18-year-old Denise Naslund, were abducted in separate instances from Lake Sammamish State Park just outside of Seattle on July 14, 1974. Later, several women at the park told investigators of a nice looking man with a cast on his arm calling himself "Ted" who asked their help in loading a sailboat onto his car. The young women's strangled and bludgeoned bodies were found on September 7, 1974, about four miles from Lake Sammamish in a remote, wooded area. The animal-gnawed remains of a third victim were found nearby. On March 1, 1975, another of Bundy's dumping grounds was discovered in a remote area of Taylor Mountain, 10 miles east of Issaquah. Bones from two other victims were found on October 12, 1974, by a deer hunter near Olympia, Washington. As police followed up on thousands of "Ted" leads, Bundy left Seattle in late August 1974 to enroll at the University of Utah Law School in Salt Lake City. Similar killings began in Utah. Four girls, ages 16 and 17, were kidnapped or killed between October 2 and November 8, 1974. A fifth woman, Carol DaRonch, 18, managed to escape from Bundy's Volkswagen on Novem-

ber 8, 1974, after he lured her out of a mall in Murray, Utah, by posing as police officer "Roseland." That same evening, 17-year-old Debra Kent disappeared from a high school parking lot in Bountiful, Utah. On January 12, 1975, the killing moved east to Colorado. Caryn Campbell, a 23-year-old nurse from Michigan, was vacationing in Aspen when she disappeared from a ski lodge. She was found bludgeoned to death five weeks later. Three more women disappeared before the killing spree ended on August 16, 1975, when Bundy was stopped by a Utah highway patrol officer for driving his Volkswagen Beetle erratically. A search of the car revealed a small crowbar, a mask made out of pantyhose, rope, an ice pick, and a pair of handcuffs. More damning, the officer found gasoline credit card receipts and maps which put Bundy near the scene of many of the "Ted Killings." Bundy was arrested on suspicion of burglary, but was soon freed on his own recognizance. Meanwhile, police worked to connect the law student to the attempted kidnapping of Carol DaRonch. On October 2, 1975, DaRonch picked Bundy out of a lineup as her attacker and he was charged with kidnapping. Tried in Salt Lake City, Bundy was convicted of aggravated kidnapping and sentenced on June 30, 1976, to 1 to 15 years in Utah State Prison.

When hairs found in Bundy's car tied him to several other recent "Ted Killings," the state of Colorado charged him with the murder of Caryn Campbell. Directing his own defense, the cocky former law student was given access to the second floor law library in the Pitkin County courthouse in Aspen. Bundled up in several layers of clothes to withstand the cool Colorado nights, Bundy escaped on June 7, 1977, by jumping from the second floor window. He was recaptured two days later. While awaiting trial for the Campbell murder in the Garfield County jail in Glenwood Springs, Bundy lost nearly 40 pounds so that he could fit through a metal plate in the ceiling of his cell. Using a hacksaw blade he somehow acquired, Bundy cut a one foot square opening in the ceiling and squeezed through to freedom on December 30, 1977. He used his 17-hour headstart to good advantage ultimately making his way to Denver by bus, to Chicago by plane, and on to Ann Arbor, Michigan, by train. Tiring quickly of the cold weather, Bundy traveled a circuitous route to Tallahassee, Florida, arriving there by bus on January 8, 1978. Bundy, as "Chris Hagen," established himself in a rooming house on the outskirts of the campus of Florida State University and began stealing credit cards to support himself.

In the wee hours of January 15, 1978, Bundy committed the atrocity for which he will always be instantly remembered in the annals of crime. Armed with a short oak log, Bundy invaded the Chi Omega sorority house at 661 W. Jefferson and in less than 15 minutes wreaked unspeakable carnage. Dead in her second floor bedroom was Lisa Levy, 20, the victim of ligature strangulation and bludgeoning. One of the young woman's nipples had nearly been bitten off and double bite marks were found on her left buttock. After death, she had been raped and sodomized with a plastic bottle of Clairol hair mist. In a nearby room, 21-year-old Margaret Bowman was found bludgeoned to death, a nylon stocking left tightly cinched around her neck. Two other young women, Karen Chandler and Kathy Kleiner, had been severely bludgeoned but lived. Within hours of the Chi Omega attacks, Bundy struck again a few blocks away bludgeoning dance student Cheryl Thomas nearly to death in her duplex apartment. Thomas survived, but sustained a permanent loss of balance. On February 9, 1978, Bundy was trolling in Lake City, Florida, when he lured 12-year-old high school student Kimberly Diane Leach into a Dodge van he had stolen three days earlier. Leach's body was subsequently found on April 7, 1978, in an abandoned hog pen in the Suwannee River State Park midway between Lake City and Tallahassee. An autopsy on her desiccated remains determined death to have been caused by "homicidal violence to the neck region."

In the meantime, Bundy had been arrested in Pensacola, Florida, on February 15, 1978, after police ran a license plate check on the stolen Volkswagen he was driving. The next day, fingerprints supplied by the FBI established the car thief's identity as escaped fugitive Ted Bundy. Still maintaining his innocence, Bundy was charged in July 1978 for the murders of Margaret Bowman, Lisa Levy, and Kimberly Leach. Tried in Miami in July 1979 for the Chi Omega killings, the former law student again insisted, over the advice of his attorneys, on taking an active role in his defense. While eyewitness testimony placed him at the scene, dental forensic evidence establishing that the teeth marks left in the buttock identically matched Ted Bundy's bite pattern sealed the case for the prosecution. On July 23, 1979, Bundy was convicted on two counts of first degree murder and sentenced eight days later to death by electrocution. In a separate trial, Bundy was convicted on February 7, 1980, of the first degree murder of Kimberly Leach and sentenced to death. A highlight of the trial occurred when Bundy, acting as his own attorney, placed lover Carole Ann Boone on the witness stand. In a vagary of Florida law, the pair were able to marry when they declared their desire to do so in open court in the presence of a notary.

For 10 years Bundy was able to use the legal system to remain alive on death row at the Florida State Prison in Starke. During that time, the convicted serial killer basked in the warm glow of publicity and granted interviews to various journalists and law enforcement officials. He even bragged of fathering a child with wife Carole Boone in the visitors' room of the prison. When it became clear in early January 1989 that all legal appeals had been exhausted in blocking his execution for Leach's murder, Bundy mounted a last ditch effort to prolong his life. Bundy, who for a decade had adamantly maintained his innocence, now offered to trade detailed confessions for time. At one point, Bundy estimated that it would take him three years to discuss unsolved cases in Utah and states in the Pacific Northwest. Florida Governor Bob Martinez refused the deal, ruefully adding that for Bundy "to negotiate for his life over the bodies of his victims [was] despicable." Scheduled to die shortly after 7:00 a.m. on January 24, 1989, Bundy confessed on January 21 to eight "Ted" murders committed in Utah, one in Colorado in 1975, and three that he could not substantiate in Washington State. Hours before his execution, Bundy granted an interview with the Reverend James C. Dobson, a Pomona, California–based religious broadcaster well known for his radio crusade against pornography. During the videotaped interview, a "repentant" Bundy told the evangelist that violent pornography had shaped his behavior and warned society that it would produce other killers like him if it was not controlled. After uttering his last words, "I'd like you to give my love to my family and friends," Bundy was electrocuted on schedule in the Q wing of Florida State Prison and pronounced dead at 7:16 a.m. While the total number of Bundy's victims may never be known, he officially confessed to 30 and hinted at two others committed in New Jersey in 1969. Law enforcement officials generally estimate Bundy's death count at between 36 and 50, while many detectives close to the case are convinced that the serial killer's victims could number well over 100.

66. Kendall, Elizabeth. *The Phantom Prince: My Life with Ted Bundy.* 1st ed. Seattle: Madrona, 1981. viii, 183 pp.; 21 cm.

Personal account by Bundy's former lover who suspected him of being the "Ted Killer."

67. Larsen, Richard W. *Bundy: The Deliberate Stranger.* Englewood Cliffs, N.J.: Prentice-Hall, 1980. ix, 303 pp.; 24 cm.

_____. [Same as 67.] New York: Pocket Books, 1986. ix, 352 pp.; 17 cm.; paperback.

Larsen, a reporter for *The Seattle Times,* first met Bundy when the university student was involved in Republican city politics. The book served as the basis for the 1986 made-for-television movie of the same title.

68. Michaud, Stephen G., and Aynesworth, Hugh. *The Only Living Witness.* New York: Linden Press/Simon & Schuster, 1983. 332 pp., [8] leaves of plates: ill.; 24 cm.

_____. [Same as 68.] New York: New American Library, 1984. 319 pp., [4] leaves of plates: ill.; 18 cm.; paperback.

_____. [Same as 68.] Updated ed. New York: New American Library, 1989. 360 pp., [8]pp. of plates: ill.; 18 cm. ("A Signet book"); paperback.

While denying his involvement in any of the murders, Bundy "speculated" on what prompted the killer to act. The authors let Bundy's supreme egotism lead him into supplying details of the murders which only the killer could know. A chilling journey into the mind of one of the most important serial killers of this century.

69. _____. *Ted Bundy: Conversations with a Killer.* New York: New American Library, 1989. xiii, 306 pp.: ill.; 18 cm. ("A Signet book"); paperback.

70. Nelson, Polly. *Defending the Devil: My Story as Ted Bundy's Last Lawyer.* 1st ed. New York: W. Morrow, 1994. 336 pp.: ill., forms; 25 cm.

Nelson was an associate with a Washington, D.C., law firm when she was given the *pro bono* project of defending Ted Bundy from execution. While she does not attempt to defend Bundy's character, she does feel that capital punishment is wrong and offers the usual arguments against it (economic, moral, etc.). Interesting if unconvincing.

71. Perry, Michael R. *The Stranger Returns.* New York: Pocket Star Books, 1992. 420 pp.; 18 cm.; paperback.

A fictional Bundy is the protagonist in this thriller novel.

72. Rule, Ann. *The Stranger Beside Me.* 1st ed. New York: Norton, 1980. 350 pp.: ill.; 24 cm.

_____. [Same as 72.] New York: New American Library, 1980. xv, 413 pp.: ill.; 18 cm. ("A Signet book"); paperback.

_____. [Same as 72.] New York: New American Library, 1981. xv, 413 pp., [4] leaves of plates: ill.; 18 cm. ("A Signet book"); paperback.

_____. [Same as 72.] New York: New American Library, 1981. xv, 442 pp., [8]pp. of plates: ill., ports.; 18 cm. ("A Signet book"); paperback.

_____. [Same as 72.] Updated ed. New York: New American Library, 1986. xv, 442 pp., [8]pp. of plates: ill.; 18 cm. ("A Signet book"); paperback.

"Updated with an afterword by the author."—Cover.

_____. [Same as 72.] Rev. and updated ed. New York: New American Library, 1989. 498 pp., [8]pp. of plates: ill.; 18 cm. ("A Signet book"); paperback.

_____. [Same as 72.] Rev. and updated ed. London: Warner, 1994. 498 pp., [8]pp. of plates: ill., ports.; 18 cm.; paperback.

Rule worked with Bundy as a volunteer at the Seattle Crisis Clinic during the time of the "Ted Killings" and her account of the case profits from this firsthand association with the man she described as "like the younger brother I had lost." Essential.

73. Winn, Steven, and Merrill, David. *Ted Bundy: The Killer Next Door.* New York: Bantam, 1979. 359 pp., 32 leaves of plates: ill.; 18 cm.; paperback.

Sensational paperback account written quickly to cash in on the case's notoriety. "Coast-to-coast horror story— The shocking true crime thriller of a brutal sex murderer."—Cover.

Buono, Angelo, Jr.

Born circa October 1944 in Rochester, New York. Auto upholsterer. Glendale, California; 10 murders (9 convictions); ligature strangulation, asphyxiation; October 17, 1977–February 17, 1978; *see also* Bianchi, Kenneth Alessio.

Busacca, Thomas F.

Born circa 1925. Died February 29, 1988. Unemployed photographer. Baldwin, Long Island, New York; 1 murder; bludgeon (bat or shovel); August 29, 1976.

"Thank you."—Busacca's response to the warden of Dannemora Prison who informed him that his dead wife's remains had been found

Precedent setting case pre-dating the conviction of Connecticut wife murderer Richard Crafts in which Thomas Busacca became only the second individual in the history of American jurisprudence to be convicted of a murder without a victim's body as evidence. Employed for only five of the 25 years he was married to wife Florence, a former opera singer who supported him and two teenaged children by giving voice lessons in their Baldwin, Long Island, home, the 51-year-old Busacca still accepted money from his parents. Florence Busacca, resentful of working while her husband spent his days watching television, shared her bed with him, but refused his sexual advances. Convinced that she had an affair while on a Paris vacation with her sister in July 1976, Busacca avoided his family and left Florence cryptic, threatening notes. Fearful for their safety, Florence initiated divorce proceedings against her unstable husband.

In the mid-evening of August 29, 1976, the Busacca children returned home to find the enclosed back porch awash in blood. The walls were spattered to a height of six feet as if, one detective noted, "someone had centered himself in the middle of the room and then from a brush made swiping motions at the walls and ceiling with red paint." Parts of an earlobe and an upper partial denture littered the floor. Blood spoor leading from the room down the porch steps ended in a pool on the driveway. Police were waiting at 1442 Circle Drive West when Busacca pulled his car into the driveway on the following morning. Busacca's face was covered with scratches and detectives noticed blood dripping from the car's trunk. When opened, it contained a bone. Placed under arrest, Busacca admitted exchanging heated words with Florence earlier in the day over his scheme to let his parents move in with them in exchange for their taking over the mortgage payments on the house. That evening the couple argued and Busacca struck his wife repeatedly in the head with a bat or a shovel after she allegedly slapped him. According to Busacca's "confession," he planned to dump her body in Lindenhurst Bay, but panicked when she started yelling and kicking from inside the trunk of the car. Instead, he drove to the nearby town of Holbrook, Long Island, and left his wife (alive and cursing) against a rail fence near a model home development.

Accompanied by Busacca, police visited the site, but found no physical evidence corroborating his story. A bloodstained shirt he claimed to have discarded was found two miles away from the scene on the shoulder of a highway. On August 31, 1976, five police agencies began a coordinated search for Florence Busacca's body. When the search ended 40 days later on October 8, 1976, police had logged in 5,000 manhours and covered hundreds of square miles. Though failing to find Florence, a piece of a blood-soaked quilt determined to belong to Busacca was recovered. The blood on the quilt, like that found at the crime scene and in Busacca's trunk, matched the rare AB negative type belonging to the victim. Armed with this physical evidence and dental records proving the partial dental plate found on the porch was Florence's, authorities took the unprecedented move of prosecuting Busacca on a charge of murder despite the fact that no one in New

York State had ever been convicted without a body.

Busacca pleaded not guilty as his trial opened in Mineola, New York, on March 2, 1977. The defense maintained that Florence was alive and living in either California or Milan and produced a witness who was "75 percent sure" that he had recently lunched with her in New York City. The chief medical examiner of Nassau County testified that given the amount of blood at the scene Florence could not possibly have survived the bludgeoning. Defense psychiatrists characterized Busacca as a longtime paranoid schizophrenic whose mind was in such an advanced state of deterioration that he lacked the rational capacity to tailor his conduct to the law. Four hours after receiving the case on March 24, 1977, a jury found Busacca guilty of second degree manslaughter. He was subsequently sentenced to not less than 8 1/3 years nor more than 25 years in prison. On November 21, 1980 (4 years, 2 months, and 21 days after the murder) an off-duty Long Island railroad police officer discovered the skeletal remains of Florence Busacca on a beach in Hampton Bays, Long Island. Busacca was released from prison in November 1986 and died of natural causes at his father's home in Brooklyn on February 29, 1988.

74. Walker, Roger W. *Silent Testimony: A True Story.* East Hampton, N.Y.: Carriage House Press, 1989. 297 pp.: ill.; 23 cm.

_____. [Same as 74.] New York: St. Martin's Paperbacks, 1990. 312 pp., [8]pp. of plates: ill.; 18 cm.; paperback.

Camb, James
(a.k.a. "Porthole Murderer," "James Clarke")

Born December 16, 1916, in Waterfoot, Lancashire, England. Died July 7, 1979. Ship's steward. At sea off the west coast of Africa; 1 murder; manual strangulation; October 18, 1947.

"I am glad to get it off my mind. What will happen about this? My wife must not know about this. If she does I will do away with myself."—Camb after admitting to authorities that Gibson died during sexual intercourse

Ship's steward convicted of murdering an actress aboard an ocean liner and disposing of her body through a porthole. Following a lengthy run starring in the Johannesburg production of Clifford Odets' play *Golden Boy*, 21-year-old British actress Gay Gibson (real name Eileen Isabella Ronnie Gibson) shipped out from Cape Town, South Africa, on October 10, 1947, aboard the Union Castle liner *Durban Castle* bound for the port of Southampton. Eight days out and nearly 150 miles off the west coast of Africa, Gibson was found missing from her cabin and feared lost in the shark-infested waters. The liner reversed course, but after a futile search continued on its journey. A night watchman stepped forward to report that at 2:28 a.m. on October 18 the bell-pushes in Gibson's cabin used for summoning a steward had been pulled for several moments. His knock on the door of cabin 126 was answered by James Camb, a 31-year-old ship's steward not assigned to B Deck. According to the watchman's testimony, Camb was wearing a sleeveless shirt and told him through a cracked door that things were "all right." Camb afterwards denied being in Gibson's cabin but now wore a long sleeve jacket, unusual in a tropical climate. An examination of Camb by the ship's surgeon revealed scratches on the steward's wrists, neck, and shoulder which Camb lamely dismissed as "heat rash."

Southampton detectives were waiting to interview the steward when the *Durban Castle* docked there on October 25, 1947. Initially denying ever having been in Gibson's cabin, Camb changed his story when authorities insisted he had been seen there. Camb admitted visiting Gibson's cabin at the actress' request where he engaged in consensual sex with her. During intercourse Gibson went into a seizure and died despite Camb's futile attempts at artificial respiration. Fearful that he would be found in a compromising position and lose his job, Camb forced Gibson's body through the cabin's porthole and into the sea. He did not know how the bell-pushes had been pulled. "The Porthole Murder Case" was tried amid great public interest at the Hampshire Assizes beginning on March 18, 1948. Physical evidence recovered from the cabin (blood, saliva, and urine stained sheets) was equally consistent with the prosecution's theory of the case (Camb raped then strangled Gibson to hide his crime) and the defense's contention that the actress died of natural causes during consensual sex. The ship's surgeon testified that the scratches on Camb's wrists were more consistent with those intentionally inflicted by fingernails during a struggle than by those wildly flailing during a seizure. Camb testified in his own defense, but his case was hurt by his insufficient answers to the questions of why he failed to summon a doctor for Gibson and, more importantly, why had he hurriedly disposed of the body which could have proven his claim of accidental death? Despite a favorable summing up by Mr. Justice Hilbery, Camb was found guilty on March 22, 1948, and sentenced to death. He was reprieved on April 30, 1948, because the "no hanging" clause of the Criminal Justice Bill (approved by the House of Commons, but defeated by the House of Lords) was then under discussion in Parliament. Camb was released from prison in September 1959. In May 1967, Camb (under the name "James Clarke") pleaded guilty to a charge of indecently assaulting an eight-year-old girl in Bishop's Stortford and was placed on probation for two years. In May 1971 Camb was employed as head waiter at the Waverly Castle Hotel in Melrose, Scotland, when he pleaded guilty to "lewd, indecent and libidinous practices" towards three pre-teenage girls staying there. Sentenced to three years, Camb returned to Wakefield Prison to serve his time. Released in 1978, the 62-year-old Camb suffered a heart attack in a pub at Leeds and died on July 7, 1979.

75. Clark, Geoffrey, ed. *Trial of James Camb: The Port-Hole Murder.* Notable British Trials. London: W. Hodge, 1949. 255 pp.: ill., ports., plans; 22 cm.

A concise introduction summarizes the case followed by extensive excerpts from Camb's trial at the Hampshire Assizes, March 18–22, 1948. Appendices include a list of trial exhibits and the text of the court of criminal appeal's dismissal of Camb's appeal on April 26, 1948.

76. Herbstein, Denis. *The Porthole Murder Case: The Death of Gay Gibson.* London: Hodder & Stoughton, 1991. xi, 259 pp., [8]pp. of plates: ill., plans, ports.; 24 cm.

_____. [Same as 76.] Sevenoaks: Coronet, 1992. xi, 259 pp., [8]pp. of plates: ill., 1 facsim., plans, ports.; 18 cm.; paperback.

Well researched, definitive account of the "Porthole Murder Case." Highly recommended.

"Camden Town Murder" *see*
Wood, Robert William
Thomas George Cavers

"Cannock Chase Murders [or]
Killings" *see* Morris, Raymond
Leslie

Carignan, Harvey Louis
(a.k.a. "Yankee," "Harv-the-
Hammer," "The Want-Ad
Killer")

Born May 18, 1927, in Fargo,
North Dakota. Gas station owner, con-
struction worker. Alaska, Washington,
Minnesota; 4 murders (suspected of
numerous others); bludgeon (hammer);
July 1949–September 1974.

"It wouldn't be the best thing for
me, but it might be for other people."—Carignan when asked by a
CNN reporter in 1983 if it would be
best for him to remain imprisoned

Serial rapist and killer whose
nickname "Harv-the-Hammer" is derived from his weapon of choice. If
there is any validity to the argument
that criminals are "made," not "born,"
then rapist-murderer Harvey Carignan
is the proof. Born a bastard during the
Depression, Carignan spent his first 11
years farmed out to relatives by a
mother who could not cope with his
stress-related facial tics and chronic
enuresis. When his bedwetting made
him unwelcome with relations, Carignan was returned to his mother who,
failing to find an orphanage, placed the
11-year-old in a reform school in Man-
dan, North Dakota, in 1939. He
remained there until 1946 when he
joined the Army. Two years later Carignan was assigned to Fort Richardson in
Anchorage, Alaska. At 21, the shy,

silent Carignan had already spent half
his life in various institutions. He had
also developed a virulent hatred of
women based upon his mother's rejection and incidents of sexual abuse committed by an adult babysitter when he
was five. On July 31, 1949, Carignan
lashed out against the sex which he felt
had always controlled and humiliated
him. After unsuccessfully attempting
to rape 40-year-old Laura Showalter
in an Anchorage park, Carignan bludgeoned her to death. Months later on
September 16, 1949, an attempted rape
of a 22-year-old woman led to his
arrest. In custody, Carignan signed a
confession to the murder of Showalter
and was tried and sentenced to death
in 1950. In a 1951 appeal to the supreme
court it was determined that in admitting the confession into evidence
Carignan's rights had been violated. He
had been illegally detained and not
promptly brought before a magistrate
on the murder charge, a violation of the
McNabb Rule. Carignan had escaped
hanging and jail time, but was subsequently convicted of the attempted
rape and assault and sentenced to 15
years in Alcatraz. After serving nine
years, the 32-year-old was paroled on
April 2, 1960.

Four months later in Duluth,
Minnesota, Carignan was arrested on
burglary, assault, and rape charges and
sentenced to 2086 days at Leavenworth. Paroled in 1964, he moved to
Seattle, Washington, where on November 22, eight months after arriving, he was arrested for second degree
burglary and sentenced to 15 years at
Walla Walla. Inherently bright and a
voracious reader, Carignan used the
time to earn a high school diploma.
Released on "good time" four years
later, he returned to Seattle where
in 1969 he married a divorcée with

children. Arrested on a parole violation and suspicion of burglary, Carignan did less than a year, but returned home to a chilly reception. It was during a violent argument with his wife that Carignan first heard "God" instruct him to kill women with a hammer. Carignan and his wife divorced and Carignan remarried another divorcée with a son and a teenage daughter in 1972. A harsh disciplinarian, he beat the son and wife and approached the daughter for sex. Both children soon left to live with their father.

On May 1, 1973, Kathy Sue Miller, 15, disappeared after answering an ad for a job at a gas station owned by Carignan. While he admitted talking to her on the phone, Carignan said she failed to make their meeting. When police pulled his rap sheet, he was put under around the clock surveillance. Days later, Miller's books were found in a parking lot in Everett, 26 miles north of Seattle. On June 23, 1973, two teenagers found the nude body of a woman wrapped in plastic sheeting on the Tulalip Indian reservation north of Everett. Two nickel-sized holes in the right rear portion of her skull suggested she had been murdered with a hammer. The next day, using dental records, police identified the remains as Kathy Sue Miller. Without probable cause, Carignan could not be arrested. He subsequently moved, without his estranged wife, to Minneapolis to escape police pressure. Shortly after his arrival, a reign of rape and murder was unleashed in and around Minneapolis. On June 28, 1973, Marlys Townsend was struck in the back of the head at a bus stop. Waking to find herself in a pickup truck, the driver told her to fondle his genitals. She was lucky enough to escape. On September 9, 1973, Carig-

nan picked up a 13-year-old hitchhiker and forced her to fellate him. After raping her with the handle of a hammer, hitting her in the head, and sodomizing her four times, he dumped her in a nearby town instructing her not to tell anyone.

In early 1974 Carignan began dating Eileen Hunley, a day-care worker heavily involved in the fundamentalist church group, "The Way." By July, however, Carignan's drinking and temper had soured the relationship and Hunley wanted out. She disappeared on August 10, 1974. Five weeks later her rotting corpse was found in a woods near Zimmerman, Minnesota. Her head was destroyed by hammer blows, and the murderer had rammed a tree branch into her vagina. On September 8, 1974, 16-year-old hitchhikers June Lynch and Lisa King were picked up by Carignan and driven to a wooded area. King escaped, but Lynch was struck seven times in the head with a hammer. She survived. Six days later, he picked up 19-year-old Gwen Burton after her car broke down. Forcing her to fellate him, Carignan raped her with the handle of a hammer, struck her in the head, and left her for dead in an alfalfa field. Hours later she was found by a farmboy. On September 18, 1974, Carignan picked up 18-year-old Sally Versoi and her girlfriend. After asking them theoretically whether they would rather be raped or killed he began beating them both. They escaped when he stopped for gas. Two days later police filed a missing persons bulletin on 18-year-old Kathy Schultz when she failed to return from class. The next day her body was found by pheasant hunters in a cornfield 40 miles outside of Minneapolis. Her skull had been shattered by hammer blows.

Acting on descriptions of the

assailant and his car given by the survivors, police picked up Carignan on September 23, 1974. All identified him as their assailant. A search of one of his former vehicles turned up maps of seven states containing 181 red circles drawn around isolated areas. Some of the circles seemed to denote body sites, while others, areas in which women were reported missing or assaulted. Though police ultimately found it impossible to correlate all the circles with bodies, they strongly suspected Carignan in the disappearance of Laura Brock near Coupeville, Washington, and in the murder of an unidentified woman at Medora, North Dakota.

Carignan went to trial for the attempted murder of Gwen Burton in the second week of February 1975. Pleading insanity, he testified that God had given him a divine mission to kill "the harlots and the whores." The attempted murder was merely "a ritual for the destruction of women." Unimpressed, the jury took less than five hours to find him guilty of aggravated sodomy and attempted murder on March 3, 1975. Carignan received 40 years, the maximum to which any criminal in Minnesota can be sentenced. The 110-year sentences passed down in the show trials for the Hunley-Schultz murders and the Billings assault were meaningless. Under the eccentricity of Minnesota law, Carignan was eligible for his first parole hearing on May 8, 1993. He was denied.

77. Rule, Ann [Stack, Andy]. *The Want-Ad Killer.* Andy Stack's True Crime Annals, vol. 2. New York: New American Library, 1983. 223 pp.; 18 cm. ("A Signet book"); paperback.

_____. [Same as 77.] Updated ed., rev. ed. New York: New American Library, 1988. xii, 229 pp., [8]pp. of plates: ill.; 18 cm. ("A Signet book"); paperback.

Ann Rule originally wrote this book in 1983 under her pseudonym "Andy Stack." Updated and revised edition (1988) notes "Ann Rule writing as Andy Stack."

Carpenter, David Joseph (a.k.a. "The Trailside Killer/ Slayer," "Mr. Stutter," "Devious Dave")

Born May 6, 1930, in San Francisco, California. Printer, novelty item salesman, former purser. San Francisco, California area; 10 murders; knife, .44 caliber Magnum pistol, .38 caliber pistol; August 1979–May 1980.

"To get away with the act of murder is the ultimate challenge."

David Carpenter, the infamous "Trailside Killer" who during a ten-month period from August 1979 through May 1980 littered parks in and around San Francisco with the bodies of ten victims, once told a woman he tried to rape that "I have this funny quirk that's got to be satisfied." The product of a mother described in a state report as an "aggressive and vicious, domineering woman" and a part-time father who regularly beat him, Carpenter developed a severe stutter at age seven which made him the object of lifelong ridicule. Though ashamed of her son's speech impediment, Carpenter's mother never sought therapy for him, preferring instead to force the uncoordinated youth to take ballet and piano lessons. Unable to communicate and barred by his mother from having friends, Carpenter's frustration expressed itself in chronic bedwetting and the torture of small animals. In 1947, the 17-year-old was sentenced to one year in the California

Youth Authority facility in Preston for molesting two cousins, an eight-year-old boy and a three-year-old girl. Paroled in 1948, Carpenter continued to commit sex offenses until his marriage on November 5, 1955. For five years he managed to suppress his high sex drive, sudden rages, and humiliation over his stuttering by having intercourse three times a night with his wife. Employed as a ship's purser by the Pacific Far East Lines, Carpenter's life seemed to be finally straightened out. On July 12, 1960, however, Carpenter picked up a 32-year-old female acquaintance and drove her to a secluded area near Crissy Field in San Francisco. When she fought his rape attempt, Carpenter struck her six times in the head with a hammer. A patrolling military policeman saved the woman's life by shooting Carpenter twice. On March 9, 1961, Carpenter was sentenced to 14 years for assault with a deadly weapon. While in prison, Carpenter's wife took their three children and divorced him.

Paroled from McNeil Island on April 7, 1969, after serving the minimum sentence of nine years, Carpenter's "funny quirk" reasserted itself near Boulder Creek, California, on January 27, 1970. Carpenter rearended 19-year-old Cheryl Lynn Smith's car, stabbed her during the subsequent rape attempt, and fled. Over the next few days the ex-con went on a rampage of attempted kidnapping, rape, and burglary before being arrested in Modesto, California, on February 3, 1970. Awaiting trial, Carpenter and four other inmates escaped from the Calaveras County Jail, but were recaptured almost immediately. Carpenter was sentenced to seven years on two counts of robbery and kidnapping. After serving his time plus an extra two-and-a-half

years for violating the terms of the 1960 conviction, Carpenter was released under parole conditions to a halfway house in San Francisco on May 21, 1979. A month later, he enrolled in a computer printing course at the California Trade School in Hayward, eventually graduating on February 22, 1980. Carpenter's free time was spent hiking on Mount Tamalpais, a Marin County peak overlooking the Golden Gate Bridge in the Point Reyes National Wilderness Area.

The so-called "Trailside Killings" began on August 19, 1979, with the murder of 44-year-old Edda Kane who was spending the day alone hiking the trails at the base of Mount Tamalpais. Kane was found the next day, the victim of a .44 caliber wound to the back of her head. The body's facedown, kneeling position suggested to police that she had been made to beg for her life before being shot execution-style. On March 8, 1980, Barbara Schwartz, 23, was hiking with her dog on the slopes of Mount Tamalpais when she was attacked and stabbed 12 times with a boning knife. The murder weapon, the only knife used in any of the "Trailside Killings," was found the next day near the scene. In early October 1980 a woman friend of Carpenter's canceled a debt she owed him by purchasing a Rossi .38 caliber five-shot revolver for the convicted felon. On October 15, 1980, the body of Anne Evelyn Alderson, 26, was found a half mile from the murder site of Edda Kane. Alderson had been raped and shot once in the head with a .38 caliber pistol. Like Kane, the position of Alderson's body suggested that the killer had possibly forced the young woman to beg before taking her life.

The carnage shifted to the 70,000-acre Point Reyes National Seashore

Park. On November 28, 1980, authorities found another of the serial murderer's killing zones. Hikers Diane
Marie O'Connell, 22, and Shauna K.
May, 23, were abducted from a trail at
gunpoint by a man fitting Carpenter's
description. Searchers found their
naked bodies the next day. Both had
been trussed up with picture frame
wire, strangled into unconsciousness,
raped, then shot in the head with a .38
caliber pistol. Ballistics determined
that the gun used in the O'Connell and
May murders was also used to kill
Alderson. On the same day, the search
for the missing hikers yielded another
grisly discovery. Missing since October 11, 1980, the decomposed bodies of
Rick Stowers, 19, and his fiancée Cynthia Moreland, 18, were found less than
half a mile from the murdered women.
Both had died from gunshot wounds to
the head. Afterwards, attendance at
Point Reyes Park dropped off by two-
thirds and signs posted on every trail
warned hikers not to hike alone.

On March 29, 1981, the killer
struck 80 miles south of San Francisco
in Santa Cruz at the Henry Cowell
Redwoods State Park. A man, later
positively identified as Carpenter,
approached 27-year-old University of
California–Davis sophomore Ellen
Marie Hanson and her boyfriend
Stephen Haertle, as they hiked in the
park only 400 yards from an observation deck. Brandishing a .38 caliber
pistol, he demanded Hansen let him
rape her and, when she defiantly
refused, shot her point blank in the
face. Haertle, shot in the neck, managed to escape to get help. Based on
his eyewitness description of the gunman combined with others who saw a
man fleeing the scene, police were able
to develop and distribute a good composite of the suspect to run in area

newspapers. On April 4, 1981, a woman
notified Santa Cruz police to report
that the man in the Identi-kit composite bore a resemblance to David
Carpenter. Twenty-six years before
while on an ocean cruise the woman
had complained to the ship's captain
about the stuttering young purser's
unwanted attention toward her daughter. Shortly after the composite appeared in the paper Carpenter began
growing a beard.

Carpenter was employed as a
computer typesetter instructor at an
agency of the trade school he graduated from when he first noticed
Heather Roxanne Scaggs, a 20-year-
old student at the school. She disappeared on May 2, 1981, after telling her
boyfriend that Carpenter was going to
help her buy a used car. When she
failed to return home, police interviewed Carpenter and were struck by
his resemblance to the composite and
his record of arrests for sexual offenses.
Following a weeklong joint surveillance conducted by local authorities
and the FBI, Carpenter was arrested
on May 15, 1981, outside the San Francisco home he shared with his aged
parents. Inside 36 Sussex Street, police
found 37 maps of local hiking areas
and guidebooks to the parks in the
area. Thirty similar maps were located
in the glovebox of his car. On May 18,
1981, Carpenter was formally charged
with the murder of Hansen and the
attempted murder of Haertle after the
lone survivor picked him out of a
lineup. The charge of murder with
"special circumstances" (a possible
death penalty offense) was added to the
indictment when hikers found the
nude and decomposed body of Heather
Scaggs six days later in Big Basin Redwoods Park. Scaggs had been raped,
then shot once through the eye with a

.38 caliber pistol. On June 16, 1981, two rock climbers in the Castle Rock State Park east of Big Basin found a human jawbone later identified through dental records as that of Anna K. Menjivar, a 17-year-old high school sophomore. Menjivar, a part-time teller at a savings and loan frequented by Carpenter, had been missing since December 28, 1980. Carpenter was subsequently charged with her murder and rape. On July 31, 1981, Carpenter was charged with five additional killings (Stowers, Moreland, O'Connell, May, and Alderson), two rapes (May, Alderson), and an attempted rape (O'Connell) after police recovered Carpenter's .38 caliber pistol which he had given to a friend.

Delayed two years by a series of defense motions and moved 300 miles from the Bay Area to Los Angeles to escape publicity, Carpenter's trial for Hansen's murder and Haertle's attempted murder began with jury selection on October 11, 1983. In a highly unusual development, two separate juries were seated: one to determine guilt and the other to determine a sentence if Carpenter was convicted. Opening arguments began six months later on May 23, 1984. The evidence laid out by the prosecution over a month-long period was overwhelming and indisputable. Carpenter's gun tied him to all the killings and Haertle's testimony identified him as the gunman. Admitting that Carpenter killed the two women, all his attorney could argue was that his client was such a "mental mess" that he could not possibly have premeditated the crimes and therefore should not be sentenced to death in the gas chamber. Carpenter was convicted on July 6, 1984. Despite hearing testimony that the murderer was psychologically "damned at an

early age" by abusive parents, a second jury recommended a sentence of death for Carpenter on October 5, 1984. On November 16, 1984, Carpenter was sentenced to die in the gas chamber at San Quentin.

Years of legal wrangling later, Carpenter faced trial in San Diego on January 5, 1988, for the five murders, two rapes, and attempted rape committed in Marin County. Again, his gun tied him to four of the five killings and documents supporting his alibi for the Stowers and Moreland murders were shown to have been "carefully" altered. Carpenter spent a week on the stand defending his innocence, but a jury needed only seven hours to find him guilty on all counts on May 10, 1988. Following the jury's recommendation, a judge sentenced Carpenter on July 19, 1988, to death. Months later, a prosecutor's worst nightmare occurred when it was determined that the foreman of the jury had told friends that she knew Carpenter had previously been convicted of murder in a "Trailside" case. Under the terms of the just concluded trial, Carpenter's past murder convictions were not allowed to be used in evidence. A juror's knowledge of them represented misconduct and was enough to have the verdict voided. On June 14, 1989, a judge calling the "evidence in (the) case overwhelming" was forced to set aside Carpenter's five murder convictions in what he called an "absolute travesty" of justice. The 11-week trial had cost Marin County an estimated $2 million. To date, Carpenter has yet to be retried for the murders.

78. Graysmith, Robert. *The Sleeping Lady: The Trailside Murders Above the Golden Gate.* 1st ed. New York: Dutton, 1990. 431 pp., [16]pp. of plates: ill.; 25 cm.

_____. [Same as 78.] New York: Onyx, 1990. xvi, 478 pp., [16]pp. of plates: ill.; 18 cm.; paperback.

Carraher, Patrick

Born October 19, 1906, in Glasgow, Scotland. Executed April 6, 1946. Thief. Glasgow, Scotland; 2 murders; knife; August 14, 1938, and November 23, 1945.

"I gave one of them a jag and ran away when the fight started."—Carraher to an acquaintance after John Gordon's murder

Scottish murderer reprieved in the killing of one soldier in 1938 only to be executed in 1946 for the murder of another military man. On August 14, 1938, soldier James Sydney Emden Shaw attempted to break up an argument between Patrick Carraher, a violent alcoholic with a long history of petty thefts, and another man on a street in the squalid Gorbals section of Glasgow. Carraher severed Shaw's jugular with an edged weapon and was arrested the next day. Found guilty of murder on September 13, 1938, Carraher escaped hanging when the jury, believing that he was intoxicated at the time of the killing, reduced the sentence to culpable homicide (manslaughter). Carraher served three years in prison and upon his release resumed a career of petty thievery. In May 1943 Carraher was again sentenced to three years for assault and razor slashing.

History repeated itself on the night of November 23, 1945, when Carraher knifed John Gordon, an 18-year veteran in the Seaforth Highlanders, during a drunken street brawl in Glasgow's Townhead section. Gordon, only recently released from a German prison camp, died hours later.

Carraher gave the murder weapon, a woodcarver's chisel with a short removable blade, to a friend who tossed it down a sewer. A few days after Carraher's arrest on November 24, 1945, police recovered the weapon which was identified as the suspect's by the shopkeeper who sold it to him.

Carraher's three-day trial commenced in Glasgow on February 28, 1946. Tied to the crime by eyewitnesses, Carraher's only hope of escaping the noose was to plead that years of chronic alcoholism had exacerbated his psychopathic personality. On March 2, 1946, a jury took only 20 minutes to unanimously reject Carraher's claim of "diminished responsibility." The two-time murderer was hanged in Glasgow's Barlinnie Prison on April 6, 1946, following the dismissal of his appeal.

79. Blake, George, ed. *The Trials of Patrick Carraher.* Notable British Trials. London: W. Hodge, 1951. xiii, 278 pp.: ill., ports., maps; 23 cm.

Carraher's two murder trials in the High Court of Justiciary, Glasgow (September 1938 and February 1946) are meticulously examined through lengthy excerpts taken from transcripts of the trials. Includes a detailed chronology, maps of the Gorbals and Townhead districts, and the text of Carraher's failed appeal.

Casteel, Dee Dyne
(a.k.a. "Dee Hostutler" [maiden name])

Born June 5, 1938, in Tampa, Florida. Waitress. Redlands, Florida; 2 murders (accomplice); razor, ligature strangulation (pantyhose); June 18, 1983, and August 6, 1983.

"I suppose I'll never understand why I did what I did. But as I think over my life, more and more I remember the day that I had that terrible fight with my father and he said, 'You're as cheap as piss.' God, that hurt me so. I don't know why, but that one moment pained me so deeply. It seemed to send me off in some bad direction."

Alcoholic waitress who acted as a go-between in arranging two murders. In June 1983, Dee Casteel, a 44-year-old waitress at the International House of Pancakes in Naranja, Florida, was asked by the restaurant's 25-year-old manager, James Allen Bryant, to set up a contract murder on his lover of eight years, Arthur Venecia, the owner of the IHOP. Casteel, in love with Bryant and fearful of losing her job, contracted the hit for $5,000 with two local gas station workers, Mike Irvine and Bill "The Joker" Rhodes. On June 18, 1983, Bryant accompanied the two men to Venecia's house in Redlands and watched as Rhodes slit the man's throat with a razor while Irvine held his arms to his sides. The next day Casteel assisted Bryant in stuffing Venecia's body into a wardrobe chest and hiding it in a barn on the property. Bryant told IHOP employees that Venecia had left the state on business, made Casteel the restaurant's assistant manager, and supported his lavish lifestyle of gay lovers and drugs by plundering both the store's cash register and his murdered lover's bank accounts. Bessie Fischer, Venecia's 84-year-old mother, lived in a trailer on her son's property and represented a potential threat to the conspirators. For seven weeks after the murder, Casteel dutifully delivered meals to the woman before agreeing with Bryant that she must be eliminated. Casteel first had a large section of land on the property backhoed, then contacted Irvine and Bryant who agreed to kill the old woman for $2500.

On August 6, 1983, the hitmen strangled Fischer to death in her trailer with a pair of pantyhose. Three days later Bryant and Casteel buried Fischer and the decomposed corpse of her son in the large hole. Casteel and the other three conspirators were arrested in early 1984 after the three-bottle-of-Scotch-a-day alcoholic confessed arranging the murders to her daughter in front of a witness. Three years after the arrest, each of the four principals were found guilty on two counts of first degree murder on July 17, 1987, and subsequently sentenced to death. On March 29, 1990, the Florida supreme court reversed all the convictions ruling that each defendant was entitled to a separate trial instead of facing a single jury. As of November 1994, Casteel and the others are in prison awaiting new trials.

80. Provost, Gary. *Without Mercy: Obsession and Murder Under the Influence*. New York: Pocket Books, 1990. 252 pp., [8]pp. of plates: ill.; 24 cm.

_____. [Same as 80.] New York: Pocket Books, 1990. viii, 305 pp., [8]pp. of plates: ill.; 17 cm.; paperback.

Cavaness, John Dale
(a.k.a. "Dr. Dale," "Napoleon")

Born October 15, 1925, in Eldorado, Illinois. Died November 17, 1986. Medical doctor. Eldorado, Illinois, and Times Beach, St. Louis County, Missouri; 2 murders; .12 gauge shotgun, .357 Magnum pistol; April 9, 1977, and December 14, 1984.

Audio: Murder in Little Egypt, a two-sound cassette, three-hour abridgement of Darcy O'Brien's book of the same title, was published in 1990 by Audio Renaissance Tapes, Inc. (Los Angeles, California) as part of their series "True Crime Audio."

"As long as I have my little black bag, I'll be just fine."—Cavaness responding to his wife's observation that his culpability in the vehicular homicide deaths of a father and his baby might cause the doctor's patients to lose confidence in him

A well respected medical doctor in Eldorado, Illinois, who murdered two of his sons for their life insurance. Cavaness, 59, though suspected in the April 9, 1977, "accidental" shotgun death of his 22-year-old son Mark, was never charged and collected $40,000. Coincidence proved too strong, however, when the doctor's heavily insured 15-year-old son Sean committed "suicide" in his presence on December 14, 1984, in an isolated area of Times Beach in Missouri's St. Louis County. Police were dubious over Cavaness' contention that he spared the family shame over Sean's suicide by shooting his son twice in the head with a .357 Magnum to make the act look like a robbery/murder. Eldorado residents stood behind their "Dr. Dale" and raised almost $38,000 for the "Dr. Cavaness Defense Fund." Following a mistrial, Cavaness was convicted of first degree murder on November 19, 1985, and condemned to death. One day after a "no suicide" clause in his life insurance policy expired, Missouri State Death Row Inmate 40 was found hanging in his cell on November 17, 1986. Surviving son Kevin spoke a fitting epitaph, "As his final act, he reamed another insurance company."

81. O'Brien, Darcy. *Murder in Little Egypt*. 1st ed. New York: Morrow, 1989. 340 pp.: ill.; 24 cm.

_____. [Same as 81.] London: Piatkus, 1990. 332 pp., [8]pp. of plates: ill., 1 map, ports.; 24 cm.

_____. [Same as 81.] New York: New American Library, 1990. 350 pp., [8]pp. of plates: ill.; 18 cm. ("An Onyx Book"); paperback.

Excellent account based on trial transcripts, police documents, and extensive interviews conducted with the surviving members of the Cavaness family. O'Brien is a graduate professor of English at the University of Tulsa.

Chambers, Robert E., Jr. (a.k.a. "The Preppy [or] Preppie Murderer")

Born circa 1967. Unemployed at time of murder. New York City, New York; 1 murder; asphyxiation; August 26, 1986.

Television: "The Preppie Murder" (1989), a two-hour, made-for-television movie, originally aired on ABC on September 24, 1989. Cast includes William Baldwin (Robert E. Chambers) and Lara Flynn Boyle (Jennifer Levin).

Audio: Wasted: The Preppie Murder, a two-sound cassette, three-hour abridgement of Linda Wolfe's book of the same title, was published in 1990 by Audio Renaissance (Los Angeles) and distributed by St. Martin's Press.

"I wasn't interested in her at all. I didn't even want to be with her."—Chambers commenting on Levin in a videotaped statement given to police at the time of his arrest

A highly publicized murder case involving alleged "rough sex" which focused negative attention on the lifestyles of New York City's affluent young adults. On August 26, 1986, the body of Jennifer Dawn Levin, 18, was found at 6:15 a.m. in Central Park behind the Metropolitan Museum of Art. Levin's clothes were disheveled and her bra was wrapped around her neck. Robert Chambers, Jr., a 19-year-old prep school graduate and Boston University dropout with a cocaine problem, was arrested and charged with second degree murder after police learned that he had left an Upper East Side bar with Levin two hours before. In a videotaped statement, Chambers explained the scratches on his face and his bitten fingers were sustained during a "rough sex" session in the park initiated by Levin. According to the 6'4" 220 pound Chambers, the 5'7" 120 pound Levin bound his hands with her panties, made him lie on the grass, and after some foreplay grabbed his testicles. Reacting in pain, he reached his left arm around Levin's throat and pulled back accidentally killing her. The autopsy seemingly contradicted Chambers' account. It fixed death as due to "asphyxia by strangulation" necessarily applied for at least 20 seconds during which time the victim would struggle violently. This key point was bitterly disputed by opposing forensic specialists during the 13 week trial. On March 25, 1988 the deadlocked jury had been out for nine days when Chambers unexpectedly agreed to a plea-bargain arrangement. He admitted intending to hurt Levin, pleaded guilty to first degree manslaughter, and agreed to serve a minimum five years of a 5 to 15 year prison sentence before being considered for parole. On May 16, 1988, the syndicated television program "A Current Affair" aired a tape made at a Manhattan apartment shortly before the start of the trial. It featured Chambers and several scantily dressed young women engaged in what the show's producer called "a lengthy slumber party." In the video, Chambers playfully twists the head off a doll during a game of charades and says, "Oops, I think I killed her." In 1988 the Levins sued their daughter's killer for damages and were awarded $25 million by default when he refused to fight the action. Chambers' first parole bid was rejected on December 17, 1992, no doubt due largely to a 50,000 signature petition opposing his release submitted by the Levins. At a December 20, 1994, parole hearing, Chambers expressed no remorse telling the board, "I guess I could also give you the party line and say I have learned my lesson; I will never do this again. But that's not how I feel at this moment, because I have a lot of conflicting emotions about the things that have occurred in my case, the politics involved, the media involvement." Chambers was denied parole, but is eligible to reapply in two years' time.

82. Taubman, Bryna. *The Preppy Murder Trial.* 1st St. Martin's Press mass market ed. New York: St. Martin's Press, 1988. vi, 293 pp., [16]pp. of plates: ill.; 18 cm.; paperback.

83. Wolfe, Linda. *Wasted: The Preppie Murder.* New York: Simon and Schuster, 1989. 303 pp., [16]pp. of plates: ill.; 25 cm.

_____. [Same as 83 minus subtitle.] New York: Pocket Books, 1989. x, 370 pp.: ill.; 18 cm.; paperback.

Chapman, George
(a.k.a. "Severin Antonovich Klosowski" [real name], "Schloski")

Born December 14, 1865, in Navgornak, Poland. Executed April 7, 1903. Tavern owner. England; 3 murders; poison (antimony); 1897–1902.

"I have none!"—Chapman when asked by an official in Wandsworth Prison if he would like to see any of his friends

Polish wife poisoner executed in

1903 who is often cited as a leading suspect in the "Jack the Ripper" murders of 1888. Son of a Polish carpenter, Severin Klosowski left his post as an assistant surgeon in Praga at 21 to enlist in the Russian Army. After serving 18 months, the "barber-surgeon" sailed for England sans wife arriving in London's Whitechapel district sometime in 1888. Known in the district as "Ludwig," Klosowski worked as a hairdresser's assistant. In 1889, Klosowski "married" Lucy Baderski and traveled with her to America. After a quarrel with her "husband," Baderski returned to England in 1891 with Klosowski following a year later. A man of strong sexual appetite, the Pole continued to either cohabit with or "marry" women as the urge moved him. In 1893, Klosowski lived for a year with a woman named Annie Chapman whose last name he appropriated in order to elude various other women with whom he was involved. "George Chapman" met his first victim, the alcoholic Mary Isabella Renton Spink, in 1895. When Chapman learned of Spink's private allowance of £600, he "married" her that October in Leytonstone. Using her funds, Chapman set up a hairdressing shop in Hastings in 1897 which featured "musical shaves." Despite the novelty of live piano music supplied by Spink, the business sagged and Chapman relocated to London where he leased the Prince of Wales Tavern. Before leaving Hastings, however, he purchased a quantity of tartar emetic signing the name Chapman in the chemist's poison book.

Soon after her arrival in London, Spink began suffering severe attacks of diarrhea and vomiting. Although Chapman showed husbandly concern throughout her ordeal, he nevertheless opened the tavern at its usual time on the day she died, Christmas Day 1897. Death was attributed to phthisis. A few months later, Chapman advertised for a barmaid eventually hiring Elizabeth (known as "Bessie") Taylor. After their "marriage," Taylor fell prey to a wasting disease. Chapman gave up the tavern and opened another called "The Grapes" in Bishop's Stortford. Taylor's health improved following an unannounced visit to a hospital, but upon her release Chapman became abusive and at one point threatened her with a gun. Chapman moved again, this time to the Monument Tavern in London's Borough district. Taylor's health worsened and her death on February 13, 1901 was officially certified as due to "exhaustion from vomiting and diarrhea." In August 1901, Chapman hired Maud Marsh, the daughter of a Croydon laborer, as a barmaid. Marsh's mother inspected the premises and was not impressed with the publican, but even less so after receiving a letter from her daughter in which she reported Chapman's threat to dismiss and send her home if he "didn't get what he wants" from her. Like the other two victims before her, Marsh knowingly entered into a bogus "marriage" with the persuasive Chapman. Still suspicious of their new son-in-law, the family asked to see a marriage certificate which was never produced.

By 1902, Marsh was suffering from vomiting, diarrhea, and chronic abdominal pains which puzzled the doctor who also attended Bessie Taylor. Marsh rallied for a time in hospital, but the illness recurred when she returned home to Chapman's devoted ministrations. As she wasted away, Chapman insisted on preparing every meal for Marsh and despite her inability to swallow made her brandy and sodas. On one occasion Marsh's mother and a nurse drank some of the mixture left in a glass and each suffered painful attacks of diarrhea and vomiting. Remarkably, no one initially suspected poisoning until the Marshes consulted their doctor who, convinced that the young woman was suffering from arsenic poisoning, contacted the attending physician. Marsh died on October 22, 1902. Now suspicious that two of Chapman's wives had died similar deaths, the doctor refused to sign the death certificate and performed an unauthorized postmortem on Marsh. Finding nothing, the doctor removed the stomach and vital organs and sent them to the Chemical Research Association for further analysis. A second autopsy revealed that death was due to antimony, not arsenic, poisoning.

Chapman was arrested on October 25, 1902, and a search of his premises uncovered white powders, documents identifying him as Klosowski, and medical books on poison. The bodies of his first two wives were subsequently exhumed and found to contain lethal levels of antimony. Tried at London's Old Bailey before Mr. Justice Grantham on March 16, 1903, Chapman's guilt was seemingly a foregone conclusion during the four day trial. On March 19, 1903, a jury needed only 11 minutes to convict him of Marsh's murder. Chapman was hanged at Wandsworth Prison on April 7, 1903. Among "Ripperologists" the murderous Pole continues to be a leading candidate for the identity of the Whitechapel serial killer based on striking coincidences between his movements in the district, anatomical knowledge, etc., and those ascribed to the unknown murderer. Chief Inspector Abberline who investigated the crimes reportedly told the police officer who arrested Chapman, "You've got Jack the Ripper at last!"

Still, the most frequent objection to Chapman being "Jack the Ripper" is the dramatic shift away from sadistically murdering his victims with knives to merely poisoning them.

84. Adam, Hargrave L., ed. *Trial of George Chapman.* Notable British Trials. Edinburgh; London: W. Hodge, 1930. x, 223 pp., [11] leaves of plates: ill., ports., plan; 22 cm.

Adam's introductory essay covers the career of Chapman and notes coincidences between his actions and those of "Jack the Ripper." Appendices include the coroner's inquest, police court proceedings on the three murders, and a translation of documents found in Chapman's possession.

Chapman, Mark David

Born May 10, 1955, in Fort Worth, Texas. Former security guard-maintenance man. New York City, New York; 1 murder; .38 caliber pistol; December 8, 1980.

Video: The Man Who Shot John Lennon (GB, 1989), a 53-minute video originally produced as a documentary film in 1989. A Yorkshire Television Production produced and written by Kevin Sim, directed by Derek Jones. Video released in 1993(?) by Wombat Film & Video (Evanston, Illinois).

"Someone had to abandon their conscience to perpetrate such a thing as I did. Even more difficult is the regaining of that conscience when you take a good, steady look at what you've done; not only to the victim, but to anyone remotely connected to him. The music, the good memories, the culture of that time. It was an end of innocence for that time. And I regret being the one that ended it."—Chapman, in a 1990 interview

Security guard suffering bipolar disorder who murdered ex–Beatle John Lennon as an alternative to suicide. On the evening of December 8, 1980, 25-year-old Mark David Chapman shot John Lennon to death as the 40-year-old musician was walking into the Dakota, the luxurious West Side Manhattan co-op where he lived with his wife, Yoko Ono, and their 5-year-old son, Sean. Chapman, a former doper, Jesus freak, and YMCA counselor, had stalked Lennon for several months since deciding that the composer had "lied" to him through the hope-filled lyrics of such songs as "Strawberry Fields Forever" and "Imagine." Suicidal and confused, Chapman sat alone in his Hawaii apartment endlessly listening to Beatles songs and praying to Satan to let demons enter his body so that he would have the strength to kill. For weeks before flying to New York, Chapman rewrote many of Lennon's most sensitive lyrics replacing them with rancorous chants of death, reflective of his inner turmoil. Hours before gunning Lennon down outside the Dakota, Chapman had talked with the musician, even shaking the hand of his young son, Sean. At their meeting, Lennon had graciously signed a copy of his "Double Fantasy" album for Chapman before going to a recording studio. Upon Lennon's return, Chapman pumped four .38 caliber slugs into the musician's back, dropped his weapon, and was calmly reading a copy of J.D. Salinger's novel *The Catcher in the Rye* when taken into custody. Awaiting trial, Chapman rejected his attorney's advice to plead not guilty by reason of insanity and instead took full responsibility for the murder. He told the judge, "I know I am guilty under God's law. I found my faith in Christ again while in jail and I know Christ wants me to plead guilty." Chapman was sentenced on August 24, 1981, to 20 years to life in prison.

85. Bresler, Fenton. *The Murder of John Lennon.* London: Sidgwick & Jackson, 1989. x, 309 pp.; 24 cm.

_____. [Same as 85, but U.S. ed. retitled: *Who Killed John Lennon?*] 1st U.S. ed. New York: St. Martin's Press, 1989. x, 309 pp., [8]pp. of plates: ill.; 22 cm.

_____. [Same as 85, but U.S. ed. retitled: *Who Killed John Lennon?*] New York: St. Martin's Paperbacks, 1990. xiv, 353 pp., [8]pp. of plates: ill.; 18 cm.; paperback.

86. Hamilton, Sue L., and Hamilton, John C. *The Killing of a Rock Legend: John Lennon. Days of Tragedy.* Bloomington, Minn.: Minneapolis, Minn.: Abdo & Daughters; Distributed by Rockbottom Books, 1989. 31 pp.: ill., ports.; 26 cm.; paper covers.

87. Jones, Jack. *Let Me Take You Down: Inside the Mind of Mark David Chapman, the Man Who Killed John Lennon.* 1st ed. New York: Villard Books, 1992. xvi, 281 pp., [8]pp. of plates: ill.; 25 cm.

_____. [Same as 87.] London: Virgin, 1993. xvi, 281 pp., [8]pp. of plates: ill., ports., facsims.; 25 cm.

_____. [Same as 87.] Warner Books ed. New York: Warner Books, 1994. xiv, 347 pp.: ill.; 18 cm.; paperback.

Chase, Richard Trenton
(a.k.a. "Dracula," "Dracula Killer," "Vampire of Sacramento," "East Area Killer")

Born May 23, 1950, in Sacramento, California. Died December 26, 1980. Unemployed (social security disability income). Sacramento, California; 6 murders; .22 caliber pistol; December 29, 1977–January 27, 1978.

Film: Rampage (US, 1987), a De Laurentiis Entertainment Group production adapted from the William P. Woods novel of the same title, directed by William Friedkin. Though made in 1987, the film was not released theatrically until 1992 due to the financial collapse of the De Laurentiis Entertainment Group. Cast includes Alex McArthur (Charles Reece/ Richard Trenton Chase) and Michael Biehn (D.A. Anthony Fraser).

"Oh, if the door is locked, that means you're not welcome."—Chase's explanation for how he chose his victims

Often referred to by the FBI as the classic example of the "disorganized serial killer," Richard Chase randomly chose then murdered six people within a mile of his Sacramento apartment. A diagnosed paranoid schizophrenic, Chase's fascination with vampirism began as a 10-year-old when he became certain that his blood was drying up within him. To replenish his dwindling supply, the youngster slaughtered neighborhood cats and drank their blood. When the blood of cats, dogs, and birds butchered in his apartment could no longer sate him, Chase turned to human beings. Following the drive-by shooting of a man on December 29, 1977, Chase established a pattern of randomly walking into a person's home, shooting them with a .22 caliber pistol, eviscerating the corpse with a knife, then drinking the blood of selected victims before removing body parts to be consumed later. Chase was arrested on January 28, 1978, one day after committing a quadruple murder in which one of the victims was a 22-month-old infant. Pleading insanity (but judged sane), Chase was convicted on six counts of first degree murder on May 8, 1979, and sentenced to die in the gas chamber. While awaiting execution at San

Quentin, Chase was found dead in his cell on December 26, 1980. The "Vampire of Sacramento" had apparently hoarded his daily doses of Sinequan, a psychotherapeutic drug for depression, and taken 36 times the normal dosage.

88. Biondi, Ray, and Hecox, Walt. *The Dracula Killer.* New York: Pocket Books, 1992. viii, 212 pp., [8]pp. of plates: ill.; 18 cm.; paperback.

_____. [Same as 88 with added subtitle: *The True Story of California's Vampire Killer.*] London: Mondo, 1992. viii, 212 pp.; 18 cm.; paperback.

Ray Biondi, chief of homicide for the Sacramento County sheriff's department and head of the Chase investigation, takes issue with the FBI's claim that psychological profiling alone was responsible for solving the case.

89. Wood, William P. *Rampage.* 1st ed. New York: St. Martin's Press, 1985. 339 pp.; 22 cm.

_____. [Same as 89.] New York: St. Martin's Press, 1986. 334 pp.; 18 cm.; paperback.

_____. [Same as 89.] London: W.H. Allen, 1988. 351 pp.; 20 cm.; paperback.

Fictional account based on the Chase case.

"Chi Omega Murders [or] Killings" *see* Bundy, Theodore Robert

Chikatilo, Andrei Romanovich

(a.k.a. "Rostov Ripper," "Butcher of Rostov," "Forest Strip Killer," "Shelterbelt Killer," "Citizen Ch.")

Born October 16, 1936, in Yablochnoye, Sumskaya province, Ukraine. Executed February 14, 1994. Supply clerk, schoolteacher. Rostov-on-Don, Russia, and various other Soviet cities. 53 murders (convicted in 52 and self-confessed in total of 55); knife, strangulation; December 1978–November 1990.

Television: "Citizen X" (US, 1995), an Asylum Films and Citadel Entertainment production in association with HBO Pictures. A made-for-television movie based on Robert Cullen's book *The Killer Department: Detective Viktor Burakov's Eight-Year Hunt of the Most Savage Killer in Russian History* which originally aired on HBO on February 24, 1995. Cast includes Stephen Rea (Det. Viktor Burakov), Donald Sutherland (Col. Fetisov), Max von Sydow (Dr. Aleksandr Bukhanovsky), and Jeffrey DeMunn (Andrei Chikatilo).

Audio: Hunting the Devil, a six-cassette, nine-hour unabridged sound recording of Richard Lourie's book of the same title read by MacDonald John, was published in 1993 by Books on Tape (Newport Beach, California).

"I am a mistake of nature, a mad beast."

Russian serial killer and cannibal whose brutal mutilation sex murders spanned 12 years and three Soviet republics. The first of Chikatilo's 53 documented murders occurred on December 22, 1978, in the town of Shakhty in the Rostov region of southern Russia. Days later, the body of a 9-year-old girl was found floating in the Grushevka River. The child had been strangled, repeatedly stabbed, and raped. Alexander Kravchenko, a 25-year-old convicted rapist and murderer, was arrested, beaten until he confessed, then executed by firing squad. The killings, however, did not stop. Beginning in September 1981 in Rostov-on-Don, police began finding bodies in the woods near train and bus stations throughout the region. The victims, children of both sexes and young women, had all been raped and horribly mutilated. The killer's savagery and blood lust even shocked a nation used to Stalin's mass butchery. The tongues of some victims had been bitten off while other bodies had been disemboweled by someone with a rudimentary knowledge of surgery. Most of the victims had been stabbed numerous times in the face and raped. The massive manhunt for the "Rostov Ripper" focused on bus and railway stations and resulted in numerous arrests including Chikatilo, who was twice questioned (1978, 1984) and released for lack of evidence. As a result of the multi-year investigation police uncovered at least 95 other murders and 245 rapes which could not be attributed to Chikatilo.

A psychological profile provided by a professor at Rostov University's medical school theorized the killer was impotent and attempted to relieve his sexual frustration by repeatedly stabbing his victims with a knife which the psychiatrist interpreted as a substitute for his penis. The profile proved remarkably accurate. Chikatilo was arrested on November 20, 1990, shortly after a body was found in the woods near a train station in Rostov. Two weeks before, Chikatilo's name had been taken down by a police officer at the station who noticed blood on the man's face and his bandaged finger. A 56-year-old married father of two with a university education, Chikatilo's job as a supply clerk necessitated his travel by train and bus throughout the Rostov region. After eight days of questioning, the former Communist Party member admitted slaughtering 55 people, led authorities to several bodies, and demonstrated his killing techniques on mannequins. Chikatilo's litany of horror included eating the sexual organs of his victims and performing Caesarian sections and amputations on many of them while they were still alive. Judged sane, Chikatilo was charged with 53 murders and tried in the Rostov Provincial Court in June 1992. Throughout the lengthy proceedings, Chikatilo sat in the courtroom under guard in a specially constructed iron cage designed to keep the victims' families in attendance from tearing him apart. On October 15, 1992, the Russian "Jack the Ripper" was convicted of 52 murders and sentenced to death. Chikatilo was executed by a single shot to the back of his head on February 15, 1994, after an 11th-hour appeal for clemency was turned down by Russian President Boris Yeltsin. Alexander Kravchenko, wrongly executed, was posthumously reprieved.

90. Conradi, Peter. *The Red Ripper.* New York: Dell Publishing, 1992. 279 pp., [8]pp. of plates: ill.; 18 cm.; paperback.

_____. [Same as 90 with added subtitle: *Inside the Mind of Russia's Most Brutal Serial Killer.*] London: True Crime, 1992. 258 pp., [8]pp. of plates: ill.; 18 cm.; paperback.

A rushed paperback account by a Moscow-based British journalist who interviewed many of the top police officials and the psychiatrist (Alexander Bukhanovsky) connected with the case. A foreword by Colin Wilson places Chikatilo in the historical tradition of other serial killers like Peter Kürten, Reginald Christie, *et al.* Includes a useful chronology of major events in Chikatilo's life and murderous career.

91. Cullen, Robert. *The Killer Department: Detective Viktor Burakov's Eight-Year Hunt for the Most Savage Killer in Russian History.* 1st ed. New York: Pantheon Books, 1993. 258 pp.: ill.; 24 cm.

_____. [Same as 91.] New York: Ivy Books, 1993. 278 pp.: ill., maps; 24 cm.

_____. [Same as 91 minus subtitle.] London: Orion, 1993. 258 pp., [8]pp. of plates: ill.; 25 cm.

_____. [Same as 91.] London: Orion, 1994. 270 pp., [8]pp. of plates: ill., maps, ports.; 18 cm.; paperback.

Cullen, one-time Moscow bureau chief for *Newsweek* and a writer covering Soviet affairs for *The New Yorker*, traces the Chikatilo investigation through the efforts of Viktor Burakov, a major on the Rostov Police Department who decided to call in a psychiatrist to profile the serial killer.

92. Krivich, Mikhail, and Olgin, Olgert. *Comrade Chikatilo: The Psychopathology of Russia's Notorious Serial Killer.* Fort Lee, N.J.: Emeryville, Calif.: Barricade Books; Distributed by Publishers Group West, 1993. 287 pp.: ill.; 24 cm.

The work of two Russian novelists writing under pseudonyms, this title was commissioned by Barricade Books through a Russian publisher and simultaneously published in New York and Moscow. Alexander Bukhanovsky, the psychiatrist who produced the uncannily accurate psychological profile of the "Rostov Ripper," is praised for his part in Chikatilo's apprehension. The only authors to have communicated directly (via letter) with the killer although they were barred by authorities from asking questions about the murders.

93. Lourie, Richard. *Hunting the Devil.* 1st ed. New York: HarperCollins Publishers, 1993. xxii, 263 pp.: ill.; 24 cm.

_____. [Same as 93 with added subtitle: *The Search for the Russian Ripper.*] London: Grafton, 1993. 280 pp., [16]pp. of plates: ill., 1 facsim., ports.; 18 cm.; paperback.

_____. [Same as 93.] First HarperPaperbacks printing. New York: HarperCollins Publishers, 1994. xxii, 298 pp.: ill.; 17 cm.; paperback.

The manhunt for Chikatilo, undertaken in 1985 by Chief Inspector Issa Kostoev, Russia's deputy head of the Department of Crimes of Special Importance, is well documented in this the best book to date on Chikatilo. Includes a detailed index. According to respected true crime writer Ann Rule's April 4, 1993, review in *The Washington Post*, the book should be "required reading" for "students of psychopathology."

"Christchurch Schoolgirl Murder" *see* Hulme, Juliet (and) Parker, Pauline Yvonne

Christie, John Reginald Halliday
(a.k.a. "Can't Do It Christie," "Reggie-No-Dick")

Born April 8, 1898, in Boothstown, Yorkshire, England. Executed July 15, 1953. Clerk. London, England; 8 murders (1 conviction); ligature strangulation; September 1943–March 1953.

Film: 10 Rillington Place (GB, 1971), a Genesis Productions–Columbia Pictures coproduction, based on Kennedy's book directed by Richard Fleischer. Cast includes Richard Attenborough (John Reginald Christie), Judy Geeson (Beryl Evans), and John Hurt (Timothy John Evans).

"The more the merrier."—Christie referring to the murders in one of his confessions

Serial sex killer who ranks as one of Britain's most notorious modern-day murderers. On March 24, 1953, a Jamaican tenant at 10 Rillington Place, London, was sounding the kitchen walls prior to installing a shelf when he discovered a hollow place. Peeling back a corner of wall paper, the tenant found that it covered a cupboard with a missing corner piece. When the man shined a flashlight into the recess he was horrified to see the naked back of a woman supported in a sitting position by a piece of blanket with one end affixed to the wall and the other knotted to a brassiere in the middle of the corpse's back. The police were notified and removed the bodies of two other women wrapped in blankets secured by electrical wire from the cupboard. Autopsies later revealed that each victim had inhaled carbon monoxide before being strangled. Sperm was also found in each victim's vagina. In the front room, police detected some loose floorboards which when removed yielded another blanket wrapped body later identified as 54-year-old Ethel Christie, the wife of the former 16-year tenant of 10 Rillington Place, John Reginald Halliday Christie. A tobacco tin containing four neatly arranged clumps of pubic hair (none from the known victims) was also recovered in the house. Police shifted their investigation to the back garden where the discovery of a human femur propping up a fence presaged the horror of unearthing two more female bodies. The discovery of six bodies on Christie's property reminded detectives that on December 2, 1949, they had been summoned to the address where the strangled bodies of tenants Beryl Evans, 19, and her 14-month-old daughter, Geraldine (Jeraldine), were found in a washhouse. At the time, John Christie was considered a prime suspect in the murders before the dead woman's husband, Timothy John Evans, a 24-year-old near mentally defective van driver, confessed to the murders. Later, Evans retracted his confession stating that the woman had died during an abortion performed by Christie, after which Christie offered to find adoptive parents for the infant. Evans was convicted of his daughter's death and hanged on March 9, 1950.

Christie, who had sublet his dwelling four days before the discovery of the bodies, became the object of a massive police manhunt and his photograph was splayed across the front pages of the London papers. On March 31, 1953, Christie was recognized by a constable on the embankment near Putney Bridge and was taken to a nearby station where he confessed to four murders, including that of his wife. According to Christie, he found his wife in convulsions from an overdose of barbiturates and unable to bear seeing her in such a pitiable state, strangled her to death with a stocking. In his initial confession, Christie also explained that the three women found in the cupboard were prostitutes that he was forced to strangle when they attacked him following violent quarrels. Francis Camps, a brilliant pathologist, did the forensic work on the victims which led to their identification and cause of death. Camps' forensic findings combined with Christie's confessions led to a clearer picture of the seemingly mild mannered clerk's nearly decade long career of murder. First to die was Ruth Marguerite Fuerst, a 21-year-old Austrian refugee missing since September 1, 1943. Christie strangled her with a rope after sex and buried her in the garden while his wife was away visiting relatives. Muriel Amelia Eady, a 32-year-old coworker of Christie's at the Ultra Radio Works at Park Royal, disappeared on October 7, 1944, while Christie's wife was away on holiday. That evening at 10 Rillington Place, Christie convinced Eady that he could cure her catarrh with his own home-made contraption. In a grim ritual that he would re-enact on three other occa-

sions, Christie plied Eady with liquor, sat her in a canopied deck chair, and had her inhale carbon monoxide from a glass tube running from a nearby gas tap. After she lost consciousness or died, Christie raped the body. Acquiring and disposing of victims became easier for Christie after he strangled his wife on or near December 14, 1952. The last three victims, prostitutes in their mid-twenties, were similarly gassed, raped, and afterwards deposited in the cupboard during January through March 1953.

Tried only for the murder of his wife in London's Central Criminal Court on June 22, 1953, Christie's plea of insanity was refuted by several psychiatrists. Psychiatric testimony, however, did reveal a chilling portrait of a sexual psychopath. Born in 1898 into a strict, loveless family, Christie grew into a weak, myopic hypochondriac whose sexual inadequacies became reflected in his nicknames "Reggie-No-Dick" and "Can't Do It Christie." Christie's sexual dysfunction became so great that, at trial, it was theorized that he gassed and killed his female victims because he was unable to have sex with a conscious woman. Turned out of the house for stealing while still a teenager, Christie joined the military and was wounded and gassed during a World War I campaign in March 1918. For the next three-and-a-half years Christie was unable to speak, a condition later diagnosed as "functional aphonia," a psychological affliction common among hysterical individuals. Christie's voice spontaneously returned at moments of great emotional stress. Marrying Ethel in 1920, Christie worked at the post office before he was caught stealing money orders and sentenced to seven months in prison. The Christies moved to 10 Rillington Place (the scene of all the murders) in 1938 and the next year Christie joined the War Reserve Police where he quickly became known as an officious martinet who cited people for minor blackout offenses. The jury rejected Christie's insanity defense and he was hanged in Pentonville Prison on July 15, 1953. Based on Christie's confession that he murdered Mrs. Beryl Evans, the home secretary appointed John Scott Henderson, Q.C., to conduct a secret inquiry to determine if Timothy John Evans had been wrongly hanged in 1950. Henderson's report, which concluded that Evans was responsible for both the deaths of his wife and child, was met with widespread criticism upon its release on July 13, 1953. Today, it is generally accepted by writers like Michael Eddowes, F. Tennyson Jesse, and Ludovic Kennedy, that Christie committed the murders for which Evans, an innocent but easily led simpleton, was wrongly executed.

94. Brabin, Daniel James. *The Case of Timothy John Evans: Report of an Inquiry by the Hon. Mr. Justice Brabin: Presented to Parliament by the Secretary of State for the Home Department by Command of Her Majesty.* Great Britain Parliament, Papers by Command; 3101. London: H.M.S.O., 1966. v, 158 pp.; 24 cm. (See 102 for the supplementary report.)

95. Bradley, Matthew. *Lay Down Dead: A Shocking, True Story Told in the Style of a Novel.* Derby Conn.: The New International Library, Inc., 1964. 126 pp.; 18 cm. ("A Gold Star book"); paperback.

Fictional account of the case.

96. Camps, Francis E. *Medical and Scientific Investigations in the Christie Case.* Foreword by the Attorney General Sir Lionel Heald. London: Medical Publications, Ltd., 1953. xxiii, 244 pp.: ill., plates (part col.), diagrams, tables; 24 cm.

Camps, a lecturer in forensic medicine at the London Hospital Medical College, was a brilliant pathologist whose study of the Christie case is essential reading. A primer for forensic pathologists, the book contains numerous crime scene photographs and Camps' excellent documentation of the case. Appendices include three statements given by Christie to authorities on March 31; June 5; and June 8, 1953. Includes bibliography and index.

97. Chance, John Newton. *The Crimes at Rillington Place: A Novelist's Reconstruction.* London: Hodder and Stoughton, 1961. vi, 190 pp.; 20 cm.

Chance believes that Christie and Evans worked in concert to kill the delivery man's wife and child.

98. Eddowes, John. *The Two Killers of Rillington Place.* London: Little, Brown, 1994. xiv, 211 pp., [8]pp. of plates: ill., ports., plans, facsims.; 23 cm.

99. Eddowes, Michael. *The Man on Your Conscience: An Investigation of the Evans Murder Trial.* London: Cassell, 1955. 280 pp.: ill., ports.; 21 cm.

Eddowes concludes "that the unpalatable truth is that Evans was innocent, and, because his accusation against the real killer was not believed, four more women were later strangled by Christie." Thought provoking study.

100. Furneaux, Rupert. *The Two Stranglers of Rillington Place.* London: Panther, 1961. 188 pp.; 18 cm. ("A Panther book"); paperback.

Noted British criminologist and true crime writer Furneaux forwards the intriguing argument that both Christie and Evans collaborated in the murder of the latter's wife and child. Appendices include Evans' first statement made at Merthyr Tydfil police station on November 30, 1949, and evidence given by Christie at Pentonville Prison on July 19, 1953.

101. Jesse, F. Tennyson, ed. *Trials of John Evans and John Reginald Halliday Christie.* Notable British Trials. London:

W. Hodge, 1957. c, 379 pp., [16]pp. of plates: ill., ports., facsims.; 22 cm.

The trials were before the Central Criminal Court, London. Evans was tried in January 1950 for the murder of his daughter Geraldine Evans; Christie was tried June 1953 for the murder of his wife Ethel Christie.

102. Henderson, John Scott. *The Case of Timothy John Evans: Supplementary Report.* Great Britain. Parliament. Papers by Command, cm.d. 8946. London: H.M.S.O., 1953. 7 pp.; 25 cm. (See 94 for the original inquiry.)

103. Kennedy, Ludovic. *Ten Rillington Place.* London: V. Gollancz, 1961. 308 pp., [8]pp. of plates: ill., maps; 23 cm.

_____. [Same as 103.] New York: Simon and Schuster, 1961. 288 pp., [8] leaves of plates: ill., map; 24 cm.

_____. [Same as 103.] London: Grafton, 1971. 335 pp.: ill., 1 map; 18 cm.; paperback.

_____. [Same as 103.] New York: Avon, 1971. 332 pp., [4] leaves of plates: ill.; 18 cm.; paperback.

A definitive study, dedicated to Evans' mother, which explores the relationship between Christie and his upstairs neighbor. Kennedy concludes that Christie committed the murders of Mrs. Evans and her child and calls for the reprieve of Timothy John Evans. Excellent.

"Clapham Commons Murder"
see Davies, Michael John

Clark, Douglas Daniel
(a.k.a. "Sunset Strip Slayer [or] Killer," "Sunset Slayer [or] Killer," "Dan Troth")

Born circa 1948 in Pennsylvania. Machinist. Los Angeles, California (Hollywood area); 6 murders (convicted, suspect in 25 others); .25 caliber pistol, knife; April–August 1980.

"Why don't you stop the bullshit and get to the sentence?"—Clark on March 16, 1983, to a judge preparing to sentence the "Sunset Slayer" to death on six first-degree murder convictions

Douglas Clark, a handsome and suave 31-year-old machinist with a prep school background, met 37-year-old Carol Bundy, a plain overweight licensed practical nurse with bad eyesight, in a North Hollywood, California country-and-western bar on December 28, 1979. By August of the next year both were arrested for the so-called "Sunset Murders," a series of killings in which at least six women (mainly prostitutes) were taken from the area around Hollywood's Sunset Strip. Bundy was additionally charged with killing then decapitating a former lover. Psychological evaluations of the pair suggested that the murders stemmed from their sadomasochistic relationship in which Clark dominated the submissive Bundy who would do anything, even repeatedly kill, in order to keep him. According to Bundy, Clark fantasized about slaughtering women and made her complicity in the carnage a test of her devotion to him. In a statement to police, Bundy admitted that "Mr. Clark had virtual control over my personality and my behavior, my wants, my desires, my dreams while I was with him."

The son of a Navy lieutenant commander turned globetrotting engineer, Clark traveled widely as a youth and attended some of the finest schools in the world. In Geneva, Switzerland, Clark attended the prestigious International School also known as the Ecolat, but applied himself more to finding sex partners among the town's girls than to his studies. He was later expelled for writing a suggestive note to a female mathematics teacher. The

16-year-old was packed off to the Culver Military Academy in Indiana where he bragged about his sexual exploits and sneaked girls into his dorm room. The cadet surreptitiously made tapes of himself having sex with the girls and played them back for his classmates. Upon graduation at 19, Clark enlisted in the Air Force decoding Russian messages in Texas and Alaska before being honorably discharged early under unexplained circumstances. He relocated to Van Nuys, California, married a woman he met at a North Hollywood rock-and-roll bar, and divorced four years later in 1976. In September 1979 Clark landed a job as a steam engineer tending a boiler at a Jergens soap factory in Burbank. He spent evenings cruising bars in North Hollywood searching for fat, lonely women to charm into letting him live with them until the rent came due. It was during one such outing in late December 1979 that he met Carol Bundy, a love- and sex-starved mother of two small boys.

One of three daughters born to an alcoholic father who sexually abused Carol on the day his wife died, Bundy was an unattractive child who suffered from diabetes and severe astigmatism. The father remarried quickly, sending Bundy and her two siblings to live in a foster home for a year before reclaiming them. Over the next 10 years, the young girl would attend 23 different schools. At 15, Bundy began peeping into neighbors' windows and started taking money for sex. Shortly afterwards, she tried unsuccessfully to take her life by ingesting iodine. To escape her father, she married a physically abusive homosexual who nevertheless fathered her two boys. They separated and Bundy moved with her children in January 1979 into an apartment complex in Van Nuys where she became infatuated with 45-year-old John Robert Murray, the married manager of the facility. Murray, an Australian born would-be singer, performed at the North Hollywood club where months later Bundy would be approached by Clark. Bundy and Murray began an affair which ultimately ended when he refused to give up his wife.

On the night they met, Clark moved in with Bundy and her two sons. A tireless and versatile lover, Clark quickly turned Bundy into his love slave. At Clark's urging, Bundy sent the children to relatives when he complained that their presence constricted him. When she could no longer physically satisfy him, Bundy consented to let Clark have sex with other women including an 11-year-old neighborhood girl. Bundy, at Clark's command, either photographed the sex or joined in. Encouraging Bundy to confide to him her darkest sexual fantasies of pain and humiliation, Clark told her that his dream was to capture young girls, torture them, and turn them into sex slaves. Later his sadistic fantasies deepened into thoughts of murder and necrophilia in which he envisioned Bundy shooting a woman straddling him during sex so he could feel her death spasms. Acting on his suggestion, Bundy purchased two .25 caliber automatic pistols in her name in May 1980. On April 27, 1980, Clark picked up 22-year-old prostitute, Charlene Andermann, on the Sunset Strip. As she was fellating him in the front seat of Bundy's blue 1973 Buick station wagon, Clark choked the woman and slashed her 26 times with a boning knife. Andermann escaped to later pick him out of a photo line-up.

On May 31, 1980, Clark took the 1976 blue Datsun Bundy bought for him out for a test drive. He drove to the Sunset Strip where he picked up 17-year-old Sacramento runaway Marnett Comer. Clark shot the teenaged prostitute three times in the head before driving her to a dump site near Foothill Boulevard. To aid in decomposition, Clark sliced the girl's stomach open to allow "the wiggly-squirmies" to work. Before eventually showing Bundy the area where he dumped Comer, Clark explained to her that the bullet holes in his car were the result of a gun cleaning accident. On June 11, 1980, Clark picked up Huntington Beach stepsisters Cynthia Chandler, 16, and Gina Marano, 15, on Sunset Boulevard. Clark shot each of the young girls in the head and spent four hours in the safety of his rental garage photographing their bodies and performing necrophilic acts with their corpses. A highway worker stumbled across their blanket-wrapped bodies the next day on an embankment near a Forest Lawn Cemetery freeway ramp.

Bundy, anxious to feel the "psychological intimacy" that sharing a murder with Clark would produce, accompanied her lover on his next outing on June 20, 1980. With Bundy in the back seat posing as his wife, Clark drove to Hollywood and picked up a teenaged hooker later identified as "Jane Doe no. 28." As the girl fellated Clark in the front seat, Bundy handed him a gun. Clark shot the teen in the head and they dumped her body in Antelope Valley north of Los Angeles where it was found on March 3, 1981. Early the next day Clark went out alone and picked up Exxie Wilson, a 20-year-old prostitute, out of a group of hookers. As she was fellating him in his parked car on Ventura Boulevard, Clark shot her in the head, decapitated

her, and dumped her body in the parking lot of a Studio City restaurant. Fearful that one of the other hookers could identify him, Clark returned to the area and picked up Karen Jones, 24. He drove Jones near the Burbank Studios, shot her in the left temple, and dumped her body on the street. At home with Bundy, Clark placed Wilson's head in the icebox and later used it as a sex toy. In her confession, Bundy admitted applying makeup to the head to make it look like a "Barbie doll." Together, they placed Wilson's head in a wooden treasure box bought by Bundy for the occasion and dumped it on June 26, 1980. It was recovered the next day. The bodies of two other "Jane Does" killed with small caliber bullet wounds to the head were found between July 25 and mid–August 1980.

Following a botched suicide attempt in late July, Bundy approached her old lover John Murray for sex. On August 3, 1980, she drunkenly confided to Murray in the North Hollywood bar where she had met Clark that they had killed several women. Frightened Murray might report them, she lured him to an after hours sex assignation in his parked van only blocks away from the bar. As he prepared for sex, Bundy shot Murray repeatedly in the head, stabbed him six times in the back, and slashed his buttocks and anus to make it appear the murder was committed by a "psycho." To avoid having the bullets lodged in Murray's skull traced, Bundy decapitated the corpse. Later that day with Clark they tossed the head in a dumpster near Griffith Park. It has never been recovered. Cracking under the emotional strain of the murders, Bundy admitted to a coworker that she and Clark were responsible for several killings. The police were notified and the pair was arrested in mid–August

1980. Two .25 caliber pistols, one linked ballistically to all the "Sunset Murder" cases where bullets were recovered, were found hidden in the soap factory where Clark worked.

Charged with the murders of Comer, Chandler, Marano, Wilson, Jones, and one of the "Jane Does," Clark maintained that Bundy and John Murray had committed the crimes, patterning them after the work of serial killer Theodore Bundy. In a five month trial that saw Clark often serving as his own attorney, Clark was unable to overcome the physical evidence against him and Bundy's damning testimony of their life together. Clark was found guilty on all six murder counts on January 28, 1983, including a charge of attempted murder and mayhem in the attack on Charlene Andermann. At his March 16, 1983, sentencing, Clark initially interrupted the judge by shouting, "Why don't you stop the bullshit and get to the sentence" then, upon receiving six consecutive death sentences, demanded they be carried out within 10 days. Clark received an additional sentence of 12 years and 8 months for the attempted murder of Andermann and the mutilation of Exxie Wilson. While awaiting numerous appeals, Clark married Kelly Keniston, an advocate for his innocence allied with the group "Information Clearinghouse on Criminal Justice." Though detectives discount Clark's claim made to Bundy that he had killed 50 people since turning 17, they believe he could be responsible for as many as 25 murders.

On May 2, 1983, the day she was set to go to trial, Bundy changed her plea of not guilty by reason of insanity to guilty in the first degree murders of John Murray and "Jane Doe no. 28." Out of consideration of her testimony against Clark and her show of remorse for her crimes, Bundy avoided the death penalty and was sentenced on May 31, 1983, to two consecutive 25 years to life terms plus two years for the use of a firearm. Her first eligible parole date is in 2012 although the prison system retains the option to keep her for life.

104. Farr, Louise. *The Sunset Murders.* New York: Pocket Books, 1992. ix, 308 pp., [8]pp. of plates: ill.; 25 cm.

_____. [Same as 104.] New York: Pocket Star Books, 1993. ix, 355 pp., [8]pp. of plates: ill.; 18 cm.; paperback.

Compelling and richly detailed account of the "Sunset Murders" based on jailhouse interviews with Clark and Bundy, police reports, 52 volumes of trial transcripts, and interviews with 80 individuals. Farr, a Van Nuys, California-based magazine writer, first heard of the case from her mother who frequented the same Northridge beauty parlor as Bundy.

Clark, Henry Lovell William

Born August 14, 1868. Executed March 26, 1913. Doctor. Agra, India; 2 murders; poison (arsenic, geselmine), sword; October 10, 1911, and November 17, 1912.

"I wish to say that I am wholly and solely to blame. Mrs. Fullam was acting under my direction. I, having the stronger will, had her under my control."—Clark's statement from the dock made at his trial for the murder of Edward Fullam; *see also* Fullam, Augusta Fairfield.

"Cleft Chin Murder" *see* Hulten, Karl Gustav (and) Jones, Elizabeth Maude

"Cleveland Torso Murders" *see* "Mad Butcher of Kingsbury Run"

"Clutter Murders" *see* Hickock, Richard Eugene (and) Smith Perry Edward

Coleman, Dennis, Jr.

Born February 23, 1968, in East Hartford, Connecticut. Country club worker. Glastonbury, Connecticut; 1 murder; ligature strangulation (pantyhose); August 5, 1987.

"To my Dreamgirl ... I will do the deed. I promise you."—Coleman in a letter to girlfriend Karin Aparo

Television: "Beyond Obsession" (1994), a two-hour, made-for-television movie based on Richard Hammer's book of the same title originally aired on ABC on April 4, 1994. Cast includes Henry Thomas (John Thompson/Dennis Coleman, Jr.), Emily Warfield (Traci DiCarlo/Karin Aparo), and Victoria Principal (Eleanor DiCarlo/Joyce Aparo).

Teenaged killer who maintained that he was manipulated by his girlfriend into murdering her physically and emotionally abusive mother. On August 5, 1987, the body of Joyce Aparo, 47, was found beneath a bridge over the Fall River in Bernardstown, Massachusetts. Clad only in a nightgown, Aparo had been strangled with a pair of pantyhose still wound tightly around her neck. Eight days later police arrested 19-year-old Dennis Coleman, Jr., the boyfriend of Joyce Aparo's 16-year-old daughter, Karin. Letters found in Coleman's room suggested Karin's possible involvement in the killing, but he protested her innocence until she gave police a letter he had written to her promising "I will do the deed." Coleman subsequently agreed to implicate Aparo in the killing in exchange for the prosecutor recommending a 42-year prison sentence. According to Coleman, he killed Joyce Aparo in the bedroom of her Glastonbury, Connecticut, condominium at Karin's instigation because her mother was trying to break up their relationship. Karin Aparo was arrested on August 28, 1987, and charged with conspiracy to commit murder and with being an accessory to murder.

Coleman pleaded guilty and on November 28, 1989, was sentenced to 34 years in prison. Jury selection in Karin Aparo's trial began in Hartford, Connecticut, on April 27, 1990. Psychiatrists characterized Coleman as Aparo's "sex slave" and agreed with his testimony in which he described their love affair as going "beyond obsession." Coleman testified that they discussed the murder and various methods of committing it for several months and planned to live together on Karin's inheritance. Aparo maintained that Coleman was driven to kill by jealousy over her relationship with a man that her mother was forcing her to date. On June 28, 1990, their ninth day of deliberations, a jury acquitted Aparo of being an accessory to murder. A mistrial was declared on the second charge of conspiracy to commit murder when the jury deadlocked 7–5 in favor of acquittal. The state of Connecticut decided to reprosecute Aparo on the conspiracy charge, but an August 10, 1992, ruling by the state supreme court prohibited some key evidence against her including parts of Coleman's testimony, from being used. As of this writing, Aparo has not been retried.

105. Hammer, Richard. *Beyond Obsession.* 1st ed. New York: Morrow, 1992. 346 pp., [6]pp. of plates: ill.; 25 cm.

_____. [Same as 105.] New York: Avon Books, 1993. x, 373 pp.: ill.; 18 cm.; paperback.

Despite the cooperation of Dennis Coleman, Jr., and his attorney, Hammer's account of the case described by police as a "complicated soap opera–type event" is hampered by Karin Aparo's refusal to allow him to quote from her journals and letters. Under new interpretations of the "fair use" laws Hammer was barred from doing so without her permission. The author suggests that Aparo did manipulate Coleman.

Collins, John Norman
(a.k.a. "John Norman Collins Chapman," "Bill Kenyon," "Don Collins," "David Johnson," "Creepy John," "Ypsilanti Ripper")

Born June 17, 1947, in Riverside, Ontario, Canada. University student. Michigan and California; 8 murders (1 conviction); gun, knife, ligature strangulation; July 1967–July 1969.

Serial rapist and killer who, like Ted Bundy, murdered female university students. A handsome 22-year-old student at Eastern Michigan University in Ypsilanti, John Norman Collins committed seven of his eight brutal murders within a 25 mile area in Washtenaw County and one near Carmel, California, while "vacationing" on the West Coast. Like his "successor," Ted Bundy, Collins preferred attractive coeds as his victims and trolled for them around the campuses of EMU and the University of Michigan at Ann Arbor. Well known and liked, the clean-cut Collins was in excellent physical shape and had once been

asked to join the Michigan State Police (many of whom he knew from hanging out with them at a local restaurant). On July 9, 1967, Mary Fleszar, a 19-year-old student, vanished while walking on the EMU campus. Nearly two months passed before her skeletal remains were found on a trash pile a few miles north of Ypsilanti. Fleszar had been stabbed 30 times and her feet and right hand were missing. A year passed before another EMU coed, 21-year-old Joan Schell, disappeared on June 30, 1968. Schell's body was found five days later on July 5, on the outskirts of Ann Arbor. The young woman had been raped, her throat cut, and she had been stabbed 25 times. Collins, who had drawn attention to himself by talking about the murder in graphic detail to coworkers, was interviewed, but discounted by police who knew him as a nice guy. On March 20, 1969, 23-year-old EMU law student Jane Mixer disappeared, her body found the next day in a cemetery in Denton Township four miles east of Ypsilanti. Shot twice point-blank in the head with a .22 caliber weapon, a nylon stocking (not the victim's) was left wound about her neck.

The attacks accelerated in frequency and brutality. On March 25, 1969, a member of a land surveying crew stumbled across the nude body of 16-year-old Maralynn Skelton in northeast Ann Arbor. The badly beaten teenager had been raped, whipped with a belt, and left spread-eagled with a stick jammed into her vagina. Thirteen-year-old Dawn Basom was found strangled with heavy electrical wire in Superior Township on April 16, 1969. Her blouse had been ripped off and jammed in her mouth. On June 9, 1969, the body of Alice Kalom, a 22-year-old EMU coed, was discovered in a vacant field near Ypsilanti. Shot once in the head with a .22 caliber weapon, Kalom had been raped, slashed across the throat, and repeatedly stabbed in the breast. Collins briefly visited northern California in June 1969. Shortly afterwards on June 30, the naked body of a 17-year-old woman wearing sandals was found in the Pescadero Canyon just north of Carmel. The teenager had been raped and strangled with the belt from her dress found wound about her neck in a pattern reminiscent of Jane Mixer, victim number three. Karen Sue Beineman, an 18-year-old freshman at EMU, was reported missing after leaving a wig shop in Ypsilanti on July 23, 1969. She was last seen by two witnesses who informed police that Beineman had ridden away with a good looking man on a motorcycle. Three days later, the teenager's nude body (except for sandals) was found tossed into a wooded gully in Ann Arbor. Like many of the other victims, Beineman had been raped, beaten, strangled, and in a twist, apparently partially scalded with some caustic chemical. The girl's panties, jammed savagely into her vagina, yielded hundreds of short clipped hairs later determined not to be the victim's.

Three days after the discovery of Beineman's body, Collins' uncle, Michigan State Police Corporal Derik Lair, returned to his Ypsilanti home from vacation. In the family's absence, his nephew John Collins had watched the house and fed the dog. Lair's wife discovered scuff marks on the kitchen floor and a bloodstained garment in the basement. Further investigation by a forensics team uncovered blood (matching Beineman's type) on the basement walls and in the front of the dryer. More importantly, investigators

found a damp rag filled with hundreds of short clipped hairs near where Mrs. Lair cut her boys' hair prior to leaving on their trip. Forensics later matched the hair clippings in the basement with those found in the victim's panties. Collins was subsequently arrested after the two witnesses identified him as the man they saw on the motorcycle with Beineman. Several other women stepped forward and told police harrowing accounts of their unsolicited sexual encounters with Collins. Through them, the picture that emerged of the handsome student was that of a violently oversexed individual who hated women, especially those who were having their menstrual period. Significantly, many of his victims were murdered during their menstrual periods. Tried in Ann Arbor for Beineman's murder, Collins was convicted on August 17, 1970, and sentenced to life imprisonment at State Prison of Southern Michigan in Jackson. In 1978, Collins and seven other inmates nearly escaped from the prison at Marquette by tunneling their way to within 35 yards of the wall. In 1982, the Canadian-born Collins (who legally changed his name in 1981 to Chapman) had the approval of the director of the Michigan Department of Corrections to serve the remainder of his sentence in Canada. The move was blocked when an angry public learned that under Canadian law it was possible that the killer could have won parole as early as 1985. In time, Collins can petition the governor of Michigan for a commutation of his life sentence; however it is highly unlikely that it will be granted.

106. Keyes, Edward. *The Michigan Murders*. New York: Reader's Digest Press: Distributed by Crowell, 1976. ix, 370 pp.; 24 cm.

Pseudonyms are used out of respect for the victims and their families.

Coppolino, Carl A.

Born circa 1933 in Brooklyn, New York. Anesthesiologist. Middletown, New Jersey, and Longboat Key, Florida; 1 murder (acquitted of 1 other); succinylcholine chloride; July 30, 1963, and August 28, 1965.

"I feel like the Tampa Bay Bucs winning the Super Bowl."—Coppolino's reaction to being granted parole after spending 12 years in prison for the murder of his wife

Anesthesiologist acquitted of killing his mistress' husband, but later convicted of murdering his first wife. Coppolino was living with his doctor-wife Carmela in Middletown, New Jersey, when he began an affair in 1963 with Marjorie Farber, the wife of Colonel William Farber. When the officer objected to the relationship, Coppolino (according to his mistress) supplied her with a lethal drug and syringe. The colonel survived a partial injection administered by his wife, but later on July 30, 1963, Coppolino allegedly smothered him with a pillow. Acting on her husband's diagnosis, Dr. Carmela Coppolino unsuspectingly signed a death certificate stating death as due to heart failure. The Coppolinos subsequently moved to Longboat Key, Florida, where the doctor took another mistress, Mary Gibson. In the meantime, Marjorie Farber had followed her lover to Florida and bought the house next door to his. Shortly after Carmela Coppolino refused to grant her husband a divorce so that he could pursue Mary Gibson, she suffered a "heart attack" on August 28, 1965. A doctor accepted Coppolino's diagnosis and

signed the death certificate. Incensed by Coppolino's marriage to Gibson, the spurned Farber told authorities that not only had the doctor murdered his wife, but also her husband. Both bodies were exhumed. A puncture mark was found on the dead woman's buttock. Exhaustive tests revealed traces of the muscle relaxant succinylcholine in her body most probably injected before death. Represented by noted attorney F. Lee Bailey, Coppolino was tried first in New Jersey for Farber's murder. A jury, bewildered by the case's conflicting and complex medical testimony, acquitted Coppolino in September 1966. Tried in Naples, Florida, for his wife's death, Coppolino was convicted of second degree murder on April 28, 1967, and sentenced to life imprisonment. A model inmate who spent his sentence tending orchids at the Avon Park Correctional Institution, Coppolino was granted parole on October 16, 1979, on the condition that he not practice medicine without the written permission of the Florida Parole and Probation Commission.

107. Coppolino, Carl A. *The Crime That Never Was.* Tampa, Fla.: Justice Press, 1980. xiii, 309 pp., [10]pp. of plates: ill., ports.; 24 cm.

108. Holmes, Paul. *The Trials of Dr. Coppolino.* New York: New American Library, 1968. 305 pp.; 22 cm.

_____. [Same as 108.] New York: Signet, 1968. 304 pp.; 19 cm.; paperback.

109. Katz, Leonard. *The Coppolino Murder Trial.* New York: Bee-Line Books, 1967. 207 pp.: ill., ports.; 18 cm.; paperback.

110. MacDonald, John D. *No Deadly Drug.* 1st ed. Garden City, N.Y.: Doubleday, 1968. xi, 656 pp.; 22 cm.

_____. [Same as 110.] 1st Ballantine Books ed. New York: Ballantine Books,

1985. xii, 562 pp.; 18 cm. ("A Fawcett
Gold Medal book"); paperback.

Corll, Dean Arnold
(a.k.a. "The Candy Man")

Born December 24, 1939, in
Waynedale, Indiana. Died August 8,
1973. Electric company worker. Houston and Pasadena, Texas; 27 murders;
ligature strangulation, gun; December
1970–August 1973.

Sadistic homosexual serial killer
who, with two teenaged accomplices,
tortured and killed 27 young boys in
the Houston area in the early seventies. Born in a suburb of Fort Wayne,
Indiana, in 1939, Dean Corll's early life
was marred by his parents' continual
bickering. Alternately punished or
ignored by his father, Corll developed
into the classic "mama's boy." Following her second divorce from Corll's
birth father, the woman remarried and
moved to east Texas in 1954. She established a candy company in which the
15-year-old Corll often worked for as
many as 12 hours a day. Drafted in 1964
despite a heart murmur, Corll spent
only 10 months in the military before
winning a hardship discharge based on
his claim that he was needed in the
family business. The Houston-based
candy company began to fail in the
summer of 1968 and Corll took a job as
a relay tester at the Houston Lighting
& Power Company. Corll, who had
become known in the poor "Heights"
section of Houston as "The Candy
Man" (for his generosity in passing out
free candy samples to children), now
actively sought out the company of
young males. While it struck some parents as odd that a 30-year-old man
would want to surround himself with
teenaged boys, Corll at least was clean-

cut, polite, and held a steady job. In
reality, Corll was offering the boys
between $5 and $10 for homosexual sex
and finding plenty of takers. Moving
frequently to avoid detection, Corll
hosted pot and glue sniffing parties
that devolved into sadomasochistic sex
sessions once the boys passed out.

Rough sex ultimately led to an
efficient routine of serial murder once
Corll recruited teenagers David Owen
Brooks and Elmer Wayne Henley to
procure him victims. Corll paid the
youths as much as $200 a head (more
if they were good looking) to lure
young boys to his home with promises
of pot smoking and paint sniffing.
According to Brooks, the earliest murder occurred in 1970 and essentially set
the pattern for those that followed. A
charming Corll plied his victim with
pot and paint and glue sniffing until
he lost consciousness. Afterwards,
Corll strapped the boy onto a homemade 8' × 3' plywood torture board,
committed oral or anal sodomy or
some other form of sexual torture
which could last for several days, then
either strangled or shot him in the
head. While Brooks would later deny
actually killing any of Corll's 27 known
victims, he admitted that he was present at some of the killings and afterwards helped his one time lover to bury
the bodies. Throughout the early seventies numerous reports of boys missing from the "Heights" were ignored
by Houston police who classified them
as runaways.

Corll's reign of terror ended on
August 8, 1973, at his home on 2020
Lamar Drive in Pasadena, Texas. The
night before, Henley had unwisely
brought along a 15-year-old girl to one
of Corll's murderous all-male parties.
Corll, the girl, Henley and another
male teenager he lured to the house,

spent the night and early morning drinking and sniffing acrylics out of paper bags. Henley awoke from a mind numbing stupor to now find himself in a position he had witnessed many times before: handcuffed and defenseless. Naked and enraged, Henley was berated by Corll for bringing the girl. Corll threatened to kill everyone in the house after he "had his fun." Henley spoke quickly, begging Corll not to kill him and promising that, if released, he would rape the girl while his friend sodomized the boy. Corll unlocked the cuffs and both went into the bedroom where the teenagers were still passed out; the girl face up on the bedroom floor, the boy strapped face down on the "torture-board." While Corll attempted to rape the boy, Henley grabbed the man's .22 pistol from atop a nearby table and shot him six times, killing him instantly. Afterwards, the tearful 17-year-old called the police.

Later that day, Henley led authorities to a Houston boat shed rented by Corll which was found to contain the bodies of 17 victims wrapped in plastic and packed in lime. The genitals on several of the bodies had been removed and separately packed. Henley's confession implicated 18-year-old David Owen Brooks who with his coprocurer pointed out two other mass burial sites. Six bodies were recovered from a beach on Mile Island with another four found buried on the shores of Lake Sam Rayburn Reservoir. Henley, convicted in July 1974 of six slayings, was sentenced to six consecutive 99 year prison terms, a total of 594 years. On March 5, 1975, Brooks received 99 years for killing 15-year-old William Lawrence. Henley's convictions were overturned on December 20, 1978, on the grounds that the trial court did not give enough consideration to a defense request for a change of venue. Retried in Corpus Christi, Henley was reconvicted on June 27, 1979. Remarkably, Henley became eligible for parole in 1983. To date, his requests have been denied. Corll was buried with full military honors in Houston's Grand View Memorial Park cemetery.

111. Gurwell, John K. *Mass Murder in Houston.* Houston: Cordovan Press, 1974. 160 pp.: ill.; 18 cm.; paperback.

A paperback account focusing on the recovery of the bodies which concludes before Henley's trial.

112. Hanna, David. *Harvest of Horror: Mass Murder in Houston.* New York: Belmont Tower, 1975. 194 pp.: ill.; 18 cm.; paperback.

Rush paperback job rife with errors including Corll's date and place of birth. Interesting in that it touches on the gay community's reaction to the crime.

113. Olsen, Jack. *The Man with the Candy: The Story of the Houston Mass Murders.* New York: Simon and Schuster, 1974. 255 pp.; 22 cm.

_____. [Same as 113.] New York: Pocket Books, 1975. 278 pp.; 18 cm.; paperback.

_____. [Same as 113.] London: Talmy Franklin, 1975. 255 pp.; 23 cm.

Olsen's readable account focuses primarily on the Heights section of Houston from which most of the lower- to middle-class victims were drawn. Not as well done as Olsen's other forays into the true crime genre, it is the best account of a sensational case that still awaits a definitive treatment.

Corona, Juan Vallejo

Born circa 1934 in Autlan, Mexico. Farm labor contractor. Yuba City, California; 25 murders; knife, machete; 1971.

"Yes, I did it, but I am a sick man and a sick man cannot be judged by the same standards as other men." — Statement attributed to Corona by Mexican consular official Jesus Rodriguez-Navarro during a 1978 prison visit with the convicted murderer

Mexican farm labor contractor convicted in two separate trials of murdering 25 migrant workers and vagrants over a six week period in 1971. On May 19, 1971, the body of a migrant farm worker was found buried in a shallow grave in a peach orchard near the Feather River five miles north of Yuba City, California. The man, later identified as Kenneth Whiteacre, had been stabbed in the chest, slashed across the head, and his skull had been bashed in. Homosexual literature found in his pocket suggested a sexual motive for the murder. Over the next few days, the bodies of eight other itinerant farm workers were found buried in shallow graves around the orchard. In each instance, the man had been stabbed to death, bore cross-like gash marks on the back of his head, and was buried face up with his arms extended over his head. Some of the corpses had their shirts pulled up over their faces, their pants pulled down, and bore evidence of homosexual anal intercourse. Juan Vallejo Corona, a well-liked, 37-year-old farm labor contractor in Yuba City, was arrested and charged with nine murders after investigators found bank and meat market receipts bearing his signature on two of the bodies. Corona, a happily married father of four daughters, initially seemed to be an unlikely suspect in what appeared to be homosexually motivated murders although it was later learned that he had been briefly institutionalized in 1956 for schizophrenia. Police, however, found blotches of blood in his car and possible murder weapons (two butcher knives, a bolo machete, and a

pistol) in his home. More incriminating was the discovery in Corona's bedroom of what the prosecution would later call a "death ledger"; a listing of 34 men the Mexican national supplied as laborers to farmers in the area. The ledger included the names of seven victims. The excavation of the orchard continued after Corona's arrest and ultimately yielded the bodies of 16 additional men killed (with some homosexually assaulted) in a similar fashion. Autopsies determined that the victims had all been murdered within the previous two months. Only four of the 25 victims could not be identified, the remainder were the types of alcoholic drifters and migrant workers from which Corona assembled his work crews.

At his trial on 25 counts of murder held in Fairfield, California, beginning in September 1972, Corona was represented by attorney Richard Hawk. The attorney suggested that Corona's half brother, Natividad, was responsible for the murders. Natividad was well known around the area of Marysville and Yuba City for offering vagrants wine and money for sex and in 1970 had been arrested for splitting open a young Mexican's head with a machete. The defense alleged that Natividad killed the men in a fit of homosexual rage triggered by his advanced case of syphilis. Unfortunately for Corona, no one could place Natividad in California during the time of the murders. Natividad was in Mexico at the time of the trial and later died in 1973. After 45 hours of deliberation, a jury found Corona guilty on all counts in January 1973. He was subsequently sentenced to 25 consecutive terms of life imprisonment. On December 2, 1973, four inmates at the California Medical Facility in Vacaville slashed and stabbed

Corona 32 times in the face, chest, and abdomen with a hobby shop knife. Corona survived the attack, but lost an eye. On May 9, 1978, the California district court of appeals unanimously reversed Corona's conviction on the ground that attorney Hawk had failed to competently represent his client by not raising "obvious alternative defenses" such as mental incompetence, diminished capacity, or legal insanity. In fact, Hawk neither called defense witnesses nor put Corona on the stand. The attorney was later disbarred for income tax evasion. Corona's retrial in Hayward, California, began in February 1982, lasted seven months, featured 1,300 exhibits, testimony from 175 witnesses, and cost the state an estimated $5 million. The recycled "Natividad Defense" failed and Corona was convicted on September 23, 1982, after a seven-man, five-woman jury deliberated 54 hours over 10 days. Afterwards, the foreman of the jury told the press that the most incriminating piece of evidence against Corona had been the so-called "death ledger" for which the labor contractor had no "reasonable explanation." Corona was sentenced to 25 concurrent terms of 25 years to life in prison. He was denied parole for the fourth time in 1993. Corona is eligible for another parole hearing in 1998.

114. Cray, Ed. *Burden of Proof: The Case of Juan Corona.* Afterword by Richard Hawk. New York: Macmillan, 1973. x, 386 pp.: ill.; 24 cm.

Cray, a professional writer who sat at the defense table during Corona's first trial, was hired by attorney Richard Hawk to serve as an investigator on the case. In its 1978 ruling which overturned Corona's conviction, the California district court of appeals found a conflict of interest in the arrangement that would pay Hawk's legal fee from exclusive rights to the farm laborer's story, *Burden of Proof,* written by Cray and published within months after the end of the trial. Excellent index.

115. Kidder, Tracy. *The Road to Yuba City: A Journey into the Juan Corona Murders.* 1st ed. Garden City, N.Y.: Doubleday, 1974. xii, 317 pp.; 22 cm.

Kidder points out the errors and incompetence of investigators and attorneys for both sides which marred the Corona case. He concludes: "I am told by a friend of an inmate at Vacaville that the prisoners sometime talk about Corona. According to this inmate, they say Corona is 'straight'—not homosexual. And apparently the story that he is innocent, was 'framed,' has gained wide circulation there."

116. Tailbitzer, Bill. *Too Much Blood.* 1st ed. New York: Vantage Press, 1978. 228 pp.: ill.; 21 cm.

The Sutter County sheriff's office provided Tailbitzer with complete access to all crime reports, correspondence, crime scene photos, personal and confidential files and memoranda pertaining to their investigation of the Corona case. The author is non-judgmental, but concludes: "If Juan Corona did not commit the murders for which he was charged and convicted, it must be said that he was the victim of one of the damndest set of coincidences that ever put a man behind bars."

117. Villaseñor, Victor. *Jury: The People vs. Juan Corona.* 1st ed. Boston: Little, Brown, 1977. xvii, 291 pp.; 21 cm.

_____. [Same as 117.] 1st ed. New York: Bantam Books, 1978. xiv, 233 pp.; 18 cm.; paperback.

Villaseñor, a Chicano, conducted extensive interviews with the 12 jurors in Corona's first trial and here presents their view of the case. Interesting.

Cottingham, Richard Francis (a.k.a. "Cott," "Carl Wilson," "Times Square Torso Murderer")

Born November 25, 1946, in Bronx, New York. Computer programmer. Hackensack, New Jersey; New York, New York; Hasbrouck Heights, New Jersey; 5 murders; ligature strangulation; December 1977–May 1980.

"I am deeply ashamed and embarrassed for getting into these episodes."—Cottingham's statement to a judge before being sentenced to 197 years in prison for the murder of one prostitute and other charges

Married father of three whose signature mutilation murders of prostitutes in New York City and New Jersey led to his arrest. Cottingham, a 33-year-old computer programmer for Blue Cross–Blue Shield of Greater New York, maintained a strict *modus operandi* throughout a string of kidnappings, rapes, and murders beginning in late 1977. He picked up prostitutes in Times Square bars, secretly drugged their drinks, then drove the semi-conscious women to motels where he bound, raped, and tortured them for hours. Maryann Carr, a 26-year-old married X ray technician living in Little Ferry, New Jersey, was Cottingham's first and only non-prostitute victim. On December 16, 1977, her body was found in the parking lot of the Quality Inn in Hackensack, New Jersey. Carr had been bound and suffocated. Cottingham's next murders, which established his *modus operandi*, even stunned case-hardened New York City detectives. On December 2, 1979, fireman responded to smoke issuing from room 417 of the Manhattan Travel Inn Motor Lodge. They entered to find the headless and handless corpses of two women who had been set on fire with lighter fluid. Their mutilated bodies confirmed that they were tortured and raped pre-mortem. Police identified one body as that of Deedeh Goodarzi, a young prostitute, but have never been able to identify her companion. On May 4, 1980, the naked and bound body of 19-year-old Manhattan prostitute Valorie Ann Street was found stuffed under a bed in a motel room in Hasbrouck Heights, New Jersey. She had been mutilated and tortured for at least six hours before being strangled. Eleven days later, 25-year-old prostitute Jean Mary Ann Reyner was found in New York City's Seville Hotel, her breasts removed with near surgical precision.

Cottingham's reign of terror ended on May 22, 1980, when he was apprehended in a hallway of a Quality Inn in Hasbrouck Heights attempting to flee the room where he spent three hours raping and torturing prostitute Leslie Ann O'Dell. Handcuffs, slave collars, pills, and surgical tape were found in his possession. In custody, Cottingham attempted suicide by breaking his glasses and cutting his wrist with a lense. He would later unsuccessfully attempt suicide two more times during his subsequent trials. Victims' personal items uncovered in a "trophy room" in Cottingham's home in Lodi, New Jersey, tied him to the murders as did latent prints found on the handcuffs binding Valorie Street. At his trial, four survivors of Cottingham's torturous attacks testified against him. On June 12, 1981, the five-week trial in Hackensack, New Jersey, ended in Cottingham's convictions for the first degree murder of Street and on other charges of kidnapping, assault, and attempted murder of the surviving prostitutes. He was sentenced to 173–197 years in prison. Cottingham received subsequent convictions on October 12, 1982, for murdering Maryann Carr (25–30 years) and on July 9, 1984, in New York for the mutilation killings of Reyner, Goodarzi, and the unidentified "Jane Doe." On August 28, 1984, Cottingham received an additional 75 years to life sentence.

118. Leith, Rod. *The Prostitute Murders: The People vs. Richard Cottingham.* 1st ed. Secaucus, N.J.: Lyle Stuart, 1983. 187 pp., [12] leaves of plates: ill.; 24 cm.

_____. [Same as 118.] New York: Pinnacle Books, 1984. xiv, 210 pp.; 18 cm.; paperback.

_____. [Same as 118, but retitled: *The Torso Killer.*] 1st ed. New York: Pinnacle Books, 1991. 239 pp., [12]pp. of plates: ill.; 18 cm.; paperback.

Leith inserts a composite detective character into an otherwise straightforward account of the case which ends with Cottingham awaiting trial in New York for the murders of three prostitutes.

Crafts, Richard Bunel
(a.k.a. "Wood Chipper Murderer")

Born December 20, 1937, in New York City, New York. Commercial airline pilot, part-time police officer. Newtown, Connecticut; 1 murder; bludgeon; November 19, 1986.

Grisly case in which a husband murdered his wife and attempted to dispose of her body by feeding it into a wood chipper. Weeks before her inexplicable disappearance on November 19, 1986, Helle Crafts confided to a friend that if she turned up missing it would be no accident. Married since 1975 to Richard Crafts, a pilot for Eastern Airlines and a part-time constable, the 39-year-old stewardess had

recently filed for divorce after learning that her husband was having an affair with a stewardess from a rival airline. Friends familiar with their domestic situation were skeptical of Crafts' explanation that Helle had abandoned him and their three children to run off with an Asian lover from Westchester County. A former marine and pilot in the CIA's Air America program, Crafts had been heard to say on more than one occasion that he would not willingly undergo a divorce.

Prompted by friends of the missing woman, police interviewed Crafts who agreed to take a polygraph examination. The test proved inconclusive, but authorities did learn that shortly before Helle's disappearance Crafts had rented an Asplundh Badger Brush Bandit 100 (a wood chipper capable of chipping logs 12 inches in diameter). He had also recently purchased a large deep freezer and replacement carpet and mattresses for the master bedroom of their stylish home in Newtown, Connecticut. The case broke when a snowplow driver told police that he remembered seeing a man on the banks of the Housatonic River feeding brush into a wood chipper in the pre-dawn hours of November 19, 1986. Police teams dubbed "mud monkeys" scoured the river bank and recovered 2660 strands of hair, slivers of bone including the tip of a thumb, and part of a gold-capped tooth. The collected evidence weighed less than an ounce and fit in the palm of one hand. Under a bridge, divers recovered a weighted chainsaw. Forensic specialists restored its abraded serial number and found it to be registered to Crafts.

Crafts was arrested on January 13, 1987, and held on $750,000 bond, the highest in Connecticut history. The publicity surrounding the case forced a change of venue from Danbury to New London where the televised trial began on April 4, 1988. The state contended that Crafts had bludgeoned Helle to death in their bedroom and then froze her body to minimize blood and tissue spew before dismembering her head and extremities with a chainsaw. Driving to the Housatonic River, he fed the dismembered parts into the Brush Bandit convinced he had committed the perfect murder. In a remarkable feat of forensic reconstruction an expert odontologist was able to state with "reasonable scientific certainty" that the recovered gold-capped tooth belonged to Helle Crafts. Similar to the gallows humor engendered by the Ed Gein case, sick jokes abounded. Explaining the crime, it was said that Crafts had loved Helle "too mulch." A popular tee-shirt sold during the trial sported the slogan "Divorce—Connecticut Style" accompanied by a drawing of a wood chipper.

In late June 1988 the case was finally sent to the jury where it remained deadlocked for 17 days. On July 16, 1988, a mistrial was declared after a lone juror, convinced that Helle had abandoned her family and was still alive, angrily walked out on deliberations. A second trial began in Norwalk almost 14 months later on September 7, 1989. After a nine week ordeal in which 380 exhibits and 115 witnesses were presented, jurors took less than three days to find Crafts guilty of first degree murder on November 21, 1988. Sentenced to 50 years in the Connecticut Correctional Institution at Somers, Crafts was led to his maximum security cell amid a prisoners' chant of "chip, chip, chip." Under Connecticut state law, Crafts must serve a minimum of 20 years before being considered for parole.

119. Herzog, Arthur. *The Woodchipper Murder*. 1st ed. New York: H. Holt, 1989. viii, 274 pp., [1] leaf of plates: ill.; 22 cm.

_____. [Same as 119.] [New, updated ed.] New York: Kensington Pub., 1990. 305 pp., [12]pp. of plates: ill.; 18 cm. ("Zebra Books"); paperback.

An updated edition including coverage of the second trial and subsequent murder conviction.

Craig, Christopher

Born May 19, 1936, in Norbury, England. Garage worker. Croydon, England; 1 murder; .45 caliber Colt revolver; November 2, 1952.

"That night I was out to kill because I had so much hate inside me for what they did to my brother."— Alleged statement made by Craig to police which he later recanted; *see also* Bentley, Derek William.

Crimmins, Craig Stephen (a.k.a. "Crimmie," "The Phantom of the Opera," "The Baby-Faced Killer")

Born March 24, 1959, in New York City, New York. Stagehand. New York City; 1 murder; victim bound then dropped from great height; July 23, 1980.

"I heard her bouncing up and down ... and that's when it happened. I went back and kicked her off."— Statement from Crimmins' confession

Young stagehand convicted of the famed "Phantom of the Opera Murder." On the morning of July 24, 1980, the nude and bound body of 30-year-old Canadian-born freelance violinist Helen Hagnes Mintik was found at the bottom of a ventilating shaft in New York City's famed Metropolitan Opera

House. Hired for 11 days to accompany the visiting Berlin Ballet, the Juilliard graduate was last seen the day before around 9:40 p.m. during an intermission prior to her performance in *Miss Julie*. When Hagnes (her professional name) failed to make her curtain call, employees searched the labyrinthine maze of backstage corridors beneath the 3,700 seat opera house before notifying police. Their search of the facility revealed evidence of a sexual assault conducted in a lower level stairwell. Investigators searching the sixth floor roof of the Met discovered Hagnes' broken body around 8:30 a.m. on a steel ledge in an airshaft at the rear of the opera house. The young musician had been stripped, possibly blindfolded, gagged, and her hands tied behind her with rope and rags matching those found in a crate on the roof. An autopsy later showed that Hagnes had been alive when hurled the 60 feet down into the fan pit. Death had resulted from skull fractures and other injuries.

In one of the largest criminal investigations in New York City history, a task force of 50 detectives systematically questioned 500 Met employees and performers who were backstage the night of the killing. The rope, a type used backstage, and the knot used to bind the victim's hands, a clove hitch commonly used by stagehands to secure scenery, led police to photograph, print, and have each stagehand fill out a detailed questionnaire charting their activities at the time of the murder. Suspicion fell on well-liked 21-year-old stagehand Craig Crimmins as inconsistencies in his questionnaire began to emerge when compared with those of his coworkers. Crimmins at first insisted that he did not miss any cues on the night of Hagnes' disappearance, but since a search party composed of stagehands had failed to find him during the second half of the show he changed his story to having passed out drunk backstage. He later convinced a fellow-stagehand to corroborate this alibi. Initially nervous and uncooperative when asked to supply prints, Crimmins finally did so. Police matched his palm print to a partial lifted from a pipe on the roof. Further inconsistencies in Crimmins' story emerged during a 16-hour interrogation session conducted on August 17, 1980. Though released afterwards, authorities closely monitored the movements of their prime suspect. Crimmins was picked up for questioning outside his apartment building on August 29, 1980, after his stagehand friend admitted lying to police in support of his alibi.

In a videotaped confession given later that day, Crimmins admitted murdering Hagnes ostensibly to cover up an unsuccessful rape attempt. On the day of the murder, Crimmins had drunk two dozen beers, popped diet pills, and smoked marijuana. According to his confession, he encountered the violinist on a backstage elevator during the intermission and crudely propositioned her. She responded by slapping him across the face and saying something "snotty and loud." He threatened Hagnes with a hammer and forced her to undress in the lower levels of the building. After trying unsuccessfully for five minutes to rape her in a stairwell Crimmins admitted rubbing himself to orgasm on her body. He herded Hagnes to the roof, tied her with rope, and was leaving the scene when she worked her way free. Recapturing her, Crimmins cut the woman's clothes off with his knife, threw them down the fan shaft, and bound and gagged her with rags found on the roof. He was again leaving when the sounds of her struggling panicked him. According to Crimmins' confession, he "went back and kicked her off."

Crimmins' family and friends reacted with shock to the arrest of the popular young man described by those who knew him well as a "regular guy." Born in Manhattan in 1959, Crimmins did not walk until age three and was not toilet trained until five. Diagnosed as a having a learning disability, the young boy struggled in school and was still in the fifth grade although 13 years old. Crimmins was later admitted to a vocational high school, but dropped out before graduating. Through his father, a backstage worker at the Metropolitan Opera House, Crimmins landed a $20,000 a year union job there as a stagehand. Engaged to a woman studying veterinary medicine, Crimmins' future looked bright. The man dubbed by police as "The Phantom of the Opera," however, had alcohol and drug problems. Crimmins routinely filled the long hours between shows at the Met drinking in local bars, smoking marijuana, and popping diet pills. Still, few believed him capable of a sexually motivated murder and several coworkers and childhood friends pooled their money to post his $50,000 cash bond.

On April 27, 1981, opening arguments began in a Manhattan courtroom where Crimmins pleaded innocent to charges of second degree murder and attempted rape. Prior to the start of the trial, the defense unsuccessfully sought to exclude Crimmins' videotaped confession as well as "enhanced" testimony of a witness police had hypnotized. Under hypnosis a dancer in the Berlin Ballet had identified Crimmins as the man she had last seen on the Met elevator with Hagnes before the musician's disappearance. The thrust of Crimmins' defense was an attack on police investigators who in their haste to get a quick arrest it was argued presented false evidence and "cut across corners in order to get their case in any way they had to." The prosecution called 33 witnesses in support of a case made almost airtight by Crimmins' confession. After being directed by the judge to not consider the uncorroborated rape charge, the jury received the case on June 3, 1981. The next day after deliberating almost 12 hours, they found Crimmins guilty of the lesser charge of felony murder, i.e. the stagehand had killed Hagnes in the commission of another crime (sexual assault). While awaiting sentencing, Crimmins was held in the infirmary at Riker's Island where his only companion was Mark David Chapman, the murderer of ex–Beatle John Lennon. Neither "media murderer" liked the other. Crimmins derided Chapman as "a nut case" while the stagehand's chain-smoking finally drove Chapman berserk and into a transfer to the Ossining Correctional Facility. On September 2, 1981, Crimmins received a 20 years to life sentence. Under the terms of his conviction he is not eligible for parole until sometime in 2001. To date, appeals filed by Crimmins to the appellate division of the state supreme court (1984) and to the New York court of appeals (1985) have both been rejected.

120. Black, David. *Murder at the Met.* Garden City, N.Y.: Dial Press, 1984. 300 pp.; 22 cm.

_____. [Same as 120.] New York: Avon, 1986. 262 pp.; 17 cm.; paperback.

"Based on the exclusive accounts of

detectives Mike Struk and Jerry Giorgio of how they solved the Phantom of the Opera case."—Title page.

Crippen, Hawley Harvey (a.k.a. "John Philo Robinson")

Born circa 1862 in Cold Water, Michigan. Executed November 23, 1910. Medical doctor, patent medicine salesman. London, England; 1 murder; poison (hyoscine); January 31, 1910.

Films: The Suspect (US, 1944), a Universal release directed by Robert Siodmak loosely based on the Crippen case. Cast includes Charles Laughton (Philip), Ella Raines (Mary), and Henry Daniell (Mr. Simmons). *Dr. Crippen* (GB, 1963), a Pathé release directed by Robert Lynn. Cast includes Donald Pleasence (Dr. Hawley Harvey Crippen), Coral Browne (Belle Crippen), and Samantha Eggar (Ethel Le Neve).

Theatre: The Distant Shore (1935), a play by Donald Blackwell and Theodore St. John. *They Fly by Twilight* (1938), a three act play by Paul Dornhorst, first produced at the People's Palace, London, on September 19, 1938. *Dearly Beloved Wife* (1938), a play by Jeanne De Casalis, presented by the London Playgoers' Club at the Vaudeville Theatre on October 30, 1938. *Belle, or the Ballad of Dr. Crippen* (1961), a "music hall musical" by Monty Norman and Wolf Mankowitz based on the play by Beverly Cross, ran for six weeks from May 4, 1961, at the Strand Theatre.

Audio: Belle, or the Ballad of Dr. Crippen, a one–sound disc, 33⅓ stereo recording of Monty Norman's "music hall musical," was published in 1960(?) by Decca (London). The recording features the original London cast of George Benson, Davy Kaye, and Virginia Vernon *et al.* The recording was re-issued in 1983 by That's Entertainment Records (London) under license from Decca International.

"In this farewell letter to the world, written as I face eternity I say that Ethel Le Neve has loved me as few women love men, and that her innocence of any crime, save that of yielding to the dictates of the heart, is absolute. To her I pay this last tribute. It is of her that my last thoughts have been. My last prayer will be that God will protect her and keep her safe from harm and allow her to join me in eternity."

American doctor and wife murderer whose trans–Atlantic flight and subsequent capture marked the first time radio technology was utilized in the apprehension of a killer. Hawley Harvey Crippen (known as "Peter") graduated from the University of Michigan and by age 25 had taken a medical degree at the Homeopathic Hospital College in Cleveland, Ohio. After the death of his first wife from apoplexy in January 1892, Crippen remarried 19-year-old Cora Turner (real name Kunigunde Mackamotzki) in Jersey City on September 1, 1892. Turner, a profoundly untalented singer, entertained pretensions of becoming a great opera diva. In this endeavor, Crippen supported her both emotionally and financially while undergoing a series of stunning career reversals. By 1897 when they moved to London, Crippen had descended into the nether regions of medical quackery selling medicine on commission for the Munyon Patent Medicine Company, co-partnering the Yale Tooth Specialist Company, and later working for an ear care business called the Aural Remedy. Turner (under the stage name "Belle

Elmore") tried unsuccessfully to launch a music hall career, but had to content herself with entertaining performers at No. 39 Hilldrop Crescent, the Crippens' home in the Kentish Town District of North London. Blaming Crippen for her failure, Turner began drinking and publicly humiliated him by taking a series of lovers. The 50-year-old Crippen turned for solace to his secretary of four years, Ethel Le Neve, 27, and the two began an affair marked by deep affection and respect.

On January 31, 1910, Turner disappeared after hosting a dinner party in their home. To cover her absence, the diminutive doctor explained that she had died while visiting friends in California. Eyebrows were raised, however, when Ethel Le Neve began openly living with Crippen at Hilldrop Crescent on March 12, 1910. After she was seen wearing the missing woman's jewelry, suspicious friends of the missing woman contacted Scotland Yard. One week later, Chief Inspector Walter Dew interviewed Crippen. The doctor readily admitted that he had concocted the story of his wife's death in order to avoid the inevitable scandal that would result if people were to learn that she had really run off with another man. Dew's search of the house revealed nothing amiss and Crippen may very well have escaped justice had he not panicked and fled with Le Neve on July 10, 1910. Learning of the doctor's flight, Dew revisited Hilldrop Crescent on July 13, 1910. After finding nothing buried in the garden, the inspector went down to the coal cellar and tested the crevices in the brick floor with a poker. When a few bricks yielded, he dug the area up with a spade to discover a reeking mass of flesh wrapped in a pajama top and covered with lime. The head, arms, legs,

and genitals had been removed so all that remained was an unidentifiable torso from which the bones and several organs had been removed with surgical-like precision. Though the fate of the missing limbs and organs was never determined, it was conjectured that some were burned in the kitchen grate while Crippen had tossed the head overboard in a handbag during a trip to Dieppe. A later autopsy determined that the remains contained a lethal dose of the drug hydrobromide of hyoscine.

Crippen and Le Neve, posing as "Mr. John Philo Robinson" and his young son "Master Robinson" were in Antwerp, Belgium, waiting to ship out on July 20, 1910, aboard the S.S. *Montrose* bound for Quebec when arrest warrants were issued for them three days after the discovery in the cellar. Police handbills and newspaper accounts of the pair featured their photographs beneath the bold face heading "Murder and Mutilation." To avoid detection, Crippen shaved off his moustache and Le Neve cut her hair and wore boy's clothes. The S.S. *Montrose* was at sea two days when Captain Harry Kendall used the ship's Marconi wireless to send a message to authorities reporting that he had identified the "Robinsons" as the wanted fugitives. On July 23, 1910, Dew set sail from Liverpool aboard the *Laurentic*, a faster ship that would arrive in Quebec on July 30, 1910, one day before the *Montrose*. Crippen, isolated aboard the ship, was unaware that the chase was front page news in every paper in England. On July 30, Dew arrived at Father Point, Canada, ahead of Crippen. Backed up by a contingent of Royal Canadian Mounted Police, Dew boarded the *Montrose* the next day and arrested Crippen and Le Neve.

Amid enormous negative publicity, Crippen's trial opened at London's Old Bailey on August 28, 1910. Instead of admitting to killing his wife during a heated argument (a tactic that certainly would have reduced the murder charge to manslaughter), Crippen unwisely maintained his innocence in the face of damning forensic evidence. Sir Bernard Spilsbury identified the mutilated remains as those of Mrs. Crippen's by connecting a scar found on the torso with that produced by an operation she had to remove an ovary. A chemist testified that days before the woman's disappearance, he had sold Crippen five grains of hyoscine and produced the poison book with the doctor's signature in it. Dr. Spilsbury had previously testified that large traces of the deadly drug had been found in the remains. Crippen was found guilty and sentenced to death on October 22, 1910, after a jury deliberated only 27 minutes. Le Neve was tried three days later as an accessory after the fact of murder, but due largely to Crippen's insistence that she had no involvement in the affair combined with a brilliant legal defense, she was acquitted. While awaiting execution, Crippen was a model prisoner who won the respect of all with his continued allegiance and devotion to Le Neve. Hanged at Pentonville Prison on November 23, 1910, Crippen was buried with a photograph of Le Neve and her letters in accordance with his last wish. Le Neve subsequently sold her story to the press, changed her name, married, and died in Dulwich in August 1967 at the age of 84.

121. Bloom, Ursula. *The Girl Who Loved Crippen.* London: Hutchinson, 1957. 189 pp.; 19 cm.
     A novel based on the Crippen murder case.

_____. [Same as 121.] Large print ed. Bath: Chivers Press, 1981. 292 pp.; 23 cm. ("A Lythway book.")

122. Constantine-Quinn, Max. *Doctor Crippen.* The Rogue's Gallery. London: Duckworth, 1935. 224 pp.; 18 cm.
     Biographical study which owes much to Filson Young's introduction to *The Trial of Hawley Harvey Crippen* (see 132). Includes chronology.

123. Cullen, Tom. *Mild Murderer.* London: Bodley Head, 1977. 223 pp., [4] leaves of plates: ill.; 23 cm.

_____. [Same as 123, but U.S. ed. retitled: *The Mild Murderer: The True Story of the Dr. Crippen Case.*] Boston: Houghton Mifflin, 1977. 223 pp., [4] leaves of plates: ill.; 22 cm.

_____. [Same as 123, but paperback ed. retitled: *Crippen: The Mild Murderer.*] Penguin True Crime. Harmondsworth: Penguin Books, 1988. 223 pp., [8]pp. of plates: ill., ports., facsims.; 20 cm.; paperback.
     A sympathetic portrait of the henpecked murderer which is by far the most readable of the many books written about the case. An appendix contains 11 letters written by Crippen to Le Neve from a condemned cell in Pentonville Prison during October 28–November 22, 1910. Also included is Crippen's "Farewell Letter to the World" printed in *Lloyd's Weekly News* on November 20, 1910.

124. Dew, Walter. *I Caught Crippen: Memoirs of Ex-Chief Inspector Walter Dew, C.I.D., of Scotland Yard.* London; Glasgow: Blackie & Son, Ltd., 1938. 242 pp.: ill., ports.; 22 cm.
     Dew, the Scotland Yard inspector who apprehended Crippen, remembers the case and his search for Jack the Ripper in an informative and charming memoir. While never doubting Crippen to be a "callously calculating murderer," Dew found "something almost likeable about the mild little fellow who squinted through thick-lensed spectacles, and whose sandy moustache was out of all proportion to his build."

125. Dornhorst, Paul. *They Fly by Twilight: A Play in Three Acts*. London; New York: Thomas Nelson, 1940. vi, 80 pp.: plan; 18 cm.

A play based on the Crippen case first performed in 1938.

126. Goodman, Jonathan, comp. *The Crippen File*. London: Allison & Busby, 1985. [96]pp.: ill.; 30 cm.; paper covers.

Reproduces facsimiles of documents and newspaper clippings covering the case from contemporary sources like the *Daily Mail*. Goodman's commentary is enlightening and this work owes much to his chapter "Accounts and Transmutations" which discusses books, plays, and films based on the Crippen case. Essential and charming.

127. Gordon, Richard. *The Private Life of Dr. Crippen: A Novel*. London: Heinemann, 1981. 184 pp.; 22 cm.

Fictional account of the sensational case.

128. Le Neve, Ethel. *Ethel Le Neve: Her Life Story*. London: John Long Ltd., circa 1910-1911; paperback.

According to Jonathan Goodman's book, *The Crippen File*, Le Neve's account was first printed in the *Lloyd's Weekly News* of November 6 and 13, 1910. John Long Ltd. published this account as a threepenny paperback "soon afterwards." Publisher Jesse Pemberton, owner of the Daisy Bank Printing & Publishing Company, Gorton, Manchester, issued an unauthorized edition of the *Life Story* a "year or so" after the Long edition. Pemberton then produced another extremely rare title, *Full Account of the Crippen Horror*, which this author has been unable to locate in any library. Goodman reproduces the title pages from these books on page 94 of his aforementioned book (see 126).

129. Meadows, Catherine. *Henbane*. London: V. Gollancz, 1934. 367 pp.; 19 cm.

_____. [Same as 129, but U.S. ed. retitled: *Doctor Moon.*] New York: G.P. Putnam's Sons, 1935. 313 pp.; 20 cm.

A novel based on the Crippen murder case.

130. Raymond, Ernest. *A Chorus Ending*. London: Cassell, 1951. 330 pp.; 21 cm.

Fictionalization based on the Crippen case.

131. _____. *We, the Accused*. London: Cassell, 1935. 629 pp.; 22 cm.

_____. [Same as 131 with added subtitle: *A Novel.*] New York: Frederick A. Stokes, 1935. 497 pp.; 22 cm.

A novel based on the Crippen murder case.

132. Young, Filson, ed. *The Trial of Hawley Harvey Crippen*. Notable British Trials. Edinburgh; London: W. Hodge, 1920. xxxv, 211 pp., [5] leaves of plates: ill., ports.; 22 cm.

_____. [Same as 132.] Notable English Trials. Toronto: Canada Law Book, 1920. xxxv, 211 pp., [5] leaves of plates: ill., ports.; 23 cm.

_____. [Same as 132.] 2nd ed. Notable British Trials. Edinburgh; London: W. Hodge, 1950. xxxv, 211 pp., [5] leaves of plates: ill., ports.; 23 cm.

_____. [Same as 132.] Special ed. The Legal Classics Library and Notable English Trials. Birmingham, Ala.: Legal Classics Library, 1985. xxxv, 211 pp., [5] leaves of plates: ill., ports.; 22 cm. (Reprint of 1920 ed. Includes "Notes from the editors" booklet as a separate publication.)

_____. [Same as 132.] Notable Trials Library. Birmingham, Ala.: Leslie B. Adams, Jr., 1991. xxxv, 211 pp., [5] leaves of plates: ill., ports.; 22 cm. (Reprint of 1920 ed.)

Young's excellent case study introduces the edited transcript of the Old Bailey trial. Appendices include Captain Kendall's message from the S.S. *Montrose*, Crippen's published statement from the *Daily Mail* of November 20, 1910, Crippen's letter to Ethel Le Neve from the *Daily Mail* of November 27, 1910, the trial of Miss Le Neve at the Old Bailey (October 25, 1910), and Crippen's appeal.

"Crowborough Chicken Farm Murder" *see* Thorne, John Norman Holmes

Crumm, James, Jr.

Born circa May 1962 in Johnson County, Kansas. High school student. Miami County, Kansas; 1 murder; shotgun; April 17, 1980.

"This is for hitting my mother and my sister, and for getting me kicked out of the house."—Statement attributed to Crumm by accomplice Paul Sorrentino seconds before the shotgun murder of Christen Hobson; *see also* Hobson, Sueanne Sallee.

Dahmer, Jeffrey Lionel

Born May 21, 1960, in Milwaukee, Wisconsin. Died November 28, 1994. Stock clerk. Bath Township, Ohio, and Milwaukee, Wisconsin; 17 murders (15 convictions); ligature strangulation; June 1978–July 1991.

Video: Jeffrey Dahmer—The Secret Life (US, 1993), a direct-to-video film coproduction of Cinema Partner Film and Flourish Productions, directed by David R. Bowen from a screenplay by Carl Crew. Cast includes Carl Crew (Jeffrey Dahmer).

"It's hard for me to believe that a human being could have done what I've done. I want you to understand that my questions regarding Satan and the devil were not to defuse guilt from me and blame the devil for what I've done, because I realize what I've done is my guilt. But I have to question whether or not there is an evil force in the world and whether or not I have been influenced by it."—From Dahmer's confession

On the night of July 22, 1991, two Milwaukee police officers cruising along the 2500 block of West Kilbourn Avenue were flagged down by an excited black man dangling a locked pair of handcuffs from one wrist. Tracy Edwards, 32, told the officers of being lured to the second floor apartment of a "big white dude" in a nearby apartment house where he was shown photos of mutilated men, propositioned, then threatened with a knife when he asked to leave. Edwards managed to escape by kicking the man in the stomach and running. Investigating the complaint, the officers drove to the four story Oxford Apartments located at 924 North 25th Street in a ghetto area of Milwaukee. As they ascended the stairs to the second floor, the policemen were struck with an overpowering stench of decomposition which grew stronger as they approached the door of Apartment 213. A handsome blond-haired man in his early thirties responded to their knock and identified himself as Jeffrey Dahmer. Inside the two-room apartment officers literally found a nightmare vision of hell. Color photos depicting mutilated bodies, body parts, and homosexual acts were found littered throughout the apartment. A search of the refrigerator yielded four human heads, five more (scraped clean) stored in a box and filing cabinet, and two additional skulls displayed on a closet shelf. In the freezer, lungs, intestines, kidneys, and a heart had been individually packaged. Decomposed hands and a male genital organ were discovered in a lobster pot. In the bedroom, a 57-gallon blue plastic drum was found to contain body parts from at least three victims awash in a chemical bath of acid and water. Later, evidence technicians garbed in oxygen masks and protective suits would remove the remains of 11 victims including five full skeletons and parts from six others.

Dahmer, only recently fired from his job as a stock clerk at the local Ambrosia Chocolate Company, was remarkably forthcoming about the murders and his motivations for them. On a personal level the 31-year-old's confessions revealed a catalog of human depravity which included mutilation, cannibalism, and necrophilia. On the social level, however, Dahmer's frank admissions revealed gross instances of incompetence, racism, and homophobia in the ranks of the Milwaukee Police Department. Of Dahmer's 17 confessed murders, only three victims were white, ten were black, and the remaining four either Hispanic, Indian, or Asian. Despite the disappearances of these 16 young men and boys from the seedier sections of Milwaukee during the period from September 15, 1987, through July 19, 1991, the police made no concerted effort to investigate. Moreover, in one heartbreaking instance they even returned a 14-year-old Laotian boy to Dahmer and his death after the youth had managed to escape from the killer's apartment. The public, then fascinated by the film *The Silence of the Lambs*, now had a true life serial killer even more horrifying than the fictional character of "Buffalo Bill."

The son of an industrial chemist, Dahmer was born in Milwaukee in 1960, but spent most of his childhood in semi-rural Bath Township, Ohio. Reportedly molested sexually at age eight by a neighborhood boy (a claim he denied), Dahmer and his younger brother grew up in a family atmosphere poisoned by his parents' constant bickering. By age 10, Dahmer was using his father's chemicals to conduct secret experiments on road kill, often dis-

solving the bones of animals or placing their skeletons in jars filled with formaldehyde. Others he buried under little white crosses in a cemetery by the side of his house. A neighbor would later tell authorities of finding the impaled carcasses of frogs, dogs, and cats staked to trees in the woods near the boy's house. At school, Dahmer was considered the classic "geek" so hungry for attention that he acted the fool by suddenly screaming out in class and walking backwards through the halls. His behavior became so outrageous and noteworthy that other students labelled any eccentric behavior by anyone as "doing a Dahmer." While other teenagers were dating, Dahmer lost himself in alcohol-fueled homosexual fantasies involving necrophilia, dissection, and taxidermy. One month after he turned 18, Dahmer's parents separated in June 1978 prior to divorcing on July 24, 1978. Under court order, Dahmer's father left the family home and moved into a nearby hotel while Dahmer's mother, a woman with a history of mental instability, was often in Chippewa Falls, Wisconsin, with her youngest son, preparing to relocate there. Abandoned and emotionally isolated, Dahmer's loneliness merged with his dark fantasies to produce the first of his self-confessed 17 murders.

On June 18, 1978, Dahmer picked up 18-year-old Steven Mark Hicks hitchhiking in Bath and took him home for a drink. When Hicks tried to leave, Dahmer struck him on the back of the head with a barbell then used the bar to strangle him to death on the floor. Dahmer kept the corpse for two days during which time he dissected the body, examined the organs, and frequently masturbated. Afterwards, Dahmer filleted the flesh off Hicks' body, dumping the pieces in trash bags. Bones were pulverized with a sledgehammer and scattered around the property. After his arrest, Dahmer produced a map directing authorities to the location of the body where some 500 bone fragments were recovered during a search of the property in late July and August of 1991. Searching for some direction in his life, Dahmer spent a semester at Ohio State University in Columbus, but instead of attending classes stayed drunk in his dorm room. At his father's suggestion, he joined the Army on December 29, 1978, and was stationed in Baumholder, West Germany, as a medic. Army buddies remembered Dahmer mixing Beefeater martinis in his barracks and drinking himself unconscious while listening to Black Sabbath records on headphones. His habitual drunkenness led to a general discharge on March 26, 1981, nearly ten months short of his three-year enlistment.

Returning to Bath to live with his father, Dahmer logged an arrest on charges of disorderly conduct and resisting arrest on October 7, 1981. Shipped off to live with his grandmother in the Milwaukee suburb of West Allis, Dahmer was cited for indecent exposure at the Wisconsin State Fair on August 7, 1982. In 1985, Dahmer was hired as an $8.75 an hour stock clerk on the graveyard shift at the Ambrosia Chocolate Company. While at his grandmother's, he stole a department store mannequin and used it for sex. Driven by fantasies of necrophilia, Dahmer visited funeral parlors searching for the bodies of attractive young men. In a confession, he admitted going to a cemetery to dig up the body of one teenager but was foiled when the ground was frozen. Dahmer became a denizen of gay bathhouses in Milwaukee where he would spike the drinks of potential sex partners with Halcion, a potent sedative, and have sex with them while they were unconscious. He was subsequently banned from one bathhouse after paramedics had to be called to revive one of his victims. Nine years after the murder of Steven Hicks, Dahmer picked up white 28-year-old Steven Walter Tuomi at a gay disco on September 15, 1987. According to Dahmer, they checked into the Ambassador Hotel where he continued to drink until he blacked out. When he awoke, Tuomi was dead. Dahmer left the room to purchase a large suitcase, stuffed Tuomi's body in it, and transported the bag by cab to his grandmother's house where he dismembered the corpse and disposed of the remains. Tuomi's body has never been recovered. Dahmer killed two other men at his grandmother's house (September 1987 and January 1988) before the unwitting old lady, concerned over the stench and mess of his "chemistry experiments," asked him to leave.

On September 25, 1988, Dahmer moved into the Oxford Apartments and lost no time in trolling for other victims. The next day, he was arrested at his apartment for attempting to fondle a 13-year-old Laotian boy to whom he had offered $50 to pose for nude pictures. Convicted on January 30, 1989, of second degree sexual assault and enticing a child for immoral purposes, Dahmer was given a five-year suspended sentence and ordered to serve one year in the Milwaukee County Jail with work release privileges which allowed him to keep his job at the chocolate factory. He served only ten months. Unhampered by the presence of others, Dahmer developed an efficient ritual that allowed him to claim an additional 13 victims between

March 1989 and his arrest in July 1991. Prior to cruising gay bars, Dahmer ground Halcion pills into a glass in anticipation of bringing a victim back to the apartment. Although he later insisted his only criterion for selecting a victim was physical attractiveness and not race, Dahmer was known to dislike blacks and a majority of the victims were non-whites. At the bar, Dahmer offered his potential victim money to pose for nude photos back at his apartment. Once there, he mixed liquor into the glass containing the sleeping pills and waited. When the man passed out, Dahmer stripped him, fondled his body while masturbating or performing anal sex, and photographed the unconscious victim in various sexual poses. Afterwards, Dahmer would drink himself into near collapse before strangling and dismembering the body with a knife or electric buzz saw. According to Dahmer, the men were murdered (as in the case of British serial killer Dennis Nilsen) so that they would not be able to leave him. Body parts, especially the head, were hoarded so that "the true essence" of the person could be kept near him forever. In at least one instance, he admitted butchering a victim and frying his bicep in a skillet with Crisco and meat tenderizer. Then, in an act reserved only for people he really liked, Dahmer ate the flesh seasoned with salt, pepper, and A-1 steak sauce. As his fantasies of control evolved, he dreamed of creating an army of compliant zombie lovers who would mindlessly do his sexual bidding. To that end, he performed crude lobotomies using an electric drill to bore holes into his victims' skulls and then injecting muriatic acid into the openings with a turkey baster in order to destroy their will.

Of all Dahmer's gruesome murders, none touched the people of Milwaukee and the nation as profoundly as that of Konerak Sinthasomphone, a 13-year-old Laotian boy whose brother had been molested by Dahmer on September 26, 1988. Dahmer was still on parole for that crime when he lured Sinthasomphone to his apartment on May 27, 1991, with the promise of paying him for posing for nude photographs. The boy was drugged, photographed, and anally raped before Dahmer performed his crude cranial surgery. When the Laotian failed to regain consciousness, Dahmer became bored and went to a local gay bar where he remained until closing time. Upon his return, Dahmer observed a dazed Sinthasomphone, naked and bleeding copiously from the rectum, sitting on a corner attended by two black females. Realizing that the youth was speaking to them in his native language, Dahmer told the incredulous pair that the boy was his friend and attempted to drag him in the direction of his apartment. The police arrived, and failing to run a check on Dahmer which would have identified him as a paroled sex offender, bought the killer's story that the incident was only a lover's quarrel. They returned the boy to Apartment 213. Sinthasomphone was strangled to death before the officers reached the street. Public outrage later reached its zenith after the Milwaukee police chief released a police audio recording in which the attending officers joked about needing to be "deloused" after leaving the boy in the apartment. The two officers were subsequently fired from the Milwaukee Police Department, but were ordered reinstated on April 27, 1994, by a Green Bay, Wisconsin, judge who called their dismissals "too harsh." In addition to their reinstatement, the officers were each awarded nearly $55,000 in back pay. Had Dahmer been apprehended at the time, the lives of Sinthasomphone and four other victims would have been spared.

Dahmer pleaded guilty but insane to 15 counts of murder committed in Milwaukee County as opening arguments began in Milwaukee on January 30, 1992. Separated from a courtroom gallery filled with the relatives of many of his victims by an eight foot tall sheet of bulletproof glass, Dahmer sat calmly while psychiatrists (in the absence of a death penalty in Wisconsin) argued whether he should spend the rest of his life in a prison or a psychiatric facility from which he might one day be paroled. After two weeks of stomach churning testimony, a jury decided on February 15, 1992, that the serial killer was sane at the time of the murders and Dahmer was sentenced to 15 mandatory life prison terms totalling 936 years. He was subsequently charged in the 1978 murder of Steven Hicks in Ohio. Incarcerated at the Columbia Correctional Institution in Portage, Dahmer refused to be isolated from the other prisoners although he knew he was a prime target for assassination. Perhaps sensing that he would not survive long in the penitentiary, Dahmer was baptized in the prison infirmary's whirlpool by Church of Christ minister Roy Ratcliff on May 10, 1994. Less than two months later on July 3, 1994, an inmate attempted to slash Dahmer's throat with a razor blade during a prison chapel service. Dahmer escaped with only a minor scratch and refused to press charges. On November 28, 1994, Dahmer and two other inmates were cleaning a bathroom near the prison gym when one of the men, Christopher Scarver, a 25-year-old black murderer, bashed the serial killer's head in with an iron bar removed from

an exercise machine. Dahmer was killed instantly. Jesse Anderson, a 37-year-old wife killer also bludgeoned by Scarver, died of massive head injuries two days later. Initial speculation that Scarver's attack on Dahmer was racially motivated was dispelled when the black prisoner announced himself to be the "Son of God." Scarver, a carpenter by trade, reasoned that since his name, "Chris," was similar to that of Christ and his mother's name was Mary, he should believe the "voices" in his head that called him "the chosen one." After the attacks, Scarver mentioned to a guard that "God told me to do it." In May 1996, relatives of Dahmer's victims accepted $407,225 from a Milwaukee civic group to keep the killer's belongings from public auction. The items will be destroyed and 11 families will get at least $32,500.

133. Baumann, Ed. *Step into My Parlor: The Chilling Story of a Serial Killer.* Chicago: Bonus Books, 1991. 305 pp., [16]pp. of plates: ill.; 23 cm.

Passable account of the murders which includes contributions by Gerson H. Kaplan, M.D., a Chicago psychiatrist, on Dahmer's psyche and by Crocker Stephenson, staff writer and assistant city editor for the *Milwaukee Sentinel*, on "Milwaukee's anguish." The photograph section features Dahmer's 17 victims in the order in which he said he killed them. Also of use is a chapter entitled "Gallows Humor" which chronicles the sick humor involving Dahmer and Wisconsin's other famous serial killer/cannibal, Ed Gein. Includes index.

134. Dahmer, Lionel. *A Father's Story.* 1st ed. New York: W. Morrow, 1994. 255 pp.: ill.; 22 cm.

_____. [Same as 134 with added subtitle: *One Man's Anguish at Confronting the Evil in His Son.*] London: Little, Brown, 1994. 255 pp.: ill., ports.; 23 cm.

Dahmer's father looks for answers which might explain how his son became a serial killer suggesting that he may have genetically passed a predisposition for violence onto his son. At the outset of the book, Lionel Dahmer announces that part of the work's proceeds will go to the families of the victims. As of January 1995, the families were still waiting and have threatened legal action.

135. Davis, Don. *The Milwaukee Murders: Nightmare in Apartment 213—The True Story.* New York: St. Martin's Paperbacks, 1991. 290 pp.: ill.; 18 cm.; paperback.

_____. [Same as 135.] Fully updated. London: True Crime, 1992. viii, 308 pp., [8]pp. of plates: ill.; 18 cm.; paperback.

Hurriedly published paperback account written primarily from media sources which covers the case up through August 22, 1991, when Dahmer was charged with an additional three murders bringing the total to 15. Includes chronology.

136. Dvorchak, Robert J., and Holewa, Lisa. *Milwaukee Massacre: Jeffrey Dahmer and the Milwaukee Murders.* New York: Dell, 1991. xii, 275 pp., [8]pp. of plates: ill.; 18 cm.; paperback.

_____. [Same as 136.] London: Hale, 1992. 188 pp., [8]pp. of plates: ill., ports.; 23 cm.; trade paperback.

Paperback original which includes a useful chronology and reproduces the criminal complaint the State of Wisconsin filed against Dahmer on August 21, 1991. The complaint provides detailed information provided by Dahmer on the victims and how they died.

137. Jaeger, Richard W., and Balousek, M. William. *Massacre in Milwaukee: The Macabre Case of Jeffrey Dahmer.* 1st ed. Oregon, Wis.: Waubesa Press, 1991. 233 pp.: ill.; 22 cm.; trade paperback.

Good account by veteran crime reporters for the *Wisconsin State Journal* in Madison. Interestingly, Jaeger covered the 1968 sanity hearing of Ed Gein, another infamous Wisconsin serial killer

and cannibal. An appendix reproduces the criminal complaint filed against Dahmer in the Milwaukee County circuit court. Includes a small bibliography and index.

138. Masters, Brian. *The Shrine of Jeffrey Dahmer.* London: Hodder & Stoughton, 1993. ix, 242 pp., [8]pp. of plates: ill., ports., 1 plan; 25 cm.

Masters, who wrote the brilliant *Killing for Company* about Dennis Nilsen (see 453), compares Dahmer with the British serial killer and concludes both killed as a way of keeping their victims with them. Essential.

139. Norris, Joel. *Jeffrey Dahmer.* New York: Windsor, 1992. 293 pp., [24]pp. of plates: ill., ports.; 18 cm. ("Pinnacle books"); paperback.

_____. [Same as 139.] London: Constable, 1992. 293 pp.; [24]pp. of plates; 20 cm.; paperback.

140. Schwartz, Anne E. *The Man Who Could Not Kill Enough: The Secret Murders of Milwaukee's Jeffrey Dahmer.* Secaucus, N.J.: Carol, 1992. x, 225 pp.: ill.; 24 cm. ("A Birch Lane Press book.")

_____. [Same as 140 with variant subtitle: *The Secret Murders of Jeffrey Dahmer.*] London: Mondo, 1992. 225 pp., [8]pp. of plates: ill., ports.; 18 cm.; paperback.

Schwartz, a journalist for the *Milwaukee Journal*, was the first reporter to enter Dahmer's apartment after police arrested him.

Dallas, Claude Lafayette, Jr. (a.k.a. "Jack Chappel," "Al Schrenk")

Born March 11, 1950, in Winchester, Virginia. Trapper. Idaho; 2 murders; .357 Magnum pistol, .22 caliber rifle; January 5, 1981.

Television: "Manhunt for Claude Dallas" (1986), a two-hour, made-for-television movie based on Jeff Long's *Manhunt: The True Story of Claude*

Dallas, originally aired on CBS on October 28, 1986. Cast includes Matt Salinger (Claude Dallas, Jr.) and Claude Akins (Bill Pogue).

Video: Outlaw, a 93-minute video version of the made-for-television movie, was released on May 1, 1991.

"I do regret what took place at Bull Camp. But I still feel, as I felt at the time, that I did the only thing I could under the circumstances." — Statement made by Dallas at his sentencing hearing

Self-styled mountain man who murdered two conservation officers and has since become a symbol to many of the rugged individualism of the Old West. On January 5, 1981, Idaho State Fish and Game Department officers Conley Elms and Bill Pogue were shot to death by Claude Dallas, 30, as they attempted to arrest him for poaching at his remote campsite in southwest Idaho near the Nevada border. Elms' body was recovered from the South Fork of the Owyhee River. In addition to two .357 Magnum pistol wounds, he had been shot twice in the head execution-style with a .22 caliber rifle. A witness to the incident admitted helping Dallas transport Pogue's body to a nearby town where the killer borrowed a truck to dispose of the corpse. Dallas, a skilled survivalist, was last seen walking into the desert carrying a backpack filled with provisions and a gun. Despite an intensive manhunt, Dallas remained at large for 15 months until an informer tipped authorities that the fugitive was hiding in a trailer near Winnemucca, Nevada. Dallas was apprehended on April 18, 1982, after being slightly wounded in a running gun battle with FBI agents. At his September 1982 first degree murder trial in Caldwell, Idaho, Dallas admitted shooting the officers, but claimed self-

defense. According to Dallas, Pogue threatened to kill him and reached for his holstered pistol. The trapper reacted by quick-drawing his .357 Magnum pistol and shooting both officers. Asked why he then shot both men twice in the head, Dallas replied, "I was a little bit out of my head at that stage ... I was wound up." Dallas fled because of the "lynch-mob attitude the state tried to cultivate." Following Dallas' directions, authorities recovered Pogue's skeletal remains in the mountains 15 miles west of Winnemucca. On October 20, 1982, a jury returned the surprisingly lenient verdict of manslaughter. Dallas, whom many in the area now revered as a folk hero, was sentenced to 30 years in prison. In November 1985, the U. S. Supreme Court upheld the conviction. On March 30, 1986, Dallas escaped from the Idaho State Prison and remained at large as one of the FBI's Ten Most Wanted until his arrest in Riverside, California, on March 8, 1987. Dallas was subsequently acquitted of the prison escape charge on September 4, 1987 after convincing a jury that he fled to escape being killed by guards. In September 1987, Dallas was transferred to a more secure Nebraska penitentiary as an escape risk. The convicted killer, described as a "mountain man born 100 years too late," could (with credit given for "good time") be released in January 2004.

141. Dozhier, Parker. *Death in the Desert: The Story of Claude Dallas.* Sutton, Neb.: Spearman, 1986. 85 pp.; 23 cm.

Dozhier, who wrote a 13-part series on the case for the monthly magazine *The Trapper*, views the tragedy as the "result of laws, regulations and decisions made by people totally removed from Idaho, the West and even the United States." The book concludes with

Dallas' 1986 escape from the Idaho State Prison.

142. Long, Jeff. *Outlaw: The True Story of Claude Dallas.* 1st ed. New York: Morrow, 1985. 239 pp.: ill., maps; 22 cm.

———. [Same as 142.] 1st McGraw-Hill paperback ed. viii, 217 pp., [8] pp. of plates : ill. ; 17 cm.; paperback.

Dallas and conservation officer Pogue are presented as modern day archetypal figures of the Old West who were destined to clash.

143. Olsen, Jack. *Give a Boy a Gun: A True Story of Law and Disorder in the American West.* New York: Delacorte Press, 1985. 333 pp., 8 pp. of plates: ill., ports.; 22 cm.

———. [Same as 143.] 313 pp., [8] pp. of plates: ill., ports.; 18 cm.; paperback.

Veteran crime writer Olsen maintains Dallas' rugged individualist image was created by his attorneys to reduce the murder charges against him. In comments made shortly after the fugitive was recaptured in California, Olsen stated "Dallas is as much of a hero as Charles Manson and as much of a mountainman as Liberace."

Daniel, Vickie Loretha
(acquitted; a.k.a. "Vickie Loretha Carroll" [maiden name])

Born circa 1947 in Baytown, Texas. Housewife. Liberty, Texas; 1 murder (acquitted); .22 caliber rifle; January 21, 1981.

Television: "Bed of Lies" (1992), a two-hour, made-for-television movie based on Salerno's book *Deadly Blessings,* originally aired on ABC on January 20, 1992. Cast includes Susan Dey (Vickie Daniel), Chris Cooper (Price Daniel, Jr.), and Fred Dalton Thompson (Richard "Racehorse" Haynes).

"He started coming down real fast. He said he was going to kill me. I didn't want him to hit me anymore. I moved back. I don't remember anything. I closed my eyes."—Excerpt from Daniel's trial testimony

Wife of an influential Texas politician acquitted of killing her husband during a domestic dispute. On January 21, 1981, police were summoned to the Price Daniel, Jr., family ranch outside of Liberty, Texas. Daniel, a 39-year-old attorney and former Speaker of the Texas House of Representatives, was found dead from a single .22 caliber rifle shot which had severed his aorta. His wife of four years, 33-year-old Vickie Daniel, was taken from the scene and hospitalized for "traumatic shock." Twice during their marriage, the former Dairy Queen worker had filed for divorce, most recently on December 31, 1980. Arrested five days after the shooting and later indicted, Vickie pleaded not guilty to the murder. While she was awaiting trial, Price Daniel's sister filed suit to gain custody of their two sons (ages ten and ten months). Vickie retained flamboyant Houston-based attorney Richard "Racehorse" Haynes who had successfully defended Fort Worth millionaire T. Cullen Davis on murder charges. The bitter six-week custody battle was highlighted by the widow's compelling allegations that the dead man was a physically abusive bisexual who molested his sons. According to Vickie's testimony, on the night of the shooting Price Daniel asked her to sign divorce papers and became enraged when she refused to do so without first letting her attorney review them. He slapped her then went to the attic to look for his stash of marijuana. When informed that she had flushed it, the former politician again became abusive. Vickie testified that she grabbed a .22 rifle, fired a warning shot, reloaded, struggled with Daniel, but could not remember firing the fatal shot. In April 1981 Vickie Daniel was permitted to retain custody of her children. The October 1981 murder trial was a virtual rerun of the testimony from the child custody battle. Shortly before Haynes completed presenting the case, Vickie waived her right to a jury trial in favor of a judge's ruling. On October 30, 1981, State District Judge Leonard Giblin, Jr., deliberated 20 minutes before acquitting her of murder.

144. Salerno, Steve. *Deadly Blessings.* 1st ed. New York: Morrow, 1987. 320 pp.; 24 cm.

_____. [Same as 144.] St. Martin's Paperbacks ed. New York: St. Martin's Paperbacks, 1988. 320 pp.; 24 cm.; paperback.

Dann, Laurie Ann
(a.k.a. "Psycho Elevator Lady," "Laurie Wasserman," "Karen Glass," "Laurie [Lori] Porter," "Melissa")

Born October 18, 1957, in Chicago, Illinois. Died May 20, 1988. Babysitter. Winnetka, Illinois; 1 murder; .357 caliber Smith & Wesson Magnum, .32 caliber Smith & Wesson revolver, .22 caliber semiautomatic Beretta; May 20, 1988.

Television: "Murder of Innocence" (1993), a two-hour, made-for-television movie based on the book of the same title by Kaplan *et al.*, originally aired on CBS on November 30, 1993. Cast includes Valerie Bertinelli (Laurie Webber/ Laurie Dann.)

Video: Community in Crisis: The Laurie Dann Case (1989), a one-hour

video featuring a minute-by-minute account of the tragedy, was produced by Skokie, Illinois-based independent producer Gerald Rogers. The tape sells for $450 and rents for $100 with profits going to the Winnetka Police Department.

"I'm going to teach you about life."—Dann to a second grade class seconds before she opened fire on them

Mentally deranged babysitter in Winnetka, Illinois, who shot several children in an elementary school before committing suicide. At 10:45 a.m. on May 20, 1988, Laurie Dann, 30, armed with three pistols, walked into the Hubbard Woods Elementary School in Winnetka, Illinois. Hours before she had left packages of food and drink laced with arsenic at houses where she had babysat and at some Northwestern University fraternities and sororities. Acting in accordance with her own bizarre timetable, she set fire to the Ravinia Elementary School in Highland Park shortly before 9:00 a.m. Half an hour later Dann was stopped by a custodian at a Jewish day-care attempting to carry a can of gasoline into the building. At 10:15 a.m. she drove to the home of the Rushe family where she babysat as "Lori Porter." Mrs. Rushe and her children were in the basement when Dann set fire to the stairway. They escaped, unharmed, through a window. Dann next drove to the Hubbard Woods Elementary School to look for one of the Rushe children who attended there. Encountering a six-year-old boy in a lavatory, she shot him in the chest. He survived to tell a teacher that a "crazy woman" was in the school. Dann then entered a second grade classroom, forced the 22 children to one side of the room, and opened fire. Five children ranging in ages from seven to nine were wounded. Eight-year-old Nicholas Corwin was killed. Dann fled the scene, forced her way into a house not far from the school, and held five hostages at gunpoint. One man suffered a gunshot wound trying to disarm her, but he and the other hostages managed to escape. Dann held police at bay for several hours before ending her life with a self-inflicted gunshot wound to the head. Subsequent inquiries revealed Dann suffered from obsessive-compulsive disorder and bipolar disorder which were being treated with the drugs anafranil (clomipramine) and lithium carbonate. In addition to being suspected of the attempted ice-pick murder of her estranged husband in September 1986, Dann had a history of aberrant behavior which manifested itself in threatening phone calls and obscene letters to suspected enemies. In May 1991 the parents of victim Nicholas Corwin won an undisclosed financial settlement in a negligence suit against the Dann family. Authorities estimate that had Dann killed everyone she attempted to shoot, burn, or poison on May 20, 1988, the death toll would have reached 50.

145. Eggington, Joyce. *Day of Fury: The Story of the Tragic Shootings That Forever Changed the Village of Winnetka.* 1st ed. New York: Morrow, 1991. 318 pp., [8]pp. of plates: ill., ports.; 25 cm.

_____. [Same as 145, but paperback ed. retitled: *Too Beautiful a Day to Die.*] New York: Berkley Books, 1992. ix, 344 pp.: ill.; 18 cm.; paperback.

An account based on approximately 150 interviews which recounts the tragedy and examines its lasting effects on the economically upscale community of Winnetka, Illinois.

146. Kaplan, Joel; Papajohn, George; Zorn, Eric. *Murder of Innocence: The Tragic Life and Final Rampage of Laurie*

Dann. New York: Warner Books, 1990. xii, 335 pp., [8]pp. of plates: ill.; 24 cm.

_____. [Same as 146.] New York: Warner Books, 1991. xii, 335 pp., [8]pp. of plates: ill.; 17 cm.; paperback.

Chicago Tribune reporters Kaplan and Papajohn expand their June 5, 1988, *Chicago Tribune Magazine* article "The Many Faces of Laurie Dann." The authors enjoyed the full cooperation of Russell Dann, ex-husband of the murderess.

Davies, Michael John
(a.k.a. "Clapham Common Murderer")

Born circa 1933 in the United Kingdom. Laborer. London, England; 1 murder; knife; July 2, 1953.

"I'm not a reformed murderer. I was never a murderer in the first place."—Davies in a post-release interview with author Tony Parker

Member of a Teddy Boy gang who many believe was wrongly convicted and sentenced to death for killing a teenager in a gang fight. To the popular 1950s British mind, "The Clapham Common Murder" (like the Derek Bentley case) came to symbolize the violent breakdown of societal values among post-war youth. On the evening of July 2, 1953, Michael John Davies, 20, and members of his gang, The Plough Boys, were on Clapham Common when a fight broke out between them and four teenagers unknown in the area. The four youths fled, pursued by Davies and eight to ten of his cronies. John Ernest Beckley, 17, and another youth made it onto a bus, but were pulled off and further beaten. Beckley broke away, but was chased down by several youths. His body, riddled with nine knife wounds, was found 100 yards away. Davies was one of six youths charged with the murder, but four gang members were cleared in a preliminary hearing. The trial of Davies and a codefendant ended in a hung jury. All but Davies were allowed to plead guilty to common assault and to serve an average sentence of nine months. Davies was retried in the Old Bailey on October 19, 1953, and convicted *solely* on the strength of one bus passenger's uncorroborated identification. He was sentenced to death and spent 92 days in a condemned cell at Wandsworth Prison before the home secretary granted him a reprieve and commuted his sentence to life imprisonment. A *cause célèbre* in Britain, Davies was released in October 1960 after spending seven years in prison. He has unwaveringly maintained his innocence and has pressed for a Queen's pardon to clear his name.

147. Furneaux, Rupert. *Michael John Davies.* Crime Documentary no. 4. London: Stevens & Sons, 1962. 152 pp., [3]pp. of plates: ill.; 23 cm.
  Resumé of the trial in transcript form.

148. Parker, Tony. *The Plough Boy.* London: Hutchinson, 1965. 270 pp., [2]pp.; 22 cm.
  Sympathetic account of "The Clapham Common Murder" which acknowledges its debt to Furneaux's earlier, more legalistic study. Parker, who interviewed Davies and other members of The Plough Boys, is convinced of his subject's innocence and offers numerous instances of alleged judicial error to support his contention.

Davis, David Richard
(a.k.a. "Rip Bell," "David Myer Bell")

Born September 27, 1944, in Flint, Michigan. Farmer, high school chemistry teacher, auto worker, commercial airline pilot. Hillsdale County, Michigan; 1 murder; succinylcholine, bludgeon (rock); July 23, 1980.
  Television: A segment on Davis coproduced by the Michigan State Police aired on the NBC television program "Unsolved Mysteries" on November 29, 1987. A rebroadcast of the program on December 28, 1988, led to Davis' apprehension. "Victim of Love: The Shannon Mohr Story" (1993), a two-hour, made-for-television movie, originally aired on NBC on November 9, 1993. Cast includes Dwight Schultz (Dave Davis) and Sally Murphy (Shannon Mohr Davis).

  "Your Honor, I would say only very briefly that I have committed no crime."—Davis addressing the court at his sentencing hearing on January 16, 1990

  Wife murderer who remained at large for several years until a segment featuring him on a television program led to his arrest. On July 23, 1980, Davis, 36, and his wife of less than a year, Shannon Mohr, were horseback riding on their farm in Hillsdale County, Michigan, when she allegedly suffered a severe fall. She was pronounced dead on arrival at a nearby hospital from head and neck injuries. At the hospital, Davis' insistence that his wife's body be cremated was met with strong opposition from her parents. Mohr was buried three days later in Toledo, Ohio. Though Davis initially denied having life insurance on Mohr, he was blocked in the courts by her parents from collecting on a $220,000 policy. Due largely to their efforts, an autopsy was performed on Mohr's exhumed body which revealed the presence of succinylcholine, a muscle relaxant that could result in suffocation if injected. Another autopsy located injection sites and bruises on Mohr's right wrist and shoulder. Mohr's death was attributed to the drug. Davis was sailing on his boat near Haiti with a new girlfriend when he learned that he had been indicted for first degree murder on October 13, 1981. He disappeared and eluded a worldwide manhunt for nearly eight years before a segment on the television series "Unsolved Mysteries" noting his wide "hammerhead thumbs" led to his arrest by FBI agents in Pago Pago on January 5, 1989. The fugitive, under the name of "David Myer Bell," had remarried and was working as a commercial airline pilot. Davis was found guilty of first degree murder on December 6, 1989, and subsequently sentenced to life in prison without the possibility of parole. The court of appeals of Michigan affirmed his conviction on May 3, 1993.

149. Hemming, Robert. *With Murderous Intent.* New York: Onyx, 1991. 352 pp., [8]pp. of plates: ill., ports.; 18 cm.; paperback.

Straightforward paperback account of the case which changes the names of several of the principals (at their request). Shannon Mohr's parents and *Detroit Free Press* reporter Billy Bowles who kept the Davis case "alive" with his October 12, 1980, cover story "Shannon Davis: Accidental Death?" cooperated fully with Hemming.

"Death Mask Murder" see LeGeros, Bernard John

DeFeo, Ronald Joseph, Jr. (a.k.a. "Butch")

Born September 26, 1951, in Brooklyn, New York. Part-time worker in a car dealership. Amityville, Long Island (New York); 6 murders; .35 caliber Marlin rifle; November 13, 1974.

Films: The Amityville Horror (US, 1979), an American International Pictures production directed by Stuart Rosenberg, based on Jay Anson's book of the same title. Cast includes James Brolin (George Lutz), Margot Kidder (Kathleen Lutz), and Rod Steiger (Father Delaney). *Amityville II: The Possession* (US, 1982), a Dino De Laurentiis Corporation production directed by Damiano Damiani, based on Han Holzer's book *Murder in Amityville.* Cast includes James Olson (Father Adamsky), Burt Young (Anthony Montelli), and Jack Magner (Sonny Montelli). *Amityville 3-D* (US, 1983), a Dino De Laurentiis Corporation production directed by Richard Fleischer. Cast includes Tony Roberts (John Baxter), Tess Harper (Nancy Baxter), and Robert Joy (Elliot West).

Videos: The Amityville Curse (US, 1990), an Allegro Films production direct-to-video release directed by Tom Berry. Cast includes Kim Coates, Dawna Wightman, and David Stein. *Amityville 1992: It's About Time* (US, 1992), a Republic Pictures Home Video direct-to-video release directed by Tony Randel. Cast includes Stephen Macht (Jacob Sterling), Shawn Weatherly (Andrea), and Damon Martin (Rusty). *Amityville: A New Generation* (US, 1993), a Ninety-Three Productions direct-to-video release directed by John Murlowski. Cast includes Ross Partridge, Julia Nickson-Soul, and David Naughton.

"I couldn't care less what happens to me or the rest of my life."—DeFeo testifying in his own defense

Family mass murderer whose unsubstantiated claims of "demonic possession" have since served as the basis for a seemingly endless stream of films, books, and videos. Sometimes in the history of homicide, the *place* where a murder was committed becomes more notorious than the deed itself. Such a place is the three-story Dutch colonial house at 112 Ocean Avenue in Amityville, Long Island, where in the early morning hours of November 13, 1974, 23-year-old Ronald DeFeo murdered his entire six-member family as they slept. Alleged parapsychological disturbances and manifestations within the house have since served as the basis of Jay Anson's bestselling book *The Amityville Horror* (1977), which chronicles the experience of the George Lutz family and how they were driven out of the home by evil spirits after spending only 28 days there. Filmed in 1979, *The Amityville Horror* has since spawned a cottage industry of films and books which have had little or nothing to do with the DeFeo case. The supernatural elements exploited by the media, however, have since sparked debate over whether DeFeo himself was possessed by a malignant entity at the time of the killings, or, as the state of New York insists, merely an anti-social personality who carefully planned the murders in the hope of finding a cashbox filled with $200,000 hidden in his parents' bedroom.

Outwardly, the DeFeo family seemed happy living in the affluent community of Amityville. Ronald DeFeo, Sr., a 43-year-old service manager in a car dealership in Brooklyn, and his wife Louise, 42, were the proud parents of five children ranging in ages from 23 (Ronald, Jr.) to seven-year-old John Matthew. According to DeFeo, his father's psychological and physical abuse of the family turned the house into a "war zone." A poor student, DeFeo was thrown out of several schools for fighting and, following an attack on his grandfather and sister, the 13 year old was placed in counseling by his father. DeFeo quit school at 16 turning to alcohol and heroin to escape the tension at home. In 1973 the usually submissive DeFeo intervened in a fight between his parents. To protect his mother, the 22 year old put a loaded shotgun to his father's head and twice pulled the trigger. DeFeo, Sr., believing that the gun's malfunctioning constituted a miracle, turned to religion. His placement of religious statues in the yard and insistence on Sunday home prayer meetings, however, did not prevent him from continuing to beat his family, according to his son.

At around 6:40 p.m. on November 13, 1974, police responded to a call placed by Ronald DeFeo, Jr., who reported that he had returned home from work to find his entire family shot to death in their beds. A pathologist used the term "bizarre" to describe how each victim lay in the exact same face-down position in bed. In all, eight shots from a .35 caliber Marlin rifle had been fired at close range into the heads or backs of the sleeping victims. Inexplicably, neighbors did not hear the gunshots even though their windows were open. The next day, DeFeo confessed to shooting his family as they slept, placing the gun and spent cartridges into a pillow case, and throwing the items into a canal near his home where they were recovered by police. During pre-trial hearings in September 1975, DeFeo recanted his confession claiming that police had beaten it out of him. In the same confession, DeFeo claimed to have been in the house watching television while the rest of the house slept. He was awakened around 3:15 a.m. by a "female" resembling his sister Dawn who entered the room carrying the gun in "black hands." He took the rifle, shot his parents to death, placed the gun on the floor of their room, then returned to the television room. Moments later he heard other shots and, realizing that Dawn had killed the children, shot her to death in a scuffle over the gun. DeFeo would continue to alter his story of the crime as he allegedly "remembered" more details of it. In its final version, he only killed sister Dawn after discovering that she had killed the family.

Opening arguments in *The People v. Ronald DeFeo, Jr.*, began in Riverhead, Long Island, on October 14, 1975. Charged with six counts of second-degree murder, DeFeo mounted an insanity defense after unsuccessfully petitioning the court to suppress his confession. A jury composed equally of men and women discounted psychiatric testimony labelling DeFeo a "paranoid psychotic" who acted under a delusion at the time of the killings and following nearly two days of deliberation found him guilty on all six counts on November 21, 1975. On December 4, 1975, DeFeo was sentenced to six concurrent 25 year to life sentences. A loss of a 1978 appeal did not stop the convicted mass murderer's attempt to get a new trial or his insistence that his rights as a prisoner be observed by the New York State Department of Corrections. On October 2, 1984, a judge awarded DeFeo $300 in compensatory damages for the "mental anguish" he suffered over being improperly "keeplocked" (locked in a cell and denied privileges) for five days at the Auburn Correctional Facility after guards in another facility found heroin taped under his bed in June 1982. DeFeo had already served nine months in his cell for the offence when an administrative error tacked five

more days onto the sentence. On November 31, 1990, DeFeo was granted a hearing on a new trial based upon his contention that he had an alibi witness who could confirm his innocence. DeFeo's inability to produce the witness, despite an intensive nationwide search through driving and credit records, prompted a judge on January 11, 1993, to deny his bid for a new trial based upon his finding that the defendant's overall testimony was "false and fabricated." DeFeo is eligible for parole in 1999 when he will be 48 years old.

150. Anson, Jay. *The Amityville Horror.* Englewood Cliffs, N.J.: Prentice-Hall, 1977. xi, 201 pp.: ill.; 24 cm. (Various eds.)

151. Holzer, Hans. *Murder in Amityville.* New York: Belmont Tower Books, 1979. 288 pp.: ill.; 18 cm.; paperback.

_____. [Same as 151.] New York: Pinnacle Books, 1982. 288 pp.: ill.; 18 cm.; paperback.

"The true story behind the sensational and horrifying new motion picture, *Amityville II: The Possession.*"—Cover.

152. Sullivan, Gerard, and Aronson, Harvey. *High Hopes: The Amityville Murders.* New York: Coward, McCann & Geoghegan, 1981. 349 pp., [8] leaves of plates: ill.; 24 cm.

_____. [Same as 152.] New York: Dell, 1982. 413 pp.; 18 cm.; paperback.

De Kaplany, Geza
(a.k.a. "The Acid Doctor," "Pierre La Roche")

Born June 27, 1926, in Mako, Hungary. Anesthesiologist. San Jose, California; 1 murder; acid; August 28, 1962.

"I realize the awful weight of that tragedy, but I do not feel any responsibility. I was crushed by forces over which I had no control." —De Kaplany at a press conference held minutes after he was sentenced to life imprisonment

Hungarian doctor convicted of the torture-murder of his wife with acid. Dr. Geza De Kaplany, born into a noted Hungarian family, graduated with honors from the University of Szeged in 1951. In his book *Doctor in Revolt*, he wrote of his daring 1956 flight from Communist Hungary. While employed as an anesthesiologist at a San Jose, California, hospital, the doctor met the strikingly beautiful Hajna (pronounced "Hoy-na") Piller, a fashion model and showgirl. Soon afterwards, they married on July 21, 1962. Five weeks later on the night of August 28, 1962, police responded to a noise complaint from neighbors tired of hearing stereo music blaring from the De Kaplany's trendy San Jose apartment at 1125 Ranchero Way. Police entered No. 30 to find the doctor clad only in a pair of shorts while his wife, naked and bound with tape and electrical cord, writhed in screaming agony on the bedroom floor. De Kaplany had slashed her left breast with a butcher's knife and then methodically applied gauze soaked in nitric acid to the wound as well as to her face, genitals, and eyes. At the scene, police retrieved a torture kit containing two knives, rubber gloves, and three types of acid. In a note written in Hungarian on a prescription pad De Kaplany warned Hajna: "If you want to live (1) Do not shout (2) Do what I tell you (3) Or else you will die."

At San Francisco's St. Francis Hospital doctors tried to neutralize the acid covering 60 percent of her body. Should she be lucky enough to live, years of plastic surgery lay ahead. In any event, her beauty was irretrievably

lost. Charged initially with attempted murder, an indifferent De Kaplany confessed to jealously attacking his wife after a meddling old neighbor woman claimed that Hajna had been unfaithful to him. De Kaplany explained, "I wanted to take her beauty away. I wanted to put fear into her against being an adulteress." Hajna protested her innocence for the remaining 795 pain-filled hours of her life. She died 33 days later on September 30, 1962. Charged with "murder by torture" at his trial in San Jose in January 1963, De Kaplany initially pleaded not guilty, but changed his plea to not guilty by reason of insanity after the court was allowed to view a morgue photo of his wife's acid scarred corpse. A defense psychiatrist posited the existence of a malevolent alter-ego named "Pierre La Roche" who periodically possessed De Kaplany at moments of extreme stress. Hajna's alleged sexual rejection of him throughout their marriage combined with his impotence on the night of the attack prompted the emergence of the demoniac personality who poured acid on the woman as punishment for her "adultery." The prosecution countered by denying that far from being a delusive paranoiac close to overt homosexuality, De Kaplany was merely a jealous husband. De Kaplany was found to be sane, convicted of murder, and sentenced to life imprisonment on March 31, 1963. In a highly controversial and inexplicable ruling the doctor was paroled in 1976, a full six months before he would have been eligible for his first hearing. Afterwards, he was thought to be practicing medicine in Taiwan.

153. Anspacher, Carolyn. *The Trial of Dr. De Kaplany*. New York: F. Fell, 1965. 296 pp.: ports.; 22 cm.

_____. [Same as 153, but U.K. ed. retitled: *The Acid Test, or, The Trial of Dr. De Kaplany*. London: Dawnay, 1966. 255 pp.: ill., ports.; 21 cm.

_____. [Same as 153.] New York: New American Library, 1967. 176 pp.; 18 cm. ("A Signet book"); paperback.

Demeter, Peter
(a.k.a. "Papitschek")

Born April 19, 1933, in Hungary. Real estate developer and contractor. Mississauga, Ontario, Canada; 1 murder; blunt object bludgeoning (murder-for-hire); July 18, 1973.

"I never realized until then that Christine had so much brains."— Demeter joking to friends about finding his wife's battered body in the garage of their home

Sensational murder-for-hire case noted at the time for being the longest criminal trial in Canadian history. Wealthy 40-year-old Hungarian-born real estate developer Peter Demeter "had it all": an expensive home in the stylish bedroom community of Mississauga on the outskirts of Toronto, a successful business, a three-year-old daughter, and a beautiful Austrian-born wife named Christine who enjoyed some success as a model. They had been married almost six years when on the night of July 18, 1973, an incident occurred which claimed the life of 33-year-old Christine Demeter and enmeshed her husband in one of the most sensational murder-conspiracy cases in Canadian history. Demeter, returning to their $100,000 home on 1437 Dundas Crescent from a shopping trip with some visiting house guests, announced the time as "exactly" 9:45 p.m. as he tripped the automatic garage door. It opened to reveal Christine splayed face

down on the floor in a pool of blood near her parked Cadillac. The upward flow of blood splattered on the car's door suggested the woman had been bludgeoned even though Demeter calmly demonstrated to police at the scene how Christine must have accidentally fallen while reaching for something in the garage. An autopsy later confirmed that the woman had died from at least seven separate blows to the head administered by a blunt object. There was no sign of forced entry, Christine had not been raped, and the killer had left unharmed the Demeter's young daughter who was watching television in the house as her mother was being beaten to death. Twenty-two miles away and in the company of friends at the time police estimated the murder occurred, Peter Demeter seemingly had an airtight alibi.

Born in Hungary in 1933, Demeter was 12 years old when Russian forces liberated Budapest. Facing two years of compulsive military service in the Russian army, the 21 year old made good on his third escape attempt in 1954 and applied for political asylum in Vienna where he became a reporter for Radio Free Europe. Demeter emigrated to Canada two years later arriving in Toronto with only $8 in his pocket. Initially supporting himself through menial jobs, the hardworking and ambitious Demeter earned a real estate license and began selling houses to fellow Hungarians. In 1962, after almost seven years of non-stop work, Demeter registered a company (Eden Gardens Limited) and began his career as a real estate developer. While visiting Vienna in 1965, Demeter became infatuated with 20-year-old model Marina Hundt and proposed marriage to her after only their second meeting. His jealousy, however, punctuated by slaps and gun threats, drove the younger woman away. In February 1967, Demeter was on the rebound from Hundt when he asked a friend for an introduction to Christine Ferrari, a statuesque "want-to-be" model who supported herself by waitressing and being the companion of successful men like film producer Franz Antel. Like Hundt, Christine suffered from Demeter's jealous rages, but married him in Toronto on November 14, 1967, nine days after her 27th birthday.

In February 1969 a key player in the Demeter affair, 29-year-old Hungarian-born Csaba Szilagyi, moved into the couple's Toronto home to work for them. The relationship between the two men slowly soured due to Demeter's nagging suspicion that Szilagyi was in reality the father of Christine's daughter born in 1970. Szilagyi moved out in the fall of 1970 and only occasionally saw his former employer. During the same time, chinks in the Demeter's "perfect marriage" began to show. Bored with Christine and frustrated with her spending, Demeter recontacted Marina Hundt in Vienna and showered her with presents. By mid–1973 the Demeters' marriage was in deep trouble and they were openly arguing in public. Prophetically, Christine wrote her parents on May 1, 1973, that "Sometimes I get this terrible *anxiety* that I'm not going to live for long." In the summer of 1983 Christine discovered that Demeter was planning a tryst with Hundt in Montreal and angrily confronted him. Demeter left anyway. Christine discussed her options with a divorce attorney and confided to a friend that she knew enough about Demeter's business dealings to put him away for 15 years. After spending a week traveling throughout Canada with Demeter, Hundt flew back to Vienna with plans to return on July 26, 1973—eight days after her "rival" would be found bludgeoned to death.

Suspicion fell on Demeter when police learned of his affair and the $1 million life insurance policy he held on Christine. The major break in the case, however, occurred when Csaba Szilagyi stepped forward with an astounding revelation. According to Szilagyi, Demeter had discussed with him as early as 1968 his desire to have him kill Christine. Over the next five-and-a-half years her death became a recurring topic of conversation between the two men and various scenarios were suggested, then rejected. These included pushing Christine off a top landing of one of Demeter's unfinished houses, electrocution, making her the victim of a false break-in, and immolating her in the garage of their home with spilled gasoline. Police tapped Demeter's phone and the wire Szilagyi wore in his meetings with the developer yielded incriminating evidence against him. At one point, Demeter cautioned Szilagyi not to take a lie detector test as he was "the only one who knows." Demeter was arrested at his home on August 17, 1973, and charged with non-capital murder.

What became the longest trial in Canadian history began with jury selection in London, Ontario, on September 23, 1974. For 51 days spread over ten weeks, revelation followed convoluted revelation as a variety of Hungarian underworld types gave conflicting testimony. A convicted arsonist/hit man testified that he refused Christine's offer of $10,000 to kill Demeter. The go-between on the deal, a petty Hungarian criminal named Laszlo Eper, allegedly argued with Christine over the money and beat her to death in the garage. As Eper was killed in a shoot-out with Toronto police on August 29, 1973, the arsonist's unsupported testimony was not as compelling as Szilagyi's story combined with Demeter's incriminating comments captured on tape. After only three hours of deliberation, a jury found Demeter guilty on December 4, 1973, and he received a mandatory sentence of life imprisonment for non-capital murder with parole eligibility after ten years served. In subsequent appeals in December 1975 and a final appeal to the Supreme Court of Canada in February 1977 the conviction was upheld.

Remarkably, the strange saga of Peter Demeter did not end with his parole from the Warkworth Institution in Campbellford, Ontario, in 1982. As a day parolee living in a halfway house in Peterborough, Ontario, the 50-year-old Demeter was arrested on October 20, 1983, and charged with three counts of arson and one of conspiracy to commit arson in relation to three fires set during the summer at the Missuaga home where Christine was murdered. Damage to the $132,000 home set up for sale to help pay Demeter's legal fees was estimated at $100,000. While in custody on the arson charges, Demeter was also charged with two counts of counselling two men to commit the murder of his 19-year-old fourth cousin, Stuart Demeter, whose father was made the legal guardian of Demeter's 13-year-old daughter. While awaiting trial, Demeter unsuccessfully attempted suicide by swallowing barbiturates and washing them down with shampoo at the Metro West Detention Centre near Toronto in March 1985. On April 15, 1985, Demeter represented himself in a Peterborough courtroom against charges of counselling two men to kidnap and murder his cousin out of hatred and revenge against members of his own family. Convicted on both counts on July 2, 1985, Demeter received two additional life sentences to run concurrently. In August 1988, the man known as one of Canada's most notorious criminals, was sentenced to yet another two additional terms of life imprisonment for conspiring to kidnap and murder the daughter of a Toronto lawyer in 1985. Though theoretically eligible for day parole on August 16, 1990, the judge recommended that Demeter never be released and told the man sentenced to five life terms, "Whether or not you are inherently evil, I do not know, but you ooze evil out of every pore and contaminate everyone around you."

154. Jonas, George, and Amiel, Barbara. *By Persons Unknown: The Strange Death of Christine Demeter.* 1st ed. New York: Grove Press, 1977. x, 349 pp., [12] leaves of plates: ill.; 25 cm.

_____. [Same as 154.] 1st paperback ed. New York: Grove Press : Distributed by Dell, 1977. 368 pp.: ill.; 18 cm.; paperback.

_____. [Same as 154.] Toronto: Macmillan of Canada, 1977. x, 349 pp., [12] leaves of plates: ill.; 24 cm.

_____. [Same as 154.] Scarborough, Ont.: Macmillan-NAL, 1978. 368 pp., [4] leaves of plates: ill., ports.; 18 cm. ("A Signet book"); paperback.

DeSalvo, Albert Henry
(a.k.a "The Boston Strangler," "Green Man," "Measuring Man")

Born circa 1931 in Chelsea, Massachusetts. Died November 26, 1973. Maintenance worker. Eastern Massachusetts; 13 murders; ligature strangulation, knife; June 1962–January 1964.

Film: The Boston Strangler (U.S., 1968), a 20th Century–Fox production based on Gerold Frank's book. Directed by Richard Fleischer. Cast includes Tony Curtis (Albert DeSalvo), Henry Fonda (John S. Bottomly), and George Kennedy (Phil DiNatale).

"See, when this certain time comes upon me, it's [a] very immediate thing. When I get up in the morning and I get this feeling and ... instead of going to work, I might make an excuse to my boss and I'd start driving and I'd start, in my mind, building this image up, and that's why I found myself not knowing where I was going."

Serial rapist and killer known as the "Boston Strangler" who was responsible for the slayings of 13 women in eastern Massachusetts in the early 1960s. The son of a violent alcoholic who once sold him and his two sisters to a farmer in Maine for $9, Albert DeSalvo's childhood was filled with violence. Among the child's earliest memories were of his father bringing prostitutes to their home, having sex with them in front of his mother, and if she complained he knocked his wife's teeth out and broke her fingers. The father abandoned the family when DeSalvo was eight, but not before teaching his son how to shoplift. As a teenager, DeSalvo amassed a hefty police record for breaking and entering. Joining the army at 17, he served in occupied Germany where he met and married a Frankfurt native. DeSalvo was transferred back to the States and was stationed at Fort Dix when he committed his first known sex offense, the molestation of a nine-year-old girl, in January 1955. The case was

not pursued and DeSalvo was honorably discharged in 1956. Hypersexual, DeSalvo pestered his wife for sex six times a day and when she ultimately refused his excessive demands, he turned to a scam which would lead him to be called the "Measuring Man." Posing as a talent scout for a modeling agency, DeSalvo went door-to-door fast-talking women anxious for a modeling career into letting him take their vital statistics as he fondled them during the process. On March 17, 1960, DeSalvo was arrested in Cambridge, Massachusetts, on suspicion of burglary and confessed to being the "Measuring Man." Sentenced to two years for attempted breaking and entering, DeSalvo was paroled for good behavior after serving only 11 months. Cut off from sex by his wife, DeSalvo launched a one man wave of sexual terror that lasted two years and claimed an estimated 300 rape victims in Massachusetts, Connecticut, Rhode Island, and New Hampshire. Known to authorities as the "Green Man" because the rapist always wore green work clothes, DeSalvo would later claim that he had raped at least 2,000 women.

With the taking of his first victim on June 14, 1962, a brutal murder which began a 19-month reign of terror that nearly paralyzed social life in eastern Massachusetts, DeSalvo laid claim to yet another nickname, the "Boston Strangler." On that date, Anna Slesers, a 55-year-old Latvian immigrant, was found strangled in her apartment, the cord from her bathrobe tied in a looping bow around her neck. Like the "Strangler's" subsequent victims, Sleser had been raped and her body spread-eagled in a pornographic pose. Two weeks later, 85-year-old Mary Mullen suffered a fatal heart attack when DeSalvo invaded her apartment.

Originally thought to be a natural death, DeSalvo later confessed that he did not rape the old lady because she reminded him of his grandmother. On June 30, 1962, the sexually insatiable DeSalvo took two lives. The nude body of 65-year-old Helen Blake was found spreadeagled facedown on the bed in her Lynn, Massachusetts, apartment. Blake had been sexually assaulted, bitten in the buttocks, and left with her nylon stockings and bra wound tightly around her neck in a bow. Later that day in Boston, 68-year-old Nina Nichols was discovered strangled in her Commonwealth Avenue apartment. DeSalvo had gained entry by posing as a maintenance worker and, after raping the elderly woman, strangled her with nylon stockings which he left around her neck. Evidence collected at the scene suggested that Nichols had also been penetrated with a wine bottle after death. For sheer grisly horror, DeSalvo's fifth murder spectacularly eclipsed the previous four. On August 19, 1962, police entering the apartment of 75-year-old Ida Irga were instantly confronted with the grotesque tableau of the elderly woman's body positioned on its back on the living room floor. Irga's nightdress had been torn up the front to expose her body and a white pillow case knotted around her neck (although she had been manually strangled). A pillow had been placed under the woman's buttocks and her legs spread and locked through the rungs of two chairs in what one reporter later described as "a parody of an obstetrical examination." Like many of the other victims, Irga had been raped and bitten. The next day DeSalvo posed as a workman and entered the Dorchester apartment of 67-year-old Jane Sullivan. Ten days later Sullivan's body was found kneel-

ing beside the bathtub, her head lolling in a few inches of water. Raped and then strangled with nylon stockings, Sullivan had also been savagely penetrated with a broom handle.

Inexplicably, the "Strangler" shifted from old to young victims for five of his final seven murders. On December 5, 1962, he raped and strangled a 25-year-old black woman named Sophie Clark. Patricia Bissette, 23, met a similar fate on December 30, 1962, a ligature formed by her blouse and stockings twisted tightly around her neck. In 1963, DeSalvo claimed an additional four victims including one in which he broke from his signature method of strangulation by using a knife. On January 4, 1964, the "Strangler" gave the terrified residents of Boston a macabre New Year's greeting. After tying up, raping, then strangling 19-year-old Mary Sullivan with her stockings, DeSalvo spreadeagled her legs and arranged the stockings in a garish bow around her neck. When police found Sullivan's body, a broom handle had been shoved up her vagina and a greeting card with the salutation "Happy New Year" had been placed against her right foot. Eleven months after the strangling, DeSalvo was picked up in November 1964 by Cambridge police after his photo was identified by a "Green Man" rape victim. While under psychiatric evaluation in the Center for the Treatment of Sexually Dangerous Persons at Bridgewater, DeSalvo was housed with George Nassar, a brutal killer with an IQ above 150, who authorities thought might also be the "Strangler." DeSalvo poured out the details of the murders to Nassar who in turn told his lawyer, F. Lee Bailey. In the monumental legal haggling that ensued, Bailey negotiated a deal in 1967 that left DeSalvo uncharged in the "Boston Strangler" slayings, but sentenced to life for rapes committed as the "Green Man." On November 26, 1973, DeSalvo was stabbed to death in his sleep by fellow inmates in his cell within the infirmary of the Massachusetts state prison at Walpole. It should be noted that many students of the case still believe that Nassar was responsible for the "Strangler" killings.

155. Banks, Harold K. *The Strangler! The Story of Terror in Boston.* New York: Avon, 1967. 238 pp.; 18 cm.; paperback.
Paperback account by a reporter for the *Boston Record American-Sunday Advertiser.* Includes transcripts of confessions DeSalvo made at Bridgewater.

156. Frank, Gerold. *The Boston Strangler.* New York: New American Library, 1966. x, 364 pp.: map (on lining papers); 24 cm.

_____. [Same as 156.] London: Jonathan Cape, 1967. 351 pp.; 22 cm.

_____. [Same as 156.] New York: New American Library, 1967. xi, 408 pp.: map; 18 cm. ("A Signet book"); paperback.

_____. [Same as 156.] London: Pan Books, 1968. 414 pp.; 18 cm.; paperback.
Definitive account of the crimes and how they affected Boston. Highly recommended.

157. Rae, George William. *Confessions of the Boston Strangler.* New York: Pyramid Books, 1967. 176 pp.: ill.; 18 cm.; paperback.

Dickman, John Alexander
(a.k.a. "John Wilkinson," "F. Black")

Born circa 1865 in England. Executed August 10, 1910. Bookmaker. Morpeth, England; 1 murder; gun; March 18, 1910.

"I declare to all men that I am innocent."—Dickman after having the death sentence passed on him

English railway killer whose execution for the murder of a bookkeeper caused a flurry of angry protest. On March 18, 1910, 44-year-old John Innes Nisbet, a bookkeeper for the Stobswood Colliery Company, left Newcastle by train in possession of a small leather bag containing £370 with which to pay wages at a colliery near Widdrington Station. At Alnmouth, the last stop on the route, Nisbet's body was found jammed face down under the seat of his compartment. He had been shot five times in the head with what police wrongly determined at the time to have been two guns instead of one. The bag containing the colliers' wages was missing. A witness' response to a reward offer of £100 posted by Nisbet's company led police to interview John Alexander Dickman, a 43-year-old bookmaker who was seen boarding the train at Newcastle with Nisbet. Dickman told authorities that he saw Nisbet at the station, but had not ridden in the same compartment with him. He had left the train at Morpeth, one stop too late, to see someone at Dovecot Colliery in Stannington. Dickman was arrested on March 21, 1910, after his statement contradicted evidence already in possession of the police. A search of Dickman's home uncovered bloodstained trousers and gloves which he explained were from a recent nosebleed. Though the stains could not be identified as either human or animal they were less than two weeks old. Nisbet, using the pseudonym "F. Black," had ordered a gun months before but denied ever having picked it up. This gun and the murder weapon were never recovered. On June 9, 1910, one month before Dickman's trial, Nisbet's bag was found at the bottom of a seldom used mine near Morpeth. It was empty save for a few coppers.

When Dickman was tried at the Newcastle Summer Assizes on July 4, 1910, thousands of booing spectators lined the road from the jail to the courthouse. Formerly the secretary for a colliery syndicate, Dickman had tried unsuccessfully for the past two years to support his wife and young daughter by gambling on horses. At the time of the murder Dickman faced massive debts and was borrowing money from lenders at 60 percent interest. Yet on the day of his arrest he inexplicably had £17 in his possession. On July 6, 1910, Dickman was found guilty on largely circumstantial evidence and sentenced to death. Many signed a petition asking for the condemned killer's reprieve and the day before his execution handbills were distributed throughout London which read, "Must Dickman be hanged tomorrow? No! No! No! Wire home secretary at once and wash your hands of complicity in the legal crime." Dickman was hanged on schedule at Newcastle Prison on August 10, 1910.

158. Rowan-Hamilton, S.O., ed. *Trial of John Alexander Dickman*. Notable British Trials. Edinburgh; London: William Hodge, 1914. viii, 208 pp.: ill., ports., map; 23 cm.

_____. [Same as 158.] Notable British Trials. Philadelphia: Cromarty Law Book, 1914. viii, 208 pp.: ill., ports., map; 23 cm.

_____. [Same as 158.] 2nd ed., rev. Notable British Trials. Introduction to edition by W. Teignmouth Shore. Edinburgh; London: William Hodge, 1926. viii, 210 pp.: ill., ports., map; 22 cm.

Notable British Trials Series entry edited by Rowan-Hamilton, barrister-at-law of Lincoln's Inn who likens Dickman to Crippen in that both controversial killers were "convicted before they were placed in the dock." In a prefatory note to the second edition, W. Teignmouth Shore notes that "no more than ... a short additional bit of introductory matter has been written in by me and a few changes of slight importance made here and there in the original text."

Dobkin, Harry

Born circa 1891 in Russia. Executed January 27, 1943. Fire-watcher, tailor. London, England; 1 murder; manual strangulation; April 11, 1941.

Russian born Jew convicted of wife-murder by the use of forensic methods first utilized in the Dr. Buck Ruxton case. On July 17, 1942, workman cleaning up the bomb-blasted Vauxhall Baptist Church in the Kennington district of East London unearthed a partially mummified skeleton of a woman buried in the cellar beneath a large paving stone. Packed in lime, the body's head and arms had been severed, its lower jaw removed, and the flesh stripped from the head to prevent identification before the corpse had been set afire. Medical investigators, sifting through four tons of earth for bone fragments, determined death as due to manual strangulation which had occurred sometime between January and July 1941. A search through missing persons reports filed during that time revealed that 49-year-old Rachel Dobkin had been reported missing by her husband Harry Dobkin on April 12, 1941. Employing methods pioneered in the Ruxton case, forensic scientists superimposed an enlarged photograph of Rachel Dobkin's face over the charred skull. The match was exact. Dental records positively identified the remains as belonging to Mrs. Dobkin.

Forty-nine-year-old Harry Dobkin, employed at the time of his wife's disappearance as an air raid fire-watcher at a paper warehouse located behind the church, had reported a fire in the cellar beneath the chapel on April 14, 1941, Easter Monday. Partly burned heaps of straw found at the scene suggested arson which Dobkin quickly denied having committed even though authorities never put the question to him. Reinterviewed on August 26, 1942, Dobkin admitted to police that his relationship with his wife had been a stormy one punctuated by his numerous physical assaults on her. She had sent him to jail on three occasions for not paying support and the pair were not living together at the time of her disappearance. Dobkin was arrested as a result of this interview and charged with his wife's murder. Steadfastly maintaining his innocence during his five-day trial at London's Old Bailey in November 1942, Dobkin's contention that he did not even know the church had a cellar was refuted by several witnesses who testified that they had seen him entering it as late as three months before the trial. Based largely on the overwhelming forensic evidence against him, a jury deliberated only 20 minutes before finding Dobkin guilty on November 23, 1942. Dobkin's appeal failed and he was hanged at Wandsworth Prison on January 27, 1943.

159. Roberts, C.E. Bechhofer, ed. *The Trial of Harry Dobkin*. Old Bailey Trial Series. London: Jarrolds, 1944. 176 pp.: ill.; 22 cm.
Installment in the Old Bailey Trial Series which summarizes the case and presents detailed transcripts from the trial. Concludes with barrister Roberts' "A Note on Capital Punishment."

Donald, Jeannie
(a.k.a. "Jeannie Ewen" [maiden name], "Cocoanut")

Born circa 1896. Housewife. Aberdeen, Scotland; 1 murder; manual strangulation (suspected); April 20, 1934.

The disappearance of eight-year-old Helen Wilson Robertson Priestly from a working class neighborhood in Aberdeen, Scotland, on April 20, 1934, launched a massive citywide search. Insane asylums were checked for missing inmates and descriptions of the missing girl were flashed on cinema screens throughout the city and outlying districts. Police lost valuable time following up a young boy's claim to have seen Priestly in the company of a middle-aged man who forced her onto a tramcar. By the time the boy confessed to making up the story, Priestly's body had been found around 5:00 a.m. the next day stuffed in a jute bag under the stairs of No. 61 Urquhart Road, a multi-family tenement near the dead girl's home. The young girl had apparently been strangled and her mutilated genitals suggested rape. Priestly had last been seen around 1:30 p.m. when her mother sent her to buy a loaf of bread from a neighborhood bakery. Two days after the discovery of the girl's body, a workman near No. 61 reported to police that he had heard a child's scream around 2:00 p.m. on the day of Priestly's disappearance.

The discovery of Priestly's body in a building next to her own home suggested the possibility that she knew her killer. Police learned in the course of their inquiries that ill will existed between the Priestly family and Jeannie Donald, 38, who with her husband and eight-year-old daughter occupied a first floor flat in No. 61. Priestly's body had been found almost literally on their doorstep. Although Mrs. Priestly and Donald had not spoken for four years their daughters occasionally played together. At the center of the controversy lay Helen Priestly. Sensing that Donald disliked her, Helen derisively referred to the woman as "Cocoanut" and routinely knocked on her door or rang the bell as she passed by No. 61. On April 25, 1934, detectives visited the Donalds and questioned them for over 13 hours as a vengeful crowd formed outside on Urquhart Road. Donald explained the source of her coolness toward the Priestlys and recounted her movements on the day of Helen's disappearance. Permission was given to search the house and a stain determined by a microscopic examination conducted at the scene to be blood was found under a split piece of linoleum in the bottom of a cupboard. Protesting their innocence, Jeannie Donald and her husband Alexander were arrested at 12:15 a.m. on April 26, 1934. A later examination of the stain found under the cupboard conclusively proved it was *not* blood.

An autopsy conducted on Priestly's body the day it was discovered fixed the time of death at just before 2:00 p.m. on the day she disappeared. As a result, Alexander Donald (who was at work during this period) was subsequently freed on June 11, 1934. The postmortem also raised other interesting observations that led to conflicting theories as to the cause of her death. It was found that Priestly had a pre-existing hereditary condition, an enlarged thymus gland, which made her more susceptible to shock than the average person. Any sudden shock could cause unconsciousness, coma, or death. The official cause of Priestly's death, however, was "asphyxiation, apparently caused by compression of the neck." Light pressure on the child's neck combined with her thymus condition could have produced unconsciousness. Priestly vomited before death, possibly as a result of the attack or in reaction to the subsequent genital mutilation, and it was conjectured that she could have choked to death. The forensic people were unanimous that rape had not occurred. The damage inflicted on the girl's private parts was done pre-mortem in an attempt to mislead the police into thinking the murder had a sexual basis.

In the absence of any witness, police realized that their sole chance of conviction lay in forging a chain of physical evidence linking Donald to the murder. They descended on No. 61 and in the course of several searches removed nearly 253 items from her home. In jail awaiting trial, police furnished Donald with a new comb and hairbrush under false pretenses. Immediately after she used them, the items were confiscated and hair strands taken from them compared with similar samples obtained from Helen Priestly's exhumed body. Local prejudice ran so high against Donald that the trial was moved to Edinburgh where it began on July 16, 1934. For six days a jury of ten men and five women listened to complex scientific evidence that even the defense noted was "unparalleled in the history of this old Court." Donald sat silently and without emotion as the prosecution introduced layer upon layer of scientific evidence against her. Although inconclusive, hairs found in a bucket under Donald's sink were "similar in all respects" to Priestly's. Fibers taken from the sack containing Priestly's body were identical in color and formation to those of a carpet in

Donald's flat. The presence of a unique type of intestinal bacilli found in the vomit on Priestly's clothes was also found on two wash cloths in Donald's home. Its occurrence in both places would be exceedingly rare. One-hundred-and-sixty-four witnesses were called including Donald's daughter who testified that a wooden box containing ashes and cinders from the fire usually kept under the sink was missing. Cinders were found lodged in the dead girl's teeth.

Unable to refute the prosecution's expert forensic evidence and hampered by Donald's lack of cooperation, the defense argued that the prosecution's case amounted to pure speculation. No point of contact between Donald and Priestly could be proven. On July 23, 1934, the jury retired at 6:01 p.m. and returned 17 minutes later with a guilty verdict (13 for guilty and 2 for not proven). Donald moaned, then swooned in the dock before temporarily regaining enough composure to hear the judge pronounce the sentence of death on her. She was carried, still moaning, from the dock. A subsequent theory advanced to explain the murder conjectured that Donald had laid in wait behind the door of No. 61 waiting for Priestly to ring the doorbell as she passed. When she did, Donald jumped from behind the door and either shook the child by the shoulders or neck to frighten her. The fright aggravated Priestly's thymus condition causing her to faint. Thinking she had killed the child, Donald panicked and inflicted genital wounds on the body to simulate rape. The pain caused Priestly to vomit leading to her asphyxiation. Donald concealed the body in a box of ashes under the sink and unable to dispose of it properly placed it under the stairs before the flat could be searched the next morning.

Donald's execution was set to occur in Aberdeen on August 13, 1934, but upon recommendation from the Scottish Office in London via the Lord Provost of Aberdeen His Majesty was asked to commute the death sentence to "penal servitude for life." On August 9, 1934, a Royal Warrant commuting the sentence to life imprisonment was promulgated and Donald was moved from Aberdeen to begin serving her sentence in Glasgow's Duke Street Prison. A persistent rumor circulated that the reprieve followed Donald's confession of the murder. A model prisoner who refused to accept visitors during her ten years of incarceration, Donald was released on special license on June 26, 1944, to be with her dying husband.

160. Wilson, John G., ed. *The Trial of Jeannie Donald.* Notable British Trials. London: W. Hodge, 1953. 305 pp.: ill.; 22 cm.

Douglas, William Henry James, Jr.
(a.k.a. "The Man," "W.H.J.D.")

Born circa 1942 in Lake Placid, New York. University professor and research biologist. Sharon, Massachusetts; 1 murder; sledgehammer; March 5, 1983.

Television: "The High Price of Passion" (1986), a two-hour, made-for-television movie based on Russell M. Glitman's book *The Ruling Passion,* aired on NBC on November 30, 1986. Cast includes Richard Crenna (William Douglas) and Karen Young (Robin Benedict).

"Children are our most important resource for the future."—Douglas speaking of his efforts on behalf of

"Smile for a Child," a prison-based program which raises funds for critically ill children

In a case likened to a modern-day American version of *The Blue Angel*, a respected professor's obsession with a $100-an-hour call girl led him to professional disgrace and murder. Prior to meeting Robin Nadine Benedict, 42-year-old Dr. William Douglas was a 16 hour-a-day workaholic whose pioneering studies in cell culture were funded by several large private and federal grants. In addition to being an associate professor of anatomy in the medical school at Tufts University, Douglas also headed his own research lab located near downtown Boston's infamous porno district, the "Combat Zone." By April 1982 Douglas was cruising the area allegedly seeking release from crushing professional responsibilities and a sexless marriage. In a hooker hangout bar called Good Time Charlie's, Douglas met Robin Benedict, a lovely 21 year old whose upper middle class background replete with loving parents and a one-time attachment to the Jehovah's Witnesses belied the fact she was making a $1000 a night as a prostitute.

Douglas became obsessed with Benedict who saw in the overweight, bookish professor a classic sucker whose awe of women could be profitably manipulated and exploited. In return for introducing him to cocaine and adventurous sex, Benedict kept Douglas "on the clock," even charging him $50 an hour to help move her out of one of her trick pads. Rapidly exhausting his personal funds, Douglas placed the one-time graphic arts student on a grant-funded payroll at $1000 a month as a "medical illustrator." On grant reports, Douglas hid expenditures incurred for oral sex, travel with Benedict, and prophylactics under humorous line item headings like "biological fluid collection units." Tufts University administrators, however, were not amused when an audit revealed Douglas had embezzled $67,400 in government grant funds. The professor was quietly called in, asked to explain himself, relieved of his duties, and allowed to resign on May 27, 1983.

By early 1983 Douglas' obsessive phone calls, letters, and stalking of Benedict led the woman to break off the affair. She demanded he pay her $5000 allegedly owed her and drove to his Sharon, Massachusetts, home on March 5, 1983, to collect. Benedict was never seen again. One day later, a man scavenging through a garbage can in a rest area on Route 95 in Mansfield near Sharon uncovered a garbage bag containing a woman's corduroy jacket, a man's blue shirt, and a two-and-a-half pound sledgehammer all smeared with blood. Tests revealed that brain matter clotted on the hammer could only have come from the "deep part" of the brain signifying a fatal blow. The jacket was later identified as Benedict's and the shirt Douglas'. A missing person's report filed by Benedict's pimp/boyfriend had already led police to Douglas who admitted seeing her on the night of the disappearance to discuss sketches for a manuscript. Douglas explained his bandaged forehead as a wound sustained in a robbery days before.

On March 19, 1983, police confronted Douglas at his home with the items and listened skeptically to his protestations of innocence. In a bedroom closet, they discovered a pair of pink panties, Benedict's coded "trick book," and her pocketbook filled with contraceptives and credit cards. Douglas feigned ignorance and accused her pimp of planting the incriminating items. More difficult to explain was his bloodstained windbreaker recovered at the scene. Unconcerned, Douglas slept as detectives continued their search. Reluctant to prosecute without an identifiable body part, the district attorney pressed police to continue their search for Benedict's missing 1982 silver Toyota Scarlet. On July 16, 1983, it was found in Manhattan's Garment District. Blood and brain matter found on the hatchback's vinyl deckmats tested similar to those on Douglas' windbreaker. Amtrak tickets and phone logs further tied Douglas to the suspected homicide.

Still vigorously protesting his innocence, Douglas was arrested on October 28, 1983, and held in jail without bail for six months while awaiting trial. In a pre-arranged plea bargain agreement, Douglas changed his innocent plea to guilty of manslaughter on the first day of the trial, April 23, 1984. Douglas admitted, in a subsequent confession, that a confrontation with Benedict in his home ended in her bludgeoning death. He insisted, however, that she had struck the first blow. He disposed of her body in a shopping center dumpster in Providence, Rhode Island. Benedict's remains have never been found. On May 7, 1984, Douglas received the maximum penalty for manslaughter and was sentenced to 18–20 years at the Massachusetts Correctional Institute at Walpole. He is eligible for parole in 12 years. Divorcing his first wife, Douglas married Bonnie-Jean Smith, a 44-year-old divorced nurse, on July 7, 1987. A model inmate who has been active in teaching fellow prisoners and in performing charity work, Douglas was moved in April 1988 to the medium-security Connecticut Correctional Institution at Enfield to be closer to his wife. Released in 1993 after serving only nine years, Douglas agreed to pay his victim's family $20,000 and to share with them half of any money he gets from his story about the case.

161. Carpenter, Teresa. *Missing Beauty: A True Story of Murder and Obsession.* 1st ed. New York: Norton, 1988. 478 pp.; 24 cm.

_____. [Same as 161 minus subtitle.] New York: Kensington, 1989. 605 pp., [16]pp. of plates: ill.; 18 cm. ("Zebra books"); paperback.

_____. [Same as 161.] London: Hamish Hamilton, 1989. 478 pp.: ill., ports.; 24 cm.

_____. [Same as 161.] London: Futura, 1991. 584 pp.; 18 cm.; paperback.

Downs, Elizabeth Diane Fredrickson

Born August 7, 1955, in Phoenix, Arizona. Part-time letter carrier. Springfield, Oregon; 1 murder; .22 caliber Ruger semiautomatic pistol; May 19, 1983.

Television: "Small Sacrifices" (1989), a two-part, four-hour made-for-television miniseries based on Ann Rule's book of the same title, originally aired on ABC on November 12 and 14, 1989. Cast includes Farrah Fawcett (Diane Downs), Ryan O'Neal (Lew Lewiston), and John Shea (Frank Joziak).

"I'm never going to see Cheryl on earth again, and I just—you can't replace children, but you can replace the effect that they give you."—Downs in May 1983 reflecting on the reason she became pregnant again

A perplexing case in which a mother shot three of her children (killing one) ostensibly because her current boyfriend did not want to be tied down with them. According to the testimony given police by 27-year-old part-time postal worker Elizabeth Diane Downs, she was driving with her three young children on a rural road near Springfield, Oregon, on May 19, 1983, when a male "bushy haired stranger" flagged her down and demanded her car keys. When she refused, the stranger sprayed the interior of the car with shots from a .22 semiautomatic pistol before fleeing the scene on foot. Downs suffered a minor arm wound, but her seven-year-old daughter Cheryl Lynn in the front seat next to her was killed. Asleep in the backseat, Christie, 9, and her three-year-old brother Stephen "Danny," survived their wounds, although Christie subsequently suffered a stroke which left her with a speech impediment. The single shot Danny caught in the back left him permanently paralyzed below the chest. Police were dubious of Downs' description of the attack when forensic evidence suggested that Cheryl Lynn had been shot once as she lay outside the car by someone *within* the vehicle. Marks found on the casings of .22 caliber cartridges uncovered in Downs' apartment matched those recovered from the scene. Perhaps as importantly, seasoned detectives doubted her story of the "bushy haired stranger," a stock character in forensic folklore which has become synonymous with the alleged perpetrator of the crime who can never be produced in court.

Downs was arrested on February 28, 1984, and charged with murder, attempted murder, and assault. As the prosecution built its case against her, a fascinating portrait began to emerge of the woman described by her ex-husband as "the only woman I know who

gets pregnant to cheer herself up." Allegedly abused sexually by her father as a pre-teen, Downs attempted suicide at 13, married at 18, and submitted to an abortion. Apparently guilt-stricken over the incident, she subsequently produced children of her own in addition to acting as a surrogate mother for $10,000 for a childless couple. Downs left her husband and moved to Arizona with her three children where she fell in love with a married man who refused to return with her to Oregon because he did not want to be around her children.

On May 7, 1984, the first day of jury selection in a Eugene, Oregon, courtroom, Downs was already eight months pregnant by an individual she identified only as a "young attractive male" who lost interest in her after she became pregnant. Surviving children, Christie and Danny, had been placed in a foster home after their mother's arrest and would ultimately be adopted by the deputy district attorney who prosecuted her. The five-week trial featured compelling forensic evidence against Downs as well as Christie's tearful testimony that she had been shot by her mother. A nine-woman, three-man jury deliberated three days before returning a guilty verdict on June 17, 1984. Downs subsequently delivered a healthy newborn daughter which was taken by the state three days after its birth. On August 31, 1984, she was sentenced to life plus 50 years. Her convictions have been upheld at state level by both the appellate and supreme court. On July 11, 1987, Downs climbed two fences and escaped from the Oregon Women's Correctional Center in Salem. Ten days later she was arrested four blocks from the medium-security facility living in a house with four men. During the time she remained at large,

Downs had become romantically involved with one of them. The man plus another resident in the house pleaded guilty to charges of hindering prosecution and received suspended sentences of three years each. On November 23, 1987, Downs was given an additional five-year prison term for the escape. Two days later, Oregon corrections officials shipped her to a maximum security prison in Clinton, New Jersey. Downs is eligible for parole consideration on June 27, 2012.

162. Downs, Elizabeth Diane. *Diane Downs: The Best Kept Secrets, Her Own True Story.* Springfield, Or.: Danmark, 1989. 318 pp., [8]pp. of plates: ill., ports.; 18 cm.; paperback.

163. Rule, Ann. *Small Sacrifices: A True Story of Passion and Murder.* New York: New American Library, 1987. 487 pp., [8]pp. of plates: ill.; 24 cm. ("An NAL book.")

_____. [Same as 163.] New York: New American Library, 1988. 494 pp., [8]pp. of plates: ill.; 18 cm.; paperback.

_____. [Same as 163.] London: Corgi, 1990. 620 pp.; 18 cm. (Originally published: New York: New American Library, 1987); paperback.

Dresbach, Ralph Wayne

Born circa 1946. High school student. Franklin Manor, Maryland; 2 murders; .22 caliber Remington automatic rifle; January 7, 1961.

"I never go to bed without remembering what I done, and there's never a day I wake up that it's not there waiting for me. Everybody pays one way or the other if they have a conscience."— Dresbach in 1978

On the morning of January 7, 1961, 15-year-old Wayne Dresbach shot and killed his adoptive parents with his father's .22 caliber rifle in their upscale waterfront home on Chesapeake Bay in Franklin Manor, Maryland. Forty-seven-year-old Harold Malone Dresbach, a respected and successful divorce attorney, was shot three times as he walked through the dining room on his way to the kitchen. Forensic evidence suggested that an additional three shots were fired into the wounded man as he lay on the kitchen floor. The nude body of his wife Shirley, 46, was found on the floor of their bedroom, the victim of five gunshot wounds to the back, chest, and elbow. Wayne placed the murder weapon under the front seat of his mother's car and left the scene intending to kill himself by running the vehicle head-on into a tree. Meanwhile, his 14-year-old brother Lee, a witness to his father's murder, notified a neighbor who contacted police. Shortly afterwards, Wayne was arrested in the company of two boys who minutes before had shared soft drinks with him in a gas station. "I shot my parents," Wayne admitted to the state trooper.

Dresbach was tried as an adult under Maryland law in 1961 which provided that juvenile status could be waived if the offender was older than 14. Public opinion ran high against the teenager, who was viewed as an ungrateful, spoiled child who abused the privileges afforded him by his wealthy adoptive parents. Wayne's uncommunicativeness with counsel, hired by relatives two months *after* his arrest and confession, reinforced the general view that he was a sullen cold-blooded killer. He was equally close-mouthed with court-appointed psychiatrists trying to determine if he was sane at the time of the double homicide. While admitting to a long history of violent arguments with his father, Wayne hid dramatic details of his family life which could possibly have mitigated the pending charges of first degree murder although the state announced prior to trial that it would not be seeking the death penalty.

At his trial in Annapolis, Maryland, on June 30, 1961, Dresbach pleaded not guilty by reason of insanity to murdering his father. He would never be tried in his mother's death. Brother Lee testified that Wayne had threatened to kill his father only days before the crime. While the defense tried to introduce testimony regarding the Dresbach's home life, the judge declared such testimony irrelevant to a defense of legal insanity strictly defined under the state's M'Naghten Rule which required only that Wayne understood the difference between right and wrong at the time of the crime. Adding his opinion to that of several other psycho-legal experts who examined Wayne, famed psychiatrist Manfred S. Guttmacher testified that while medically the teen was a disordered individual he was not by legal definition insane. The all-male jury retired at 6:02 p.m. after hearing seven hours of complex legal and psychological testimony. They returned 12 minutes later in the quickest guilty verdict ever rendered in a Maryland murder trial. On July 7, 1961, Dresbach received an automatic life sentence in the Maryland Penitentiary. In 11 years he would be eligible for his first parole hearing. A petition filed by his attorney sent Dresbach instead to the Patuxent Institute where he was identified as a "defective delinquent." At Patuxent, Dresbach faced an indeterminate sentence although his would be reviewed annually. Shortly after arriving, he unsuccessfully attempted suicide by ingesting barbiturates.

After years of psychotherapy at Patuxent, Dresbach confessed to psychiatrists the years of mental and physical abuse inflicted upon the family by his father. Twice a candidate for the Maryland General Assembly and a seeming pillar of the community, attorney Harold Dresbach was stated to be a sexually sadistic, wife-beating alcoholic who privately terrorized his family. Bragging to friends about the way he wanted to die, Dresbach stated, "I'd like to croak in jail at age ninety-nine, awaiting trial for rape." With wife Shirley, Dresbach orchestrated sexual orgies in their home often photographing the participants' antics while the children, ordered never to come downstairs when there was "company," slept upstairs. Wayne found hundreds of pornographic Polaroid snapshots in his father's desk depicting scenes of sadism, bestiality, sodomy, and group sex often involving his parents. These same photos and "other devices" were confiscated by police during their investigation of the crime scene. A devoted nudist who imposed this interest on his reluctant sons, Harold Dresbach was barred from several camps for trying to smuggle in a camera.

While no family member escaped Dresbach's abuse, Wayne was singled out as his favorite target. When severe eye trouble caused the boy to fail all his courses in the ninth grade Dresbach beat him bloody with a garrison belt. As further punishment, the boy was forced to stay inside for an entire summer and only allowed out to cut grass and fetch drinks for his parents sunbathing nude on the back patio. Once while accompanying his drunken father on a duck hunt, Wayne objected to the man's shooting of a swan. As punishment, Dresbach forced his son to pluck, clean, and eat the bird. When a larger boy bloodied his nose, Wayne reluctantly told his father who reacted to his weakling son by knocking him unconscious. When not physically abusing Wayne, Dresbach verbally humiliated the boy, often comparing him unfavorably to his athletic younger brother in front of embarrassed company. A frequent runaway, Wayne was referred to counseling where he was diagnosed as a child suffering from severe emotional problems. The father attended only one family therapy session and refused to acknowledge the counselor's suggestion that there might be a connection between his son's behavior and their home life. Unable to endure any further abuse, Wayne Dresbach killed his parents on January 7, 1961.

At the Patuxent Institute Dresbach avoided homosexual rape by cultivating a tough guy image. He had a fellow-inmate tattoo him, developed his body through weightlifting, and traded on his reputation as a killer. On April 27, 1962, the court of appeals of Maryland turned down Dresbach's appeal and any hope of further legal recourse was ended in the fall of 1963 when a court ruled he could not inherit from his parents' estate. Dresbach earned his certificate of high school equivalence in August 1965 and five years later was granted work-release status. On February 18, 1971, the 25 year old was granted parole. In 1980 it was reported that Dresbach was working as a salesman for a Baltimore ship chandler.

164. Mewshaw, Michael. *Life for Death.* 1st ed. Garden City, N.Y.: Doubleday, 1980. 281 pp.; 22 cm.

_____. [Same as 164.] New York: Avon, 1983. 280 pp.; 18 cm.; paperback.
Dresbach cooperated with writer and childhood friend Mewshaw in this well written and researched account which documents the emotional and physical abuse allegedly prompting the teenager to murder his parents. Called by the *New York Times* (August 24, 1980) "a sobering cautionary tale for zealous advocates of adult punishment for juvenile offenders."

Einhorn, Ira Samuel (a.k.a. "The Unicorn," "The Mayor of Powelton," "Ian Morrison," "Grace O'Malley," "Ben Moore")

Born May 15, 1940, in Philadelphia, Pennsylvania. Lecturer, writer, consultant. Philadelphia, Pennsylvania; 1 murder; bludgeon; September 1977.

"The sacred mystery of another must be preserved—only death can do that."—Entry in Einhorn's diary dated late June 1962

Hippie/New Age philosopher and social activist who fled the United States in order to avoid prosecution on a charge of murdering his lover. For decades Ira Einhorn, a name synonymous with the counterculture in Philadelphia, had focused his genius level intellect (an IQ above 140) on raising that city's consciousness by organizing a series of happenings beginning in 1967 with a Be-In and extending through 1978's Sun Day festivities. "The Unicorn," a self-given nickname derived from his surname (Einhorn, in German, "one horn") had also run for mayor of Philadelphia on the Planetary Transformation ticket in 1971. By the late seventies, Einhorn's interest in the New Age philosophies of UFOs, the paranormal, and other fringe sciences had been embraced by the Establishment. Pennsylvania Bell underwrote the cost of Einhorn's weekly mailings of articles and clippings on topics in the field of New Age paranormal research to a worldwide network of researchers and scholars he dubbed the "psychic mafia." Still sporting his tied-back ponytail from the sixties and wearing dashikis, the unconventional Einhorn was appointed a fellow of the Institute of Politics at the Kennedy School of Government at Harvard in the fall of 1976.

Einhorn's lover, 31-year-old Helen "Holly" Maddux, had been missing since September 1977 when police, acting on information supplied to them by private investigators working for her family, served a search warrant on the New Age guru at his second floor apartment in Powelton Village, the Bohemian section of Philadelphia near the University of Pennsylvania campus on March 28, 1979. Questioned at the time of Maddux's initial disappearance, Einhorn informed investigators that he had not seen his lover of five years since she failed to return to the apartment from a food buying trip at a local co-op. According to Einhorn, Maddux phoned days later to inform him that she had decided to cut all ties with her past life. Out of respect for her wishes, he refused to help private investigators at the time try to locate her. Police currently searching Einhorn's apartment forced open a locked closet door on an enclosed porch overlooking the backyard of the property. Inside they found boxes marked "Maddux," a suitcase, and a steamer trunk which emitted a foul odor. The trunk contained Maddux's handbag, driver's license, social security card, and a woman's body desiccated down to 37 pounds covered in styrofoam and plastic bags. Fingerprints and dental records established the corpse's identity as Holly Maddux. An autopsy determined death due to

"cranio-cerebral injuries to the brain and skull" caused by a minimum of six and possibly as many as 14 crushing blows from a blunt object.

Einhorn's arrest for first degree murder was met with disbelief by friends who were among the most influential people in Philadelphia. While many dismissed Einhorn's claim to have been framed as part of a joint CIA-KGB effort to stop his dissemination of sensitive information on psychotronic weaponry through his network, none believed him capable of committing murder. At Einhorn's April 3, 1979, bail hearing, the crush of friends and supporters anxious to attest to his excellent character was so great that there was not room for all of them to testify. "The Unicorn" retained Arlen Specter, former two-term Philadelphia district attorney and later elected to the Senate from Pennsylvania, to represent him. Specter, more recently of Anita Hill/Clarence Thomas fame, was instrumental in having Einhorn's bail reduced from $100,000 to a mere $40,000. Wealthy friends put up the $4,000 (10 percent of the bond) while Einhorn's parents assumed the remaining $36,000 liability. When Einhorn failed to appear for a pre-trial hearing on January 21, 1981, an arrest warrant was issued and his parents forfeited the money. Authorities traced Einhorn to Dublin, Ireland, which in 1981 had no extradition treaty with the United States. He was joined there by his current lover Jeanne Marie Morrison who returned to the United States in late 1986 after breaking up with Einhorn. Although granted immunity, Morrison's testimony failed to help locate her former lover.

Fearful that several key witnesses would either die or move away before Einhorn's capture, the district attorney tried the fugitive in absentia on September 20, 1993. Witnesses testified to his stormy relationship with Maddux, a former high school cheerleader and Bryn Mawr graduate he met in 1972. Einhorn was found guilty on September 23, 1993, and immediately sentenced to life imprisonment. In October 1993 Einhorn's defense attorney filed a motion for a new trial based on the absence of his client who was unable to defend himself. Since jumping bail "The Unicorn" has continued to remain at large by living under assumed names in England, Ireland, and Spain. Einhorn was last spotted in Stockholm, Sweden, in 1988.

165. Levy, Steven. *The Unicorn's Secret: Murder in the Age of Aquarius: A True Story.* 1st ed. New York: Prentice Hall Press, 1988. ix, 352 pp., [8]pp. of plates: ill.; 25 cm.

_____. [Same as 165.] New York: New American Library, 1990. 397 pp., [8]pp. of plates: ill.; 18 cm. ("An Onyx book"); paperback.

Levy documents two earlier incidents in which the guru of non-violence assaulted women who attempted to end affairs with him, the incident authorities believe prompted Einhorn to murder Maddux. The author speculates that Einhorn's abuse of ketamine, a sister drug of PCP ("angel dust") which acts on the cerebral cortex and produces a "strong dissociation from one's environment," is a possible explanation for the reason he was able to keep a corpse in his apartment for 18 months.

Ellis, Ruth
(a.k.a. "Ruth Neilson" [maiden name], "Ruth Hornby")

Born October 9, 1926, in Rhyl, North Wales. Executed July 13, 1955. Night club manager, prostitute. Hamp-

stead, London, England; 1 murder; .38 caliber Smith & Wesson revolver; April 10, 1955.

Film: Dance with a Stranger (GB, 1985), a Samuel Goldwyn Company release of a First Film Company production for Goldcrest and the National Film Finance Corporation, directed by Mike Newell. Cast includes Miranda Richardson (Ruth Ellis) and Rupert Everett (David Blakely).

"An eye for an eye, a life for a life. I took David's life, and I don't ask you to save mine. I don't want to live." — Ellis to her attorney

The last woman to be hanged in Britain. Tragically unlucky in love, Ruth Ellis possessed a genius for becoming involved with the wrong type of man. Pregnant at 16 by a married French-Canadian soldier, Ellis kept the child and supported herself by posing nude for photographers. At 19 she began working as a hostess in a night club in Mayfair where she drifted into casual prostitution. A marriage to club regular George Ellis, an alcoholic dentist with a violent temper, ended abruptly when he requested a divorce on the grounds of mental cruelty. In October 1953 Ruth Ellis became manager of the Little Club, a night spot in Knightsbridge, living rent free in a two room flat above the club. Members of a motor racing fraternity, the Steering Wheel Club, often drank there and Ellis soon became sexually attracted to David Moffett Drummond Blakely, a hard drinking 24-year-old racecar driver. Within two weeks of meeting, Blakely was sharing Ellis' flat. While both continued other sexual affairs, Ellis seemed genuinely to love Blakely and even remained with him after paying to abort his baby at the end of 1953. The relationship, however, was volatile and by late 1954 Ellis was all but keeping Blakely. A violent drunk, Blakely routinely beat Ellis and following a particularly brutal attack on March 7, 1955, she suffered a miscarriage.

On the night of April 10, 1955 (Easter Sunday), Blakely was drinking with a male friend at the Magdala, a pub on the edge of Hampstead Heath. Ellis and Blakely had quarreled earlier in the evening and the racecar driver had refused to see her when she tried to intercept him at a friend's house in Hampstead. As Blakely left the Magdala and was attempting to open his car door Ellis approached and fired six shots from a .38 caliber Smith & Wesson revolver point blank at her lover. Two of the four shots striking Blakely proved instantly fatal. One errant shot ricocheted off the pavement and wounded a passerby in the hand. Arrested at the scene, Ellis told interrogators at Hampstead police station, "I intended to find David and shoot him." While awaiting trial in Holloway Prison, Ellis requested a Bible and a photograph of Blakely. The platinum blond was cool and unrepentant as her two-day trial opened at the Old Bailey on June 20, 1955. Ellis' counsel pleaded her not guilty and argued that the 28 year old had been driven to kill by the sufferings Blakely had inflicted upon her. The case was effectively lost, however, when Ellis admitted to the prosecution that "I wanted to kill him." On June 21, 1955, a jury needed only 27 minutes to return a guilty verdict with no recommendation for mercy. Against Ellis' wishes, her solicitor wrote a seven-page letter to the home secretary outlining why she should be spared the death penalty. The reprieve was refused and Ellis was hanged at Holloway Prison on July 13, 1955. In 1971 construction at Holloway necessitated the moving of the remains of all the executed women buried on the grounds. On April 1, 1971, Ellis was reburied at St. Mary's, Haversham, under the name "Ruth Hornby." Ten years after her controversial execution, Home Secretary Lloyd George (Lord Tenby then) admitted to a writer that he refused Ellis' reprieve because she had wounded a passerby in her attack on Blakely.

166. Farran, Denise. *The Trial of Ruth Ellis: A Descriptive Analysis.* Studies in Sexual Politics; no. 24. Manchester: Sociology Department, University of Manchester, 1988. 108 pp.; 30 cm.; unbound.

167. Goodman, Jonathan, and Pringle, Patrick. *The Trial of Ruth Ellis.* Celebrated Trials Series. Newton Abbot: David & Charles, 1974. 156 pp.: ill., map; 22 cm.

_____. [Same as 167.] Bath: Chivers, 1990. [152]pp.: ill.; 21 cm.

Succinct, well presented case study compiled from official and unofficial sources. Appendices include the article "Should Ruth Ellis Hang?" by "Cassandra" (William Connor) which appeared in the *Daily Mirror* on June 30, 1955, letters published in the London *Evening Standard* June 30–July 12, 1955, and the leading article "The Death Penalty" in *The Lancet* (July 23, 1955) with resultant correspondence. The authors conclude that Ellis' hanging played "a major part in bringing about the abolition of capital punishment" in England.

168. Hancock, Robert. *Ruth Ellis: The Last Woman to Be Hanged.* London: A. Barker, 1963. 208 pp.: ill.; 21 cm.

_____. [Same as 168.] London: Weidenfeld and Nicolson, 1989. 192 pp., [8]pp. of plates: ill., ports.; 20 cm.; paperback.

_____. [Same as 168.] London: Orion, 1993. 192 pp., [8]pp. of plates: ill., ports.; 18 cm.; paperback.

Hancock originally covered the case in the spring of 1955 in a series of articles for the now defunct British newspaper *Woman's Sunday Mirror*. Includes material based on the author's conversations with Desmond Cussen, described at the trial as Ellis' "alternative lover," and the individual some feel supplied her with the gun that killed Blakely.

169. Marks, Laurence, and Van Den Bergh, Tony. *Ruth Ellis: A Case of Diminished Responsibility?* London: Macdonald and Jane's, 1977. v, 178 pp., [8]pp. of plates: ill., facsims., ports.; 23 cm.

_____. [Same as 169.] London; New York: Penguin, 1990. 215 pp., [8]pp. of plates: ill., ports.; 18 cm.; paperback.

Engleman, Glennon E.
(a.k.a. "The Killing Dentist")

Born February 6, 1927, in St. Louis, Missouri. Dentist. Missouri; 5 murders (5 convictions, prime suspect in 2 others); gun, bomb; December 17, 1958–January 14, 1980.

Television: "Beyond Suspicion" (1993), a two-hour, made-for-television movie, originally aired on NBC on November 22, 1993. Cast includes Corbin Bernsen (Dr. Glennon Engleman), Markie Post (Joyce Engleman), and Kelsey Grammer (Bill Garvey).

"My sister did my horoscope 15 years ago. It said that one day I would have to go and live with people of the underworld." — Engleman's comment after being sentenced to 50 years to life for the 1976 murder of Peter J. Halm

St. Louis dentist with a hypnotic control over women credited with orchestrating the murder for profit and revenge slayings of seven people from 1958 through January 1980. In a case illustrative of his *modus operandi*, Engleman persuaded Carmen Miranda, his dental assistant, to marry his patient Peter J. Halm so that he could later be killed for his life insurance. On December 4, 1980, Engleman shot Halm to death as the man walked with his wife in a wooded area near Pacific, Missouri. Miranda later gave Engleman $10,000 of the $40,000 insurance settlement. In the only case not to involve a woman confederate or dupe, Engleman had dynamite placed in the car of Sophie Marie Berrera, the owner of a dental supply office in St. Louis, because she had filed suit against him to collect $14,500 he owed her. Berrera was blown to bits on January 14, 1980. Convicted in federal and state courts on charges stemming from the Halm and Berrera murders, Engleman was serving two life sentences plus 60 years in the Missouri State Penitentiary when he was linked to three other murder-for-profit killings which he arranged in 1977 and 1979. Engleman pleaded guilty to the murders on June 18, 1985, and was given three additional life terms. He continues to be the prime suspect in two unsolved murders, a shooting in 1958 and a bombing in 1963. Prison officials have denied Engleman's request that he be allowed to practice dentistry on fellow inmates.

170. Bakos, Susan Crain. *Appointment for Murder: The Story of the Killing Dentist.* New York: G.P. Putnam's Sons, 1988. 286 pp.; 24 cm.

_____. [Same as 170 minus subtitle.] New York: Pinnacle Books, 1989. 384 pp.; 18 cm.; paperback.

Erler, Robert John, Jr.
(a.k.a. "The Catch Me Killer," "Bruce Strickland")

Born July 1, 1944, in Adam, Massachusetts. Police officer. Hollywood, Florida; 1 murder; .22 caliber pistol; August 11, 1968.

"Something just clicked and I said, 'Kill her!' It was like retreating back in my mind and watching myself do it. The little girl started screaming, so I shot her too."

Hollywood, Florida, police officer who, after shooting a woman and her daughter, anonymously phoned police and begged them to catch him. On August 11, 1968, Erler, a 24-year-old former Green Beret, was running on the beach to relieve stress when he encountered 42-year-old drifter Dorothy Clark and her daughter, Merilyn, 12, sleeping there. Recently estranged from his wife, Erler invited the pair back to his trailer to spend the night.

When Clark refused his sexual advances, Erler pumped six shots from a .22-caliber pistol point blank into her head then turned the gun on the girl. After dumping them in separate locations, Erler "discovered" the body of Dorothy Clark in an industrial park. Remarkably, the woman survived the attack and would later identify him as her attacker. The body of Merilyn Clark, shot five times in the head, was found a couple of miles away. Later that day, Officer Erler anonymously phoned police headquarters and told the dispatcher, "Please catch me! Come and get me. I may kill tonight too!" One day after the shooting, Erler quit the force citing "personal reasons" and moved to Phoenix, Arizona, where he was arrested on September 15, 1968. A jury composed of six fathers found the "Catch Me Killer" guilty of second degree murder on January 31, 1969, and Erler was sentenced to 99 years and 6 months hard labor at the state prison in Raiford, Florida.

At Raiford, the ex-cop's refusal to be segregated from the general prison population resulted in numerous inmate attacks in which he lost several teeth, sustained a broken jaw, and suffered a head injury that required over 100 stitches. Already a Golden Gloves boxing champion, Erler turned to karate and achieved the rank of black belt. Transferred to the medium security Bell Glade Correctional Institute on Lake Okeechobee, Erler escaped across an alligator-infested swamp in 1973 and fell in with the mob in Miami. On March 31, 1973, Erler was arrested following a high speed car chase near Mathiston, Mississippi, where he was spotted at a post office attempting to pick up a mail-order .357 Magnum. Reincarcerated, Erler underwent a religious conversion, confessed to the attack on the Clarks, and dropped his pending appeal. At Florida State Prison Erler became the head of the Christian Men's Fellowship and organized a Jaycee chapter. Erler continued his evangelical activities at the Arizona State Prison where he transferred in 1977 to be closer to his family. While there, he baptized more than 100 fellow convicts in an irrigation ditch on the prison grounds. Erler has since been licensed as a minister by the North Phoenix Baptist Church whose associate pastor describes him as "a rocket that just needs to be aimed." In 1978 the Arizona parole board recommended Erler's release, but the state of Florida ruled he must serve 25 years before being considered for parole. Nevertheless, Erler was paroled on July 19, 1983, and as of September 1994 was still under the supervision of an Arizona department of corrections' parole officer.

171. Erler, Bob, and Souter, John C. *The Catch Me Killer.* Wheaton, Ill.: Tyndale House, 1980. 220 pp.; 24 cm.

_____. [Same as 171, but paperback reprint retitled: *They Call Me the Catch*

Me Killer.] Wheaton, Ill.: Tyndale House, 1982. 220 pp.; 18 cm.; paperback.

Erler's spiritual autobiography chronicles the murder, his violent prison experiences, and the religious awakening which has led to his prison ministry. In a "Postscript," Souter, a freelance writer, maintains that "Bob Erler is for real, both as a man and as a Christian" and argues that his continued incarceration is "a great injustice."

Essex, Mark James Robert (a.k.a. "Mata," "Howard Johnson Sniper")

Born circa August 1949 in Emporia, Kansas. Died January 7, 1973. Former Navy man. New Orleans, Louisiana; 10 murders; rifle; January 1–7, 1973.

"Hate white people—Beast of the Earth."—Slogan found painted on the wall of the apartment used by Essex

Black racist whose hatred of whites exploded in mass murder and arson in a New Orleans hotel in 1973. Mark Essex, born in Emporia, Kansas, in 1949, learned to hate whites while in the Navy. Discharged in February 1971 for "unsuitable character and behavior," Essex steeped himself in revolutionary black philosophy adopting the name "Mata," Swahili for "hunter's bow." Armed with a .44 caliber Magnum Ruger Deerslayer carbine, Essex relocated to New Orleans, Louisiana, in August 1971. In the racially divided city, the 22-year-old focused his anger on the police. On New Year's Eve 1972, Essex attacked the Central Lockup of the New Orleans Police Department killing two officers, one of them black. A week later, on January 7, 1973, Essex shot a white grocery store owner, stole a car, and drove to the Downtown

Howard Johnson's Hotel five blocks from the French Quarter. Over the next several hours, Essex roamed the halls shooting guests and police, torching rooms, and sniping at passers-by. In the chaos that followed, Essex worked his way to the roof of the 17-story structure and barricaded himself into a concrete bunker. Essex maintained his position against a barrage of police firepower (including a helicopter gunship) for over seven hours yelling occasional taunts at his attackers. Shortly before 9:00 p.m. Essex broke cover and ran across the roof shouting, "Come and get me!" He was hit from a steady stream of gunfire from the helicopter and surrounding police which lasted for four minutes. One officer commented that "the bullets caught him and held him up, sort of like when you shoot at a pie plate and keep it rolling." In the course of his two attacks, Essex had killed ten and wounded twelve. Two days later, police visited the revolutionary's apartment and found the words "My destiny lies in the bloody death of racist pigs" scrawled on the walls amid other anti-white slogans.

172. Hernon, Peter. *A Terrible Thunder: The Story of the New Orleans Sniper.* 1st ed. Garden City, N.Y.: Doubleday, 1978. 288 pp., [12] leaves of plates: ill.; 22 cm.

Evans, Gwynne Owen (a.k.a. "John Robson Walby" [real name], "Owen Evans," "Ginger," "Sandy")

Born April 1, 1940, in Maryport, Cumberland, England. Executed August 13, 1964. Dairyman, kitchen porter, driver, elevator operator, railway worker. Workington, Cumberland

England; 1 murder; bludgeon, knife; April 7, 1964.

"I don't know anything about a knife. I don't have to use a knife to kill a man—I'm an expert at Judo and Karate. I never hit Jack—it was Peter that did all the hitting."—Evans in a statement to police

Mentally deficient killer who with accomplice Peter Anthony Allen shares the dubious distinction of being the last criminal to be hanged in Britain. On April 7, 1964, the body of John Alan West, a 53-year-old van driver for Lakeland Laundry, was found in his home at No. 28 Kings Avenue in Workington after neighbors, responding to suspicious noises coming through a common wall, summoned police. West's skull had been shattered by repeated blows from a metal tube encased in rubber (recovered at the scene) and he had been stabbed once through the heart. In the victim's bedroom police found a raincoat containing a Royal Life Saving Society medallion inscribed with "G. O. Evans" and an Army Memorandum Form with the name of an unmarried female factory worker in Liverpool. Police located the 17-year-old girl who admitted briefly dating a man known as "Ginger Owen Evans." She identified the raincoat and medallion as belonging to her former beau. Peter Anthony Allen, 21, and his lodger Gwynne Owen Evans, 24, were picked up on April 8, 1964, after police traced them through withdrawals they made from West's bank in Workington dated *after* his murder. At the time of his arrest in Manchester, Evans (real name John Robson Walby) was carrying the wristwatch presented to West by his firm in appreciation of his 25 years of service.

Both killers presented strikingly similar backgrounds and psychological profiles. Allen, plagued as a child by hearing and speech impediments, was discharged from the Army at 16 for a lack of intelligence. Drifting from job to job, he was inevitably fired for chronic absenteeism or lying on his timecard. Evans manifested mental problems at age ten and for two years was treated in a mental institute where he was diagnosed as "showing a vivid imagination which was in part due to the lack of toys supplied to him as a child." Enlisting in the military on at least three occasions, Evans was each time declared "mentally unfit under existing standards" and discharged early. Like Allen, he too was incapable of holding any job. In January 1964 Evans began lodging with Allen, his wife and two children at their home at No. 2 Clarendon Street in Preston. Their string of petty thefts was soon interrupted when they were collared for breaking and entering and car theft. Given two months by the court to either pay the hefty fines or go to prison, Evans remembered John Alan West, a former coworker he knew often kept money at home.

Not surprisingly, in their confessions Allen and Evans accused the other of killing West. Both agreed, however, that they drove to Workington in a stolen car to ask West for a loan and that Evans initially entered the house alone to speak with West while Allen waited outside in the car with his wife and children. According to Evans' statement, Allen afterwards burst into the house and beat West to death with a cosh. Allen admitted striking the man in the face with his fist, but insisted that Evans killed West with the pipe. A day after their arrest, Allen's wife led police to the weapon (a kitchen knife with a three-and-one-half inch blade) in Windermere where she said Evans dumped it after the murder. Authorities generally believed that Allen did most of the battering while Evans stabbed West. The pair's trial commenced at the Manchester Assizes in July 1964 and over the next six days 40 witnesses testified in the case. On July 7, 1964, both men were found guilty of capital murder after a jury deliberated just over three hours. Their appeal denied, Allen was hanged at Liverpool and Evans at Manchester on August 13, 1964.

173. Jones, Elwyn. *The Last Two to Hang.* New York: Stein and Day, 1966. 160 pp., [4]pp. of plates: ill.; 22 cm.

_____. [Same as 173.] London: Macmillan, 1966. 101 pp., [3]pp. of plates: ill.; 23 cm.

_____. [Same as 173.] London: Pan Books, 1968. 123 pp.; 18 cm.; paperback.

Jones focuses on the investigation that resulted in the arrest of Allen and Evans less than 48 hours after their murder of John Alan West. It is suggested that West's killing may have had homosexual overtones.

Evans, Timothy John

Born November 20, 1924, in Merthyr Vale, Wales. Executed March 9, 1950. Van driver. London, England; 1 murder (convicted); ligature strangulation; November 8 or 10, 1949.

"I had nothing to do with it. My wife was dead when I got home ... Christie done it." *See also* Christie, John Reginald Halliday.

Eyler, Larry W.
(a.k.a. "The Highway Killer")

Born December 21, 1952, in Crawfordsville, Indiana. Died March 6, 1994. House painter, liquor store clerk, attendant in state-licensed home for developmentally disabled children. Indiana, Illinois; 21 murders (2 convictions, self-confessed in 19 others); knife, awl; October 1982–August 21, 1984.

"I ask God to forgive me because I can never forgive myself."—Conclusion of Eyler's December 4, 1990, statement in which he confesses to and describes the murder of Steven Agan

Sadistic homosexual torture-killer who is often compared to another Illinois serial murderer, John Wayne Gacy. The bodies of young men and boys aged 14 to 28 began turning up in the rural fields of Illinois and Indiana in late 1982. In each instance, the victim had been repeatedly stabbed, mutilated, and found with their pants pulled down around their ankles. Twelve bodies had been recovered by August 1983 when a caller to the Central Indiana's Gay Homicide Task Force hotline alerted authorities to Larry Eyler, a 30-year-old house painter who commuted between residences in Terre Haute, Indiana, and Chicago. The caller noted that Eyler "projected violence during sex," a fact verified by several gay men who had encounters with him. Eyler had been under police surveillance for over two months when an Indiana State Trooper detained him shortly before 7:00 a.m. on September 30, 1983, for illegally parking his pickup truck along a northern Indiana highway. The young male hitchhiker in the truck with the suspected serial murderer told officers that Eyler had offered him $100 to let him tie him up and have sex. A search of the truck revealed handcuffs, a bloodstained knife, rope, tape, and a pair of boots whose soles matched footprints left in a Lake County, Illinois, cornfield where the tortured and mutilated body of

28-year-old Ralph E. Calise was found on August 31, 1983. Eyler was charged with Calise's murder, but freed on $10,000 bond on February 6, 1984, after a judge ruled that police had illegally searched his truck, thus making the incriminating evidence found in it barred from any trial. During the time the Calise case was being resolved, authorities found seven more bodies scattered throughout Wisconsin, Indiana, and Illinois.

On August 21, 1984, Eyler was arrested at his apartment on the North Side of Chicago after the dismembered body of 15-year-old prostitute Daniel Bridges was found in eight plastic garbage bags in a dumpster behind the building. A janitor witnessed Eyler disposing of the bags and police found bloodstains throughout the apartment. Eyler was convicted of Bridges' murder on July 9, 1986, and subsequently sentenced to death. In November 1990, Eyler agreed to cooperate with authorities in Indiana investigating some of the 24 killings attributed to him throughout the Midwest in exchange for their assurance that he would not be executed. He admitted the torture-mutilation slaying of 23-year-old Steven Agan at an abandoned farmhouse one mile north of Newport, Indiana, on December 28, 1982. In a graphic confession, Eyler related how he stabbed and mutilated the bound Agan while longtime friend and companion Robert David Little, the 53-year-old Chairman of the Department of Library Science at Indiana State University in Terre Haute, took photographs and masturbated over the bondage scene. Eyler was sentenced to 60 years for Agan's murder. Little was arrested on the strength of Eyler's confession and with no physical or other evidence to back up the killer's allega-

tions was acquitted on April 17, 1991. Eyler's offer to clear up to twenty homicides in exchange for being taken off death row in Illinois was rejected by the Cook County State's Attorney. The so-called "Highway Killer" died of AIDS at the Pontiac Correctional Center's prison infirmary on March 6, 1994, after confessing to his attorney that he committed 21 murders, four with an accomplice who remains at-large.

174. Kolarik, Gera-Lind, and Klatt, Wayne. *Freed to Kill: The True Story of Larry Eyler.* 1st ed. Chicago, Ill.: Chicago Review Press, 1990. v, 379 pp., [16]pp. of plates: ill.; 24 cm.

_____. [Same as 174 with variant subtitle: *The True Story of Serial Murderer Larry Eyler*]. New York: Avon, 1992. 423 pp., [16]pp. of plates: ill.; 18 cm.; paperback.

Coauthor Kolarik was responsible for recognizing the pattern between the Indiana and Illinois killings and her book is credited with prompting Indiana officials to reopen the 1982 murder investigation of victim Steven Agan. The paperback edition contains an afterword reporting on Little's 1991 acquittal on a charge of helping Eyler murder Agan.

"Fatal Vision Murders" *see* MacDonald, Jeffrey Robert

Fernandez, Raymond Martinez
(a.k.a. "The Lonely Hearts Murderer [or] Killer," "Charles Martin")

Born December 17, 1914, in Hawaii. Executed March 8, 1951. Dock worker, sailor, confidence man. Spain, Illinois, Long Island, New York, Michigan; 5 murders (1 conviction);

drugs, ligature strangulation, gun, drowning, bludgeon (hammer); November 1947–March 1949.

Film: The Honeymoon Killers (US, 1970), a Roxanne/Cinerama production written and directed by Leonard Kastle. Cast includes Shirley Stoler (Martha Beck), Tony LoBianco (Ray Fernandez), and Mary Jane Higby (Janet Fay).

"I am going to die. As you know that is something that I've been prepared for since 1949. I'm going to die like a man."—Fernandez in a statement issued shortly before his execution

The "Lonely Hearts Murders," one of the most famous cases of the early 1950s. Martha Beck was 27 in November 1946 when she received a pamphlet from "Mother Dinene's Family Club for Lonely Hearts." As a cruel joke, an acquaintance had submitted her name to the club which promised to show those looking for love "the road to happiness." Beck sent in a profile of herself, a description of her dream man, and $5, neglecting to mention that she was a 250 pound divorcée with two small children. But then the man who responded to her letter, 34-year-old Raymond Martinez Fernandez, failed to tell Beck that he made his living out of bilking lonely women. Their perverse relationship would result in at least three murders, foster sensational tabloid headlines, and afford a tragic glimpse into the depths of human loneliness and cruelty. The woman described by the yellow press as "an overweight ogress whose mind and heart were shaped only for murder" was an unwanted child whose dominating mother openly disliked her. A pituitary-ovarian gland disorder swelled her body to massive proportions and accelerated her sex drive. By nine she was already men-

struating, developing breasts, and being noticed by men. While the glandular disorder increased her sex drive, a genital malformation prevented Beck from experiencing much pleasure from "normal" sexual intercourse. At 13, she was raped by a 17-year-old brother who, threatening to kill her if she told, raped her again ten days later. Finally confiding in her mother, the woman blamed Beck for the incident, whipped her, and kept an even closer watch on the "sinful" girl.

Beck turned to academics for the approval denied her at home and after completing high school in Milton, Florida, was admitted into the Pensacola School of Nursing. In March 1942 she placed first in her class, but her appalling physical appearance barred her from securing hospital employment in the area. As a last resort, she worked for a local mortician preparing female bodies for burial. Romance novels and true confession magazines brought temporary respite from the horrors of life and Beck immersed herself in them. Unable to endure the funeral home job, she moved to Napa, California, and worked by day as a floor nurse at an Army base hospital. At night, Beck cruised bus stations and railway depots to pick up soldiers on war leave. Six months after arriving in California, she became pregnant by a Vallejo bus driver. Only the man's attempted suicide ended Beck's demands that he marry her. Following the incident, she was hospitalized for hysteria and suffered total amnesia for days. Alone and pregnant, Beck bought a wedding ring to conceal her plight and returned to Pensacola to look for work.

Beck spoke often to Florida acquaintances about her fictional "husband," a Navy officer on duty in the

Pacific. All shared her grief when a telegram announcing his death in action arrived shortly before the birth of "their" child. In early January 1944 she resumed her California pattern; days spent working in a hospital, nights spent trolling for men at the Pensacola bus depot. By the time knowledge of her lifestyle prompted the hospital to dismiss her on May 31, 1944, Beck had met bus driver Alfred William Beck. Although he reluctantly married her on December 14, 1944, the pregnant woman filed for divorce in May 1945. Lonely, unemployed, grotesquely obese and saddled with two small children, Beck spent hours reading romance novels and repeatedly seeing the films of her dream man, actor Charles Boyer. On February 15, 1946, Beck was hired as a nurse by the Pensacola Crippled Children's Home and six months later became its superintendent. Romance, in the form of a man described as "a seedy Charles Boyer," would soon enter her life.

Raymond Martinez Fernandez, born in Hawaii in 1914 to Spanish parents, was dominated by a father who saw in the sickly boy he despised, a source of cheap labor. Moving the family to Bridgeport, Connecticut, when Raymond was three, the elder Fernandez had to be compelled to let the child attend school. Shortly after graduating grade school, Raymond had his first and only brush with the law, before sustaining the head injury which seemingly launched his criminal career. The teenager was caught stealing chickens for the holiday table after his father refused to buy the family a Thanksgiving turkey. Unwilling to speak on his son's behalf, Raymond received sixty days imprisonment in the county jail. His confinement coincided with a growth spurt which transformed the

frail youth into a strikingly handsome, powerfully built man. Released, Fernandez travelled to Spain to work on an uncle's farm and at 20 he married a woman his father disliked. The feeling was mutual and their bickering made Fernandez's life intolerable. During World War II, he worked on the docks in Gibraltar and supposedly served as a small-time spy and informer for the British government. After the war, he secured a berth as an ordinary seaman on an oil tanker. In late 1945, a falling hatch struck Fernandez on the head causing a deep three inch indentation in the skull high on the forehead and a scar on the tissue of his brain. Within months, Fernandez's behavior underwent a startling transformation. Racked with recurring migraine headaches, his sex drive increased, and he inexplicably attempted to leave ship in Mobile, Alabama, with a duffel bag stuffed with dirty government issue linen. Fernandez was sentenced to a year in Tallahassee federal prison for the attempted theft.

Serving time in Florida with large numbers of Caribbean prisoners, Fernandez became fascinated by their talk of voodoo and black magic and steeped himself in occult practices. The judge's decision to reduce his sentence to six months convinced the budding occultist that he possessed the power to hypnotize from a distance. When released on December 3, 1946, he went to Brooklyn to live with a sister. Nearly bald, emaciated, and plagued by headaches, Fernandez began writing to women through lonely hearts clubs bragging to his friends that he could make love from a distance to his correspondents by rubbing his letters with a sexually exciting "commanding power." Initially, his interest in these women was purely sexual. He would request fetish items from them like a lock of hair or fingernail clippings and use them to adorn miniature dolls of the women. During the two years following his release, Fernandez corresponded with hundreds of women and conducted simultaneous affairs with as many as 15 of them at a time. Several, he later bilked out of large sums of money.

In early 1947, Fernandez (wearing a toupee to cover his scar) met divorcée Jane Lucilla Wilson Thompson through a lonely hearts club. Posing as man and wife, they sailed to Spain on October 2, 1947. In La Linea, Fernandez introduced his real wife and their four children to Thompson who seemingly accepted the situation for a week. On November 7, 1947, the "honeymooners" quarreled and Fernandez left the hotel. He returned next morning to find Thompson dead in her room, the official victim of "cardiac collapse during acute gastroenteritis." It was subsequently learned that Fernandez had earlier purchased a bottle of digitalis from the hotel pharmacy. By the time Spanish police charged him, Fernandez was on trial in Brooklyn for another murder. Back in New York, Fernandez presented a will to Thompson's elderly mother which named him as the sole beneficiary of her daughter's estate. He magnanimously allowed the old woman to share the Brooklyn apartment with him.

In late 1947, Fernandez ran across 26-year-old Martha Beck's ad in Mother Dinene's pamphlet. Representing himself as a successful Spanish businessman, he wooed Beck in a series of love letters. On December 28, 1947, he travelled to Pensacola to meet the woman who had so totally misrepresented herself in their correspondence. Though taken aback by her appearance

and two kids, Fernandez quickly charmed the infatuated woman. That night, Beck experienced sexual fulfillment for the first time. From that moment, she was psychically enslaved to a man who initially looked upon her devotion as troublesome. Leaving Florida, he posted a cool letter to her breaking off the affair. Beck attempted suicide. Brushing aside his objections, she packed up her children and moved into his New York apartment, displacing the aged mother of Fernandez's first victim. His ultimatum: She could stay, but the kids must go. Obediently, she shipped the kids off to her mother in Florida, never to see them again.

Fernandez explained his "line of business" to Beck and she agreed to help him fleece other women on the condition that he refrain from having sex with any of them. He bigamously married a Pennsylvania woman on February 28, 1948, with Beck posing as his sister-in-law. Again on August 14, 1948 he married a woman in Chicago, feeding her barbiturates when she complained about the omnipresent Beck. She would die days later from "cerebral hemorrhage and liver inflammation." Posing as "Charles Martin," Fernandez began writing Janet Fay, a 66-year-old New York widow, in late 1948. On December 30, Fernandez with his "sister" in tow arrived in Albany to meet the woman. Over the next several days, Fay closed out her savings accounts, cashed bonds, and wrote herself a check for $1500. The pair transported the "soon to be married" widow to their apartment at 15 Adeline Street in Valley Stream, Long Island. Under a pretense of notifying friends about the wedding, Fernandez tricked Fay into signing her name on blank sheets of paper. Reports conflict on what happened later that night,

January 3, 1949. Fernandez went to sleep in another room leaving Beck and Fay to discuss him. Jealous over the widow's fondling of Fernandez, Beck argued with Fay who threatened not to let the "sister" live with them once they married. Enraged, Beck "blacked out" and hit Fay in the temple with a ball-peen hammer. Fernandez tied a scarf around Fay's neck and used the handle of the hammer to slowly tighten the ligature until the woman strangled to death. The body languished in a trunk for days as they liquidated the dead woman's assets and searched for a place to bury her. Eight days after the murder, on January 11, they rented a house at 133-15 149th Street, South Ozone Park, Queens. The next day, Fay's body was buried in the cellar and cemented over. Four days later they gave possession of the house back to the realtor.

On the day of the murder, "Charles Martin" received a letter from Delphine Downing, a 41-year-old widow with a young daughter named Rainelle. Weeks later she was thrilled to learn that he and his sister would come to Byron Center, a suburb of Grand Rapids, Michigan, to visit them. Promising Beck he would not sleep with Downing, Fernandez soon swept the widow off her feet. Love-struck, she constructed a story which explained their living with her. Less than a month after the Fay murder, Fernandez was engaging in sex with the widow and promising her marriage while Beck fumed and tried to keep the couple apart. Downing's assets had been converted to cash by February 1949 when the widow caught Fernandez sans toupee. Shocked by his baldness and ugly scar, she tearfully condemned his deceit and threatened to cancel the marriage. On March 1, 1949, tension in the house reached its peak.

Downing, fearful that she was pregnant, asked Beck to abort the fetus. The former nurse supplied Downing with sleeping pills, assuring the woman that the "abortion tablets" would terminate her pregnancy. Drugged, Downing collapsed into bed. Beck attempted to strangle into silence the cries of 20-month-old Rainelle, but was stopped by Fernandez. To prevent Downing from reporting the assault to police, Fernandez shot the woman twice in the head. Like Fay, Downing's body was buried in the cellar and cemented over. A dog was bought to appease the terrified child, but when the infant still refused to come near them, Martha drowned her in a washtub. Instead of leaving the state, they attended a movie in Grand Rapids. Police, called by suspicious neighbors, arrested the duo upon their return to the house. In custody, they confessed to the Fay and Downing murders. A bitter extradition battle ensued between New York, where they faced execution for the Fay murder, and Michigan, a state with no death penalty. On March 16, 1949, Michigan extradited the pair to New York with the stipulation that they be returned to stand trial for the Downing murders if not executed.

Fueled by inflammatory press headlines, the trial of "The Lonely Hearts Murderers" captured the popular imagination. Throughout the 44 days of the trial, women packed the courtroom to catch a glimpse of the "virile" Fernandez. No day passed that he did not receive letters from women offering sex and marriage, despite the fact he had already bigamously married six or more times. Beck too received marriage offers and was thrilled to find that men finally "wanted" her. Ever the masochist, Beck attempted to shield Fernandez from the first degree murder charge. The defense initially argued that the "mentally unbalanced" Beck was solely responsible for Fay's unpremeditated murder and that Fernandez was only an accessory after the fact. This strategy soon proved futile and Fernandez changed his plea to "not guilty" by reason of insanity. The defense contended that the pair's sexual abnormalities and perversities made it "impossible for them to act as normal individuals." The jury needed less than 13 hours to find the lovers guilty of first degree murder on August 18, 1949. Their appeal denied, the pair was scheduled to be electrocuted in Sing Sing on March 8, 1951. Two hours before the execution, Fernandez sent Beck a note proclaiming his undying love for her. The executions of two teenaged murderers preceded Fernandez's death at 11:12 p.m. Twelve minutes later, Beck was led into the chamber to face the final indignity of her life; she had to awkwardly squeeze her massive frame into the electric chair. Four jolts later, Beck joined her lover.

175. Brown, Wenzell. *Introduction to Murder: The Unpublished Facts Behind the Notorious Lonely Hearts Killers, Martha Beck and Raymond Fernandez.* New York: Greenberg, 1952. 232 pp.; 21 cm.

_____. [Same as 175.] London: A. Dakers, 1953. 232 pp.; 21 cm.

Fish, "Albert" Hamilton Howard

(a.k.a. "Frank Howard," "James W. Pell," "Bobby or Robert E. Hayden," "Robert Fiske," "Thomas Sprague," "The Gray Man")

Born May 19, 1870, in Washington, D.C. Executed January 16, 1936. House painter, handyman, janitor. Brooklyn and Westchester County, New York; 2 murders (confessed, estimated total of 15); knife, manual strangulation; circa 1910–1928.

"If only pain were not so painful."

Religious fanatic and murderous pedophile whose cannibalism predates that of Ed Gein and Jeffrey Dahmer. The sex life of Albert Fish, according to defense psychiatrist Frederic Wertham, was one of "unparalleled perversity" and included (among 19 known perversions) frequent acts of pedophilia, cannibalism, coprophagia, and castration. Enshrined in abnormal psychology textbooks, Fish manifested nearly a dozen more perversions than previously identified by alienists prior to 1936. Grandfatherly in appearance with kind blue eyes, gray mustache, bowlegs, and stooped shoulders, Fish appeared to be a harmless 64 year old as he sat in a New York courtroom charged with the murder, dismemberment, and cannibalization of a ten-year-old-girl. Born Hamilton Fish in 1870, he was five when his father died and his destitute mother was forced to place him temporarily in an orphanage. At New York City's St. John's Refuge Fish was introduced into an environment of strict religious dogma, corporal punishment, and homosexuality. Shortly before leaving the facility, he and other boys doused a horse in kerosene and set it ablaze. Fish returned home at seven and sustained a fall from a tree which resulted in a lifelong history of headaches and dizzy spells. When classmates taunted him about his first name, his mother "changed" it to Albert in memory of an earlier child who died at birth. After completing first grade, Fish apprenticed as a house painter and thought of becoming an evangelist, an odd calling for a boy who collected newspaper clippings of bizarre crimes for masturbatory purposes.

At 17, Fish moved to New York City and indulged his passion for homosexuality and boy rape until a visit from his mother convinced him he could resist such temptation by marrying. Momentarily repentant, he wed 19-year-old Anna May Hoffmann and fathered six children by her, but returned to homosexuality during a one- to five-year stretch in Sing Sing for petty larceny. Released after a couple years, Fish returned home to find Anna having an affair. He forgave her, but the break became irrevocable when he discovered that she was keeping the man hidden in the attic of their home. Though never divorced, Fish took custody of the children. In 1918, the 48 year old began hearing voices from "God" instructing him to leave his family to become an itinerant worker. Fish deposited them in cheap lodgings and from 1918 to 1928 wandered through 23 states securing employment in institutions where children were present. During this period it is estimated that he raped one hundred boys. In St. Louis, Missouri he picked up a mentally defective boy and played sadomasochistic sex games with him for weeks before partially castrating him and attempting to drink his blood. Fish later atoned for his bouts of wickedness by beating his own naked buttocks with a nail studded paddle. The voices increased in November 1927 and acting under their urgings Fish kidnapped four-year-old Billy Gaffney from a Brooklyn tenement house. In a foul parody of Abraham sacrificing his son Isaac, Fish slaughtered the Gaffney boy with a knife in the Riker Avenue Dumps.

On May 28, 1928, Fish, posing as wealthy Long Island farmer "Frank Howard," responded to a newspaper ad placed by 18-year-old Edward Budd who was seeking a "position in the country." Arriving at the Budds' basement apartment at 406 West 15th Street in Manhattan, Fish convinced mother Delia he had farm jobs for her son and his friend. A week later Fish sent the boy a telegram misaddressed to "William" explaining he would be delayed until Sunday, June 3, 1928. That morning, Fish left his wrapped "implements of hell" at a nearby newsstand prior to visiting the family. The bundle contained a saw, a cleaver, and a butcher's knife. Fish was at the Budd home when their ten-year-old daughter Grace returned from Mass shortly after noon. She reacted to Fish's obvious interest in her by jumping in the old man's lap and hugging him. Fish gave the boys $2 to see a movie, explaining he had to attend a birthday party for his sister's child before leaving for the farm. Grace's parents were happy to have her accompany Fish to the party at the fictitious uptown address he gave them. Before catching a train to Westchester County, Fish retrieved his package from the newsstand. Ironically, as the pair were getting off the train Grace reminded the absent-minded Fish not to leave his bundle on the seat. A short walk brought them to remote Wisteria Cottage, a ramshackle house Fish lived in with his family in 1922. He left her in the yard picking flowers and went to an upstairs room to spread a canvas, unwrap his cutlery, and undress. He called for Grace. When she reached the top of the stairs, Fish jumped out and dragging her into the room, choked her to death. Dismembering her body, he placed her head and shoes in an outhouse. He returned four days later to bury the rotting body parts behind a stone wall.

Within the four week period following the murder, Fish was arrested three times for larceny but always released. He wandered for two years living off women he met through lonely hearts clubs, bigamously marrying three times. In November 1930 a conviction for sending "letters of indecent character" through the mail landed Fish in Bellevue for three weeks of psychiatric examinations. Diagnosed as a sexual psychopath, the court handed him a six month suspended sentence. He was released January 16, 1932, judged "disturbed but sane." In 1934, Fish as "Robert E. Hayden," penned a series of obscene letters to a woman covertly asking her to spank him. Fearful of arrest, he soon stopped. That November he took a room in a flophouse at 200 East 52nd Street where he received a monthly check from a son. While there, he read a newspaper account on Grace Budd and using a monogrammed envelope found in a closet, posted a letter to her mother. In it, he admitted to killing Grace and to consuming her body over a nine day period. Delia Budd gave the unopened letter to Detective Will King who had worked unceasingly on the case for six years. King noted that the writing in the letter was identical to "Frank Howard's" signature and traced the monogrammed company envelope to a former tenant of the flophouse who admitted leaving some stationery in a closet there. Fish moved in the interim, but still returned monthly to pick up his check. King staked out the roominghouse for three weeks until Fish surfaced on December 12, 1934.

Taken into custody, Fish attacked King with straight razors but did no harm. His pockets were stuffed with razors and blades and his trunk contained a new clipping on homosexual murderer-cannibal Fritz Haarman and the complete works of Edgar Allan Poe. Fish immediately confessed and ascribing the murder to his "lust for blood," admitted that before seeing Grace, Edward Budd had been his intended victim. In Fish's twisted mind, Grace's death ensured that she would forever remain a virgin. Notations in Fish's address book implicated him in at least four other murders although only the remains of Grace were recovered at Wisteria Cottage. Fish later confessed to the murder-cannibalization of Billy Gaffney. While in custody, Fish complained of severe stomach pains and x-rays taken on December 28, 1934 revealed 27 sewing needles in his abdomen and pelvis. He had inserted them over a ten year period of self-torture and expiation for the pain he had caused others. Doctors decided not to remove them as they posed no immediate health risk.

The question of Fish's sanity became the central issue in his trial which began in the second week of March 1935 in White Plains, New York. Fish sat impassively throughout the proceedings, face buried in hands, listening to 55 witnesses lay bare his bizarre life. Defense psychiatrist Frederic Wertham eloquently argued that Fish's lifelong history of aberrant behavior clearly marked him as insane and unresponsible for his actions. His contentions were bolstered by the accounts of family members who testified that Fish once proclaimed himself to be Jesus Christ while inserting needles into his body. The prosecution agreed that while Fish was a psychopathic personality, the Budd murder showed clear premeditation and his subsequent acts to elude capture demonstrated that he knew the difference between right and wrong. On March 22, 1935, the case was given to an all-male jury, all but one of whom was a parent. They needed only three-and-a-half hours to sentence the 65 year old to the electric chair. Fish thanked them. A few days later he attempted suicide by slashing his abdomen with a pork chop bone sharpened on the floor of his cell. A subsequent appeal was rejected in November 1935 and an execution date of January 16, 1936, was set. Waiting for death in Sing Sing, Fish amused himself by writing an autobiography authorities condemned as pornographic filth. As the date drew near, Fish enthused "What a thrill it will be if I have to die in the electric chair. It will be the supreme thrill—the only one I haven't tried." Calm and self-possessed, Fish was electrocuted at 10:30 p.m. on January 16. A first charge of electricity, presumably shorted out by the needles in his body, failed to kill him. Seconds later a second jolt ended his life. Four days later, the oldest man ever to be executed in America was buried in an unmarked grave.

176. Angelella, Michael. *Trail of Blood: A True Story*. Indianapolis, Ind.: Bobbs-Merrill, 1979. ix, 205 pp.; 24 cm.

———. [Same as 176.] New York: New American Library, 1981. ix, 181 pp.; 18 cm. ("A Signet book"); paperback.

177. Heimer, Mel. *The Cannibal*. New York: L. Stuart, 1971. 154 pp.; 22 cm.

———. [Same as 177.] London: Xanadu, 1988. 154 pp.; 23 cm.

———. [Same as 177.] New York: Pinnacle, 1991. 167 pp., [8]pp. of plates: ill.; 17 cm.; paperback.

178. Schechter, Harold. *Deranged: The Shocking True Story of America's Most Fiendish Killer!* New York: Pocket Books, 1990. 306 pp., [8]pp. of plates: ill.; 18 cm.; paperback.

———. [Same as 178.] London: Warner, 1992. 306 pp., [8]pp. of plates: ill., ports.; 18 cm.; paperback.

Wonderful account of Fish's bizarre life and crimes which owes much to the cooperation of James Dempsey, the cannibal killer's defense attorney. The 89-year-old gave Schechter unrestricted access to his files and the result is the most factual book to date on one of America's most fascinating murderers. Excellent selection of photographs.

Fitzsimmons, George Kearon Joseph

(a.k.a. "The Karate Chop Killer," "The Buffalo Ripper," "George Smith")

Born May 7, 1937, in Cleveland, Ohio. Salesman. Amherst, New York and Roulette, Pennsylvania; 4 murders; karate, hunting knife; January 12, 1969, and November 18, 1973.

"Not insane. I did not do the incidents. Not guilty."—Fitzsimmons on the murder of his aunt and uncle

Paranoid schizophrenic who murdered his parents with karate blows in Amherst, New York, on January 12, 1969. Found "not guilty by reason of insanity," Fitzsimmons spent less than three years in the Buffalo State Hospital before being declared "no longer any danger" to society. He was released on March 22, 1973, to the care of an elderly aunt and uncle in Roulette, Pennsylvania. When Fitzsimmons became convinced that the 80 year olds were poisoning his food he slaughtered the pair in their home with a hunting knife on November 18, 1973. The ex-mental patient used $40,000 of the money he inherited from his parents to retain famed criminal attorney F. Lee Bailey, but bitterly clashed with his counsel's strategy of mounting an insanity defense. Fitzsimmons deluged the judge with stacks of letters in which he voiced his opposition to the defense and insisted that he was "mentally and physically ready to stand trial." On December 20, 1976, three years after the double homicide, Fitzsimmons was convicted on two counts of first degree murder and sentenced to two natural life terms to run concurrently. The convictions have since been upheld by both the Pennsylvania and U.S. supreme courts.

179. Heimel, Paul. *No Longer Any Danger: The Fitzsimmons Story.* Coudersport, Penn.: Enterprise Publishing Association, 1981. 133 pp.: ill., ports.; 23 cm.; paperbound.
   Privately produced, small print run account of the case.

Fox, Sidney Harry
(a.k.a. "Cupid")

Born circa January 1899 in Great Fransham, Norfolk, England. Executed April 8, 1930. Forger, confidence man. Margate, England; 1 murder; manual strangulation; October 23, 1929.

"My Lord, I never murdered my mother."—Fox's statement to Mr. Justice Rowlatt after being sentenced to death

British petty thief and con man who elaborately murdered his mother in order to collect her life insurance. Sidney Harry Fox used his earnest face and affable demeanor to cover numerous forgeries, petty frauds, and confidence scams which nevertheless landed

him in prison for most of 1919 and 1920. A devoted son, Fox was supported in his criminal lifestyle by his mother Rosaline Fox. In 1927, Fox and his mother struck up a relationship with a middle-aged Australian woman named Mrs. Morse and lodged with her in Southsea. Although a homosexual, Fox saw the potential for profit in seducing the married woman. They began an affair and the charming confidence man convinced the lovestruck woman to make her will out in his favor while (unknown to her) he took out a £3000 insurance policy on her life. Shortly afterwards, Mrs. Morse awoke in the middle of the night to find her room filled with gas. Authorities told the shaken woman that the gas had been purposely turned on. Mrs. Morse terminated the affair and Fox left the shared flat with his mother after stealing his former lover's jewelry. Apprehended for the theft, Fox was sent to prison for 15 months in March 1928.

Upon his release, Fox, accompanied by his mother, moved throughout England staying in the finest hotels then leaving without paying the bill. Sensing that he had perhaps exhausted every moneymaking scam at his disposal, Fox convinced his ailing mother on April 21, 1929, to make out a will leaving everything to him. Nine days later he took out life insurance on the woman after asking the agent if the policy covered accidental death by drowning or poisoning. On October 16, 1929, Fox took rooms for himself and his mother at the Hotel Metropole in Margate. Two days later he traveled to Ramsgate to take out another £1000 accidental death policy on the 63-year-old woman. Concerned over his mother's health, Fox had the hotel manager move her to a room (No. 66) with a gas fire while he took an adjoining room without one. The next day Fox traveled to London and arranged policies totaling £3000 to be paid if his mother died before midnight on October 23, 1929. In an amazing coincidence which later proved to be a cornerstone of the prosecution's case against him, Fox raised the Hotel Metropole at 11:40 p.m. on October 23, 1929, with cries that his mother's room was on fire. A guest of the hotel fought through the dense black smoke in No.66, found Mrs. Fox crossways on her bed naked save for a small vest, and dragged her into the hall. She failed to respond to artificial respiration and her death was later ruled accidental due to shock and suffocation. A burning armchair near the gas fire was initially assumed to be the cause of the fatal blaze.

Though emotionally devastated by her death, Fox left the hotel without paying and lived off a small cash advance from the insurance company while awaiting full payment on the policies. Suspicious that Mrs. Fox died 20 minutes before the policies on her life would have expired, the insurance company conducted tests on the burned objects in the room. They concluded that the fire could not have been accidental, a finding bolstered by the fact that a wide strip of unburned carpet lay between the fireplace and the armchair disproving any connection between them. Pending a murder charge, Fox was arrested on six counts of fraud in Norwich on November 3, 1929. Following the exhumation of Mrs. Fox's body at Great Fransham on October 29, 1929, and a detailed post mortem examination by renowned pathologist Sir Bernard Spilsbury, the original charges were altered to murder on January 9, 1930. Conflicting expert medical evidence highlighted Fox's trial which opened at Lewes on March 12, 1930. Spilsbury maintained that the lack of soot in Mrs. Fox's air passages combined with the absence of carbon dioxide in her blood suggested that she was dead before the fire started. A recent bruise found at the back of her larynx pointed to death by manual strangulation. Two other medical experts disagreed with Spilsbury and claimed that Mrs. Fox's death was due to heart failure caused by her waking to see the room ablaze. They dismissed the bruised larynx as nothing more than a patch of discoloration due to the body's putrefaction. A jury needed only 70 minutes on March 21, 1930, to find Fox guilty. The son Mrs. Fox called "Cupid" was hanged, without confessing, at Maidstone Gaol on April 8, 1930.

180. Jesse, F. Tennyson, ed. *Trial of Sidney Harry Fox.* Notable British Trials. Edinburgh; London: W. Hodge, 1934. xii, 299 pp., [9] leaves of plates: ill., ports.; 22 cm.

_____. [Same as 180.] Notable British Trials. Toronto: Canada Law Book, 1934. xii, 299 pp.: ill.; 22 cm.

Jesse's concise summary introduces the transcript of Fox's trial.

Franklin, George Thomas, Sr.

(*conviction overturned;* a.k.a. "Mr. Flirty-Flirty")

Born circa 1939 in Bassett, Virginia. Fireman, real estate speculator. Foster City, California; 1 murder (conviction overturned); bludgeon (rock); September 22, 1969.

Television: "Fatal Memories" (1992), a two-hour, made-for-television movie based on Eileen Franklin's book *Sins of the Father: The Landmark Franklin Case: A Daughter, a Memory, and a Murder*, originally aired on NBC on November 9, 1992. Cast includes Shelley Long (Eileen Franklin-Lipsker), Duncan Fraser (George Franklin, Sr.), and Dean Stockwell (Bob Morse).

"I'm not guilty of the crime with which I've been charged."—Franklin addressing the court at his sentencing on January 29, 1991

Controversial landmark legal case in which a father was convicted of a child murder he committed 20 years earlier based on his daughter's repressed memory of the event. In September 1988 28-year-old Eileen Franklin-Lipsker was playing at home with her two children when she flashed back to the afternoon of September 22, 1969. In her repressed memory, the woman saw her childhood friend, eight-year-old Susan Kay Nason, splayed on the ground looking up with terrified eyes at the trusted man who had raped her and now held a rock in both hands over his head. Two blows shattered the child's skull. For Eileen Franklin-Lipsker it had taken 20 years to realize in an instant that the murderer was her father, George Thomas Franklin, Sr. As memories flooded back to Franklin-Lipsker, she remembered growing up in a home dominated by her tyranni-cal and drunken father, a San Mateo, California, fireman. In 1968, Franklin purchased a Volkswagen van and cus-tomized it with curtains and a remov-able mattress. On days off, he left his family without a word and cruised alone in his "motorized bedroom" look-ing for "adventure." Eileen Franklin-Lipsker would later testify in court that following Susan Nason's death her father began to sexually abuse her and a sister. In one particularly vivid mem-ory recalled by the woman, Franklin held the 11-year-old down while a god-father raped her. Another daughter was such a frequent target of abuse that Franklin allegedly kept a jar of vase-line near her bed.

On September 22, 1969, eight-year-old Susan Nason disappeared after school in Foster City, California, a town 18 miles south of San Francisco. The Franklin family lived five houses away from the Nasons and the 30-year-old firefighter joined in the mas-sive search for his eight-year-old daughter's best friend. On December 3, 1969, a San Mateo water department employee discovered Nason's decom-posed corpse under a rotting bedspring in a wooded canyon around Crystal Springs Reservoir some ten miles west of Foster City. A rock covered with some strands of hair lay near the child's crushed head. A ring on her right hand had been "broken" as a result of her attempt to shield her head from the blows. A sock matching the one remaining on her foot was found hang-ing at eye level in a bush near the body. Recalling the murder some 20 years later, Franklin-Lipsker contacted the San Mateo district attorney's office in November 1989 and discussed the case with an investigator. According to the woman, she was riding in her father's van on September 29, 1969, when they stopped to give Susan Nason a ride. Franklin drove to Crystal Springs Reservoir while the girls played on the mattress in the back of the van. Park-ing, he joined them and raped Nason as his daughter cowered in the front seat. Afterwards, Franklin beat Nason's head in with a rock and blamed Eileen for the murder reasoning that the girl would still be alive if she had not invited her for a ride. He would kill her if she talked. After comparing the physical evidence in the case against her detailed recollection, investigators concluded that Franklin-Lipsker must have been an eyewitness to the murder.

Franklin, 50, was arrested in the Sacramento suburb of Carmichael on November 28, 1989, and charged with first degree murder. A search of his apartment uncovered child pornography, articles on father-daughter incest, and newsletters from a pedophile organization. Unable to post the $2 million bail, Franklin sat in jail for nearly a year awaiting trial. When opening arguments were finally heard in a Redwood City courtroom on October 31, 1990, cameras were barred from recording the precedent setting event. Beyond determining Franklin's guilt or innocence, the legitimacy of repressed memory as a credible form of testimony was also on trial. In arguing Franklin's innocence, the defense attempted to cast doubt on the reliability of Franklin-Lipsker's repressed memory. A Stanford University professor of psychiatry testified that victims of violence are as likely to recall a false memory as an accurate one when their memory is triggered. The so-called "facts" recalled by the witness contained nothing that could not have been learned from reading news accounts of the crime. Describing her memory as a "free-floating" tale, the defense also maintained that Franklin's daughter stood to gain financially from already signed book and movie deals if her father was convicted. The prosecution insisted that Franklin-Lipsker had supplied details of the murder not in the public domain and noted that another of Franklin's daughters had five years earlier identified her father to police as a suspect in Nason's death. Franklin's former wife testified that a

few days after the murder he had given her a bloodstained shirt to launder.

Six weeks and 61 witnesses later the case went to the jury on November 29, 1990. Following eight hours of deliberation the eight-woman, four-man jury found Franklin guilty of first degree murder the next day. At his sentencing on January 29, 1991, Franklin reiterated his innocence to an unmoved judge who pronounced him to be "a wicked and depraved man" fully deserving of the death penalty. However, under an anomaly of the law as it existed in 1969 when the crime was perpetrated, Franklin could only be sentenced to life imprisonment. In the absence of the death penalty, Franklin is eligible for parole in seven years. In March 1991, he was also considered a suspect in the stabbing deaths of two Pacifica, California, teenagers in 1976, but was never charged. In a stunning reversal, Judge Lowell Jensen of federal district court in San Francisco overturned Franklin's conviction on April 4, 1995, based on two serious constitutional errors committed in the 1990 trial. First, the prosecution was wrongly allowed to introduce evidence of a visit Franklin received in jail from Franklin-Lipsker in which she urged her father to "tell the truth" about the Nason killing. Franklin remained silent and Judge Jensen noted that the prosecution should have been prevented from arguing that the suspect's silence was proof of guilt. Second, Judge Jensen noted that the trial judge had wrongly prevented Franklin's attorneys from introducing evidence that supported their contention that details of the killing recalled by Franklin-Lipsker had been reported in the press. The prosecution argued that only an eyewitness could have provided the specifics of the murder. The San Mateo

County district attorney has 90 days to decide how to proceed with the case. As of this writing, Franklin is scheduled to be retried in September 1996.

181. Franklin, Eileen, and Wright, William. *Sins of the Father: The Landmark Franklin Case: A Daughter, a Memory, and a Murder.* 1st ed. New York: Crown, 1991. 353 pp.: ill.; 24 cm.

_____. [Same as 181 minus subtitle.] Edinburgh: Mainstream, 1992. 353 pp., [8]pp. of plates: ports.; 24 cm.

_____. [Same as 181.] 1st Ballantine ed. New York: Fawcett Crest, 1993. 341 pp., [8]pp. of plates: ill.; 18 cm.; paperback.

_____. [Same as 181 with variant subtitle: *A Daughter, a Memory, a Murder.*] London: Pan, 1993. 353 pp., [8]pp. of plates: ports.; 18 cm.; paperback.

182. MacLean, Harry N. *Once Upon a Time: A True Story of Memory, Murder, and the Law.* 1st ed. New York: HarperCollins, 1993. viii, 485 pp.: ill.; 25 cm.

_____. [Same as 182.] New York: Dell, 1994. viii, 566 pp.: ill.; 18 cm.; paperback.

Friedgood, Charles Edward
(a.k.a. "Charlie Boy," "Chief," "The Magnificent Deceptor," "Daddy," "Konge")

Born circa 1918 in Toledo, Ohio. Medical doctor. Kensington, Long Island, New York; 1 murder; Demerol; June 18, 1975.

"I'm innocent ... I know in my heart I'm not guilty, and God knows it in Heaven."—Friedgood at a pre-sentencing hearing in which he received the maximum 25 year sentence

Medical doctor convicted of the Demerol injection murder of his wife. Good looking and self-assured, Dr.

Charles Friedgood parlayed a tireless energy for self-promotion into staff appointments at prestigious institutions like the University of Pennsylvania Hospital and Brooklyn's Maimonides Hospital. Neither facility renewed the doctor's contract and chose not to report to the appropriate medical boards his numerous infractions which ran from performing unnecessary operations to billing patients for free services. In 1960 Friedgood entered private practice finding a devoted clientele among the Hasidim. Indicted in 1964 on eight counts of abortion, Friedgood escaped prosecution when witnesses refused to testify. Friedgood's second marriage in 1948 to Sophie Davidowitz, a millionaire's daughter, resulted in six children but life in their 14-room brick house at 47 Beverly Road in the stylish Kensington section of Long Island was marred by their continual bickering over money. In 1967 Friedgood met Harriet Boell Larsen, a 28-year-old Danish nurse who became his office manager, mistress, and mother of his two illegitimate children. Despite money problems at home, Friedgood set his mistress up in a luxury apartment and gave her a $1000 a month allowance. Under pressure from Larsen to leave his wife, Friedgood hesitated because he had earlier placed all his assets in her name to protect himself against bankruptcy. Shortly before her death, Sophie's suspicions concerning Friedgood's infidelity were confirmed when she found a cache of nude photos of Larsen among love letters written to her husband by the younger woman.

According to the medical examiner's reconstruction of the crime, Sophie was lying in bed on the night of June 17, 1975, when Friedgood attacked her with a syringe filled with the pain-killing drug Demerol. In the ensuing struggle the doctor injected her in the armpit, thigh, and buttock. When the drugged woman still clung to life, the doctor plunged the needle into her chest penetrating the liver. Friedgood returned the syringe to a filing cabinet in his office and slept the rest of the night next to his dead wife. That morning before leaving the house Friedgood instructed a day house-keeper not to disturb the ailing Sophie. Her body, already turning blue, was found that afternoon. Police sum-moned a distraught Friedgood who explained that his wife had a history of strokes and high blood pressure. He produced and signed a death certificate (conveniently on his person) certifying the cause of death to be a "cerebral vas-cular accident." He further informed authorities that Jewish law dictated she must be buried by sundown tomorrow and that burial was scheduled to take place the next day at Sophie's family plot in Hazelton, Pennsylvania.

Friedgood's rush to bury Sophie combined with the highly questionable ethics of a doctor signing a death certificate on a family member led police to petition for an autopsy. On June 19, 1975, officers from the Nassau County police department took a state-ment from Friedgood at the funeral home in Hazelton while a local coro-ner performed an on-site autopsy. "No detectable cause of death" was found. However, the coroner did note six dime-sized bruises on the woman's buttock, thigh, chest, and beneath both arms which could be injection sites. Undigested food in Sophie's stomach suggested that death did not occur after 9:00 a.m. on the morning of her death as Friedgood contended, but sev-eral hours earlier. A preliminary test

revealing death due to an overdose of Demerol was later confirmed after the body was exhumed on July 11, 1975, and found to contain twice the fatal dosage of the drug. Police searched Fried-good's home on June 22, 1975, looking for the syringe and Demerol, but failed to find the evidence. Under his direc-tion, Friedgood's daughter (an attor-ney) concealed the items in her under-pants.

Police, acting on a tip from Fried-good's son-in-law, removed the doctor from a British Airway's plane at Ken-nedy Airport on July 25, 1975, where he was en route to Denmark to meet his mistress. A satchel containing $650,000 in negotiable bonds and a quantity of his wife's jewels was in his possession. Friedgood was arrested on August 5, 1975, and charged with mur-der and theft from his wife's estate. Released on $250,000 bond, Friedgood pleaded not guilty before a Nassau County court in Mineola, New York, in early October 1976. Charges of con-cealing evidence and obstructing jus-tice were dropped against Friedgood's daughter in exchange for her testimony concerning the syringe and Demerol. Evidence showed Friedgood had forged Sophie's signature on docu-ments permitting him access to over $600,000 in negotiable bonds held in trust for their children. Friedgood was found guilty of second degree murder and grand larceny on December 15, 1976. He was given the maximum 25 years to life sentence on January 26, 1977. In 1978 the New York state leg-islature passed legislation popularly known as "the Dr. Friedgood Bill" pro-hibiting doctors from signing death certificates for relatives. In November 1977 Friedgood established the first prison clinic in the country for the treatment of handicapped and elderly prisoners at the Fishkill Correction Facility. In a bid for freedom vehemently opposed by the Nassau County district attorney's office, the 66-year-old doctor presented a petition for clemency signed by 28 congressmen to Governor Mario Cuomo in June 1989. In it, Friedgood expressed a desire to travel to Africa to provide medical care to drought-stricken famine victims. Though Cuomo rejected an earlier bid for clemency in 1985, Friedgood's latest petition has been "accepted for review" by the governor's executive clemency bureau.

183. Levitt, Leonard. *The Healer.* New York: Viking Press, 1980. x, 261 pp.; 24 cm.
_____. [Same as 183.] New York: Avon, 1981. x, 261 pp.; 24 cm.; paperback.
    Levitt, who originally covered the case in a series of articles for the Long Island paper *Newsday*, indicts the medical profession whose unspoken "code of silence" protected Friedgood, an incompetent doctor, for many years.

Fry, John Carl
(a.k.a. "Lucky")

Born August 31, 1946. Pimp, thief. Detroit, Michigan; 1 murder; bludgeon (baseball bat); July 13, 1985.
    "I cut his throat to try and get some of the blood out of him ... I don't know why. It just seemed like a good idea at the time."
    Violent pimp who bludgeoned a noted psychologist to death over a prostitute. Dr. Alan W. Canty, a respected and highly published psychologist, built a flourishing practice in Detroit which earned him $150,000 annually. Using the alias "Dr. Al Miller," the workaholic 51 year old began in November 1983 to cruise Detroit's Cass Corridor, the skid row

area north of downtown featured in the 1986 Eddie Murphy movie *Beverly Hills Cop.* Known locally as the Motor City's mecca for drug addicts and prostitutes, it was a world away from the fashionable Grosse Pointe section where Canty lived with his psychologist wife of nearly 11 years. In this unlikely setting on his birthday, November 30, Canty picked up a fresh-faced 18-year-old prostitute named Dawn Marie Spens. A one-time high school honor student, Spens worked the streets at $50 a trick to support a $200 a day heroin habit as well as the $1,000 a day habit of her 37-year-old live-in boyfriend, pimp John "Lucky" Fry. The street-wise pimp manipulated Canty's obsession with Spens to squeeze the psychologist for nearly $140,000. Described by police as a "sick, sadistic, psychopathic gnome," former biker John Fry managed to marry and divorce three times in between stints of imprisonment totaling ten years in six federal and state penitentiaries. Drafted into the Army in 1965, he was court-martialed twice for desertion and did time in Michigan, Indiana, and Minnesota for nonviolent crimes ranging from bad checks and counterfeiting to breaking and entering. Deemed a model prisoner by prison officials despite escaping on three occasions, Fry used his time in confinement to pump iron, tattoo his massive arms with biker and white supremacist designs and slogans, and to earn a high school degree.
    "The Pinhead," as Fry derisively referred to the trick known as "Al Miller," quickly became Spens' major source of revenue. "Miller" often gave her $200 an hour (which she dutifully gave to Fry for dope) just to spend time with him. By Christmas 1983, Canty was spending over $1,000 a week on

the prostitute and running up huge credit card debts. Anxious not to lose the "sucker," Fry hid the nature of his relationship with Spens from Canty. At the pimp's urging, she easily extracted money from Canty for their rent, utilities, and groceries. Aware of her drug habit, Canty supplied her with money for heroin and increased his payments to her so she could stop prostituting. By April 8, 1984, Canty had figured out the relationship between Spens and Fry and agreed to give the pimp $5,000 and a plane ticket if he would bow out of her life. Fry agreed, blew the money on drugs, temporarily moved into a neighbor's apartment, but still directed the "squeeze" on Canty. Ironically, Canty asked Fry to move back in with Spens to protect her after the ex-con foiled a robbery attempt against her.

By mid–1985, Canty realized the vulnerability of his position and sought to regain control over his life. Broke and aware that Fry knew his true identity and could blackmail him, the psychologist maneuvered to break the financial ties chaining him to the pair. To decrease their financial dependence on him, Canty enrolled the pair in a $100-a-week methadone treatment program to wean them from heroin. A resentful Fry just ordered Spens to turn more tricks to compensate for the lost income and issued dark threats against Canty to his friends. On July 13, 1985, Canty drove to the couple's home where Fry demanded nearly $30,000 from the psychologist so that he could start a new life with Spens in California. In the ensuing argument, Fry shattered Canty's head with at least four blows from a Louisville Slugger baseball bat. Ordering Spens out of the house to turn some tricks, Fry dragged Canty's body into the bathtub, shot up with cocaine laced with heroin,

stripped, and dismembered the corpse with a Ginsu steak knife. According to Fry's version of the events later revealed after he had shielded Spens from prosecution on a mutilation charge, the prostitute returned to the house and helped him wrap the body parts in newspaper. The pair loaded up Canty's car with garbage bags and a satchel containing body parts and along with the bat and Ginsu knife disposed of them in various dumpsters on Detroit's southside. Heading to a friend's cabin in Alanson, Michigan, Fry dumped a bag of body parts along I-75 in Auburn Hills 25 miles north of Detroit. Aided by his friend, Fry buried the satchel containing Canty's head, hands, and feet in an animal boneyard in rural Emmett County near Petoskey, Michigan.

Fry and Spens returned to Detroit, tried unsuccessfully to sell Canty's car, and later burned it to destroy fingerprints. Police recovered the burned-out hulk in a vacant westside lot on July 16, 1985. An informant's tip led to the pair's apprehension on July 20, 1985. The pimp readily confessed to the murder and directed police to Canty's remains near Petoskey. The next day the garbage bag containing Canty's left leg was recovered off I-75. On July 22, 1985, Fry was charged with first degree murder and mutilation of a dead body. Spens was charged with being an accessory to murder after the fact and mutilation. While awaiting trial, Fry and two other inmates were caught attempting to break jail on September 9, 1985.

A jury of twelve women and two female alternates was impanelled on December 3, 1985, to hear the case against Fry and Spens in a Detroit courtroom. The trials were set to run concurrently with Spens' defense to begin after Fry's verdict. As the defendant had confessed, the only question facing the court was whether the murder was premeditated. Fry, the only witness in his defense, maintained that he killed Canty in a rage when he learned that the psychologist had reintroduced Spens to drugs. Arguing for a manslaughter conviction, Fry's attorney accused Canty of using the pair's drug dependency to manipulate them like "guinea pigs" while he watched with scientific detachment. On December 11, 1985, the jury deliberated less than three hours before finding Fry guilty of first degree murder and mutilation. He was sentenced to life without the possibility of parole on December 23, 1985. Spens was tried the next day and bolstered by Fry's statement that she was not present during the mutilation, was found innocent of that charge on December 17, 1985. She was, however, found guilty of being an accessory to murder after the fact and was referred for psychiatric evaluation prior to sentencing. On January 2, 1986, a judge disregarded the recommendation of the probation department and psychiatric clinic that Spens be sentenced to five years in prison. Believing her to be a "retrievable human being," he placed her on probation for three years with the stipulation that after her release from jail she enter a drug rehabilitation program and remain until discharged. Spens was released from jail on March 19, 1986. She and Fry no longer correspond.

184. Cauffiel, Lowell. *Masquerade: A True Story of Seduction, Compulsion, and Murder.* 1st ed. New York: Doubleday, 1988. xiv, 343 pp., [8]pp. of plates: ill.; 24 cm.

_____. [Same as 184 minus subtitle.] New York: Kensington, 1988. 472 pp.,

[8]pp. of plates: ill.; 18 cm.; paperback.

Well researched and written account based on police records, trial testimony, and hundreds of hours of interviews with key witnesses. Unlike many lesser true crime authors, Cauffiel crosschecks reconstructed dialogue with documents and testimony. Cauffiel is an excellent writer who could well be the genre's heir apparent to Jack Olsen.

Fugate, Caril Ann

Born July 30, 1943. Student. Bennet, Nebraska; 1 murder (convicted, involved in 9 others); gun; January 28, 1958.

"Did he tell the truth before he died?"—Fugate's reaction upon hearing that Starkweather had been executed; *see also* Starkweather, Charles Raymond.

Fullam, Augusta Fairfield
(a.k.a. "Mrs. Clarkson")

Born June 23, 1875, in Calcutta, India. Died May 28, 1914. Agra, India; 2 murders; poison (arsenic, geselmine), sword; October 10, 1911, and November 17, 1912.

"How God has worked out all things so beautifully and brought us two most devoted and loving sweethearts close together, and given us freely to each other!"—Fullam in a letter to her lover Henry Clark after they murdered her husband

Crime passionnel in which illicit lovers conspired to murder their spouses in British colonial India. Augusta Fairfield Fullam, 35, was married to husband Edward, a deputy examiner in the military accounts department stationed in India, for 15 years when she fell in love with Lt.

Henry William Lovell Clark in 1909. A Eurasian doctor assigned to the India Subordinate Medical Service, the 42-year-old married father of four was well known in the English communities of India for his numerous extramarital affairs. Fullam, bored with her colorless husband, and Clark, openly contemptuous of his "damned swine" of a wife, began a torrid affair fueled by a voluminous and passionate correspondence. In a letter to his lover dated April 20, 1911, Clark outlined a plan to poison Edward Fullam with a "tonic" powder he would supply her. The "tonic" (arsenic) simulated heatstroke and would not arouse suspicion in a country where temperatures routinely hit 115 degrees. Fullam agreed to the plan, dutifully sprinkled arsenic in her husband's food and drink, and in letters to Clark meticulously documented its effects on the unsuspecting man. When Edward Fullam seemed to be thriving on the diet of arsenic poisoning, the impatient lovers substituted a liquid mixture of atropine and cocaine. He fell violently ill, was hospitalized on August 17, 1911, and when released in October was declared no longer fit to work by the medical board. Remarkably, in light of Edward Fullam's jealousy and dislike of Clark, he agreed to move into a bungalow owned by the doctor in Agra (pronounced Argra). On October 8, 1911, Fullam poisoned her husband's food. As he lay retching in bed, Clark injected him with the deadly alkaloid poison geselmine. In the absence of an autopsy, Fullam's death was registered as a heatstroke.

The killers now turned their full attention to the sole remaining impediment to their happiness—Mrs. Clark. Aware that her husband had made two previous attempts on her life by employing native servants to poison her food, Mrs. Clark was seriously considering moving in with her son when she was murdered. On the night of November 17, 1912, four native assassins employed by Dr. Clark for the sum of 100 rupees entered Mrs. Clark's bedroom in Agra and slaughtered the sleeping women with swords. Her 10-year-old daughter in bed next to her was unharmed. As the strained relations between the husband and wife were a staple of local gossip, Dr. Clark became an immediate suspect. Clark's weak alibi, that he dined with Mrs. Fullam on the night of the murder, brought police to her home. During their investigation, authorities found a tin dispatch box under the widow's bed containing some 400 letters written by Fullam to Clark (and initialled by her lover) carefully tied up in packets of 50. The incriminating documents led to the conpirators' arrest for Mrs. Clark's murder and prompted the exhumation of Edward Fullam's body which was found to contain a small quantity of arsenic.

The pair's trial for Fullam's murder opened at the high court of Allahabad on February 27, 1913. Damned by their correspondence, Clark attempted to shield his paramour by claiming sole responsibility. Fullam, who offered to turn "King's evidence," claimed that she acted under his hypnotic influence. Both were convicted on March 1, 1913, after a jury deliberated only two minutes. At a second trial for the murder of Mrs. Clark, the pair was convicted of having aided and abetted in the commission of the crime. On March 13, 1913, the lovers were sentenced to death for both murders. Fullam, pregnant with Clark's child, was subsequently spared hanging and resentenced to life imprisonment. Clark was hanged in Naini Prison at Allahabad on March 26, 1913, his last request to see Fullam before dying denied by his lover. Fullam gave birth to Clark's child in the same prison where she ironically died of heatstroke on May 28, 1914.

185. Walsh, Cecil. *The Agra Double Murder*. London: Ernest Benn, 1929. 254 pp.: ill., double facsims.; 20 cm.

In lieu of presenting excerpts from the transcripts of their two trials, Sir Cecil Henry Walsh, K.C., instead sets the case in the form of a connected narrative which draws heavily on extracts taken from their voluminous correspondence. Includes a facsimile letter written by Augusta Fairfield Fallum to the joint magistrate in which she offers to turn "King's evidence" against her paramour, Dr. Henry William Lovell Clark. Walsh, an appellate court judge in India, tends to moralize and to manifest the English sense of colonial superiority in regard to indigenous populations.

186. Whittington-Egan, Molly. *Khaki Mischief: The Agra Murder Case*. Classic Crime Series. London: Souvenir, 1990. 255 pp.: ill., facsims., 1 map, ports.; 22 cm.

_____. [Same as 186.] Melbourne: Australian Large Print, 1991. 377 pp.: ill., ports.; 24 cm. (This edition cased; also published in paperback.)

Definitive account of the case by the solicitor-wife of respected true crime writer Richard Whittington-Egan. First rate on all counts.

Fuller, Thomas Charles, II

Born circa 1950. High school student. Mattoon, Illinois; 5 murders; gun; April 27, 1968.

Illinois high school student convicted of murdering five members of his girlfriend's family. Thomas Fuller, an 18-year-old senior at Mattoon High School, systematically shot to death five Cox family children, ranging in ages from five to sixteen, on April 27, 1968. Placing the bodies in and near a corncrib on the family farm eight miles northwest of Mattoon, Fuller bolted and was arrested after an 11-hour manhunt, walking down the center line of the highway running through nearby Charleston, Illinois. Prosecutors offered anger or jealousy as two possible motives for the mass murder. Fuller, described by classmates as "polite" and "clean-cut," had asked Edna Louise Cox, the twin sister of one of his victims, to marry him. Although the teen's parents liked Fuller and agreed to the marriage, they asked the couple to wait until she graduated from high school. Another possible motive involved Fuller's jealousy over the amount of time his girlfriend spent looking after her younger siblings. Shortly before opening arguments were set to begin, Fuller changed his plea to guilty. It was suggested at the time that the legal maneuvering was either an attempt to avoid the death penalty, or more cynically, a deal cut by the prosecution to avert a costly trial. Fuller was sentenced on December 10, 1968, to five terms of 70 to 99 years, with two of the sentences to run consecutively to the other three sentences. A model prisoner, Fuller was denied parole in 1978 and when he reapplied on December 19, 1979, was opposed by the remaining members of the Cox family who initiated a statewide petition to block his release. The more than 32,000 signatures they collected were forwarded to the parole board which ruled against Fuller. Eligible to reapply every two years, he is incarcerated as of 1996.

187. Sawyer, Diane. *The Mattoon Murders*. [S.l.]: D. Sawyer, 1982. 108 pp.: port.; 21 cm.; paperback.

Based on her study of the case and

interviews conducted with Fuller, reporter Sawyer believes that he should one day be granted parole. Sawyer writes of Fuller, "He has good reason to keep his parole plans secret. A real threat does exist: the possibility that someone, either a relative of the Cox family or a self-styled vigilante, may try to kill him. In prison, he's relatively safe. In the free world, he may not be safe. He may very well lose his life shortly after release."

Gacy, John Wayne (a.k.a. "Jack Hanley," "The Killer Clown," "Pogo the Clown," "Patches")

Born March 17, 1942, in Chicago, Illinois. Executed May 10, 1994. Building contractor. Norwood Park, Illinois; 33 murders; ligature strangulation, knife; January 1972–December 1978.

Television: "To Catch a Killer" (1992), a two-part, four-hour series produced by the Canadian-based CTV Television Network, originally aired during the window of May 11–31, 1992. Cast includes Brian Dennehy (John Wayne Gacy), Michael Riley (Detective Joe Kozenczak), and Meg Foster (City Attorney Leslie Carlson).

"Execute Justice ... Not People!!!"—Letterhead on Gacy's prison stationery

Homosexual serial killer of 33 young men and boys in Chicago, Illinois, during the 1970s. One of the twentieth century's most notorious serial killers, John Wayne Gacy (like Ted Bundy) shattered the comfortable public myth that multiple victim murderers could be recognized by the "way they looked." Gacy, a successful building contractor in Chicago, was politically connected, active in the community, and generally well liked by those who knew him. Through his business,

PDM (an acronym for painting, decorating, maintenance), Gacy seemingly provided employment opportunities to unskilled young men and boys just breaking into the work force. Only after his arrest in December 1978 and the excavation of the crawlspace beneath his home at 8213 West Summerdale Avenue in Norwood Park, an unincorporated suburb northwest of Chicago, did the world learn that John Wayne Gacy, a man who entertained hospitalized children as "Pogo the Clown," was in fact a sadistic homosexual who systematically committed 33 sex-inspired murders over a seven-year period from 1972 through 1978. Feeding on street hustlers, runaways, and strays he later contemptuously described to detectives as "worthless little queers and punks," Gacy might have continued killing indefinitely had he not chosen Robert Piest, a 15-year-old boy from a close family, as his 33rd victim on December 11, 1978. The subsequent police investigation of Piest's disappearance which resulted in Gacy's arrest and confession led to what is arguably (along with the horror found in Jeffrey Dahmer's apartment) the single most shockingly memorable event in the history of twentieth century murder; the discovery and removal of the decomposed bodies of 27 young men from the crawlspace beneath Gacy's ranch style brick house.

Born in Chicago on St. Patrick's Day 1942, Gacy was the second of three children and the only son of John Stanley Gacy, the machinist son of Polish immigrants. A quick tempered alcoholic who demanded perfection from everyone, the elder Gacy routinely beat his wife and children. However, he reserved a special contempt for his son John, a sickly overweight child who inevitably failed to measure up to his father's high standards and expectations. Any mistake the boy made earned him his father's verbal taunts of "dumb" and "stupid." His mother's ineffectual attempts to act as a buffer between them only resulted in more verbal abuse from his father who accused the woman of turning their son into a "mama's boy," or worse, a "queer" or "he-she." At five, Gacy suffered seizures for no apparent organic cause although five years later a doctor diagnosed him with a form of psychomotor epilepsy. His father dismissed the episodes as the boy's attempts to get out of school or gain attention. At nine, Gacy was caught with a bag containing his mother's underwear and whipped by his father. His usually understanding mother tried to humiliate him out of further thefts of her lingerie by making him wear them to school under his clothes. Anxious to win his father's approval, Gacy took on a variety of odd jobs and became active in school. The old man, however, remained unimpressed and continued to avoid his family by declaring the basement off-limits and retiring there after dinner to drink and conduct loud conversations with himself in two voices. Gacy's first heterosexual experience at 18 was marred when he inexplicably passed out when she was taking off her clothes. The incident added fuel to the elder Gacy's speculation that his soft, doughy, unathletic son was a homosexual.

Gacy dropped out of school during his senior year in 1961 and following a bitter argument with his father ran away from home. Months later, the 19 year old turned up in Las Vegas, Nevada, where he worked on an ambulance crew at a funeral home before being reassigned to the mortuary. Gacy cleaned bodies for three months, sleep-

ing on the premises behind the embalming room. He later quit after the funeral director suspected that he was undressing the corpses and "experimenting" with them. Returning home, Gacy graduated from a year long business course and in 1963 the 21 year old became a management trainee for the Nunn-Bush shoe company at a department store in Springfield, Illinois. Always the overachieving workaholic, the fast-talking Gacy launched himself into the Junior Chamber of Commerce (Jaycees), a group of under-30 businessmen, and through dogged determination won the Key Man award for April 1964. Around this time, Gacy (who would later call himself a bisexual) had his first homosexual experience with an older man he allowed to fellate him. In September 1964, however, he married Marlynn Myers, a fellow department store worker whose father was a wealthy Kentucky Fried Chicken franchiser. Offered the opportunity to manage three of his father-in-law's chicken franchises in Waterloo, Iowa, Gacy moved there with his pregnant wife and soon distinguished himself by working 14-hour days. Nor did he slacken his pace when a son was born in 1966 and a daughter in 1967. In addition to managing the restaurants, Gacy continued his involvement in the Jaycees and was voted the outstanding member for 1967 while also serving as the chaplain of the local organization.

The first public crack in Gacy's persona of devoted husband, father, and pillar of the community occurred in late summer 1967. Gacy's wife was out of town when he offered Donald Voorhees, the 15-year-old son of a fellow Jaycee, a ride. They went to Gacy's house where the man showed the teen a stag movie then talked him into performing oral sex. The relationship continued (with Gacy sometimes paying the youth) until March 1968 when Voorhees told his father. During a subsequent grand jury investigation of the incident, jurors learned that Gacy had offered a ride to another boy, 16-year-old Edward Lynch, in late August 1967. Lynch, an employee at one of Gacy's restaurants, went to his employer's home where the older man showed him stag movies, tied him up with a chain and padlock, strangled him into unconsciousness, then tried to force him to commit oral sex at knifepoint. The boy escaped, but was fired from his job a few days later. Gacy subsequently pleaded guilty to the Voorhees sodomy and was sentenced on November 17, 1968, to 10 years in the Iowa State Reformatory for Men at Anamosa. His wife divorced him that day. At Anamosa, Gacy characteristically launched himself into a flurry of activity. By the time he was paroled as a model prisoner on June 18, 1970, after serving only 18 months of his sentence, Gacy had earned his high school equivalency diploma, taken college courses in psychology, become active in the prison's Jaycee chapter, and constructed a miniature golf course for the prisoners. Paroled, Gacy returned to Chicago to live with his mother (his father had died of cirrhosis of the liver on Christmas Day in 1969) and was hired as a cook at Bruno's, a downtown restaurant often frequented by players on the Chicago Blackhawks and cops. Eight months later in October 1971, Gacy was unconditionally released from parole.

On August 15, 1971, Gacy and his mother moved into the house at 8213 West Summerdale in Norwood Park which also served as the headquarters for his new business venture, PDM. When not working, Gacy cruised Chicago's gay areas looking for street hustlers and quick sex. One night around New Year's 1972 when his mother was away, Gacy picked up a 16-year-old (later identified as Timothy J. McCoy) near the downtown Greyhound bus station. He drove the boy back to the house on West Summerdale and after several drinks and sex fell asleep. According to Gacy's later confession, he awoke to find the boy standing near him with a butcher's knife. The pair struggled and Gacy was slightly wounded before managing to wrest the knife away from the teen and stab him to death with it. Afterwards, Gacy lowered McCoy's body through a trapdoor into the crawlspace where it would ultimately be joined by 26 others. Cleaning up in the kitchen, Gacy saw a slab of uncut bacon on a countertop and realized too late that the teen was only planning to make him breakfast, not attack him with the knife. Seven months after the murder, Gacy married Carol Hoff, a recent divorcée with two little girls, and his mother moved out of the house. Almost immediately Hoff commented on the nauseating stench rising from the crawlspace, which Gacy dismissed as "sewer problems." Marriage, however, did nothing to dull Gacy's preference for gay sex. Hoff soon found gay porno mags and semen-stained male bikini underwear hidden beneath the bed in their room. On one occasion, she witnessed Gacy pulling out of the garage late at night in the company of a blond boy. Upon closer investigation, Hoff found a crumpled semen-stained blanket on the garage floor. Finally, on Mother's Day 1975 Gacy told his wife that there would be no more sex between them.

Though devoting himself full time to PDM, Gacy also made time to solidify his position in the community by allying himself with local Democratic politicians, hosting extravagant theme parties at his home, and visiting area hospitals to entertain sick children or the elderly as "Patches" or "Pogo the Clown." Gacy, however, continued to lead a double life fuelled by a large intake of Valium washed down with Scotch. In addition to being a lucrative business, PDM also served to bring Gacy into contact with young victims. On July 31, 1975, John Butkovich, an 18-year-old PDM employee, disappeared after a quarrel with Gacy. Gacy later confessed that he had awakened in his home after a night spent drinking heavily with Butkovich to find the teen dead on the floor wearing a pair of handcuffs. The contractor buried Butkovich in the garage covering the tomb with concrete. His divorce from Hoff in 1976 gave Gacy even more time to troll for victims in Chicago's gay areas. Often passing himself off as homicide detective "Jack Hanley" (the last name of a detective he met while working as a chef at Bruno's) Gacy cruised the night in his black Oldsmobile festooned with an official looking red light and a vanity license plate marked "PDM 42."

Gacy killed at least ten times in 1976 burying all his young victims in the crawlspace beneath his home. Eight more victims had already been taken by Gacy in 1977 when, posing as an undercover cop, he ordered 19-year-old Robert Donnelly into his car in late December of that year. Gacy drove Donnelly to his house in Norwood Park where he subjected the teen to a night of rape and torture. Donnelly was released after assuring Gacy that he would not tell the police. When he did, Gacy insisted to the authorities that the sex was consensual and no charges were filed. Three months later on the

night of March 21, 1978, Jeff Rignall, a 26-year-old homosexual, accepted a ride from Gacy in the New Town section of Chicago. Gacy chloroformed Rignall who awoke back at the contractor's house naked and strapped helplessly to a homemade pillory. According to the account in his book, *29 Below*, Rignall was repeatedly raped with various objects and sodomized by Gacy and another individual he later was unable to identify. Gacy later dumped Rignall, bleeding from the rectum and damaged internally by the chloroform, in a park near where he was picked up. Rignall doggedly tracked Gacy down, but when police learned that the assault victim was a homosexual little was done to proceed against the successful contractor with political clout. Rignall filed a civil suit against Gacy who later settled out of court for $3,000 just "to make it go away."

Throughout 1978 Gacy continued to engage in high profile social activities highlighted by his serving as director of the Polish Constitution Day parade where he was photographed shaking hands with First Lady Rosalyn Carter. Unable to pack more corpses into a crawlspace already overflowing with 27 dead young men and boys, Gacy was forced to toss his last four 1978 victims off the I-55 bridge into the Des Plaines River. On December 11, 1978, Gacy broke with his usual pattern of selecting victims who would not be missed, a crucial mistake that led to his capture. That night, Gacy was at the Nisson Pharmacy in Des Plaines where Robert Piest, a 15-year-old part-time worker there, asked the contractor about the possibility of working for him. Before leaving with "a contractor," Piest told his waiting mother that he would soon return after speaking with him. When he did not, she notified the police. By the time authorities arrived at Gacy's home and took his statement in which he denied seeing the boy, the serial killer had already strangled Piest and hid his body in the attic. Later that night before talking to police at headquarters, Gacy dumped Piest's body into the Des Plaines River. After detectives found a photo receipt in Gacy's house linking him to Piest, the contractor was put under around the clock surveillance. On December 19, 1978, Gacy invited the two officers tailing him inside his house to warm up. While one detective was in Gacy's bathroom, the furnace came on forcing the putrid stench of rotting flesh up through a floor duct.

Gacy was arrested two days later, confessed to murdering 33 victims, and provided a detailed map to the location of 27 bodies in the crawlspace and two others on the West Summerdale property. The grisly excavation revealed that many of the bodies had ropes wrapped around their necks, some had underwear jammed down their throats, while others had foreign objects inserted into their anuses. Eight of the corpses found in the crawlspace would never be identified. In custody, Gacy demonstrated his murderous technique using a rosary and pen provided by detectives. After tricking the young men into putting handcuffs on, Gacy performed the "rope trick" which consisted of looping a rope around the victim's neck, inserting a hammer handle through the loop, and then turning it to tighten the noose as he ostensibly had sex with the dying victim. Gacy initially blamed the murders on his alter-ego, "Jack Hanley," but a jury refused to believe that Gacy, a man who ran a successful business, actually had 33 separate instances of insanity during which he was not responsible for the murders he committed. After deliberating for only 1 hour and 50 minutes, a jury convicted Gacy on 33 counts of murder on March 13, 1980. He subsequently received 12 death sentences for the young men he killed after Illinois reinstituted capital punishment in 1977 and life terms for the other 21.

True to form, Gacy continued to be the overachieving workaholic during the 14 years he spent on death row at the Menard Correctional Center in southern Illinois. Now vigorously protesting his innocence, Gacy maintained that several of his employees had keys to the house on West Summerdale and that forensic evidence proved he was out of town when many of the murders were committed. According to Gacy, his only crime was in being so "trusting and gullible." Gacy took his case to the people, developing a voluminous correspondence with hundreds of individuals worldwide. Many traveled to the prison nestled atop a hill overlooking the Mississippi River and spoke directly with Gacy in cramped interview rooms where the handcuffed former contractor would explain in great detail how he was actually the "34th victim." As the appeals process moved with glacial speed towards his inevitable execution, Gacy taught himself how to paint and, ever the entrepreneur, began selling self-portraits of himself as "Patches" and "Pogo the Clown" through the mail. Other favorite subjects of Gacy's oil painting included generic clown studies, death's heads, Disney characters, and birds. Shortly before his appeals ran out, Gacy opened up a 900 telephone line where for $1.99 a minute callers could hear him speak for 12 minutes about his innocence and how "the facts don't match the fantasy, and it raises the doubt who John Gacy really is…" Conjointly, he sought a publisher for his book *A Question of Doubt*, a rambling narrative in which Gacy "refuted" point-by-point the State's case against him. Amid a flurry of last minute filings by his attorneys, Gacy was helicoptered from Menard to the Stateville Correctional Center near Joliet where he was scheduled to die by lethal injection shortly after midnight on May 10, 1994. Following a last meal of Kentucky Fried Chicken, butterfly shrimp, fresh strawberries, and Diet Coke, Gacy and Nic Howell, a spokesman for the Illinois department of corrections, took a stroll around the prison courtyard each puffing a cigar. Afterwards, Gacy was strapped onto a gurney and wheeled into the execution chamber where he calmly told prison officials and witnesses that his execution was unjust and amounted to his murder. Due to a problem with the chemicals, Gacy's execution took 18 minutes rather than the expected 10. William Kunkle, a witness at the execution and the attorney who prosecuted the serial killer, spoke for many when he said, "He got a much easier death than any of his victims."

188. Cahill, Tim, and Ewing, Russ. *Buried Dreams: Inside the Mind of a Serial Killer*. New York: Bantam, 1986. x, 372 pp.; 24 cm.

_____. [Same as 188.] Bantam paperback ed. New York: Bantam, 1987. ix, 353 pp.; 18 cm.; paperback.

_____. [Same as 188.] London: Fourth Estate, 1993. ix, 353 pp.; 20 cm.

A collaboration between journalist Cahill and Ewing, a reporter for WLS in Chicago, which is probably the most widely read book on the Gacy case. Based

in part on over 100 hours of interviews with Gacy (which he vehemently denied ever giving), the book cites instances in which the condemned killer "became" his murderous alter-ego, "Jack Hanley," during their discussions at Menard Correctional Center.

189. Gacy, John Wayne. *More Letters to Mr. Gacy*. Baton Rouge, La.: MYCO Associates, 1992. 1 v. (unpaged): ill.; 28 cm.

Gacy's first book of letters (see 191) sold so well that he compiled another collection. More of the same in which he condemns the press for portraying him a "media monster" and maintains that he is an innocent victim.

190. _____. *A Question of Doubt: A Commentary on the Arrest and Trial of John Wayne Gacy*. 1st ed. Hannibal, Mo.: MYCO, 1993. 323 pp.: ill.; 29 cm.

According to James Turanto, the literary and artistic executor of Gacy's estate, this independently produced and pirated edition was limited to 500 hardbound copies published shortly before Gacy's execution and without the killer's permission. Turanto suggests that the print run may not have been as extensive as the publisher stated.

191. _____. *They Call Him Mr. Gacy: Selected Correspondence of John Wayne Gacy*. Compiled by C. Ivor McClelland. Brighton, Col.: McClelland Associates, 1989. 1 v. (unpaged): ill.; 29 cm.; paperback.

_____. [Same as 191.] Hannibal, Mo.: MYCO Associates, 1989. 1 v. (unpaged): ill.; 28 cm.

Reproduces Gacy's letters in response to individuals and institutions requesting information about him. The serial killer conducted a voluminous correspondence with people all over the world and his letters, in general, have one theme: his innocence. The book's success prompted Gacy to release another collection of letters (see 189).

192. _____. *The 34th Victim*. Los Angeles: Princeton Publications West, 1995(?).

(issued with an audiotape of Gacy discussing his case); paperback.

Unpublished as this book went to press, Gacy's volume is essentially the same as *A Question of Doubt* (see 190) with added material covering the motions and appeals in the case. According to James Turanto, Gacy's literary executor who is responsible for its publication, the book is an authorized edition which will also contain numerous previously unpublished examples of Gacy's art work. Destined to be highly collectable.

193. Kozenczak, Joseph, and Henrikson, Karen. *A Passing Acquaintance.* New York: Carlton, 1992. 192 pp.: ill.; 21 cm. ("A Hearthstone book.")

Lt. Kozenczak was the commander of the criminal investigation department of the Des Plaines police department who led the inquiry into the disappearance of Robert Piest.

194. Linedecker, Clifford L. *The Man Who Killed Boys.* New York: St. Martin's Press, 1980. 250 pp., [6] leaves of plates: ill.; 22 cm.

_____. [Same as 194.] New York: St. Martin's Press, 1980. 250 pp., [4] leaves of plates: ill.; 17 cm.; paperback.

_____. [Same as 194.] New York: St. Martin's Paperbacks, 1986. 250 pp., [8]pp. of plates: ill.; 18 cm.; paperback.

Early account marred by Linedecker's inability (due to a court order) to interview law enforcement officials connected with the case. As such, the book is a rehash of newspaper articles.

195. Rignall, Jeff. *29 Below: An Encounter with John Wayne Gacy.* Chicago: Wellington Press, 1979. 257 pp.; 22 cm.

Rignall's firsthand account of his abduction and torture at the hands of Gacy makes for fascinating reading. A self-professed homosexual, Rignall's claims were dismissed by police who seemingly never bothered to check Gacy's past sodomy conviction in Iowa.

196. Sullivan, Terry, and Maiken, Peter T. *Killer Clown.* New York: Grosset & Dunlap, 1983. 345 pp., [8]pp. of plates: ill.; 24 cm.

_____. [Same as 196.] New York: Pinnacle Books, 1984. 375 pp.; 18 cm.; paperback.

_____. [Same as 196 with added subtitle: *The John Wayne Gacy Murders.*] New York: Pinnacle, 1991. 375 pp.; 18 cm.; paperback

Sullivan was the State's attorney who directed Gacy's prosecution.

Gallego, Gerald Armand (a.k.a. "Stephen Feil," "Stephen Styles")

Born July 17, 1946, in Sacramento, California. Bartender, truck driver. California, Oregon, Nevada; 10 murders; .25 caliber revolver, bludgeon, manual strangulation; September 1978–November 1980.

"I can honestly tell you—and I'm not bragging—if I had a problem with girls, it's not because I didn't have enough. It is because I had too many."—Excerpt from Gallego's closing statement in his trial for the murders of Mary Beth Sowers and Craig Miller

A husband and wife serial killer team who kidnapped, raped, and murdered throughout three states in order to find young girls to fulfill a sadistic sex slave fantasy. The son of an executed murderer, Gerald Gallego had already notched 23 arrests and served time for motel robbery before marrying his fifth wife Charlene Williams in September 1978. Two weeks prior to the ceremony in Reno, Nevada, Gallego had convinced Williams to help him realize his fantasy of finding the perfect sexual partner. On September 11, 1978, Williams lured teenagers Kippi Vaught, 16, and Rhonda Scheffler, 17, out of a mall in Sacramento, California, to the parking lot where Gallego waited in his van. Gallego intimidated the pair with a .25 caliber revolver, bound them, and drove to a rural area in nearby Baxter, California. After raping the teenagers, Gallego shot them both execution-style in the back of the head. Their bodies were found two days later. The Gallegos next struck at the Washoe County Fair in Reno, Nevada, on June 24, 1979. Using a similar ploy, Williams convinced Brenda Judd, 14, and her friend Sandra Colley, 13, to accompany her to the van. Gallego raped the pair as Williams drove to a desert outside Lovelock, Nevada. Although their bodies have never been recovered, Williams later testified that Gallego used a hammer or shovel to beat the girls to death. Seventeen-year-old Stacy Ann Redican and Karen Chipman Twiggs met a similar fate on April 24, 1980. Williams picked them up in a Sacramento mall and their bodies were found three months later in Limerick Canyon near Lovelock, Nevada. Both had been killed with a hammer. With victim number seven, Linda Aquilar, the Gallegos changed their usual pattern of abduction. On June 27, 1980, the pair picked up the 21-year-old pregnant mother of a two-year-old son as she hitchhiked near Gold Beach, Oregon. They drove her to a secluded stretch of beach near the town where Gallego bludgeoned her into unconsciousness with a rock before burying her alive in the sand where she suffocated. Aquilar's body was found 12 days later. On July 16, 1980, 34-year-old cocktail waitress Virginia Mochel was abducted from the parking lot of the bar where she worked in West Sacramento, California. Gallego, posing as "Stephen Feil," had spent the night drinking at the bar with Wil-

liams. Mochel's body, her feet and hands bound by fishing line, was eventually found by fisherman near Freeport, California, on October 2, 1980. Death was attributed to manual strangulation.

On November 2, 1980, the Gallegos abducted 22-year-old Craig Miller and his date Mary Beth Sowers, 21, at gunpoint as they left a fraternity dance in Sacramento. The abduction was observed by a friend of Miller's who noted the license plate. Gallego, now driving a car registered to Williams, drove to a secluded area 15 miles east of Placerville where he shot Miller in the back of the head and dumped his body near Bass Lake. With Williams in tow, Gallego returned to their apartment and repeatedly raped Sowers before driving her to a horse pasture in Placer County where he executed her in the fashion of Miller. Both bodies were ultimately recovered. Police traced the license plate to Williams and learned of Gallego's long criminal history. Bullets taken from the bodies of Miller and Sowers proved to be from the same gun Gallego once fired into the ceiling of a North Sacramento bar he tended to wake up sleeping patrons. On November 17, 1980, the fugitive Gallegos were captured by FBI agents in Omaha, Nebraska as they tried to pick up money in a Western Union office wired to them by Williams' parents.

In mid–1981 Charlene Williams cut a deal with authorities in which she agreed to testify against Gallego in exchange for being allowed to plead guilty to second degree murder in the killings of Redican and Twiggs. Under the terms of the plea bargain, Williams would serve a maximum prison sentence of 16 years and 8 months making her eligible for release in August 1997.

As Gallego had never bothered to obtain a divorce from an earlier wife, he was not legally married to Williams and she was free to testify against him. Gallego acted as his own attorney in the Sowers-Miller trial in Martinez, California, which lasted from November 1982 through April 1983. Based largely on Williams' testimony and the forensic evidence against him, Gallego was found guilty and sentenced on May 24, 1983, to die in the gas chamber at San Quentin. As it appeared unlikely that the convicted killer would ever be executed in California, the State of Nevada successfully extradited Gallego in January 1984 to face charges of murdering Redican and Twiggs. Nevadans donated an unprecedented $25,000 to defray the cost of his prosecution. After a five week trial, Gallego was found guilty on June 7, 1984, and sentenced five days later to die by lethal injection. As of this printing he is still awaiting execution.

197. Biondi, Ray, and Hecox, Walt. *All His Father's Sins: Inside the Gerald Gallego Sex-Slave Murders.* Edited by Bruce B. Henderson. Rocklin, Calif.: Prima Publishing and Communications, 1988. 197 pp., [8]pp. of plates: ill.; 23 cm.

_____. [Same as 197 with variant subtitle: *The Shocking Truth About California's Most Gruesome Serial Killer.*] Edited by Bruce B. Henderson. New York: Pocket Books, 1990. 221 pp.: ill.; 18 cm.; paperback.

Biondi, head of the homicide unit of the Sacramento County sheriff's department, focuses on the police investigation leading to the arrest of the Gallegos.

198. Van Hoffmann, Eric. *A Venom in the Blood.* New York: Donald I. Fine, 1990. xxii, 322 pp.: ill., map; 24 cm.

_____. [Same as 198.] New York: Kensington, 1991. 338 pp.: map; 18 cm. ("Zebra Books"); paperback.

_____. [Same as 198.] London: Futura, 1992. xii, 322 pp., [8]pp. of plates: ill., facsims., 1 map, ports.; 18 cm.; paperback.

A former police officer's overwritten account of the case which is marred by extensively "recreated" dialogue.

Gardiner, William George Last

(acquitted; a.k.a. "The Peasenhall Mystery," "Holy Willie")

Born December 22, 1866, in Bulcamp, England. Died 1941. Foreman carpenter. Peasenhall, Suffolk, England; 1 murder (acquitted); knife; May 31 or June 1, 1902.

Pious churchgoer and devoted father of six twice tried and acquitted of murdering his suspected paramour in what is known in the annals of British crime as "The Peasenhall Mystery." Known as "Holy Willie" in Peasenhall, an isolated village in Suffolk, Gardiner was a choirmaster and elder of the Primitive Methodist Connexion in nearby Sibton. On May 11, 1901, Gardiner was called before representatives of the Sibton Chapel to answer charges of impropriety leveled at him by two teenagers who claimed that on May 1 they overheard him discussing in personal detail a sexual passage in Genesis with Rose Anne Harsent, a flirtatious 23-year-old choir member and live-in servant at Providence House, the home of a Baptist deacon and his wife situated some 200 yards from Gardiner's home. Gardiner vehemently denied the charge and though not sanctioned by the church agreed never again to place himself in a position with Harsent that could be similarly misinterpreted. However, like Harold Greenwood, Gardiner became the object of vicious local gossip and was thereafter romantically linked with Harsent in the minds of many of the villagers.

On the morning of June 1, 1902, following a thunderstorm Rose Harsent's body was found in Providence House lying on the kitchen floor in a pool of blood with a trail leading up to her room. Harsent's throat had been slashed ear to ear and attempts made to burn her nightdress from a nearby paraffin lamp had resulted in the charring of the flesh on her thighs and buttocks. Remarkably, authorities initially considered the case a suicide until finding an unsigned note postmarked May 31st in which a secret meeting had been set with Harsent for midnight. Suspicion settled on Gardiner after a broken medicine bottle labeled for his children was found near the woman's body as was a copy of the *East Anglian Daily Times* which Harsent's brother insisted he had earlier delivered to Gardiner. The discovery that Harsent was six months pregnant at the time of her death solidified public opinion against the 34-year-old master carpenter.

Arrested on June 3, 1902, Gardiner was tried in Ipswich the following November. Gardiner denied writing the note of assignation found in Harsent's room and his alibi for the evening of the murder was supported by his wife. Mrs. Gardiner testified that she gave Harsent the medicine bottle bearing her children's prescription after the servant complained of having a cold. Gardiner's counsel suggested (not too convincingly) that Harsent's fatal injury could have been sustained by her having fallen down the darkened stairs and severing her windpipe on the broken glass of the lamp. When the jury failed to agree on a verdict (11 for conviction, 1 for acquittal) Gardiner was retried at the Suffolk Assizes in Ips-

wich in January 1903. On January 24, 1903, a jury again failed to reach a verdict (11 for acquittal, 1 for conviction). Prospects for a third trial were quashed on January 29, 1903, after the director of public prosecutions lodged a *nolle prosequi*, the rough equivalent of the Scottish "not proven" verdict which allows for another proceeding if new evidence arises. Gardiner was subsequently freed and, with his wife, opened a general store in Norwood. He died in 1941.

199. Fido, Martin, and Skinner, Keith. *The Peasenhall Murder.* Stroud: Sutton, 1990. xiii, 202 pp., [16]pp. of plates: ill., facsims., ports., 1 map; 24 cm.

_____. [Same as 199.] Wolfeboro Falls, N.H.: A. Sutton, 1991. xiii, 202 pp., [16]pp. of plates: ill.; 24 cm.

"Ripperologists" Fido and Skinner's collaboration stands as the definitive account of the Peasenhall mystery. A meticulously researched investigation, the authors conclude that "Gardiner's innocence is incontrovertible" and that the case is insoluble. Appendices include a time-chart of the events of May 31–June 1 compiled by Stewart P. Evans. Includes bibliography and index.

200. Henderson, William, ed. *Trial of William Gardiner (The Peasenhall Case).* Notable British Trials. London; Edinburgh: W. Hodge, 1934. x, 332 pp., [4] leaves of plates: ill., port.; 22 cm.

_____. (Same as 200.) Notable British Trials. Toronto: Canada Law Book, 1934. 332 pp.: ill., front., ports., facsim.; 22 cm.

Transcript of Gardiner's second trial at the Suffolk Assizes, Ipswich, January 1903 for the murder of Rose Harsent. The first trial, resulting in a disagreement of the jury, was held in November 1902. Includes a chronology of dates in the Peasenhall case.

201. Packer, Edwin. *The Peasenhall Murder.* Yoxford: Yoxford Publications, 1980.

54 pp.: ill., 1 map, 2 ports.; 22 cm.; paperback.

202. Rowland, John. *The Peasenhall Mystery.* London: J. Long, 1962. 174 pp.: front.; 22 cm.

Rowland, reconstructing the case from its coverage in the *East Anglian Daily Times* and courtroom records, concludes that Gardiner murdered Harsent during an argument over their unborn child. Includes bibliography and index.

Garrow, Robert F.

Born circa 1937. Died September 11, 1978. New York; 4 murders; knife, bludgeon; July 1973.

Television: "Sworn to Silence" (1987), a two-hour, made-for-television movie based on Alibrandi and Armani's book *Privileged Information*, originally aired on ABC on April 6, 1987. Cast includes Peter Coyote (Sam Fischetti), Dabney Coleman (Marty Costigan), and Liam Neeson (Vincent Cauley).

Serial rapist and murderer gunned down in 1978 during a prison break in New York State. The son of physically abusive alcoholics, Garrow began having sex with animals when he was 11, and had already served eight years in prison for rape when he committed his first known murder on July 11, 1973. Sixteen-year-old high school student Alicia Hauck was walking home from school in Syracuse, New York, when Garrow picked her up. He raped Hauck in a nearby cemetery, stabbed her to death with a knife, and hid her body beneath some underbrush near a maintenance shed. Nine days later on July 20, 1973, Garrow tortured then murdered 21-year-old Daniel Porter with a knife, leaving his body tied to a tree in a woods near Weverton, New York. He abducted the man's camping

companion, Susan Petz, and repeatedly raped her for three days before stabbing and bludgeoning her to death then jamming her body down a mineshaft in Mineville, New York. On July 29, 1973, Garrow, 36, confronted four campers in the Adirondacks State Park. At gunpoint, he tied the three males to trees out of sight of one another and was preparing to rape their female friend when two of the men managed to work free. When they returned to the scene they found Philip Domblewski, 18, dead from knife wounds. After an 11 day search through rugged mountain terrain, Garrow was severely wounded during a capture by authorities near his sister's home in Witherbee, New York, on August 9, 1973. Awaiting trial for Domblewski's murder in Lake Pleasant, New York, Garrow told his attorneys of the whereabouts of Hauck and Petz so that they could essentially use the girls as chips in a plea bargain agreement. The attorneys visited the locations, photographed the bodies, and bound by the rule of attorney-client privilege were legally unable to divulge the information to authorities. Garrow's attorneys were severely criticized when the information became known although both were later absolved of any criminal or professional wrongdoing by a grand jury and the American Bar Association. The issue became moot, however, after the women's bodies were found in December 1973, months before the start of Garrow's trial in June 1974. Garrow's insanity plea failed and he was convicted of first degree murder on June 27, 1974. He was subsequently sentenced to 25 years to life. In March 1975 Garrow's official body count rose to four when he pleaded guilty to the murders of Hauck, Porter, and Petz under an agreement which provided for the dropping of all other charges. On September 8, 1978, Garrow escaped from the Fishkill Correctional Facility in southeast New York armed with a .32 caliber Gaztanaga Destroyer pistol smuggled into the prison by his son in a bucket of fried chicken. For three days the convicted killer eluded capture by lying in the dense underbrush some 500 yards from the prison fence until he was shot to death on September 11, 1978, after wounding an officer. Garrow was later buried in the Syracuse cemetery where he hid Alicia Hauck's body.

203. Alibrandi, Tom, and Armani, Frank H. *Privileged Information.* New York: Dodd, Mead, 1984. 215 pp.; 25 cm.

_____. [Same as 203.] New York: HarperPaperbacks, 1991. xii, 318 pp., [8]pp. of plates: ill., map; 18 cm.; paperback.

Vivid account cowritten by Frank H. Armani, an attorney for Garrow who was roundly criticized for refusing to violate his client's confidence by revealing the location of two of his murder victims.

204. New York (State). Dept. of Correctional Services. *The Escape of Robert F. Garrow.* Albany: State of New York, Department of Correctional Services, 1978. 48 leaves; 28 cm.

Gates, Wyley
(*acquitted;* a.k.a. "Coyote," "The Computer Whiz Kid")

Born circa 1966 in Craryville, New York. High school student. Canaan, New York; 4 murders (acquitted); Walther PPK .380 semi-automatic pistol; December 13, 1986.

"I did it for no big emotional reason."—Statement attributed to Gates by a Columbia County sheriff's deputy

Unusual case in which a brilliant high school student confessed to murdering four family members, but was convicted only on a conspiracy charge. Despite being a member of the National Honor Society and student government vice president, 17-year-old Wyley Gates was ridiculed by his father and older brother because he was more interested in computers than cars and sports. According to the prosecution, Gates and his 16-year-old friend and classmate Damian Rossney plotted their murder (code named "Infierno," the Spanish word for hell) as part of an elaborate fantasy computer game. On December 13, 1986, Gates allegedly shot his father, the woman who lived with him, his brother, and a three-year-old cousin in their log cabin home in Canaan, New York. Afterwards, Gates left the gun with Rossney and the pair attended a showing of the Clint Eastwood movie *Heartbreak Ridge.* Arrested the next day, Gates admitted the crime but authorities failed to record the confession which was obtained in the absence of the teenager's attorney even though he was present at police headquarters. Rossney was subsequently arrested and charged with hindering prosecution. Gates pleaded not guilty and amid conflicting psychiatric testimony maintained that he had confessed to the murders out of a psychotic loyalty to protect his friend. Following 42 hours of deliberation spread over six days, Gates was acquitted of the killings on October 6, 1987, but found guilty of second degree conspiracy to commit the murders. Jurors, troubled by the lack of a taped confession, had simply not considered it in their deliberations. Nevertheless, in December 1989 an upstate appeals court refused to suppress the confession despite the irregularities that originally led local jurors to disregard it. On November 9, 1987, Gates received the maximum sentence of 8⅓ to 25 years in prison. He has since continued his education at Elmira Correctional Facility taking college level courses in technical mathematics and life science administered by Corning Community College. Gates' acquittal weakened the case against Rossney who was tried only for the murders of the father and son. Rossney was acquitted on December 7, 1988, but like Gates, was found guilty of conspiracy and given the same maximum sentence. As of this writing, no other suspects have been charged in the four murders.

205. Gelb, Alan. *Most Likely to Succeed: Multiple Murder and the Elusive Search for Justice in an American Town.* New York: Dutton, 1990. 415 pp., [16]pp. of plates: ill.; 24 cm.

_____. [Same as 205.] New York: St. Martin's Paperbacks, 1991. 415 pp., [8]pp. of plates: ill.; 18 cm.; paperback.

Gelb, a novelist and neighbor of the Gates family, examines the case and its legal ramifications.

Gein, Edward Theodore
(a.k.a. "The Mad Butcher of Plainfield," "The Plainfield Head Collector," "The Shy Ghoul," "Ghastly Gein")

Born August 27, 1906, in La Crosse, Wisconsin. Died July 26, 1984. Handyman. Plainfield, Wisconsin; 2 murders (1 conviction, strongly suspected of at least 5 others); .32 caliber pistol, .22 caliber rifle; December 1954–November 1957.

Films: While no film has been made specifically on Gein (*Deranged* comes closest), the following have been suggested or inspired by the case: *Psy-*

cho (US, 1960), a Universal Pictures production based on Robert Bloch's book of the same title, directed by Alfred Hitchcock. Cast includes Anthony Perkins (Norman Bates), Janet Leigh (Marion Crane), John Gavin (Sam Loomis), Vera Miles (Lila Crane) and Martin Balsam (Milton Arbogast). *Psycho II* (US, 1983), a Universal Pictures production from an idea by Robert Bloch, directed by Richard Franklin. Cast include Anthony Perkins (Norman Bates), Vera Miles (Lila Loomis), and Meg Tilly (Mary). *Psycho III* (US, 1986), a Universal Pictures production directed by Anthony Perkins. Cast includes Anthony Perkins (Norman Bates), Diana Scarwid (Maureen), and Jeff Fahey (Duane Duke). Also: *Deranged* (US, 1974), an American International Pictures production directed by Jeff Gillen and Alan Ormsby. Cast include Roberts Blossom (Ezra Cobb), Cosette Lee (Ma Cobb), and Leslie Carlson (Narrator). *The Texas Chainsaw Massacre* (US, 1974), a Vortex-Henkel-Hooper production directed by Tobe Hooper. Cast includes Marilyn Burns (Sally), Allen Danziger (Jerry), Paul A. Partain (Franklin), and Gunnar Hansen (Leatherface). *The Texas Chainsaw Massacre 2* (US, 1986), a Cannon Films, Inc. production directed by Tobe Hooper. Cast includes Dennis Hopper (Lt. "Lefty" Enright, Texas Ranger), Caroline Williams (Vanita "Stretch" Brock), and Bill Johnson (Leatherface). *Leatherface: The Texas Chainsaw Massacre III* (US, 1990), a New Line Cinema/Nicholas Entertainment production directed by Jeff Burr. Cast includes Ken Foree (Benny), Kate Hodge (Michelle), and R.A. Mihailoff (Leatherface). *The Silence of the Lambs* (US, 1991), an Orion Pictures release of a Strong Heart/Demme production based on Thomas Harris' book of the same title, directed by Jonathan Demme. Cast includes Jodie Foster (Clarice Starling), Anthony Hopkins (Dr. Hannibal Lecter), Scott Glenn (Jack Crawford), and Ted Levine (Jame Gumb/Buffalo Bill).

Television: "Psycho IV: The Beginning" (1990), a 96-minute, made-for-cable television movie, originally aired on Showtime on November 10, 1990. Cast includes Janet Leigh (Host), Anthony Perkins (Norman Bates as an adult), and Henry Thomas (Norman Bates as a child).

"When I made these masks, you see, I stuffed them all out with paper so they would dry. On the vagina I did, you know, sprinkle a little salt." —From Gein's confession

Diminutive, soft spoken Wisconsin killer-cannibal whose monstrous acts inspired the 1960 Alfred Hitchcock film *Psycho* and the seemingly endless series of *Texas Chainsaw Massacre* movies. Long before the mind-numbing evidence of dismemberment, necrophilia, cannibalism, and body part "trophies" were found in the Milwaukee apartment of his fellow Wisconsinite Jeffrey Dahmer, Ed Gein (pronounced "Geen"), in a lonely farmhouse six miles west of Plainfield, Wisconsin, was establishing himself as the yardstick by which mental aberration is measured. The product of a textbook dysfunctional family, Gein and his older brother, Henry, were physically and verbally abused by an alcoholic father and dominated by a fanatically religious mother, Augusta, who taught them that sex was an evil and contaminating influence which should be avoided. Moving in 1914 from La Crosse to a remote 195-acre farm near Plainfield, the Gein family quickly established themselves as the oddest in

the area. While Augusta refused to associate with the neighbors, her out-of-work husband remained in a near constant state of alcoholic stupor. At school, classmates taunted Gein for his effeminate manner and the shy 16 year old dropped out of school after graduating from the eighth grade. The death of his father in April 1940 followed by the inexplicable loss of his brother while fighting a marsh fire near their home in May 1944 left the budding psychopath alone with his beloved mother. Her death in late December 1945 at the age of 67 accelerated Gein's freefall into total madness. He carefully cleaned the dead woman's room, folded her clothes, then boarded up the room as a permanent shrine to her memory.

Alone in the dilapidated farmhouse, Gein spent his days working as a handyman around Plainfield where he was considered by most of its residents as little more than an eccentric, but harmless, village idiot. Shy and soft-spoken, Gein related better to children than adults, often entertaining them for hours with stories of head-hunters and cannibals culled from his dog-eared collection of true crime magazines. On a few occasions, Gein invited some children into his trash-strewn house to view his treasured collection of shrunken heads. The heads, he told them, were from the South Seas sent to him by a cousin who fought in the Philippines during World War II. On December 8, 1954, Mary Hogan, 51, disappeared from her tavern in Pine Grove, Wisconsin seven miles from Plainfield. A spent .32 shell casing was found on the floor near a pool of blood. A thin blood trail leading across the floor and out into the parking lot suggested that Hogan's attacker had loaded her into a vehicle. History seemingly repeated itself three years later when 58-year-old Bernice Worden disappeared from her hardware store in downtown Plainfield on November 16, 1957. Blood found on the floor trailed out to the parking lot where it abruptly ended. The discovery at the scene of a handwritten receipt for antifreeze focused immediate suspicion on Gein who had inquired about its cost the day before. In darkness, authorities drove out to Gein's farmhouse to search the premises by flashlight. Moments after arriving, Bernice Worden's headless body was founded suspended by the ankles from the rafters of a summer kitchen attached to the rear of the house. The woman's body had been dressed out like a deer's, gutted, and the genitals removed. The gruesome discovery was only a prelude to even greater horror. Inside the cluttered house, searchers found a soup bowl made from the sawed off top of a human skull. Two other skulls were perched atop the posts of the handyman's filthy, unmade bed. A shoebox contained nine vulvas, one quite fresh, while another box was filled with four noses. A belt fashioned out of female nipples laid near chairs upholstered in human skin. Several searchers vomited when they realized that the "masks" they found in Gein's bedroom had literally been peeled off the skulls of nine women. A face with hair still attached recovered from a paper bag was identified as the missing Mary Hogan. Even this paled, however, with the discovery of Gein's "skin wardrobe." One item, a vest fashioned from the upper torso of a middle-aged woman, still had breasts and genitals attached. The sexually confused Gein later admitted that he sometimes wore the mammary vest and danced in the moonlight. Worden's heart was found in a plastic bag near a pot-bellied stove,

her warm entrails wrapped in a newspaper, her head in a burlap bag sandwiched between two stained mattresses. Nails driven through the ears and picture wire strung between them would permit the head to be wall-mounted. In all, parts from 15 women were found in the house.

In custody, the 51-year-old confessed in Madison, Wisconsin, to the murders of Hogan and Worden explaining that he had collected the other body parts found in the farmhouse in a string of over 40 grave robberies committed from 1947 through 1954. To confirm Gein's seemingly outlandish story, authorities decided to open the grave of 52-year-old Eleanor Adams who had died six years before and was buried in Plainfield Cemetery next to Gein's mother. The exhumation on November 23, 1957, revealed that Adams' corpse had been stolen from her coffin. In its place, diggers found a 12-inch crowbar. Moving to the nearby grave of 69-year-old Mabel Everson (dead since April 1951), investigators found it too had been violated. Bones found outside the casket confirmed Gein's story that he had excised certain parts of the woman's body and taken them back with him to the farmhouse. Gein, whose own ambiguous sexuality compelled him to wear the external sex organs of women, insisted that he never engaged in sex with the corpses ("they smelled too bad") preferring to masturbate instead. He also denied eating the women's flesh, a claim difficult to accept in light of his other well documented perversions. Declared by psychiatrists to be a schizophrenic who had been living in "his own little world" since the death of his mother 12 years before, Gein was declared mentally ill at a hearing in Wisconsin Rapids on January 6, 1958. He was committed to an indeterminate period at the Central State Hospital for the Criminally Insane in Waupun. On March 20, 1958, ten days before a scheduled auction of his meager possessions, Gein's farmhouse was burned to the ground by unidentified arsonists. The auction, attended by 2,000 people, proceeded on schedule at Gein's farm with a sideshow exhibitor from Rockford, Illinois, paying the top price of $760 for the handyman's 1949 maroon Ford which he used to transport Worden's body. The entrepreneur later exhibited "Ed Gein's Crime Car" in carnivals throughout the Midwest charging patrons a quarter a look.

A decade after Gein used a .22 caliber rifle to kill Bernice Worden, psychiatrists pronounced the mental patient competent to stand trial for her murder. Tried before Circuit Judge Robert Gollmar, Gein was found guilty of first degree murder on November 14, 1968. In a penalty phase of the trial conducted hours later, he was declared not guilty by reason of insanity and recommitted to Central State Hospital. In February 1974 Gein filed a petition with the Waushara County clerk of courts claiming that he had fully recovered his mental health and should not be hospitalized. Gein's petition was rejected on June 27, 1964. The quiet little man who later served as the film inspiration for "Norman Bates" in *Psycho* and "Buffalo Bill" in *The Silence of the Lambs* died of respiratory failure on July 26, 1984, in the geriatric ward of the Mendota Mental Health Institute in Madison at the age of 78. Fittingly, Gein was later secretly buried in an unmarked plot in Plainfield Cemetery next to his mother.

206. Bloch, Robert. *Psycho*. New York: Simon and Schuster, 1959. 185 pp.; 18 cm.

("An Inner Sanctum Mystery"); paperback. (Various eds.)

207. _____. *Psycho II*. Binghamton, N.Y.: Whispers, 1982. 317 pp.; 18 cm.; paperback. (Various eds.)

208. _____. *Psycho House*. 1st ed. New York: T. Doherty Associates, 1990. 217 pp.; 22 cm. ("A Tor book.")

209. Gollmar, Robert H. *Edward Gein, America's Most Bizarre Murderer*. Delavan, Wis.: C. Hallberg, 1981. 236 pp.: ill.; 24 cm.

_____. [Same as 209 minus subtitle.] New York: Pinnacle Books, 1984. xxi, 226 pp., [8]pp. of plates: ill.; 18 cm. (Note: also 1984 and 1990 printings); paperback.

Gollmar, the presiding judge at Gein's 1968 murder trial, bases his account on the transcript of those proceedings, trial notes, official medical reports, conferences with trial counsel and police officers involved in the case, and a personal visit with the killer at Central State Hospital. Both the foreword and an appendix on "Gein Humor" are by George Arndt, M.D., a fellow of the American Psychiatric Association. Contains graphic photos of Bernice Worden's body dressed out like a deer's.

210. Schechter, Harold. *Deviant: The Shocking True Story of the Original "Psycho."* New York: Pocket Books, 1989. xi, 274 pp., [8]pp. of plates: ill.; 18 cm.; paperback.

_____. [Same as 210.] London: New English Library, 1989. xi, 274 pp.; 18 cm.; paperback.

_____. [Same as 210.] London: Coronet, 1993. xi, 274 pp.; 18 cm.; paperback.

A readable and accurate paperback original on one of America's most fascinating serial killers. From the cover: "His crimes went beyond your very worst dreams."

211. Woods, Paul Anthony. *Ed Gein—Psycho!* London: Annihilation Press, 1992. [112]pp.: ill.; 21 cm.; paperback.

"Genesee River Killings" *see*
Shawcross, Arthur John

Gillette, Chester Ellsworth
(a.k.a. "Carl Grahm," "Charles
George," "Charles Gordon")

Born August 9, 1883, in Wickes,
Montana. Executed March 30, 1907.
Stock clerk. Herkimer County, New
York; 1 murder; bludgeon (oar or ten-
nis racquet), drowning; July 11, 1906.

Films: An American Tragedy (US,
1931), a Paramount production directed
by Josef von Sternberg. Cast includes
Phillips Holmes (Clyde Griffiths),
Sylvia Sidney (Roberta Alden), and
Frances Dee (Sondra Finchley). *A Place
in the Sun* (US, 1951), a Paramount pro-
duction directed by George Stevens.
Cast includes Montgomery Clift
(George Eastman), Elizabeth Taylor
(Angela Vickers), and Shelly Winters
(Alice Tripp).

Video: Murder on Big Moose? (US,
1988), a one-hour video produced by
Bob Payton. Describes the Gillette
murder case, the inspiration for Theodore Dreiser's novel *An American Tragedy*. The authors of *Adirondack Tragedy*
(Joseph W. Brownell) and *Murder in
the Adirondacks* (Craig Brandon) provide commentary on the case and on
the ensuing literary and dramatic interpretations of it.

Handsome 25-year-old social
climber whose murder of his pregnant
mistress in 1906 formed the basis for
Theodore Dreiser's novel *An American
Tragedy* and the film *A Place in the Sun.*
Chester Gillette, the son of Salvation
Army officers, spent his early life traveling in the Northwest with his parents
as they preached in the slum districts
of cities like Spokane, Washington. As
a teenager, the likable Gillette went to

boarding school and later to a prep
school in Ohio connected with Ober-
lin College. An average student, he
quit in June 1903 without graduating.
In April 1905 Gillette moved to Cortland, New York, to work for a wealthy
uncle at the Gillette Skirt Company.
With promises from his uncle that he
could rise in the company through hard
work, Gillette was given a lowly stock
room clerk's job paying $10 a week. By
the early summer of 1905 Gillette
had won the affections of 18-year-old
Grace "Billie" Brown, a $6 a week in-
spector at the company. To protect
both their reputations and jobs, the
pair kept their relationship secret
although it became the source of much
gossip among Brown's coworkers. By
fall 1905, Gillette was making love to
Brown twice a week in the parlor of
her roominghouse after the landlady
had gone to bed. Being the nephew of
a socially prominent man, Gillette had
the opportunity to move in the upper
levels of Cortland society. During the
time Gillette was surreptitiously having sex with Brown, he met Harriet
Benedict, the 18-year-old daughter of
a prominent local attorney. While the
two never became lovers, to Gillette
the beautiful young woman and the
others like her that he dated represented the exalted social class he hoped
to one day attain.

In the spring of 1906 Billie Brown
shattered Gillette's rosy dream of
entering high society by announcing
that she was pregnant with his child.
To hide her condition, she left the factory and lived with her parents in
South Otselic, New York, where she
anxiously awaited word from her lover
that he would marry her. Certain that
he would be disowned by his uncle and
ostracized by his upper class friends
should he marry the factory girl,

Gillette bought time with infrequent, but placating letters to Brown. She replied in a series of pleading and pathetic letters to Gillette which were later read with great effect at his trial. In July 1906, Gillette arranged to have Brown meet him in a motel in Utica, New York. After spending the night together, the pair moved on at Gillette's suggestion to find a hotel near a lake that rented small boats. Arriving at the Glenmore Hotel on Big Moose Lake in the Adirondacks on July 11, 1906, Gillette signed for a room using the alias "Carl Grahm." Amazingly, he checked Brown in under her real name. Without stopping to dispose of their luggage, Gillette signed for a 17-foot canoe at a boathouse again using his alias and Brown's real name. According to the various official versions, Gillette then paddled Brown to a secluded area of the lake where he either struck her in the head with an oar or his tennis racket. The canoe capsized and Brown, who could not swim, drowned. Later that day, Gillette was observed walking in the woods with a suitcase toward Eagle Bay six miles from the scene of the crime. Brown's submerged body, a gash across her face, was found the next day near the capsized canoe. Gillette was subsequently arrested on July 14, 1906, at the Arrowhead Hotel in Inlet Bay, New York.

Opening arguments in Gillette's trial were heard in the Herkimer County Courthouse on November 17, 1906. Financially abandoned by the Cortland Gillettes, the accused killer had been forced to sell copies of his photos to the press at $10 each in order to buy a new suit for the trial. Pleading not guilty, Gillette testified that Brown committed suicide by jumping out of the canoe after he informed her of his intention to tell her father of the

pregnancy. In this scenario, Gillette was not a murderer but merely what his attorney called a "moral coward." Gillette was quickly found guilty of first degree murder on December 4, 1906, and sentenced to death. His mother, who had accepted a deal with the *New York Journal* to report on the trial in exchange for her travel fare to Herkimer, now campaigned to raise money for her son's appeal. The elderly woman put together a lecture program entitled "Chester Gillette—Guilty or Not Guilty—A Mother's Plea for Her Son" and managed to speak in only a few cities before monetary losses forced it to close. During the 16 months he spent in Auburn Prison awaiting the outcome of his appeal, Gillette filled his time by taking correspondence courses in engineering. His appeal denied, Gillette was electrocuted at Auburn on March 30, 1907.

212. Brandon, Craig. *Murder in the Adirondacks: "An American Tragedy" Revisited.* 2nd ed. Utica, N.Y.: North Country Books, 1986. xii, 380 pp.: ill.; 24 cm.

Excellent case history by Brandon, a reporter and columnist for *The Daily Express* in Utica, New York. In addition to reporting on the case, Brandon examines the sensational journalism generated by the murder, Dreiser's *An American Tragedy*, and dedicates a chapter to films and folklore inspired by the crime. Includes bibliographic notes and index.

213. Brown, Grace. *Grace Brown's Love Letters: Read in the Herkimer Court House, November 20, 1906, at the Trial of Chester E. Gillette Charged with Her Murder.* Herkimer, N.Y.: Citizen, 1906. 23 pp.; 22 cm.

214. Brownell, Joseph W,. and Wawrzaszek, Patricia. *Adirondack Tragedy: The Gillette Murder Case of 1906.* Interlaken, N.Y.: Heart of the Lakes, 1986. 215 pp.: ill., geneal. tables; 23 cm.

Brownell spent years revisiting the key sites of the case and conducted exhaustive research in the Cortland County Historical Society and the Herkimer County Historical Society. Includes bibliographic notes and the family trees of Grace Brown and Chester Gillette on the lining papers.

215. Dreiser, Theodore. *An American Tragedy.* New York: Boni and Liveright, 1925. 2 v.; 20 cm. Vol. 1: [8], 431, [1]p. (last page blank); vol. 2: [10], 409, [1]p. (first 2 pp. and last p. blank). (Various eds.)

A masterpiece of fiction based on the Gillette trial which Dreiser attended.

216. Ingraham, Granville S. *History Gillette Murder Trial and Grace Brown's Love Letters.* Herkimer, N.Y.: Published by Charles E. Garlock, 1907. 76 pp.: ill., ports.; 22 cm.

Cover title: *Gillette Murder Trial and Grace Brown's Love Letters.*

217. Samuels, Charles. *Death Was the Bridegroom.* Gold Medal Books Series no. 466. New York: Fawcett, 1955. 157 pp.; 19 cm. ("A Gold Medal original"); paperback.

Craig Brandon in his excellent study of the case (see 212), notes that this fictionalized account of the case offers no new research and is primarily based on the original trial transcript and the *New York Sun* newspaper account.

Gillies, Jesse James
(a.k.a. "Chess Gillees")

Born circa 1960. Stablehand, horse wrangler. Arizona; 1 murder; bludgeon (rock); January 29, 1981.

"All that just for killing that bitch?"—Gillies' reaction when told by a Phoenix detective that the gas chamber was the mode of execution in Arizona

Drifters Michael David Logan, 27, and Jesse James Gillies, 20, first met in Phoenix, Arizona, in January 1981

while employed as wranglers at the Weldon Riding Stables. Logan, posing as "Mike Richardson," had escaped from Jackson State Penitentiary north of Detroit in August 1980 and, if apprehended, faced a 15 year sentence for violating the terms of his parole on a 1977 conviction for attempted robbery. Raised in a predominantly black suburb in Detroit, the white Logan quickly learned how to survive on the street. His membership in the "Crazy Mother Fuckers," a Detroit-based teenage motorcycle club, gave the 15 year old an avenue by which to indulge his taste for violence, alcohol, and drugs. Reasoning that if he never sobered up he would never have a hangover, Logan spent much of his life in a narcotic and alcoholic haze. Dropping out of school at 16, Logan briefly married and spent two years drifting across America working at racetracks as a "hot-walker." Arrested in December 1977 for an attempted robbery in Detroit, he was sentenced to 3 to 15 years, but gained trustee status at Jackson State Penitentiary by attending Alcoholics Anonymous meetings and passing a high school equivalency test. After serving 27 months, the 25-year-old was released to a halfway house in the community. Logan soon resumed his heavy drinking of 30 to 40 beers a day, began selling drugs and guns, and was returned to prison. In August 1980, he escaped from Jackson State Penitentiary and arrived by bus in Phoenix, Arizona, on Labor Day. Logan was planning the one big "score" he needed to finance his escape to Australia when he met Jesse James Gillies.

Like Logan, Gillies was no stranger to violence, alcohol, drugs, or prison. An unwanted child born to an unwed mother, Gillies spent much of his early life shunted back and forth between his mother, grandparents, and foster homes. At school, Gillies started fires, bullied other children, and was a habitual runaway. Arrested in 1976 for burglary and possession of marijuana, the 16 year old raved in custody that he was "Jesus Christ." A year later while working construction in San Francisco, Gillies prophetically told a coworker, "When I get angry I really don't give a fuck anymore." Soon afterwards, he raped the 17-year-old daughter of a woman who had let him live in her home. Broke, addicted to alcohol and drugs, Gillies was arrested and did time in mid-to-late 1979 for various incidents of burglary, petty theft, and passing bad checks. On June 19, 1980, while working in his uncle's stables in Litchfield Park, Arizona, Gillies beat up and extorted money from a retarded man who stabled his horse there. As part of a plea bargain arrangement, Gillies agreed to admit to theft in exchange for probation and only a year of county jail time. A judge set aside the agreement and sentenced Gillies to one and a half years in prison. Due to prison overcrowding in Arizona, however, Gillies was placed in the state's Fort Grant Training Center where he was released on work furlough on December 26, 1980 and granted permission to work in a riding stable in Phoenix.

On the night of January 28, 1981, around 11:00 p.m. a broke Gillies and Logan were looking for drunks to roll outside of a bar in a seedy area of Phoenix when they noticed that an attractive young woman across the street at a convenience store had locked her keys in her Pinto. Twenty-six-year-old Suzanne Rossetti, former cheerleader and National Honor Society member, was on her way to meet her visiting parents when she stopped at the store to buy a pack of gum. She accepted the two men's offer of help and Gillies unlocked the car using a screwdriver borrowed from the store's manager. Rossetti thanked the pair and asked if she could do something for them in return. At Logan's suggestion, she bought them a six pack of beer and was preparing to leave when they asked her for a ride to the stable where they worked. Whether she willingly gave them a ride or was forced to is a matter of contention, but after driving 300 yards Gillies struck her in the head twice, pushed her out of the car, and raped her on the desert road while Logan looked through her purse for money. Finding only $34, they tied Rossetti with strips torn from a towel and drove to her condominium in Scottsdale.

Inside the apartment, Gillies again raped the woman while Logan smoked dope and searched for valuables. He found her ATM card to a bank account containing about $4,000, the big "score" he needed to finance his escape to Australia. Exchanging places, Logan raped Rossetti as Gillies smoked dope and listened to loud rock music. Around 2:10 a.m. on January 29, 1981, they drove to an automatic bank teller machine and tried to deplete Rossetti's entire account, but learned to their dismay that only $250 per 24-hour period could be withdrawn. Logan's dream was within reach, but he needed time to plunder Rossetti's savings. Unknown to the pair, a hidden camera snapped their picture which would later be used in evidence against them. Fearful that Rossetti would report the sexual assault, they drove her to a deserted road on Fish Creek Hill in the Superstition Mountains where they again took turns raping her. When she refused to jump off a cliff, Logan kicked her off the steep embankment and she fell 40 feet crushing the left side of her face. Although she pleaded for mercy, Rossetti was pushed off another cliff. Finally, one of the men (both claimed it was the other) repeatedly bashed Rossetti's head in with a rock. They spent an hour covering the body with rocks and afterwards sat on the grave smoking a cigarette which was recovered by authorities. An autopsy report determined that Rossetti had died of compound causes: exsanguination, aspiration of blood, and head injuries. In short, the young woman had been alive when buried and choked to death in her own blood.

Following leads supplied by coworkers and friends of the murderers, authorities were able to locate Rossetti's stolen car in the parking lot of the Phoenix zoo. Inside was a laundry receipt bearing the name "Chess Gillees" dated after Rossetti's disappearance. On February 2, 1981, Gillies was arrested at the Weldon Riding Stables after confiding to coworkers that he and Logan were involved in the rape/murder. In his possession were a pair of Rossetti's panties and one of her credit cards. Logan, who had stayed in Phoenix to use Rossetti's ATM card and bet at the dog races, was arrested in a cheap hotel the next day. Informed that Gillies had implicated him in the murder, Logan pointed the finger at his partner as the killer. As no one in the history of Arizona had ever been convicted of murder in the absence of a body, the county attorney offered both men a deal that would free them from the death penalty in exchange for their aiding police in the recovery of Rossetti's remains. Logan quickly accepted the offer and led police to the Superstition Mountains where Ros-

setti's body was found on February 5, 1981.

Under the terms of the plea agreement, Logan pleaded guilty on August 3, 1981, to charges of first degree murder, sexual assault, kidnapping, aggravated robbery, and first degree computer fraud and on August 31, 1981, was sentenced to life imprisonment plus 67 years. Gillies pleaded not guilty to murder, insisting that Logan was the perpetrator, and his trial began in Phoenix on August 21, 1981. One witness testified that Gillies had commented to Logan, "Wasn't the Superstitions fun?" The jury received the case at 3:10 p.m. on August 27, 1981, and needed only until 5:00 p.m. to find Gillies guilty on all counts. On September 28, 1981, Gillies was given the death penalty plus 72 years on four other charges. An execution date has been set twice (1983 and 1985), but a federal court has intervened in each instance on appeal. Gillies, who claims to have been "born again," has logged numerous rule violations in the Arizona State Prison by threatening both guards and inmates. On May 30, 1988, he tried to commit suicide by slitting the arteries in his forearms. A suicide note containing the words "Everybody dies" was found in his cell. Gillies awaits execution in the gas chamber. By contrast, Michael Logan has been a model prisoner and prison staff have repeatedly recommended that he be reclassified and transferred from Arizona State Prison to a less secure institution. To date, senior corrections officials have refused to do so.

218. Watkins, Ronald J. *Evil Intentions: The Story of How an Act of Kindness Led to a Senseless Murder*. 1st ed. New York: W. Morrow, 1992. 296 pp.; 24 cm.

Gilmore, Mark Gary

Born circa November 1940 in Texas. Executed January 17, 1977. Career criminal. Orem and Provo, Utah; 2 murders; pistol; July 19–20, 1976.

Television: "The Executioner's Song" (1982), a two-part, four-hour miniseries adapted by Norman Mailer from his book of the same title, originally aired on NBC on November 28–29, 1982. Cast includes Tommy Lee Jones (Gary Gilmore), Rosanna Arquette (Nicole Baker), and Christine Lahti (Brenda Nicol).

Audio: The Executioner's Song, a two-cassette, three-hour abridgement of Mailer's book read by Michael McConnohie, was published by Audio Renaissance Tapes (Los Angeles) in 1990. *Shot in the Heart*, a four-cassette, four-hour abridgement of Gilmore's book read by Will Patton, was published by Bantam Doubleday Dell Audio Pub. (New York) in 1994.

"Let's do it."—Gilmore's last words

Double murderer whose 1977 execution was the first in the United States in nearly a decade. By age 35, Gary Gilmore had spent more than half of his life in prison for offenses ranging from repeated break-ins to armed robbery. Paroled from the federal penitentiary in Marion, Illinois, in April 1976, Gilmore was ill-equipped to deal with the outside world. The ex-con began shoplifting, drinking heavily, and making unwanted sexual advances to every woman he met. Only three months after his release, Gilmore committed the two senseless murders in Utah which brought him to national prominence. On July 19, 1976, in Orem, Gilmore held up a gas station manned by Max Jensen, a 24-year-old Brigham Young University student. After ordering Jensen to empty his pockets,

Gilmore forced him into the men's room, made him lie face down on the floor, then pumped two rounds in the back of the man's head at close range. The next night, Gilmore drove to Provo where he robbed the City Center Motel. He forced the night attendant, 25-year-old Bennie Bushnell, into a back room, and following the ritual he established with Jensen's murder, shot the man in the back of the head. The robbery-murder netted Gilmore $125. The ex-con was quickly apprehended by authorities, convicted of Bushnell's murder in October 1976, and sentenced to death. The case would have excited little national attention had Gilmore not insisted that Utah make good on its sentence and actually execute him. Executions in the United States had been suspended for nearly ten years when the media learned that Gilmore not only demanded to die, but had exercised his right under Utah law to choose a firing squad as the means. The resulting publicity made the misfit a celebrity as did two suicide attempts, a hunger strike, and his spirited legal battles against those who tried to block his execution. On January 17, 1977, Gilmore was taken to the cannery of the Utah State Prison in Provo and strapped into a chair in front of a backstop of sandbags and a mattress. After telling the warden, "Let's do it," Gilmore was executed by a five member firing squad and pronounced dead two minutes later from four .30 caliber slugs to the heart. Afterwards, the killer's body was taken to the University of Utah Medical Center where it was dissected for scientific purposes or use in transplant operations.

219. Gilmore, Mikal. *Shot in the Heart.* 1st ed. New York: Doubleday, 1994. xii, 403 pp.: ill.; 25 cm.

_____. [Same as 219.] London: Viking, 1994. xi, 403 pp.: ill.; 24 cm.

Gilmore's brother, a successful rock writer, outlines his tormented family's history which included an abusive alcoholic father and an intensely superstitious mother. According to the author, older brother Gary received most of his father's physical abuse because the man believed him not to be his own, but rather the child of his grown-up son. Gilmore's final words to his younger brother: "Don't be proud of me. I'm just going to be shot to death for something that never should have happened."

220. Mailer, Norman. *The Executioner's Song.* 1st ed. Boston: Little, Brown, 1979. 1056 pp.; 24 cm.

_____. [Same as 220.] London: Hutchinson, 1979. 1056 pp.; 24 cm.

_____. [Same as 220.] New York: Warner Books, 1980. 1024 pp.; 18 cm.; paperback.

_____. [Same as 220.] London: Arrow, 1980. 1056 pp.; 18 cm. (Various printings); paperback.

_____. [Same as 220.] London: Vintage, 1991. 1056 pp.; 20 cm.; paperback.

_____. [Same as 220.] 1993 Modern Library ed. New York: Modern Library, 1993. x, 1002 pp.; 22 cm.

Television producer Larry Schiller bought the rights to Gilmore's life and persuaded Mailer to write this incredible book which one reviewer called "an epic-scaled psychopathic reverie." Often compared to Truman Capote's masterpiece, *In Cold Blood*, this "true life novel" depicts the nine month period of Gilmore's life beginning with his parole from the federal penitentiary at Marion, Illinois, on April 9, 1976, through his execution in the Utah State Prison. Based on hundreds of hours of interviews and court documents. In 1980, Mailer was awarded the Pulitzer Prize in Fiction for this remarkable achievement.

Graham, Gwendolyn Gail (a.k.a. "Bunny Foo Foo." Known in conjunction with Catherine May Wood as "The Dykes of Death")

Born August 6, 1963, in Santa Maria, California. Nurse's aide. Warren, Michigan; 6 murders (suspected of 8); suffocation (wash cloth or towel); January–April 1987.

"I am not guilty of killing anybody. This was just a joke that got carried too far." —Graham quoted in a pre-sentence report prepared by the Michigan department of corrections prior to her sentencing on November 1, 1989; *see also* Wood, Catherine May.

Graham, Lewis Texada, Jr.

Born September 24, 1940, in Lafayette, Louisiana. Research scientist, university professor and administrator. Shreveport, Louisiana; 1 murder; bludgeon (sledgehammer); March 31, 1980.

"I finally got a little mercy from a system that never gave me justice." —Graham's reaction to the commutation of his life sentence to 25 years in prison with the possibility of parole

A case strongly reminiscent of that of Dr. Jeffrey (*Fatal Vision*) MacDonald's. Dr. Lewis Graham, 39, claimed that on the night of March 31, 1980, intruders broke into his Shreveport, Louisiana, home, dragged him from the bed he shared with Kathleen, his wife of 17 years, and stabbed him once in the chest and hand before knocking him out against their bedroom wall. The Louisiana State University Medical Center research scientist woke to find the room awash in blood and his wife's skull shattered by at least five blows from a sledgehammer. This weapon and a hunting knife found at the scene were later identified as Graham's. The biochemist's apparent lack of emotion over his wife's brutal murder combined with his own superficial wounds led police to consider him a prime suspect. He was arrested on July 15, 1980, after authorities learned that his recent affair with a coworker had jeopardized his marriage. Tried in Shreveport in July 1981 the case hinged largely on circumstantial evidence bolstered by testimony from a top forensics expert who asserted that the minute bloodstains found on the front of Dr. Graham's underwear and the back of his tee-shirt were consistent with the splatter patterns produced by the type of arching blows used to bludgeon the victim. He was convicted of second degree murder on August 2, 1981, and subsequently sentenced to life imprisonment at hard labor without either the possibility of parole, probation, or suspension. Graham's conviction was subsequently upheld by the Louisiana Supreme Court and the U.S. Supreme Court has refused to hear the case. On February 3, 1988, outgoing Louisiana governor Edwin Edwards commuted Graham's life sentence to 25 years based on a 3–2 vote recommendation from the state pardon board. Now eligible for a parole hearing every six months, Graham has been denied parole twice since applying for it in November 1989. The Reverend David Laverty, foreman of the jury that convicted him, has regularly attended the hearings to oppose Graham's release. As of August 1992, Graham has been incarcerated at the State Police Barracks in Baton Rouge, Louisiana.

221. Lewis, Craig A. *Blood Evidence: A Story of True Crime in the Suburban South.*

1st ed. Little Rock, Ark.: August House, 1990. 271 pp.; 23 cm.

_____. [Same as 221 minus subtitle.] Berkley ed. New York: Berkley Books, 1992. xii, 273 pp.: ill., map; 18 cm. ("A Berkley book"); paperback.

Based on the 25-part series that Lewis wrote on the case for the *Shreveport Journal.*

Gray, David Malcolm

Born November 20, 1956, in Port Chalmers, New Zealand. Died November 14, 1990. Unemployed. Aramoana, New Zealand; 13 murders; Norinco .223 caliber semiautomatic rifle; November 13, 1990.

"If you want mercy, ask it from God for you shall find none at the hands of man."—Excerpt from a letter written by Gray to a gun magazine on the day of the rampage

Paranoid schizophrenic whose 13 killings rank as the largest mass murder in New Zealand history. David Gray, a sullen loner with a fascination for guns and militaria, lived in a cabin called "Hlidskjalf" (named after the high seat in the palace of Odin, the Norse god of war) in the isolated seaside resort village of Aramoana 17 miles north of Dunedin. As Gray's paranoia deepened, he cut himself off from his neighbors, spending hours in his cabin reading *Soldier of Fortune* magazine, drawing knives and bombs, and writing articles on survival tactics. By mid–1990 Gray began assembling an impressive arsenal and huge stores of ammunition. One month before the rampage, he crossed out the mystical symbols painted on the door of "Hlidskjalf." Just before 8:00 p.m. on November 13, 1990, a day immortalized in New Zealand criminal history as "Black Tuesday," Gray shot neighbor Gary

John Holden and his 11-year-old daughter to death with a semiautomatic assault rifle and torched their home. During the next 22 hours, Gray (outfitted in khaki camouflage with his face blackened commando-style) went house-to-house through the darkened neighborhood killing anyone he found. New Zealand police, who traditionally do not carry guns, sealed the area and called in anti-terrorist squads from Timaru, Christchurch, and Invercargill. At 5:52 p.m. the next day, authorities confronted Gray in a deserted house and shot him to death as he emerged firing and hysterically shouting, "Kill me, fucking kill me!" During the standoff, Gray killed 13 people (including a police officer and a six-year-old child) and wounded six. On November 17, 1990, angry townspeople burned "Hlidskjalf" to the ground.

222. Bensemann, Paul. *Tragedy at Aramoana*. Whatamongo Bay, N.Z.; Cape Catley; Tatia, N.Z.: Inprint, 1991. 259 pp.: ill., facsim., map, plans, ports.; 22 cm.; trade paperback.

Bensemann covered the event for the New Zealand Press Association.

223. O'Brien, Bill. *Aramoana: Twenty-two Hours of Terror*. Illustrated by Simon Blake. Auckland, N.Z.: Penguin Books, 1991. 221 pp., [16]pp. of plates: ill., facsims., maps, ports.; 20 cm.; paperback.

Firsthand account by a senior sergeant of the New Zealand police responsible for handling media inquiries concerning the mass murder. Highly favorable of the police handling of the case.

Gray, Henry Judd
(a.k.a. "Lover Boy," "Bud," "The Putty Man")

Born July 8, 1892, in Cortland, New York. Executed January 12, 1928.

Corset salesman. Long Island, New York; 1 murder; bludgeon (sash weight), manual strangulation; March 20, 1927.

"Momie, Momie, for God's sake help me!"—Gray's plea to Snyder during the murder of her husband; *see also* Snyder, Ruth May.

"Green Bicycle Murder" *see* Light, Ronald Vivian

"Green River Killer"

Unknown. Areas in and around Seattle and Tacoma, Washington and Portland, Oregon; 49 murders; ligature and manual strangulation; 1982–1984.

Unknown serial killer responsible for the largest and longest series of unsolved murders in the United States. On July 15, 1982, the body of Wendy Lee Coffield, a 16-year-old runaway linked to prostitution, was found snagged on an old piling in the Green River south of Seattle, Washington. Coffield, reported missing from a foster home eight days earlier, had been strangled. Within the next two months, the remains of five other women between the ages of 16 and 31 were found scattered along the banks of the Green River near where Coffield was recovered. Like the teenager, the victims had been strangled and the majority of them were prostitutes with links to the "Sea-Tac Strip," a two mile stretch of seedy bars, motels, and hotels near the airport serving Seattle and Tacoma. Nicknamed "The Green River Killer," the unknown serial murderer continued to dump the bodies of dead runaways, hitchhikers, and prostitutes in secluded woodland areas around Seattle and Tacoma despite the formation in January 1984 of the Green River Task Force which would ultimately spend an estimated $15 million trying to capture him. Hampered by the reluctance of prostitutes and street people to cooperate with them, investigators were able to do little more than compile names of missing persons matching the killer's target victims and visiting body sites which were being found with alarming regularity.

As the death toll mounted into the double digits, two suspects were questioned early in the investigation but discounted after one passed a polygraph test and physical evidence failed to link the other to the murders. The discovery of four bodies in Portland, Oregon, in mid–1987 brought the known dead to 46. On September 18, 1987, the *Seattle Times* printed a revised version of the Green River Killer's psychological profile originally prepared by FBI special agent John Douglas in 1982, shortly after the first victims were found. The profile depicted the murderer as a white male high school dropout between the ages of 25 and 35, the product of a broken home, who more than likely was raised by a nagging single mother. Douglas characterized the killer as having "very strong personal feelings of inadequacy" and had probably been jilted by a woman for another man. Feeling that women would prostitute themselves for any reason, the killer was angered by the sight of streetwalkers and posed as a police officer to make contact with them. Douglas concluded, "He is an angry individual who demonstrates power over his victims and enjoys the publicity he is receiving." Another "viable suspect" was questioned in July 1989 when the death toll peaked at 49, but he too was ultimately released. The highly criticized multi-agency Task

Force disbanded in 1990 amid massive budget cuts and political infighting. Many writers familiar with the case believe that the killer may have left the Sea-Tac area in 1984 relocating to Southern California where at least ten similar unsolved killings were reported in San Diego in 1985.

224. Smith, Carlton, and Guillen, Thomas. *The Search for the Green River Killer.* New York: Onyx, 1991. xvi, 479 pp., [16]pp. of plates: ill.; 18 cm. ("An Onyx book"); paperback.

Two reporters for the *Seattle Times* criticize the Green River Task Force for its inefficiency and incompetence citing as examples their loss of key evidence and a reluctance to follow up on missing persons reports filed on prostitutes. The authors are very effective in illustrating the role politics can play in a serial murder investigation. The book's publisher offered a $50,000 reward for information leading to the capture and conviction of the serial killer and maintained a 24-hour hotline between March 1 and May 1, 1991, to collect tips.

Greenwood, Harold
(acquitted; a.k.a. "Pilkington")

Born circa 1874 in Ingleton, Yorkshire, England. Died January 17, 1929. Solicitor. Kidwelly, Carmarthenshire, Wales; 1 murder (acquitted); poison (arsenic); June 16, 1919.

"It is a fearful, unbelievable thing to be tried for your life."—From Greenwood's article "Armstrong's Fight for Life," published in *John Bull* (April 22, 1922)

Forty-five-year-old solicitor tried and acquitted of the arsenic poisoning of his wife in one of the most sensational trials of 1920. Harold Greenwood lived with his wife, the former Mabel Bowater, and his four children in Rumsey House, Kidwelly, Carmarthenshire in South Wales. A solicitor in the nearby town of Llanelly, Greenwood was moderately successful but could never have afforded the spacious 14-room home without his wife's private income of nearly £700 a year left to her in trust by her deceased father. The family was outwardly happy although dark rumors circulated in the township that the handsome solicitor often flirted with women. On June 15, 1919, Mrs. Greenwood, who had a long history of poor health, became seriously ill after eating lunch at which she drank burgundy from a bottle labeled "Real Pure Wine." A doctor was summoned who gave the 47-year-old woman morphia pills for her severe diarrhea and vomiting. Mrs. Greenwood died early the next day and her death was certified as due to valvular disease of the heart. Rumors, more than likely started by the attending nurse, now ran rampant through the district and were exacerbated by Greenwood's hasty marriage to 30-year-old Gladys Jones less than four months after his first wife's death. Greenwood's 21-year-old daughter Irene was not told of the marriage until two days before the event and left immediately afterwards to live with relatives in London. Not long after returning from his honeymoon, Greenwood was interviewed at Llanelly police station and gave authorities permission to exhume his wife's body on April 16, 1920. The subsequent postmortem revealed no evidence of valvular heart disease but the coroner did find a quarter grain of arsenic, the minimum fatal dose, in Mrs. Greenwood's organs. Interviewed afterwards by the *Daily Mail*, Greenwood commented on the poisonous atmosphere surrounding the case: "I am the victim of village gossip, of village scandal, and, if you know Welsh village life, you will know what that means." On June 16, 1920, a coroner's inquest found that the woman's death had been caused by arsenic poisoning administered by Greenwood. Authorities who earlier in the day had placed the solicitor in protective custody formally charged him with his wife's murder the next day.

An international press corps descended on Guildhall, Carmarthen, as the trial opened before Mr. Justice Shearman on November 2, 1920. Pleading not guilty, Greenwood was brilliantly defended by Sir Edward Marshall Hall who cast doubt on the medication given to Mrs. Greenwood by her attending physician. The doctor, who at the inquest testified that he had given the woman morphia pills, now claimed that they had been opium pills. Hall suggested the possibility that the doctor had mistakenly confused the medicines in his dispensary and inadvertently poisoned Mabel Greenwood. The case properly ended, however, when Irene Greenwood destroyed the prosecution's contention that the solicitor had placed arsenic in the burgundy bottle from which only his wife had partaken at dinner. Under oath, the daughter (who had not been interviewed by police) testified that she too had drunk from the same burgundy bottle at both lunch and supper on the day prior to her mother's death. Perhaps as important, Hall showed that Greenwood had no motive for murdering his wife. Upon her death, the solicitor stood to lose her £700 yearly income which would be automatically placed in a trust for her children. On November 9, 1920, the jury was out less than three hours before returning a verdict of not guilty. A rider attached to the verdict and not made public at the trial stated that although the jury found that "a dangerous dose of arsenic was administered to Mabel Greenwood" they were neither satisfied that it was the immediate cause of death nor was the evidence presented sufficient to satisfy them "as to how, and by whom, the arsenic was administered...." His reputation destroyed and legal practice lost, Greenwood won a libel action in March 1922 against a waxwork firm who placed his effigy on display amidst a grouping of notorious murderers. Greenwood subsequently attended and reported on the sensational poisoning trial of fellow-solicitor Herbert Rowse Armstrong in the South Wales county adjacent to Carmarthenshire for the April 22, 1922, issue of *John Bull*. Living in obscurity under the assumed name "Pilkington," Greenwood died a penniless and broken man at Walford, Ross-in-Wye, Herefordshire, on January 17, 1929, eight years and two months after his acquittal.

225. Duke, Winifred, ed. *Trial of Harold Greenwood*. Notable British Trials. Edinburgh; London: W. Hodge, 1930. xi, 347 pp., [8] leaves of plates: ill., ports., fold. plan, facsim.; 22 cm.

_____. [Same as 225.] Notable British Trials. Edinburgh: W. Hodge; Sydney, N.S.W.: Butterworth, 1930. xi, 347 pp., [8] leaves of plates: ill., ports., fold plan, facsim.; 22 cm.

_____. [Same as 225.] Notable British Trials. Toronto: Canada Law Book, 1930. xi, 347 pp., [8] leaves of plates: ill., ports., fold plan, facsim.; 22 cm.

Greenwood's trial within the Guildhall, Carmarthen, Carmarthen Assizes, November 1920, for the murder of his wife, Mabel Greenwood. Appendices include the coroner's inquest, police court proceedings, list of exhibits, interviews with Greenwood, a brief account of the

judge and counsel, and a list of the jurymen.

Gregg, Troy Leon

Born circa 1948 in Georgia. Died circa July 28, 1980. Drifter. Gwinnett County, Georgia; 2 murders; gun; November 21, 1973.

Double murderer whose death sentence was at issue when the U.S. Supreme Court upheld Georgia's death penalty law in 1976. On November 21, 1973, Troy Gregg, 25, and a 16-year-old traveling companion were picked up hitchhiking north in Florida by Fred Edward Simmons and Bob Durwood ("Tex") Moore. According to the prosecution's theory of the case, the men stopped around 11:00 p.m. to rest at the intersection of Georgia Highway 20 and I-85 in Gwinnett County, Georgia. While Simmons and Moore were urinating by the side of the road, Gregg shot the pair, fired an additional bullet into the skull of each man, robbed them of around $400, then rolled their bodies into a drainage ditch before driving off in their car. A Georgia jury, disbelieving his claim of self-defense, convicted Gregg and he was sentenced to death in February 1974. Gregg was appealing his sentence when he and three other inmates escaped from the Georgia State Prison in Reidsville on July 28, 1980. Later that same day, the convicted killer twice called a reporter for the *Albany Herald* to report the escape. In one of the telephone conversations Gregg reportedly said, "We had to get out. We couldn't stand it any longer. We all decided we'd rather be dead than stay here another day. Conditions here are inhuman." Two days later, swimmers in Mountain Island Lake in Gaston County, North

Carolina, found Gregg's body submerged in seven feet of water shortly before the three remaining fugitives were recaptured by FBI agents in a lakefront home 12 miles away. Evidence indicated that escapee Timothy McCorquodale, a 27-year-old convicted murderer sentenced to die for the 1974 torture-slaying of a 17-year-old Virginia woman, had helped the other prisoners stomp Gregg to death.

226. Davis, Christopher. *Waiting for It.* 1st ed. New York: Harper & Row, 1980. ix, 182 pp.; 22 cm.

227. Gregg, Troy Leon (petitioner). *Troy Leon Gregg [petitioner] Versus State of Georgia [respondent]: Petition and Briefs.* Criminal Law Series; v. 7, no. 36. New York: Law Reprints, 1975. 526 pp.; 22 cm.

Griffiths, Peter
(a.k.a. "The Blackburn Baby Murderer")

Born circa 1926. Executed November 19, 1948. Flour mill packer, Irish Guardsman. Blackburn, Lancashire, England; 1 murder; bludgeon; May 14-15, 1948.

"I hope I get what I deserve."— The final words of Griffiths' signed confession given to police on August 14, 1948

A textbook example of scientific criminal investigation which marked the first time an entire city's male population was fingerprinted in order to apprehend a sadistic child killer. In the early hours of May 15, 1948, police responded to a call from the Queen's Park Hospital in Blackburn, Lancashire, reporting that June Anne Devaney, almost four, was missing from her crib. Shortly afterwards, Devaney's body was found at the base of a nine-foot stone wall some 283 feet from where she had been abducted from the babies' ward. The young girl's attacker had raped her before grabbing her by the ankles and repeatedly swinging her head against the wall. Scotland Yard was immediately notified and turned up two pieces of vital physical evidence at the scene. Footprints left by the intruder on the ward's recently waxed floor contained fibers from his socks. More importantly, a large Winchester bottle containing sterilized water was found beneath Devaney's crib. When dusted for fingerprints it yielded 20 sets. Prints taken from the 2,017 people who had legitimate access to the ward during the past two years left only the killer's prints unidentified. His obvious familiarity with the ward's layout suggested to police a local man.

In an unprecedented move, authorities fingerprinted every male in Blackburn between the ages of 16 and 70, roughly half the city's population of over 110,000. A mayoral appeal combined with an assurance that the prints would be publicly pulped after the investigation ensured almost unanimous public cooperation. Officers, going house-to-house, collected 500 sets of fingerprints a day. By the end of June 1948 prints taken from more than 46,000 area men had failed to produce a match. Similarly, circulars of the suspect's prints sent to all police agencies in Great Britain and every fingerprint agency in the world proved unsuccessful. In all, the murderer's fingerprints had been compared to nearly ten million prints worldwide. According to ration card records, some 800 men who lived in Blackburn during the war still had not come forward to be printed. To determine those who still resided in the area, an officer visited Number

31 Birley Street on August 12, 1948, the home of Peter Griffiths. A slightly built man of 22 who lived with his parents, Griffiths did not speak as police printed him. The next day he was arrested in the street near his home when his prints (number 46253) were found to be identical to those on the bottle. Griffiths initially denied murdering Devaney until told of the fingerprint evidence against him. The suit he wore the night of the murder was retrieved from a pawnshop and the blood on the fly of the trousers matched the dead child's type. Fibers from the trousers were identical to those found on Devaney's nightdress.

Griffiths pleaded not guilty by reason of insanity at the start of his trial at the Lancaster Autumn Assizes on October 15, 1948. The defense offered a compelling portrait of the prototypical individual who, suffering from a lifelong condition of "dementia praecox" (schizophrenia), was subject to brief, inexplicable episodes of violence sandwiched between longer periods of apparent normalcy. Griffiths was the son of a schizophrenic father and at age six had sustained a serious head injury. When discharged from the Welsh Guard in 1948 it was ascertained that the 22 year old possessed an IQ of 48 (significantly less than the average of 100). According to his counsel, Griffiths' latent violence was brought to the fore on the night of the murder by drunkenness and a recent argument with his girlfriend. A jury needed only 25 minutes on October 18, 1948, to find him guilty. Griffiths denied police allegations that he was responsible for the rash of other child assaults and one murder in Lancashire. He was hanged in Liverpool's Walton Gaol on November 19, 1948.

228. Godwin, George, ed. *The Trial of Peter Griffiths: The Blackburn Baby Murder.* Notable British Trials. London: W. Hodge, 1950. 219 pp., [16]pp. of plates: ill., ports. plan., facsim.; 22 cm.

Excellent entry in the Notable British Trials Series edited by barrister-at-law Godwin. Appendices include essay "Schizophrenia and Other Mental Disorders of Medico-Legal Import" by C. Stanford Read, M.D., consulting psychiatrist to the West End Hospital for Nervous Diseases and late lecturer in psychopathology to the Royal Bethlem Hospital.

Griggs, Ronald Geeves
(acquitted)

Born circa 1900 in Franklin, Tasmania. Wesleyan clergyman. Omeo, Australia; 1 murder (acquitted); arsenic; January 3, 1928.

"True as God, I never committed the crime. It just shows you how easily circumstantial evidence may convict a man."—From a statement made by Griggs to *Smith's Weekly* in Sydney and published in that paper on August 4, 1928

Wesleyan clergyman acquitted of poisoning his wife after two sensational trials. Melbourne-educated Ronald Geeves Griggs was 26 years old when he arrived in the small isolated town of Omeo, Australia, in May 1926 to assume a church post. Griggs' 20-year-old wife of one month, the former Ethel Constance White, accompanied the field preacher and set up housekeeping in the parsonage. Aloof and unsociable, the preacher nevertheless struck up a friendship with John Condon, a devout Methodist who lived with his family at Tongio ten miles from the Omeo parsonage. Griggs was a frequent visitor to the house and often stayed overnight when traveling through the district on his motorcycle. In December 1926, Condon's 19-year-old daughter Lottie Elizabeth was staying at the parsonage at the request of Mrs. Griggs. The preacher became infatuated with the outgoing, energetic girl and by Christmas had begun an affair. Sensing her husband's attraction to the girl, the seven months pregnant Mrs. Griggs asked the girl to leave. In January 1927 Condon went to stay with an aunt in Wagga some 400 miles away. Eight weeks after his wife gave birth to their child on February 2, 1927, Griggs was riding his motorcycle to visit his lover. Following an argument with his wife over the suspected relationship, the preacher suggested that she take the baby and visit her mother in Tasmania. The unhappy woman left in mid–July 1927 and during her five-and-a-half-month absence the affair began in earnest. Meeting illicitly in the parsonage and in her bedroom at her parents' home, Griggs and Condon were also a common sight on the streets of Omeo where their constant togetherness started rumors flying.

Notified by his wife that she would return on December 31, 1927, Griggs told no one except Condon in a secret late night meeting at her home in Tongio. Shortly after Mrs. Griggs returned home at 9:00 p.m. on December 31, 1927, she became violently ill and died 53 hours later on January 3, 1928. During her ordeal, Griggs did get the sick woman a prescription but waited until a day before her death to call a doctor who arrived too late to save her. Death was attributed to cardiac failure caused by "hyperemesis and exhaustion" and 20-year-old Ethel Constance Griggs was subsequently buried without an autopsy. Rumors of

the preacher's marital infidelity, however, kept the case alive and prompted Condon's father to ask authorities for a full inquiry. Griggs initially denied a relationship with the girl, but later admitted to it when police produced a signed statement from Lottie Condon detailing their improprieties. Griggs was arrested on February 2, 1928, after a postmortem conducted on his dead wife's exhumed body revealed arsenic poisoning. Tried at Sale, Victoria, from March 7 through 9, 1928, Griggs admitted having access to arsenic, but denied the poisoning. Offering an alternative explanation of the woman's death, his counsel argued that the distraught woman committed suicide over the affair. The jury deadlocked ten to two in favor of conviction and Griggs was retried 39 days later in Melbourne on April 17, 1928. With public support now in his favor, Griggs was acquitted on April 19, 1928, after a jury deliberated just over six hours. Under an assumed name, the preacher subsequently found a temporary position as an assistant minister to a pastorate in South Australia, but was dismissed when his identity became known.

229. Buchanan, A.J., ed. *The Trial of Ronald Geeves Griggs*. Famous Australian Trials. Sydney: The Law Book Company of Australia, 1930. vi, 321 pp., [12] leaves of plates: ill.; 23 cm.

Patterned after the Notable British Trial Series, Barrister-at-Law Buchanan's short summary of the controversial case precedes transcripts from the two trials. Appendices include Lottie Condon's January 18, 1928, statement to authorities and the full text of Griggs' post-acquittal statement published in the August 4, 1928, issue of the Sydney newspaper *Smith's Weekly*.

Gunness, Belle
(a.k.a. "Brynhild Paulsdatter Storset" [maiden name], "Mistress of Murder Hill," "Lady [or] Female [or] Madame [or] Modern Bluebeard," "The Hog Butcher of Indiana," "The Black Widow," "Borgia of the Cornfields," "Bucolic [or] Modern Borgia," "The Merry Widow," "Queen of the Abattoir," "Belle, the Butcher," "The Mail-Order Circe," "The Sorceress of Murder Farm")

Born November 11, 1859, in Selbu, Norway. Died 1908? (exact date unknown). Hog farmer, sausage-maker. LaPorte, Indiana; 16 murders known (estimates range from 28 to 42); poison (strychnine, arsenic), bludgeon (cleaver, hatchet); circa 1896-1908.

Without question, Belle Gunness, "The Hog Butcher of Indiana," stands alone as the 20th century's most prolific and brutal female serial killer. In a murderous career spanning an estimated 13 years (circa 1896–1908), Gunness is credited with dispatching at least 16 victims, mostly men, by using strychnine poisoning coupled with meat cleavers and hatchets. Dismembered skeletal remains found near her farmhouse in LaPorte, Indiana, have led some sources to number the victims of "the Lady Bluebeard" as high as 28 or more. To lure potential victims to her "Murder Farm," the widow Gunness placed ads in the matrimonial columns of large city newspapers: "Personal—Comely widow who owns a large farm in one of the finest districts in LaPorte County, Indiana, desires to make acquaintance of a gen-tleman equally well provided, with view of joining fortunes. No replies by letter considered unless sender is willing to follow answer with personal visit." Belle introduced the steady stream of wealthy suitors around LaPorte as her "brothers" or "cousins." Few ever left the small northwestern Indiana town alive. Most were drugged with strychnine, bludgeoned, dismembered in the cellar with a meat cleaver, then buried in a pigpen behind the house. Belle pocketed their money and placed another ad.

Born Brynhild Paulsdatter Storset in the small Norwegian fishing village of Selbu in 1859, Gunness' early life was one of extreme poverty. In 1883 the 24 year old emigrated to Chicago to be near an older married sister, anglicized her name to "Belle," and married Norwegian Max "Mads" Sorensen the next year. Belle's criminal career began in 1897 after she burned down her Chicago confectioners store for the insurance. She used the money to buy a house in the suburb of Austin which also mysteriously burned in 1898 as did a subsequent home. Belle collected on each house. Ironically, during this period two of her four children, both insured, also died of some type of poisoning. After 17 years of marriage to Belle, Mads Sorenson died on July 30, 1900, from a supposedly "enlarged heart" although prior to his death he manifested the classic symptoms of strychnine poisoning. No autopsy was performed and Belle used the $8,500 insurance money to buy a 48 acre farm on the outskirts of LaPorte, Indiana. She moved there in November 1901 with her two surviving children (Myrtle and Lucy) and a ward Jennie Olsen. Once used as a bordello, the house was insured by Belle who quickly collected a claim when the unused carriage house and boat pavilion burned to the ground.

In April 1902 Belle married Norwegian farmer Peter Gunness who less than a year later became the victim of a bizarre "accident." On December 16, 1902, the unfortunate man was seated at the kitchen table when the handle of a sausage grinder fell from a shelf above him striking him on the head. An inquest ruled his death from brain hemorrhage accidental. Belle again collected insurance. In 1903 the unwed widow gave birth to a son possibly fathered by one of the endless stream of suitors and handymen who appeared and disappeared regularly at the hogfarm. In September 1906 many of LaPorte's 10,000 residents began commenting on the fact that Belle's 14-year-old ward Jennie Olsen had not been seen for months. Belle explained that the girl had gone to Los Angeles to attend school. Less than two years later Olsen's body along with those of her three adopted siblings would be discovered buried on the grounds of Belle's farmhouse.

A matrimonial ad placed by Belle in a Norwegian language newspaper in 1906 brought Ole B. Budsburg, an elderly widower from Iolo, Wisconsin, to LaPorte in May 1907. He was not seen again until retrieved from the hogpen behind Belle's farmhouse. John Moo, a Norwegian farmer from Elbow Lake, Minnesota, met a similar end as did hired hands Eric Gurhold and Olaf Lindblom. These men, along with Belle's final kill, Andrew Helgelein, were the only positively identified male victims of the "Lady Bluebeard" although 12 other men were last seen heading towards LaPorte with money in their pockets to answer Belle's advertisements. After a 16-month correspondence with Belle, Andrew Hel-

gelein, a Norwegian rancher and wheat grower from Aberdeen, South Dakota, arrived in LaPorte in early 1908. He disappeared shortly after withdrawing all his money from the local bank.

In the early morning hours of April 28, 1908, Belle's McClung Road farmhouse burned to the ground. In the structure's smoking basement the bodies of Belle's three children (Myrtle, Lucy, and Philip) as well as the headless corpse of a woman presumed to be Belle Gunness were found. To the surprise and horror of the LaPorte County sheriff, the basement yielded still more grisly remains. Scattered among personal items like men's watches were the bodies of an unidentified woman, at least four more men, and masses of bone fragments. On May 5, 1908, Andrew Helgelein's brother, Asle, discovered still more human remains, including his brother's, wrapped up in lye-filled gunny sacks buried in a garbage-filled hogpen behind the main house. An ex–gold prospector, cheered on by hundreds of onlookers, was hired to sift through the ashes for evidence. Belle's dentures were found in the rubble on May 19, 1908 although many still believed that the headless female body found in the farmhouse was not hers. Widow Gunness stood nearly 5'8" and weighed close to 250 pounds while the recovered corpse was that of a woman not more than 5'3" and weighing only 150 pounds.

The arrest of Ray Lamphere, Belle's former lover and handyman, on murder and arson charges raised even more questions. Belle hired Lamphere in 1906 and fired him in February 1907 after an argument. According to the official police version, Lamphere murdered the family and set fire to their farmhouse as an act of revenge. In custody, Lamphere insisted that Belle was alive and the headless corpse in the basement was that of a woman Belle had picked up to use as a stand-in for faking her own death. Belle murdered her children and with the handyman's help torched the house. Lamphere drove her to a railway station in Stillwell, Indiana, where she effected her escape. The pair planned to meet later. The final inquest report filed on May 20, 1908, concluded that the headless body was Belle's and that she had met her end through "felonious homicide" committed by an unknown perpetrator.

At his trial in LaPorte, Indiana, in November 1908, Ray Lamphere was charged with four counts of murder and one count of arson. A neighbor of Belle's testified that she had seen the widow on July 8, 1908—almost *one month* after her supposed death. Believing that Belle could still be alive, the jury acquitted Lamphere of the murder on November 26, 1908, choosing only to find him guilty of arson. Until his death from tuberculosis in the Northern Indiana State Prison in 1909 Lamphere continued to insist that Belle was alive and that she had killed at least 49 people during the years 1903–1908. In all, Belle's matrimonial/murder scheme had netted her more than $100,000. According to Lamphere, Belle drugged her victims' coffee, bludgeoned them to death, dismembered them in the cellar, tied the parts into gunny sacks, then buried the remains in her yard. While he had never assisted in the killing, Lamphere admitted helping the widow bury "several bodies." Jennie Olsen and Belle's children were murdered for "knowing too much."

Belle Gunness sightings have been numerous since her disappearance on April 28, 1908. Among the most interesting occurred in Los Angeles where in the spring of 1931 a deputy district attorney contacted the LaPorte sheriff concerning a suspect, Mrs. Esther Carlson. The elderly woman was being held for the fatal poisoning of August Lindstrom, a wealthy 81-year-old lumberman, who was in her care. Mrs. Carlson bore a striking resemblance to Belle and at the time of her arrest had in her possession pictures of children bearing an uncanny resemblance to Myrtle and Lucy Sorenson and Philip Gunness. As LaPorte authorities lacked the funds to send a representative to Los Angeles during the Depression, the mystery was destined to remain unsolved. Carlson died of tuberculosis in jail while awaiting trial for the murder of Lindstrom in order to get his $2,000 bank account.

As a testament to the enduring legacy of her myth and legend, Belle Gunness has achieved a place in popular culture and folklore accorded to only a few other female criminal figures, most notably the nineteenth century murder suspect Lizzie Borden. Like her infamous predecessor, Belle has also been immortalized in doggerel verse and ballads: "Now some say Belle killed only ten, And some say forty-two; It was hard to tell exactly, But there were quite a few."

230. De La Torre, Lillian. *The Truth About Belle Gunness.* New York: Fawcett, 1955. 175 pp.; 19 cm.; paperback.

Surprisingly well researched paperback account of the case to which Langlois' more complete study often refers. Rare, but highly recommended.

231. Langlois, Janet L. *Belle Gunness: The Lady Bluebeard.* Bloomington: Indiana

University Press, 1985. xi, 174 pp.: ill.; 25 cm.
Excellent, meticulously documented study of Gunness which not only reports on the murders, but as importantly discusses the rich folklore which has grown up around the case. A reworking of Langlois' doctoral dissertation, *Belle Gunness, the Lady Bluebeard: Community Legend as Metaphor*, Indiana University, Department of Folklore, 1977.

Haigh, John George
(a.k.a. "Acid Bath Murderer," "Vampire Killer," "Smiling Killer," "Old Corpus Delecti," "Chinky," "Ching," "Sonnie," "Haighie," "J. McLean," "William Cato Adamson")

Born July 24, 1909, in Stamford, Lincolnshire, England. Executed August 10, 1949. Engineer, advertising and insurance man, salesman, dry-cleaner. London and Crawley, England; 6 murders (confessed to three other unsubstantiated murders); bludgeon (pinball table leg), gun; September 9, 1944–February 18, 1949.

"All men who are freed from a sense of guilt are happy. I take the view that the world's a happy hunting-ground full of mugs who were born to be exploited by blokes like me. They are rabbits on which we feed."—Haigh to a police officer

Self-confessed "Acid Bath Murderer" who methodically slaughtered for personal gain yet at trial maintained that he was the helpless instrument of an unseen spirit commanding him to kill, then drink the blood of his victims. Raised by devoutly religious parents, Haigh rebelled against their strict discipline by becoming an artful forger

and an inveterate liar. According to Haigh, his "taste for blood" developed in early childhood, the result of being spanked on the hands with a hairbrush by his mother. The bristles drew blood which he licked off. Soon Haigh was deliberately cutting his finger to suck blood. An altar boy, Haigh began dreaming of the bloodied, crucified Christ. After sustaining a head injury later in life, Haigh alleged that he was plagued by dreams in which a man offered him a cup filled with blood to drink. The dream cycle presaged and prompted each murder. As Haigh explained to skeptical authorities, "I was impelled to kill by wild blood dreams. The spirit inside me commanded me to kill." His claim of drinking his own urine since age 11 was similarly viewed as an attempt to escape the noose by feigning insanity.

Convicted of conspiracy to defraud and forgery in 1934, Haigh was released on December 8, 1935, and went to work as a chauffeur/secretary for W. D. McSwan, owner of a pinball factory and some saloons. Haigh, quickly tiring of honest employment, left to set up a phony solicitor's office which resulted in a four-year prison sentence for fraud. Upon his release in August 1940 Haigh became a fire-watcher in war-time London, but was arrested for theft and sentenced in June 1941 to 21 months hard labor. While working in the tinsmith's shop at Lincoln Prison, Haigh began experimenting with sulfuric acid. For a price, fellow-inmates supplied him with field mice which he placed in jars of acid to gauge their decomposition. Released on September 17, 1943, Haigh worked a year for a Crawley-based light engineering firm during which time he acquired the use of a basement room as a workshop at No. 79 Gloucester Road.

In 1944, Haigh offered to show William Donald McSwan, the son of his former employer, how to avoid national service as he had done. On September 9, 1944, McSwan went to Haigh's workshop where he was bludgeoned to death with the leg of a pinball table. Haigh supposedly opened a vein in McSwan's neck and drank a cup of blood before disposing of the man with acid. Haigh informed the man's parents that their son had gone "underground" to avoid the draft. A few days later they received a letter from their son (forged by Haigh) postmarked from Glasgow requesting money for his upkeep be given to Haigh. Impatient over the small sums of money he was milking from them, Haigh lured the father to Gloucester Road on July 2, 1945, on the pretext of meeting his fugitive son. There, he battered McSwan to death and when the elderly corpse allegedly did not produce enough blood to satisfy him, Haigh brought the mother to the workshop and murdered her. Both were disposed of by acid. Posing as the junior McSwan, Haigh forged a power of attorney and gained the family's estate.

Deeply in debt by August 1947, Haigh befriended Dr. Archibald Henderson and his wife, Rose, under the pretext of buying their house. Haigh misrepresented himself to the couple as a manufacturer who owned a factory in Crawley. In actuality, Haigh was permitted by the managing director of an engineering firm to use a storeroom as a workshop on the factory grounds. On February 15, 1948, Haigh invited Dr. Henderson to the storeroom where he used the man's gun to shoot him in the head. Later that day he murdered Rose at the site and disposed of their bodies in tanks of acid. He sold off their possessions, keeping Dr. Henderson's glasses for reading.

By February 1949 Haigh had gambled away the proceeds from the Henderson murders. He next focused his attention on 69-year-old Mrs. Olivia Durand-Deacon, a fellow resident of the Onslow Court Hotel. On February 18, 1949, Haigh lured the wealthy widow to his "factory" and shot her in the back of the head. After allegedly taking his customary glass of blood, Haigh donned a rubber mackintosh and gloves before tipping the 196-pound woman headfirst into a 45-gallon drum of sulfuric acid. Returning the next day, Haigh emptied the greasy remains onto a rubbish heap and applied more acid. Forensic specialists sifting through the sludge later found 28 pounds of melted body fat, three gallstones, part of a left foot, and dentures positively identified as Durand-Deacon's. Haigh quickly pawned much of the dead woman's jewelry and showed concern over her disappearance when questioned by police.

When a background check revealed his past convictions, Haigh was reinterviewed by police who confronted him with pieces of Durand-Deacon's jewelry recovered from pawnshops. The usually unflappable Haigh then asked the artless question which cast doubt on his subsequent claim of insanity, "Tell me, frankly, what are the chances of anybody being released from Broadmoor?" Mistakenly believing he could not be prosecuted for murder if a corpse could not be produced, Haigh confessed to killing Durand-Deacon and in a later written confession, also admitted murdering the McSwan family, the Hendersons, and three other individuals. Police, however, discounted the latter three killings when Haigh could offer only vague details.

Pleading not guilty by reason of insanity, Haigh toiled in the dock over the *Daily Telegraph* crossword as his trial for the murder of Durand-Deacon commenced in Lewes on July 18, 1949. Presided over by 82-year-old Mr. Justice Travers Humphreys, the oldest judge in England, the trial was a media event par excellence with the tabloid, *News of the World*, paying for Haigh's defense. Even the headline hungry Haigh complained of the droves of housewives who crushed forward to see him. The prosecution argued that the matter before the jury was "a simple case of a man not mad but bad." Haigh's claim to have been insane at the time of the murder and "working under the guidance of and in harmony with some vital principle" above the law was merely a hastily constructed strategy designed to spare him from the gallows. When the one psychiatric expert offered by the defense to substantiate Haigh's insanity claim was forced to admit that he felt Haigh knew that murder was "punishable by law" and therefore "wrong by the law" of England, the case was lost. It took the jury less than 20 minutes on July 19, 1949, to find Haigh guilty of murder. He was sentenced to death by hanging.

Awaiting death at Wandsworth Prison, Haigh distinguished himself in the annals of British crime by petitioning the governor of the prison for a rehearsal of his own execution. The request was denied. His last days were spent playing chess with warders and worrying that the wax effigy already being planned for inclusion in Madame Tussaud's Chamber of Horrors would not be accurate or correctly dressed. At 9:00 a.m. on August 10,

1949, Haigh was hustled from the condemned cell to the execution shed and dispatched in the astonishing elapsed time of 11 seconds. His request that Madame Tussaud's receive the Lovat green suit and foulard tie he wore at trial was granted.

232. Byrne, Gerald. *John George Haigh, Acid Killer: The Whole Astounding Story with Pages of Letters and Pictures.* Headline Books Series. London: J. Hill, 1954. 143 pp.: ill.; 19 cm.; paperback.

233. Dunboyne, Lord Patrick, ed. *The Trial of John George Haigh (The Acid Bath Murder).* Notable British Trials. London: W. Hodge, 1953. 271 pp., [21]pp. of plates: ill.; 22 cm.

An excellent case summary introduces lengthy excerpts from Haigh's trial at the Sussex Summer Assizes in July 1949 for the murder of Mrs. Durand-Deacon. Appendices include the text of the contempt of court case brought by the Crown against the London tabloid *Daily Mirror* for publishing a story on Haigh "Vampire—A Man Held" in their March 4, 1949, issue which might have potentially prejudiced the case against the defendant. Also includes the essay "The Medical Aspects of the Case of John George Haigh" by Clifford Allen, psychiatrist to the Seamen's Hospital, Greenwich.

234. Jackson, Stanley. *John George Haigh.* Famous Criminal Trials Series. London: Odhams Press, 1953. 127 pp., [8]pp. of plates: ill., ports.; 19 cm.; paperback.

Concise retelling of "The Acid Bath Murder" case. Jackson, who believes Haigh "was simply a murderer who committed his ghastly crimes for gain," compares him to mentally deranged killers Neville Heath and John Thomas Straffen in a postscript. Includes an index.

235. La Bern, Arthur J. *Haigh: The Mind of a Murderer.* London; New York: W.H. Allen, 1973. 187 pp., [16]pp. of plates: ill., ports.; 23 cm.

_____. [Same as 235.] London: Star Books, 1974. 187 pp., [12]pp. of plates: ill., facsims., ports.; 18 cm.; paperback.

Includes a psychiatric analysis of Haigh by Dr. Noel C. Browne, a Dublin psychiatrist and former minister of health in the Eire government, and six pages of letters written by the serial killer while in prison awaiting trial then execution. Includes an index.

Hall, Archibald Thomson (a.k.a. "Roy Fontaine," "Roy Thomson Hall," "Donald Stewart," "Thurlby," "The Monster Butler")

Born July 17, 1924, in Glasgow, Scotland. Butler. Scotland and London, England; 5 murders; .22 caliber rifle, suffocation, bludgeon (spade, poker), drowning; May 1977–January 1978.

"Well, it's fate, isn't it?"—Hall's explanation for his criminal behavior

Certified "criminally insane" on three separate occasions by Scottish courts, career criminal Archibald Thomson Hall, a.k.a. "Roy Fontaine," ranks with serial killer Peter Manuel as Scotland's most notorious murderer. Born in Glasgow in 1924 to a seemingly normal port-office sorting clerk and his wife, Hall manifested aberrant behavior at an early age. As an adolescent he spent hours making dresses for his sister's dolls. His arrest at 13 for malicious mischief signalled a lifelong pattern of criminal conduct which netted him sentences totalling 41½ years before he committed the first of his five murders. Good looking, suave, and sophisticated, Hall spent his periods of incarceration for housebreaking, theft, and forgery avidly reading books on etiquette, jewelry, and antiques. The assumption of the alias "Roy Fontaine,"

inspired by his devotion to film star Joan Fontaine, completed Hall's persona as the well-bred "gentleman's gentleman." Armed with self-written glowing references, the fast-talking confidence man first secured employment as a butler in the homes of the landed gentry in mid–1963. From his position of trust, Hall stole jewelry from his employers until caught and sentenced on January 13, 1964, to 10 years preventive detention in Blundeston, Lowestoft, Suffolk. Hall escaped and remained at large for two years before his arrest in May 1966 in Edinburgh on new charges of theft and fraud. In prison, Hall's bisexual nature emerged and even after being paroled on January 31, 1972, he continued to correspond with his homosexual lover.

Hall met David Wright, a 26-year-old Birmingham crook, in Long Lartin Prison while serving time in 1973 for receiving stolen property. In 1977 Hall was employed as a butler on the Scottish estate of Lady Peggy Hudson in Dumfriesshire when, based on his recommendation, she hired Wright as a handyman. Wright pressed Hall to rob the old woman, but the butler was seemingly content with his position as a trusted servant. In May 1977 Hall discovered that Wright had stolen a valuable ring from Lady Hudson. In the ugly scene that ensued, the drunken small time thief fired a rifle at Hall, then threatened to expose the man's criminal background unless he agreed to help rob the woman. The next day, Hall lured Wright onto a secluded corner of the estate on the pretext of hunting rabbit and shot the blackmailer four times in the back of the head with a .22 caliber rifle. Hall later returned to the murder site and hid the body in a stream under some large rocks. Wright's skeletal remains were not recovered until January 21, 1978, when Hall's confession directed them to the burial site near Waterbeck, Dumfriesshire. Lady Hudson fired Hall on September 7, 1977, after she learned of his prison record from an ex-girlfriend.

Hall again faked his references and in November 1977 secured employment as a butler for 82-year-old former member of parliament, Mr. Walter Travers Scott-Elliot, and his 62-year-old wife, Dorothy. Their London home was a veritable treasure trove of priceless antiques, jewels, and art. Determined to rob them, Hall met later that month with Mary Coggle and her 39-year-old lover Michael Anthony Kitto in the Lancelot Public House in Knightsbridge to discuss the job. Described by police as a clearinghouse for stolen credit cards and checks, the 51-year-old mother of eight had known Hall for seven years. Kitto, the illegitimate son of a chemist's shop assistant, spent his early years in and out of foster homes until entering the military in 1956. While serving in the rifle brigade in Germany, Kitto was arrested for a robbery with assault and court-martialed in 1960. He continued to be arrested periodically for assault, robbery, and theft up to the time of his initial meeting with Hall in November 1977.

On the evening of December 8, 1977, Kitto visited Hall at the Scott-Elliot's home on 22 Richmond Court, Sloane Street, to admire the items they planned to steal. The aged former PM was asleep in his room and Mrs. Scott-Elliot was thought to have been spending a few days in a nursing home. Opening the door to her room, Hall was astonished to find the woman there. Panicking, he knocked Mrs. Scott-Elliot down while Kitto, attempt-ing to muffle her screams, suffocated the elderly woman with a pillow. Mary Coggle was called upon to assume the murdered woman's identity while Mr. Scott-Elliot was fed a steady diet of sleeping pills to befuddle his senses. The next night, the woman's body was loaded into the trunk of a car and the drugged man placed on the back seat next to his "wife," Mary Coggle wearing a blonde wig and the dead woman's expensive fur and jewelry. Driving to Scotland, Hall and Kitto stopped long enough to buy a spade and fork before burying Mrs. Scott-Elliot in a shallow grave near Braco, Perthshire. Mr. Scott-Elliot was fed more drugs to make the trip to Hall's cottage in Newton Arlosh where they spent the night.

Over the next couple of days the group drove around Scotland staying in hotels paid for by checks signed by the drugged man. On December 14, 1977, they drove Scott-Elliot to a remote road in Glen Afric and when strangling him with a scarf failed to kill him, they beat him to death with the spade used to bury his wife. Disposing of him in a shallow grave, they drove to Edinburgh to sell articles stolen from the couple's home. Mary Coggle's refusal to part with the dead woman's fur coat, jewelry, and clothes marked her for death. Fearful that the conspicuous items would lead to their arrest, Kitto held Coggle's arms behind her while Hall bludgeoned her with a fireplace poker at his home in Newton Arlosh on December 17, 1977. After binding her hands behind her back with a tie, they placed a plastic bag over her head, and went out for a drink. They later drove to the country village of Middlebie, dumped Coggle's body off a bridge, and hid the poker in a nearby hedge. Her body was not found until Christmas Day.

In London, Hall and Kitto systematically looted the treasures in the Scott-Elliot home and used the proceeds to dine in the finest restaurants. Mutually distrustful, when together one murderer kept the gun while the other held the bullets. The relationship was further complicated with the arrival on the scene of Hall's younger brother, Donald, recently released from prison after serving three years for housebreaking. Hall, 17 years Donald's senior, hated his brother's slovenly appearance, lack of education, and pedophilic inclinations toward young girls. When Donald Hall began asking embarrassing questions about the pair's bankroll they decided to eliminate him. In the early morning hours of January 15, 1978, an inebriated Donald Hall bragged to his brother and Kitto that he could free himself from any binding. Eager to demonstrate how he could escape the knots, Donald urged them to bind his hands behind him with a pajama cord. Once helpless, Archibald Hall pressed a chloroform soaked rag over his brother's face. Donald broke free, but the pair caught him, choked him, then held him face down in a bathtub filled with water. Like two other victims before him, Donald's body was stuffed into the trunk of the rented car as they drove around in search of a dumping ground.

Later that day, their suspicious behavior in a North Berwick hotel prompted the manager to notify police. The next day, January 16, authorities detained Hall and Kitto after finding that the license plate on their car was registered to another vehicle. Before the trunk containing his brother's body could be opened, Hall was permitted to use the restroom at police headquarters. He escaped through an open window, flagged down a cab, but was arrested hours later at a roadblock where he was informed that the body had been found. Placed in a detention cell at Musselburgh police station, Hall made the first of two suicide attempts. A routine search had failed to reveal the packet of librium capsules Hall had secreted in his anus. He was able to ingest several of them before having his stomach pumped out at the Edinburgh Royal Infirmary. Days later, Hall used the same cache of pills in another unsuccessful suicide attempt.

Directed by Hall and Kitto's series of confessions, authorities were able to recover the bodies of all their victims as well as physical evidence (the poker and chloroform) linking them to the murders. On May 2, 1978, Hall was sentenced in an Edinburgh court to life imprisonment for the murders of Mr. Walter Travers Scott-Elliot and David Wright. An added stipulation mandated that "the Monster Butler" serve not less than 15 years. Kitto was given life imprisonment for his role in the murder of Mr. Scott-Elliot. At a hearing on November 1, 1978, Hall received an additional life sentence for the murders of Mary Coggle and Donald Hall. Hall pleaded not guilty to murdering Mrs. Dorothy Scott-Elliot and to spare the enormous expense of a public trial the charge was left on file. Kitto, arguing that he was under Hall's influence, pleaded guilty to manslaughter and was given a 15-year prison term. Although the judge recommended that he never be given parole except in the case of "serious infirmity," Hall is optimistic that the passage of time combined with changing public attitudes may one day see his release.

236. Copeland, James. *The Butler.* London: Granada, 1981. 204 pp., [8]pp. of

plates: ill.; 18 cm. ("A Panther book"); paperback.

237. Lucas, Norman, and Davies, Philip. *The Monster Butler*. London: Arthur Barker, 1979. 159 pp., [4] leaves of plates: ill.; 23 cm.

_____. [Same as 237.] London: Mirror Books, 1979. 159 pp., [8]pp. of plates: 1 ill., ports.; 19 cm.; paperback.

_____. [Same as 237.] London: Weidenfeld and Nicolson, 1991. 159 pp.: ill., ports.; 20 cm.; paperback.

Straightforward account of the crimes which portrays Hall/Fontaine as "a Walter Mitty character who dreamed of ending his days beneath the brilliant Brazilian sunshine under a new name…"

"Hammersmith Nudes Murders" *see* "Jack the Stripper"

Hansen, Robert C.

Born February 15, 1939, in Pocahontas, Iowa. Baker. Anchorage, Alaska; 17 murders (admits killing 20 and is suspected of more); knife, .223 caliber rifle; 1973–1983.

Audio: Butcher, Baker: A True Account of a Serial Murderer, an audio cassette version of Gilmour and Hale's book of the same title, was released in 1991 by the Iowa Department for the Blind in Des Moines.

"I was just seeing everybody else get theirs, and it was my turn to have fun now."—Hansen's explanation for why he killed at least 17 women

Described by a prosecutor as "an extreme aberration of a human being … who has walked among us for 17 years, serving us donuts … and hot coffee," Robert C. Hansen, a baker and devoted family man, methodically murdered 17 women in and around Anchorage, Alaska, over a 10 year period beginning in 1973. A champion

hunter who held several world bow and arrow records, Hansen selected his human prey from the ranks of prostitutes and topless dancers in "the Tenderloin," the red-light district in Anchorage. Posing as a doctor or lawyer, Hansen offered scores of women hundreds of dollars to pose nude or to have lunch with him. Those accepting were kidnapped, taken to remote areas, bound, raped, and if they did not resist, set free. On June 13, 1983, Hansen picked up a 17-year-old prostitute and brought her to his home at 7223 Old Harbor Road. Over her objections, he handcuffed the girl and raped her. Hansen's plan to fly her in his private plane to a wilderness cabin for more sex was thwarted when she broke free at the air field and escaped. She subsequently identified his plane to authorities and picked him out of a lineup. Hansen's home was searched, and while it matched her description of it, police were more inclined to accept the alibi of a well-connected businessman than the unsupported accusation of a teenaged prostitute.

Beginning in 1980, Anchorage authorities had noted a disturbing three-year pattern of working girls reported missing from the Tenderloin. All were either prostitutes or topless dancers, fitting a general physical profile, and had been offered big money for a "date" by a stranger shortly before they disappeared. On September 12, 1982, two off-duty police officers hunting moose on the Knik River 25 miles north of Anchorage discovered the partially clothed body of 24-year-old Sherry Morrow (a.k.a. Graves) buried in a sand bar. A topless dancer at a downtown club, Morrow had vanished in November 1981. Her head was wrapped in an ace bandage and a spent .223 caliber shell casing normally used in a high-powered rifle was found in her grave. She died from a gunshot wound to the head. Almost a year later on September 2, 1983, the body of Paula Goulding, a 31-year-old topless dancer, was found near Morrow's grave on a remote part of the Knik River accessible only by boat or plane. Missing since April 1983, Goulding had also been shot through the head. A shell casing identical to one found in Morrow's grave was recovered from the scene. When the FBI determined that both casings had been fired from the same gun, alarmed authorities realized that a serial killer was at work in Anchorage who had the means to dump his victims in wilderness areas.

The striking similarities between the cases of the missing prostitutes and the teenager who escaped from Hansen intrigued authorities. A broader background check on the baker revealed an extensive criminal record of kidnapping, assault, and rape dating from 1971. In December of that year Hansen attempted to rape an 18-year-old real estate receptionist and, while awaiting trial for that offense, kidnapped and raped a prostitute at gunpoint. Hansen pleaded no contest on the attempted rape and did less than two years in prison. The kidnapping charge was reduced to assault with a dangerous weapon and Hansen was sentenced to five years on March 24, 1972. He was on parole in 1975 when he abducted a topless dancer and drove her to Chugach State Park where he forced her at gunpoint to fellate him. He reportedly told the woman that she would not be a good witness against him "because you're a nude dancer and a prostitute." Hansen later denied raping the woman insisting that they had only argued over price. The woman refused to testify against him. In 1979,

Hansen kidnapped another topless dancer who, naked, managed to escape from his truck. He told investigators that the woman became upset and fled after he refused to pay her for sex. No charges were ever filed.

At the request of Anchorage authorities, the FBI's Behavioral Science Unit prepared a profile of the unknown serial killer which proved to be a remarkably accurate portrait of Robert Hansen. Based on material provided them, the FBI concluded that the killer was probably a respected and hardworking man married to a religious woman who was unaware of his activities. He probably stuttered, was an excellent hunter, kept a murder kit, and liked to keep mementos of his kills to relive the fantasy of murder. Hansen, the son of a domineering father and weak mother, developed a lifelong stutter possibly resulting from his father's insistence that he be right-handed. An acne-scarred social outcast, Hansen was continually derided by his father as worthless and was disliked in school. In 1961 after returning from army basic training, he burned down a school bus barn in his hometown of Pocahontas, Iowa, and was placed in the Men's Reformatory in Anamosa for three years. His first wife divorced him shortly afterwards. Following a 1972 assault conviction, Hansen underwent a psychiatric examination in which he admitted that "he fantasized about doing all sorts of harmful things to girls who rejected him." At that time, he was diagnosed as suffering from periodic schizophrenic episodes of psychotic dissociation. Hansen remarried a devoutly religious woman and moved with her to Alaska in the early 1970s.

On October 27, 1983, Hansen was arrested for the kidnapping and rape of the teenage prostitute after his alibi admitted covering for him. Bail was set at $500,000. A stash of mementos including the .223 caliber rifle used in the murders of Morrow and Goulding, some victims' jewelry, and an aviation map meticulously dotted with 24 X-marks were found hidden beneath the insulation in the attic of his home. Investigators, fearful that the X-marks were not hunting areas as Hansen insisted but rather the burial sites of more victims, began matching dozens of old missing persons cases with the markings. Two of the marks were in the exact Knik River locations where the bodies of Morrow and Goulding had previously been recovered. Ostensibly to protect his wife and child from the humiliation of numerous murder trials, Hansen agreed on February 16, 1984, to "clear the decks." One week later, the 45-year-old man signed an Agreement of Understanding with the State of Alaska in which he agreed to confess to the 17 murders he committed and lead authorities to the bodies in exchange for being charged with only the five murders they knew about.

In his 12-hour confession, Hansen calmly described a 10-year reign of rape and murder that he termed "a summertime project." Drawing a sharp distinction between "good" women like his wife and "bad" women like prostitutes and topless dancers, Hansen felt justified in killing women that he considered "inferior" and "lower" than himself. As long as he enjoyed total control over the women he drove or flew to the wilderness to rape they were brought back "unharmed." If they struggled, Hansen shot them (many believed after first hunting them) and "they stayed." The first murder occurred in summer 1979 near Lake Eklutna. The young unidentified woman dubbed "Eklutna Annie" was not found until July 17, 1980. Unlike the other 16 victims who were shot, Hansen used the woman's own knife to kill her. As the body sites of his victims were spread out over hundreds of square miles of Alaskan wilderness, Hansen was taken by helicopter on February 25, 1984, to several of the locations marked on his map. He identified 12 burial sites that officers marked with fluorescent spray paint. They returned after the spring thaw and recovered 11 bodies by the end of summer 1984.

On February 27, 1984, Hansen pleaded guilty in an Anchorage superior court to the slaying of the four women whose bodies had been recovered as well as 13 others still buried in shallow graves throughout Alaska. Hansen also admitted to the kidnapping and rape of over 30 women he did not kill. In the absence of the death penalty, the prosecution recommended that the serial killer be sentenced to the maximum period of 461 years plus life in a federal institution for charges that included four murders, kidnapping, rape, felony weapons possession, and theft. Before following the recommendation, the judge noted that Hansen's case represented "an indictment" of the entire judicial system. The killer had been arrested three times over the past 12 years for charges associated with kidnapping or sexual assault and each time permitted to go free. Ironically, had Alaska's most prolific serial murderer received the maximum penalty of five years for one of these crimes he would have been in prison during the time three of the four murders he was formally charged with were committed. Hansen's record sentence of 461 years was eclipsed on July 7, 1984, by computer programmer Louis Hastings who received 634 years for methodically hunting down and murdering six people

in the small Alaskan town of Mc-
Carthy.

In February 1984, Seattle, Washington, police discounted the apparent
similarities between the killings committed by the Green River Killer and
those confessed to by Hansen. Even
though the Seattle prostitute killings
stopped about the time of Hansen's
arrest, the Green River Killer strangled
his victims instead of shooting them.
In prison, Hansen has written several
humorous short stories and plans to
publish an autobiography. Two publishers have already contacted him for
the rights. In spring 1990 corrections
officers in Juneau discovered a cache of
stamps and an aviation map of southeast Alaska in Hansen's cell. He has
since been transferred to a maximum
security prison near Seward.

238. Du Clos, Bernard. *Fair Game.* St.
Martin's paperback ed. True Crime
Series. New York: St. Martin's Paperbacks, 1993. 179 pp., [8]pp. of plates: ill.;
18 cm.; paperback.

_____. [Same as 238 with added subtitle:
Alaska's Most Notorious Serial Killer.]
London: Mondo, 1993. 284 pp., [8]pp. of
plates: ill.; 18 cm.; paperback.

A paperback original based on
police and court records (1961–1984),
transcriptions of interviews (1983–1984),
and interviews with persons connected
to the Robert Hansen case. Du Clos
recreates some scenes and dialogue and
uses a pseudonym for Hansen's second
wife.

239. Gilmour, Walter, and Hale, Leland
E. *Butcher, Baker: A True Account of a Serial Murderer.* New York: Onyx Books,
1991. 342 pp., [8]pp. of plates: ill., map;
18 cm.; paperback.

Though based on interviews and
court and police transcripts, the book also
contains several scenes which have been
dramatically recreated by the authors. In

the midst of conflicting versions of
events, they "have sought to provide the
version which in their opinion is the most
credible." A paperback original. "The
savage sex slayer who bloodied the
Alaskan landscape."—Cover

Harris, Jean Struven

Born circa 1923 in Cleveland
Heights, Ohio. Headmistress. Purchase, New York; 1 murder; .32 caliber
pistol; March 10, 1980.

Television: "People vs. Jean Harris" (1981), a two-part, three-hour
made-for-television movie, originally
aired on NBC on May 7–8, 1981. Cast
includes Ellen Burstyn (Jean Harris),
Martin Balsam (Joel Arnou/Herman
Tarnower), and Richard Dysart (Judge
Russell R. Leggett). "They're Doing
My Time" (1989), a television documentary exploring what happens to
children when their mothers are incarcerated. Narrated by Jane Alexander,
the program features an interview with
prison inmate Harris who is active in
educating prison mothers.

A case in which the high profile
murder of a renowned physician by his
long time mistress helped fix intellectual debate on the social position of
aging women and the relations between
the sexes. On March 10, 1980, Jean
Harris, the 57-year-old headmistress
of the exclusive Madeira School for
Girls in McLean, Virginia, confronted
her lover of 14 years, Dr. Herman Tarnower, in the bedroom of his $500,000
home in Purchase, New York. The 69-
year-old cardiologist, author of the
runaway best seller *The Complete Scarsdale Diet*, had recently begun an affair
with his assistant, a woman 20 years
younger than Harris. At her subsequent trial, Harris maintained that she
intended to kill herself over Tarnower's

involvement with the younger woman, but the .32 caliber pistol discharged four times into the doctor's body when he struggled to take it from her. The prosecution convinced a jury in Westchester County that Harris killed Tarnower in a jealous rage and she was convicted of second degree murder on February 24, 1981. Sentenced to a minimum of 15 years to life in prison, Harris was a model prisoner at the maximum security Bedford Hills Correctional Facility in Westchester County situated 15 miles from the site of the murder. During her incarceration, Harris helped set up a center where children born to women prisoners could spend a year with their mothers. Harris had been denied clemency on three occasions by New York Governor Mario Cuomo when she suffered a heart attack in the prison's infirmary in December 1992. On December 29, 1992, hours before she was to undergo quadruple bypass surgery, Cuomo granted the 69-year-old clemency based largely on her tireless work with women prisoners and their infants. During the 11 years, ten months, and six days Harris served in prison, she wrote three books. In one, *Stranger in Two Worlds* (1986), she told her version of the events leading up to Tarnower's murder. Harris currently lives alone in a New Hampshire log cabin on a retirement fund from her 36 years of teaching.

240. Alexander, Shana. *Very Much a Lady: The Untold Story of Jean Harris and Dr. Herman Tarnower.* 1st ed. Boston: Little, Brown, 1983. xvi, 316 pp., [8]pp. of plates: ill.; 24 cm.

_____. [Same as 240 minus subtitle.] New York: Dell Books, 1986. xii, 372 pp.; 17 cm.; paperback.
Includes a new postscript.

241. David, Jay. *The Scarsdale Murder.* New York: Leisure Books, 1980. 254 pp.: ill.; 18 cm.; paperback.

242. Harris, Jean. *Stranger in Two Worlds.* New York: Macmillan, 1986. xxv, 388 pp., [16]pp. of plates: ill., ports.; 25 cm.

_____. [Same as 242.] New York: Kensington Publishing Corp., 1987. 560 pp., [16]pp. of plates: ill., ports.; 18 cm. ("Zebra books"); paperback. (Various dated printings.)

_____. [Same as 242.] G.K. Hall Large Print Book Series. xxxiii, 581 pp. (large print); 25 cm.

243._____. *They Always Call Us Ladies: Stories from Prison.* New York: Scribner's: Special Sales Director, Macmillan [distributor], 1988. vii, 276 pp.; 24 cm.

_____. [Same as 243.] New York: Kensington, 1990. 318 pp.; 18 cm. ("Zebra books"); paperback. (Various dated printings.)

244. Harris, Jean, and Alexander, Shana. *Marking Time: Letters from Jean Harris to Shana Alexander.* New York: Toronto: New York: Charles Scribner's Sons; Maxwell Macmillan Canada; Maxwell Macmillan International, 1991. xiii, 189 pp.; 24 cm. ("A Robert Stewart book.")

_____. [Same as 244 minus subtitle.] New York: Kensington, 1993. 252 pp.; 18 cm. ("Zebra books"); paperback.

245. Spencer, Duncan. *Love Gone Wrong: The Jean Harris Scarsdale Murder Case.* New York: New American Library, 1981. 281 pp., [8]pp. of plates: ill., ports.; 18 cm. ("A Signet book"); paperback.

246. Trilling, Diana. *Mrs. Harris: The Death of the Scarsdale Diet Doctor.* 1st ed. New York: Harcourt Brace Jovanovich, 1981. 341 pp.; 25 cm.

_____. [Same as 246.] Harmondsworth; New York: Penguin Books, 1982. 438 pp.; 19 cm.; paperback.

Hatcher, Charles Ray
(a.k.a. "Albert Ralph Price," "Richard Lee Price," "Richard Martin Clark," "Richard Mark Clark," "Ronald Springer," "Richard Harris," "Richard Lee Grady," "Earl L. Kalebough," "Carl L. Kalebough," "Albert Aire," "Charles Marvin Tidwell," "Hobart Prater," "Dorison Mullins," "Dorison Mullins Travis," "Dorison Mullins Jarvis," "Dwayne Lee Wilfong")

Born July 16, 1929, in Mound City, New Jersey. Died December 7, 1984. Drifter. Missouri, Illinois, California; 16 murders (self-confessed); manual asphyxiation, knife; 1978-1982.

"I kill on impulse. It's an uncontrollable urge that builds and builds over a period of weeks until I have to kill. It doesn't matter if the victims are men, women or children. Whoever is around is in trouble."—Hatcher to FBI agents in an August 3, 1983, interview

In a 35-year, 8-state criminal career highlighted by child molestation and 16 self-confessed murders, Charles Ray Hatcher repeatedly manipulated the penal and mental health systems designed to identify and segregate violent sexual psychopaths. Described by one prosecutor as being as "close to evil as a human being can come," Hatcher adroitly avoided prison by feigning insanity to be placed instead in the less restrictive atmosphere of psychiatric units. Once there, he either escaped or won early release by convincing doctors that he was "cured." During a period of violent criminal activity between the fall of 1978 and the spring of 1982, Hatcher was involved in a series of molestations, attempted abductions, and attempted murders in Nebraska and Iowa. Remarkably, he never spent a day behind bars during that period. Arrested in Bettendorf, Iowa, on July 16, 1981, for the attempted abduction of an 11-year-old boy, Hatcher feigned insanity and spent only 49 days in a mental hospital before winning release. Perhaps even more disconcerting, law enforcement agencies in Nebraska and Iowa never bothered to run his fingerprints. Had they done so, officials would have realized that they were dealing with a career criminal whose record dated back to October 1947.

Born in New Jersey in 1929, Hatcher's early life was one of extremes characterized by drunken beatings administered by an ex-con father and excessive attention lavished on him by an unstable mother. Some psychiatrists theorize that Hatcher's fascination with death stemmed from having witnessed at age six his older brother's electrocution while flying a kite. By ten, the boy's family had relocated over a dozen times to escape creditors. The 16 year old moved with his mother and her third husband to St. Joseph, Missouri, and in 1947 received a two-year suspended sentence for stealing a truck. His probation was revoked in 1948 for auto theft and on February 7, 1948, Hatcher began serving a two-year sentence in the Missouri State Penitentiary where he was gang raped the first week. Enjoying the first of many breaks given him over the years by the corrections system, Hatcher was released a year early in August 1949, but was back inside before the year was out for forging a $10 check. Between February 1948 and September 1955 Hatcher was incarcerated six times for forgeries, car thefts, and repeated escape attempts. By age 42, he had spent nearly half his life in Missouri jails and prisons.

Released on March 18, 1959, Hatcher's violent side emerged. Armed with a butcher knife, he attempted to abduct a 16-year-old newspaper boy in St. Joseph, Missouri, on June 26, 1959. The teenager escaped and Hatcher was arrested driving a stolen car and sentenced to five years in the Missouri State Penitentiary. Penal authorities there strongly suspected Hatcher of the rape and stabbing murder of an inmate in the prison kitchen on July 2, 1961. The case was never officially solved and Hatcher was released from prison on August 24, 1963. Using the alias "Albert Ralph Prince," Hatcher resurfaced in San Francisco on August 29, 1969, where he abducted, raped, and savagely beat a five-year-old Mexican boy. He was arrested at the scene when a passerby notified police that a man was forcing a boy to fellate him. In custody, Hatcher refused to talk and attempted suicide by slashing his wrist with a razor blade. Fingerprints established Hatcher's true identity and revealed that during the years between the attempted abduction of the newsboy in St. Joseph and the rape of the child in San Francisco, "Prince" had logged four escapes from jails and prisons in Missouri, Kansas, and California.

Facing charges of assault with intent to commit sodomy and kidnapping, Hatcher convinced court-appointed psychiatrists that he was insane and unable to stand trial. He was ordered to the California State Hospital at Atascadero for observation, the first of five instances in which Hatcher avoided prison in California by feigning mental illness. Between August 1969 and December 1972 when he was finally tried, Hatcher success-fully manipulated the system by undergoing eight different psychological exams during the period. On June 2, 1972, he escaped from San Francisco General Hospital where he was undergoing treatment. Hatcher, "Richard Lee Grady," was arrested a week later in Colusa, California, but acted so strangely that he was committed to Atascadero where nurses recognized him as "Albert Prince." In August 1972, Hatcher was transferred to San Quentin. Two days later, fearful of being killed by a prisoner he had snitched on at another institution in 1969, Hatcher wrote a letter to his attorney declaring himself fit for trial. Psychiatrists now agreed and more than three years after the attack on the child he was convicted on December 17, 1972, of lewd and lascivious behavior and committed for treatment to Atascadero as a mentally disordered sex offender. Facing an indeterminate sentence of one year to life in the medical facility, Hatcher reacted to their recommendation that he be transferred to Folsom Prison by slashing his wrist and neck with a razor blade. He ultimately convinced doctors at Vacaville that he had significantly improved and was released to a halfway house in San Francisco on May 20, 1977. Five days later Hatcher bolted.

On May 26, 1978, a man fitting Hatcher's description abducted four-year-old Eric Scott Christgen from a mall playground in St. Joseph, Missouri. The next day the boy's body was found in a ravine near the bank of the Missouri River. Christgen had been sexually abused and the coroner determined that death had resulted from asphyxiation during oral sodomy. Police interviewed several suspects (one died of a heart attack while being questioned) before making 25-year-old

Melvin Lee Reynolds, an unemployed cook, their prime suspect. While he bore no physical resemblance to the description of the abductor supplied by two witnesses, Reynolds was a troubled man who was a known homosexual. After several hours of intense questioning by St. Joseph police, Reynolds confessed to Christgen's murder on February 14, 1979, and was subsequently sentenced to life imprisonment in the Missouri State Penitentiary, Hatcher's alma mater.

During the years following his 1977 flight from San Francisco, Hatcher roamed the Midwest logging arrests under assumed names for attempted abductions, assaults, and molestations. In each instance Hatcher used the system to escape prison, gain admittance to psychiatric hospitals, then be miraculously "cured" of insanity in order to continue what one California official called a "one-man crime wave." In the last week of July 1982 Hatcher surfaced in St. Joseph where he tried unsuccessfully on successive days to abduct a 19-year-old woman and a 10-year-old girl. The next day, July 29, Hatcher abducted 11-year-old Michelle Steele from a downtown drugstore. Her nude body was found the next day under bushes on the bank of the Missouri River less than a mile downstream from where Eric Christgen's body had been discovered. Steele, who had been beaten and raped, died of asphyxiation caused when she lost consciousness in a position in which she was unable to breathe. The night before the discovery of the child's body Hatcher, identifying himself as "Richard Harris," had been questioned by a reserve deputy sheriff less than 100 yards from where Steele's body was found. On July 30, 1982, Hatcher as "Richard Clark" checked himself into

the St. Joseph State Hospital complaining of voices in his head. An alert hospital employee hearing a description of "Harris" on police band radio notified authorities about "Clark." Hatcher was charged with Steele's murder on August 3, 1982, after his two other potential victims picked him out of a photo lineup.

In custody, Hatcher laid in a fetal position for ten days refusing to speak with authorities. On September 12, 1982, he pleaded not guilty by reason of mental disease to the murder, but a court-appointed psychiatrist did not buy his story of hearing inner voices compelling him to "sacrifice a maiden" and ruled Hatcher competent to stand trial. Hatcher contacted the FBI in May 1983 and days later supplied an agent with a map and detailed handwritten instructions on where to find a concealed body. The map led agents to the decomposed remains of James L. Churchill, 28, buried beneath rocks on the Mississippi River near the Rock Island arsenal in Illinois. Hatcher admitted stabbing his drinking buddy 10 to 12 times on June 20, 1981. During the same interview session, Hatcher also confessed to the strangulation murder of 12-year-old William J. Freeman in Antioch, California, on August 28, 1969. Hatcher's next admission rocked the city of St. Joseph and set off a firestorm of controversy. The serial murderer, supposedly feeling guilty over Melvin Lee Reynolds' unjust imprisonment, confessed to the murder of Eric Christgen and provided details of the crime which could only be known to the killer. On October 13, 1983, Hatcher pleaded guilty to the Christgen murder and was sentenced to life imprisonment with no possibility of parole for 50 years. Reynolds, after serving almost four years for a crime he did not commit, was released the next day. Hatcher later recanted his confession in the Christgen murder.

Two years and 50 days after Michelle Steele's murder, Hatcher faced a capital murder charge in a Warrensburg, Missouri, courtroom on September 17, 1984. Hatcher was convicted five days later and in the separate penalty phase of the trial the jury disregarded the child killer's impassioned plea to be executed and instead sentenced him to life imprisonment without the possibility of parole for 50 years. On December 7, 1984, Hatcher was found hanged in his cell at the Missouri State Penitentiary. He left no suicide note. Hatcher's death officially closed the books on the 1969 murder of 12-year-old William Freeman in Antioch, California. After family members refused to claim his body, Hatcher was buried on December 11, 1984, in an unmarked grave in Longview Cemetery on the outskirts of Jefferson City, Missouri. Death, however, did not end the controversy surrounding Missouri's first convicted serial murderer. In January 1985 area residents protested the planned inclusion of the electrical cord and the three-foot-long shoelace Hatcher used to commit suicide in "A Century of Crime in St. Joseph" exhibit at the Jesse James Museum. The idea was later dropped after the local PTA voted against it and the museum's board of directors received a 5,000 signature petition protesting the inclusion of the suicide items in the display.

247. Ganey, Terry. *St. Joseph's Children: A True Story of Terror and Justice.* New York: Carol Pub. Group, 1989. 237 pp., [8]pp. of plates: ill.; 23 cm. ("A Lyle Stuart book.")

_____. [Same as 247, but paperback ed. retitled: *Innocent Blood: A True Story of Terror and Justice.*] St. Martin's paperback ed. New York: St. Martin, 1990. x, 302 pp.: ill.; 18 cm.; paperback.

A veteran reporter's detailed account based on extensive interviews, court transcripts, police reports, and Hatcher's mental health records. Includes a detailed chronology entitled "The Violent Odyssey of Charles Hatcher."

Hauptmann, Bruno Richard (a.k.a. "Lindbergh Baby Kidnapper," "John," "Cemetery John")

Born circa 1899 in Kamenz, Germany. Executed April 3, 1936. Carpenter. Hopewell, New Jersey; 1 murder; unknown (fall suspected); March 1, 1932.

Film: Miss Fane's Baby Is Stolen (US, 1934), a Paramount film suggested by the Lindbergh baby kidnapping directed by Alexander Hall. Cast includes Dorothea Wieck (Madeline Fane), Alice Brady (Mrs. Molly Prentiss), Baby LeRoy (Michael Fane), and William Frawley (Capt. Murphy).

Theatre: Hauptmann (1986), a play by John Logan directed by Terry McCabe, premiered at Chicago's Stormfield Theatre on September 13, 1986. Cast includes Denis O'Hare (Bruno Richard Hauptmann), Layne Beamer, and Donna Powers.

Television: "The Lindbergh Baby Kidnapping Case" (1976), a three-hour, made-for-television movie, originally aired on NBC on February 26, 1976. Cast includes Anthony Hopkins (Bruno Richard Hauptmann), Cliff DeYoung (Charles Lindbergh), and Joseph Cotten (Dr. John Francis Condon).

"The poor child has been kidnapped and murdered, so somebody must die for it. For is the parent not the great flyer? And if somebody does not die for the death of the child, then always the police will be monkeys. So I am the one who is picked out to die."—Hauptmann on death row, 1936

German immigrant executed for the Lindbergh baby kidnapping which H.L. Mencken called "the biggest story since the Resurrection." In 1932 Colonel Charles A. Lindbergh, the first man to fly solo across the Atlantic (1927), was arguably the greatest hero in the United States and was even more popular than Babe Ruth. To escape the glare of publicity, "Lucky Lindy," his wife Anne Morrow Lindbergh, and their 18-month-old son Charles Augustus, Jr., moved to a recently built 14-room house on their estate in East Amwell Township near Hopewell, New Jersey, in the Sourland Mountains. At 10:00 p.m. on March 1, 1932, the Lindbergh's nursemaid entered the second floor nursery and discovered the child missing from his crib. The abductor's ransom note, riddled with misspellings, demanded $50,000 for the boy's return. A crudely made ladder, believed to have been used by the kidnapper to remove the baby through the second story window, was found on the grounds near the house. The country was stunned and outraged by the kidnapping. Colonel H. Norman Schwarzkopf, chief of the New Jersey state police and father of the army general who commanded the international forces during the Gulf War, headed up the nationwide manhunt. President Herbert Hoover announced, "We will move Heaven and Earth to find out who is this criminal that had the audacity to commit a crime like this." As ransom demands began to pour in, 72-year-old Dr. John

F. Condon, a lecturer in education at Fordham University, agreed to act as an intermediary between the kidnapper and the Lindberghs. Using the code name "Jafsie" (based on his initials J.F.C.), the eccentric Condon placed a series of ads in the *Bronx Home News* which led to a meeting with the kidnapper on March 12, 1932. The man, calling himself "John," upped the ransom to $70,000 and gave Condon the missing child's sleeping suit to prove his authenticity.

The ransom payoff was set to take place in St. Raymond's Cemetery in the Bronx on the night of April 2, 1932. Two bundles of gold certificates were prepared, one containing $50,000 and the other $20,000. Earlier, the FBI had spent hours recording the serial numbers of each of the bills. That night, as Lindbergh waited in a parked car outside the cemetery gates, Condon entered the graveyard and gave "John" the bundle containing $50,000. In exchange, Condon was given an envelope directing him to the location of the child, on a boat somewhere off the coast of Massachusetts between Horseneck Bay and Gay Head near Elizabeth Island. Coast Guard cutters scoured the area for weeks, but found nothing. On May 12, 1932, the body of Charles Augustus, Jr., his skull fractured, was found in a shallow grave in the woods five miles from the Lindbergh estate. The body's advanced state of decomposition led a local pathologist to conclude that the boy must have been dead since the night of the kidnapping. In fact, the body's decomposition was so pronounced that its sex, let alone its identity, could not be firmly established although both Lindbergh and the boy's governess verified the remains as those of the missing child. The Lindberghs' pediatrician, who examined the body in the funeral home shortly before the corpse was cremated, said, "If you were to lay ten million dollars on that table and tell me it was mine if I said positively this was the Colonel's son, I'd have to refuse the money."

Almost three years after the child's abduction and murder, authorities got their first solid lead in the case. On September 15, 1934, a man used a $10 gold certificate to purchase gas in a Manhattan service station. In April 1933, President Franklin Delano Roosevelt had ordered all holders of gold-backed notes to exchange them for silver certificates. The government had also distributed 250,000 circulars giving the serial numbers of the gold certificates used in the Lindbergh ransom payoff. The gas station attendant, Water Lyle, wrote the car's license plate on the back of the note and checked it against the circular sent out by the U.S. Treasury Department. It matched. On September 19, 1934, authorities arrested Bruno Richard Hauptmann, a 35-year-old German immigrant, at the apartment in the Bronx he shared with his wife Anna, and their infant son. Hauptmann, a carpenter by profession, had served three years in a German prison for burglary and armed robbery before arriving in New York as a stowaway in 1924. Police found $14,600 in ransom bills hidden in the German's garage and dismissed his explanation as to how the money had come into his possession. According to Hauptmann, his friend and business partner Isidor Fisch left a shoe box in his care without telling him its contents before returning to Germany for a visit. Hauptmann put the box on a shelf in the broom closet and forgot about it. Sometime later word came from Germany that Fisch had died of a tuber-

cular condition. Still Hauptmann did not open the shoe box until a leak developed in the closet and drenched the parcel. Discovering the money, Hauptmann decided to keep some of it to settle a debt Fisch owed him and to bury the rest in the garage until such time as he could return the balance to his partner's relatives when they came to the United States to settle the estate. New Jersey Attorney General David Wilentz, the prosecutor in the case, would later contemptuously call Hauptmann's account a "Fisch story." An equally damning piece of evidence was found in Hauptmann's attic. At the time of the child's abduction, a rung of a ladder had been found at the scene. Arthur Koehler, a forestry department expert, traced the wood used in fashioning the rung of the kidnap ladder to a gap in the floor of Hauptmann's attic. Additionally, seven handwriting experts agreed that the ransom notes had been written by the German carpenter.

The eyes of the nation were on Flemington, New Jersey, as Hauptmann's kidnap-murder trial opened in the Hunterdon County Courthouse on January 2, 1935. As press and spectators daily jammed the courtroom, street merchants peddled miniature 10 cent replicas of the kidnap ladder which many wore pinned to their lapels. In exchange for exclusive access to the suspected killer and his wife, newspaper magnate William Randolph Hearst paid for Hauptmann's legal defense. Though Hauptmann continued to maintain his innocence, he was crushed by a flood of evidence. Prosecutor Wilentz carefully outlined the state's "lone wolf kidnapper" theory of the case arguing that the child died of a fractured skull sustained in a fall when the ladder bearing him and

Hauptmann broke under their combined weight. Eyewitnesses placed Hauptmann at or near the scene of the crime; handwriting experts testified that he wrote the ransom notes; an expert on wood technology matched the rung on the kidnap ladder with a board found in Hauptmann's attic; and both Condon and Lindbergh testified that it was the German's voice they heard in the cemetery on the night of the ransom payoff. On February 13, 1935, the 32nd day of the trial, Hauptmann was found guilty and sentenced to death. Outside the courtroom, an ugly crowd of 10,000 screamed, "Kill Hauptmann! Kill the German!" Hours before his execution at the New Jersey State Prison in Trenton, Hauptmann scrawled a letter to New Jersey Governor Harold Hoffman and, indirectly, to the prosecutor. He wrote: "My writing is not in fear of losing my life, this is in the hands of God, it is His will. I will go gladly, it means the end of my tremendous suffering. Only in thinking of my dear wife and my little boy, that is breaking my heart … Mr. Wilentz, with my dying breath I swear by God that you convicted an innocent man. Once you will stand before the same Judge, to whom I go in a few hours. You know you have done wrong on me … I beg you, Attorney General, believe at least a dying man. Please investigate, because this case is not solved, it only adds another dead to the Lindbergh case." Hauptmann was electrocuted on April 3, 1936.

Hauptmann's death has not ended the controversy surrounding the verdict or dispelled the odious cloud of racism that continues to enshroud this case. Anna Hauptmann, the convicted killer's widow, continued her tireless campaign to clear her husband's name filing various lawsuits against the state of New Jersey alleging suppression of evidence (a claim many scholars of the case believe to be true). In 1986 one such case made it all the way to the U.S. Supreme Court where it was dismissed without comment. Mrs. Hauptmann, 96, died on October 10, 1994, her 69th wedding anniversary, at a hospital in Lancaster, Pennsylvania. Recently declassified FBI documents cast strong suspicion on Hauptmann's guilt and call into grave question the handling of the case by every law enforcement agency which investigated the Lindbergh baby kidnapping.

248. Behn, Noel. *Lindbergh: The Crime.* 1st ed. New York: Atlantic Monthly Press, 1994. x, 464 pp.: ill.; 24 cm.

_____. [Same as 248.] New York: Onyx, 1995. 496 pp., [16]pp. of plates: ill.; 18 cm.; paperback.

The novelist of *The Kremlin Letter* (1966) and *Big Stick-Up at Brinks!* (1977) strongly suggests, based on interviews with Harry Green, an attorney hired to investigate the case after Hauptmann's conviction, that the child was not kidnapped from his crib or murdered by his abductor. Instead, he was murdered several days earlier by his aunt, Elisabeth Morrow, because she sought revenge on her sister Anne Morrow Lindbergh for winning the affections of Charles Lindbergh. "Lucky Lindy" devised the false kidnap plot to protect his family from public stigma. Undocumented hearsay.

249. Brant, John, and Renaud, Edith. *True Story of the Lindbergh Kidnapping.* New York: Kroy Wen, 1932. 275 pp.: ill., front., ports.; 20 cm.

250. Condon, John F. *Jafsie Tells All! Revealing the Inside Story of the Lindbergh-Hauptmann Case.* New York: Jonathan Lee, 1936. ix, 238 pp.: ill., ports.; 22 cm.

Dr. Condon discusses his role as intermediary between the kidnapper and the Lindbergh family.

251. Demaris, Ovid. *The Lindbergh Kidnapping Case: The True Story of the Crime That Shocked the World.* Monarch Americana Series, MA307. Derby, Conn.: Monarch Books, 1961. 144 pp.; 19 cm.

252. Dutch, Andrew K. *Hysteria: The Lindbergh Kidnap Case.* Philadelphia: Dorrance, 1975. xi, 222 pp.: ports.; 22 cm.

253. Fisher, Jim. *The Lindbergh Case.* New Brunswick, N.J.: Rutgers University Press, 1987. vii, 480 pp.: ill.; 26 cm.

_____. [Same as 253.] New Brunswick, N.J.: Rutgers University Press, 1987. xxii, 480 pp.: ill.; 26 cm.; trade paperback.

Fisher, a former FBI agent and professor of criminal justice at Edinboro State College, concludes: "I can confidently write that Hauptmann was not unfairly framed and railroaded. I've spent four years studying more data than any other researcher up to now." According to Fisher, he wrote the book "as a vindication of the slander that the New Jersey State Police have undergone" and insists that the Lindbergh investigation was "a high point in the history of criminal investigation and forensic science."

254. Haldeman-Julius, Marcet. *The Lindbergh-Hauptmann Kidnap-Murder Case.* Girard, Kan.: Haldeman-Julius, 1937. 100 pp.; 22 cm. (Softcovers.)

255. Haring, J. Vreeland. *The Hand of Hauptmann; The Handwriting Expert Tells the Story of the Lindbergh Case.* Plainfield, N.J.: Hamer, 1937. 361 pp.: ill., ports., facsims.; 23 cm.

_____. [Same as 255.] Plainfield, N.J.: Hamer; Montclair, N.J.: Distributed by Patterson Smith, 1937. 361 pp.: ill., ports., facsims.; 23 cm.

[Note: Bookseller Patterson Smith purchased the author's inventory and is distributing the original 1937 edition.]

256. Heatter, Gabriel. *Word Pictures of the Hauptmann Trial.* [S.l.: s.n., 1935?] 31 pp.: ports.; 22 cm.

Photo essay of the Hauptmann trial.

257. Kennedy, Ludovic. *The Airman and the Carpenter: The Lindbergh Kidnapping.* London: Collins, 1985. x, 438 pp., [32]pp. of plates: ill., ports., facsims.; 24 cm.

_____. [Same as 257 with variant subtitle: *The Lindbergh Kidnapping and the Framing of Richard Hauptmann.*] New York: Viking, 1985. x, 438 pp., [32]pp. of plates: ill.; 25 cm.

_____. [Same as 257 with variant subtitle: *The Lindbergh Case and the Framing of Richard Hauptmann.*] London: Fontana, 1986. x, 438 pp., [32]pp. of plates: ill., ports., facsims.; 20 cm.; paperback.

_____. [Same as 257 with variant subtitle: *The Lindbergh Kidnapping and the Framing of Richard Hauptmann.*] New York: Penguin Books, 1986. xvii, 438 pp., [16]pp. of plates: ill.; 20 cm.; paperback.

Kennedy convincingly argues that Hauptmann was innocent and paints a vivid picture of press and legal misconduct at the time of the trial. Appendices include an extract from FBI report 62-3057 on the method of kidnapping, a note on the identification of Charles Lindbergh, Jr.'s body, extracts from the report of Gunter P. Haas (British handwriting expert), and a letter from Richard Hauptmann to his mother dated December 27, 1935. Includes chronology, bibliography, and index. An important book.

258. O'Brien, P.J. *The Lindberghs: The Story of a Distinguished Family.* Philadelphia: International Press, 1935. 352 pp.: ill., ports., facsims., maps; 22 cm.

_____. [Same as 258.] London: J. Long, 1936. viii, 285 pp.: ill., ports., facsims., maps; 24 cm.

259. Pease, Frank. *The "Hole" in the Hauptmann Case?* New York: F. Pease, 1936. 51 pp.; 23 cm.

260. Scaduto, Anthony. *Scapegoat: The Lonesome Death of Bruno Richard Hauptmann.* New York: Putnam, 1976. 512 pp., [8] leaves of plates: ill.; 24 cm.

_____. [Same as 260 with variant subtitle: *The Truth About the Lindbergh Kidnapping.*] London: Secker & Warburg, 1977. 512 pp.; 24 cm.

Scaduto, formerly a reporter for the *New York Post*, maintains that the government concealed evidence that would have supported Hauptmann's alibi on the day of the kidnapping and the day that the ransom money was passed by Dr. Condon. Tirelessly researched and documented, this book methodically picks apart the prosecution's case against the German immigrant. Essential reading and a necessary starting point for any consideration about the Lindbergh baby kidnapping.

261. Shoenfeld, Dudley D. *The Crime and the Criminal: A Psychiatric Study of the Lindbergh Case.* New York: Covici-Friede, 1936. vii, 411 pp.; 22 cm.

262. Vernon, John. *Lindbergh's Son.* New York: Viking, 1987. 279 pp.; 22 cm.

Fictionalized account based on the premise that the body found near the Lindbergh home on May 12, 1932, was not that of Lindbergh's child.

263. Vitray, Laura. *The Great Lindbergh Hullabaloo: An Unorthodox Account.* New York: W. Faro, 1932. 190 pp.: ill., front., map; 21 cm.

264. Waller, George. *Kidnap: The True Story of the Lindbergh Case.* New York: Dial Press, 1961. vi, 597 pp., [16]pp. of plates: ill.; 24 cm.

_____. [Same as 264 with variant subtitle: *The Story of the Lindbergh Case.*] London: Hamilton, 1961. xi, 594 pp., [8] leaves of plates: ill., facsims., fold. plan, ports.; 23 cm.

_____. [Same as 264 minus subtitle.] Giant Cardinal ed.; GC-774. New York: Pocket Books, 1962. 691 pp., [8] leaves of plates: ill.; 18 cm.; paperback.

265. Wendel, Paul H. *The Lindbergh-Hauptmann Aftermath.* Police ed. Brooklyn, N.Y.: Loft, 1940. 255 pp.: ill., ports.; 21 cm.

266. Whipple, Sidney B. *The Lindbergh Crime.* New York: Blue Ribbon Books,

1935. 341 pp.: front., plates; 22 cm. ("Erratum" slip mounted on p. 89.)

_____. [Same as 266.] London: Methuen, 1935. 294 pp.; 19 cm.

267. _____, ed. *The Trial of Bruno Richard Hauptmann.* 1st ed. Garden City, N.Y.: Doubleday, Doran, 1937. vii, 565 pp.: ill., plates, ports.; 24 cm.

_____. [Same as 267.] Special ed. Notable Trials Library. Birmingham, Ala.: Notable Trials Library, 1989. vii, 565 pp., [7] leaves of plates: ill.; 24 cm.

An account of proceedings in the case of Bruno Richard Hauptmann charged with the murder of Charles A. Lindbergh, Jr., in the township of East Amwell, New Jersey.

Heath, Neville George Clevely

(a.k.a. "Group Captain Rupert Brooke," "Captain Bruce Lockhart, M.C.," "Captain James Selway, M.C.," "Captain James Robert Cadogan Armstrong," "Blyth," "Denvers," "Graham," "Diamond Jim from J'Burg," "Lord Dudley")

Born June 6, 1917, in Ilford, Essex, England. Executed October 16, 1946. Former military airman. London and Bournemouth, England; 2 murders; knife; June 20 or 21, 1946, and July 3, 1946.

"My only regret at leaving the world is that I have been damned unworthy of you both."—Heath in a prison letter written to his parents

Sexual sadist hanged in 1946 for the murder of a woman at a British seaside resort. Strikingly good-looking and roguishly self-confident, former Royal Air Force Officer Neville Heath was never at a loss for female companionship. Bored with "normal love,"

Heath sought the "primitive" in a life-long orgy of sadism involving bondage, whippings, beatings, and ultimately, murder. His sadistic impulses emerged early. While still at school, Heath thrashed an eight-year-old girl with a teacher's cane so severely that she required hospitalization. Numerous affairs with teenaged girls ensued with at least one known to have been assaulted and partially strangled. Heath left school at 17 and embarked upon a military career in aviation blighted by fraud, deception, bad checks, and three separate court-martials. Dismissed from the Royal Air Force Fighter Command in 1937 for being chronically Absent Without Leave, the summer of 1938 found him sentenced to Borstal for three years on numerous convictions of petty fraud. On the outbreak of World War II Heath was released to join the Royal Army Service Corps and transferred to the Middle East as a second lieutenant in March 1940. In October 1941 he was again court-martialed, this time for drawing double pay and passing bad checks. Resurfacing in Durban, South Africa, Heath lived by defrauding women and banks. In 1942 he married an heiress to the DeBeer's diamond fortune, but she divorced him years later when he was unable to explain to her satisfaction the charred remains of a young nurse found in the burnt out wreckage of his car. Though police did not believe Heath's story that he was thrown from the wreckage, murder could not be proved. A three year stint in the South African Air Force ended when he was seconded to the RAF and later court-martialed in 1946 for "conduct prejudicial to Air Force discipline." During this time, the sadistically brutalized body of a young Air Force woman was found near Oxford-shire where Heath served. The crime was never solved.

Heath arrived in London in January 1946 where his drinking and sexual escapades quickly brought him under police scrutiny. Workmen at London's Strand Hotel reported hearing moans and blows coming from a guest's bedroom. Investigating, they found a semi-conscious nude woman bound spreadeagled on a bed and a naked Heath flagellating her with a whip. Fearing publicity, the bleeding woman refused to press charges. A similar incident occurred in May 1946 when Mrs. Margery Aimee Brownell Gardner, the 32-year-old estranged wife of a police officer serving abroad, consented to have sex with Heath at a West End hotel. Reacting to a woman's screams, the hotel detective opened their room with a passkey to find the nude and bleeding Gardner tied spread-eagled to a bed by silk handkerchiefs. Naked and shaking with rage, Heath had to be physically restrained from continuing the beating. Gardner, a masochist who enjoyed pain, refused to press charges.

A month later on June 20, 1946, Gardner's search for masochistic sex ended in death. Apparently still on good terms with Heath, she met him in the bar at the Trevor Arms hostelry in Knightsbridge. Heath had already drunk 24 pints of beer that day. Together, they left for Heath's room at the Pembridge Court Hotel in Notting Hill Gate. A chambermaid discovered Gardner's blood smeared body the next day. Partially clothed, it lay on its back. Both nipples had been practically bitten off and 17 lashes administered with a leather thong scarred the body. Hands and feet were bound with handkerchiefs and the killer had washed her face after death. An autopsy revealed a seven-inch wound inside the vagina apparently inflicted by the rough insertion of a fire poker savagely rotated while she was still alive. Death was due to suffocation. Intercourse had not taken place. A check of the hotel's register revealed the room had been let to "Lieutenant-Colonel and Mrs. N.G.C. Heath." Photos of Heath were circulated throughout the country and police later recovered from his luggage a heavy metal-tipped leather whip and a blue scarf containing hair and blood stains similar to Gardner's. A day after the crime, Heath wrote a letter to police stating that although he let Gardner use the room he was not with her. He described a man he saw with her and admitted discovering the body when he returned to the room later that night. He promised police to send them the beating instrument.

The next day, Heath checked into Bournemouth's Tollard Royal Hotel as "Group Captain Rupert Brooke." While there, he met 21-year-old Doreen Marshall who accepted his dinner invitation for the evening of July 3, 1946. That evening she disappeared. Again Heath felt compelled to communicate with police. Arriving at the station to identify a photograph of Marshall, Heath was detained when a constable noted his resemblance to the suspect photo circulated in the Gardner murder. A search of Heath's room turned up a cloakroom ticket for a suitcase at a railway station. It contained a blood-stained leather whip and handkerchiefs. Police later determined Heath had pawned Marshall's ring for £5 and sold her watch to a local jeweler for £3. On July 8, 1946, Marshall's body was found in Branksome Dene Chine, a secluded Bournemouth beauty spot overlooking the sea. Hidden beneath a clump of rhododen-

drons, the body was naked except for her left shoe. Marshall's throat had been cut and her pudenda and breasts mutilated postmortem with a pocket knife. A sharpened tree branch had been inserted and rotated in her vagina. Heath denied committing the murder, but later insisted that if he had it was done during a "blackout." An address book confiscated by police contained the phone numbers of 177 women.

Heath pleaded "not guilty by reason of insanity" to the Margery Gardner murder on September 24, 1946, at London's Old Bailey. While examining psychiatrists agreed that Heath knew what he was doing, they disagreed over whether or not he knew that it was wrong. In fact, Heath showed no remorse and wondered what all the furor was about. The "moral insanity" defense failed and a jury took only an hour to find Heath guilty. Sentenced to death by hanging, he was removed to Pentonville Prison to await his October 16, 1946, date with state hangman Pierrepoint. At dawn on the appointed day, a composed Heath requested a double whiskey and was hung wearing the designer suit he had specially made for the trial.

268. Byrne, Gerald. *Borstal Boy: The Uncensored Story of Neville Heath.* Headline Books Series. London: J. Hill, 1954. 144 pp.: ill.; 21 cm.

269. Critchley, Macdonald, ed. *The Trial of Neville George Clevely Heath.* Notable British Trials. London: W. Hodge, 1951. 238 pp., [13]pp. of plates: ill., ports., map (fold); 22 cm.

_____. [Same as 269.] [New ed.] Notable British Trials. London: W. Hodge, 1955. 238 pp., [13]pp. of plates: ill., ports., map (fold); 22 cm.

Entry in the Notable British Trials Series chronicling in detail Heath's trial for the murder on June 20 or 21, 1946, of Mrs. Margery Aimee Brownell Gardner, held in the Central Criminal Court, London, Sept. 24–26, 1946.

270. Hill, Paull. *Portrait of a Sadist.* London: N. Spearman, 1960. 208 pp.: ill.; 23 cm.

_____. [Same as 270.] New York: Avon Books, 1960. 160 pp.: ill.; 20 cm.; paperback.

Readable account of the case written by an attorney who briefly met Lieutenant Heath in 1941 during the time he was court-martialed from the Royal Army Service Corps for conduct unbecoming an officer. As the title suggests, the book focuses on Heath's sexual sadism.

271. Selwyn, Francis. *Rotten to the Core?: The Life and Death of Neville Heath.* Crimes of the Century. London: Routledge, 1988. xii, 248 pp.; 23 cm.

Well researched biography featuring much detail on Heath's early life and checkered military career. Includes a select bibliography.

Heidnik, Gary Michael
(a.k.a. "Madman of Marshall Street," "Gary Bishop")

Born circa November 1943 in Eastlake, Ohio. "Minister," stock investor. Philadelphia, Pennsylvania; 2 murders; asphyxiation, electrocution; February–March 1987.

Audio: Cellar of Horror, a two-cassette, three-hour abridgement of Ken Englade's book of the same title read by Michael McConnohie, was published in 1991 by Audio Renaissance Tapes (Los Angeles, California) as an entry in their "True Crime Audio" series.

"As you may know after so many failed suicide attempts on my part I´ facetiously label myself an expert on the subject."

Schizophrenic "minister" who made sex slaves out of the black prostitutes and mentally retarded women he kidnapped in order to create his own race. Born to an alcoholic mother who would commit suicide in 1970 and an emotionally distant father he described as an "Archie Bunker type," Gary Heidnik was too young at two to remember their messy divorce. Heidnik and his brother lived with their mother until reaching school age when they were shipped off to be with their recently remarried father. Called "football head" by classmates due to a childhood head injury, Heidnik eventually dropped out of the Staunton Military Academy in Virginia and enlisted in the army one week after his eighteenth birthday. After scoring high marks in his medical training at Fort Sam Houston in San Antonio, Texas, Heidnik was posted as an orderly in a military hospital in Landstuhl, West Germany, in May 1962. By October 1962, Heidnik was transferred back to the States and placed in a military hospital in Valley Forge, Pennsylvania, suffering from dizzy spells, blurred vision, and hallucinations. On January 23, 1963, 14 months into a 36-month enlistment, Heidnik was honorably discharged from the military following an Army board of review's diagnosis that the young soldier was suffering from a schizoid personality disorder. Heidnik was given a 100 percent service-related disability rating and awarded a full pension of almost $1,400 a month. After his arrest, Heidnik would later claim that the military had used him as a guinea pig in their covert LSD experiments.

In and out of various Pennsylvania mental institutions over the next 25 years, Heidnik did manage during that time to earn a licensed practical nurse degree in 1964 and intern at the Philadelphia General Hospital. Combining his paycheck from the hospital with his disability income, Heidnik purchased a three-story house in 1967 and rented out two floors to tenants. Around this time, he began ingratiating himself to the staff of the Elwyn Institute, a local mental health facility primarily catering to retarded female clients of black or Hispanic ethnicity. Heidnik was allowed to check the women out on day passes for picnics, shopping trips, and movies while in reality taking them to his house for sex. According to Heidnik, God told him in the spring of 1971 to found the "United Church of the Ministers of God," a ministry solely devoted to the care of the mentally and physically handicapped that he found at the Elwyn Institute. On a less spiritual level, by founding a church "Bishop Heidnik" was able to take advantage of tax breaks accorded to religious institutions. An astute investor with a genius level IQ of nearly 140, Heidnik was able to parlay an initial investment of $1,500 placed with Merrill Lynch in 1975 into a stock portfolio worth $545,000 at the time of his arrest. Heidnik later claimed that Jesus routinely gave him stock market tips.

Heidnik's increasingly bizarre behavior manifested itself in 1976 when he barricaded himself in the basement of his home with two weapons. A black tenant was shot in the face as he tried to register a complaint with his landlord, but the charge of aggravated assault was later dismissed. Heidnik later moved from the house and afterwards the new owner discovered that someone had chipped through the basement's concrete floor

and dug a three foot hole in the earth. In 1978 Heidnik fathered a child by an illiterate and retarded black woman and in May of that year kidnapped the girl's 34-year-old sister from a mental institution. The woman (with an IQ of a three-year-old) was found in the basement of Heidnik's home. Heidnik was later arrested, charged with rape, kidnapping and other related charges, convicted, and sentenced to three to seven years in prison. Released on April 12, 1983, after serving four years and two months, Heidnik purchased a two story house on Marshall Street in a seedy area of North Philadelphia. On October 3, 1985, Heidnik married a Filipino woman that he had been corresponding with for two years. She soon left him after Heidnik raped her and forced her to watch him have sex with black prostitutes. Charged with spousal rape and other charges, Heidnik dodged prosecution after the frightened woman failed to appear at a preliminary hearing.

Anxious to prevent any other woman from ever leaving him, Heidnik set into motion his insane plan to amass a harem of 10 women by which he planned to father and raise in his basement a race of children unstained by the outside world. On November 26, 1986, Heidnik picked up 25-year-old half black, half Puerto Rican prostitute Josefina Rivera, took her to his home, choked her into unconsciousness, then placed her in a pit dug into the floor of the basement, and covered it over with a weighted plywood board. Heidnik raped Rivera daily, keeping her barely alive on a diet of bread, water, and dog food. On November 29, 1986, Heidnik abducted Sandra Lindsay, a 25-year-old black retarded woman, and chained her to an exposed beam in the basement where, like

Rivera, she was turned into an unwilling sex slave. Lisa Thomas, a black 19 year old, was abducted on December 22, 1986, quickly followed by black prostitutes Deborah Johnson Dudley, 23, on January 1, 1987, and Jacquelyn Askins, 18, on January 18, 1987. When the women failed to conceive after his repeated rapings, Heidnik beat them and jammed a screwdriver into the ears of those he felt were conspiring against him. On February 7, 1987, Sandra Lindsay died of suffocation after being hanged for several days by a shackled hand from a basement ceiling beam as punishment for trying to escape. Heidnik dismembered Lindsay with an electric saw in an upstairs bathroom, ground up her flesh in a food processor, and fed her remains in dog food to his remaining prisoners. On March 18, 1987, Heidnik electrocuted the uncooperative Deborah Dudley by hooking electrical wires to her shackles while she stood in a pit filled with muddy water. Heidnik and Rivera later dumped the woman's nude body in Wharton State Forest near Camden, New Jersey. On March 23, 1987, Heidnik kidnapped his final captive a 24-year-old black prostitute named Agnes "Vickie" Adams who worked in a strip club with Rivera.

The next day, Rivera convinced Heidnik to let her visit her children in exchange for a promise to procure fresh women for his harem. Once free, Rivera notified police who, upon entering the house, found 24 pounds of Lindsay's plastic-wrapped body parts in the freezer and parts of her charred ribs in a roasting pan. Malnourished, chained, and naked from the waist down, officers found Thomas, Askins, and Adams huddling in terror in the basement. Heidnik was arrested the next day, March 25, cruising the neigh-

borhood in one of his luxury cars. Based on information provided by Rivera, the body of Deborah Dudley was retrieved from its shallow grave in Wharton State Forest. While awaiting trial on two counts of first degree murder and numerous other charges, Heidnik attempted to hang himself with a tee-shirt in the shower at the Philadelphia Detention Center on April 2, 1987. The trial opened in Philadelphia on April 4, 1988, before a jury selected in Pittsburgh in order to minimize the taint of pre-trial publicity. Heidnik's plea of not guilty by reason of insanity was rejected by the jury when they learned that he was sane enough to have built a small stock market investment into a half million dollar portfolio. Convicted on two murder counts, five rapes, four aggravated assaults, and six counts of kidnapping on July 1, 1988, Heidnik was condemned to death two days later and given a cumulative prison sentence of between 150 and 300 years. On January 1, 1989, the double murderer attempted suicide in his cell at the State Correctional Institution in Pittsburgh by overdosing on Thorazine, a strong anti-depressant drug. Heidnik remained comatose for several days, but survived. The Pennsylvania Supreme Court rejected Heidnik's automatic appeal of his two death convictions on March 7, 1991. The so-called "Madman of Marshall Street" has since instructed his attorney not to pursue any other appeals on his behalf and has requested the U.S. Supreme Court to speed up the execution process.

272. Apsche, Jack. *Probing the Mind of a Serial Killer*. Foreword by Charles Peruto, Jr. Morrisville, Penn.: International Information Associates, 1993. 232 pp.: ill.; 22 cm.

Fascinating psychological study of

Heidnik with a foreword by Peruto, the attorney who defended the serial killer. Includes the "Constitution of the United Church of the Ministers of God" and several of Heidnik's letters. Includes bibliography and index.

273. Englade, Ken. *Cellar of Horror*. 1st St. Martin's Press mass market ed. New York: St. Martin's Press, 1989. 277 pp., [8]pp. of plates: ill.; 17 cm.; paperback.

_____. [Same as 273 with added subtitle: *The True Story*.] London: Angus & Robertson, 1989. 227 pp., [8]pp. of plates: ill., ports.; 18 cm.; paperback.

_____. [Same as 273 with added subtitle: *The True Story*.] London: Grafton, 1993. 227 pp., [8]pp. of plates: ill.; 18 cm.; paperback.

Well done paperback original by a veteran true crime writer. Englade concludes: "Twenty-one times Gary Heidnik entered mental health facilities. Twenty-one times he was discharged. Even when he said he wasn't ready to go. Even when he begged to stay. The truth is, Gary Heidnik should never have been free."

Heirens, William George
(a.k.a. "George Murman," "The Lipstick Killer")

Born November 15, 1928, in Evanston, Illinois. University student. Chicago, Illinois; 3 murders; knife, manual strangulation, gun; June 1945–January 1946.

"I wish to express my deep humbleness. I'm sorry for the acts I committed. I'm still very bewildered by some of this, but everything seems to have worked out all right." —Heirens' statement before receiving three life sentences

Sexually aberrant University of Chicago student whose murder and dismemberment of a six-year-old girl in 1946 stands as one of the most sen-

sational cases in that city's history. William Heirens (pronounced Hirens) first came to the notice of Cook County authorities in 1942 when at the age of 13 he was arrested for carrying a loaded gun into his parochial school. Chicago police visited the affluent home of his father, an executive at a steel company, and turned up a small arsenal hidden throughout the house. Heirens admitted 11 burglaries and six arsons, but because of his youth and excellent family background was sent on probation to the Gibault School in Terre Haute, Indiana. A brilliant student and model resident, Heirens was released in 11 months. Unknown to school psychologists, however, Heirens' burglaries and thefts were part of an aberrant sexuality which would become even more elaborate and deadly as he aged. Warned by a puritanical mother that "all sex was dirty," Heirens had developed a furtive fantasy life centering around stolen female underwear. According to some psychiatrists familiar with his case, the boy wore the garments while looking at a homemade scrapbook he filled with pictures of Nazi leaders. Back in Chicago, Heirens continued to burgle houses, was caught, and this time sent away to a correctional school in Peru, Illinois. He remained there for a year and a half before entering the University of Chicago as a sophomore in 1945 after passing a special examination for academically accelerated 16 year olds. Shortly after his arrival on campus, Heirens began burgling apartments on the North Side of Chicago as much to experience the sexual release of surreptitiously entering a stranger's dwelling as to actually steal.

On June 5, 1945, Heirens was burgling the fifth floor apartment of 43-year-old Josephine Alice Ross at 4108

N. Kenmore Avenue in Chicago when the widow surprised him. The teenager panicked, slashed Ross' throat with a hunting knife, then tried to bandage the dead woman. During the three hours he spent in the apartment experiencing multiple orgasms, Heirens stole $12, and washed Ross' body. During the next months, Heirens continued to invade apartments for sexual release, and when confronted by an occupant, brutally attack them. On October 5, 1945, Heirens entered the Midway-Drexel Apartment Hotel on 6020 Drexel and after trying several locked doors moved to the penthouse where 27-year-old former army nurse Evelyn Peterson was cleaning her sister's apartment. Heirens smashed Peterson in the head with a metal bar, bound her with a lamp cord to a chair, took $150, then attended his class at the University of Chicago. On December 10, 1945, Heirens gave Chicago a foretaste of the horror that was to come. That day, he entered the sixth floor apartment of Frances Brown, a 33-year-old secretary, at 3941 N. Pine Grove Avenue on the North Side of Chicago. Surprising Brown in her bath, Heirens bludgeoned the woman with the butt of his .38 caliber pistol, shot her twice point blank in the head, then retrieved a butcher knife from the kitchen and repeatedly stabbed her in the neck. When police investigated the scene, they found Brown's freshly washed corpse draped over the side of the tub with its genitals exposed, the knife still sticking in the neck. Scrawled in lipstick on the wall above her bed was the hastily written plea, "For heaven's sake, catch me before I kill more. I cannot control myself."

Heirens, however, made no attempt to give himself up and on the night of January 7, 1946, committed one of the most shocking murders in the long and colorful history of Chicago crime. Using a ladder found in a nearby street, Heirens entered the first floor bedroom of six-year-old Suzanne Degnan at 5943 N. Kenmore Avenue. To muffle the child's frightened screams, Heirens strangled Degnan to death and carried her corpse to the basement of a nearby building at 5901 N. Winthrop Avenue. There he used a hunting knife to decapitate and dismember his small victim in a laundry tub. Carefully wrapping up the remains in paper bundles, Heirens distributed the body parts in five sewers and catch basins near the girl's home. Sometime during the carnage, Heirens wrote a bogus ransom note demanding $20,000 for the girl's return and placed it in her room. The discovery by authorities of the bloody laundry tub ultimately led to the recovery of Degnan's body parts over the next few days. Almost seven months after the murder on June 26, 1946, Heirens was knocked unconscious with a stack of flowerpots by an off-duty policeman as he tried to flee from a burglarized apartment in Rogers Park. Three days later the state's attorney announced that the 17-year-old University of Chicago student had been tied to the Degnan murder by fingerprints left on the ransom note. A search of his dorm room yielded guns and stolen items linking him to the murders of Ross and Brown. Nearly 40 pairs of women's panties found hidden in the attic of his parents' home prompted Heirens to admit that he was a sexual fetishist who was only able to experience orgasm by entering a strange house through a window.

Under the influence of "truth drugs" administered without Heirens' permission, the teenager told psychiatrists about his dominant alter ego, "George Murman" (*Murder Man*), who he maintained actually committed the crimes. At least one prominent psychiatrist dismissed Heirens' claim of "split personality" which perhaps motivated the youth's counsel to seek a plea bargain arrangement for their client. On August 6, 1946, Heirens' attorneys cut a deal with the office of the state's attorney which stipulated that in exchange for his full confessions to the murders of Ross, Brown, and Degnan the state of Illinois would not seek the death penalty. Afterwards, Heirens confessed to the murders during a marathon eight-hour interrogation session. On the afternoon of his formal sentencing hearing, September 5, 1946, the 17 year old attempted to hang himself with a bed sheet in his cell in the Cook County Jail. Uninjured, Heirens attended the hearing and was sentenced to three consecutive life sentences. In 1965 Heirens was placed on institutional parole for the Degnan murder, but continues to serve his two remaining life sentences. Heirens distinguished himself in February 1972 by becoming the first prisoner in Illinois history to earn a bachelor's degree. After taking 25 years of correspondence, television, and prison courses, Heirens graduated from Lewis College. In recognition of exemplary behavior, Heirens was transferred to the minimum security Vienna Correctional Center in 1975 after serving 24 years in various maximum security prisons. He currently serves as clerk to the facility's Catholic chaplain. Heirens now claims that he never committed any of the murders and only pleaded guilty in 1946 on the advice of his attorneys who convinced him that the "lynch atmosphere" in Chicago would surely result in his execution should he be tried. To date, Heirens

has been rejected for parole 30 times and has served more years in prison than any other inmate in Illinois penal history.

274. Cauldwell, David Oliver. *William Heirens Notorious Sex Manic* [sic]. Girard, Kan.: Haldeman-Julius, 1948. 31 pp.; 22 cm. (Haldeman-Julius, B677). (Paper covers.)

275. Downs, Thomas. *Murder Man*. New York: Dell, 1984. 188 pp.; 18 cm.; paperback.

Passable paperback account of the case which includes excerpts from Heirens' confession.

276. Freeman, Lucy. *"Before I Kill More..."* New York: Crown, 1955. 316 pp.: ill.; 22 cm.

_____. [Same as 276.] New York: Award Books, 1955. 380 pp.; 18 cm.; paperback.

_____. [Same as 276.] New York: Pocket Books, 1955. x, 374 pp.; 18 cm. ("A Kangaroo book"); paperback.

_____. [Same as 276.] Cardinal ed. New York: Pocket Books, 1956. 357 pp.; 17 cm. (cover title: *Catch Me Before I Kill More*); paperback.

Earliest book length examination of the case accepts Heirens' insanity plea as fact.

277. Kennedy, Dolores. *William Heirens: His Day in Court*. 1st ed. Chicago, Ill.: Bonus Books, 1991. xv, 408 pp.: ill.; 24 cm.

Kennedy, a legal secretary, was instrumental in establishing the Parole for Heirens Committee, a group of supporters who believe the convicted triple killer has been rehabilitated and that his further imprisonment is unnecessary and inhumane. She argues, with some merit, that press coverage at the time probably precluded the possibility of Heirens receiving a fair trial and that his attorneys conspired with the prosecution to coerce a confession. Kennedy, however, seems to be on shakier ground when she suggests that Heirens could be innocent. Appendices include a chronology of events leading to Heirens' imprisonment and the transcript of his murder confessions. Includes bibliography and index.

Henley, Elmer Wayne

Born circa 1956. Procurer. Houston, Texas; 6 murders; ligature strangulation, gun; circa 1970–August 1973; *see also* Corll, Dean Arnold.

Herrin, Richard James
(a.k.a. "Richard James")

Born December 16, 1953, in Los Angeles, California. University graduate student. Scarsdale, New York; 1 murder; bludgeon (hammer), manual strangulation; July 7, 1977.

Controversial murder case in which an organized religion became actively involved in the court proceedings. On July 7, 1977, Richard Herrin, 23, bludgeoned his girlfriend, Bonnie Joan Garland, 20, with a hammer and then strangled the unconscious woman to death in her parents' upscale home in Scarsdale, New York. The brutal murder capped a stormy relationship which had begun at Yale University in November 1974 when Herrin, a poor Chicano on academic scholarship at the prestigious school, met Garland, the daughter of a successful Yale-educated attorney. Garland's grades began to suffer and her concerned parents encouraged her to see other men. When Herrin left Yale in 1975 to pursue graduate studies in geology at Texas Christian University, Garland joined the Yale Glee Club as a featured soprano. Through the group, Garland became interested in another man and was trying to break free from Herrin when he accepted her invitation to stay

with her at her parents' home for a few days. Shortly before the murder, Garland informed Herrin that she wished to date other men and that her parents disapproved of their exclusive relationship. On the night of July 7, 1977, Herrin entered Garland's bedroom and beat the girl senseless with a claw hammer before manually strangling her to death. After driving aimlessly for hours, Herrin eventually wound up at a Catholic Church in Coxsackie, New York, where he confessed the murder to a priest and later to local authorities. A few minutes before 8:00 a.m., Scarsdale police roused the unsuspecting Garland household. Upstairs in a pool of blood, the young woman had clung to life for more than six hours. Twenty hours after the attack, she died following a three-hour operation at White Plains Hospital. She was buried in her Glee Club outfit.

Sister Ramona Pena of St. Thomas More House, the center for Roman Catholics in the Yale community where Herrin was well known and respected, and the confessed killer's former roommate at Yale organized a defense fund and letter writing campaign to "salvage" the killer's life. A top criminal lawyer was hired with the $50,000 raised and the judge was deluged with letters attesting to Herrin's good character. If granted bail, he would reside in Albany with the Fratres Scholarum Christianarum, an order of unordained Catholic clergy. Noting that Herrin's bail application was the most impressive he had ever seen, the judge set bail at $50,000 on August 11, 1977. Pending trial, he lived with the brothers, worked at a gift shop under an assumed name, and even took classes at a local university until found out by the school's administration. The involvement of the Church in the case prompted an outraged letter from Garland's parents to the chancellor of the Archdiocese of New York. In protest over the support afforded Herrin by some Yale faculty members and alumni, Paul Garland terminated his relationship with the university except for the establishment of the Bonnie Garland Music Fund to help students further their singing careers.

The second degree murder trial began on May 15, 1978, in White Plains. Pleading "not guilty" by reason of insanity, the defense sought to prove that at the time of the murder Herrin was suffering from "transient situational reaction," an acute reaction to overwhelming environmental stress. During 12 days of testimony, 29 witnesses and 5 psychiatrists laid bare the soul of Richard Herrin as Sister Pena, eyes closed, sat praying in the second row fingering her rosary. The case went to the jury on June 16, 1978. Thirty-six hours later on Father's Day, Herrin was acquitted of second degree murder, but convicted on the lesser charge of first degree manslaughter, a crime carrying a sentence of 8–25 years. In the week following the verdict, the judge received over 1,000 letters complaining it was too lenient. At the July 27 sentencing, Herrin received the maximum 25 years after declaring he wished to dedicate the remainder of his "life to serving others in Bonnie's memory." Bonnie's mother observed that "If you have a $30,000 defense fund, a Yale connection, and a clergy connection, you're entitled to one free hammer murder." In a 1981 interview Herrin subsequently declared himself to be an atheist. Herrin, 40, was automatically released on January 12, 1995, after serving 17 years of his sentence without a blemish.

278. Gaylin, Willard. *The Killing of Bonnie Garland: A Question of Justice.* New York: Simon and Schuster, 1982. 366 pp., [8]pp. of plates: ill.; 22 cm.

_____. [Same as 278.] New York: Penguin Books, 1983. 374 pp., [8]pp. of plates: ill.; 20 cm.; paperback.

279. Meyer, Peter. *The Yale Murder.* 1st ed. New York: Empire Books: Distributed by Harper & Row, 1982. 302 pp.; 24 cm.

_____. [Same as 279.] Berkley ed. New York: Berkley Books, 1983. 325 pp.; 18 cm.; paperback.

Meyer received the cooperation of the two opposing attorneys in the case and spent 30 hours interviewing Herrin at the Eastern Correctional Facility in Napanoch, New York.

"Hi-Fi Killings" *see* **Pierre, Dale Selby (and) Andrews, William A.**

Hickock, Richard Eugene (a.k.a. "Tracy Hand")

Born June 6, 1931, in Kansas City, Kansas. Executed April 14, 1965. Drifter. Holcomb, Kansas; 4 murders; shotgun, knife; November 15, 1959.

Film: In Cold Blood (US, 1967), a Pax Enterprise/Columbia production based on Truman Capote's book of the same title, written, produced, and directed by Richard Brooks. Cast includes Robert Blake (Perry Smith), Scott Wilson (Dick Hickock), and John Forsythe (Det. Alvin Dewey).

Audio: Truman Capote Reads Scenes from In Cold Blood, a 12-inch, 33⅓ RCA Victor record (New York, 1966). *In Cold Blood*, a two–sound cassette, three-hour abridgment of Capote's book read by Michael McConnohie, was published in 1991 by Audio Renaissance (Los Angeles).

"Well, what's there to say about capital punishment? I'm not against it. Revenge is all it is, but what's wrong with revenge? It's very important. If I was kin to the Clutters ... I couldn't rest in peace till the ones responsible had taken that ride on the Big Swing."

Misfit drifter who, with accomplice Perry Smith, committed the shocking mass murder of a prominent Kansas farm family chronicled in Truman Capote's Edgar Award–winning "nonfiction novel" In Cold Blood. Richard "Dick" Hickock, the son of a poor, but honest farm couple in Olathe, Kansas, earned As in high school and lettered in several sports before embarking on a criminal career which included writing bad checks and thievery. He was serving time in the Kansas State Prison in Lansing when he met Perry Smith, the half-breed son of an Irish father and a Cherokee mother who partnered in a rodeo act. When the couple separated, Smith lived with his mother who quickly degenerated into an alcoholic prostitute while his father knocked around the country. In and out of detention homes and orphanages throughout his youth, Smith joined the Merchant Marines at 16, enlisted in the army in 1948, and won a Bronze Star in Korea. Shortly after mustering out in 1952, Smith wrecked his motorcycle, breaking his legs in five places. To kill the pain, he gobbled aspirins, quickly becoming addicted to them. Aggressive and violent, Smith was arrested for larceny and other charges and sentenced to 5 to 10 years in Lansing. Hickock, looking to "score" big when he got out, listened carefully as his cellmate, Floyd Wells, passed the long prison hours by telling him about a wealthy Holcomb, Kansas, wheat farmer named Herbert William Clut-

ter. Wells, a former employee at the farm serving time for theft, spun an exaggerated tale about Clutter's wealth and lied when he told Hickock that the farmer kept $10,000 in cash on hand in a house safe. Hickock persuaded Smith to help him rob Clutter. After their parole they met in Kansas City to buy rope, tape, and gloves.

In the early Sunday morning hours of November 15, 1959, Hickock and Smith entered the Clutters' isolated farmhouse in Holcomb through an unlocked side door. Armed with a shotgun and a hunting knife, the pair tied up Herbert Cutter, 48, his invalid wife Bonnie, 45, and their two children, 15-year-old son Kenyon and daughter Nancy, 16. While Smith accepted Herb Clutter's truthful explanation that there was no safe in the house, Hickock continued to threaten to hurt the man's family if he did not produce the cash. At Clutter's offer to write him a check, Hickock exploded into rage. Herb Clutter and Kenyon were herded down into the basement where the father was forced to lie on the floor while the son was placed facedown on a sofa in another room. As Hickock shined a flashlight on Herb Clutter's face, Smith slit the man's throat ear to ear then blew his head apart with a shotgun blast. Moving quickly to the other room, Smith shot the teenager in the head before he and Clutter walked upstairs where the women waited in terror. Hickock wanted to rape Nancy Clutter, but Smith prevented him. According to one of Smith's early confessions, he refused to kill the women and held the flashlight on the victims' faces as Hickock first shot the daughter then the mother. Smith would later say, "It was like picking off targets in a shooting gallery." A little over an hour after entering the house, the killers left with less than $50 in cash.

As Hickock and Smith wandered across North America in a stolen car stopping in Miami, Florida, Acapulco, Mexico, back to Kansas and finally Las Vegas, Nevada, police worked nonstop to solve the crime. Floyd Wells was sitting in his cell in the Kansas State Prison when he heard a radio news flash about the Clutter murders. He contacted the warden and told him that Hickock's plan to rob Herb Clutter had evolved out of their earlier conversations about the farmer. The killers were subsequently traced to Las Vegas, Nevada, and arrested there on December 30, 1959. Hickock was the first to confess, insisting that Smith alone had killed the entire family. Smith, when informed that his partner had implicated him solely in the slaughter, admitted killing the men but fingered Hickock as the killer of the women. Before their trial commenced in Garden City, Kansas, in March 1960, Smith accepted full blame for the murders "out of consideration for Hickock's parents" adding "that it might be some comfort for her [Hickock's mother] to know Dick never pulled the trigger." At trial, Wells testified about his conversation with Hickock and was rewarded for his testimony with an early release from the penitentiary. After deliberating only 40 minutes, the jury found each defendant guilty of murder and sentenced them to death by hanging. As they were leaving the courtroom, Smith laughingly turned to Hickock and said, "No chicken-hearted jurors, they!" The pair languished on death row at the Kansas State Prison for five years and five months while three separate appeals were heard and denied by the United States Supreme Court. Smith used the

time to improve his mind by reading 15–20 books a week while Hickock read popular sex novels and tried his hand at jailhouse lawyering. Their appeals exhausted, the pair ordered identical last meals of shrimp, french fries, garlic bread, ice cream, strawberries and whipped cream. Shortly after midnight on April 14, 1965, Hickock was the first to be hanged after telling the assembled witnesses, "You people are sending me to a better world than this ever was." Smith soon followed, uttering in a barely audible voice from the scaffold, "It would be meaningless to apologize for what I did. Even inappropriate. But I do. I apologize." The pair were buried side-by-side in a private cemetery near the penitentiary.

280. Capote, Truman. *In Cold Blood: A True Account of a Multiple Murder and Its Consequences.* New York: Random House, 1965. 343 pp.; 22 cm. (Also a 1966 ed.)

_____. [Same as 280.] Garden City, N.Y.: International Collectors Library, 1965. 326 pp.; 22 cm.

_____. [Same as 280.] New York: The Modern Library, 1965. 343 pp.; 19 cm. (Also a 1968 ed. in the publisher's "The Modern Library of the World's Best Books Series" [ML48] and a 1992 "Modern Library ed.")

_____. [Same as 280.] New York: New American Library, 1965. 384 pp.; 18 cm. ("A Signet book"); paperback. (Also a 1980 ed.)

_____. [Same as 280.] London: H. Hamilton, 1966. 284 pp.; 23 cm.

_____. [Same as 280.] Harmondsworth, Eng.: Penguin Books, 1966. 343 pp.; 19 cm.; paperback.

_____. [Same as 280.] London: Sphere, 1981. 335 pp.; 18 cm.; paperback.

_____. [Same as 280.] Falmouth, Cornwall: Abacus Books, 1986. xii, 336 pp.; 20 cm.

_____. [Same as 280.] 1st Vintage International ed. New York: Vintage Books, 1994. 343 pp.; 21 cm.

Capote's landmark case study is still considered by most to be the finest book yet written in the so-called "true crime" genre and continues to be the yardstick by which others are judged. Capote researched the book (originally serialized in *The New Yorker*) for six years during which time he literally lived in Holcomb and Garden City, Kansas, while interviewing everyone connected with the case. After the killers' conviction, he conducted hundreds of hours of interviews with Hickock and Smith in their death row cells at the Kansas State Prison in Lansing. Refusing to take notes in front of his subjects or use a tape recorder because he felt it would make them self-conscious, Capote trained himself to memorize the interviews in their entirety, later transcribing them with remarkable accuracy. Capote's self-proclaimed "nonfiction novel" became a huge best seller and generated almost universal critical acclaim. Absolutely essential reading.

Hilley, Audrey Marie
(a.k.a. "The Black Widow," "Audrey Marie Frazier," "Lindsay Robbi Hannon [or] Homan," "Robbi L. Homan," "Teri Martin")

Born June 4, 1933, in Anniston, Alabama. Died February 26, 1987. Secretary, office manager. Anniston, Alabama; 2 murders (convicted of 1); poison (arsenic); May 1975–January 1977.

Television: "Wife, Mother, Murderer—The Marie Hilley Story" (1991), a two-hour, made-for-television movie, originally aired on ABC on November 10, 1991. Cast includes Judith Light (Marie Hilley), David Dukes (Joe Hubbard), and David Ogden Stiers (John Homan).

Audio: Black Widow, a two-cassette, three-hour abridgement of R. Robin McDonald's book of the same title read by Michael McConnohie, was published in 1990 by Audio Renaissance (Los Angeles).

Unusual case involving family poisonings and an assumed identity. Born in Depression-era Alabama to overworked and underpaid linen mill workers, Audrey Marie Hilley's formative years were spent being raised by a neighbor who also took in orphans. Convinced she was unloved and demeaned by the commonness of life around her, Hilley became obsessed with attaining wealth and social position. In May 1951 she married high school sweetheart Frank Hilley who was then serving in the Navy. Shortly after the marriage, the first warning signs of Marie's troubles with money appeared. Instead of banking the paycheck Hilley sent from his duty station in Guam, Marie spent it on clothes. Following his discharge, the Hilleys settled in Anniston, Alabama, where he worked at a foundry, taking college classes at night, and Marie worked as a secretary for the town's social elite. Outwardly, the marriage was a happy one producing two children, a son and a daughter named Carol Marie born on January 14, 1960.

Unknown to Frank Hilley, Marie continued to live well beyond her means. Shortly after noticing items disappearing from the house he became ill. His health progressively deteriorated throughout the early months of 1975 as baffled doctors disagreed over a diagnosis. Concerned, Marie injected him with what she claimed to be an anti-nausea drug. In reality, it was a solution of liquid arsenic, the *coup de grâce* in an ongoing campaign to poison her husband for his life insurance. One week later, three weeks after their 24th wedding anniversary, Frank Hilley died on May 25, 1975. The autopsy, which failed to test for poison, assigned death to infectious hepatitis. Marie collected $31,140 in insurance and promptly went on a spending spree. In the months and years to follow, Marie collected on several claims ranging from the mysterious loss of her house by fire to a series of unexplained thefts. When her mother, Lucille Frazier, died from cancer on January 4, 1977, Marie collected on a $600 burial policy. Toxicologists later examining the exhumed woman's body noted levels of arsenic in her liver ten times greater than normal.

On July 27, 1978, Hilley took out a $25,000 life insurance policy on her 17-year-old daughter, Carol, which included a $5,000 accidental death benefit. Almost four years after the death of her father, Carol became ill and had to be hospitalized on May 6, 1975. As her daughter's weight dropped from 107 pounds to 87 during a five-month period, Hilley led doctors to believe that Carol was anorexic. Deeply in debt to creditors, Hilley attempted to hasten Carol's death by injecting her with liquid arsenic. The teenager's hands and feet went numb, prompting a doctor at the University Hospital in Birmingham, Alabama, to suspect arsenic poisoning. Tests run on her urine and hair revealed levels of arsenic 100 times higher than the normal level. While relatives of the sick woman were pressing Anniston police to investigate their poison claims against her mother, Hilley was arrested on September 19, 1979, on unrelated charges of passing bad checks. Remarkably, Hilley consented to the coroner's request to exhume her husband's body on October 3, 1979. Three days later, her sister-in-law stumbled across a pill bottle containing liquid arsenic in a house Hilley once occupied. On October 8, 1979, Hilley was arrested and charged with the attempted murder of her daughter. That same day the state toxicologist announced that Frank Hilley's body contained a lethal level of arsenic. The next day, Lucille Frazier was exhumed and was determined to have died from arsenic poisoning.

Hilley was free on $14,000 bond and awaiting trial in Birmingham when she jumped bail in November 1979. During her absence she was charged with the murder of her husband. The object of a three-year nationwide FBI manhunt, Hilley assumed the name of "Lindsay Robbi Hannon" and began a relationship with John Homan, a 33-year-old boat builder, in Ft. Lauderdale, Florida, in 1980. The pair moved to Marlow, New Hampshire, and married on May 29, 1981. Claiming that her health was deteriorating, Hilley moved alone to Houston, Texas, for its warmer climate. While there, she launched an incredible scheme to assume another identity. After dying her hair blonde and losing 30 pounds, Hilley called Homan on November 9, 1982, posing as "Teri Martin," his wife's twin sister, to announce that his spouse had died. For proof, "Teri Martin" produced an obituary and an announcement declaring that the dead woman's body had been donated to science. To complete the bizarre charade, Hilley reappeared in New Hampshire to offer condolences to the bereaved and gullible John Homan. On January 12, 1983, the FBI finally arrested Hilley in Brattleboro, Vermont.

Tried in Anniston on May 30, 1983, Hilley pleaded not guilty to the murder of husband Frank Hilley and the attempted murder of daughter Carol. The defense attempt to portray Hilley as a mentally unstable drug addict who was not responsible for her actions was seriously damaged by Carol's testimony that on three separate occasions her mother had injected her with an unknown "milky white" substance. Testimony from Priscilla Lang, a former cellmate of Hilley's at the Calhoun County jail, provided yet another motive for the poisonings besides the collection of insurance money. According to Lang, Hilley admitted poisoning Carol because she was a lesbian and Frank Hilley because he defended her. The woman the prosecutor likened to a "black widow" was convicted on both counts on June 8, 1983, and received maximum concurrent sentences of life (murder) and 20 years (attempted murder). On February 22, 1987, the 54-year-old Hilley was declared a fugitive after failing to return from a three-day furlough from the Julia Tutwiler Prison for Women in Wetumpka. Police, responding to a call about a suspicious person, found Hilley unconscious on the back porch of a home in north Anniston on February 26, 1987. Later that day, Hilley was declared dead from a combination of exposure, hypothermia, and cardiopulmonary arrest. Ironically, Hilley was buried in a grave next to the husband she murdered.

281. Ginsburg, Philip E. *Poisoned Blood: A True Story of Murder, Passion, and an Astonishing Hoax.* New York: Scribner, 1987. xv, 462 pp., [16]pp. of plates: ill.; 24 cm.

_____. [Same as 281 minus subtitle.] New York: Warner Books, 1989. xv, 462 pp., [16]pp. of plates: ill.; 17 cm.; paperback.

_____. [Same as 281.] London: O'Mara, 1992. ix, 462 pp., [8]pp. of plates: ill., ports.; 23 cm.

282. McDonald, R. Robin. *Black Widow: The True Story of the Hilley Poisonings.* Far Hills, N.J.: New Horizon Press; New York: Distributed by Macmillan, 1986. 409 pp., [16]pp. of plates: ports.; 24 cm.

_____. [Same as 282 minus subtitle.] St. Martin's Press Nonfiction. New York: St. Martin's Press, 1987. 414 pp., [16]pp. of plates: ports.; 17 cm.; paperback.

Firsthand local account of the case by the police reporter who covered the case for the *Anniston Star.*

"Hillside Strangler" see Bianchi, Kenneth Alessio (and) Buono, Angelo, Jr.

Hindley, Myra
(a.k.a. "Myra Hess," "Veronica," "Myra Spencer," "Betty Busybody," "The Moors Murderer")

Born July 23, 1942, in Gorton, Manchester, England. Shorthand typist. Manchester, England area; 5 murders (convicted of 2); strangulation, gun, knife, hatchet; July 1963–October 1965.

"If 'life means life' and that goes for everyone, I understand. But I have watched child murderers come and go, people who actually killed while I only lured, and I am still here. It was a horrendous thing and I accept any adjectives you choose to apply to my name, but some of the reason I'm still here is because my release would be a political vote loser."—Hindley in a December 18, 1994, *Sunday Times* interview with Lesley White expressing frustration over the perceived injustice she sees in having to serve life in prison; *see also* Brady, Ian Duncan.

Hirasawa, Sadamichi (a.k.a. "Dr. Shigero Matsui," "Dr. Jiro Yamaguchi")

Born circa 1891 in Japan. Died May 10, 1987. Painter. Tokyo, Japan; 12 murders; potassium cyanide; January 26, 1948.

"Thirty four years darkness in life has continued. But justice will never be crushed."

Japanese mass murderer convicted of the "Imperial Bank Incident" who subsequently spent more years on death row than any other condemned prisoner in history. On January 26, 1948, a man wearing the arm band of a health official entered the Shiinamachi branch of the Teikoku Bank in downtown Tokyo shortly after closing time. He was admitted after presenting a calling card identifying himself as "Dr. Jiro Yamaguchi." The official explained that a man infected with dysentery had been in the bank earlier that day and to prevent an epidemic everyone present must take an oral dose of vaccine. Sixteen persons, including two children, stood obediently in line as the doctor filled their teacups with the vaccine, then at his order, drank the solution. Almost immediately they fell to the floor in agony, victims of a deadly mixture of potassium cyanide. As 12 of the group died, the murderer grabbed 160,000 yen (roughly $500 at the 1948 exchange rate) and fled. The four survivors gave police a description of the poisoner that set into motion an intensive manhunt which ended on August 21, 1948, with the arrest of Sadamichi Hirasawa in Otaru on the northernmost main island of Hokkaido. In what police believed was a dry run for the Teikoku Bank job a man fitting Hirasawa's general description had left the calling card of a Dr. Shigero Matsui at

the Yasuda Bank in November 1947. The 56-year-old painter had exchanged cards with the real Dr. Matsui several months before the crime, but was unable to produce it for authorities. Three days after the killings Hirasawa deposited 80,000 yen in a Tokyo bank and was unable to provide police with a plausible explanation as to how he came by the money. Five days after his arrest Hirasawa attempted suicide in his cell by slashing his wrist with the point of a pen, writing in blood on the wall, "I am innocent." The painter ultimately confessed to the murders after 32 interrogations, but recanted his confession at trial claiming police coercion. On July 25, 1950, Hirasawa was convicted in the Tokyo District Court of twelve murders and four attempted murders and sentenced to death by hanging. While awaiting the outcome of a supreme court appeal, Hirasawa's wife divorced him in 1952 and his five children disowned him. On April 6, 1955, the supreme court upheld his conviction.

Hirasawa continued to maintain his innocence throughout his 35 years on death row, the most time ever served by a prisoner awaiting execution. Despite his sentence, 33 successive justice ministers declined to sign his execution order. A "Save Hirasawa Committee" composed of lawyers, human rights activists and others petitioned for his release. In 1982 a Washington-based freelance writer, William Triplett, used the Freedom of Information Act to unearth United States military documents that established that Japanese police and U.S. occupation officers believed at the time that a link existed between the "Imperial Bank Incident" and "Unit 731," a top secret regiment in the Japanese Imperial Army concerned with germ warfare experiments. After the war, the U.S. granted immunity to members of the unit in exchange for their data on biological warfare experiments conducted on Chinese, Soviet, and American prisoners of war featuring human vivisection, germ infections, and cyanide poisonings. According to Triplett's theory, embraced by those supporting Hirasawa's innocence, the real killer was probably a veteran of the unit. Fearful the secret immunity deal would be made public, Americans quashed the investigation into the link. Equally anxious to save their public standing, the Japanese police railroaded Hirasawa. On May 10, 1987, the 95-year-old Hirasawa died of pneumonia in the Hachioji Prison Hospital outside of Tokyo. At the time of his death, he had filed 18 separate requests for a retrial, five requests for a special pardon, and one for revocation of his death sentence—all denied. Nearly blind after spending 37 years on death row, Hirasawa produced over 1300 tempera paintings during his incarceration. Hirasawa's adopted son continues to try to clear his father's name. On February 5, 1992, Hirasawa's defense lawyers filed their nineteenth request for a retrial based on new evidence they maintain can prove his innocence.

283. Triplett, William. *Flowering of the Bamboo.* Kensington, Md.: Woodbine House, 1985. 263 pp., [16]pp. of plates: ill., facsims., ports.; 24 cm.
    Compelling study that argues Hirasawa was a victim of the conspiracy between U.S. occupation authorities anxious to hide their immunity deal with a unit of the Imperial Army conducting biological warfare and the Japanese police. While Triplett believes the murderer was actually a veteran of "Unit 731," he concludes that his identity "will probably remain a point of conjecture."

Appendix includes declassified U.S. government documents obtained by the author under the Freedom of Information Act.

Hobson, Sueanne Sallee
(a.k.a. "Sueanne Sallee" [maiden name], "Sueanne Sallee Crumm")

Born circa 1945 in Prairie Village, Kansas. Housewife. Miami County, Kansas; 1 murder; shotgun; April 17, 1980.

"After all I've done for you, can't you do this one little thing for me? If you loved me, you would do it."—According to son James Crumm, Jr., a statement made by Hobson to persuade him to kill her stepson

A mother convicted of hiring her birth son and his friend to murder her stepson. On April 17, 1980, 13-year-old Christen Hobson was reported missing from the Overland Park, Kansas, home he shared with his father and stepmother Sueanne Hobson. Police initially suspected that Hobson had run away when inquiries revealed a tumultuous history of ill will between the teenager, his stepmother and her two children from a previous marriage (James Crumm, Jr., 17, and teenaged Suzanne Crumm). On May 3, 1980, Hobson's body was found in a shallow grave on the banks of Big Bull Creek in a remote area of Miami County. Death had resulted from four shotgun blasts delivered at close range. The case broke when a classmate of 16-year-old Paul Sorrentino, a high school acquaintance of James Crumm, allowed police to tape a telephone conversation between them in which Sorrentino admitted helping Crumm murder the youth. Crumm's confession of May 4,

1980, identified his mother as the architect of the murder. According to Crumm, Sueanne Hobson blamed her stepson for the dissension in their homelife and for months prior to the murder had badgered him to "get rid of" Hobson. She had even made two previous attempts on the teen's life: once by putting six Quaaludes in his ice cream and then later by lacing a stick of gum with cocaine. When Crumm failed to shoot his stepbrother on a hunting trip, his mother pressed him to find someone to do the job. Paul Sorrentino, who openly told classmates that he aspired to become a Mafia hit man, accepted the "contract" after Hobson agreed to pay him $350 for repairs to his motorcycle. She allegedly promised to buy her son a new car. Sueanne Hobson was arrested but charges were dropped on July 11, 1980, due to a lack of available witnesses. The father of the dead boy divorced Hobson in August 1980, but remarried her in December after she convinced him of her innocence.

Insisting that his mother had driven him to murder, James Crumm was convicted on May 1, 1981, and sentenced to life imprisonment with no chance of parole for 15 years. Under the terms of a plea bargain agreement Sorrentino pleaded guilty to first degree murder and was given a life sentence with a chance at parole after 7½ years in exchange for his testimony against Hobson. She was subsequently arrested on June 22, 1981, but numerous legal maneuverings and a botched suicide attempt postponed the trial until the end of April 1982. Crumm and Sorrentino testified to being hired by Hobson and told in chilling detail how they made the teenager dig his own grave prior to murdering him. Hobson admitted knowing about the killing,

but never told her husband out of fear that Crumm would make good his threat to kill them both. On May 7, 1982, Hobson was convicted of first degree murder and conspiracy to commit murder and subsequently sentenced to life imprisonment. The Kansas Supreme Court upheld Hobson's conviction on December 3, 1982, and on April 5, 1985, denied another appeal. Hobson's husband remains convinced of her innocence and faithfully visits her in prison.

284. O'Donnell, Thomas J. *Crazymaker.* New York: HarperPaperbacks, 1992. 480 pp., [8] pp. of plates: ill.; 18 cm.; paperback.

Overlong, but meticulously detailed account of the case by a professor of English at the University of Kansas.

Hoffman, Barbara
(a.k.a. "Queen of the Massage Parlors," "Linda Millar")

Born June 15, 1952. Office worker, prostitute. Madison, Wisconsin; 1 murder (tried and acquitted on one other); poison (cyanide); December 23, 1977, and March 25, 1978 (acquitted).

"I did not commit the crime of which I was accused and of which I was convicted."—Hoffman's statement at her sentencing hearing

Former massage parlor prostitute convicted of murdering one of her "fiancés" for his insurance. On December 25, 1977, Gerald Thomas Davies, a 31-year-old mail room worker in the department of audio-visual instruction at the University of Wisconsin, led police to the naked body of a man buried in a snowdrift outside of Madison. The victim, later identified as Harry Berge, a 52-year-old forklift operator at a local tire plant, had been viciously bludgeoned about the head and genitals before death had resulted from a lethal dose of cyanide. The gullible Davies told police that he helped his fiancée, Barbara Hoffman, dispose of the body after she returned to her Madison apartment and found it dumped in her bathroom. Police questioned Hoffman, a former massage parlor prostitute currently employed as an office worker, but held off arresting her after an initial search of her apartment failed to turn up any physical evidence. A subsequent search yielded banking records and a social security number in the name of "Linda Millar," an alias used by Hoffman after quitting work at the massage parlor. Two months before his death, Berge had altered his will making fiancée "Linda Millar" the sole beneficiary of life insurance policies totaling $69,500. Hoffman was arrested on January 18, 1978, after police found blood matching the victim's in the snow near a dumpster next to her apartment.

Hoffman was out on bail when her other "fiancé," Gerald Davies, was found dead in his bathtub on March 27, 1978, from an apparent suicide. In a letter postmarked two days earlier, Davies had written to a local crime reporter that Hoffman had nothing to do with Berge's murder. Investigators learned that although Davies earned less than $10,000 a year he had taken out a $750,000 life insurance policy in November 1976 naming Hoffman (who paid the hefty premium) as the sole beneficiary. An autopsy later revealed that Davies died from acute cyanide poisoning. Hoffman was charged with the murder after police learned that she not only had access to the poison while a chemistry student at the University of Wisconsin, but that Davies had also purchased syringes and

cyanide from a lab in Milwaukee. The 28-year-old "masseuse" faced two counts of first degree murder as opening arguments began in her trial at Madison on June 19, 1980. One witness testified that Hoffman, while under the influence of drugs at a party, confided to him that after marrying Davies she planned to eliminate him with the homegrown poison Botulinum toxin, the lethal agent in food poisoning. Arguing against the obvious motive of insurance money, Hoffman's counsel maintained that Davies killed his rival Berge then committed suicide. On June 28, 1980, Hoffman was acquitted of murdering Davies, but convicted of the Berge killing. She subsequently received an automatic life sentence, and as of February 1994 was incarcerated at the Taycheeda Correctional Institute.

285. Harter, Karl. *Winter of Frozen Dreams*. Chicago: Contemporary Books, 1990. x, 261 pp., [12]pp. of plates: ill.; 24 cm.

_____. [Same as 285.] New York: Windsor, 1992. 337 pp., [12]pp. of plates: ill.; 17 cm. ("Pinnacle Books"); paperback.

Based on interviews with the investigating detectives, lawyers, newspaper coverage, and individuals familiar with the massage parlor scene in Madison, Wisconsin.

Hoolhouse, Robert William

Born circa 1917. Executed May 26, 1938. Farm laborer. Wolviston, England; 1 murder; knife; January 18, 1938.

Television: A dramatic recreation of the case entitled "Shadows of Doubt" appeared on the Granada produced British television program "In

Suspicious Circumstances" on March 16, 1993. Narrated by Edward Woodward, the cast includes Michael Yeaman (Robert Hoolhouse) and Nicola Duffett (Margaret Dobson).

Controversial case in which a British farm laborer was executed for the rape-murder of an elderly woman on purely circumstantial evidence. On January 18, 1938, the body of 67-year-old Margaret Jane Dobson was found along a grass verge off a farm track near the village of Wolviston in the English county of Durham. Dobson had been viciously beaten, raped, then fatally stabbed in the chest and neck. Within 36 hours police interviewed 20-year-old laborer Robert Hoolhouse at his home at Number 6 Pickering Street in Haverton Hill. Years earlier the Hoolhouse family had occupied the laborer's quarters on Dobson's "High Grange Farm" before being ordered to leave and cautioned never to return after Hoolhouse's father was accused of milk tampering. Hoolhouse was arrested and charged with murder after circumstantial evidence began to pile up against him. He roughly fit the description of a man seen riding a bicycle with "drooped handlebars" near the scene at the time of the murder and admitted owning such a bike. Hoolhouse explained that the fresh scratches on his right cheek were due to a biking accident and the blood on his clothes (the type of which matched both the victim's and his own) came from a shaving cut. While his pocket knife was judged capable of inflicting the wounds found on Dobson's body, an insufficient quantity of blood found in its groove precluded a test to determine its type. Significantly, bloodstains on the fly of Hoolhouse's trousers were not accompanied by semen stains. Neither could a footprint found near the body be tied to Hoolhouse.

Few believed the farm laborer would be convicted as his trial opened at the Leeds Assizes on March 28, 1938. Hoolhouse's counsel, certain of acquittal, confidently argued that there was not a case to go to the jury. He subsequently called no witnesses or offered any evidence supporting his client's alibi or innocence. When the case went to the jury on March 30, 1938, most courtroom spectators expected a verdict of not guilty. Hoolhouse's parents even had a taxi waiting to take him home. Four hours later the all-male jury, visibly shaken, found Hoolhouse guilty of Dobson's murder. His appeal was rejected on May 9, 1938, as was a petition filled with 14,400 signatures requesting a reprieve. Hoolhouse was hanged at Durham Gaol on May 26, 1938.

286. Furneaux, Rupert. *Robert Hoolhouse.* Crime Documentaries no. 2. London: Stevens, 1960. vii, 189 pp., [5]pp. of plates: ill.; 22 cm.

Furneaux presents the official trial transcript in narrative form and concludes that Hoolhouse was a "probably innocent man" who was doubtfully convicted and executed "on evidence on which few Englishmen would hang a cat." Appendix: The Evidence Relating to the Footprints and the Scientific Evidence.

Hosein, Arthur
(a.k.a. "King Hosein," "Mafia Group 3," "M3")

Born August 18, 1936, in Dow Village, Trinidad. Tailor. Stocking Pelham, England; 1 murder; gun; circa January 1, 1970.

"Believe me, I have great sympathy for the McKay family. I have a mother myself. I am no murderer ever if I am found guilty. These hands are artistic, not destructive. I believe in the preservation of Man. That is what I am living for!"—Hosein's address to the court given during his testimony

Convicted for the first kidnapping for ransom case in contemporary British history. On October 3, 1969, Arthur Hosein, a 33-year-old Trinidad-born tailor in England since 1955, watched a television interview featuring newspaper magnate Rupert Murdoch. Seeing an opportunity to realize his lifelong dream of becoming a millionaire, Hosein enlisted the aid of younger brother Nizamodeen (Nizam) in a plot to kidnap Murdoch's wife Anna and hold her for a one million pound ransom. The brothers learned where they *thought* Murdoch lived by staking out the publisher's *News of the World* office in London and following his blue Rolls Royce to a residential address in Wimbledon. Unknown to the kidnappers, however, Anna Murdoch had left England on holiday with her children on December 13, 1969. During their absence, the Rolls was being used by Murdoch's deputy chairman, Alick McKay, who resided with his wife Muriel Florence on Arthur Road, Wimbledon. On the evening of December 29, 1969, Alick McKay returned home to find a page of a Sunday newspaper littering the drive, the front door unchained, the television on, and the contents of his wife's handbag scattered on the stairs in the entry hall. On a table lay a billhook, twine, and an open can of adhesive bandages. A quick search of the house revealed that the phone had been disconnected, its number disc removed, and that money and jewelry had been taken. There was no sign of Mrs. McKay or a note left to explain her suspicious absence.

On December 30, 1969, an individual with a markedly "black" or American voice contacted Alick McKay from a phone booth in Epping. Identifying himself as a member of "Mafia Group 3," an organized crime outfit from the United States, the kidnapper demanded one million pounds in a few days or else Mrs. McKay would be killed. Numerous letters (some written by Mrs. McKay) and phone calls followed until a ransom drop was finally set up for February 1, 1970, in London. Police flooded the area and the wary kidnappers were scared off. Another round of negotiations followed in which the date of February 5, 1970, was set up for the ransom drop. The kidnappers demanded that two suitcases filled with the money be delivered to a garage in Bishop's Stortford by McKay and his chauffeur. Detectives, doubling as the men, dropped the money off, but the kidnappers drove off in a Volvo when they spotted a concerned citizen picking up the unattended bags to turn in to local police. A police surveillance team took down the car's license plate and Scotland Yard identified the vehicle as the Hoseins. An intensive search of Arthur Hosein's 10 acre "Rook's Farm" in Stocking Pelham failed to turn Mrs. McKay's body but did yield physical evidence tying the brothers to the kidnapping.

Both brothers pleaded not guilty as their kidnapping/murder trial opened at the Old Bailey on September 14, 1970. A palm print found on the newspaper in McKay's driveway was identified as Arthur Hosein's. Mrs. McKay's ransom letters were written on leaves of paper found in Nizam's room. Finally, authorities identified Nizam as the driver of the Volvo seen at Bishop's Stortford during the abortive ransom pickup. Both brothers were convicted on all charges after a nine man, three woman jury deliberated for four hours. The jury, however, unanimously recommended leniency toward Nizam feeling that the 22 year old was clearly under the influence of his older, more aggressive brother. Both received life imprisonment for murder, with an additional 25 years given to Arthur and 15 to Nizam for kidnapping. According to the most widely held theory on the case, police believe the Hoseins shot Mrs. McKay at Rook's Farm around New Year's Day, dismembered her corpse, and fed the remains to the pigs which had been sold for slaughter before their arrest. Released from prison in 1990, Nizamodeen Hosein was deported, permanently barred from Britain, and as of March 1992 worked for the Trinidad Environment Ministry. On March 16, 1992, the *Evening Standard* reported that he recently married Lela Ramadeen, Haringey's deputy education director who has twice been voted Britain's Woman of the Year.

287. Cooper, William. *Shall We Ever Know? The Trial of the Hosein Brothers for the Murder of Mrs. McKay*. London: Hutchinson of London, 1971. 224 pp.: ill.; 22 cm.

_____. [Same as 287, but U.S. ed. retitled: *Brothers: The Trial of the Brothers Hosein for the Murder of Mrs. McKay*.] 1st U.S. ed. New York: Harper & Row, 1971. xi, 220 pp.; 22 cm.

Cooper attended the trial and presents a day-by-day summary of the events interspersed with his comments. Appendices include dates, times, and extracts from the letters and telephone calls placed by the kidnappers to the McKay family.

288. Deeley, Peter, and Walker, Christopher. *Murder in the Fourth Estate: An Investigation into the Role of Press and*

Police in the McKay Case. London: Gollancz, 1971. 192 pp., 4 plates: ill., map (on lining papers), ports.; 23 cm.

_____. [Same as 288 minus subtitle.] 1st U.S. ed. New York: McGraw-Hill, 1973. 186 pp.: ill.; 22 cm.

A thought-provoking examination of the relationship between the media and the police in the McKay case which concludes that while the authorities need to increase their trust in the media, they in turn must not exploit that trust.

289. O'Flaherty, Michael. *Have You Seen This Woman?* London: Corgi, 1971. 208 pp., 8 plates: ill., facsims., ports., map; 18 cm.; paperback.

Hosein, Nizamodeen (a.k.a. "Shariff Mustaph," "Mafia Group 3," "M3")

Born July 1, 1948, in Dow Village, Trinidad. Tailor. Stocking Pelham, England; 1 murder; gun; circa January 1, 1970.

"I'd rather *die* than be charged with murder!"; *see also* Hosein, Arthur.

Hulme, Juliet (a.k.a. "Anne Perry" [legal name change])

Born October 28, 1938, in Liverpool, England. Student. Christchurch, New Zealand; 1 murder; bludgeon (brick); June 22, 1954.

Film: Heavenly Creatures (NZ, 1994), directed by Peter Jackson, a Miramax International presentation of a Wingnut Films/Fontana Film Productions coproduction in association with the New Zealand Film Commission. Cast includes Melanie Lynsky (Pauline Parker), Kate Winslet (Juliet Hulme), and Sarah Peirse (Honora Parker).

"After the first blow was struck, I knew it would be necessary to kill her."—From Hulme's confession

Sensational New Zealand case with lesbian overtones in which a pair of schoolgirls murdered one of their mothers. Juliet Hulme, 15, and Pauline Parker, 16, first met at high school in Christchurch, New Zealand, in 1953. Brought together by a shared belief in their own intellectual superiority, the pair expressed their love for one another in a series of romantic letters and a diary kept by Parker. When a tubercular condition confined Hulme to a sanatorium for four months, Parker devotedly wrote every day vowing her eternal love. The relationship reached its crisis in the spring of 1954 with the announcement by Hulme's father that he had accepted a teaching position in a university in England. News that Hulme would soon be leaving for England via South Africa threw the girls into a panic. They begged Mrs. Honora Mary Parker, Pauline's mother, to let her daughter accompany the Hulmes to England, but concerned over the pair's unwholesome attachment to one another, she refused. Viewing Mrs. Parker as the sole impediment to their togetherness, the pair planned the woman's murder as meticulously documented in Parker's diary. On June 22, 1954, the pair lured Mrs. Parker to the Cashmere Mountains near Christchurch on the pretext of sharing a farewell outing. Hulme dropped a brightly colored stone on the path in front of Mrs. Parker and when the woman bent down to examine it her daughter bludgeoned her in the head with a half-brick knotted into a stocking. Hulme later admitted striking the woman at least once. Investigators, who found a bloody sock at the scene, immediately discounted the girls' story that Mrs. Parker had repeatedly struck her head in an accidental fall. An autopsy determined that the woman had been struck 47 times in the head and shoulders. Both girls subsequently confessed and Parker's diary provided the key to the murder.

Tried amid unprecedented publicity in Christchurch in August 1954, the prosecution characterized the pair as "precocious and dirty minded little girls" whose "unhealthy devotion to one another" led to the "coldly and callously planned murder." Two defense psychiatrists testified that the girls were insane at the time of the murder and suffered from a mental condition known as *folie à deux* (communicated insanity between two persons with similar mental weaknesses). The prosecution contended, "They are not incurably insane. They are incurably bad." The pair was convicted by an all male jury but spared the death penalty under the Capital Punishment Act of 1950 which allows a person under 18 to be detained indefinitely "at Her Majesty's pleasure." The pair served their sentences at different institutions and were released with new identities in 1960. Parker converted to Roman Catholicism while in prison and it was reported in 1994 that she was working in an Auckland, New Zealand, bookstore. While researching an article on a film about the case (*Heavenly Creatures*), a reporter for New Zealand's *Sunday News* revealed in August 1994 that mystery novelist Anne Perry, author of two successful Victorian detective series, was in actuality Juliet Hulme. A devout Mormon, the unmarried Perry was living in the quiet Scottish fishing village of Portmahomack near her aged mother. In a television interview aired in New Zealand on September 19, 1994, Perry denied having shared a lesbian relationship with Parker and blamed a weak character as the reason she took part in the murder. "I didn't have the strength to say no, this is wrong, no matter what, and to just walk away," she stated. As of this writing, the pair had not seen or corresponded with each other since their 1954 conviction.

290. Glamuzina, Julie, and Laurie, Alison J. *Parker & Hulme: A Lesbian View.* Auckland: New Women's Press, 1991. 214 pp.: ill., ports.; 22 cm.; trade paperback.

Glamuzina, a tutor in information technology, and Laurie, a lecturer in the women's studies department at Victoria University, explore the killers' alleged homosexuality in the context of mid–1950s New Zealand and examine the surrounding issues of social control and gender. A controversial social history employing pro–lesbian/feminist theory, the book contains a detailed reconstruction of the crime based on the Supreme Court trial transcripts, the coroner's reports, entries in Parker's diary, and on interviews with some of the participants.

291. Gurr, Tom, and Cox, H.H. *Obsession.* London: Frederick Muller Ltd., 1958. 254 pp.; 21 cm.

A documentary novel in which all details of the crime are accurate, but which substitutes fictitious names for the participants. Actual quotes from Parker's diary entries are used as well.

Hulten, Karl Gustav
(a.k.a. "Cleft Chin Murderer," "Inky Finger Murderer," "Richard John Allen")

Born March 3, 1922, in Stockholm, Sweden. Executed March 8, 1945. U.S. Army soldier. Staines, England; 1 murder; Remington automatic pistol, October 6, 1944.

"She said she would like to do something exciting like becoming a 'gun moll' like they do back in the States."—Hulten, after his arrest, describing Jones' personal aspirations

Fatal pairing of a U.S. army deserter with a striptease artist in wartime England which resulted in what the press called the "Cleft Chin Murder." On October 7, 1944, the body of a man with a markedly cleft chin and ink-stained fingers was found in a roadside ditch in Staines, England. The victim, subsequently identified as 34-year-old hired driver George Edward Heath, had been shot in the back of the head at close range. Heath's Ford V-8 car was located in southwest London on October 9, 1944. As police staked out the vehicle a young American Army officer entered it on the driver's side. The soldier, who gave his name as "Second Lieutenant Richard John Allen," was detained and a search of his person yielded an automatic weapon. He admitted deserting and a check of military records established his identity as Karl Gustav Hulten, a 22-year-old soldier born in Sweden, raised in the United States, and currently attached to the Army's 501st Parachute Infantry. Hulten initially maintained that he had found the car abandoned the previous afternoon and at the time of the murder was asleep in a truck at Newbury. Under intense questioning, the young soldier changed his story. In the new version, he stole the car and spent the night of the murder with a striptease artist named "Georgina Grayson" at her home in Hammersmith. "Grayson," the stage name of 18-year-old Elizabeth Maud Jones, supported Hulten's alibi until a casual remark she made to a war reserve policeman led her to confess that she was with her lover when he shot Heath. Jones had known Hulten for only six days before the murder, but was impressed by his boasts of being a Chicago gangster who was the leader of a gang of black marketers in London.

Enraged by her confession, Hulten denied the gangster story and implicated Jones in the murder. According to him, the stripper wanted to do "something dangerous" and aspired to an exciting life as a gun moll. Their brief time together had been spent in random acts of robbery and violence which included the attempted drowning of a young girl in the Thames River at Runnymede. Though they had intended to rob Heath, his killing was an accident, and Jones *had* helped to dump the body. The decision of the United States to waive its rights to prosecute Hulten under the Visiting Forces Act cleared the way for the soldier's case to be tried in a British court. The highly publicized trial for the "Cleft Chin Murder Case" began in London's Old Bailey on January 16, 1945, and lasted six days. Jones insisted throughout the proceedings that she acted solely in fear of Hulten and his threats of violence. No witnesses substantiated her claim. On January 23, 1945, the nine-man, three-woman jury was out only 75 minutes before finding the pair guilty, but with a recommendation for mercy for Jones. Two days before Hulten's hanging at Pentonville Prison on March 8, 1945, the home secretary granted Jones a reprieve. She was released from prison in May 1954.

292. Roberts, C.E. Bechhofer, ed. *The Trial of Jones and Hulten*. The Old Bailey Trial Series. London: Jarrolds, 1945. 238 pp.: ill.; 22 cm.

Roberts, a barrister of Gray's Inn and the South-Eastern Circuit, intro-

duces excerpts from the trial's transcript with a brief, but illuminating summary of the case. An appendix includes the text of The United States of America (Visiting Forces) Act, 1942.

Hume, Brian Donald

(a.k.a. "The Flying Smuggler," "Captain D. B. Hulme," "The Fuse," "Donald Brown," "John F. Lea," "John Stephen Bird," "Johnny Bird," "John Stanislaw," "Donald Brown" [legal name change])

Born December 1919 in Swanage, Dorset, England. Electrical company owner. Golders Green, England, and Zurich, Switzerland; 2 murders; German S.S. dagger and pistol; October 4, 1949, and January 30, 1959.

"I was born with a chip on my shoulder, large as an elephant. I've got a grudge against society." — Excerpt from Hume's confession serialized in the *Sunday Pictorial* during June 1958

British double murderer who sold his confession to one of the killings to the *Sunday Pictorial*. The illegitimate son of a schoolmistress who hid his parentage from him, Hume was fascinated from childhood with the adventure of flying. In 1939 he joined the Royal Air Force Volunteer Reserve, but was declared unfit for duty after sustaining a severe head injury in a practice flight in 1940. As a civilian, Hume used his position as a firespotter in Acton to turn in false air raid alarms. While others sheltered, he pilfered tinned food from shops to sell on the black market. Arrested in June 1942 for passing bad checks, Hume used his time in prison to study electrical engineering and when released opened his own radio and electrical shop in Golders Green in 1943. By 1947, thanks to the design and manufacture of his own "Little Atom" toaster, Hume was prospering. However, when the post-war pinch began hurting business Hume once again started dealing on the black market.

In early 1949 Hume began stealing cars for Iranian-born Stanley Setty (real name Sulman Seti), a successful 44-year-old car dealer specializing in selling stolen cars on the black market and laundering money. Setty also utilized Hume's skill as a pilot to have him deliver guns to the Middle East. Despite the mutually beneficial arrangement, neither man liked or trusted the other. In August 1949 an incident occurred which marked the end for Setty. Hume's beloved dog, Tony (half–husky, half–Alsatian), scratched the paint on Setty's car and the dealer kicked the animal. Hume, convinced that Setty was also seeing his wife, brooded over the kick. On October 4, 1949, Setty visited Hume at his maisonette at 620 Finchley Road in Golders Green to discuss business. According to Hume's later newspaper confession, the men argued and Hume killed Setty with a German S.S. dagger declaring in print, "Now, those S.S. initials stood for ... Stanley Setty." Hume dismembered the corpse with a hacksaw and lino knife, wrapped the pieces in three bundles, and over the next couple of days dropped the parcels out of a plane over the English Channel. On October 21, 1949, a farm laborer at Tillingham, Essex, found a parcel floating in the Dengie marshes which contained a legless, headless human torso which had been stabbed five times in the chest. Fingerprints established Setty's identity. Other post-mortem injuries suggested that the body had been dropped from a plane.

Official inquiries at airports led police to Hume when a worker at a flying club in Elstree remembered seeing him place two parcels into a hired plane on October 5, 1949.

In custody, Hume denied killing Setty and told a story of being approached by three men named "Mac," "Greenie," and "the Boy" to drop parcels into the sea. Not by chance, Hume's description of the trio bore a remarkable resemblance to the detectives who interrogated him. Under questioning, Hume finally admitted that he suspected the parcels might have contained Setty's dismembered remains. Hume pleaded innocent to Setty's murder at his weeklong trial which began in the Old Bailey on January 18, 1950. Despite having passed some of Setty's money which he later admitted in his confession to finding in the dead man's clothes, a jury deliberated two and a half hours on January 26, 1950, before notifying the court that they could not agree on a unanimous verdict. The murder charge against Hume was dropped, but he pleaded guilty to being an accessory after the fact and was sentenced to 12 years. Released early on account of good conduct on February 1, 1958, Hume sold his confession to the *Sunday Pictorial* for £2,000 knowing that he could not be tried again for Setty's murder because of the double jeopardy law.

Legally changing his name to Donald Brown, Hume used the money to establish himself in Zurich, Switzerland. Over the next year, Hume used a variety of aliases while robbing banks in England and Zurich. On January 30, 1959, Hume robbed the Gewerbe Bank in Zurich and shot a cashier. During his escape, he shot and killed 50-year-old taxi driver Arthur Maag before being captured by an angry crowd. Hume used the time before the start of his trial at Winterthur, Switzerland, on September 24, 1959, to write a 60,000 word novel about gangsters and their molls entitled *The Dead Stay Dumb*. During the same time, a psychiatrist examined the double murderer and declared him to have been legally sane at the time of Maag's killing. On September 30, 1959, Hume was convicted and sentenced to life imprisonment at hard labor in Regensdorf Prison. Over the years, Hume's mental state deteriorated to the point that Swiss authorities considered him violent and dangerous. After being examined by two psychiatrists at London's Heathrow Airport on August 20, 1976, Hume was formally admitted to Broadmoor Hospital under the Mental Health Act of 1959.

293. Butler, Ivan, ed. *Trials of Brian Donald Hume*. Celebrated Trials Series. Newton Abbot; North Pomfret, Vt.: David and Charles, 1976. 128 pp., [4]pp. of plates: ill., map, plan, ports.; 23 cm.
    A succinct review of the case featuring day-by-day coverage of Hume's separate trials for the murders of Stanley Setty and Swiss taxi driver Arthur Maag. Includes a list of "Principal Dates" noting the highlights of Hume's life and criminal career.

294. Williams, John. *Hume: Portrait of a Double Murderer*. London: Heinemann, 1960. 248 pp.: ill.; 21 cm.
_____. [Same as 294.] London: Hamilton, 1961. 191 pp.: ill.; 18 cm.; ("Panther books"); paperback.
    An excellent and highly readable study which features exclusive material from Mirror Features, London, as well as liberal quotes from Hume's public statements. A wonderful selection of photographs includes a reconstruction showing Hume accompanied by his dog Tony

in the air over the English Channel pitching the bundle containing Setty's torso from the plane.

Hunt, Joe
(a.k.a. "Joseph Henry Gamsky" [birth name], "The Godfather of the Brat Pack")

Born October 31, 1959, in Chicago, Illinois. Commodities trader. Beverly Hills, California; 2 murders (1 charge dropped); .22 caliber pistol, suffocation; June 6, 1984, and July 30, 1984.

Television: "The Billionaire Boys Club" (1987), a two-part, four-hour made-for-television miniseries based on Sue Horton's book of the same title, originally aired on NBC on November 8 and 9, 1987. Cast includes Judd Nelson (Joe Hunt), Ron Silver (Ron Levin), and Frederic Lehne (Chris Fairmont).

Charismatic founder and leader of the "Billionaire Boys Club," a Los Angeles investment group and social fraternity, whom authorities credit with masterminding two murders for profit. On June 6, 1984, Hunt and Jim Pittman, the BBC's director of security, murdered 42-year-old Ron Levin in his Beverly Hills home after forcing him to make out a check to the group for $1.5 million. Levin, a well-connected con man, had earlier duped Hunt in a business deal which cost the 25 year old millions of dollars. According to Pittman's later confession aired in May 1993 on the television program "A Current Affair," he murdered Levin and, with Hunt, disposed of the body in Soledad Canyon, a wilderness area about an hour from downtown Los Angeles. To date, Levin's body has not been found. When Levin's check bounced, Hunt allegedly seized upon another idea to secure big money to cover the club's debts. On July 30, 1984, Hedayat Eslaminia, the wealthy father of a BBC member, was kidnapped by his own son, beaten, and locked into a steamer trunk until he agreed to sign over $30 million in assets to the organization. Before he could do so, the 56 year old suffocated and was dumped in Soledad Canyon. Hunt was convicted of Levin's murder on April 22, 1987, and sentenced to life in prison without the possibility of parole. Representing himself in the Eslaminia murder, the trial ended in a hung jury in Redwood City, California, on December 9, 1992. The charge was later dropped. On April 10, 1993, Hunt married a paralegal who helped win the mistrial.

295. Horton, Sue. *The Billionaire Boys Club.* 1st ed. New York: St. Martin's Press, 1989. xii, 354 pp., [6]pp. of plates: ill.; 24 cm.

_____. [Same as 295.] New York: St. Martin's Paperbacks, 1990. xii, 354 pp., [8]pp. of plates: ill. 18 cm.; paperback.

"Inky Fingers Murder" *see* **Hulten, Karl Gustav (and) Jones, Elizabeth Maude**

"Jack the Stripper"
(a.k.a. "The Hammersmith Nudes Murders")

Unknown. London, England area; 8 murders; asphyxiation, manual strangulation; June 1959–January 1965.

Unknown serial killer of prostitutes whose career is often likened to that of Jack the Ripper's. Dubbed "Jack the Stripper" by the press, the killer claimed his first victim on June 17, 1959. The body of a woman later

identified as 21-year-old prostitute Elizabeth Figg was found propped up against a tree at Duke's Meadow on the banks of the Thames near the Chiswick Bridge. Figg's dress was torn down the front and her underwear, shoes, and handbag were missing. She had engaged in sex shortly before being manually strangled to death. On November 8, 1963, the headless body of Gwynneth Rees, a 22-year-old prostitute from Bethnal Green, was found in a rubbish heap at Mortlake near the Thames naked save for one stocking. After the discovery of a third dead prostitute (Hannah Tailford, 30) floating in the Thames at Hammersmith on February 2, 1964, the police and the press realized the serial nature of the crimes and thereafter referred to them as the "Nude Murders." Tailford's panties were found stuffed in her mouth, her stockings around her ankles. Two months later on April 8, 1964, the nude body of another prostitute, 26-year-old Irene Charlotte Lockwood, was found floating in the Thames 300 yards from where Tailford was discovered. Lockwood was four months pregnant at the time she drowned. Later that month, a 54-year-old caretaker named Kenneth Archibald confessed to Lockwood's murder, but the case against him fell apart at trial when he recanted his confession.

The first solid lead in the ongoing investigation of the killings occurred on April 24, 1964, with the discovery of a woman's nude body facedown on a garbage heap near a sports ground at Acton one mile from the Thames. Identified through fingerprints as Helene Catherine Barthelemy, four of the 22-year-old prostitute's teeth had been forced out. One was retrieved from her throat. Death was due to asphyxiation and the sperm found in her throat led authorities to conjecture that the killer had murdered his victim during the act of fellatio, literally choking her to death with his penis. Barthelemy's body had been stripped after death and microscopic metallic flecks of spray paint on it suggested that it had been stored in a garage for a day before being dumped on the garbage heap. On July 14, 1964, Mary Fleming's nude body was found propped up against the door of a garage near a private residence in Acton. Like Barthelemy, Fleming had died of asphyxiation during oral sex and the paint flecks found on her body identically matched those found on the other prostitute. Margaret McGowan, a 21-year-old prostitute missing since October 23, 1964, was found naked atop a trash heap in Kensington on November 25, 1964. Asphyxiated during fellatio or orally raped after death, McGowan's throat contained sperm and a dislodged tooth. On February 16, 1965, "Jack the Stripper's" last victim was found in weeds on the Heron Trading Estate in Acton. Identified as Bridget Esther O'Hara, a 27-year-old prostitute living in Hammersmith, the woman's partially mummified body had been stored for a month before it was dumped. Missing teeth, sperm in the throat, and paint flecks linked the woman to Barthelemy and McGowan. Two hundred detectives checked out all the spray paint operations and garages within a 24 square mile radius of London and questioned all 7,000 workers on the Estate. Lacking a viable suspect, the police decided to use the media to apply pressure on the killer by announcing that their list of suspects had dwindled to ten. Within a month of O'Hara's murder a night security guard on the Heron Estate gassed himself to death in his van. In a

suicide note, he wrote, "I cannot stand the strain any longer." To date, the only "proof" of the unidentified man's guilt is that the murders stopped after his death.

296. McConnell, Brian. *Found Naked and Dead.* London: New English Library, 1974. 190 pp.; 21 cm.

_____. [Same as 296.] London: New English Library, 1975. 190 pp.; 18 cm.; paperback.

Jahnke, Richard John, Jr.

Born June 27, 1966, in Fort Ord, California. High school student. Cheyenne, Wyoming; 1 murder; .12 gauge shotgun; November 16, 1982.

Television: "Right to Kill?" (1985), a two-hour, made-for-television movie, originally aired on ABC on May 22, 1985. Cast includes Frederic Forrest (Richard Jahnke, Sr.), Christopher Collet (Richard Jahnke, Jr.), and Justine Bateman (Deborah Jahnke).

"I thought about killing him ever since I was a little kid, but I always chickened out."

A case of patricide credited with bringing the issue of child abuse to the national consciousness. On November 16, 1982, Richard C. Jahnke, Sr., 38, a special agent for the Internal Revenue Service, and his wife Maria pulled into the driveway of their home in the fashionable area north of Cheyenne, Wyoming, after spending the evening celebrating the 20th anniversary of their meeting. Before they left, Jahnke had violently argued with his 16-year-old son Richard and ordered him not to be there when he returned. As the elder Jahnke moved to open the garage door, his son fired six shotgun blasts through it striking his father four times in the chest and killing him instantly. The boy's 17-year-old sister, Deborah, waited with a .38 carbine in the living room in case the father killed his son. Her brother later testified that Deborah suggested they kill their mother as well before they fled the house. Richard Jahnke subsequently pleaded innocent to charges of first degree murder and conspiracy while Deborah entered an identical plea to charges of aiding and abetting a murder and conspiracy. Richard was tried as an adult at a February 1983 trial in Cheyenne where a picture of the all–American family gone wrong emerged in graphic detail. Testimony from friends and family portrayed Jahnke, Sr., as an ultra-strict disciplinarian who had physically abused both his children since they were two. A former career army sergeant with a gun fixation, his explosive temper was directed at his children and wife for the smallest "infractions." Both children received regular beatings for coughing at the dinner table or for scraping their plates with their forks. Richard testified to once witnessing his father fondling his sister. The defense emotionally argued that the boy acted in self-defense to end the life of a man who for 14 years had been slowly emotionally killing the entire family. Jahnke was convicted of a lesser charge of voluntary manslaughter and acquitted of conspiracy on February 19, 1983. His sister was convicted in March 1983. Prior to their sentencing, public support for the battered teens ran high and intensified after Richard received 5–15 years on March 18, 1993, and Deborah 3–8 years in April. The case received national attention when it was featured on the CBS television news magazine "60 Minutes" and letters to Wyoming governor Ed Herschler ran 95 percent in favor of reducing or commuting their sentences. Eight days after the Wyoming State Supreme Court upheld the boy's conviction, Herschler commuted Jahnke's sentence to three years to be served in the Wyoming Industrial Institute in Worland. He similarly commuted Deborah's sentence and ordered the teen be placed on one year's probation five days after the State Supreme Court upheld her conviction. In a final act of compassion, Herschler signed an order freeing Jahnke on October 17, 1985. Under the terms of the order the 19 year old was placed on supervised parole until age 21.

297. Prendergast, Alan. *The Poison Tree: A True Story of Family Violence and Revenge.* New York: Putnam's, 1986. 350 pp.; 23 cm.

_____. [Same as 297 with variant subtitle: *A True Story of Family Terror.*] New York: Avon, 1987. 326 pp.; 17 cm.; paperback.

Prendergast, who originally covered the Jahnke case in a August 19, 1982, *Rolling Stone* article entitled "It's You or Me Dad," presents a sympathetic account focusing on the cycle of abuse which led to patricide.

Jenkins, Steven Todd
(a.k.a. "Steven Todd Anderson" [adopted name])

Born circa 1965. Construction worker. Ruthton, Minnesota; 2 murders; M-1 carbine; September 29, 1983.

"I am sorry that this happened. Please forgive me and Daddy."— Jenkins, at the time of arrest, writing to his mother on the back of his Minnesota fishing license

The tragic double murder of two bankers near Ruthton, Minnesota, on September 29, 1983, by a dispossessed farmer and his 18-year-old son is open to interpretation. It can be viewed either as symbolic of the clash in rural America between local banking institutions and financially hard-pressed farmers during hard economic times or as a straightforward case of vengeance-motivated murder committed by a father and his son. By 1980, 44-year-old James Lee Jenkins' life was falling apart. A divorce and the near loss of his son Steven in a motorcycle accident was capped off by his inability to continue making the payments on a 10-acre, 60-cow dairy farm three miles north of Ruthton. In October 1980, the Buffalo Ridge State Bank foreclosed on the property. Jenkins' failure to make another dairy farm financially viable near Hoffman, Minnesota, seemingly confirmed the general consensus that he was a born failure in business matters. Jenkins left Minnesota for Texas in the summer of 1982, finding $3.90 an hour work as a janitor and night watchman for the Brownwood, Texas, school district. Working nearly around the clock from August 1982 through July 1983, Jenkins saved money by living in a cramped trailer on the school grounds and dreamed of the day he would have enough money to return to Minnesota and start another dairy farm. Months after moving to Texas, Jenkins was joined by his devoted teenaged son, Steven.

Like his father, Steven Jenkins was a loner. Fascinated by the military from an early age, Steven's lifelong dream was to join the Marines. As a four-year-old, he painted "U. S. Army" on a wagon and a photo taken around the time of his tenth birthday party shows him dressed in full military costume. He received his first rifle at 11. As an adolescent, an interest in weaponry, especially guns, became the focal point of his life. Steven trained himself to be a crack shot and wore a Bowie knife strapped to his leg. Steven's dream of becoming a Marine ended in 1981 when he was rejected due to a spleen ruptured in a motorcycle accident in 1980. At 17 Steven bought an M-1 carbine (the murder weapon) with his father's permission. The gun seldom left Steven's side and when not hanging in the window rack of his father's truck was propped in a corner of his bedroom. Rejected by the Marines, Steven affected all the trappings of military life. He wore fatigues, close-cropped his hair, tattooed his arms, and set up an obstacle course on his grandparents' farm complete with a target dressed in a man's clothes. In Texas, Steven met the "real thing," a Vietnam combat veteran who trained him in the art of running and shooting the M-1 in full combat gear. Steven, during this period, was later described by the superintendent of the Texas construction company where he worked as "a goofball who was always talking about blowing someone's head off."

Father and son returned to Minnesota in mid–1983 with the idea of starting up a dairy farm with the money they had saved. James Jenkins rented a small farm near Hardwick in Rock County, but with his bad credit history was repeatedly denied financing from lending institutions and cattle lessors. On September 28, 1983, a Long Prairie cattle dealer refused to extend Jenkins credit when informed by Rudolph Blythe, president of Buffalo Ridge State Bank, that the would-be dairyman had filed bankruptcy in 1980. Convinced Blythe was purposely giving him bad credit references, Jenkins, posing as prospective buyer "Ron Anderson," set up a 10:00 a.m. meeting with the banker at the old Jenkins' farm near Ruthton the next

morning, September 29. Jenkins allegedly told son Steven that he planned
"to go there and rob (Blythe) and ...
scare the hell out of him." Together
they loaded up the trunk of James
Jenkins' pickup truck with Steven's
mini-arsenal: an M-1 carbine, a .12
gauge shotgun, a sawed-off .410 shotgun with makeshift silencer and bayonet attached, a nine-shot .22 caliber
pistol, ammunition, knives, a machete,
three defused hand grenades, and a
kung-fu style throwing star.

The next day, Rudolph H. Blythe,
Jr., 42, accompanied by the bank's chief
loan officer Deems A. Thulin, 37,
arrived unexpectedly early at the farm
and noticed a white truck. Minutes later
Blythe's wife drove on the scene and was
instructed by her husband to call the
sheriff because trespassers were about.
The shooting started shortly after she
drove away. First to die was Thulin
seated behind the wheel of his car. The
first of three shots fired from a high-
powered rifle struck Thulin in the throat
killing him instantly. Blythe, hiding
behind the car, was struck in the shoulder and fled 100 yards across the front
yard toward the main road with the gunman pursuing him. He was overtaken
and shot to death in a ditch. Leaving the
scene in a white pickup truck bearing a
Texas plate, father and son drove to a
nearby town and bought ammunition.
Steven Jenkins later admitted firing
three rounds from his M-1 at a pursuing
police car. A six-state, three-day search
for the fugitives ensued which culminated in James Jenkins' shotgun suicide
in Paducah, Texas, on October 3, 1983.
Steven led police to his father's body that
day. Jenkins' suicide note, belatedly
found on January 6, 1984, read: "I Killed
Rudy Blythe / The S O B / Steve Leaving / Won't Listen Anymore / A Guy
Just As Well Be Dead."

Extradited back to Minnesota,
Steven insisted at his April 10, 1984,
trial in Ivanhoe that James Jenkins had
committed the murders and that he
had only participated out of fear of his
father. This contention was seriously
damaged by testimony which presented the elder Jenkins as an infirm,
barely ambulatory diabetic who could
not possibly have run 100 yards after
the wounded Blythe. More importantly, the prosecution argued, Jenkins'
poor eyesight would have prevented
him from sighting the rifle which killed
Thulin at long range. The Marine vet
who trained Steven in run and shoot
techniques in Texas testified to the
teen's proficiency with an M-1. Particularly damning was Steven's grand jury
testimony in which he admitted only
weeks before the murders asking an
acquaintance about the type of caliber
bullet needed to penetrate the bulletproof glass used in banks. After ten
hours of deliberation conducted over
two days, a jury on April 26, 1984,
handed down two murder convictions
against Jenkins; first degree for Blythe
and second degree for Thulin. Awaiting sentencing, Jenkins was adopted by
his attorney Swen Anderson and
appeared as "Steven Todd Anderson"
at his sentencing hearing on May 22,
1984. In the absence of the death
penalty in Minnesota, Anderson was
awarded concurrent sentences of mandatory life imprisonment for Blythe's
murder and 8 years and 4 four months
for Thulin's. Anderson/Jenkins is eligible for parole consideration in 2001
after serving 17 years of his sentence.

298. Amato, Joseph. *When Father and
Son Conspire: A Minnesota Farm Murder.*
1st ed. Ames: Iowa State University Press,
1988. xiv, 226 pp., [8]pp. of plates: ill.; 23
cm.

Amato, a history professor at Southwest State University in Marshall, Minnesota, and the former director of that school's rural studies program, views the killings as "the final outcome of a broken family and broken identities." He disagrees with the thesis outlined in Andrew Malcolm's book (see 299) which links the killings to the farm crisis. According to Amato, James Jenkins failed as a farmer several years before the farm crisis reached its peak.

299. Malcolm, Andrew H. *Final Harvest: An American Tragedy.* 1st ed. New York: Times Books, 1986. xiv, 320 pp.: map; 25 cm.

_____. [Same as 299.] Signet Nonfiction. New York: New American Library, 1987. xiv, 337 pp.: map; 18 cm. ("A Signet book"); paperback.

Malcolm covered the case for the *New York Times* and saw a direct link between the killings and the dire economic crisis which faced American farmers at the time.

Jones, Elizabeth Maude
(a.k.a. "Cleft Chin Murderer," "Inky Finger Murderer," "Georgina Grayson," "Elizabeth Marina Jones")

Born July 5, 1926, in Wales. Stripper. Staines, England; 1 murder (accomplice); Remington automatic pistol; October 6, 1944.

"If you had seen somebody do what I have seen done, *you* wouldn't be able to sleep at night."—The casual remark made to an acquaintance by Jones which led her to confess her involvement with Karl Gustav Hulten in the sensational "Cleft Chin Murder"; *see also* Hulten, Karl Gustav.

Jones, Genene Ann
(a.k.a. "Death Nurse," "Genene

Ann DeLany" [former married name], "Genene Ann Turk" [married name at time of arrest])

Born July 13, 1950, in San Antonio, Texas. Licensed vocational nurse. San Antonio and Kerrville, Texas; 1 murder (convicted, suspected of at least 15 others); succinylcholine; 1978– 1982.

Television: "Deadly Medicine" (1991), a two-hour, made-for-television movie adapted from Moore and Reed's book of the same title, originally aired on NBC on November 11, 1991. Cast includes Susan Ruttan (Genene Jones), Veronica Hamel (Dr. Kathy Holland), and Stephen Tobolowsky (Ron Sutton).

"I'm not just anybody young lady. I'm the nurse that killed all those babies."—Statement attributed to Jones by Kathy Engelke, a woman placed in a jail holding cell with her

On May 25, 1983, Genene Jones, a 32-year-old licensed vocational nurse, was indicted on one count of murder for the death of 15-month-old Chelsea Ann McClelland. The infant died of respiratory failure on September 17, 1982, after receiving treatment by Jones in the Kerrville, Texas, office of pediatrician Kathleen M. Holland. During the six weeks Jones worked for Dr. Holland (August through late September 1982), seven children had suffered seizures after visits to the office. On the weekend of September 25-26, 1982, Jones brought Dr. Holland a vial of succinylcholine, a synthetic muscle relaxant, which the nurse had earlier reported missing. Jones was subsequently fired after she could not explain the vial's disappearance or the puncture holes in its permanent rubber cap. McClelland's body was exhumed and an autopsy revealed that an injection of succinylcholine had simply stopped her breathing. More ominously, the special grand jury that recommended indicting Jones in the McClelland case had also reviewed compelling evidence which suggested she had been involved in perhaps as many as 47 deaths while working in the pediatric intensive care unit at the Bexar County Hospital in San Antonio, Texas. During Jones' employment there from October 30, 1978, through March 1982, code blue emergencies on her 3:00 p.m. to 11:00 p.m. shift skyrocketed. The increase in multiple infant deaths was so dramatic that hospital officials conducted three separate inquiries into the seemingly inexplicable deaths occurring in their pediatric intensive care unit. Despite a state law governing the reporting of suspicious deaths to the medical examiner, no one affiliated with the hospital ever contacted that office. A later Centers for Disease Control study of the pediatric unit of the medical facility for the years 1981–1982 revealed a 178 percent increase in that unit's death rate when compared with other units in the hospital. More compellingly, the study suggested that infants in the unit were 10.7 percent more likely to die when "Nurse 32" (generally assumed to be Jones) was working than when she was not. This finding would seem to be supported by testimony given by Susanna Maldonaldo at Jones' 1984 trial for injuring four-week-old Rolando Santos. Maldonaldo, a coworker, compiled a list of 42 infants who died on Jones' shift between January 1981 and March 1982.

Tried in Georgetown, Texas, on January 15, 1984, Jones pleaded not guilty to murdering McClelland and to seven additional counts of injuring children by injection of drugs in Kerrville and San Antonio. The prosecutor argued that Jones was a supreme egotist who injected children under her care with life threatening drugs in order to focus attention on herself while she heroically fought to save their lives. One psychiatric explanation later forwarded to explain her bizarre behavior was the rare disorder Munchausen syndrome which causes its sufferer to derive emotional satisfaction from inflicting injury on others then subjecting them to medical treatment. The defense maintained that not only was McClelland a chronically sick child, but that Jones was being made the scapegoat for the incompetence of Dr. Holland. It was further argued that the sophisticated test used for finding the presence of succinylcholine in the child's body was unreliable. Testimony concerning other cases of sudden infant respiratory seizures, however, clearly demonstrated Jones' pattern of involvement. The medical charts of five infants showed that after Jones had injected them they had stopped breathing and had to be mechanically resuscitated. Jones was found guilty of first degree murder on February 15, 1984, and sentenced to 99 years in prison. Tried in San Antonio in October 1984 for injecting 4-week-old Rolando Santos with the anticoagulant heparin, Jones was convicted by a district court judge on October 24, 1984, and sentenced to a concurrent term of 60 years. Suspected in as many as 15 other murders, Jones continues to maintain her innocence.

300. Elkind, Peter. *The Death Shift: The True Story of Nurse Genene Jones and the Texas Baby Murders*. New York: Viking, 1989. xiii, 351 pp., [8]pp. of plates: ill., ports.; 24 cm.

_____. [Same as 300.] New York: Penguin, 1990. xiii, 400 pp.: ill.; 18 cm. ("An Onyx book"); paperback.

_____. [Same as 300.] London: Corgi, 1990. 447 pp.; 18 cm.; paperback.

Elkind, who first reported on the case in an August 1983 article in *Texas Monthly*, portrays Jones as a crisis junkie and condemns administrators at the Bexar County Hospital for failing to expose her. Fearing litigation, they gave Jones a letter of recommendation for her next job despite the knowledge that coworkers suspected her of harming children.

301. Moore, Kelly, and Reed, Dan. *Deadly Medicine.* 1st ed. New York: St. Martin's Press, 1988. x, 465 pp.: ill.; 22 cm. ("A Joan Kahn book.")

_____. [Same as 301.] 1st rev. St. Martin's Press mass market ed. New York: St. Martin's Press, 1989. xiii, 561 pp., [8]pp. of plates: ill.; 18 cm.; paperback.

Called by the authors "a true-life allegory about the nature of human evil and the possibility of choice," the book is based on personal interviews, letters, declarations, courtroom transcripts, secret grand jury testimony, and medical records.

Jones, James Warren

Born May 13, 1931, in Lynn, Indiana. Died November 18, 1978. Preacher. Jonestown, Guyana; 918 murders; poison (cyanide), gun; November 18, 1978.

Film: Guyana: Cult of the Damned (MEX, SP, PAN, 1979), a Re-Al Productions release of a 90 minute film docudrama directed by Rene Cardona, Jr. Cast includes Stuart Whitman (The Reverend James Johnson/Jim Jones) and Gene Barry (Congressman Lee O'Brien/Leo J. Ryan).

Television: "Guyana Tragedy: The Story of Jim Jones" (1980), a four-hour, two-part made-for-television miniseries based on Charles A. Krause's 1978 book *Guyana Massacre: The Eyewitness Account*, originally aired on CBS on April 14 and 15, 1980. Cast includes Powers Boothe (the Reverend Jim Jones), Ned Beatty (Congressman Leo J. Ryan), and Irene Cara (Alice Jefferson).

"I tried. I tried. I tried. Mother! Mother!"—Jones' last words before committing suicide

A charismatic cult leader who ordered the single largest mass-suicide of the 20th century. Preaching his first sermon at age 12 to schoolmates, Indiana-born Jim Jones married in 1947 and opened a small interdenominational church in Indianapolis in 1953. The unordained minister's strong advocacy of civil rights attracted great numbers of poor blacks to his church, but alienated many white parishioners. Following a break with the Methodists, Jones established the Peoples Temple Full Gospel Church, a group affiliated with the Disciples of Christ. In 1961 Jones was named director of the Indianapolis Human Rights Commission, spent 1961 through 1963 as a missionary in Belo Horizonte, Brazil, and was ordained as a Disciples of Christ minister in 1964. Targeted as a "nigger lover" by the more radical elements in Indianapolis, Jones endured acts of vandalism directed against his home and church. In 1963, Jones announced to his congregation that God had instructed him to move the church to either Northern California or Brazil: the only two places on earth which would be safe from an imminent nuclear holocaust which had been foretold to him in a divine vision. Joined by nearly 100 followers, Jones convoyed his congregation across the country in minivans finally settling in 1965 in Ukiah, California, a town in Redwood Valley 100 miles north of San Francisco. Jones, a charismatic speaker with a penchant for flashy ties and dark glasses, quickly attracted converts from the ranks of ex-convicts, poor blacks, and down-and-outers. Using money donated by his parishioners, the Reverend Jones invested heavily into real estate and other business ventures.

After moving the church headquarters to San Francisco in 1970, Jones became a powerful figure in local politics. Political luminaries like California governor Edmund G. Brown, Jr., and San Francisco mayor George Moscone visited the church which at its height averaged 5,000 for a Sunday service. Despite this support, however, the first sinister signs of unrest within the Peoples Temple began to emerge in August 1977 with the publication of a startling news account in the magazine *New West*. In the story, reporters Marshall Kilduff and James Tracy quoted ten former church members who described beatings and death threats made to those attempting to leave or discredit the church. Articles in the *San Francisco Examiner* further detailed that the Peoples Temple's estimated worth of $5 million had been largely built upon welfare fraud. Converts to the church were ordered to sign away all their worldly goods to the Temple at the time they joined. Jones especially targeted welfare recipients and the elderly who received monthly Social Security benefits. After converting them, the reverend quietly funneled the checks (an estimated $65,000 a month) into secret overseas bank accounts. In 1977 public outcry over the alleged excesses of the Peoples Temple forced Jones to leave the United States with nearly 1,000 of his followers and relocate to a 27,000-acre settlement in Guyana purchased earlier with church money. For months before the move, Jones had carefully brainwashed his congregation telling the black members that if they failed to follow him to Jonestown, Guyana, then the enemies of the church would put them into concentration camps and kill them. Jones convinced white members that their names were on a secret list of enemies of the state maintained by the CIA and that they would be captured, tortured, then executed if they did not flee with him.

Parents, friends, and siblings of Jonestown residents inundated the state department with complaints about the self proclaimed messiah. In May 1978 25-year-old Deborah Layton Blakely, a top aide of Jones and the Temple's treasurer, managed to leave the cult and in a June 15, 1978, affidavit detailed conditions at Jonestown. Characterizing Jones as a "paranoid" obsessed with "traitors," Blakely described public beatings ordered by the reverend and executed by a loyal squad of 50 armed guards who watched over the camp at all times. On average, Jones broadcast his paranoiac message six hours a day over loudspeakers positioned throughout the compound. During nightly marathon meetings with his flock, Jones harangued his followers telling them he was the reincarnation of Lenin and Christ. As a possessor of mystical powers, he could read their minds and heal the sick. At least once a week, according to Blakely, Jones conducted "White Night," an emergency drill in which residents of Jonestown lined up and were given a small glass of red liquid. Jones told them it was laced with a poison that caused death within 45 minutes of drinking it. Such an act of "revolutionary suicide" was essential, Jones maintained, because invaders in the jungle would torture them if they were captured alive. After 45 minutes passed with no one dying, Jones informed the group that the exercise had been a test of their loyalty, but that one day it might become necessary for them to take their lives.

Alarmed by these unsettling reports, California congressman Leo J. Ryan visited Jonestown on a fact-finding mission in November 1978. During Ryan's stay, a visibly nervous Jones entertained the congressman and a contingent of reporters under an open air pavilion in the heart of the Jonestown compound. On the morning of November 18, 1978, several members of the church asked Ryan to take them back to the States with him. As the congressman was leaving, one church member tried to attack him with a knife. Ryan was not injured, but intimated to Jones that the incident would be reflected negatively in his report. After Ryan's departure with 14 defectors, Jones told an aide, "They never stop. This is the finish. It's finished." As Ryan and his entourage were boarding two chartered planes on the Port Kaituma airstrip eight miles from Jonestown, a commune tractor pulling a trailer moved onto the runway. Gunmen aboard the tractor-trailer opened fire on the group killing Ryan, three newsmen, one defector, and wounding 12 others. Back at Jonestown, the self-styled messiah had ordered the "White Night" ritual to begin. As Jones addressed his faithful over the loudspeaker on the "beauty of dying," the congregation was herded into the large open aired pavilion where a tub filled with strawberry-flavored Kool-Aid laced with tranquilizers and cyanide had been placed by the Temple's medical staff. Some drank the mixture willingly, others at gun point. Guards pulled babies from the arms of reluctant mothers and let

"nurses" spray "the potion" down the infants' throats with hypodermic syringes. Jones, from his seated position on the pavilion stage, watched as his followers gasped and retched on the ground then shot himself in the temple. Some Jonestown residents managed to escape the carnage by bolting into the dense jungle surrounding the compound and notifying Guyanese authorities. Guyanese troops arrived first on the scene and likened the sight of the bloated and festering dead to a Hitlerian death camp. Initial estimates of 400 dead were soon revised after the arrival of a team of grave-registration and body identification experts from the United States. To their horror they found the bodies of several children beneath those of their mothers. While the total body count at the Jonestown compound came to 913, including Jones, authorities were never able to compile a complete list of the dead. A search of the camp revealed a trunk crammed with 803 U.S. passports, scores of uncashed Social Security checks, and more than $1 million in cash. A mass grave in Oakland, California, holding the bodies of 421 members of the Peoples Temple bears the inscription, "In memory of the victims of the Jonestown tragedy, November 18, 1978, Jonestown, Guyana."

302. Alinin, S.F.; Antonov, B.G.; Itskov, A.N. *The Jonestown Carnage: A CIA Crime.* Translated from the Russian by Nadezha Burova and Sergei Chulaki. Moscow: Progress, 1987. 186 pp., [20]pp. of plates: ill.; 20 cm.

303. Carpozi, George. *The Suicide Cults.* New York: Manor Books, 1978. 255 pp.; 18 cm.; paperback.

304. Chidester, David. *Salvation and Suicide: An Interpretation of Jim Jones, the Peoples Temple, and Jonestown.* Religion

in North America. Bloomington: Indiana University Press, 1988. xv, 190 pp.; 24 cm.

_____. [Same as 304.] 1st Midland Book ed. Religion in North America. Bloomington: Indiana University Press, 1991. xv, 190 pp.; 24 cm.; trade paperback.

305. Deukmejian, George, and Moy, John B. *Report of Investigation of People's Temple.* Sacramento, Calif.: Office of the Attorney General, 1980. iv, 104 pp.; 28 cm. (Also a "corrected ... second printing, December 1981.") (Paper covers.)

306. Dieckmann, Ed. *The Secret of Jonestown: The Reason Why.* Torrance, Calif.: Noontide Press; Decatur, Ga.: Historical Review Press, 1981. 176 pp.: ill.; 20 cm.; paperback.

307._____. *Beyond Jonestown: Sensitivity Training and the Cult of Mind Control.* 2nd ed. Torrance, Calif.: Noontide Press, 1985. 191 pp.: ill., ports.; 22 cm.
Reprint, with addendum, of *The Secret of Jonestown.*

308. Endleman, Robert. *Jonestown and the Manson Family: Race, Sexuality, and Collective Madness.* New York: Psyche Press, 1993. xvii, 211 pp.; 22 cm. (Also in a paperback ed.)

309. Feinsod, Ethan. *Awake in a Nightmare: Jonestown, the Only Eyewitness Account.* 1st ed. New York: Norton, 1981. 222 pp.; 22 cm.
A chronological account based in part on interviews with two surviving Jonestown residents.

310. Hall, John R. *Gone from the Promised Land: Jonestown in American Cultural History.* New Brunswick, N.J.: Transaction Books, 1987. xx, 381 pp.; 24 cm.

_____. [Same as 310.] Paperback ed. New Brunswick, N.J.: Transaction, 1989. xx, 381 pp.; 23 cm.; trade paperback.

311. Hamilton, Sue L. *The Death of a Cult Family: Jim Jones.* Edited by John C. Hamilton. Days of Tragedy. Blooming-

ton, Minn.: Abdo & Daughters; Minneapolis, Minn.: Distributed by Rockbottom Books, 1989. 32 pp.: ill., port.; 26 cm.
A brief biographical account of Jones and a description of his church and the mass suicide which he inspired.

312. Jackson, George. *Cuname, Curare & Cool Aid: The Politics That Spawned and Nurtured Jonestown.* 1st ed. New York: G.D. Jackson Associate, 1986. 147 pp.; 22 cm.

313. Kerns, Phil, and Wead, Doug. *People's Temple, People's Tomb.* Plainfield, N.J.: Logos International, 1979. xi, 288 pp.: ill.; 18 cm.; paperback.

314. Kilduff, Marshall, and Javers, Ron. *The Suicide Cult: The Inside Story of the Peoples Temple Sect and the Massacre in Guyana.* New York: Bantam Books, 1978. xvi, 201 pp., [16] leaves of plates: ill.; 18 cm.; paperback.
Kilduff, one of the authors who first alerted the media to the excesses of the Peoples Temple in his *New West* magazine article, offers a fascinating look at the tragedy. Staff correspondents of the *San Francisco Chronicle* also contributed to this paperback original.

315. Klineman, George; Butler, Sherman; Conn, David. *The Cult That Died: The Tragedy of Jim Jones and the Peoples Temple.* Research by Anthony O. Miller. New York: Putnam, 1980. 372 pp.; 24 cm.

316. Knerr, M.E. *Suicide in Guyana.* New York: Belmont Tower Books, 1978. 175 pp.: ill.; 18 cm.; paperback.

317. Krause, Charles A.; Stern, Laurence M.; Harwood, Richard. *Guyana Massacre: The Eyewitness Account.* Commentary by Frank Johnston. New York: Berkley, 1978. 210 pp., [16]pp. of plates: ill., map; 18 cm. ("A Washington Post book"); paperback.

318. Landau, Nathan. *Heavenly Deceptor: The True Story Behind the Jonestown Massacre Including Connections to the Kennedy & King Assassinations.* [United

States]: N. Landau, 1991. 223 pp.; 19 cm.

_____. [Same as 318 minus subtitle.] Brooklyn, N.Y.: Sound of Music, 1992. 230 pp.; 22 cm.
"The true story behind the Jonestown Massacre, including connections to the Kennedy and King assassinations; based upon newly discovered secret documents."—Cover.

319. Lane, Mark. *The Strongest Poison.* New York: Hawthorn Books, 1980. x, 494 pp.; 25 cm.

320. Levi, Ken, ed. *Violence and Religious Commitment: Implications of Jim Jones's People's Temple Movement.* University Park: Pennsylvania State University Press, 1982. xv, 207 pp.; 24 cm.

321. Maguire, John, and Dunn, Mary Lee. *Hold Hands and Die!: The Incredibly True Story of the People's Temple and the Reverend Jim Jones.* New York: Dale Books, 1978. 271 pp.: ill.; 18 cm.; paperback.

322. Meiers, Michael. *Was Jonestown a CIA Experiment?: A Review of the Evidence.* Lewiston, N.Y.: E. Mellen Press, 1988. vii, 575 pp., [128]pp. of plates: ill.; 24 cm.

323. Mills, Jeannie. *My Six Years with God: Life Inside Reverend Jim Jones's Peoples Temple.* New York: A & W, 1979. 319 pp.: ill.; 24 cm.

324. Moore, Rebecca. *A Sympathetic History of Jonestown: The Moore Family Involvement in Peoples Temple.* Studies in Religion and Society; vol. 14. Lewiston, N.Y.: E. Mellen Press, 1985. 456 pp.: ill.; 24 cm.

325. Moore, Rebecca, and McGehee, Fielding M., eds. *The Need for a Second Look at Jonestown.* Studies in American Religion; vol. 41. Lewiston, N.Y.: E. Mellen Press, 1989. 244 pp.; 24 cm.

326. _____. *New Religious Movements, Mass Suicide, and Peoples Temple: Scholarly Perspectives on a Tragedy.* Studies in American Religion; vol. 37. Lewiston, N.Y.: E. Mellen Press, 1989. 251 pp.: ill.; 24 cm.

327. Naipaul, Shiva. *Black and White.* London: H. Hamilton, 1980. 215 pp.; 24 cm.

_____. [Same as 327.] London: Abacus, Sphere Books, 1981. 279 pp.; 20 cm.; paperback.
Also published under title: *Journey to Nowhere: A New World Tragedy.*

_____. [Same as 327, but U.S. ed. retitled: *Journey to Nowhere: A New World Tragedy.*] New York: Simon and Schuster, 1981. 336 pp.; 22 cm.

_____. [Same as 327, but U.S. ed. retitled: *Journey to Nowhere: A New World Tragedy.*] New York: Penguin, 1982. 336 pp.; 20 cm.; paperback.

328. Nichols, Norma. *Pot-Pourri with a Taste of Cult.* Georgetown, Guyana?: s.n., 1979 or 1980. 30 pp.: ill.; 23 cm.; paperback.

329. Nugent, John Peer. *White Night.* 1st ed. New York: Rawson, Wade, 1979. 278 pp.; 24 cm.

330. Reiterman, Tim, and Jacobs, John. *Raven: The Untold Story of the Rev. Jim Jones and His People.* 1st ed. New York: Dutton, 1982. xvii, 622 pp., [32]pp. of plates: ill.; 25 cm.

331. Reston, James. *Our Father Who Art in Hell.* New York: Times Books, 1981. xiii, 338 pp.; 25 cm.

332. Rose, Steve. *Jesus and Jim Jones.* New York: Pilgrim Press, 1979. 232 pp.; 22 cm. (Also in paperback ed.)

333. Thielmann, Bonnie, and Merrill, Dean. *The Broken God.* Elgin, Ill.: David C. Cook, 1979. 154 pp., [8]pp. of plates: ill., ports.; 21 cm.

334. United States. Congress. House. Committee on Foreign Affairs. *The Death of Representative Leo J. Ryan, People's Temple, and Jonestown: Understanding a Tragedy.* Washington: U.S. Govt. Print. Off., 1979. iii, 61 pp.; 23 cm. (Paper covers.)
Hearing before the Committee on Foreign Affairs, House of Representatives, Ninety-sixth Congress, first session, May 15, 1979.

335. United States. Congress. House. Committee on Foreign Affairs. Staff Investigative Group. *The Assassination of Representative Leo J. Ryan and the Jonestown, Guyana, Tragedy: Report of the Staff Investigative Group to the Committee on Foreign Affairs, U.S. House of Representatives.* Washington: U.S. Govt. Print. Off., 1979. xv, 782 pp.: ill.; 24 cm.

House document, 96th Congress, 1st session, no. 223.

336. Weightman, Judith Mary. *Making Sense of the Jonestown Suicides: A Sociological History of Peoples Temple.* Studies in Religion and Society; vol. 7. New York: E. Mellen Press, 1984. 220 pp.; 24 cm.

337. White, Mel; Scotchmer, Paul; Shuster, Marguerite. *Deceived.* Old Tappan, N.J.: Spire Books, 1979. 231 pp.: ill.; 18 cm.; paperback.

238. Wooden, Kenneth. *The Children of Jonestown.* 1st McGraw-Hill paperback ed. New York: McGraw-Hill, 1981. ix, 238 pp., [4] leaves of plates: ill.; 21 cm.; paperback.

Wooden argues that the Jonestown calamity was largely facilitated by a failed social welfare system that enabled Jones to build a financial empire through welfare fraud.

339. Yee, Min S., and Layton, Thomas N. *In My Father's House: The Story of the Layton Family and the Reverend Jim Jones.* 1st ed. New York: Holt, Rinehart, and Winston, 1981. xx, 361 pp.: ill.; 24 cm.

_____. [Same as 339.] New York: Berkley, 1982. xv, 335 pp.: ill.; 18 cm.; paperback.

Joubert, John J.
(a.k.a. "Sarpy County Killer")

Born July 2, 1963, in Portland, Maine. Airman First Class United States Air Force. Maine, Nebraska; 3 murders; strangulation, knife; August 1982–December 1983.

Convicted homosexual serial child killer whose execution in Nebraska has been indefinitely delayed by legal debate over the wording of that state's capital punishment statute. John Joubert told a court-appointed psychiatrist he could not remember a time when fantasies of murder and cannibalism had not consumed him. Even as a six year old he dreamed of murdering the babysitter who urged his devoutly Catholic, strong-willed mother to leave her weak, "no good" husband. They separated when he was eight and Joubert, a younger sister, and his mother relocated to Portland, Maine, from Lawrence, Massachusetts. Small, frail, and painfully shy, Joubert joined the Boy Scouts in a bid to fit in with classmates, but became the butt of their cruel jokes. One seemingly changed his life. Asked by a classmate if he was "gay," Joubert, unaware that the term meant homosexual, replied yes. His naïve response spread quickly throughout the school, further isolating him. By the time he earned the rank of Eagle Scout at 17, Joubert's sexual fantasies had expanded to include the true crime detective magazines he voraciously read. Masturbating three times a day, Joubert later told a reporter that he was attracted to their covers because they depicted "people in … helpless situations." At 18, a brief college career failed when Joubert, more interested in video games than class, left Norwich University in Vermont after completing only 10 credits in his freshman year.

Joubert's violent fantasies emerged into reality on August 22, 1982. Eleven-year-old Ricky Stetson disappeared while jogging in the Portland area of Back Cove. The next day, his partially clad body was found under a footbridge across I-295. He had been strangled, stabbed numerous times in the chest, and bitten on a calf. During the year it took to arrest, try, and acquit a suspect, Joubert had enlisted in the Air Force, attained the rank of airman first class, and was serving as a radar technician at Offutt Air Force Base near Omaha, Nebraska. Volunteering as an assistant scoutmaster in the nearby community of Bellevue, Joubert's civic dedication prompted the mayor to call him "an asset to the community." On September 18, 1983, he kidnapped 13-year-old paperboy Danny Joe Eberle off a street in Bellevue. Binding the boy with rope he used to demonstrate knot tying techniques at scout meetings, Joubert drove to a secluded field south of town. Searchers found Eberle's partially clothed body three days later. The boy had been stabbed repeatedly in the back, chest, and neck. Bite marks were found on a leg and upper shoulder. His ankles had been bound postmortem. Joubert later confessed (he has since recanted) that following the murder he returned to his quarters at Barracks 400, Room 113, and consummated the scene by masturbating.

Seventy-nine days later on December 2, 1983, 12-year-old Christopher Paul Walden, son of an Air Force meteorologist, was abducted while walking to school in Papillion, Nebraska. Like the Eberle boy, Walden's body was found by bird hunters in similar disarray in a plum grove northwest of town three days later. Stabbed repeatedly in the back, his throat had also been slit. An investigator ironically noted that a starlike design carved into the boy's chest resembled the Boy Scout's insignia. On January 11, 1984, Joubert decided to respond to a sheriff's media taunt that if the killer was a "real man" he would pick on someone "his own size." Driving a rented Chevy Citation to a Bellevue preschool, Joubert at-

tempted to accost the school's director, but panicked when she fled past him. The woman memorized the license plate and police confronted Joubert in his quarters at Offutt. A search of his room yielded a rope with colored strands identical to those found binding Eberle's ankles. More rope and a filet knife were found in Joubert's car.

Arrested that night, Joubert confessed to murdering the two boys and attempting to rob the woman for car repair money. In a July 3, 1984, hearing before a panel of three judges at the Sarpy County Courthouse, Joubert was found guilty on two counts of first degree murder and sentenced on October 9, 1984, to death by electrocution. Portland police, noting the similarities in the Stetson and Nebraska murders, obtained hair samples and teeth impressions from Joubert in February 1985. On January 10, 1986, Joubert was indicted in Maine for the 1982 "intentional and knowing murder" of Richard Stetson. Following years of jurisdictional debate between Maine and Nebraska, Joubert was tried and convicted in Wiscasset, Maine, on October 15, 1990. Sentenced to life imprisonment without possibility of parole on January 1, 1991, Joubert tried unsuccessfully to remain in Maine which does not have a death penalty. Joubert, who has since recanted his confessions and has twice been turned down on appeal by the United States Supreme Court, won a legal victory of sorts on October 11, 1994, when a judge in the U.S. district court in Omaha overturned the killer's two death sentences. Judge William Cambridge ruled that Joubert should be resentenced because part of Nebraska's capital punishment statute, which uses the phrase "exceptionally depraved," has been ruled unconstitutionally vague. Joubert could be resentenced to death as long as the next sentencing meets constitutional tests. Nebraska attorney general Don Stenberg has vowed to continue his efforts to have the death penalty reinstated.

340. Pettit, Mark. *A Need to Kill.* 1st ed. Lincoln, Neb.: Media Publications, 1990. 198 pp., [16]pp. of plates: ill.; 24 cm.

_____. [Same as 340.] 1st Ballantine Books ed. New York: Ballantine, 1991. 202 pp., [16]pp. of plates: ill.; 18 cm. ("Ivy books"); paperback.

Pettit, a television anchorman for KMTV, Channel 3 in Omaha, interviewed Joubert, the victims' families, and had unrestricted access to the case file.

Judd, Winnie Ruth
(a.k.a. "Tiger Woman [or] Lady," "The Blond Butcher," "Trunk Murderess [or] Slayer," "Velvet Tigress," "Wolf Woman," "Winnie Ruth McKinnell" [maiden name], "Marian Burke," "Marian Lane")

Born January 29, 1905, in Oxford, Indiana. Medical secretary. Phoenix, Arizona; 2 murders (convicted of 1); .25 caliber Colt automatic; October 16, 1931.

Theatre: Tiger Lady (1992), a drama by Layce Gardner.

Audio: The Trunk Murderess, a two-cassette, three-hour abridgement of Jana Bommersbach's book of the same title read by Jane Alexander, was published in 1992 by Simon & Schuster (New York).

"I visited a lot of dark caves when I lived in Mexico and wasn't afraid, but this dark place scares me to death."— Judd's reaction upon first seeing death row in the Arizona State Prison in Florence

Sensational "Tiger Woman" trunk case of the thirties in which a 26 year old was convicted of murder and dismemberment. Winnie Ruth Judd, a petite and attractive blond, was employed as a medical secretary at the Grunow Clinic in Phoenix when she separated from her doctor-husband in the spring of 1931. Judd moved into a bungalow at 2929 North Second Street with two friends she met through the clinic. Agnes Anne LeRoi, a 27-year-old X ray technician at Grunow's, and her best friend Hedvig "Sammy" Samuelson, a 25-year-old tuberculosis patient, initially welcomed Judd into their group, but relations between the women soon soured. In October 1931, Judd moved into an apartment within walking distance of the clinic. While conflicting testimony would later obscure the events of the night of October 16, 1931, this much is known. Judd was at her friends' bungalow when an argument erupted between them. As a result, both LeRoi and Samuelson were shot to death with Judd sustaining a .25 caliber gunshot wound to the hand. According to the prosecutor's theory of the case, Judd argued with the women over the attention they were paying to her boyfriend, a wealthy Phoenix lumber man. The quarrel ended when Judd shot both the women. Judd would later claim that Samuelson shot her in the hand and in the ensuing struggle she killed the women in self-defense. In any case, Judd arrived in Los Angeles by train three days later with two large steamer trunks she said contained her husband's medical books. The trunks were subsequently opened by L.A. detectives after a baggage handler noticed they were emitting a foul odor and leaking a dark, sticky fluid. Inside, shocked authorities found the surgically dismembered remains of LeRoi and Samuelson. Over 2,000 police officers throughout the West entered into the search for the missing woman which ended on October 23, 1931, when Judd, responding to a newspaper appeal by her husband, gave herself up to authorities in the basement of a Los Angeles mortuary.

Charged only in the murder of LeRoi, Judd pleaded not guilty as her trial opened in Phoenix on January 19, 1932. The all-male jury disbelieved her claim of self-defense and Judd was found guilty and sentenced to death. On December 12, 1932, the Arizona State Supreme Court upheld the conviction, but Judd was given another opportunity to tell her story before the Maricopa County Grand Jury on December 28, 1932. While reiterating her claim of self-defense, Judd denied dismembering the body. This was done, she testified, by her lumber man boyfriend, Jack Halloran. Judd did admit, however, that she placed body parts in the trunks. The grand jury disbelieved Judd's story and the complaint against Halloran was dismissed. At an insanity hearing conducted days before she was set to be hanged on April 28, 1933, Judd's courtroom hysterics shocked the jury. Doctors testifying to Judd's emotional instability and well-documented history of family mental illness were interrupted by her shrieks of "You bullies! You gangsters! Quit torturing me!" Judd was declared to be insane and committed to the Arizona State Hospital for the Insane in Phoenix until such time as she was pronounced "cured" and could be returned to prison and executed.

During the nearly 30 years "The Tiger Woman" spent in the asylum she managed to escape seven times. On October 8, 1962, Judd escaped and remained at large until June 27, 1969, when her fingerprints, found on a suspect car in a murder investigation, led to her arrest in Danville, California. Judd, as "Marian Lane," had spent nearly seven years of freedom as a housekeeper/cook for Dr. and Mrs. John Blemer. The wealthy family was so impressed by Judd that they assured the parole board that should she ever be released, her old job would be waiting for her. Judd was serving her sentence in the Arizona State Prison when the parole board, acting on Governor Jack Williams' recommendation, granted the 66 year old parole on December 22, 1971. Judd, under an assumed name, returned to California to work for the doctor and his wife until the death of Ethel Blemer in January 1982. Evicted from the Blemer household by relatives, Judd filed a $408 million suit against the estate. In it, she claimed that the Blemers had kept her as an "indentured servant" without formal wages since her release from prison. Judd remained silent concerning the working arrangement out of fear that her parole would be revoked if she complained. In December 1982 Judd was awarded a $225,000 settlement which included a monthly stipend of $1,250 for life.

341. Bommersbach, Jana. *The Trunk Murderess, Winnie Ruth Judd: The Truth About an American Crime Legend Revealed at Last.* New York: Simon & Schuster, 1992. 270 pp.: ill.; 25 cm.

_____. [Same as 341 minus subtitle.] Berkley ed. New York: Berkley, 1994. 298 pp.: ill.; 17 cm.; paperback.

Bommersbach concludes that Judd acted in self-defense and that J.J. "Happy" Halloran, a Phoenix lumber man with political clout, either dismembered the bodies or had a doctor-friend do it. She charges Phoenix police with concealing evidence that supported Judd's claim of self-defense and Halloran's involvement in the case. Nominated by the Mystery Writers of America for a 1993 Edgar Allan Poe Award.

342. Dobkins, J. Dwight, and Hendricks, Robert J. *Winnie Ruth Judd: The Trunk Murders*. New York: Grosset & Dunlap, 1973. viii, 248 pp.: ill.; 22 cm.

Unspectacular account of the case which concludes with Judd's parole.

Judy, Steven Timothy
(a.k.a. "Ricky Kelly," "Creek Murderer")

Born May 24, 1956, in Indianapolis, Indiana. Executed March 9, 1981. Truck driver, construction worker. Morgan County, Indiana; 4 murders (self-confessed suspect in at least 7 other unsubstantiated murders); ligature strangulation, drowning; April 28, 1979.

"I'm telling each one of you now, you'd better vote for the death penalty for me, because I will get out, one way or another, and it may be one of you next or one of your family. That goes for you, too, judge. That's it." — Judy addressing the jury prior to the sentencing phase of his trial

Twenty-two-year-old rapist and murderer of a mother and her three children who subsequently fought all attempts to prevent his execution. The son of an abusive alcoholic and a lascivious mother who had sex with men in front of him, Judy was early profiled by a psychiatrist as "having unresolved hostilities toward females." A burglar, voyeur, and assaulter of young girls, Judy was in and out of juvenile institutions throughout his teens. On April 17, 1970, the 13-year-old raped a woman in her Indianapolis, Indiana, apartment, stabbed her 42 times with a knife, and

tried to finish the job with a hatchet. Released from a mental hospital two years later, Judy continued to assault women at knife and gunpoint in Illinois and Indiana before committing the most shocking murder in the history of Morgan County, Indiana. On April 28, 1979, the naked body of 22-year-old Terry Lee Chasteen was found by mushroom hunters along the bank of White Lick Creek near Mooresville. She had been raped and strangled. The drowned bodies of her three children, the oldest being five, were found floating in the creek. Judy was arrested the next day after a witness identified his truck near the site. His insanity defense failed and a jury recommended the death sentence on February 16, 1980. While resisting any appeals on his behalf, Judy bragged about his criminal record which he claimed included 200 burglaries, 12–15 rapes and the murders of at least seven women throughout Indiana, Texas, Louisiana, and California. None were ever verified. After willing his body to science and apologizing for the murders, Judy was electrocuted at the Indiana State Prison in Michigan City on March 9, 1981. At his own request, he was buried with a bottle of bourbon at Floral Park Cemetery in Indianapolis.

343. Nunn, Bette. *Burn, Judy, Burn*. Martinsville, Ind.: B. Nunn, 1981. 232 pp.: ill.; 18 cm.; paperback.

Small press run case history written by the reporter who covered the local trial.

Kallinger, Joseph Michael
(a.k.a. "Joseph Renner Scurti" [birth name], "Crazy Joe," "Door-to-Door Killer," "The Shoemaker")

Born December 11, 1936, in Philadelphia, Pennsylvania. Died March 26, 1996. Shoemaker. Philadelphia, Pennsylvania, and Leonia, New Jersey; 3 murders; suffocation, knife, drowning; July 1974–January 1975.

"My home is my castle and I pray nothing evil will ever come cross my door."—Kallinger poem entitled "My Home"

Schizophrenic shoemaker who with his son murdered three people, including another son, in an insane attempt to bring about the destruction of everyone on earth. Born to an unwed mother who put him up for adoption when he was 22 months old, the infant "Joseph Renner Scurti" was adopted by the Kallingers, a married couple of Austrian-Catholic immigrants who operated a family shoemaking business out of their home in Philadelphia. Ultra-strict parents, the Kallingers physically and emotionally abused the boy warping his psychosexual development with threats of emasculation. Kallinger was nearly seven when an incident occurred which many psychiatrists feel triggered his lifelong psychosis and provided the sexual basis of his crimes. After undergoing a hernia operation, Kallinger was told by his parents that the surgeon had also "fixed" his penis by removing the "evil spirit" that lived in it. Thereafter, it could never again become "big" and get himself or others in trouble. Alternately abused, neglected, and threatened by his parents with being returned to the orphanage if he misbehaved, Kallinger developed a persecution complex and retreated into a hallucinatory world in which he believed God spoke directly to him. Kallinger married at 17 and produced 10 children before his wife left him for another man in September 1956. He remarried

in April 1958 and over the next decade attempted suicide, spent time in a mental institution, and set fire to his home seven times, ultimately being acquitted of arson charges in 1968 and collecting $26,000 in insurance.

In January 1972 the shoemaker was living with his family in the home formerly owned by his parents when God commanded him to punish his 12-year-old daughter Mary Jo and his son Joe, Jr., then 11. In a rite of purification, Kallinger branded the girl on the thigh with a hot spatula and handcuffed his son to a bed. Charges were filed against him although both children later recanted their testimony. His daughter now insisting that the three inch burn on her leg was from chafing blue jeans and his son stating that he was handcuffed to help break a thumb sucking habit. Kallinger was convicted on child abuse charges and placed on four years' probation. By 1974, the self-employed shoemaker's psychosis was full blown and during frequent bouts of auditory hallucinations spoke with a disembodied head named "Charlie" who spurred him on to commit acts of sadism. Under personal orders from "God," Kallinger set out to fulfill his divine mission of killing every human being on earth. In late June 1974, Kallinger confided his plan to his 13-year-old son Michael who eagerly agreed to help him set the cosmic plan into action. On July 8, 1974, Kallinger and son picked 10-year-old José Collazo out of a group of kids at a neighborhood pool and lured him into an abandoned rug factory. There, the pair bound and gagged the child before lopping off his penis with a leather cutting tool. Collazo's body was found weeks later with suffocation ruled as the official cause of death. On July 28, 1974, after two earlier attempts to kill his son Joseph Jr., had failed, Kallinger and Michael lured the boy to a demolition site, chained him to a ladder, and pushed him face down into the flooded basement of a demolished building. One month before the murder, Kallinger had taken out a $74,000 life insurance policy on the boy, an act which later went far to convince a judge that the shoemaker was not insane, just greedy.

Beginning in late 1974 police in New Jersey, New York, Pennsylvania, and Maryland were confronted with a rash of burglaries and rapes committed by an older man in the company of an adolescent boy. In many instances, the boy posed as a door-to-door salesman and after initiating contact with the female victim at her home returned with a man armed with a knife and gun. The pair then forced their way into the home, tied the housewife to the bed where the man raped her, then left with cash and jewels. On January 8, 1975, father and son invaded a home in Leonia, New Jersey, where eight persons had assembled for a party. After binding their captives, 21-year-old practical nurse Maria Fasching was dragged down into the basement where Kallinger slashed and repeatedly stabbed the woman after she refused his order to bite off another captive's penis. Fleeing the scene with $80 in cash and jewelry, Kallinger discarded a bloodstained shirt blocks from the scene which investigators were able to trace back to him through a laundry mark. The pair were arrested on January 17, 1975, although Michael, ruled "salvageable" by a judge, was never charged with the murders. In return for his guilty plea to robbery counts, murder charges against the teenager were dropped and he was placed on probation until the age of 25.

Kallinger's first trial in Harrisburg, Pennsylvania, in May 1975 on charges stemming from a robbery committed in that town on December 3, 1974, was declared a mistrial after a 70-year-old sheriff's matron told sequestered jurors that she considered Kallinger guilty and informed them of other charges facing him. Pleading innocent at a second trial in September 1975, Kallinger denied the crime informing the court that he was 1,000 years old and had been a butterfly before receiving his present bodily form. He was found guilty in less than one hour on September 18, 1975, and sentenced to 30 to 80 years in prison. Extradited to New Jersey to face charges of murdering Fasching, robbery, and contributing to the delinquency of a minor, Kallinger pleaded innocent by reason of insanity. Shortly after opening statements began in Hackensack on September 24, 1976, Kallinger had to be subdued by deputies after pulling a jagged piece of glass from his pocket. Earlier in his cell, the shoemaker had tried to slash open his wrists with his pants zipper. Kallinger was convicted of all charges on October 12, 1976, and sentenced to life imprisonment with the term to run consecutively with his Pennsylvania conviction. In a subsequent trial in Camden, New Jersey, for breaking and entering and the rape of a Lindenwold woman, Kallinger was given an additional 42 to 51 years.

Following the publication of Flora Rheta Schreiber's 1983 book *The Shoemaker: The Anatomy of a Psychotic* in which Kallinger confessed to murdering Collazo and son Joseph, Jr., the convicted killer was charged with and tried for their murders before a judge in Philadelphia. Kallinger again pleaded insanity, but was convicted of both murders on January 31, 1984, after the judge determined that the father had killed his son to collect life insurance. Sentenced to two more consecutive life sentences, Kallinger has continued his suicide attempts in prison while simultaneously expressing his continued desire to realize "Godhood" by slaughtering everyone on the planet. On June 22, 1990, Kallinger began fasting after he told prison authorities of experiencing a vision of the Holy Spirit in his toilet bowl. The next month, a common pleas court judge ruled that the triple killer could pursue his wish to starve himself to death without state interference. The ruling was overturned by a commonwealth court judge who ordered on July 18, 1990, that Kallinger be force fed through a nasal tube into his stomach until a higher court made a final ruling in the matter. Two months later, Kallinger attempted suicide by placing some 70 elastic bands around his arms and legs to cut off his circulation. In September 1990, doctors at Pennsylvania's Fairview State Hospital for the Criminally Insane found several paperclips and staples in the killer's stomach during a routine X-ray examination. Kallinger, 59, choked to death on his own vomit on March 26, 1996, in the infirmary of the Pennsylvania State Correctional Institute at Cresoon.

344. Downs, Thomas. *The Door-to-Door Killer.* True Crime Series. New York: Dell, 1984. 174 pp.; 18 cm.; paperback.

345. Schreiber, Flora Rheta. *The Shoemaker: The Anatomy of a Psychotic.* New York: Simon and Schuster, 1983. 342 pp.: ports.; 22 cm.

_____. [Same as 345.] New York: New American Library, 1984. 406 pp.; 18 cm. "A Signet book"); paperback.

_____. [Same as 345.] New York: Penguin Books, 1984. 406 pp.; 18 cm. ("A Signet book"); paperback.

Excellent study by a noted writer who perhaps became too close to her subject. Includes poems by Kallinger as well as general and psychological indexes.

Kemper, Edmund Emil, III (a.k.a. "The Co-Ed Killer," "Guy," "Big Ed," "Forklift")

Born December 18, 1948, in Burbank, California. Highway worker. North Fork, Berkeley, and Santa Cruz, California; 10 murders; .22 caliber rifle, .22 caliber Ruger automatic pistol, hammer, knife, manual and ligature strangulation; August 27, 1963, and May 1972–April 1973.

"What do you think, now, when you see a pretty girl walking down the street? One side of me says, 'Wow, what an attractive chick. I'd like to talk to her, date her.' The other side of me says, 'I wonder how her head would look on a stick?'"—Kemper in an interview with Marj von Beroldingen published in *Front Page Detective*, March 1974

If not the most prolific of the Santa Cruz, California, killers of the early 1970s (Herbert Mullin murdered 13 and John Linley Frazier 5), Ed Kemper was certainly the most psychologically complex and self-aware of the trio. From May 1972 through April 1973, the so-called "Co-ed Killer" murdered, raped, cannibalized, and dismembered six female college students in the area as well as his mother and her best friend. In 1963, the 15-year-old had used a rifle to kill his grandparents. Unlike his intellectually stunted killer counterparts, Kemper's hulking 6'9", 285 pound frame housed an intellect that matched his oversized body. His IQ (measured at the near-genius level of 136), combined with the insights and psychiatric jargon he learned during five years of incarceration in the Atascadero State Hospital for the Criminally Insane where he memorized the correct responses to 28 psychological tests, made Kemper a particularly articulate and thoughtful commentator on his crimes which in their depravity beggar the imagination. When briefly held in an adjoining cell to Mullin's in the San Mateo county jail Kemper showed his disdain for the paranoid schizophrenic by deriding him as "a no-class killer."

Kemper was born in Burbank, California, in 1948 and experienced a childhood characterized by parental rejection and verbal abuse. His father, a 6'8" electrician, left the family when the boy was nine and Kemper's mother, Clarnell, coped with the divorce by becoming an alcoholic. At five Kemper confessed to his older sister that he wanted to kiss her teacher. When urged by her to do so, Kemper replied, "I can't. I would have to kill her first." At ten Kemper's apparent sexual interest in his 13-year-old-sister prompted his mother to move him into a drab basement room. There, the young boy gave free reign to bloody fantasies focusing on torture and mutilation. In acts that presaged his later ritual murders, Kemper mutilated small animals and dolls. Once he buried a cat alive in his backyard later returning to decapitate the dead animal. He placed its head on a makeshift altar in his room and prayed to it that everyone in the world but him might be killed. At 13, Kemper slaughtered his pet Siamese cat with a machete when he felt it was showing more attention to his sisters than to him. He buried some of the remains in the backyard, keeping others in his closet.

Emotionally starved for parental attention and affection, the teenaged Kemper tried to re-establish a connection with his father who had relocated to southern California and was remarried with an infant son. Kemper visited the man, but was sent away when his stepmother took an instant dislike to him. Following an argument with his mother at Christmas, Kemper ran back to his father who deposited the unwelcome intruder with his parents, Edmund and Maude Kemper, at their isolated seven-acre farm at North Fork, California, in the foothills of the Sierra Mountains. To avoid further contact with his son, he got an unlisted telephone number. Clarnell Kemper's emotional deprivation of her son paralleled that of her ex-husband's except that it was played out against a backdrop of demeaning sarcasm. Branding Kemper, "a real weirdo," she berated him for his size and shunted him off to his grandparents whenever she could no longer stand the sight of him.

Edmund Kemper, 72, and his wife Maude, 66, were similarly disconcerted by their troubled grandson who often sat around the farm for hours staring off into space. Conversely, Kemper was intimidated by his grandmother who he felt was little more than an elderly version of his own domineering mother. Feeling isolated and abandoned, Kemper happily accepted the gun his grandfather gave him to cheer him up and proceeded to turn it on birds and small animals. On August 27, 1963, Kemper's anger over his grandmother's attempts to "emasculate" him and his grandfather exploded into violence. As she was sitting at the kitchen table, the 6'4" 15 year old shot her in the head and stabbed her three times in the back with a kitchen knife. When his grandfather returned from the grocery, Kemper was waiting in the yard and shot the old man in the head. The teenager later told psychiatrists at the Atascadero State Hospital where he was remanded by the California Youth Authority that he "just wondered how it would feel to shoot grandma." In 1969 Kemper was released over the objections of his doctors after serving five years at the facility. The 6'9", 285 pound giant went to live with his mother in Aptos, California. Now divorced for the third time, Clarnell Strandberg worked as an administrative assistant to the provost at the University of California–Santa Cruz.

Kemper, the man who had spent the formative years of his sexual development isolated from females in a mental hospital, now lived with a mother who reminded him daily that the coeds he saw walking on campus were just the types of women he could never hope to have as a wife. When not arguing with her, Kemper hung out at a local bar frequented by police officers where "Big Ed," as he was known to the clientele, listened intently whenever discussions turned to police procedure. From 1970 to 1971 Kemper picked up an estimated 150 female hitchhikers while cruising the highways around Santa Cruz and Berkeley. During this period prior to the first "coed killing" Kemper familiarized himself with his "kill zone" and learned how to appear nonthreatening to his potential victims. Fanned by his contact with female hitchhikers, Kemper's fantasies revolved around murdering several select women and having sex with their corpses. As he later confessed to a detective, "Taking life away from them, a living human being, and then having possession of everything

that used to be theirs. All that would be mine. Everything."

Kemper's "dry runs" ended on May 7, 1972, when he picked up two 18-year-old Fresno State College roommates off Ashby Avenue in Berkeley. Anita Luchessa and Mary Ann Pesce had hoped to hitch a ride to Stanford University, but once in Kemper's car he pulled a 9mm Browning automatic from under the seat. He drove the pair to a secluded area near Livermore, California, and after locking Luchessa in the trunk tried to suffocate the handcuffed Pesce with a plastic bag. When she refused to die quickly, Kemper stabbed her repeatedly with a pocket knife then slit her throat. He used a buck knife he nicknamed "the General" to stab Luchessa to death in the trunk. Kemper transported the bodies to his apartment in Alameda, removed their heads and hands, engaged in sex with various body parts, then photographed the remains for future masturbatory use. He bagged and buried Pesce's body parts in a shallow grave in the Loma Prieta area of the Santa Cruz Mountains and later admitted to investigators that he often visited the site just to be "near her." Kemper kept the "trophy" heads for sex toys before tossing them down a ravine in the mountains. Pesce's head was recovered on August 15, 1972. Luchessa's remains have never been found.

Kemper next felt "little zapples" (his term for the "torqued up" feeling he experienced prior to a kill) on September 14, 1972. On that day he picked up 15-year-old Aiko Koo hitchhiking in Berkeley. Pinching her nostrils shut with his fingers, Kemper raped the teenager as she lost consciousness. He used Koo's scarf to finish the job of strangulation before dissecting her body in his apartment. Ironically, Koo's head was in the trunk of Kemper's car the next day when he met with state psychiatrists whose positive report on his mental state ("no longer any danger") officially sealed his juvenile record. Afterwards, Kemper buried Koo's hands and head in a shallow grave near a religious camp above Boulder Creek in the Santa Cruz Mountains. On May 17, 1973, body parts recovered earlier from the area were identified as Aiko Koo's.

Kemper picked up Cabrillo College coed Cindy Schall on January 8, 1973, as she was hitchhiking around the UC-SC campus. After driving her to the secluded hill area around Freedom, California, he forced her into the trunk of his car where he shot her in the head. While his mother was at work, Kemper hid the corpse in the closet of his room in her apartment at 609-A Ord Drive in Aptos. The next day, he had sex with the body, dissected it with an axe and "the General," and placing the remains in a plastic bag tossed them over a seaside cliff south of Carmel. The body parts (minus Schall's head) were found less than 24 hours later. Kemper had buried the head in the backyard of his mother's home facing his window where, as he told investigators, "I said affectionate things [to it] ... like you would say to a girlfriend or a wife."

Following a vicious argument with his mother on the evening of February 5, 1973, Kemper promised himself that "the first girl that's halfway decent I pick up, I'm gonna blow her brains out." On the nearby UC-SC campus he picked up 23-year-old coed Rosalind Thorpe, then moments later, Alice Liu. He shot both women to death and placed their bodies in the trunk where they remained while he ate supper with his mother. When his mother retired for the evening, Kemper decapitated both the women in the trunk and the next day while his mother was at work carried their bodies to his room where he had sex with Liu's headless corpse on the floor and later severed her hands. To cover the evidence of his necrophilia, Kemper washed Liu's body and disposed of the pair off Eden Valley Road near Highway 580 in Alameda County.

On Easter weekend 1973, Kemper directed his fury at the individual he later identified as being the cause of his murderous attacks against women—his mother. Kemper entered her bedroom as she slept and bashed her head in with a claw hammer. Armed with the pocket knife he used to kill Mary Ann Pesce, Kemper slit her throat, excised her larynx, and raped the corpse. As a final payoff for what Kemper termed as his mother's years of "bitching" and "screaming" at him, he forced her larynx into the garbage disposal and used her severed head as a dart board. Sara Hallett, her best friend, called later that day and Kemper invited her to a surprise dinner in honor of his mother. Shortly after her arrival, Kemper choked Hallett to death and decapitated her. He placed her body on his bed and spent the night in his mother's room before leaving in the morning on a three-day, 1500-mile odyssey that ended on April 23, 1973, when he called authorities in Santa Cruz from a phone booth in Pueblo, Colorado, and confessed his crimes. Kemper, strung out from dropping No-Doz for three straight days, waited in his car until local authorities arrived to take him into custody.

Kemper's detailed confessions of murder, necrophilia, dismemberment, and cannibalism shocked even the most case-hardened detectives. At one point the serial murderer observed, "Oh, Jeez, wouldn't this make a good horror story on tape?" He led police to the burial sites of several of his victims and explained that the decapitated heads he kept for his sexual pleasure could be equated with the "exalted" feeling a hunter experienced when displaying the trophy of his kill. The fact that three psychiatrists found him sane did not prevent Kemper from pleading not guilty by reason of insanity to eight charges of first degree murder. While awaiting his October 23, 1973, trial, Kemper twice tried to commit suicide by slashing his wrists. His testimony on November 1, 1973, offered a stunned courtroom a post-graduate lecture on abnormal psychology. "I wanted the girls for myself—as possessions," he explained. "They were going to be mine; they are mine." On November 8, 1973, a six-man, six-woman jury deliberated five hours before pronouncing their verdict: "Guilty, sane, and first degree" to all counts. Kemper, who had stated that the only just punishment for him would be torture, was sentenced to eight concurrent life terms. In pronouncing the sentence, the judge recommended "in the strongest terms possible" that Kemper never be released.

At the California Medical Facility State Prison at Vacaville 65 miles northeast of San Francisco, Kemper as of 1988 headed up a 12-convict group known as the Volunteers of Vacaville. The "Blind Project," as it is known to inmates, makes tape recordings of books requested by and for the blind. As of January 1987 Kemper had been with the program for ten years and had spent more than 5,000 hours in a sound booth reading hundreds of books onto cassette tape. With more than four million feet of cassette tape to his credit, Kemper has produced more books for the project than any other prisoner. He is paid $36 a month. Referring to the "extraordinary degree of violence" of his crimes and citing negative prison psychological reports, a three-member Board of Prison Terms panel in June 1988 denied Kemper parole for the sixth time. As of this writing, the "Co-ed Killer" is still incarcerated.

346. Cheney, Margaret. *The Co-Ed Killer*. New York: Walker, 1976. xv, 222 pp.; 24 cm.

_____. [Same as 346, but updated, slightly revised, and retitled: *Why—The Serial Killer in America*.] Saratoga, Calif.: R & E, 1992. xiii, 222 pp.; 23 cm.; trade paperback.

Interesting and factual account based on interviews with authorities, the courtroom testimony of medical witnesses, and transcripts of Kemper's taped confessions. Cheney views Kemper's crimes as rooted in society's patriarchal attitudes toward females. Recommended.

Kennedy, William Henry
(a.k.a. "Patrick Michael William," "William Herbert," "Henry le Fevere," "Henry Jones," "Michael Sullivan," "Two-Gun Pat," "The Fairhaired Sniper")

Born circa 1884 in Ayrshire, Scotland. Executed May 31, 1928. Compositor, garage manager. Stapleford Abbotts, Essex, England; 1 murder; Webley revolver; September 26, 1927.

"I say it in no mere spirit of bravado when I say I am not afraid to die, but I meet it willingly, because I have the certain knowledge that in the hereafter I will be re-united for all eternity to the one darling girl who has stuck to me all through this trouble."—

Kennedy's statement to Mr. Justice Avory after having the sentence of death passed on him; see also Browne, Frederick Guy.

Kitto, Michael Anthony

Born circa August 1938. Confidence man, thief. Scotland and London, England; 4 murders; suffocation, bludgeon (spade, poker), drowning; December 1977–January 1978; see also Hall, Archibald Thomson.

Klenner, Frederick Robert, Jr. (a.k.a. "Fritz," "Der Fritzer," "Doctor Crazy")

Born July 31, 1952, in Durham, North Carolina. Died June 3, 1985. Medical doctor (imposter). Prospect, Kentucky, and Old Town and Summerfield, North Carolina; 9 murders (including himself); gun, bayonet, bomb; July 1984–June 1985.

Television: "In the Best of Families: Marriage, Pride and Madness" (1994), a two-part, four-hour miniseries based on Jerry Bledsoe's book *Bitter Blood: A True Story of Southern Family Pride, Madness, and Multiple Murder*, originally aired on CBS on January 16 and 18, 1994. Cast includes Harry Hamlin (Fritz Klenner), Kelly McGillis (Susie Sharp Newsom), and Keith Carradine (Tom Leary).

"If things get really bad you can always take something worthless, like people, and make something valuable out of the raw materials, like fertilizer."—Klenner speaking to a fellow survivalist circa 1980

Bizarre case set in the American South in which family tensions caused by a bitter child custody battle resulted in the deaths of nine members of two prominent families. "Fritz" Klenner worshipped his father, Dr. Frederick R. Klenner, a renowned, but eccentric physician who claimed that the megadoses of vitamins he injected into patients in his Reidsville, North Carolina, clinic could cure anything from polio to multiple sclerosis. While still a boy, Klenner decided to become a doctor like his father. He also accepted as gospel the man's ultra right wing political philosophy that preached the world's problems were caused by communist conspiracies, blacks, and Jews. Armageddon was imminent and only those who hoarded guns and food would survive the Apocalypse. Inseparable companions, a favorite father-son activity centered on setting off dynamite charges in a family-owned woods to unearth the lair of the "Wampus Cat," a Bigfoot-type creature Dr. Klenner believed lived there.

Considered "strange" and "secretive" by classmates, the friendless boy wore military clothing to school and defended Hitler as a victim of "bad press." In 1969 Klenner transferred from public to private school to avoid as he put it "having to sit next to a nigger." At the Woodward Academy, a former military school near Atlanta, Klenner flourished under the mock-military program. In 1970 he entered the pre-med program of the University of Mississippi, but four years later had not earned a degree. While at the university, Klenner's fantasy life burgeoned. He carried a concealed pistol to class, claimed to be an undercover narcotics officer, and spoke archly of paramilitary training sessions in the bayou. Lying to his family about graduating, Klenner announced in 1976 his acceptance to Duke University Medical School, his father's alma mater. He maintained the deception by living weekdays in Durham to "attend classes" and commuting to Reidsville on weekends to assist in the clinic. In Durham, Klenner passed himself off as a CIA contract operative to various paramilitary and survivalist groups. A December 1978 marriage failed to prevent him from conducting at least five affairs with older, emotionally troubled women. The marriage ended in spring 1981 when his wife caught him cheating. Before leaving, she informed Dr. Klenner that his son was not enrolled at Duke. Remarkably, the man continued to permit "young Dr. Fritz" to masquerade as a physician in his clinic.

Klenner may have remained just a bigoted eccentric had he not become involved with first cousin Susie Newsom Lynch and her young boys, John and James. Lynch, attempting to recover from a bitter divorce with Tom Lynch, began visiting her uncle's clinic in 1980. Dr. Klenner diagnosed multiple sclerosis and placed her on a megadose regimen of vitamin B injections. Fritz listened sympathetically to his cousin's paranoiac fears focusing on Tom Lynch's efforts to expand his visitation rights with his boys. By 1982, Klenner's fantasy life had enveloped Susie and he began to manipulate her paranoia. Through his "CIA connections" he "learned" that Tom Lynch was in actuality a drug dealer who owed the Mafia vast sums of money. With the death of his father on May 20, 1984, and the subsequent state-ordered closing of the clinic, Klenner's tenuous hold on reality ended. He used most of the $25,000 insurance payment he received to buy weapons and supplies for the approaching Armageddon.

By mid–1984, Klenner's influence over Susie's life had extended to the point that the boys' even dressed in camouflaged outfits like their beloved "Uncle Fritz." Florence Newsom, Susie's mother, disliked Klenner as did Tom Lynch's mother, Delores. The 68-year-old millionaire's insistence that her son petition the court for more visitation time signed her death warrant. On July 22, 1984, armed with an assault rifle, Klenner murdered Delores Rodgers Lynch, 68, and her daughter Jane Lynch, 39, at their home in Prospect, Kentucky. The killings were so efficient that police believed them to be a professional "hit." Klenner convinced Susie that Tom Lynch had his mother killed in order to collect a $250,000 inheritance he could use to pay off drug dealers and press his case for more access to the children. He vowed to protect his lover.

In March 1985 Klenner moved into Susie's Greensboro, North Carolina, apartment and quickly converted it into an armed bunker. Shortly before a May 23, 1985, custody hearing, Susie's father Robert Newsom, Jr., told his daughter that his testimony would support Tom Lynch. Klenner swung into action. He duped long-time friend Ian Mark Perkins into accepting him as a CIA contractor who needed the college student's help as a getaway driver in a "hit" to eliminate KGB-connected drug smugglers. Perkins, a CIA want-to-be anxious to impress the "Company," agreed to help. On May 18, 1985, they drove to Old Town, North Carolina, and while Perkins waited in the car Klenner entered the house containing the suspects. Inside, Susie's parents Robert and Florence Newsom and her grandmother Hattie were watching television. Klenner shot each repeatedly, stabbing and slitting Florence's throat. Police likened the scene to a terrorist's vengeance raid.

Klenner told Susie that the killings were further proof that Lynch would stop at nothing to get her children. Investigations into both sets of murders pointed to Klenner, the "weird cousin," as the common link. On May 22, 1985, State Bureau of Investigation agents interviewed Susie in her apartment with Klenner present. The booby-trapped front door and the survival knife worn by Klenner aroused their suspicion. Ian Perkins, interviewed by SBI agents on May 30, 1985, cracked and discredited Klenner's alibi for the night of the Newsom murders. Realizing he had been duped, Perkins agreed to wear a wire in future meetings with the prime suspect. In a June 3, 1985, meeting between the two heavily monitored by police, Klenner abruptly broke off the conversation and returned to Susie's apartment to pack.

Authorities watched as Klenner and Susie Lynch loaded the black K-5 Blazer with automatic weapons, sleeping bags, supplies, and her two sons. A four mile chase through Greensboro into nearby Summerfield ensued with Klenner spraying his pursuers with intermittent bursts of 9mm Uzi submachine gun fire. Three officers were wounded. At 3:07 p.m., the Blazer stopped and two shots were heard. Seconds later, Klenner activated an explosive device rigged under the car which blew it more than 100 feet into the air. Noone survived. A subsequent autopsy revealed that John and James Newsom had both been fed cyanide and shot in the head at close range. A later SBI report named Susie as the shooter. Ian Perkins was subsequently convicted of being an accessory after the fact to the Newsom murders and served four months of a six-year prison sentence.

347. Bledsoe, Jerry. *Bitter Blood: A True Story of Southern Family Pride, Madness,* *and Multiple Murder.* 1st ed. New York: Dutton, 1988. x, 468 pp., [16]pp. of plates: ill.; 25 cm.

_____. [Same as 347.] New York: New American Library, 1989. viii, 573 pp., [16]pp. of plates: ill.; 18 cm. ("An Onyx book"); paperback.

_____. [Same as 347.] New York: Penguin, 1989. 573 pp., [16]pp. of plates: ill.; 18 cm.; paperback.

348. Newsom, Robert W., and Trotter, William R. *Deadly Kin: A True Story of Mass Family Murder.* Greensboro, N.C.: Signal Research, 1988. 217 pp., [8]pp. of plates: ports.; 22 cm.

Knighten, Greg Spencer (a.k.a. "Sparky")

Born circa 1971. High school student. Midlothian, Texas; 1 murder; .38 caliber pistol; October 23, 1987.

"Oh God, forgive me of my sins and what happened tonight. I'm so scared. And I'm sorry." —Knighten expressing remorse in a prayer session with his girlfriend hours after murdering an undercover police officer

High school student and adopted son of a police officer who murdered an undercover narcotics officer posing as a classmate. George William Raffield, Jr., 21, had been on the Red Oak, Texas, police department only three months when he was assigned to investigate teenage drug use in Midlothian, Texas, a bedroom community of 7,500 thirty miles south of Dallas. Posing as "William George Moore," Raffield enrolled as a senior in Midlothian High School in the fall semester of 1987. As school administrators were unreceptive to an outside agency policing their institution, Raffield was placed undercover in the school without their knowledge. Though younger looking than his age, Raffield quickly aroused suspicion among the student population by his eagerness to fit in and his mature demeanor. Raffield's willingness to drive his pickup to drug buys brought him to the attention of sophomore Greg Knighten, the 16-year-old adopted son of a 17-year-old veteran on the Dallas police department. As a child, Knighten's hyperactivity, foul mouth, aggressive behavior, and mistreatment of animals forced his parents to move when neighbors no longer permitted their children to play with him. He was later expelled from an alternative school. The Knightens' move to rural Midlothian to escape drugs failed to prevent Greg from becoming a "doper." In October 1987, he met 17-year-old Richard Goeglein at school. Months earlier Goeglein had moved to Midlothian from Red Lake, Arizona, where he had witnessed a 19-year-old friend bludgeon a 16-year-old boy nearly to death with a baseball bat. Goeglein was never charged, but testified against his friend in a preliminary hearing. Combining drug use and satanism with a devotion to heavy metal bands like Slayer, Goeglein wore a black heart-shaped amulet around his neck which he believed contained the spirit of a dead girl he once knew. "Terry the Heart" answered all Goeglein's questions and permitted him to predict the future for up to three days. Goeglein and Knighten became fast friends.

Raffield was building cases against both youths when another student ripped him off on a drug buy. To maintain his cover, Raffield angrily confronted the boy who, calling him a "narc," slapped him in the face. Raffield did not fight back and afterwards confided to his mother that he feared his cover might be blown. His position was further compromised on October

21, 1978, when Knighten took him to Cynthia Fedrick's apartment to smoke dope. A heavy drug user since age 14, the twice divorced 23 year old observed Raffield closely, then called Knighten into another room to tell him that his friend was not inhaling the smoke and looked too old to be a teenager. The undercover cop's fate was sealed when they returned to the living room to find him casually looking at a serial number on the back of a stolen stereo later confiscated by police. At school the next day, an enraged Knighten was overheard telling his friend Jonathan Jobe, 17, and Goeglein that he was going to kill Raffield. Later that night in Knighten's bedroom, Goeglein used his amulet on a Ouija board to confirm that Raffield was indeed a police officer.

On the evening of October 23, 1987, Knighten and Goeglein lured Raffield to a remote pasture eight miles outside Midlothian near Venus on the pretext of buying crank. Knighten, seated on the tailgate of the truck with Raffield while Goeglein sat in the cab, shot the officer twice in the head with his father's borrowed .38 Special. Goeglein took the dead man's wallet and Knighten used one of the several tee-shirts he wore to wipe the pickup clean of fingerprints. Jobe picked them up on the highway where they split the $18 found in Raffield's wallet. Afterwards, they drove to Fedrick's apartment and informed her of the shooting. Knighten destroyed Raffield's identification, but when the wallet failed to burn, Fedrick threw it in a garbage bin. It was later retrieved by police. Remorseful, Knighten went to his girlfriend's house and prayed with her for hours. The three conspirators were arrested the next day after Goeglein called a friend in Arizona and described the killing.

The friend's father notified Texas authorities who picked up Jobe and Goeglein. Jobe led police to the body. Knighten was arrested around 10:00 p.m. while on a hayride.

As the case was prepared for trial, police were stunned to learn that most of Midlothian's teenagers knew of the murder plot, but said nothing. Knighten was certified to stand trial as an adult as his friends, Goeglein and Jobe, each cut deals with the prosecution guaranteeing reduced sentences in exchange for their testimony against Knighten as the shooter. Opening arguments in the capital murder trial began in a Waxahachie, Texas, courtroom on May 31, 1988. Knighten pleaded not guilty insisting that Goeglein, not he, pulled the trigger. The defense strategy focused on portraying the state's star witness as a drug-crazed satanist who killed Raffield as part of an occult ritual. At least four witnesses pointed to Knighten as the murderer, while only the boy's policeman father testified on his behalf. Knighten was found guilty on June 8, 1988, and the jury sentenced he and Goeglein each to 45 years in prison of which they must serve a minimum of 15 years before being considered eligible for parole. Underscoring the senselessness of the murder, authorities conceded that had Raffield been successful in arresting Knighten and Goeglein on minor drug charges each would probably have received probation if convicted.

349. Stowers, Carlton. *Innocence Lost.* New York: Pocket Books, 1990. x, 291 pp.: ill.; 25 cm.

_____. [Same as 349.] New York: Pocket Star Books, 1990. xii, 391 pp.: ill.; 17 cm.; paperback.

Knowles, Benjamin
(acquitted)

Born circa 1885. Died October 1933. Doctor. Beckwai, Ashanti, West Africa; 1 murder (acquitted); gun; October 20, 1928.

"If my wife rolls up, I will be hung by the neck until I am dead."

British doctor in West Africa tried and convicted of murdering his wife in the absence of a jury, sentenced to death, but later acquitted on appeal. The medical officer of health in the Beckwai district of the Gold Coast territory of Ashanti, Dr. Benjamin Knowles lived in a bungalow with his wife, Harriet Louise Knowles, the former music hall singer Madge Clifton. The pair argued continually and Knowles, an alcoholic drug abuser, had on more than one occasion threatened to shoot his nagging wife. Shortly after the conclusion of a luncheon party at the couple's bungalow on the afternoon of October 20, 1928, their native houseboy reported hearing a gunshot from the structure followed by Mrs. Knowles' cry of pain. The district commissioner, present at the party, investigated and was told by Dr. Knowles that nothing was amiss. The next day a contingent of officials, including the provincial commissioner and a surgeon specialist, called on Knowles. Drunken and confused, the doctor admitted there had been a "domestic fracas" in which his wife had bruised his legs with an Indian club. An examination of Harriet Knowles revealed that she had suffered a gunshot wound in the abdomen which her husband had treated with iodine. Mrs. Knowles was rushed to the Colonial Hospital in Kumasi where she dictated a deposition clearing her husband of any involvement in the shooting. Swearing on a Bible, the dying woman related to authorities that she had placed her husband's cocked gun on a chair, then inadvertently sat on it. The gun discharged when she tried to remove it from under her. Harriet Knowles died on October 23, 1928. Police discovered two more bullet holes in the bungalow and detained Dr. Knowles even after an acquaintance told authorities that one of the holes had been there for a long time.

Knowles was tried before an acting circuit judge at Kumasi in November 1928 in accordance with the law of Ashanti. No jury was present, Knowles was denied legal counsel, and the commissioner of police acted as prosecutor in the case. After a nine day trial, Knowles was found guilty on November 23, 1928, and sentenced to hang. The governor of the Gold Coast later commuted the sentence to life imprisonment. Knowles was brought to England for an Appeal to the King where, on November 19, 1929, the judicial committee of the Privy Council quashed the verdict. Surprisingly, the committee based their decision not on the absence of a jury, but rather on the grounds that the judge had erred in not considering the lesser charge of manslaughter as a sentencing option. Knowles died in London in October 1933 at the age of 48.

350. Lieck, Albert, ed. *Trial of Benjamin Knowles*. Notable British Trials. Edinburgh; London: W. Hodge & Company, Ltd., 1933. 215 pp., [6] leaves of plates: ill.; 22 cm.

_____. [Same as 350.] Notable British Trials. Toronto: Canada Law Book, 1933. 215 pp., [6] leaves of plates: ill.; 22 cm.

Edited transcript of the trial of Dr. Knowles within the Chief Commissioner's Court of Ashanti, Kumasi, November 1928 for the murder of his wife, Harriet Louise Knowles, and appeal to the King in Council. Appendices include the laws of Ashanti and the Gold Coast colony and reprints of press comments on the case from *The Times* (London) and the *Daily Telegraph*.

Knowles, Paul John
(a.k.a. "Casanova Killer," "Lester Daryl Golden," "L.D.," "Bob Williams," "PJ," "Mad Dog")

Born April 17, 1946, in Orlando, Florida. Died December 18, 1974. Welder, drifter. Florida, Georgia, Ohio, Nevada, Texas, Alabama, Connecticut, Virginia; 18 murders (claims 35); strangulation, gun, knife; July 1974–November 1974.

"If I die tomorrow it wouldn't matter that much."

In a taped diary given to his attorney, 28-year-old Paul John Knowles described killing 16 people for notoriety and sex over a four month, eight state murder spree. Bragging that he would one day be as famous as Dillinger, Knowles ultimately confessed to 35 murders in 37 states although police could verify his involvement in only 18. Seldom random, the murders often took place after Knowles had indulged in some heterosexual or homosexual experience. Discounting the bike he stole at seven, Knowles' criminal career began at 18 when he kidnapped a Jacksonville, Florida, police officer at gunpoint after the patrolman had stopped him for questioning in a traffic incident. Knowles released the officer unharmed, but was arrested and given five years for kidnapping on April 21, 1965. Over the next ten years Knowles averaged seven months each year in prison on burglary-related charges. While serving three years in Raiford, Knowles began corresponding with California divorcée Angela Covic after running across her name in an astrology magazine. She visited Knowles in prison, accepted his proposal of marriage, arranged a job for him as a sign painter, and paid for a lawyer to secure his release. Paroled on May 14, 1974, Knowles went to San Francisco to marry Covic, but she inexplicably dumped him four days after his arrival. Deeply hurt, Knowles confessed to murdering three people that night, a claim unverified by police.

Returning to Florida, Knowles knifed a bartender in a barfight in Jacksonville Beach on July 26, 1974, and was jailed. Later that night, he kicked his way out of a detention cage and escaped to begin a bloody reign of terror. The next night, Knowles ransacked the Jacksonville home of Alice Curtis, leaving the bound and gagged 65-year-old retired school teacher to choke to death on her dentures. On August 1, 1974, while dumping the stolen Curtis car, Knowles kidnapped 11-year-old Lillian Annette Anderson and her seven-year-old sister Mylette Josephine after recognizing them as friends of his mother who might later be able to identify him. Their strangled bodies were found buried in a swamp in January 1975. The next day, 49-year-old Marjorie Howie was found strangled to death with a knotted nylon stocking in her Atlantic Beach apartment. Knowles next raped and strangled an unidentified teenaged girl hitchhiker near Macon, Georgia. On August 23, 1974, Knowles forced his way into the Musella, Georgia, home of Kathy Sue Pierce and strangled her to death with a telephone cord while her three-year-old son watched. The child was left unharmed.

On September 3, 1974, Knowles' murderous rampage spread to Ohio. After sharing a few drinks with 32-year-old William V. Bates in a bar outside of Lima, Knowles bound and strangled the man in a nearby woods. Bates' nude body was not found until months later on Thanksgiving Day. Using his victim's credit cards and Chevrolet, Knowles drove virtually non-stop throughout the West and Midwest, seldom staying longer than a day in any state. On September 18, 1974, he murdered elderly Emmett and Lois Johnson in their camper in Ely, Nevada. Both were trussed up and shot behind the left ear. He used their credit cards to make his way to Seguin, Texas, where on September 23, 1974, he met 42-year-old widow Charlynn Hicks stopped by the roadside to admire the view. Her body was found four days later. Knowles had raped and strangled the woman with her own pantyhose before dragging her through a barbed wire fence. Restlessly moving into Alabama in late September or early October 1974, Knowles met 49-year-old Anne Dawson in Birmingham. He strangled the woman days later presumably dumping her unrecovered body in the Mississippi River. On October 15, 1974, Knowles checked into a motel in Mystic, Connecticut. The next day, the bound bodies of 35-year-old Karen White and her 16-year-old daughter Dawn were found raped and strangled with nylon stockings in their rural home near Marlborough. A tape recorder and a small religious statue had been taken.

Knowles headed south to Woodford, Virginia, on October 18, 1974, and murdered Doris Hovey, 53, with a rifle he took from her husband's study. Stopped for a traffic violation in Key West, Florida, Knowles was let off with a warning. Shaken, he consulted his Miami-based attorney and gave him a set of tapes in which he confessed to 16 murders. On November 6, 1974, the bodies of Carswell Carr and his 15-year-old daughter Mandy were found in their home in Milledgeville, Georgia. Carr's bound and nude body was stabbed 27 times with a pair of scissors. Mandy was strangled with a nylon stocking and another was jammed so far down her throat it took a doctor 15 minutes to remove it. The position of her body and the absence of semen suggested that Knowles was unsuccessful in raping her corpse. Most of Carr's clothes and credit cards were stolen. Police also suspect that Knowles murdered hitchhikers Edward Allen Hillard and Debbie Griffin while in the Macon area.

On November 7, 1974, British *Daily Express* writer Sandy Fawkes met Knowles ("Daryl Golden") in a bar in Atlanta. They spent the next three days together with Knowles often unable to maintain an erection during their lovemaking. When they separated three days later in West Palm Beach, Florida, Knowles attempted to rape Fawke's friend, Susan MacKenzie, but she escaped. Knowles abandoned his car and posing as an IRS man, entered the home of 31-year-old cerebral palsy victim Beverly Mabee. Abducting the invalid's sister, Barbara Tucker, he forced her to drive to Fort Pierce, Florida, where he released her unharmed. On November 16, 1974, Knowles kidnapped 35-year-old Florida highway patrolman Charles E. Campbell when the officer pulled him over near the town of Perry, Florida. The same day, Knowles used the police car to abduct James E. Meyer, a 29-year-old Delaware businessman. Transferring his hostages to Meyer's car, Knowles headed into Georgia where

they were spotted by a gas station attendant. Later that day near Perry, Georgia, Knowles handcuffed the two men around a tree and shot each in the head. Despite a massive search, their bodies were not found until November 21, 1974.

On November 17, 1974, Knowles crashed through a police roadblock outside of Stockbridge, Georgia, and fled into a Henry County woods where he eluded capture for four hours. In custody, Knowles' mention of the tapes set into motion a legal battle that saw his attorney jailed for contempt for initially refusing to produce them, although he later relented. Asked the number of murders he committed, Knowles wrote "18" on his palm, but boasted of as many as 35. Unafraid of death, Knowles said the only thing he would miss would be "the enjoyment of watching them [the police] making idiots out of themselves." The serial killer was shot to death on December 18, 1974, by a Georgia Bureau of Investigation agent while attempting to escape in Douglasville, Georgia, during a car transfer to another facility. The man described by his own attorney as "the most heinous murderer in history" was buried in Jacksonville, Florida, in a ceremony attended only by his family and the girlfriend who dumped him.

351. Fawkes, Sandy. *Killing Time.* London: Owen, 1977. 180 pp., [8]pp. of plates: ill., facsim., ports.; 23 cm.

_____. [Same as 351.] Feltham: Hamlyn, 1978. 180 pp., [8]pp. of plates: ill., facsim., ports.; 18 cm.; paperback.

_____. [Same as 351.] Markham, Ont.: PaperJacks, 1978. 180 pp.; 18 cm.; paperback.

_____. [Same as 351.] 1st American ed. New York: Taplinger, 1979. 167 pp.; 22 cm.

British journalist Fawkes had a short personal relationship with Knowles and offers some interesting insights into his personality. She concludes, "Paul John Knowles was as much a victim as any of the eighteen people he killed ... May his poor, demented soul rest in peace."

Kraft, Randy Steven
(a.k.a. "The Score Card Killer")

Born March 19, 1945, in Long Beach, California. Computer programmer and consultant. California, Oregon, Michigan; 16 murders (convicted, suspected of killing 67); ligature strangulation; 1971–1983.

"The ultimate orgasm is in death."—Statement attributed to Kraft by a close friend

Homosexual torture slayer whose sadistic murders of an estimated 67 young men rank him among the most prolific serial killers of all time. At 1:10 a.m. on May 14, 1983, two California highway patrol officers working Interstate 5 in Mission Viejo pulled over a Toyota Celica which was being driven erratically. The driver was Randy Steven Kraft, a 38-year-old computer programmer from Long Beach. On the seat next to him, apparently asleep, was a young Marine later identified as Terry Lee Gambrell, 25, stationed at El Toro, California. Closer examination of the "sleeping" soldier revealed that Gambrell had been strangled with his own belt. A jacket thrown over his lap concealed hands tied with his own shoelaces and pants pulled down to his knees. A search of the vehicle uncovered a packet of 47 color photographs of several young men, many nude, who appeared to be lifeless. A sheet of paper found in the car's trunk, later called a "death list" and a "score card" by pros-

ecutors, contained coded entries for a suspected 61 murder victims. A search of Kraft's Long Beach apartment yielded more color photographs of men found dead in the area between 1972 and 1979 and clothes later determined to have belonged to several of the victims. A background check on the likable computer programmer revealed that in 1966 he had been arrested on suspicion of lewd conduct in Huntington Beach (charge dismissed) and again in June 1975 in a beach restroom in Long Beach. The 1966 charge was dismissed, but Kraft pleaded guilty to having sexual activity with another man in the 1975 charge, spent five days in jail, and paid a $125 fine. In between time, Kraft graduated from Clermont Men's College in 1967 with a degree in economics and spent one year in the Air Force before being honorably discharged on grounds related to homosexuality. Kraft's name had first surfaced in connection with a murder investigation in 1975 when he was questioned in the March 29, 1975, disappearance of 19-year-old Keith Daven Crotwell. The youth's severed head was found a little more than a month later near a jetty in Long Beach harbor. Kraft admitted being with Crotwell the night of his disappearance but police, lacking any further evidence, did not charge him. Crotwell's skeletonized remains (minus hands) were found near El Toro on October 18, 1975. On the "death list" he was referred to as "parking lot," the last place he was seen before disappearing. Aided by the photographs and the so-called "death list," authorities began meticulously tying Kraft to a string of 16 strangled and sometimes mutilated bodies often found dumped along freeways in Orange County. As a result of their investigation, police became convinced that not only had Kraft murdered for over a decade throughout California, he had also killed in Oregon and Michigan while on business trips in those states. After a five year delay, Kraft's trial for the 16 murders he allegedly committed in Orange County opened in Santa Ana on September 26, 1988. The prosecution maintained that Kraft's murders followed a precise ritual often involving young male hitchhikers. Kraft usually took the intended victim to his Long Beach home where he administered "the combo": a combination of drugs and alcohol designed to render the man unconscious. The victim would then be molested, perhaps mutilated, strangled, photographed, then dumped. The genitals of many of the victims had been sliced off, and foreign objects like pens, combs, and socks, had been roughly inserted into their body cavities. During the 13 month trial, the longest in Orange County history, the prosecution matched victims with the coded notations on the "score card" found at the time of Kraft's arrest. Entry "EUCLID," it was argued, stood for Scott Michael Hughes, an 18-year-old Marine (one of six soldiers among the 16 victims) found on April 16, 1978, on the shoulder of the Euclid Street on-ramp to the eastbound Riverside Freeway in Anaheim. Hughes had been strangled and emasculated. Following 11 days of deliberation, Kraft was convicted on each of the 16 first degree murder counts on May 12, 1989. A four month penalty phase resulted in a jury recommendation on August 11, 1989, that Randy Kraft die in California's gas chamber. Continuing to maintain his innocence, Kraft was formally sentenced to death on November 29, 1989. In sentencing the serial killer, Judge Donald A. McCartin commented on

Kraft's mutilation of the victims: "I can't imagine doing these things in scientific experiments on a dead person, much less someone alive." While the cost of Kraft's trial has been officially sealed by court order, it is estimated that his defense cost Orange County $5 million, a sum which may be overshadowed only by the McMartin Pre-School molestation trial in Los Angeles County. Kraft is currently on San Quentin's death row awaiting the outcome of an appeals process which could take 10 years. According to news reports, Kraft passes the time playing bridge with fellow death row inmates William Bonin, the "Freeway Killer" of 14 young men and boys, Douglas Clark, the "Sunset Strip Killer" convicted of murdering six prostitutes and runaways, and Lawrence "Pliers" Bittaker, who in 1979 raped and murdered five women while tape recording their screams.

352. McDougal, Dennis. *Angel of Darkness*. New York: Warner Books, 1991. xiv, 336 pp., [16]pp. of plates: ill.; 24 cm.

_____. [Same as 352.] New York: Warner Books, 1991. 381 pp., [16]pp. of plates: ill.; 18 cm.; paperback.

_____. [Same as 352.] London: Warner, 1991. xv, 381 pp., [8]pp. of plates; 18 cm.; paperback.

In his novelization of the case based on extensive research, *Los Angeles Times* reporter McDougal maintains that Kraft committed 67 murders, more than any other serial killer in the United States. In May 1993, Kraft filed a $60 million libel suit against McDougal claiming that the book not only portrayed him unfairly as a "sick, twisted man," but also destroyed his chances for future employment. The case was thrown out by the supreme court of California in June 1994, but not before McDougal spent a rumored $25,000 in legal fees.

Krenwinkel, Patricia Dianne (a.k.a. "Katie," "Marnie Reeves," "Big Patty," "Mary Ann Scott")

Born December 3, 1947, in Los Angeles, California. Cult member. Los Angeles, California; 7 murders (7 convictions); gun, knife, bludgeon; August 9–10, 1969.

"You have just judged yourselves." — Krenwinkel's reaction to the jury recommendation that she be sentenced to death; see also Manson, Charles Milles.

Kürten, Peter (a.k.a. "Franz Becker," "Fritz Baumgart," "Monster of Düsseldorf," "Düsseldorf Vampire," "Ripper")

Born circa 1883 in Köln-Mulheim, Germany. Executed July 2, 1931. Sand moulder. Germany; 15 murders (convicted of 9); scissors, knife, bludgeon (hammer), strangulation; May 1913–November 1929.

Films: M (GER, 1931), a Nero Film/Film Star production directed by Fritz Lang. Cast includes Peter Lorre (Franz Becker/Peter Kürten), Otto Wernicke (Inspector Karl Lohmann), and Gustav Grundgens (Schraenker). M (US, 1951), a Columbia production directed by Joseph Losey. Cast includes David Wayne (Martin Harrow/Peter Kürten), Howard Da Silva (Carney), Luther Adler (Langley), and Raymond Burr (Pottsy).

"No, I have no remorse. As to whether recollections of my deeds make me feel ashamed, I will tell you. Thinking back to all the details is not at all unpleasant. I rather enjoy it." — Kürten discussing his crimes with medico-legal expert Karl Berg

Called by one judge, "the King of Sexual Delinquents," Peter Kürten, the infamous "Monster of Düsseldorf," occupies a unique place within the annals of 20th century murder. Unlike other serial sex killers who confined their slaughter solely to men or women (e.g., John Wayne Gacy and Ted Bundy, respectively), Kürten indiscriminately killed both sexes, even animals, in a singleminded drive to release sexual tension. The sadistic act of murder committed using a knife, scissors, hammer, or by strangulation was often sufficient to produce "eruptions" (orgasms) within Kürten. In time, Kürten's fantasy life became so rich that merely contemplating acts of individual carnage or scenarios in which he instigated mass poisonings, arsons, or deadly train wrecks was enough to bring him to orgasm. In custody, the 47-year-old confessed that his principal satisfaction in life was derived from tasting the warm blood of his victims as it gushed from their wounds into his mouth.

For 15 months, between February 3, 1929, through his arrest on May 24, 1930, the fastidious and well-mannered factory worker conducted a reign of terror against the German city of Düsseldorf and surrounding areas that resulted in 11 killings and at least 30 attempted murders. Despite public outcry over the inability of the Düsseldorf police to capture the elusive killer, local authorities in conjunction with Berlin-based crime specialists followed-up 1,200 clues, questioned 9,000 people in Düsseldorf, received over 600 letters purportedly from the murderer, worked through hundreds of phony confessions and accusations, and distributed throughout Germany 60,000 copies of an ill-conceived brochure justifying their delay in catching the killer, whom, based on the different weapons used in the attacks and murders, they believed to be four separate men. When the seemingly genteel and mild-mannered Kürten was finally apprehended, medico-legal specialists were afforded an unprecedented opportunity to study an anomalous psychological type who was eager to share his early life and describe his crimes in shocking detail.

Born into crushing poverty in Köln-Mülheim, Germany, in 1883, Kürten was one of 13 children violently abused by an alcoholic father. While Kürten adored his mother, he was powerless to protect her from his father's abuse. In an attempt to discover possible causes of Peter Kürten's aberrant behavior, researchers later traced his family tree and discovered that while his mother's side of the family was "normal," his father's side boasted an almost unbroken line of alcoholics and psychopaths extending back over generations. In 1897, the elder Kürten was jailed for 15 months for attempted incest with his daughter. Ironically, son Peter would also be jailed for attempting incest with the same girl. In Köln-Mülheim, the Kürten family shared lodgings with the town dog-catcher who introduced the young Peter into the perverse joys of animal torture. The pained screams of animals excited Kürten and he began practicing bestiality with dogs, sheep, goats, and pigs always experiencing orgasm when he stabbed the animal to death. Kürten's sadism soon evolved to encompass brutality towards other children. He committed his first murders at age nine by pushing a boy off a raft into the Rhine River. When another child attempted to save the boy, Kürten kept them both off the raft until they drowned.

As an adolescent, Kürten added pyromania to his growing list of sexual perversions, often achieving orgasm while watching the numerous fires he set. He wandered throughout Germany attacking and robbing young girls and women before running away to Coblenz to live with a prostitute who indulged his sadomasochistic leanings. Arrested for theft, Kürten began serving the first of what ultimately would amount to over 20 years' imprisonment for a variety of offenses including forgery, military desertion, and violence. In prison, Kürten often committed minor infractions in order to be placed in solitary confinement. Alone in his cell, he would masturbate while reading of the exploits of his hero "Jack the Ripper" and fantasize about blowing up bridges or poisoning the water supplies of large cities. Released in 1899, Kürten lived with a masochistic prostitute twice his age. Kürten spent the next 13 years in and out of prison until he was drafted into military service. He quickly deserted and wandered the countryside burning barns.

Kürten's first verifiable murder occurred in Cologne on May 25, 1913. As 13-year-old Christine Klein lay asleep in her bed, Kürten crept into the room and slit her throat. Though he inadvertently dropped a handkerchief with a "P.K." monogram, the initials matched those of the child's father. Suspicion for the crime settled on the man's brother, Otto Klein, with whom he had quarreled earlier on the day of the murder. Klein was tried for the murder, acquitted, and later killed in World War I before having his name cleared by Kürten's subsequent confession. Kürten told his interrogators that he had attended Klein's trial and was mightily entertained by the proceedings. Though he continued his attacks on women, Kürten married in Altenburg in 1923. While Kürten's bride was initially reluctant to marry him, she acquiesced after he threatened to kill her if she refused. The marriage seemingly "calmed" Kürten's dark urges for several years although he confessed to authorities that he managed to sustain "normal" sexual relations with his wife only by fantasizing about blood and death during the act.

Residing with his wife on the Mettmannerstrasse in Düsseldorf, Kürten's reign of terror began in earnest in early 1929. On February 3, 1929, he attacked Frau Kuhn with a pair of scissors, stabbing the woman 24 times and stopping only after their point broke off in her head. Kuhn survived. Ten days later on the outskirts of Düsseldorf, Kürten stabbed to death 45-year-old Rudolf Scheer, plunging a pair of scissors 20 times into the man's temples. On March 8, 1929, the body of eight-year-old Rose Ohliger was found next to a building site on the outskirts of Düsseldorf. The child had been strangled, stabbed 13 times in the left side and temples, then doused in paraffin and burned. Kürten attempted to strangle four more women in March and July before meeting Maria Hahn at the city zoo on August 8, 1929. Kürten lured Hahn into a woods where he strangled and stabbed her to death. The sex killer subsequently returned to the murder site as many as 30 times achieving orgasm each time by fingering the earth where he buried her. Kürten later confessed to murdering a girl named "Anni" that same month and to dumping her body in the river where it was never recovered.

Kürten changed his weapon from scissors to a knife to commit his next offenses, the stabbing of two women and a man in August. All survived. On August 24, 1929, the bodies of foster sisters Gertrude Hamacher, 5, and Luise Lenzen, 14, were discovered near their home in Flehe. Both girls had been strangled and their throats cut. Returning to Flehe the next day, Kürten basked in the villagers' reaction to his bloody handiwork. On August 26, 1929, Kürten attempted to rape 26-year-old Gertrude Schulte and during the ensuing struggle inflicted multiple stab wounds in the woman's neck, shoulder, back, and temples. Schulte survived and supplied a good description of the man calling himself "Fritz Baumgart." After the attack, Kürten disposed of his knife in favor of a hammer for the twofold purpose of convincing police that more than one criminal was at work in the area and, perhaps the more compelling reason, his belief that wielding the new weapon would afford him "still greater satisfaction."

Kürten's one-man crime spree continued throughout August and September with non-lethal attacks on three women. On September 30, 1929, Kürten picked up Ida Reuter walking along the Oberkassel and beat her to death with a hammer. In an almost identical attack ten days later (October 11), Kürten repeatedly hammered Elisabeth Dorrier in the temple. Though still breathing when found, Dorrier died without regaining consciousness. Kürten rounded out October with two other non-lethal hammer attacks before directing his sexual fury against five-year-old Gertrude Albermann. Reported missing from her home in Flingern on November 7, 1929, Albermann's body was discovered two days later near a brick wall surrounding a factory. The child had been strangled and stabbed 36 times with a pair of scissors. Toying with police,

Kürten sent a letter directing them to the corpses of Albermann and an earlier victim, Maria Hahn. Hahn's body was recovered from beneath a stone in Pappendelle on November 14, 1929, and bore 20 stab wounds to the temples, throat, and breast identical to those inflicted on Albermann.

Kürten ushered in 1930 with at least seven attempted strangulations and numerous hammer attacks directed against young girls. On May 14, 1930, Kürten picked up 20-year-old Maria Budlick and took her back to his flat for a meal. Afterwards while walking in the Grafenberg woods, Kürten attempted to strangle the young woman. Inexplicably, he released Budlick after she assured him that she did not remember where he lived. Budlick notified police and the "Monster of Düsseldorf" was arrested at his flat on May 24, 1930. Theatres, cabarets, and cinemas halted performances to announce his arrest. Kürten, anxious to talk and concerned only that his sexual infidelities might cause his wife pain, offered authorities, between May 25 and June 1, 1930, one of the most detailed confessions in criminal history. He remembered every ghastly detail of his crimes and enjoyed shocking hardened homicide detectives by recounting tales of blood drinking and other perversions.

Following the most extensive psychological examination of a murderer up to that time, Kürten went on trial in Düsseldorf on April 13, 1931. Kürten's father, survivors of his attacks, and medico-legal experts testified for eight days in a trial that held Germany enthralled. On April 21, 1931, a jury deliberated only an hour and a half before finding Kürten guilty of nine murders, seven attempted murders, and an attempted rape. Sentenced to death by decapitation, Kürten was moved from Düsseldorf Prison to Cologne's Klingelputz Prison shortly before his July 2, 1931, execution date. He spent his last hours writing letters to the relatives of 13 of his victims in which he asked for their forgiveness and prayers. Unafraid of the guillotine (he confessed to one psychiatrist that his greatest thrill would be to hear his own blood gushing from his severed neck), Kürten dined heartily on *two* last meals of wienerschnitzel, fried potatoes, and bottles of white wine. At 6:00 a.m. Kürten was led into the inner courtyard of the prison and beheaded.

353. Berg, Karl. *The Sadist.* Authorized translation by Olga Illner and George Godwin. Library of Abnormal Psychological Types, vol. 1. Edited by George Godwin. London: Acorn Press, 1938. 177 pp.: plates; 22 cm.

_____. [Same as 353.] Authorized translation by Olga Illner and George Godwin. Library of Abnormal Psychological Types, vol. 1. Edited by George Godwin. London: Heinemann, 1945. 177 pp.: ill., ports.; 22 cm.

354. Berg, Karl. *The Sadist: An Account of the Crimes of a Serial Killer* (together with) *Peter Kürten: A Study in Sadism.* Authorized translation of Berg title by Olga Illner and George Godwin. Definitive ed. Introduction to definitive ed. by Candice A. Skrapec. Patterson Smith Series in Criminology, Law Enforcement, and Social Problems; publication no. 144. Montclair, N.J.: Patterson Smith, 1996. 352 pp.: ill., maps; 22 cm.

Berg, professor of forensic medicine in the Düsseldorf Medical Academy and the medico-legal officer of the Düsseldorf criminal court, had unlimited access to Kürten and the result is a classic text on the sexual criminal. Includes photographs of the victims, a list of Kürten's offenses drawn from his own statement, a table of his throttling cases, and a table of postmortem findings. Essential.

355. Godwin, George. *Peter Kürten: A Study in Sadism.* London: Acorn Press, 1938. 58 pp.: ports.; 23 cm.

_____. [Same as 355.] London: William Heinemann Medical Books, 1945. 58 pp.: port.; 23 cm. (Re-issue of 1938 publication.)

Originally intended as the introduction to Berg's *The Sadist,* Godwin's sketch draws heavily from this more complete account.

356. Wagner, Margaret Seaton. *The Monster of Düsseldorf: The Life and Trial of Peter Kürten.* London: Faber & Faber, 1932. 248 pp., [9] leaves of plates: ill., port., facsims., plan; 21 cm.

_____. [Same as 356.] New York: Dutton, 1933. 248 pp., [9] leaves of plates: ill., port., facsims., plan; 21 cm.

The most readable account of the case. Useful.

Landru, Henri Désiré
(a.k.a. "The French Bluebeard," "The Red Man of Gambais," "Morel," "Clichet," "Raoul Dupont," "Diard," "Fremyet," "Lucien Guillet," "Georges Petit," "Forest de Barzieux," "Cuchet")

Born circa 1869 in Paris, France. Executed February 23, 1922. Confidence man. Vernouillet and Gambais, France; 11 murders; ligature strangulation (waxed cord—suspected); April 1915–January 1919.

Films: Monsieur Verdoux (US, 1947), a Chaplin/United Artists production written and directed by Charles Chaplin. Cast includes Charles Chaplin (Henri Verdoux, *et al.*), Martha Raye (Annabella Bonheur), and Isobel Elsom (Marie Grosnay). *Bluebeard's Ten Honeymoons* (GB, 1960), an Anglo Artists production directed by W. Lee Wilder. Cast includes George Sanders (Landru), Corinne Calvet (Odette), and Patricia Roc (Mme. Dueaux). *Landru* (FR/IT, 1963), a Rome-Paris/CC Champion production directed by Claude Chabrol. Also known as *Bluebeard.* Cast includes Charles Denner (Henri-Désiré Landru), Michele Morgan (Celestine Buisson), and Danielle Darrieux (Berthe Heon). *Bluebeard* (FR/IT/GER, 1972), a Barnabe/Gloria/Geiselgasteig production directed by Edward Dmytryk. Cast includes Richard Burton (Bluebeard/Baron Von Sepper), Raquel Welch (Magdalena), and Joey Heatherton (Anne).

"Eh bien! It is not the first time that an innocent man has been condemned."—Landru's last words to his attorney

Infamous French serial killer who often placed matrimonial ads in order to meet the lonely, unmarried women he afterwards killed for their possessions. Arrested seven times for fraud before committing his first murder in January 1915, Henri Désiré Landru seemingly exercised a hypnotic effect over a certain type of woman who was easily seduced by his personal charm, bald head, and pointed brown beard. Posing as engineer "M. Diard," Landru seduced 39-year-old widow Mme. Jeanne Cuchet and in April 1915 went to Vernouillet to live in the villa she shared with her 16-year-old son. Soon after his arrival the Cuchets disappeared. Throughout the remainder of 1915 Landru made the villa his base of operations killing two other women who traveled to Vernouillet to meet (as his ad billed him) the "affectionate" widower with a "comfortable income." In December 1915, Landru as "Dupont," an engineer from Rouen, relocated to the Villa Ermitage in the village of Gambais. It was there until his arrest in January 1919 that Landru systematically strangled at least seven of his paramours, dismembered their corpses, and fed some of their remains into a coal-burning stove. Afterwards, Landru converted his victims' furniture into cash, signed over their bank accounts to his alias, and lived off the proceeds. Landru was finally arrested on April 12, 1919, after relatives of two of the missing women notified police in Gambais. At the time of his arrest, Landru carried a black notebook filled with the names of his 11 victims, the money he spent on them, and the times at which he killed them. A search of the Villa Ermitage uncovered the bodies of three dogs and near the kitchen stove charred bone splinters and teeth from the bodies of three people.

An uncooperative Landru was disdainful of the 11 murder charges against him, believing that in order to be convicted the bodies of his alleged victims had to be produced. More than two years after his arrest Landru's trial opened at the La Cour d'Assises in the Palais de Justice at Versailles on November 7, 1921. Ironically, women jammed the overflowing courtroom and many openly flirted with the man dubbed "The French Bluebeard" by the sensational press. Experiments conducted with the stove found in the Villa Ermitage determined that it was capable of consuming a large quantity of flesh in a short time period. In a desperate attempt to overcome the damning evidence contained in his client's notebook, Landru's counsel put forth the dubious contention that the missing middle-aged women had not been murdered, but rather spirited away by the "white slaver" Landru to brothels in South America. Landru was found guilty on November 30, 1921, and despite the jury's petition for clemency was guillotined on February 25, 1922. Immediately after his execution, a handwritten letter from Landru was delivered to the prosecutor. It concluded, "Farewell, *monsieur*, our common history will doubtless die tomorrow. I die with an innocent and quiet mind. I hope respectfully that you may do the same."

357. Bardens, Dennis. *The Ladykiller: The Life of Landru, the French Bluebeard.* London: P. Davies, 1972. 221 pp., [8]pp. of plates: ill., facsim., ports.; 23 cm.

Definitive study of Landru which lists in tabular form the chronological order of disappearances and names of his 11 victims and a chronology of the killer's addresses and aliases taken from the records of the Prefecture de Police, Paris. Includes a detailed index.

358. Mackenzie, F.A., ed. *Landru.* Famous Trials Series. London: G. Bles, 1928. v, 244 pp., [4] leaves of plates: ill., ports.; 23 cm.

Mackenzie focuses primarily on Landru's trial in this entry in the Famous Trials Series.

359. Masson, Rene. *Landru.* 1st ed. Garden City, N.Y.: Doubleday, 1965. 448 pp.; 22 cm.

Fictionalized account of the case.

360. _____. *Number One: A Story of Landru.* Translated from the French by Gillian Tindall. London: Hutchinson, 1964. 448 pp.; 22 cm.

Translation of *Les roses de Gambais.*

361. Wakefield, H. Russell. *Landru: The French Bluebeard.* London: Duckworth, 1936. 174 pp.; 19 cm.

Wakefield draws heavily on Bolitho's essay "The Poetry of Désiré Landru" in demythologizing the French serial killer. A lifelong academic who spoke several languages, Wakefield seldom translates the numerous French quotations to be found in this dated study.

Larzelere, Virginia Gail

(a.k.a. "Virginia Gail," "Virginia Gail Antley," "Virginia Gail Matheny," "Virginia Gail Mathis," "Virginia Gail Serry," "Virginia Gail Ferry," "Virginia Gail Surrey")

Born December 27, 1952, in Lake Wales, Florida. Bookkeeper, office manager. Edgewater, Florida; 1 murder; shotgun (accomplice in a murder-for-hire); March 8, 1991.

"They say I did it to get about $1.5 million in life insurance ... but I'd rather have my husband back and only two cents."—Virginia Larzelere on March 27, 1991, refuting police claims that she is the prime suspect in the death of her husband

On March 8, 1991, a tall thin man wearing a ski mask and toting a sawed off .12 gauge shotgun entered the Edgewater, Florida, office of Dr. Norman "Doc" Larzelere shortly after 1:00 p.m. Attempting to hide from the gunman, the 39-year-old dentist fled into an office, but was mortally wounded by a single blast that tore through the closed door of the room. The gunman fled past three people in the office (Larzelere's 38-year-old wife, Virginia, a patient in the waiting room, and a dental assistant) before speeding off in a car driven by an accomplice. As Larzelere lay bleeding to death on the floor, his wife of over six years cradled his head in her lap and kissed him until paramedics arrived. Larzelere died in a helicopter en route to a Daytona Beach medical center. Less than two months later, Virginia Larzelere and her 18-year-old son from a previous marriage, Jason, were arrested for the first degree murder of Norman Larzelere, her fourth husband and Jason's adoptive

father. The ensuing trials which featured sensational revelations about alleged incest, murder-for-hire plots, greed, and the rapacious sexual exploits of Virginia Larzelere shocked southern Florida and commanded national attention.

Born into a working class family in Lake Wales, Florida, in December 1952, Virginia Larzelere née Antley was sexually molested by her father while still a teenager. Intelligent and sexually attractive, Larzelere employed both qualities to escape the poverty of her background. Though only 17, she married electrician Henry J. Mathis and bore him two children, Jason and Jessica, both later adopted by Norman Larzelere. While working in 1970 as an office manager for a small business, Larzelere was caught embezzling $16,000 and only escaped prosecution by agreeing to reimburse the money in monthly installments. Five years later in 1975, she was accused of embezzling $5,000 from an engineering firm where she worked. In exchange for agreeing to pay back the money, Larzelere pleaded "no contest" to forgery and larceny charges and was placed on five years probation. On April 21, 1975 (in what in retrospect appeared to be a forerunner of the successful "hit" on Norman Larzelere), Henry Mathis received a call from Virginia informing him that his cousin's car had broken down in a remote citrus grove on the outskirts of Lake Wales. Mathis drove to the site and encountered a man with a .32 caliber pistol who shot at him four times. Hit once in the scalp and right arm, Mathis escaped into the grove. Unknown to him, Virginia had earlier taken out a $300,000 life insurance policy on him. Questioned in the hospital's emergency room, Larzelere refused to cooperate with police on the advice of her attorney. Though strongly suspecting the woman of the set-up, police lacked enough evidence to charge her. The pair divorced in 1978.

A traffic accident in May 1982 led to a meeting between Larzelere and her future second husband, Florida highway patrol trooper James O. Matheny. They married two months later, but Larzelere's erratic behavior prompted fellow deputies to show Matheny the 1975 police report on the Mathis shooting. The officer's search of their home uncovered several of his wife's aliases, and a computer check revealed her history of bad checks, outstanding warrants, and larceny. Three months after the marriage, Matheny moved out and divorced her in February 1983. The divorce had not been finalized when she married Frank Finley Ferry in a biker bar on February 7, 1983. About a month later she called the sheriff to report that Ferry had struck her and threatened her with a shotgun. Authorities arrived at her home to find her unconscious on the bedroom floor with a front tooth broken out. Ferry was arrested, but bargained aggravated assault and battery charges down to a misdemeanor. At Larzelere's request, the marriage was annulled in August 1983.

Virginia met Dr. Norman Larzelere in Daytona Beach in 1985 and easily persuaded the successful dentist that she and her children had been abused by her past husband. Employed as a bookkeeper in a construction company, Virginia was charged with embezzling $50,000 from the firm, fired, and was in the process of having criminal charges filed against her when she married Larzelere in DeLand, Florida, on June 14, 1985. The dentist bought her out of prosecution by paying the company $34,000 in restitution. The respected dentist's generosity, however, did not

end there. He formally adopted Virginia's children and lavished expensive presents on stepson Jason. Chronically in trouble, Jason was expelled from numerous private schools, sold and used drugs, and was greatly bothered by his homosexuality. More unsettling, perhaps, was his relationship with his mother which sister Jessica described as more "like man and wife." (She later recanted this testimony.) Though a teenager, Jason allegedly still slept with his mother and often bought her sexy lingerie. Following the birth of Larzelere and Virginia's son, Benjamin, in May 1986, many people hinted darkly that Jason was the child's true father.

Shortly after Virginia assumed the position of business manager in Larzelere's Edgewater practice, formerly contented patients began complaining about billing irregularities. Besides billing for work not performed, she also forged the doctor's name on prescriptions for valium and amphetamines. Virginia used the embezzled money to have her breasts enlarged, began openly having affairs with several men, and admitted to her family that she wished Larzelere would die. At her trial, some of her lovers testified that she tried to solicit their aid in having her husband killed. Bowing to patients' complaints, the Florida Department of Professional Regulation recommended that Dr. Larzelere be fined and have his license suspended or revoked. Stunned, Larzelere decided to file for divorce in late 1989, but withdrew the petition after his second son David was born in November 1989.

Almost immediately after Larzelere's murder, Virginia became the prime suspect when her description of the gunman and his movements following the crime differed radically from other witnesses in the office who described the masked killer as tall and thin rather than heavy-set. Police looked closely at Jason (6'1", 135 pounds) after several people claimed he could walk unaided even though he was allegedly partially crippled as a result of an earlier car accident. Throughout the weeks following the murder, Virginia tried unsuccessfully to claim some money from her husband's $2.1 million life insurance policy. In an attempt to rouse public sympathy for her family, Virginia held press conferences in which she berated the Edgewater police for discounting her version of the murder. Police were similarly dubious over her contention that an unknown gunman had fired three shots at her on April 2, 1991.

The case broke on May 2, 1991, when 19-year-old Steven Heidle, a paid companion to Jason, admitted under questioning that he and Kristin Palmieri, a worker in Larzelere's office, knew Virginia and Jason committed the murder. According to Heidle, Virginia agreed to pay Jason $200,000 after he pulled the trigger on his stepfather. Acting under her instructions, Heidle and Palmieri poured muriatic acid on a shotgun and a pistol to destroy fingerprints and encased the weapons in concrete. Heidle led authorities to the bridge over Interstate 95 from which he had tossed the block into the tidal basin and divers recovered the weapons. Virginia was arrested at her home in DeLand on May 4, 1991. Jason turned himself in two days later. Both were charged with first degree murder and held without bond.

On October 4, 1991, a judge ruled the pair could be tried separately and after numerous delays jury selection began in Virginia's trial in Daytona Beach on January 27, 1992. Arguing

that Virginia masterminded the murder and Jason carried it out, the prosecution bolstered their case against the widow by calling her ex-lovers who testified she offered them money to have her husband killed. Granted immunity from prosecution, Heidle and Palmieri's testimony was damning. According to Palmieri, Virginia claimed to have kissed her dying husband to prevent him from calling out Jason's name and thereby identifying him as the gunman. Afterwards, Jason allegedly joked about the killing and reenacted his stepfather's terrified flight through the office. Attempting to discredit the prosecution's star witnesses, the defense accused them of committing the murder. On February 24, 1992, the jury retired at 2:34 p.m. and returned with a verdict of guilty that evening at 8:55 p.m. The jury recommended by a vote of 7–5 that Virginia be sentenced to death. Formal sentencing was postponed pending the outcome of Jason's first degree murder trial.

Convinced of his son's innocence, Jason's birth father, Henry Mathis, mortgaged his house to hire a new defense team to represent the teenager. The trial was moved to Palatka, Florida, where a jury was empaneled on August 21, 1992. Jason's new attorney skillfully raised the spectre of reasonable doubt by pointing the finger at Heidle and Palmieri as the killers of the Edgewater dentist and by questioning the description of the gunman as being "like Jason" which was offered by a witness to the shooting. Larzelere, he contended, was killed either by the state's witnesses, a South Florida hitman, or an unknown gunman. The jury received the case on September 19, 1992, and the next day at 7:10 p.m. Jason was acquitted of being the triggerman in the killing. Describing Virginia Larzelere as a "conniving and manipulative" woman who murdered "to satisfy her greed for money," a judge on May 11, 1993, sentenced her to death by electrocution. On March 28, 1996, the Florida Supreme Court unanimously upheld her conviction.

362. Butcher, Lee. *For a Mother's Love.* New York: Windsor, 1992. 372 pp., [10]pp. of plates: ill.; 18 cm. ("Pinnacle Books"); paperback.
    "The shocking true story of twisted love and murder behind the death of Dr. Norman Larzelere."—Cover.

Legere, Allan Joseph
(a.k.a. "The Monster [or] Madman of the Miramichi," "Fernand Savoie")

Born February 13, 1948, in Chatham Head, New Brunswick, Canada. Thief. Canada's Miramichi River area; 5 murders (suspected of several others); knife, ligature strangulation, bludgeon, asphyxiation; June 1986– November 1989.
    "Up yours, judge."
    Canadian-born serial rapist and killer who terrorized towns in the Miramichi River area in the late 1980s. Allan Legere, 41, was serving a life sentence for a June 1986 torture-killing when he escaped from prison guards on May 3, 1989, during a visit to a hospital in Moncton, New Brunswick. Exploiting his detailed knowledge of the hills surrounding his boyhood home in the communities around the Miramichi River, the muscular Legere launched a seven-month campaign of terror in northeastern Canada which claimed four lives. On May 29, 1989, three weeks after Legere's escape, firefighters answered an alarm in Chat-

ham and discovered the brutalized body of 75-year-old shopkeeper Annie Flam in the smoldering ruins of her house. Her sister-in-law, who survived being strangled, beaten with a chain, raped twice, and burned, could not identify her masked assailant. On October 14, 1989, firemen were called to a blaze in Newcastle, directly across the Miramichi from Chatham. Inside the two-story frame house, the bodies of Donna and Linda Daughney, sisters aged 45 and 41, were found in an upstairs bedroom. One woman had been raped while both were beaten to death and their faces slashed beyond recognition. Finally, on November 16, 1989, Royal Canadian Mounted Police officers discovered the beaten and stomped body of the Reverend James Smith, a 69-year-old Roman Catholic priest, in the church rectory in Chatham Head near Newcastle. Fear swept through the area and one of the largest manhunts in Canadian history was launched to catch the so-called "Monster of the Miramichi." The seven month chase ended on November 29, 1989, near Nelson-Miramichi when Legere, who had been living in the area's dense woods, was apprehended driving a tractor-trailer truck towards the airport in Chatham. Legere's trial on four counts of first degree murder began in Burton on August 28, 1991. In the main, the prosecution based its case against Legere primarily on the DNA evidence recovered from the semen found on two of the female victims and the woman who survived the sexual assault. When the DNA in the semen was compared with that in blood and hair samples taken from Legere it was determined that there was just a one-in-310 million possibility that the matching genetic patterns could have come from anyone but the defendant. In addition, glasses found at the scene of one of the murders perfectly matched Legere's prescription. Two months, several outbursts by Legere, and 243 prosecution witnesses later, a jury found the "Monster of the Miramichi" guilty of all counts on November 3, 1991. The trial judge, not known for commenting on jury decisions, told jurors: "Don't lose any sleep over your verdict." On January 15, 1993, Legere was granted leave by the New Brunswick court of appeal to appeal his convictions on the grounds of the admissibility of the DNA "fingerprinting." While in the exercise yard of Ste. Anne des Plaines, a federal penitentiary near Montreal, Legere was stabbed with a homemade knife by another inmate on November 27, 1994. Treated and released for superficial wounds, Legere refused to make a statement to investigators. Depending upon the outcome of his appeal, Legere is eligible for parole in 2015.

363. Fraser, Raymond, and Matchett, Todd. *Confessions of a Young Criminal: The Story Behind Allan Legere and the Murder at Black River Bridge*. Fredericton, N.B.: New Ireland Press, 1994. [Physical description unavailable at press time.]

364. MacLean, Rick, and Veniot, André. *Terror: Murder and Panic in New Brunswick*. Toronto: McClelland & Stewart, 1990. 189 pp., [8]pp. of plates: ill.; 18 cm. ("An M&S paperback"); paperback.

365. MacLean, Rick; Veniot, André; Waters, Shaun. *Terror's End: Allan Legere on Trial*. Toronto: McClelland & Stewart, 1992. 358 pp., [16]pp. of plates: ill.; 18 cm. ("An M&S paperback original"); paperback.

366. Mitchell, Sandra. *The Miramichi Axe Murder: Was Robbie Cunningham the Scapegoat for Allan Legere?* Halifax, N.S.:

Nimbus, 1992. xii, 218 pp.: ill., map, ports.; 18 cm.; paperback.

LeGeros, Bernard John (a.k.a. "The Death Mask Murderer")

Born April 6, 1962. Art gallery employee. Tomkins Cove, Long Island, New York; 1 murder; AR-7 rifle; February 23, 1985.

"When the flames shot up, it was as if the gates of Hell had opened up and I was the Keeper."—A statement allegedly made by LeGeros to a friend in which he described the burning of Vesti's body

Homosexual son of a United Nations official convicted of the sado-masochistic sex killing of a male model in what the press dubbed "The Death Mask Murder." On March 17, 1985, hikers on the wooded grounds of an estate in Rockland County, Long Island, owned by United Nations official John LeGeros found the charred skeletal remains of a man wearing only a hooded leather bondage mask hidden in a Revolutionary War-era smokehouse on the property. The victim, identified by a ring as Eigel Dag Vesti, a 26-year-old Norwegian student at Manhattan's Fashion Institute of Technology and part-time model, had been reported missing weeks before. A frequenter of homosexual sadomasochistic clubs on the Lower West Side, Vesti had been shot twice in the back of the head with a .22 caliber rifle, then burned. Police arrested Bernard John LeGeros, the 22-year-old son of the U.N. official, on March 24, 1985, after he provided them with theories concerning the murder. In a detailed written confession, LeGeros admitted killing Vesti and implicated his 39-year-old employer, Andrew Crispo, the owner of a Manhattan art gallery bearing his name. According to LeGeros, they lured Vesti to the estate where they alternately engaged in sadomasochistic sex and beat the model for hours. Afterwards, they led Vesti (naked except for the leather mask) on a dog leash to the smokehouse where they forced him to kneel and beg for his life. LeGeros then shot him twice in the head and set the corpse on fire with gasoline. Eight days later, LeGeros returned and torched the body again using twigs and logs. Acting on LeGeros' directions, police recovered the murder weapon from an air conditioning unit in Crispo's East 57th Street gallery. Crispo denied any part in the killing and under state law his employee's confession could not be used against him.

Opening statements in LeGeros' second degree murder trial began in New City, New York, on September 3, 1985. According to the prosecution's theory of the case Vesti was murdered by LeGeros as part of a bizarre sadomasochistic sex ritual. A confidant of the accused testified that LeGeros had admitted cutting Vesti's chest open, removing the heart, and drinking his blood. The defense argued that the uncharged Crispo was the mastermind behind the sex murder who manipulated LeGeros like a slave by supplying his cocaine addiction. At the time of the murder, LeGeros was so high on the drug that he was not responsible for his actions, a view supported by two defense psychiatrists. LeGeros was found guilty on September 27, 1985, and was subsequently sentenced to the maximum term of 25 years to life. In November 1985 Crispo was convicted of income tax evasion and served three

years in prison. While still serving time, he was charged with the unrelated sodomy and sexual torture of a New York University graduate student. Although LeGeros testified against him, Crispo was acquitted on October 16, 1988, after a jury deliberated six days. On July 22, 1989, Crispo's $2.5 million home in Southampton filled with his $7 million art collection was leveled by a gas leak explosion. Crispo subsequently sued the Long Island Lighting Company and was awarded $8.6 million damages in February 1991. Although technically still a suspect in the Vesti killing, Crispo has at the time of this writing not been charged.

367. France, David. *Bag of Toys: Sex, Scandal, and the Death Mask Murder.* New York: Warner Books, 1992. 350 pp., [8]pp. of plates: ill.; 24 cm.

_____. [Same as 367.] New York: Windsor, 1994. 470 pp., [8]pp. of plates: ill.; 18 cm. ("Pinnacle Books"); paperback.

Unflinching look at the sensational "Death Mask Murder" that places it within the context of Manhattan's homosexual sadomasochistic club scene. The "Bag of Toys" of the title refers to the sexual devices Crispo often carried with him. France, a senior editor at News Inc. and a winner of the Gay Press Association Award for feature writing, reconstructs dialogue from police notes, court depositions, and other published sources. Andrew Crispo, who France suggests escaped justice, refused to be interviewed for the book. Includes an excellent index.

Leonski, Edward Joseph (a.k.a. "The Singing Strangler," "The Brown-Out Strangler")

Born December 12, 1917, in New York, New York. Executed November 9,

1942. American soldier. Melbourne, Australia: 3 murders; strangulation; May 1942.
"She had a lovely voice. I wanted that voice. I choked her."—From Leonski's confession

American soldier stationed in Australia during World War II who strangled three women during a 15-day period. Shortly after the first contingent of U.S. soldiers landed on Australian soil, the infamous "Brown-Out Murders" (so-called because the streets of Melbourne were dimly lighted as a precaution against Japanese air raids) began on May 4, 1942, with the discovery of the body of 40-year-old Ivy Violet McLeod in a doorway in the Albert Park district. McLeod, strangled in what appeared by the savage disarray of her clothes to have been a sex crime, had not been raped. Pauline Buchan Thompson, 31, the wife of a police constable, was the second victim. Her body was found on the front steps of her boarding house on May 9, 1942. Like McLeod, Thompson had been strangled and displayed, but not raped. Similarities in the murders suggested to Australian authorities the work of one man. They focused their investigation on American servicemen after a witness reported seeing Thompson drinking with one shortly before her body was found. On May 18, 1942, the strangled and displayed body of Gladys Lillian Hosking, 40, was found lying in wet yellow clay by an air-raid trench near Camp Pell, an American installation. An Australian soldier reported seeing a U.S. serviceman covered in the distinctive clay the night before the body was found. Inquiries led U.S. and Australian officials to Edward Joseph Leonski, a 24-year-old soldier well known for his alcoholic binges and feats of physical strength.

Clay found on his uniform and bunk matched that at the murder scene. Leonski subsequently confessed under interrogation to murdering all three women. In an unprecedented move, the Australian government agreed to let the United States military try Leonski even though the crimes violated the criminal law of the Commonwealth. Tried in July 1942, Leonski pleaded not guilty to the murders. Psychiatric testimony suggested that although Leonski was a psychopath who confessed to killing his victims in order to take their voices, he was sane at the time of the murders. The son of alcoholic parents, Leonski's acute alcoholism was discussed as possibly motivating his murderous aggression. On July 17, 1942, a jury of ten officers found Leonski guilty and sentenced him to death by hanging. General Douglas MacArthur affirmed the order and Leonski was hanged at Pentridge Prison in the suburbs of Melbourne on November 9, 1942. Originally buried in the "isolated section" of Melbourne's Springvale Cemetery, Leonski's body was disinterred numerous times before being permanently buried on April 14, 1949, in the Post Cemetery at Schofield Barracks, Honolulu, Hawaii.

368. Chapman, Ivan. *Private Eddie Leonski: The Brownout Strangler.* Sydney, N.S.W.: Hale & Ironmonger, 1982. xiv, 253 pp.; ill.; 23 cm. (Also in paperback.)
Chapman interviewed several of the extant principals in the Leonski case in this well balanced account which also discusses the complex legal issue of jurisdiction involving U.S. military personnel accused of violating Australian criminal law.

369. Mallon, Andrew. *Leonski: The Brownout Murders.* Collingwood, Vic.: Outback Press, 1979. 202 pp.; 22 cm.

Mallon created characters and changed the names of many of the principals in this turgid "docu-novel."

Leopold, Nathan Freudenthal, Jr.

(a.k.a. "Babe," "George Johnson," "Morton D. Ballard")

Born November 19, 1904. Died August 30, 1971. University student. Chicago, Illinois; 1 murder; bludgeon (chisel); May 21, 1924.

Films: Rope (US, 1948), a Transatlantic production directed by Alfred Hitchcock based on the Patrick Hamilton play *Rope's End*. Cast includes James Stewart (Rupert Caldell), John Dall (Shaw Brandon), and Farley Granger (Philip). *Compulsion* (US, 1959), a 20th Century–Fox film directed by Richard Fleischer based on Meyer Levin's book of the same title. Cast includes Orson Welles (Jonathan Wilks/ Clarence Darrow), Dean Stockwell (Judd Steiner/Nathan Leopold), and Bradford Dillman (Artie Straus/ Richard Loeb). *Swoon* (US, 1992), an Intolerance Productions and American Playhouse Theatrical Films coproduction directed by Tom Kalin. Cast includes Daniel Schlachet (Richard Loeb), Craig Chester (Nathan Leopold, Jr.), Paul Connor (Bobby Franks), and Robert Read (Clarence Darrow).

Theatre: Rope a.k.a. *Rope's End* (1929) by Patrick Hamilton. *Compulsion* (1959) by Meyer Levin based on his novel of the same title. *Never the Sinner* (1985), a play by John Logan directed by Terry McCabe, premiered at Chicago's Stormfield Theatre on September 10, 1985. Cast includes Denis O'Hare (Nathan Leopold, Jr.), Bryan Stillman (Richard Loeb), and Richard Burton Brown (Clarence Darrow).

"Why should we have to be told what to do by a bunch of illiterate farmers? They're nothing but little Hitlers."—Leopold referring to prison guards

A senseless thrill killing committed by two brilliant university students who were convinced of their own intellectual superiority. Nathan "Babe" Leopold, a 19-year-old University of Chicago law student with an IQ of 210, and Richard "Dicky" Loeb, an 18-year-old student at the same university, were both the pampered sons of wealthy German-Jewish parents living in Chicago. Leopold, who graduated from the University of Chicago at 18 and spoke five languages fluently, was a devotee of the German philosopher Friedrich Nietzsche and embraced the thinker's notion that men of superior intellect, the so-called Übermensch, were above the laws of the common run of man. Loeb, handsome and charming, with an interest in committing the "perfect crime," perfectly fulfilled Leopold's vision of the Nietzschean superman. The pair began their criminal career with a series of burglaries and supposedly when Leopold wanted to stop stealing, Loeb held him in thrall by granting the genius sexual favors. As proof of their intellectual superiority, the pair (apparently at Loeb's instigation) meticulously planned the "perfect" kidnapping/murder, selecting at the very last moment as their victim 14-year-old Bobby Franks, the son of a millionaire pawnshop owner and reportedly a distant relative of Leopold. On May 21, 1924, the pair rented a car, drove to the southside Chicago suburb of Kenwood and parked near a school where they selected Franks off the street. Franks accepted Loeb's offer of a ride and sat with him in the backseat as Leopold drove. Without warning,

Loeb smashed Franks four times in the face with a cold chisel purchased the day before from a hardware store. Loeb tied up the dying boy, stuffed pieces of cloth into his mouth, covered him with a robe, and left him on the floor of the car as he and Leopold stopped for sandwiches. Under cover of darkness, the pair drove the dead boy to a secluded area called Panhandle Tracks where a swamp drained into a culvert. Stripping Franks, they poured hydrochloric acid over the boy's face and genitals to hinder identification then stuffed his body into a drain pipe.

Later that night they phoned Franks' father informing him that his son had been kidnapped and to expect a ransom demand by post the next day. The ransom note, typed on a typewriter Loeb had stolen from the University of Michigan while a student there, demanded $10,000 for the return of the child and gave detailed instructions on how to drop the money. The note was signed "George Johnson." Before Mr. Franks could respond to the demand, his son's body was found by workmen on May 22, 1924. Nearby, police found a pair of horn-rimmed spectacles that Leopold had inadvertently dropped from the pocket of his coat as he was helping Loeb dispose of the body. As part of the massive search for the boy's killer which ensued, investigators traced the glasses back to the manufacturer. Though the glasses were a common prescription with a popular frame-type, the hinge connecting the earpiece to the nosepiece was a unique item present on only three frames sold in the area. After clearing the other two owners of the identical glasses, police questioned Leopold who was unable to produce his pair. Loeb was also questioned and while initially bluff with police, later confessed to the mur-

ders naming Leopold as the actual killer. Hearing himself named as the murderer, Leopold confessed, fingering his friend and lover as the killer. When the pair was reunited, Loeb allegedly said to Leopold, "We're both in for the same ride, Babe, so we might as well ride together."

The boys' wealthy fathers retained noted defense attorney Clarence Darrow, then 67, at a reported fee of $1 million. Charged with two capital crimes (murder and kidnapping for ransom), the thrill killers were damned by a public eager to see them executed for their senseless and arrogant crime. As the "trial of the century" opened in Chicago on July 21, 1924, Darrow opted to forego a jury trial in favor of convincing a lone judge that the killers were suffering from mental illness at the time they murdered Bobby Franks. Darrow used the trial as a forum to attack the practice of capital punishment and his eloquence succeeded in persuading the judge to spare the lives of Leopold and Loeb. Noting the young age of the defendants, the judge on September 10, 1924, sentenced the pair to life imprisonment for the murder and 99 years for the kidnapping. The convicted killers were initially sent to the Illinois State Prison where Leopold was first assigned to the rattan factory then later made a clerical worker in the shoe factory. Loeb was put to work in the chair factory and later named straw boss over other inmates cleaning up the prison yard. Both men were ultimately transferred to the prison at Stateville where in January 1932 they started a school for prisoners. Loeb directed the school and taught English composition, history, and Spanish while Leopold ran the prison library. Both men adjusted well to life behind bars, but on January 28,

1936, Loeb was attacked in the prison shower by James Day, his former cellmate who was serving ten years for robbery. Loeb was slashed 58 times with a straight razor and died, with Leopold by his side, in the prison infirmary. Day later told a guard that he attacked Loeb because of the man's homosexual advances, but a more plausible explanation seems to be that the convicted robber was angry at Loeb for no longer sharing his provisions with him. Day was subsequently tried for Loeb's murder and acquitted. After his friend's death, Leopold took several college courses, became an X ray technician, and volunteered to work with a team of University of Chicago research scientists searching for a cure for malaria. After serving 33 years in prison, he was granted parole on March 13, 1958. Sponsored by the Church of the Brethren, Leopold went to a hospital in Puerto Rico operated by that organization and worked as an X ray technician. Two years later, he earned an M.S. at the University of Puerto Rico, taught math courses there, and conducted research on leprosy for the school of medicine while writing a book on the birds of Puerto Rico. He married in 1961 and when his parole ended in 1963 traveled extensively. Leopold, who died in San Juan at the age of 66 on August 31, 1971, willed his body to the University of Puerto Rico for research purposes.

370. Darrow, Clarence. *Attorney Clarence Darrow's Plea for Mercy and Prosecutor Robert E. Crowe's Demand for the Death Penalty in the Leopold-Loeb Case, the Crime of the Century.* Chicago: Wilson, 1924. 163 pp.; 23 cm.

371. _____. *Clarence Darrow's Plea in Defense of Loeb and Leopold: August 22, 23, and 25, 1924.* Big Blue Book no. B-

20. Girard, Kan.: Haldeman-Julius, 1926. 69 pp.; 22 cm.; pamphlet.

372. _____. *Clarence Darrow's Sentencing Speech in State of Illinois v. Leopold and Loeb.* Classics of the Courtroom; vol. 8. Hopkins, Minn.: Professional Education Group, 1988. iii, 89 leaves; 21 cm.

373. Gertz, Elmer. *A Handful of Clients.* Chicago: Follett, 1965. xv, 379 pp.; 22 cm.

Gertz was the attorney responsible for obtaining parole for Leopold and also represented him in an unsuccessful libel suit against Meyer Levin, the author of the fact-based, but fictionalized account of the case *Compulsion* (see 376).

374. Higdon, Hal. *The Crime of the Century: The Leopold and Loeb Case.* New York: Putnam, 1975. 380 pp., [8] leaves of plates: ill.; 24 cm.

Authoritative, well-researched account of the pair's relationship and the murder that sprung from it. Includes extensive bibliographic notes and an index. Highly recommended.

375. Leopold, Nathan F., Jr. *Life Plus 99 Years.* Introduction by Erle Stanley Gardner. 1st ed. Garden City, N.Y.: Doubleday, 1958. 381 pp.; 25 cm.

_____. [Same as 375.] Introduction by Erle Stanley Gardner. New York: Popular Library, 1958. 415 pp.; 18 cm.; paperback.

_____. [Same as 375.] Introduction by Erle Stanley Gardner. Westport, Conn.: Greenwood Press, 1974. 381 pp.; 23 cm. (Reprint of 1958 Doubleday edition.)

Leopold's prison autobiography does not talk too much about the "Crime of the Century," but rather dwells on his adjustment to prison life. The book concludes on November 19, 1957, with the 53 year old being turned down for parole. Interesting for Leopold's assessment of Loeb, a man who "didn't have the faintest trace of conventional morality" and never "to the day of his death, felt truly remorseful for what we had done."

376. Levin, Meyer. *Compulsion.* New York: Simon and Schuster, 1956. 495 pp.; 22 cm. (Various eds.)
Well known and highly regarded fictionalized account of the crime. Leopold subsequently sued Levin for libel, but lost.

377. McKernan, Maureen, ed. *The Amazing Crime and Trial of Leopold and Loeb.* Introduction by Clarence Darrow and Walter Bachrach. Chicago: The Plymouth Court Press, 1924. 380 pp.: ill.; 20 cm.

_____. [Same as 377.] Introduction by Clarence Darrow and Walter Bachrach. New York: New American Library, 1957. 300 pp., [8]pp. of plates: ill.; 18 cm. ("A Signet book"); paperback.

_____. [Same as 377.] Introduction by Clarence Darrow and Walter Bachrach. The Notable Trials Library. Birmingham, Ala.: Leslie B. Adams, Jr., 1989. 380 pp., [14] pp. of plates: ill.; 20 cm.
An early account which excludes much of the case's sexual material as well as Loeb's confession, though not Leopold's. McKernan similarly edits many of the other more sensational documents relating to the case.

378. Sellers, Alan V. *The Leopold-Loeb Case: With Excerpts from the Evidence of the Alienists and Including the Arguments to the Court by Counsel for the People and the Defense.* Brunswick, Ga.: Classic, 1926. 321 pp.; ill.; 20 cm.

379. Urstein, Maurycy. *Leopold and Loeb: A Psychiatric-Psychological Study.* New York: Lecouver Press, 1924. 132 pp.; 21 cm.

380. Yaffe, James. *Nothing but the Night.* 1st ed. Boston: Little, Brown, 1957. 336 pp.; 21 cm. ("An Atlantic Press Monthly book.")

_____. [Same as 380.] London: Cape, 1958. 294 pp.; 21 cm.

_____. [Same as 380.] Boston: Bantam Books, 1959. 248 pp.; 19 cm. ("A Bantam giant"); paperback.
A novel suggested by the Leopold-Loeb murder case.

Light, Ronald Vivian (*acquitted;* a.k.a. "The Green Bicycle Murderer," "Leonard Estelle")

Born October 19, 1885, in Leicester, Leicestershire, England. Died May 15, 1975. Mathematics instructor. Little Stretton, Leicestershire, England; 1 murder (acquitted); gun; July 5, 1919.

"Damn and blast that canal."

Former military man invalided out of the army for shell shock; acquitted in "the Green Bicycle Murder." On July 5, 1919, the body of Annie Bella Wright, a 21-year-old tire factory worker from Stoughton, was found lying near her bicycle along Gartree Road outside of Little Stretton in Leicestershire, England. Wright had been shot once in the head and a spent .455 caliber shell casing was found nearby. Earlier that day, Wright was seen in the company of a man riding a green B.S.A. bicycle. Police circulars, describing the man and his bicycle, posted throughout Leicestershire failed to produce a suspect even after authorities raised the original £5 reward to £20. On February 23, 1920, more than seven months after the murder, a horse-drawn barge on the Old River Soar near the factory where Wright had been employed churned up the frame and front wheel of a green B.S.A. bicycle. Later, a revolver holster and ammunition of the type believed to have killed Wright was dredged up from the industrial canal. Although an effort had been made to file off the bicycle's serial numbers, an expert in Leicester was able to detect a second serial on the bike's front fork. Armed with this information, police traced ownership to Ronald Vivian Light, a 34-year-old mathematics master at Dean Close School in Cheltenham. Interviewed on March 4, 1920, Light stated that he did not know Wright and initially denied ever owning a green bicycle. Eventually, after being picked out of a police identity parade, Light admitted that the bicycle was his and that he had met Wright on the day of her death. Later reading of her murder, Light panicked and disposed of his bike, army holster, and ammunition.

Light's murder trial began on June 9, 1920, at the Leicester County courthouse. Though the circumstantial evidence against the defendant seemed insurmountable, Sir Edward Marshall Hall was able to raise doubt as to the caliber and source of the bullet which killed Wright. He argued that a .455 caliber bullet fired at close range would leave a much larger wound than the one found above the victim's left cheek. An admission from a firearms expert that the bullet could have been fired from a rifle *or* a pistol was expanded by Hall into a suggestion that a stray rifle shot could have accidentally killed Wright. Light proved to be an excellent witness in his own defense during the five hours he spent in the box. While admitting that he was wrong to initially deny ownership of the bicycle, Light convincingly maintained that his further acts of concealment were designed to protect his invalid mother from shock. In his closing speech, Hall noted that Wright had not been sexually molested, the only apparent motive Light could have had for killing a woman he met only hours before. Light was acquitted on July 11, 1920. The 90-year-old died on May 15, 1975, at the home of his stepdaughter at Kingsdown, Sittingbourne.

381. East, C. Wendy. *The Green Bicycle Murder.* Stroud: Alan Sutton, 1993. xiii, 202 pp.: ill., 1 facsim., 1 map, ports.; 26 cm.

_____. [Same as 381.] Dover, N.H.: Alan Sutton, 1993. xiii, 202 pp.: ill., 1 facsim., 1 map, ports.; 26 cm.

Definitive study of the case debunks the widely held myth that Light was an "officer and a gentleman" and concludes that he more than likely murdered Bella Wright. Includes bibliography and index.

382. Wakefield, H. Russell. *The Green Bicycle Case.* London: P. Allan, 1930. 152 pp.: ill., facsim., ports.; 23 cm.

Wakefield, then bishop of Birmingham, relied on contemporary newspaper accounts of the case and the cooperation of Detective Superintendent Taylor who showed him about the Leicester district. Wakefield's assessment of the defendant: "It is beyond dispute that Ronald Light behaved most foolishly, that he hopelessly lost his head and jeopardized his neck, but his punishment was out of all proportion to his failings, for to be tried for his life and all that that fearful phrase denotes is the direst fate an innocent man can suffer, except the fate of being actually condemned to death, in such circumstances."

"Lindbergh Baby Kidnapping"
see Hauptmann, Bruno Richard

List, John Emil
(a.k.a. "Robert Peter Clark")

Born September 17, 1925, in Bay City, Michigan. Accountant, insurance salesman. Westfield, New Jersey; 5 murders; .22 caliber Colt revolver and a 1918 German 9mm Steyr semiautomatic; November 9, 1971.

Television: "Judgment Day: The John List Story," a two-hour, made-for-television movie, originally aired on CBS on February 23, 1993. Cast includes Robert Blake (John List) and Beverly D'Angelo (Helen List).

"It may seem cowardly to have

always shot from behind, but I didn't want any of them to know even at the last second that I had to do this to them."—Excerpt from List's letter left at the scene of the murders

Mass murderer of his family who remained a fugitive for 18 years until a segment on a popular television program led to his arrest. On November 9, 1971, John List, a 46-year-old unemployed accountant, methodically shot to death his aged mother, 85, his sick wife, 45, and his three teenaged children in their heavily mortgaged 18-room Victorian mansion home in Westfield, New Jersey. Leaving his mother's body in a third floor hallway (she was too heavy to move), List carefully arranged his wife and three children on Boy Scout sleeping bags in the ballroom, turned the heat down to preserve their bodies, switched on several lights, tuned the radio to a classical station, and then left the house to begin a new life as "Robert Peter Clark." Their bodies were found 28 days later along with a five page confessional letter written by the devoutly religious List to his Lutheran minister. According to the handwritten document, List murdered his family not only to save them from the embarrassment of having to go on welfare, but also because he feared that they were falling away from their Christian faith. He added, "Of course, Mother got involved because doing what I did to my family would have been a tremendous shock to her at this age."

Two days after the discovery, December 9, 1971, List's car was traced to New York's Kennedy Airport where the trail went cold for over 18 years. List had fled to Denver, Colorado, after the murders and worked for several years as a cook before meeting divorcée Delores Cook at a church-spon-

sored singles social in spring 1977. Unaware of his true identity, Cook married "Clark" in November 1985 and they relocated to Midlothian, Virginia, in 1989 where List found work in an accounting firm in nearby Richmond. On May 21, 1989, the popular television program "America's Most Wanted" aired a segment on the 1971 List murders which featured a bust of the wanted man as he might presently look rendered by Frank A. Bender, a Philadelphia forensic sculptor. Recognition by a former Denver neighbor of "Robert Clark" led to List's arrest by FBI officers at his Richmond office on June 1, 1989. Initially denying that he was List, the murderer's identity was verified by fingerprints and a mastoidectomy scar. On April 12, 1990, after seven days of testimony, List was found guilty in an Elizabeth, New Jersey, courtroom of five first degree murders and subsequently ordered to serve five consecutive life sentences. In imposing the maximum sentence, the judge told the mass murderer "The name of John Emil List will be eternally synonymous with concepts of selfishness, horror, and evil." In June 1993 the New Jersey appeals court upheld List's 1990 conviction.

383. Benford, Timothy B., and Johnson, James P. *Righteous Carnage: The List Murders.* New York: Scribners; Toronto: Maxwell Macmillan Canada; New York: Maxwell Macmillan International, 1991. vii, 310 pp.: ill.; 24 cm.

In the best of the books on the case, the authors portray List as an obsessive-compulsive whose inability to effectively deal with people led to the loss of his job and ultimately the mass murder of his family. The photographs section includes a floor plan of the List home marking the location and methodical placement of the bodies in "Breeze Knoll," the List's mansion at 431 Hillside Avenue in Westfield, New Jersey. Well written and documented with access to the text provided through an excellent index.

384. Ryzuk, Mary S. *Thou Shalt Not Kill.* Popular Library ed. New York: Popular Library, 1990. xvii, 509 pp.: ill.; 17 cm.; paperback.

Lengthy novelization of the case based on police files and newspaper accounts. Includes an extensive bibliography primarily comprised of New Jersey and New York newspaper coverage.

385. Sharkey, Joe. *Death Sentence: The Inside Story of the John List Murders.* New York: Penguin Group, 1990. viii, 305 pp., [16]pp. of plates: ill.; 18 cm. ("A Signet book"); paperback.

Uninspired account of the List murders quickly written so as to be published immediately after his 1990 conviction. As such, the trial is dealt with in an "Epilogue."

Loeb, Richard R.
(a.k.a. "Dickie," "Louis Mason," "Morton D. Ballard")

Born June 11, 1905. Died January 28, 1936. University student. Chicago, Illinois; 1 murder; bludgeon (chisel); May 21, 1924.

"If I were going to murder anybody, I would murder just such a cocky little son of a bitch as Bobby Franks."—Loeb's statement to a Chicago detective prior to being arrested for the boy's murder; *see also* Leopold, Nathan Freudenthal, Jr.

Logan, Michael David
(a.k.a. "Indian," "Mr. Clean," "George [and] Mike Richardson")

Born circa 1953 in Detroit, Michigan. Stablehand, horse wrangler. Ari-

zona; 1 murder; bludgeon (rock); January 29, 1981; *see also* Gillies, Jesse James.

"Lonely Hearts Killings (or) Murders" *see* Fernandez, Raymond Martinez (and) Beck, Martha Jule (Seabrook)

Lonergan, Wayne Thomas

Born circa 1917 in Toronto, Ontario, Canada. Died January 2, 1986. Royal Canadian Air Force Cadet. New York City, New York; 1 murder; strangulation, bludgeon; October 24, 1943.

Bisexual social climber convicted after a sensational trial in 1944 of murdering his heiress wife. On October 24, 1943, Wayne Lonergan, a 25-year-old cadet in the Royal Canadian Air Force, strangled then bludgeoned his wife Patricia Burton Lonergan, heiress to the Burton-Bernheimer beer fortune, to death with a silver candelabra. Her naked body was found in her luxurious Manhattan triplex apartment on East 51st Street. Weeks before the murder, the heiress had filed for divorce and moved to cut Lonergan out of her will. Lonergan's confession, obtained after a marathon interrogation session, painted a decadent picture of New York "cafe society." An arraignment in early 1944 resulted in a mistrial before a single juror was seated. A second trial before the General Sessions Court in March 1944 attracted international newspaper coverage in which lurid details of Lonergan's bisexuality and drunken carousings were minutely detailed. Lonergan blamed an overly possessive mother with forcing him into occasional homosexual periods and in fact, a male companion testified that the would-be playboy came to his apartment immediately after the murder to change clothes. Found guilty of second degree murder on March 31, 1944, Lonergan was sentenced to 35 years to life. In Sing Sing, he instituted legal action to claim a part of his wife's $7 million estate, but a court ruled that because of his life sentence he was considered legally dead. In 1954, Lonergan's son inherited the Bernheimer fortune originally intended for his mother. Lonergan was paroled in 1967 on condition that he return to his native Canada. On January 2, 1986, the 67-year-old died of cancer in Toronto.

386. Heimer, Mel. *The Girl in Murder Flat.* New York: Fawcett, 1955. 141 pp.; 18 cm. ("A Gold Medal original"); paperback.

387. Perry, Hamilton Darby. *A Chair for Wayne Lonergan.* New York: Macmillan, 1971. xii, 290 pp.: ill.; 22 cm.

Pro-Lonergan account written to encourage a reconsideration of his case.

Lucan, Lord
(a.k.a. "Richard John Bingham," "Lucky")

Born December 18, 1934, in London, England. Socialite, professional gambler. London, England; 1 murder; bludgeon; November 7, 1974.

Television: "Murder in Belgravia— The Lucan Affair" (1994) aired on BBC1 on November 2, 1994. "The Trial of Lord Lucan" (1994), an ITV production, aired in November 1994. Cast includes Julian Wadham (Lord Lucan) and Lynsey Baxter (Lady Lucan).

"The most ghastly circumstances arose last night. The circumstantial evidence against me is so strong that V (Lady Veronica) will say it is all my doing and I will lie doggo for a while, but I am only concerned about the children ... and V has demonstrated her hatred for me in the past and would do anything to see me accused."— Lucan in a letter to a friend shortly after the murder

British peer whose disappearance after mistakenly murdering his children's nanny during an attempt on his wife's life has sparked endless speculation on whether he is still alive. Richard John Bingham, 7th Earl of Lucan, 3rd Baron Bingham, 13th Baronet Bingham was a direct descendant of the man who ordered the ill-fated charge of the Light Brigade during the Crimean War. Eton-educated and an officer in the Coldstream Guards, Lucan was later placed by an influential relative into a trainee management post with the merchant bank of William Brandt. On November 20, 1963, the handsome Lucan married 25-year-old Veronica Duncan, a model and secretary, who bore him three children. Even before his marriage, Lucan became a nightly habitué of the Clermont Club, a private gaming establishment where he thought little of losing thousands of pounds on the turn of a card. Called "Lucky" (with some little irony) by his friends, Lucan had run up massive gambling debts by the time he separated from Lady Veronica in 1973. His desperate financial woes were further compounded by a bitter custody battle in which he spent £40,000 in an unsuccessful bid to keep his children. Lady Veronica continued to live with the children in the family's five-story mansion at 46 Lower Belgrave Street in the heart of London's fashionable Mayfair district while Lucan moved to a furnished flat at 72A Elizabeth Street two blocks from the house.

On the night of Thursday, November 7, 1974, Lady Lucan was watching television in her third floor living room with Sandra Rivett, 29, nanny to the estranged couple's three children. Rivett, who usually had Thursday off, remained in because of a cold. Shortly after 9:00 p.m., Rivett went to the basement kitchen to make tea. When she did not return straightaway, Lady Lucan investigated and noticed that the light in the kitchen was not working. As she reached the bottom of the winding kitchen stairs, Lucan attacked her with a length of lead pipe wrapped in surgical tape. Bludgeoned and bleeding from head wounds which would require 70 stitches, the countess managed to escape and run to a nearby pub, the Plumbers Arms, where she barged in screaming, "He's murdered the nanny!" Scotland Yard rushed to the mansion and found Rivett in the kitchen battered to death and partially stuffed into a mailbag. According to the official reconstruction of the crime, investigators believed that Lucan let himself into the house, removed the light bulb in the basement kitchen and waited in the darkness for his wife to prepare her usual evening cup of tea. Rivett was accidentally killed by Lucan who mistook her for his wife in the darkness. The mailbag she was found stuffed in was to be used to dump the body in the English Channel. Interviewed in October 1994, Lady Lucan denied that her husband's near fatal attack on her was due to any bad feeling between them. "The murder was about money. It was purely financial. He decided he was about to go bankrupt and he had to save the family reputation. The only way he could do that was either to win a terrific amount at the table, which he couldn't—or to get hold of the house and sell it as fast as he could. Since I was firmly in place, he had to get rid of me. It was a calculated act. There was no personal feeling involved."

Following the murder, Lord Lucan telephoned his mother and told her that he had interrupted a fight in his basement between an intruder and his wife in which she and the nanny had been hurt. By midnight Lucan had motored to a friend's country mansion in Uckfield, 40 miles south of London. Over the next two days Lucan set his affairs in order and explained his actions in a series of phone calls and letters to friends. In one letter, Lucan wrote that he had bolted the scene out of fear that Lady Veronica's animosity toward him would lead her to accuse him of the murder. On November 10, 1974, Lucan's borrowed Ford Corsair was found abandoned at the south coast port of Newhaven, a departure point for ferries to France. Blood on the steering wheel and driver's seat were of the same group as Rivett's and Lady Lucan's. A length of lead pipe was found in the trunk. After authorities established that no ferry had transported Lucan, Scotland Yard spearheaded a massive search for the missing Lord. Interpol alerted the police of 120 nations, frogmen combed the English Channel near the port for Lucan's body, and the homes of his wealthy friends were systematically searched. At an inquest in June 1975 a coroner's jury determined that Lord Lucan had murdered Sandra Rivett. To date, Lucan's body has not been found, a fact which has fuelled much speculation over "Lucky's" fate. Many believe, including Lady Veronica, that Lucan committed suicide by taking a small boat into the Channel, weighting his body, then sinking the vessel. Others feel that Lucan's wealthy friends (dubbed the "Eton Mafia" by investigators) set him up with a new identity and relocated him in a foreign country. Since his disappearance, Lucan "sightings" have been made on four continents including the countries of France, the Netherlands, Ireland, South Africa, Mozambique, Australia, and Brazil.

388. Lucas, Norman. *The Lucan Mystery.* London: W.H. Allen, 1975. 156 pp., [8] leaves of plates: ill.; 22 cm.

389. Marnham, Patrick. *Trail of Havoc: In the Steps of Lord Lucan.* London: Viking, 1987. xix, 204 pp.: ill.; 23 cm.

_____. [Same as 389.] 1st American ed. New York: Viking, 1988. xix, 204 pp., [24]pp. of plates: ill., ports.; 22 cm.

_____. [Same as 389.] London: Penguin, 1988. xix, 204 pp., [24]pp. of plates: ill., 3 facsims., 1 map, ports.; 19 cm.; paperback.

_____. [Same as 389.] New York: Penguin Books, 1988. xix, 204 pp., [24]pp. of plates: ill.; 18 cm.; paperback.

_____. [Same as 389.] Bath: Chivers, 1989. [209]pp. (large print); 23 cm. ("A Lythway book.")

Marnham theorizes that Lucan hired a man to murder his wife who instead mistakenly killed Rivett instead.

390. Moore, Sally. *Lucan: Not Guilty.* London: Sidgwick & Jackson, 1987. 271 pp., [8]pp. of plates: ill., maps, ports.; 24 cm.

_____. [Same as 390.] London: Fontana/ Collins, 1988. 364 pp.; 18 cm.; paperback.

British tabloid journalist Moore maintains that Lucan is innocent and suggests that either Rivett's boyfriend or a police officer is the real murderer. Includes a facsimile of the letter Lucan wrote at Uckfield to his friend Bill Shand Kydd. Includes index.

391. Ranson, Roy, and Strange, Robert. *Looking for Lucan: The Final Verdict.* London: Smith Gryphon, 1994. xiv, 210 pp., [16]pp. of plates; 22 cm.

Ranson, the Scotland Yard chief who led the hunt for Lucan, believes his quarry is still alive and living somewhere in Africa. In July 1994 the *Daily Mail* serialized the book and in conjunction with the publisher offered a reward of £100,000 to anyone providing information that leads Lord Lucan to justice. The reward expires on June 30, 1995. Includes a computer enhanced photo of Lucan as he might look in 1994.

392. Ruddick, James. *Lord Lucan: What Really Happened.* London: Headline, 1994. 214 pp., [12]pp. of plates; 18 cm.; paperback.

Lucas, Henry Lee

Born August 23, 1936, in Blacksburg, Virginia. Tecumseh, Michigan, and at least 25 other states; 13 murder convictions (self-confessed to 360, authorities estimate at least 110); knife, gun, bludgeon, strangulation, ax; January 11, 1960, and 1976–1982.

Film: Henry: Portrait of a Serial Killer (US, 1986), a Maljack Productions release written, produced, and directed by John McNaughton. Cast includes Michael Rooker (Henry), Tom Towles (Ottis), and Tracy Arnold (Becky).

Video: Confessions of a Serial Killer (US, 1987), a Concorde production direct-to-video release directed by Mark Blair, based on the Lucas case. Cast includes Robert A. Burns (Daniel Ray Hawkins) and Dennis Hill (Moon Lawton).

Theatre: The Road (1988), a play by David Earl Jones based on the exploits of Lucas and Toole, was performed in Los Angeles in August 1988. Cast includes Craig Stout (Henry) and Kelly Edwards (Ottis).

"I had no feelings for the people themselves, or any of the crimes. ... I'd pick them up hitchhiking, running and playing, stuff like that. We'd get to going and having a good time. First thing you know, I'd killed her and throwed her out somewhere."

One-eyed drifter considered by many to be the most prolific serial killer of all time but dismissed by others as the biggest liar in the history of 20th century murder. With his July 11, 1983, arrest in Stoneburg, Texas, on a charge of illegally possessing a firearm, 46-year-old Henry Lee Lucas began a litany of confession which implicated him and his simpleminded homosexual lover Ottis Elwood Toole in over 300 murders committed in some 26 states over a seven-year period. While Lucas has since recanted many of his confessions and law enforcement officials have discounted numerous others, the controversial killer nevertheless remains one of this century's most intriguing murderers. Born in a tar-papered cabin in the backwoods of Montgomery County, Virginia, on August 23, 1936, Lucas' mother Viola, a half Chippewa Indian, was a 50-cent-a-trick hooker and bootlegger. A mean alcoholic, the woman openly had sex with clients in front of Lucas, his older brother, and her husband, a former train worker who had lost both legs in a railroad accident. According to Lucas, "First thing I can remember was when my mom was in bed with another man in the house, and she made me watch it. I just couldn't stand there and watch. I had to turn my back and walk out of the house, and after I did that, she beat me, 'cause I didn't watch it." On one occasion, the woman struck her five-year-old son in the head with a board knocking him out for three days. Lucas' lifelong headaches, dizzy spells, and blackouts date from this injury. Finally, the woman's tyranny became too much for her drunken legless husband. After watching her have sex in

their bed with a neighborhood man, he dragged himself out into the snow, contracted a deadly case of pneumonia, and died. On Lucas' first day of school in 1943, Viola dressed him up as a girl and sent him off to class to endure the ridicule of his schoolmates. Later that year, Lucas suffered a knife wound to his left eye which was further aggravated by a classroom injury to the area. His eye was removed and inexpertly replaced with a glass one which left him with a permanently drooping eyelid.

As a teenager, Lucas was introduced to bestiality by his mother's live-in lover who captured dogs and sheep, stabbed them, then had sex with their bloody lifeless bodies. Lucas followed suit adding voyeurism, murder, and ultimately necrophilia to his grab bag of sexual aberrations. If Lucas is to be believed, he strangled his first victim, a young girl playmate, at 14, mainly because "I wanted to try the sex I'd been watching." Concurrently, Lucas began stealing, logging his first jail time at 15 after being arrested on June 12, 1952, for burglarizing an appliance store. The teen served two years in a reformatory before being released in 1954. Months later, Lucas was rearrested on felony charges and sentenced to four years in the state penitentiary in Staunton, Virginia. The 20 year old escaped from a prison road gang on May 28, 1956, stole a car, and was re-arrested in Clinton, Michigan, on June 19, 1956. Released from prison on September 2, 1959, Lucas was living near his half-sister in Tecumseh, Michigan when his 74-year-old mother arrived in town for a visit. Following a heated argument with his mother on January 11, 1960, Lucas fatally stabbed the woman in the neck and was subsequently convicted of second degree murder and sentenced to 20 to 40 years in the state prison of Southern Michigan at Jackson. Twice attempting suicide by slashing his wrists, the convict was transferred to the state mental institution in Ionia where he remained until April 1966. Lucas served ten years for murdering his mother, winning parole on June 3, 1970. His freedom was shortlived. Arrested for the attempted kidnapping of two teenage girls, Lucas was convicted and served three-and-a-half years of a five-year sentence. Paroled over his own objections in August 1975, Lucas relocated to Pennsylvania where he briefly worked on a mushroom farm and met and later married Betty Crawford. The couple and her two young daughters from a previous marriage moved to Port Deposit, Maryland. Lucas abandoned the family in July 1977 after his wife accused him of sexually molesting her daughters.

According to Lucas, he had already begun crisscrossing the country indiscriminately killing people before meeting Ottis Elwood Toole in a Skid Row rescue mission in Jacksonville, Florida in late 1976. Toole, a 29-year-old simpleminded grade school dropout, was introduced to sex before he was ten by an older sister who also dressed him up as a girl. Initiated into homosexual sex around the same time by a neighbor, Toole began incorporating arson into his sexual fantasies. The boy set a string of fires in Jacksonville and masturbated as he watched the flames. Dressing in drag, Toole haunted the city park and rescue mission looking for gay sex. By the time he met Lucas in 1976, Toole had served hard time in Kentucky for car theft and was supposedly a serial killer in his own right. Each immediately recognized in the other a kindred spirit and, brought

together by their murderous tastes, became lovers. After Lucas walked out on his wife to avoid child molestation charges, he drifted to Jacksonville where Toole welcomed him into the family home. If Lucas is to be believed (an increasingly difficult task according to many law enforcement officials), he and Toole embarked on a cross country murder and rape spree that lasted from 1978 until 1982. During that time, the pair took to the highway, sleeping in their car, and working at odd jobs only long enough to earn gas money. By their own estimation, they claimed the lives of several hundred people in every conceivable manner except poison. Lucas, who had used his time in the state penitentiary at Jackson to study prisoners' records, educated Toole on the proper way to kill and avoid detection. "He was doing his crimes all one way," Lucas said. "I started to correct him in his ways, in doing the crime where he wouldn't leave information." Toole, the cannibal, even removed a part of a victim's leg, "filleted" it, then ate it with barbecue sauce. Lucas later denied joining his lover only because "I don't like barbecue sauce."

While living at Toole's home, Lucas fell in love with Frieda "Becky" Powell, the 12-year-old daughter of the sister who had molested Toole as a child. Following the death of Toole's mother in May 1981, Lucas, Toole, Powell and her brother hit the road. In January 1982, Lucas ran off with Becky Powell leaving Toole in Florida to continue alone his string of arsons and murder. Wandering through Texas, Lucas and his "child bride" ended up in a pentecostal religious commune near Stoneburg called the House of Prayer. The group's leader, a roofing contractor, hired Lucas and let the odd couple live in a shack on the grounds of the commune. Bowing to Powell's wish to return home to Florida, Lucas was hitchhiking with the teenager off Interstate 35 near Denton, Texas, on August 24, 1982, when she made the mistake of slapping him during a heated argument. Lucas plunged a carving knife into Powell's chest, raped the corpse, decapitated it and cut the body into nine pieces, and scattered the parts over a field. Less than a month later on September 16, 1982, Lucas stabbed 80-year-old Kate Pearl Rich at her home in Ringgold, Texas. After sexually violating her body, Lucas stuffed the old woman in a drain pipe. Months later he moved the body to his home where he dismembered and burned it in a wood stove. On June 11, 1983, while under police surveillance in the disappearance of Rich, Lucas was arrested for illegal possession of a firearm. Four days later, Lucas not only confessed to Rich's murder, but also Becky Powell's, as well as over 100 others. Over the next 18 months, Lucas inflated the death count to over 300 which he and Toole (serving 20 years in a Florida penitentiary on arson charges) allegedly committed in over 20 states. In time, Lucas would take credit for 600 killings, confess to being a member with Toole of a satanic cult called the "Hand of Death," and take a perverse satisfaction in shocking law enforcement officials from all over the country who made a beeline to Texas to discuss unsolved murders in their states with him.

Lucas was ultimately convicted of 13 murders in Texas and at this writing awaits execution by lethal injection for the October 31, 1979, rape and murder of an unidentified woman whose body was found along I-35 near Georgetown, north of Austin. Police tagged the victim "Orange Socks" based on the only article of clothing the woman was wearing. Toole's death penalty conviction for the arson-murder of a 64-year-old Jacksonville, Florida, man in January 1982 has since been vacated and he was resentenced to life in prison. In September 1991, Toole received four additional life sentences for the murders in Florida of three women and the father of a Jackson County sheriff in 1980–1981. Lucas was also charged in the murders, but Florida never prosecuted because of the prohibitive cost of supplying counsel for the convicted killer. It should be noted that serious doubt has been cast on the majority of Lucas' confessions which by September 1994 had "cleared" 214 murders in several states. Lucas has confirmed accusations that the Texas Rangers and other police organizations have fed him information about the killings in order to solve outstanding cases, but at this point it is impossible to believe anything the condemned killer says. As of November 1985, police in at least 18 states had reopened 90 cases that the drifter had confessed to, but Lucas seems "good" for the remaining 110 or so. Adding another bizarre twist to the case, a woman claiming to be murder victim Frieda "Becky" Powell turned up in Cape Girardeau, Missouri in October 1992. Lucas, eager to escape execution, backed up the woman's story claiming that the only reason he had confessed to Powell's murder in the first place was to embarrass authorities. The hoax unravelled when it was learned that "Powell" was in actuality Phyllis Kathleen Wilcox, a 41-year-old diagnosed schizophrenic who had also corresponded with killers John Wayne Gacy and Charles Manson. It is extremely doubtful, given Lucas' penchant for lying and Toole's substandard intelligence, that any definitive body count will ever be finalized.

393. Call, Max. *Hand of Death: The Henry Lee Lucas Story.* Lafayette, La.: Prescott Press, 1985. 187 pp.: ill.; 24 cm.

Call, a "born again" religious writer, accepts every word that Lucas told him as truth. The result is a fascinating fiction which presents Lucas and Toole as members of a deadly international satanic cult called the "Hand of Death." Call also details Lucas' conversion to Christianity. According to Michael Newton's 1988 monograph *Mass Murder: An Annotated Bibliography,* the book was recalled by the publisher after Lucas recanted his confessions and reissued with new advertising which identified Call's claims as only a "possible" solution to the case.

394. Cox, Mike. *The Confessions of Henry Lee Lucas.* New York: Pocket Books, 1991. xii, 306 pp., [8]pp. of plates: ill.; 18 cm. ("Pocket Star Books"); paperback.

_____. [Same as 394.] London: Warner, 1992. xii, 306 pp., [8]pp. of plates: ports.; 18 cm.; paperback.

The best account of the case written by journalist Cox who in 1985 was public information officer for the Texas Department of Public Safety. In regard to Lucas' claims that he only murdered three people (his mother, Powell, and Rich), Cox concludes that it is difficult to believe given the drifter's extensive travels.

395. Norris, Joel. *Henry Lee Lucas: The Shocking True Story of America's Most Notorious Serial Killer.* New York: Kensington, 1991. 303 pp.: ill.; 18 cm. ("Zebra Books"); paperback. (Also published with an audiocassette tape entitled "Henry Lee Lucas Confesses.")

_____. [Same as 395.] London: Constable, 1993. 303 pp., [16]pp. of plates: ill., ports.; 18 cm.; paperback.

Lundgren, Jeffrey Don

Born circa 1950 in Independence, Missouri. Cult leader. Kirtland, Ohio; 5 murders; gun; April 18, 1989.

Audio: *Prophet of Death,* a two-cassette, three-hour abridgement of Earley's book of the same title read by Victor Garber, was published in 1992 by Simon & Schuster Audio (New York).

"I will say unto you, Mr. Avery sought to lead people to false ends, and yes, I put him to death ... I cannot say I'm sorry, for I did what God told me to do."—Lundgren testifying at his murder trial

Self-proclaimed prophet of a breakaway religious cult convicted of the human sacrifice murders of a five-member family of his congregation. Ousted from the lay ministry of the Reorganized Church of Jesus Christ of Latter Day Saints in 1988, Jeffrey Lundgren, 39, established a commune with about two dozen of his followers on a 15-acre farm near Kirtland, Ohio. Under Lundgren's direction, the new congregation gave all their money and property to the new prophet. Anticipating the coming holocaust, Lundgren stockpiled semiautomatic weapons, outfitted his followers in uniforms, and drilled them in paramilitary exercises in preparation for the group's exodus to salvation. However, before they could leave their Kirtland commune Lundgren told his followers that a spiritually cleansing human blood sacrifice must first be performed to enable them to find a "golden sword" in the wilderness of West Virginia. Lundgren believed that with the sword he would find writings containing the wisdom he needed to convert the entire world to his teachings. On April 18, 1989, Lundgren and his followers "sacrificed"

Dennis Avery, his wife, and three daughters (ranging in ages from 6 to 15) partly because they were not considered as devout as other members. The family was bound and gagged with duct tape, shot execution-style by cult members on Lundgren's order, and buried in a barn off Ohio 6. The congregation left two days later. The killings went undetected for almost nine months before a tip led agents from the Bureau of Alcohol, Tobacco and Firearms to recover the bodies on January 3 or 4, 1990. Several cult members were subsequently arrested throughout the country. On January 7, 1990, Lundgren, his wife Alice, and 19-year-old son Damon were apprehended ten miles from the Mexico border in National City, California. Lundgren was convicted of five counts of aggravated murder and kidnapping on August 29, 1990. Armed with a Bible, a Book of Mormon, and the Doctrine of Covenants, Lundgren told a sentencing hearing, "I will say unto you, Mr. Avery sought to lead people to false ends, and yes, I put him to death … I cannot say I'm sorry, for what I did God told me to do." Lundgren was sentenced to death in the electric chair. Following a divorce, Lundgren married 41-year-old Kathy Johnson, the divorced wife of a former cult member and mother of his four-year-old daughter, in a brief ceremony at the Lucasville prison in June 1994.

396. Earley, Pete. *Prophet of Death: The Mormon Blood-Atonement Killings.* 1st ed. New York: Morrow, 1991. 448 pp.: ill.; 25 cm.

_____. [Same as 396.] New York: Avon Books, 1993. 422 pp., [16]pp. of plates: ill.; 18 cm.; paperback.

397. Sasse, Cynthia Salter, and Widder, Peggy Murphy. *The Kirtland Massacre.* New York: D.I. Fine, 1991. x, 302 pp.: ill.; 24 cm.

_____. [Same as 397.] New York: Zebra Books, 1992. 430 pp.: ill; 18 cm.; paperback.

McCollum, Ruby

Born circa 1915. Housewife. Live Oak, Florida; 1 murder; .32 caliber Smith & Wesson; August 3, 1952.

"I do not know whether I did right or wrong when I killed Dr. Adams."

A racially charged case in which a black woman was convicted and sentenced to death by an all white Southern jury for the murder of a respected white doctor with political connections. Ruby McCollum, a 37-year-old black woman married to a wealthy local racketeer, entered the Live Oak, Florida, office of Dr. Clifford LeRoy Adams on August 3, 1952, and shot the fiftyish physician four times in the back. Adams, a highly respected doctor whose political star was on the rise, died at the scene. According to the prosecution, the murder was prompted by an argument between the pair over the price of the drugs he was selling her. At the trial in Suwannee County, circuit judge Hal Adams (no relation to the victim) prevented the jury from hearing of McCollum's six year affair with Adams which produced one daughter and had the woman three months' pregnant on the day she murdered him. She miscarried while awaiting trial. McCollum was convicted by an all white jury in 1952 and sentenced to death by electrocution. Writer and civil rights advocate William Bradford Huie became involved in the case and was largely responsible for prompting the Florida State Supreme Court to grant McCollum a new trial set for

August 1954. Fearful that a racist jury would deliver the same result, McCollum's defense team pressed to have her declared insane and committed to a mental institution. In September 1954 a psychiatrist determined that McCollum was suffering from "prison psychosis" and she was sent to the Florida State Hospital in Chattahoochee for observation and treatment. She was never retried. Huie was subsequently convicted of criminal contempt for tampering with a witness in the case and fined $750. The Florida State Supreme Court declared McCollum innocent by reason of insanity in 1974 and she was released from Chattahoochee to the care of her daughter. In 1981 the 70 year old, described by a psychiatrist as an "apathetic schizophrenic," was living in a foster home in Silver Springs, Florida.

398. Huie, William Bradford. *Ruby McCollum: Woman in the Suwannee Jail.* 1st ed. New York: Dutton, 1956. 249 pp.: ill.; 21 cm.

_____. [Same as 398.] New York: American Library, 1957. 157 pp.: ill.; 18 cm.; paperback.

_____. [Same as 398, but U.K. ed. retitled: *The Crime of Ruby McCollum.*] London: Jarrolds, 1957. 206 pp.; 22 cm.
First published in U.S. under title: *Ruby McCollum: Woman in the Suwannee Jail* (1956).

_____. [Same as 398.] Rev. ed. New York: New American Library, 1964. 190 pp.: ill., port.; 18 cm. ("A Signet book"); paperback.
Noted novelist and social historian Huie examines the political/racial aspects of the case first brought to his attention by black author Zora Neale Hurston who covered the trial for the *Pittsburgh Courier.* Controversial at the time of its publication, the book was banned in Suwannee County for many years. Huie died in 1986 and his personal papers (including all the legal documents, court transcripts, and notes concerning the case) are archived at Ohio State University in Columbus.

MacDonald, Jeffrey Robert

Born circa 1944. Physician. Fayetteville, North Carolina (Fort Bragg); 3 murders; paring knife, ice pick, bludgeon (club); February 17, 1970.

Television: "Fatal Vision" (1984), a two-part, four-hour made-for-television miniseries based on Joe McGinniss' book of the same title, originally appeared on NBC on November 18 and 19, 1984. Cast includes Gary Cole (Jeffrey MacDonald), Karl Malden (Freddy Kassab), and Eva Marie Saint (Mildred Kassab).

Audio: Fatal Vision, a two-cassette, three-hour abridgement of Joe McGinniss' book of the same title read by Christopher Reeve, was published in 1992 by Simon & Schuster Audio (New York).

"I'll just stay here in my little concrete condo."—MacDonald commenting on what he would do if the U.S. Supreme Court would not give him a hearing. On November 30, 1992, the Supreme Court released a statement saying it would not review the case. MacDonald remains in prison.

Green Beret doctor convicted of murdering his family whose case has become widely known through the book, and later film, *Fatal Vision.* In the early morning hours of February 17, 1970, military police at Fort Bragg outside of Fayetteville, North Carolina, received an urgent phone call from Green Beret Captain Dr. Jeffrey MacDonald who managed to painfully gasp out news of a stabbing at his home at 544 Castle Drive before losing consciousness. MPs arrived to find MacDonald lying on the floor of his bedroom next to his 26-year-old pregnant wife Colette. The dead woman had been stabbed with a knife nine times in the neck, seven times in the chest, and stabbed 21 times in the chest with an ice pick. Her head had been shattered by at least six blows from a club and both arms were broken. On the headboard of their bed the word "PIG" had been written in blood. Dead in another bedroom was MacDonald's five-year-old daughter Kimberly. She had been hit at least three times in the head and stabbed once in the throat. Her two-year-old sister, Kristen, was found in the bedroom across the hall dead from 33 stab wounds to her chest and back and some 15 ice pick punctures inflicted on her chest. MacDonald, suffering from a collapsed lung caused by four ice pick wounds to his chest, told MPs of struggling with four intruders (two white men, a black man, and a hippie woman in a blonde wig and floppy hat) who broke into his home and attacked his family. He remembered the woman standing over him as he was being beaten chanting, "Kill the pigs. Acid is groovy." The Army's Criminal Investigation Division (the CID) almost immediately discounted the 26-year-old doctor's claim that he was attacked by hippies because he refused to supply them with drugs primarily because the lack of disorder at the crime scene belied MacDonald's claim that he violently struggled with the four intruders. In a four month investigation marked by incredibly shoddy police work, the CID pronounced the charges of murder against MacDonald to be "not true." MacDonald subsequently received an honorable discharge from the military, relocated to Southern California, worked

in the emergency room of a San Diego hospital, and generally lived what many have described as "life in the fast lane."

Alfred "Freddy" Kassab, Colette MacDonald's 62-year-old stepfather, refused to let the case drop. Poring over the 153 pages of MacDonald's testimony at the Army hearing, Kassab noted inconsistencies and became convinced that his son-in-law was a pathological liar. MacDonald would later attribute Kassab's vehemence towards him as based in large part upon his decision to leave the East and relocate to the West Coast. More likely, however, is MacDonald's contention that he intentionally lied to Kassab about his finding and "taking care" of the killers with some Green Beret buddies. According to MacDonald, the lie was designed to give Kassab some sense of closure about the murders. Instead, Kassab became a zealot personally traveling to Washington, D.C., and discussing the case with every member of Congress. Kassab's persistence paid off when the justice department reopened the case in 1974. A grand jury was convened in Raleigh, North Carolina, and after meeting for six months, indicted MacDonald on three counts of murder in January 1975. MacDonald appealed and in January 1976 the 4th circuit court of appeals overturned the indictment and dismissed all charges ruling that the doctor's right to a speedy trial had been violated. The legal wrangling continued and in May 1978 the U.S. Supreme Court reversed the ruling and ordered MacDonald to stand trial.

In July 1979, nine and one-half years after the murders, MacDonald finally stood trial in Raleigh, North Carolina. The prosecution based its case largely on physical evidence found at the scene (fibers, skin, bloodstains, position of the bodies) which they maintained contradicted MacDonald's account of the events of February 17, 1970. According to the prosecution's theory of the case, the murder occurred around 2:00 a.m. after five-year-old Kimberly, asleep in the MacDonalds' bed, wet it. MacDonald argued with his wife and during his attack on her inadvertently struck and killed the child with a club. MacDonald then murdered Kristen in her bed, made the murders look like a hippie attack, and carefully wounded himself before reporting the killings. Helena Stoeckly, the female intruder in the blonde wig and the floppy hat who had earlier confessed to at least six people about her involvement in the MacDonald family murders, was called to testify, but the aging hippie was so burned out by years of drug abuse that she could remember nothing. Barred by the judge's ruling that the people she confessed to could not be called as witnesses, MacDonald's defense crumbled. In May 1981, Stoeckley would resurface in the case to tell an investigator working on MacDonald's defense team that her group killed the doctor's family because he refused to supply them with drugs. After a seven week trial, MacDonald was convicted on August 29, 1979, on one count of first degree murder (Kristen) and two counts of second degree murder (Colette and Kimberly). The doctor, still vigorously protesting his innocence, was subsequently sentenced to three life sentences. To date, MacDonald's various appeals at the appellate and supreme court levels based on new pieces of physical evidence, the confessions of others, and corroborating statements have been turned down. Eligible for parole since 1991, MacDonald has chosen not to apply since he feels to do so

would be tantamount to an admission of guilt. Before dying of emphysema on October 24, 1994, Alfred Kassab left several documents and a videotaped statement for the parole board in which he argues against ever granting his son-in-law early release from his life convictions. *Fatal Justice*, a 1995 book on the case based on nine years of research, purports to introduce compelling new evidence withheld at the time of the trial which at the least, its authors contend, should give MacDonald a new trial if not exonerate him. At this writing, MacDonald is serving his sentence at the federal prison in Sheridan, Oregon.

399. McGinniss, Joe. *Fatal Vision*. New York: Putnam, 1983. 663 pp.; 25 cm.

_____. [Same as 399.] New York: New American Library, 1984. 654 pp., [4]pp. of plates: ill.; 18 cm. ("A Signet book"); paperback.

_____. [Same as 399.] London: Deutsch, 1984. 665 pp.; 25 cm.

_____. [Same as 399.] New York: New American Library, 1985. 659 pp., [8]pp. of plates: ill.; 18 cm. ("A Signet book"); paperback.
   Includes a new afterword by McGinniss.

_____. [Same as 399.] Abridged ed. London: Sphere, 1985. 533 pp.: 1 plan; 18 cm.; paperback.

_____. [Same as 399.] Newly updated ed. New York: New American Library, 1989. 684 pp., [8]pp. of plates: ill., ports.; 18 cm. ("A Signet book"); paperback.
   Includes McGinniss' 1985 afterword and the 1989 epilogue.

_____. [Same as 399.] Newly updated ed. New York: Penguin Books, 1989. 684 pp., [8]pp. of plates: ill., ports.; 18 cm. ("A Signet book"); paperback. (Includes McGinniss' 1985 afterword and the 1989 epilogue.)
   Bestselling book marred by accusa-

tions that McGinniss befriended Mac-Donald under false pretenses in order to get the inside scoop on the case. Originally a supporter of the doctor, McGinniss turned on his subject when he supposedly "realized" that MacDonald was guilty. McGinniss' ethics in the Jeffrey MacDonald case have always been troubling, but especially now in light of the charges of plagiarism levelled at the writer for his 1993 book on Edward Kennedy, *The Last Brother.*

400. Malcolm, Janet. *The Journalist and the Murderer.* 1st ed. New York: Knopf: Distributed by Random House, 1990. 161 pp.; 21 cm.

401. Potter, Jerry Allen, and Bost, Fred. *Fatal Justice: Reinvestigating the Mac-Donald Murders.* New York: W.W. Norton, 1995. 463 pp.: ill.; 25 cm.

Fascinating book which calls into serious question the government's case against MacDonald and how the prosecution kept important evidence from the defense and jury. Bost is an ex–Army and Pentagon investigator. Important.

402. Stephens, Melinda. *I Accuse: The Torturing of an American Hero.* U.S.: American Ideal, 1987. 285 pp.: ill.; 23 cm.

Stephens, a strong MacDonald supporter, offers an interesting argument for his innocence.

Mackay, Patrick David
(a.k.a. "Franklin Bollvolt the First," "Pluto," "Peter McCann," "Hammond")

Born September 25, 1952, in Middlesex, England. Unemployed gardener. England; 3 murders (convicted, suspected of 8 others); knife, ax; February 1974–March 1975.

"These murders were so solemn when I think of them, yet so quick, so fast to take place." — Patrick Mackay in a statement to police made on November 2, 1975

British psychopath with an obsession for Nazism whom authorities suspect murdered 11 people throughout England in the mid–1970s. Patrick David Mackay was still in the womb when an alcoholic father kicked his pregnant mother in the stomach. After his birth, the woman continued to suffer the brunt of her violent husband's physical abuse until the boy reached an age where he became the preferred object of his father's regular weekend beatings. The senior Mackay's alcoholism so financially devastated the family that sympathetic neighbors allowed the boy and his two younger sisters in their homes to take hot baths. The 11-year-old boy showed little emotion when his father died on November 8, 1962, at age 42; however, Mackay's delinquency dates from his father's death. Assuming his father's role as family tyrant, the boy violently abused his mother and sisters to the point that his mother suffered a nervous breakdown in 1963 which necessitated a yearlong hospitalization during which the children were placed in a foster home. The family was reunited in early 1964, but Mackay's tyranny over the group continued unabated.

When not terrorizing his family, Mackay bullied younger children at school and tortured small animals. In one particularly cruel act, the boy methodically roasted his pet turtle alive on an open fire. Dead birds became his favorite playthings and Mackay took to wondering aloud if the bones of his dead father had yet rotted away. Mackay's first recorded offense dates from age 11 when on July 8, 1964, he was accused of 21 counts of theft and setting a fire in a Catholic Church. Found guilty on July 22, 1964, the boy was placed on three years' probation. Mackay's violence against his family accelerated as he entered adolescence. At 13, after demolishing his mother's home in Gravesend during an argument, Mackay was placed in a psychiatric adolescent unit attached to a hospital in nearby Chartham. He proved to be so incorrigible that he was sent to a work farm for adolescent offenders. On January 7, 1967, Mackay attempted to commit suicide, the first of several unsuccessful attempts at self destruction throughout his life. Released to his mother, Mackay was arrested in Dartford for attempting to strangle a young boy. A home office psychiatrist who examined the 15 year old at the time described Mackay as "a cold psychopathic killer" with an "explosive temper." Despite the diagnosis, Mackay was imprisoned for only one day, then sent to a psychiatric hospital outside Liverpool where he was officially certified as a psychopath. Mackay's mother successfully argued for his release over the objections of hospital staff (as she did on numerous occasions) and the disturbed teenager was allowed to return home in her custody.

There, he indulged his alcoholism, experimented with drugs, and predictably, battled with his mother and sisters. In early 1970, Mackay became obsessed with Nazism and Adolf Hitler. Over the years, he plastered the walls of his room with Nazi photos and memorabilia, stole books on the subject from the local library, and passionately advocated the extermination of Jews, euthanasia, and eugenics. To complete the fantasy, Mackay made a Nazi uniform and demanded to be called "Franklin Bollvolt the First" a name he insisted was "to be feared and remembered, like Hitler's." In May 1973 Mackay met Father Anthony Crean, a 63-year-old Roman Catholic chaplain to a convent of Carmelite nuns operating an old persons' home in the Kent village of Shorne. Crean befriended the disturbed 20 year old who within two weeks of their meeting broke into the priest's house and stole a check. He was arrested over the priest's objection and thanks again to his mother's intervention was given only a small fine, ordered to repay Crean, and placed on two years' probation. Mackay was employed as a groundsman at the Tudor Sports Field in the outer London suburb of Barnet when he met 84-year-old widow Isabella Griffiths in Chelsea in February 1974. A friendship between the pair resulted when Mackay carried the elderly woman's groceries to her stylish home at 19 Cheyne Walk. Afterwards, Mackay often did Griffiths' grocery shopping for her. On February 14, 1974, Mackay dropped by the widow's house and, when she refused him admittance, broke the chain lock. He strangled Griffiths in the hall and dragged her into the kitchen where he stabbed her in the stomach with a 12-inch knife he left in the body. Before leaving, he crossed her arms, closed her eyes, and placed a chair cover over the corpse. Griffiths' body was found 12 days later.

Released from London's Wormwood Scrubs Prison on November 22, 1974, after serving four months for burglary, Mackay committed a three-month-long series of muggings against elderly women which netted him over £600. Mackay was drinking heavily around Belgrave Square on March 10, 1975, when he noticed 89-year-old Adele Price. He followed the elderly woman to her flat in nearby Lowndes Square and, feigning illness to gain access to her rooms, strangled Price in her bedroom. On March 21, 1975, Mackay travelled to Shorne to visit his old friend Father Crean who was startled by the troubled man's appearance. When Mackay started beating Crean with his fists the priest broke away and locked himself in the bathroom. Armed with an ax found under the stairs in the house, Mackay broke open the bathroom door and in the process knocked Crean into the bathtub. He repeatedly stabbed the priest in the neck and head with a knife until the top of Crean's head bent the blade. Mackay continued the assault with the ax. Explaining to authorities afterwards that "something in me ... just exploded," Mackay filled the tub and sat for an hour watching Crean's body float in the bloody water.

Mackay was arrested on March 23, 1975, less than 48 hours after Crean's killing, when a detective remembered that in May 1973 the priest had interceded for a burglar with a long history of mental illness. Within half an hour of his arrest Mackay confessed to Crean's murder and subsequently confessed to the series of muggings as well as the murders of Isabella Griffiths and Adele Price. Investigators, however, were convinced that Mackay was responsible for at least eight other murders beginning with that of Heidi Mnilk, a 17-year-old West German *au pair* girl living in Bromley, Kent, on July 8, 1973. While leaving London Bridge Station, Mnilk was stabbed in the throat and thrown from the train. Mackay bragged about the killing in Brixton Prison, but witnesses were unable to pick him out of a lineup. Twelve days later on July 20, 1973, Mary Hynes, 73, was found bludgeoned to death in her flat in Kentish Town. The killer had stuffed Hynes' panties in her mouth and covered the body with an eiderdown quilt. Mackay was charged, but the case was subsequently left on file as part of a plea agreement.

On January 4, 1974, the bodies of Stephanie Britton, 57, and her four-year-old grandson Christopher Martin were discovered at her luxury home on Hadley Green, Hertfordshire. Britton had been pinned to the floor with a knife. Mackay allegedly confessed the crime to a fellow-prisoner, but denied the murders to police. Mackay did confess, however, to pushing an old tramp into the Thames River off London's Hungerford Bridge in January 1974. Due to lack of evidence, he was not charged. On June 13, 1974, the body of 62-year-old tobacconist Frank Goodman was found in his Finsbury Park shop in northern London. Goodman sustained 14 blows to the head with a lead pipe and his overcoat was placed over his feet. Mackay told police where to find the bloody boots he wore during the crime, but when recovered, the stains on them proved too old for analysis. Mackay was charged, but the case was left on file as part of a plea agreement. The body of 92-year-old Sarah Rodwell was discovered in her flat in Ash Grove, Hackney, on December 23, 1974. She had been beaten to death with a blunt object while trying to unlock the door of her home. Mackay denied responsibility for the murder. On February 9, 1975, Ivy Davis was found hacked to death with an ax on the settee of her home in Southend-on-Sea, Essex. Mackay also denied committing this murder.

The battery of court-appointed psychiatrists who interviewed Mackay while he was on remand in Brixton Prison unanimously agreed that he suffered from a "severe psychopathic disorder." Nevertheless, he was judged fit and sane to plead and charged with five murders (Griffiths, Price, Crean, Hynes, and Goodman) at his trial in the Old Bailey on November 21, 1975.

The prosecution agreed to withdraw charges in the Hynes and Goodman murders when the certified psychopath agreed to plead guilty to three counts of manslaughter by reason of diminished responsibility in the remaining killings. Mackay was sentenced to life imprisonment to be served in a penitentiary rather than in a mental institution.

403. Clark, Tim, and Penycate, John. *Psychopath: The Case of Patrick Mackay.* London: Routledge & K. Paul, 1976. vii, 140 pp., 8 leaves of plates: ill.; 23 cm.

"Mad Butcher of Kingsbury Run"
(a.k.a. "The Head Hunter [or] Phantom of Kingsbury Run," "The Horrible Headhunter," "Cleveland Butcher [or] Torso Murders")

Unknown. Cleveland, Ohio, and Pittsburgh, Pennsylvania; 16 murders (suspected of as many as 40); butcher knife; 1934–1940.

Unidentified serial torso killer who terrorized Cleveland, Ohio, during the Depression. Kingsbury Run, an ancient creek bed cutting through the heart of Cleveland, Ohio, is a nexus of railroad tracks serving downtown factories and the suburb of Shaker Heights. During the Depression, the dingy area was a favorite playground for children and the site of a sprawling hobo jungle. For seven years in the thirties it also became the favored killing ground for a brutal serial killer dubbed by the press "The Mad Butcher of Kingsbury Run." On September 5, 1934, the lower portion of a woman's body was found partially buried in the sand at Euclid Beach

some eight miles east of downtown Cleveland. The unidentified woman's legs had been severed at the knees and a chemical preservative applied to her torso. On September 23, 1935, a 16-year-old boy playing in Kingsbury Run found the headless, emasculated corpses of two men. Their heads were found buried nearby. The coroner later determined that the decapitations (one estimated to have been done three weeks before, the other four days before discovery) had been accomplished with a heavy butcher knife skillfully wielded by an individual with a knowledge of dissection. The chemical preservative found staining the torso of the older victim was identified as identical to that found on the "Jane Doe" recovered from Euclid Beach. Fingerprints identified the body of the younger man as 28-year-old Edward A. Andrassy, a one-time orderly at Cleveland City Hospital arrested four years before for carrying a concealed weapon. The dismembered remains of the killer's fourth victim, 41-year-old prostitute Florence Sawdey Polillo, were found near Kingsbury Run in two burlap bags and a half bushel basket on January 26, 1936. Various missing parts of Polillo's body, minus the head, were found 13 days later in a vacant building.

On June 5, 1936, two boys playing near the Run chanced across the severed head of a man. His heavily tattooed torso was found the next day, but failed to lead to an identification. The killer crossed the Cuyahoga River to claim his sixth victim in the West Side suburb of Brooklyn. On July 22, 1936, a man's headless nude body was found floating in Big Creek. He too was never identified. The dismembered and rotting remains of victim seven were found on September 10, 1936, floating in a pool of stagnant water beneath the

East Thirty-fourth Street bridge in Kingsbury Run. The man's severed head, arms, and genitals were never found. On February 23, 1937, the hacked upper torso of a young woman was found washed up from Lake Erie onto the same stretch of Euclid Beach as the first victim. The unidentified victim's lower trunk was found in another part of the city on May 5, 1937, although her head, arms, and legs were never recovered. A skeleton was found beneath the Lorain-Carnegie Bridge on June 5, 1937, later identified through dental records as that of 40-year-old Cleveland resident Rose Wallace. On July 6, 1937, dismembered parts of a man's body were fished out of the Cuyahoga River. The victim's head was never found. The severed leg of the "Mad Butcher's" eleventh victim was found floating in the river on April 8, 1938. A month later a burlap bag containing her left foot, thighs, and headless torso were recovered from the river. Victims twelve and thirteen (a male and female, killed on different dates) were found on August 16, 1938, in a dump near downtown Cleveland's business district. The female's torso (hacked into nine pieces and all recovered) was found beneath rocks, her head nearby wrapped in brown paper. The hair-covered skull and about 40 bones from a "John Doe" were also recovered from the scene.

In January 1939, the *Cleveland Plain Dealer* published a letter which had been received by the chief of the Cleveland police department. Purportedly written by the "Head Hunter" and posted from Los Angeles, the letter stated that he had moved on to "sunny California" to continue his scientific research on the "laboratory guinea pigs [he] found on any public street." The letter, signed "X," related another mur-

der and gave the location of the victim's severed, but faceless head, buried between two streets in Los Angeles. A search by L.A. authorities yielded nothing. On July 5, 1939, Cleveland detectives arrested Frank Dolezal, a 52-year-old Bohemian immigrant and bricklayer, on suspicion of being the serial killer. Following a brutal marathon interrogation session, Dolezal "confessed" to the murders of Andrassy and Polillo. Cleveland police later "corrected" several discrepancies in his statement to firm up their case against him. Dolezal later retracted his confession, accused the detectives of beating him, and the incriminating bloodstains found in his rented room were soon identified as belonging to an animal. On August 24, 1939, Dolezal used strips of cleaning rags to hang himself in his cell in the Cuyahoga County Jail. Experts on the case no longer consider Dolezal to be a serious suspect, just an unfortunate lunatic. The fire-scorched bodies of two men and one woman were found on May 3, 1940, in box cars in McKees Rocks, Pennsylvania, a Pittsburgh suburb. All were headless, two had been severed at the hips and shoulders while one body was intact. A victim identified as James David Nicholson, a 30-year-old vagrant from Chicago, had the word "NAZI" (with the Z inverted) carved into his chest. Cleveland authorities unanimously agreed it was the work of the Mad Butcher. A decade later, on July 22, 1950, the headless, dismembered, and emasculated body of Robert Robertson, a 44-year-old vagrant suspected of being a homosexual, was found near a Cleveland factory. According to the coroner who had worked on the earlier Head Hunter victims, Robertson's murder bore "the Kingsbury technique," but could have been a copycat killing. Several researchers have since speculated that compelling links exist between the Kinsgbury Run killings and a series of decapitation murders committed around New Castle, Pennsylvania, between 1925 and 1939. The Mad Butcher case remains officially unsolved.

404. Nickel, Steven. *Torso: The True Story of Eliot Ness and the Search for a Psychopathic Killer.* Winston-Salem, N.C.: J.F. Blair, 1989. 231 pp., [18]pp. of plates: ill.; 24 cm.

_____. [Same as 404 with variant subtitle: *The Story of Eliot Ness and the Hunt for the Mad Butcher of Kingsbury Run, a True Story.* New York: Avon Books, 1990. 247 pp., [8]pp. of plates: ill.; 18 cm.; paperback.

Excellent book on the unsuccessful efforts of Eliot Ness, former "Untouchable" and Cleveland's public safety director during the time of the murders, to apprehend the Mad Butcher of Kingsbury Run. An important contribution to true crime writing. Includes bibliography and index.

Mahon, Patrick Herbert
(a.k.a. " J. Waller," "J. Rees," "Pat Derek Patterson," "Douglas Horsfall")

Born circa 1889 or 1890 in Liverpool, England. Executed September 9, 1924. Sales manager. Eastbourne, England; 1 murder; bludgeon; April 15, 1924.

"I wonder if you realize how terrible a thing it is for one's body to be active and one's mind to fail to act."— Statement made by Mahon to detectives on the day of his arrest

A philandering husband apprehended for the dismemberment murder of his mistress after his Gladstone bag containing a knife and bloody clothes were found in a Waterloo Station cloakroom. Mahon, a sales manager in a factory at Sunbury, began an affair in early 1923 with Emily Beilby Kaye, a 38-year-old typist at the firm. Although no stranger to marital indiscretions, Mahon was unable to disentangle himself from the persistent Kaye and feared she would compromise his professional position. Upon learning of her lover's past criminal record (forgery, embezzlement, and a five-year imprisonment for assaulting a woman with a hammer) Kaye possibly used the knowledge to blackmail Mahon into traveling with her under the assumed name of "Waller" to a bungalow on a remote beach between Eastbourne and Pevensey Bay to conduct what she called " a love experiment." On April 12, 1924, days before his rendezvous with Kaye at "Officer's House," Mahon purchased a saw and a 10-inch chef's knife. According to Mahon's later confession, the pair argued at the bungalow on April 15, 1924, over Kaye's pregnancy and his refusal to start a new life with her in South Africa. In the ensuing struggle, Kaye struck her head against a coal cauldron and died. Few believed Mahon's account as he had made a date with another woman for the next day and even entertained her in the house with Kaye's body locked in another room covered by a fur coat.

Mahon dismembered the corpse, burning its head, feet and legs in the sitting room grate until the smell was too overpowering to continue. Seizing on a novel way to dispose of the remainder of his murdered mistress, he boiled her flesh into small lumps, placed them in a Gladstone bag, and tossed them off a train as he traveled around London. Mahon was arrested on May 2, 1924, after his wife found a ticket for a Waterloo Station cloakroom in his clothes. Suspicious that he was having an affair, she asked a friend with connections to the railway police to investigate and when the Gladstone bag containing a knife and bloody clothes were found Mahon was taken into custody as he tried to claim it. After first insisting that he was carrying dog meat in the bag, Mahon later confessed. A search of "Officer's House" yielded body parts, 37 pieces of flesh in a hat box, and part of a large intestine in a biscuit tin. Mahon was tried at the Sussex Summer Assizes on July 15, 1924, and his claim that Kaye was accidentally killed during a domestic quarrel was damaged when it was learned that he spent £500 of Kaye's money. While not committing to a cause of death noted pathologist Sir Bernard Spilsbury definitively ruled out head trauma as responsible for Kaye's death and suggested she had been strangled. After a 45-minute deliberation on July 19, 1924, a jury found Mahon guilty and he was sentenced to death. Mahon was hanged at Wandsworth Prison on September 9, 1924, following a failed appeal.

405. *The Case of Patrick Mahon.* Criminological Studies no. 1. London: G. Newnes, Ltd., 1932. 128 pp.; 18 cm.

406. Wallace, Edgar, ed. *The Trial of Patrick Mahon.* Introduction by Edgar Wallace. Famous Trials Series. General editor: G. Dilnot. London: G. Bles, 1928. 286 pp.: ill.; 23 cm.

_____. [Same as 406.] Introduction by Edgar Wallace. Famous Trials Series. General editor: G. Dilnot. New York: Charles Scribner's, 1928. 286 pp.: ill.; 23 cm.

A concise and lively introduction by Edgar Wallace, a British novelist of popular thrillers and motion picture screen-

plays, prefaces lengthy excerpted transcripts from Mahon's murder trial and unsuccessful appeal.

Manson, Charles Milles (a.k.a. "No Name Maddox," "Jesus Christ," "God," "The Devil," "Soul," "Charles Willis Manson")

Born November 12, 1934, in Cincinnati, Ohio. Car thief, cult leader. Los Angeles, California; 9 murders (possible involvement in as many as 40); bludgeon, gun, knife; July–August 1969.

Film: Manson (US, 1972), a 93-minute documentary directed by Robert Hendrickson and Laurence Merrick (Merrick International Pictures). Cast includes Charles Manson, Susan Atkins, Patricia Krenwinkel, Charles "Tex" Watson, and Jess Parsons (narrator).

Theatre: Charles Manson, a.k.a. Jesus Christ: A Rock-Musical Tragedy (1972), book by Fabian Jennings and music by Allan Rae, was performed in Toronto, Canada, in 1972 by the Playwrights Co-op. *The Manson Family: Helter Five-O* (1990), an avant-garde opera by John Moran, was performed in New York City's Alice Tully Hall on July 17 and 18, 1990. The work was commissioned by Serious Fun!, Lincoln Center's annual avant-garde festival. Released by Point Music (New York) on compact disk in 1992 as *The Manson Family: An Opera.*

Television: "Helter Skelter" (1976), a two-part, four-hour made-for-television movie based on Bugliosi's book of the same title, originally aired on CBS on April 1 and 2, 1976. Cast includes George DiCenzo (Vincent Bugliosi), Steve Railsback (Charles

Manson), Nancy Wolfe (Susan Atkins), Marilyn Burns (Linda Kasabian), Christina Hart (Patricia Krenwinkel), Cathey Paine (Leslie Van Houten), and Bill Durkin (Charles "Tex" Watson).

Video: Sharon Tate, the Victim … Charles Manson, the Convicted Serial Killer (US, 1990). Doris Tate, the murdered woman's mother, discusses the case in a 50-minute video manufactured and distributed by ATI Mark V Products, Inc.

"I'm willing to get out and kill a whole bunch of people. That's one reason I'm not really too fast on getting out. Because if I got out, I'd feel obligated to get even. It would be an honorable thing."—Manson in an August 1989 interview

Hippie cult leader often viewed as the prototype of the predatory guru (*see* Jim Jones) whose "Family"-directed murders marked the symbolic end of the 1960s era of innocence and free love. Born "No Name Maddox" to a 16-year-old prostitute in Cincinnati, Ohio, on November 12, 1934, Manson never met his father. Taking his surname from a man his mother briefly married, the young child spent his early life shuffled between relatives and foster homes. In 1939 Manson's mother was convicted of armed robbery and during her imprisonment the five year old was sent to live with a strict, religious aunt and her violent husband. To "toughen up" the youngster, the man forced Manson to wear a dress to school on the first day of class. Released from prison after serving five years, Manson's alcoholic mother reclaimed the boy but soon tired of having him underfoot. Once in a drunken stupor, she reportedly "gave" Manson to a barmaid in payment for a drink. In 1947 at the age of 12, Manson was placed in

the first of many institutions, the Gibault School for Boys in Terre Haute, Indiana. Ten months later he fled, making his way on the streets by stealing. In the next several years, Manson received his early instruction in criminal behavior at a variety of institutions including Father Flanagan's Boy's Town and the reform school at Plainfield, Indiana. In his book, *Manson in His Own Words*, the killer graphically described his hellish three-year stay at Plainfield where, if he is to be believed, he was routinely raped and beaten by the other inmates. Escaping from Plainfield in February 1951, Manson was recaptured and spent most of the fifties and sixties in and out of state and federal institutions for crimes ranging from homosexual assault, car theft, forging and cashing stolen U.S. Treasury checks, pimping and transporting prostitutes across state lines.

On March 21, 1967, Manson was paroled from Terminal Island Prison in San Pedro, California, after serving a long term for car theft and pimping at the federal prison McNeil Island in the state of Washington. Prophetically, the 32-year-old Manson realized that the 19 years he had spent behind bars had rendered him ill-equipped to adapt to the outside world and he asked authorities to permit him to remain in jail. They refused and with $35 in his pocket Manson drifted north to San Francisco, then the center of the Hippie movement. Thoroughly schooled in the "jail house con," the charismatic Manson soon realized that there was a place for him in San Francisco's Haight-Ashbury district. A budding musician/songwriter (Alvin "Creepy" Karpis of the Ma Barker gang had taught him to play guitar in prison), Manson used his music combined with an addled messianic philosophy buttressed with marijuana and mind-altering drugs to attract a coterie of young middle-class white women who had dropped out of society looking for "truth." Manson used his "young loves" to attract to his "Family"-disaffected males who possessed the skills he needed to make his cult self-sufficient; a handiness with weapons and automobile mechanics. With his Family in tow, Manson relocated to the Los Angeles area where he settled his commune at Spahn Ranch, an old film set and horse ranch in Simi Valley. In exchange for care and sex from Manson's women, George Spahn, the 81-year-old owner, permitted the Family to stay there free. Manson used the ranch as a base from which to sell drugs and to convert stolen cars into dune buggies.

At Spahn Ranch, Manson solidified his total control over the 30 or so members of his cult. Feeding them a steady stream of marijuana and LSD, the guru orchestrated sexual orgies designed to rid his followers of any of their "hang-ups." Calling himself "Jesus Christ" and "God," the 5'2" ex-convict preached his version of the upcoming apocalypse which combined his bizarre interpretation of the biblical book of Revelation with the unimagined depths of meaning he found in the Beatles' *White Album*, more specifically the song "Helter Skelter." According to Manson's paranoid reasoning the coming race war between the blacks and the whites was inevitable. In the ensuing struggle, the blacks would emerge victorious but lack the intelligence to rule the world. At this point, Manson and his followers would emerge from their "Bottomless Pit," a place of safety in California's Death Valley to which they had fled to avoid the carnage, and take over the planet. Tired of waiting for "Helter

Skelter," the day of the Apocalypse, Manson decided to instigate the event by sending out four of his most devoted disciples to kill prominent members of the white Establishment, then plant evidence implicating black revolutionaries. Terry Melcher, the record producer son of Doris Day and then boyfriend of actress Candice Bergen, was selected as a victim because a year earlier he had refused to give Manson a recording contract. At that time, Melcher was living at 10500 Cielo Drive in the West Los Angeles Benedict Canyon area. Unknown to Manson, Melcher had recently sub-let the house to Polish film director Roman Polanski and his wife of eight months actress Sharon Tate. The beautiful actress was eight-and-a-half months pregnant and waiting for her husband to return from shooting a film in England. On the night of August 8, 1969, Manson assembled his "hit team" telling its appointed leader Charles "Tex" Watson, a 23-year-old one-time "A" student and high school football star, that "You're going out on the Devil's business tonight" and to "kill everyone inside" the house. Accompanying Watson were 21-year-old topless dancer Susan Atkins (known in the Family as "Sadie Mae Glutz"), Patricia Krenwinkel, the 21-year-old daughter of a middle-class insurance salesman, and Linda Kasabian, the group's drug-addicted 20-year-old driver and lookout who had left her home in the Midwest to look for God.

Shortly after midnight, Watson and the three women invaded the Cielo Drive home of actress Sharon Tate. First to die was Steven Earl Parent, 18, who was visiting the caretaker who lived in a cottage on the grounds. Watson shot Parent four times at close range with a .22 caliber pistol as the teenager sat in his parked car in the driveway. Entering the house, Watson, accompanied by Atkins and Krenwinkel ultimately herded the occupants into the living room. Visiting the 26-year-old actress that night were Wojiciech (Voytek) Frykowski, a 32-year-old Polish emigré playboy and drug dealer, his lover Abigail (Gibby) Folger, 25-year-old heiress to the Folger's coffee fortune, and Jay Sebring, 35, Tate's former lover and a famous name in the recently invented field of men's hairstyling. In the ensuing carnage Frykowski was stabbed 51 times, shot twice, and pistol whipped with such force by Watson that the handle of his gun broke off. His body was found on the front yard of the estate. Folger was stabbed 28 times with a bayonet by Watson and Atkins before dying near Frykowski. Sebring was shot in the back and stabbed seven times. Last to die was Sharon Tate who, after pleading for the life of her unborn baby, was told by Atkins, "Look bitch … I don't care if you're going to have a baby … You're going to die and I don't feel anything about it." The group stabbed the actress 16 times. Per Manson's instructions, Watson tossed a rope over an exposed ceiling beam and wrapped the ends around the necks of Tate and Sebring. Atkins, who actually tasted Tate's blood, wanted to cut out the woman's unborn fetus and take it to Manson for ritualistic purposes, but was told by Watson it was time to leave. Before doing so, Atkins daubed a towel in Tate's blood and scrawled the word "PIG" on the front door.

The next night, August 10, Manson accompanied Watson, Atkins, Krenwinkel, Kasabian, and Leslie Sue Van Houten, 19, on a raid in the Los Feliz section of Los Angeles 15 miles from the site of the Tate massacre. Alone and armed with a gun, Manson entered the home of Leno and Rosemary LaBianca at 3301 Waverly Drive. He tied up the 44-year-old supermarket tycoon and his 38-year-old wife assuring them both as he left that they would not be harmed. Returning to the car, Manson ordered Watson, Krenwinkel, and Van Houten to kill the bound pair. When Leno LaBianca was later found, he had been stabbed 26 times and the word "WAR" and several crosses had been carved into his chest. A knife and a fork were found protruding from his body. His wife was strangled with an electric cord and stabbed 41 times. "DEATH TO PIGS" and "RISE" were written on the living room wall in the the victims' blood as was the slogan "HEALTER SKELTER" [sic] found scrawled across the door of the refrigerator. Acting on Manson's instructions, the killers dropped the wallet of one of their victims in a black neighborhood in the hope that someone there would be caught by police using a credit card thereby leading them to believe that the murders were racially motivated. As public pressure mounted to solve the crimes (initially believed not to be linked), Manson had relocated his Family to Barker Ranch on the edge of Death Valley where he was arrested with 22 members of his group in October 1969 on charges of grand theft auto and arson.

The killers were identified as suspects in the Tate-LaBianca murders after Susan Atkins, held at the Sybil Brand Institute as a suspect in the Manson-ordered torture-murder of Malibu music teacher Gary Hinman a few days before the Tate-LaBianca killings, told her cellmates about slaughtering the people on Cielo Drive on "Charlie's" order. She also bragged about Manson's future plans to shake up the Establishment by murdering well-known celebrities like Frank Sinatra, Tom Jones, and Elizabeth Taylor. At a police press conference in Los Angeles held on December 1, 1969, authorities announced that the Tate-LaBianca case was solved. In a spectacular nine-month trial in which Linda Kasabian turned state's evidence in exchange for immunity from prosecution, Manson, Atkins, Van Houten, and Krenwinkel were convicted of murder on March 29, 1971, and subsequently sentenced to death. Tried separately, Charles "Tex" Watson received a similar verdict and sentence. Manson and two other Family members were also convicted in the murder of Donald "Shorty" Shea, a would-be actor and hand on the Spahn Ranch. The death sentences, however, were overturned and commuted to indeterminate life sentences in 1972 after the California Supreme Court invalidated the existing capital punishment statute. All the principals in the Manson case have been eligible for parole since 1978, but their petitions have been consistently denied due largely to the efforts of Sharon Tate's family. Van Houten was subsequently retried in 1976 because her attorney, Ronald Hughes, disappeared during the first trial. His remains were found four months later in a mountain wilderness prompting many to speculate that he was killed by Family members because he refused to follow Manson's defense strategies. A second trial for Van Houten ended in a hung jury, but she was finally convicted in 1978. Watson married, fathered two children during prison conjugal visits, served as an assistant Protestant pastor at the California Men's Colony at San Luis Obispo, and currently runs his own prison ministry.

The women convicted in the case have since taken advanced educational degrees and counsel new female inmates.

Manson, still sporting the swastika he carved into his forehead, continues to be a figure of fascination for the media who hungrily hang on his every word. Realistic enough to know that he will never be released from prison, he now only occasionally attends his parole hearings. On September 25, 1984, Manson was hanging about the hobby shop in the California Medical Facility at Vacaville when he argued with fellow-inmate Jan Holmstrom over the man's constant recital of Hare Krishna chants. Holmstrom, a 36-year-old devotee of the sect doing life for the 1974 shotgun murder of his father, doused Manson with paint thinner and tossed a match on him. Manson survived, but was treated for second and third degree burns over his face, scalp, and hands. In 1993, the convicted killer was again thrust into the public spotlight when the enormously popular Los Angeles-based rock band Guns N' Roses featured his song "Look at Your Game, Girl" as the 13th and final cut on their *The Spaghetti Incident* album. Though the song was not cited on the album's play list, the name "Charlie" appears in the credits and lead singer Axl Rose thanks "Chas" at the end of the song. Depending on record sales, Manson could have earned as much as $62,000 in royalties. However, based on a judgment obtained in 1971 it was ruled that Manson's royalties would go to the son of Voytek Frykowski. To deflect public criticism, Axl Rose promised to donate any royalties the band received from the song to an environmental group that helps dolphins. To many, Rose further served to popularize the killer by wearing a tee-shirt bearing Manson's likeness while performing. Manson's image has been officially licensed by Zooport Riot Gear, a surf-wear company based in Newport Beach, California, which pays him 10¢ a shirt. Writers on the case have since speculated that Manson was part of a murderous satanic organization which included "Son of Sam" killer David Berkowitz and also that many of the murders were drug-related "hits."

407. Atkins, Susan, and Slosser, Bob. *Child of Satan, Child of God.* Plainfield, N.J.: Logos International, 1977. vii, 290 pp., [3] leaves of plates: ill.; 22 cm.

_____. [Same as 407.] Plainfield, N.J.: Logos International, 1977. vii, 287 pp., [4] leaves of plates: ill.; 18 cm.; paperback.

_____. [Same as 407.] New York: Bantam Books, 1978. 269 pp., [4] leaves of plates: ill.; 18 cm.; paperback.

_____. [Same as 407.] London: Hodder and Stoughton, 1978. [9], 290 pp.; 18 cm.; paperback.

Like many convicted killers, Atkins experienced a religious conversion in prison and, at the time of this book, was ministering to inmates at the California Institution for Women. According to Atkins' account of the Tate murder, she did not kill the actress, but did taste her blood. Many cynical commentators on the case firmly believe that "Sexy Sadie's" newfound religion is a transparent attempt to one day win parole.

408. Baer, Rosemary. *Reflections on the Manson Trial: Journal of a Pseudo-Juror.* Waco, Tex.: Word Books, 1972. 175 pp.: ill.; 23 cm.

409. Bishop, George. *Witness to Evil.* Illustrated by Bill Lignante. Los Angeles: Nash, 1971. xii, 431 pp.: ill.; 23 cm.

_____. [Same as 409.] Illustrated by Bill Lignante. Foreword by Art Linkletter. New York: Dell, 1972. 347 pp., [4] leaves

of plates: ill., ports.; 18 cm.; paperback.

410. Bugliosi, Vincent, and Gentry, Curt. *Helter Skelter: The True Story of the Manson Murders.* 1st ed. New York: Norton, 1974. xvii, 502 pp.: ill.; 24 cm.

_____. [Same as 410.] New York: Bantam, 1975. xix, 676 pp., [64]pp. of plates: ill., ports.; 18 cm.; paperback.

_____. [Same as 410, but U.K. ed. retitled: *The Manson Murders: An Investigation into Motive.*] London: Bodley Head, 1975. [8], 502 pp., [50]pp. of plates: ill., facsims., 2 maps, 1 plan, ports.; 24 cm.

_____. [Same as 410, but U.K. ed. retitled: *The Manson Murders: An Investigation into Motive.*] Abridged ed. Harmondsworth: Penguin, 1977. 623 pp., [16]pp. of plates: ill.. maps, 1 plan, ports.; 19 cm.; paperback.

_____. [Same as 410, but U.K. ed. retitled: *The Manson Murders: An Investigation into Motive.*] London: Penguin, 1989. 502 pp.; 20 cm.; paperback.

_____. [Same as 410.] London: Arrow Books, 1992. xix, 676 pp.: ill.; 18 cm.; paperback.

_____. [Same as 410.] 25th Anniversary ed. with a new afterword by Vincent Bugliosi. New York: W.W. Norton, 1994. xvii, 528 pp., [26]pp. of plates: ill., maps; 24 cm.

The most popular of the many books on Manson written by the prosecutor of the Tate-LaBianca trials. Excellent index.

411. Cohen, Scott. *The Charles Manson Index.* [S.l.]: Full Court Press, 1971. 1 v. (unpaged); 28 cm.; paper covers.

412. Cooper, David E., ed. *The Manson Murders: A Philosophical Inquiry.* Cambridge, Mass.: Schenkman, 1974. viii, 141 pp.; 22 cm.

_____. [Same as 412.] Rochester, Vt.: Schenkman Books, 1994. vii, 141 pp.; 22 cm.

413. Endleman, Robert. *Jonestown and the Manson Family: Race, Sexuality, and*

Collective Madness. New York: Psyche Press, 1993. xvii, 211 pp.; 22 cm.

414. Gilmore, John, and Kenner, Ron. *The Garbage People.* Los Angeles: Omega Press, 1971. 185 pp.; 21 cm.; paperback.

The authors conducted extensive interviews with Manson at the Los Angeles County Jail. The book's title is derived from the following Manson quote: "Where does the garbage go, as we have tin cans and garbage alongside the road, and oil slicks in the water, so you have people, and I am one of your garbage people."

415. Harrington, William. *Columbo: The Helter Skelter Murders.* 1st ed. New York: Forge, 1994. 295 pp.; 23 cm. ("A Tom Doherty Associates book.")

Fictionalization of the case featuring the television detective Lt. Columbo.

416. Livsey, Clara. *The Manson Women: A Family Portrait.* New York: Richard Marek Publishers, 1980. 244 pp.; 24 cm.

Psychoanalytic study of Atkins, Krenwinkel, Van Houten, Lynette "Squeaky" Fromme, and Sandra Good.

417. Manson, Charles, and Emmons, Nuel. *Manson in His Own Words.* 1st Grove Press ed. New York: Grove Press, 1986. 232 pp., [16]pp. of plates: ill., ports.; 24 cm.

_____. [Same as 417, but U.K. ed. retitled: *Without Conscience: Charles Manson in His Own Words.*] London: Grafton, 1987. 221 pp., [16]pp. of plates: ill., ports.; 24 cm.

_____. [Same as 417.] 1st Evergreen ed. New York: Grove Press, 1988. 232 pp., [16]pp. of plates: ill., ports.; 24 cm.; paperback.

_____. [Same as 417, but U.K. ed. retitled: *Without Conscience: Charles Manson in His Own Words.*] London: Grafton, 1988. 276 pp., [16]pp. of plates: ill., ports.; 18 cm.; paperback.

418. Murphy, Bob. *Desert Shadows: The Bizarre and Frightening True Story of Charles Manson.* Billings, Mont.: R. Murphy, 1986. ix, 125 pp.: ill.; 22 cm.; paperback.

_____. [Same as 418 with variant subtitle: *A True Story of the Charles Manson Family in Death Valley.*] Updated ed. Montana: R. Murphy; Morongo Valley, Calif.: Distributed by Sagebrush Press, 1993. ix, 133 pp.: ill., maps; 22 cm.

419. Perry, Michael R. *Skelter.* New York: Pocket Star Books, 1994. 408 pp.; 18 cm.; paperback.

Fictionalization.

420. Russell, J.D. *Chronicle of Death.* Woodbridge, Conn.: Apollo Books, 1971. 179 pp.; 18 cm.; paperback.

Fictionalization.

421. Sanders, Ed. *The Family: The True Story of Charles Manson's Dune Buggy Attack Battalion.* 1st ed. New York: Dutton, 1971. 412 pp.: maps; 22 cm.

_____. [Same as 421 with variant subtitle: *The Story of Charles Manson's Dune Buggy Attack Battalion.*] Rev. ed. New York: Avon, 1972. 415 pp.: maps; 19 cm.; paperback.

_____. [Same as 421 with subtitle: *The Story of Charles Manson's Dune Buggy Attack Battalion.*] London: Hart-Davis, 1972. 412 pp.: 3 maps; 23 cm.

_____. [Same as 421 with variant subtitle: *The Story of Charles Manson's Dune Buggy Attack Battalion.*] St. Albans: Panther, 1973. 348 pp.: maps; 18 cm.; paperback.

_____. [Same as 421 with variant subtitle: *The Manson Group and Its Aftermath.*] Rev. and updated ed. New York: New American Library, 1989. xi, 496 pp., [8]pp. of plates: ill.; 18 cm. ("A Signet book"); paperback.

Highly regarded study of Manson and the Family which focuses on the group's occult influences.

422. Schiller, Lawrence and Atkins, Susan. *The Killing of Sharon Tate: With the Exclusive Story of the Crime by Susan Atkins (Confessed Participant in the Murder of Film Star Sharon Tate.)* New York: New American Library, 1970. 126 pp., [8]pp. of plates: ill.; 18 cm. ("A Signet book"); paperback.

423. Schreck, Nikolas, ed. *The Manson File*. New York: Amok Press, 1988. 197 pp.: ill., ports.; 22 cm.; paperback. "The unexpurgated Charles Manson as revealed in letters, photos, stories, songs, art, testimony, and documents."—Cover.

424. Taylor, James. *Satan's Slaves and the Bizarre "Underground" Cults of California*. 1st NEL ed. London: New English Library, 1970. 127 pp.: ill.; 18 cm.; paperback.

425. Terry, Maury. *The Ultimate Evil: An Investigation into America's Most Dangerous Satanic Cult*. 1st ed. Garden City, N.Y.: Doubleday, 1987. xiii, 512 pp., [8]pp. of plates: ill., ports.; 24 cm. ("A Dolphin book.")

_____. [Same as 425 with variant subtitle: *An Investigation into a Dangerous Satanic Cult*. New York: Bantam Books, 1989. xiii, 640 pp., [16]pp. of plates: ill., ports.; 18 cm.; paperback.

Terry links Manson and "Son of Sam" killer David Berkowitz to a satanic cult called the Process which he contends was responsible for a series of ritual murders.

426. Watkins, Paul, and Soledad, Guillermo. *My Life with Charles Manson*. New York: Bantam Books, 1979. 278 pp.; 18 cm.; paperback.

427. Watson, Tex, and Hoekstra, Ray. *Will You Die for Me?* Old Tappan, N.J.: F.H. Revell, 1978. 223 pp., [8] leaves of plates: ill.; 24 cm.

_____. [Same as 427.] Dallas: International Prison Ministry, 1978. 216 pp., [8] leaves of plates: ill.; 18 cm. ("A Spires book"); paperback.

Watson, the leader of the Manson murder squad in both the Tate and LaBianca murders, chronicles his religious conversion.

428. Wizinski, Sy. *Charles Manson: Love Letters to a Secret Disciple: A Psychoanalytical Approach*. Terre Haute, Ind.: Moonmad Press, 1976. iv, 219 pp.: ill.; 22 cm.

Some sources cite author Wizinski as "S. Rosenthal."

429. Zaehner, R.C. *Our Savage God*. London: Collins, 1974. 319 pp.; 22 cm.

_____. [Same as 429 with added subtitle: *The Perverse Use of Eastern Thought*.] New York: Sheed and Ward, 1975. 319 pp.; 22 cm.

430. Zamora, William. *Trial by Your Peers*. New York: M. Girodias Associates; Secaucus, N.J.: distributed by L. Stuart, 1973. 483 pp.; 24 cm.

_____. [Same as 430, but abridged ed. retitled: *Blood Family*.] A Zebra/Lyle Stuart book; 211. New York: Kensington, 1976. 507 pp.; 18 cm.; paperback.

Manuel, Peter Thomas Anthony
(a.k.a. "The Man Who Talked Too Much")

Born March 15, 1927, in New York, New York. Executed July 11, 1958. Woodworker, railway worker, burglar. Glasgow, Scotland, area and Newcastle, England; 9 murders (suspected in at least 3 others); bludgeon, .38 caliber revolver, knife; ligature strangulation; January 1956–January 1958.

"My family is just an ordinary family—nice people. I have given them a lot of trouble. I have given them a terrible life."

Scotland's most infamous modern serial murderer, Peter Manuel is crime's classic example of the killer whose inflated ego and need for attention led directly to his apprehension and execution. Manuel's criminal career began at 12 with housebreaking and gradually evolved to encompass robbery with violence, rape, and ultimately multiple homicides. Before committing his first murder in early 1956, Manuel spent his adolescence learning the craft of crime in ten Borstal institutes. By 1946, Manuel's career as a rapist was temporarily halted by a six-year prison term for that crime. Upon release, Manuel tried to marry but his prison record and refusal to attend confession scared the woman off. An unsuccessful prosecution for indecent assault in October 1955 left him free to begin a two-year murder spree which claimed several lives.

On January 4, 1956, the bludgeoned body of 18-year-old Anne Knielands was found dumped off the fifth tee of the East Kilbride golf course near Glasgow. Nearby in a patch of blood-soaked earth, 15 fragments of her skull were recovered. While her pants had been torn from her, no sexual assault had occurred. Manuel, his face covered in scratches, was questioned by police, but his alibi held. Several months later on September 17, 1956, Manuel broke into the bungalow of the Watt family in High Burnside, Rutherglen, near Glasgow and shot two sleeping sisters to death in the bed they shared before beating and shooting Mrs. Watt's teenage daughter. Police again suspected Manuel, but could prove nothing. Suspicion shifted to the vacationing William Watt, husband and father of the victims, and the hapless man was arrested on September 27, 1956, and detained in Barlinnie Prison for 67 days. One week later, Manuel arrived there to serve 18 months for robbery.

Psychically incapable of distancing himself from the crime's notoriety, Manuel contacted Watt's attorney claiming to know the identity of the real killer. His detailed description of the Watt home convinced the lawyer that he had been present at the murders. Watt was freed on December 3, 1956, and accompanied by his attorney met with Manuel days after the mur-

derer's release a year later. Manuel responded to Watt's accusation that he was involved in the murders by fingering an old enemy as the killer. Days later Manuel travelled to Newcastle where he shot and slashed taxi cab driver Sydney Dunn to death. Ironically, Manuel was charged with the murder on July 28, 1958—17 days *after* his execution.

On December 28, 1957, 17-year-old Isabelle Cooke disappeared while walking through a woods on her way to a dance in Uddingston. A massive search yielded some articles of her clothing, but no body. Once in custody, Manuel later confessed to strangling the teen with her own brassiere and led police to her body buried in a freshly ploughed field. The first week of the new year brought fresh horror to Uddingston as the bodies of the Peter Smart family were found shot to death in the bedrooms of their home. Days earlier, Manuel had destroyed the three on New Year's Day, stole £25 in fresh blue bank notes, and for days afterwards had used the death house as a base of operations. He was arrested on January 14, 1958, after police traced the distinctive bills back to him. In custody, he traded his written confession to the Knielands, Watt, Cooke, and Smart murders for the dropping of burglary charges against his father.

An international press corp descended on Glasgow for the May 12, 1958, murder trial. Midway through the proceedings, Manuel fired his attorneys and represented himself (excellently according to the judge). Portraying himself as an innocent victim of a police conspiracy, Manuel denied confessing to any murders. In a moment of supreme irony, the killer accused William Watt of murdering his own family during a brutal cross-examination of the bereaved widower. Convicted on May 28, 1958, of all charges except the Knielands murder (lack of corroborative evidence), Manuel was hanged at Glasgow's Barlinnie Prison on July 11, 1958. Authorities believe that the serial killer was responsible for at least three other murders.

431. Bingham, John, and Muncie, William. *The Hunting Down of Peter Manuel, Glasgow Multiple Murderer.* London: Macmillan, 1973. 223 pp.: ill.; 21 cm.

_____. [Same as 431 minus subtitle.] St. Albans: Panther, 1975. 224 pp., [8]pp. of plates: ill., ports.; 18 cm.; paperback.

Bingham, in association with detective chief superintendent William Muncie of the Lanarkshire county police, focuses on Manuel's apprehension. Appendixes document Manuel's mental condition and correlate his murderous attacks with lunar phases.

432. Wilson, John G. *The Trial of Peter Manuel: The Man Who Talked Too Much.* London: Secker and Warburg, 1959. 238 pp.: ill.; 23 cm.

Wilson's account neatly summarizes the over 700,000 word transcripts produced by Manuel's 16-day trial and 2-day appeal.

Merrett, John Donald
(a.k.a. "Ronald John Chesney," "John Donald Milner," "Chief," "Leslie Bernard Treville Chown")

Born August 17, 1908, in Levin, North Island, New Zealand. Died February 17, 1954. Smuggler. Edinburgh, Scotland, and Ealing, England; 3 murders; pistol, drowning, bludgeon, ligature strangulation (silk stocking); March 17, 1926 and February 10–11, 1954.

"I have seen so much of prisons I have no wish to return to there even for a day and the prospect of being hanged appeals to me even less."— Merrett in a letter to his solicitor written ten hours before his suicide

New Zealand–born smuggler and confidence man who murdered three women 28 years apart using two different names. Fearful that his mother would learn of the checks he forged against her account, John Donald Merrett, 17, shot the woman in the right ear on March 17, 1926, in their Edinburgh, Scotland, home. Initially believed to be a suicide attempt, authorities prosecuted Merrett for murder and forgery on February 1, 1927. Though the murder charge against Merrett was officially ruled as "not proven," he was unanimously convicted for forgery and sentenced to 12 months' imprisonment. Released after serving only eight months, Merrett assumed the name "Ronald John Chesney" and embarked on a 17-year career of smuggling drugs, liquor, and diamonds that made him known to the authorities of Britain, France, Germany, Switzerland, and Belgium. Long estranged from his wife and desperate for the nearly £10,000 marriage settlement he would realize upon her death, Merrett murdered the woman and her mother on the night of February 10–11, 1954, in their jointly owned retirement home in Ealing. Forensic evidence tied Merrett to the crime and, with arrest imminent, the 46-year-old walked into a wooded park in Cologne, Germany, on the morning of February 17, 1954, and shot himself in the mouth with a Colt .45 automatic. Merrett was buried in Cologne under the name "Ronald John Chesney."

433. Roughead, William, ed. *Trial of John Donald Merrett.* Notable British

Trials. Edinburgh; London: William Hodge & Company, Limited, 1929. x, 326 pp.: ill., ports., facsims.; 22 cm.

_____. [Same as 433.] Notable British Trials. Sydney: Butterworth, 1929. x, 326 pp.: ill., ports., facsims.; 22 cm.

_____. [Same as 433.] Notable British Trials. Toronto: Canada Law Book, 1929. x, 326 pp.: ill., ports., facsims.; 22 cm.

Exhaustive transcript coverage of Merrett's February 1927 trial in Edinburgh, Scotland, on charges of murdering his mother and "uttering" forged checks upon her bank account. Essential.

434. Tullett, Tom. *Portrait of a Bad Man.* London: Evans Brothers, 1956. 196 pp.: ill.; 21 cm.

_____. [Same as 434.] New York: Rinehart, 1956. 196 pp., [9] leaves of plates: ill.; 21 cm.

Florid account of Merrett's criminal career as "Ronald John Chesney" written by Tullett, ex–criminal investigations detective at Scotland Yard and present chief of the *Sunday Pictorial* (London) crime staff. Based on interviews with Merrett's women, criminal associates, and detectives.

Miller, James William
(a.k.a. "Truro Murders")

Born February 2, 1940, in Adelaide, Australia. Drifter. Truro, Australia; 7 murders (convicted of 6); knife; December 23, 1976–February 1977.

"Why fate chose that I should have become involved in this madness and why I should live when my two dearest friends died are just two questions surrounding Truro for which I do not know the answers."

Australian career criminal convicted of killing seven women in 1977 in what has become known as the "Truro Murders." Miller, a 34-year-old

petty thief with no record of violence, met Christopher Robin Worrell, 20, in Adelaide Gaol in 1974. After their release, the pair continued their homosexual relationship although Worrell was also attracted to women. On December 23, 1976, the pair picked up a young woman and drove her to the hills outside of Adelaide. According to Miller, he left Worrell and the woman in the car to have sex while he wandered off. He returned to find the woman stabbed to death. Miller, under a death threat from Worrell, helped his lover bury the body near Truro. The scenario was repeated six times over an eight-week period whenever Worrell, by Miller's account, had one of his "satanic moods." The serial killings ended abruptly on February 19, 1977, when Worrell and his girlfriend died in a car crash. Miller was barely scratched. Throughout 1978 and 1979 the skeletonized bodies of girls reported missing in 1977 began being discovered on the road to Truro. A sizable reward resulted in Miller's arrest in Adelaide in May 1979. Tried for seven murders before the South Australian Supreme Court in Adelaide in February 1980, Miller was found guilty of having acted "in concert" with Worrell to commit the murders and was sentenced to life imprisonment for six of the seven killings. An appeal based on new evidence showing that Worrell suffered from documented violent mood swings was denied on May 21, 1984.

435. Miller, James William. *Don't Call Me Killer!* Hawthorn, Vic.: Harbourtop Productions, 1984. 200 pp.: ill., ports.; 20 cm.; paperback.

Miller proclaims his innocence of the Truro murders in notes, writings, and audio tapes made in his cell at Yatala Labor Prison and edited into book form by Dick Wordley. In a preface Miller writes, "I was there at the time and I helped bury the girls. For that I am guilty of an unforgivable felony and fully deserve the life sentence I am currently serving in prison."

Milo, Frederick P.

Born July 22, 1944. Beauty supply company manager. Bath Township, Ohio; 1 murder (accomplice); .32 caliber automatic pistol; August 10, 1980.

A "murder-for-hire" fratricide masterminded by a greedy brother anxious to gain control over the lucrative family business. On August 11, 1980, 41-year-old Constantine R. "Dean" Milo, president of the multi-million dollar Milo Beauty and Barber Supply Corporation, was found dead inside the front door of his fashionable home in the Akron, Ohio, suburb of Bath Township. Clad only in his underwear, Milo had been shot twice in the head at close range. Police initially termed the murder "just another suburban killing" until evidence obtained by Dallas, Texas, private investigator William C. Dear (hired by Milo's widow) convinced them that they were dealing with a contract killing resulting from a family blood feud. Under an agreement set up by their parents in 1975, Dean Milo, his younger brother Frederick, and a sister were given equal ownership of the company with Dean having the firm's sole voting share. In August 1979, Dean Milo fired his brother and sister contending that they had converted $300,000 in corporate funds to their private use. After Dean Milo's death, brother Frederick assumed co-control of the corporation with his sister. Following a meticulous investigation, Frederick Milo was arrested on December 20, 1980, and charged with

working through former employees of the beauty supply corporation to hire a three man hit squad to kill his brother. Ultimately, ten other conspirators (including a go-go dancer and an attorney) were arrested and sentenced to prison terms ranging from four years to life. Frederick Milo's first trial for aggravated murder ended in a hung jury in Columbus, Ohio, on May 19, 1981. Retried in July 1981, Milo again pleaded not guilty by reason of insanity and psychiatric evidence was offered to support his claim that in the throes of a psychotic delusion he paid to have an "imitation" of his brother eliminated. Milo was found guilty on July 29, 1981 and sentenced to life imprisonment. His conviction was unanimously upheld by the Franklin County court of appeals on September 30, 1982.

436. Dear, William C., and Stowers, Carlton. *"Please—Don't Kill Me": The True Story of the Milo Murder.* Boston: Houghton Mifflin, 1989. ix, 245 pp., [8]pp. of plates: ill., ports.; 22 cm.

_____. [Same as 436.] New York: Ballantine Books, 1990. xi, 225 pp.: ill.; 18 cm.; paperback

Behind the scenes account of the case written by Dear, the private investigator hired by Milo's widow, and true crime writer Stowers.

437. Moldea, Dan E. *The Hunting of Cain: A True Story of Money, Greed, and Fratricide.* 1st ed. New York: Atheneum, 1983. xx, 287 pp., [4] leaves of plates: ill.; 22 cm.

_____. [Same as 437.] 1st St. Martin's Press mass market ed. New York: St. Martin's Press, 1988. xx, 292 pp.: ill.; 17 cm.; paperback.

Moldea, a specialist in organized crime, focuses on the unfolding criminal investigation in the Milo case. Meticulously researched.

"Miramichi Murders" *see* Legere, Allan Joseph

Montgomery, Candace Lynn
(acquitted)

Born circa 1950. Bible school teacher, housewife. Wylie, Texas; 1 murder (acquitted); ax; June 13, 1980.
Television: "Killing in a Small Town" (1990), a two-hour, made-for-television movie based on Bloom and Atkinson's book of the same title, originally aired on CBS on May 22, 1990. Cast includes Barbara Hershey (Candy Morrison/Montgomery), Brian Dennehy, and Hal Holbrook.
"I hit her, and I hit her, and I hit her, and I hit her."—Excerpt from Montgomery's trial testimony
Thirty-year-old Bible school teacher acquitted of the ax murder of her former lover's wife. The Montgomerys and Gores met through their involvement in choir and committee work at the United Methodist Church of Lucas, Texas. Candace "Candy" Montgomery, the married mother of two children, initiated an affair with Allan Gore in December 1978. The pair met in motels twice a week for ten months when Montgomery's daughter was in Bible class. Gore terminated the affair in October 1979. Montgomery was babysitting Betty Gore's young daughter on June 13, 1980, when she dropped by the 30-year-old schoolteacher's house in Wylie, Texas, to pick up a swimsuit for the child. Gore confronted Montgomery about the affair with her husband which she apologetically acknowledged. According to Montgomery's later testimony, Gore fetched a three-foot ax from the garage and forced her into a laundry room. During a struggle, Montgomery wrested the ax from Gore fatally striking her 41 times. "I hit her, and I hit her, and I hit her, and I hit her," she later admitted. Montgomery turned herself in to authorities 13 days later. Tried for murder in McKinney, Texas, in October 1980, Montgomery testified before a hostile courtroom gallery that she had acted in self-defense; a contention supported by lie detector tests which suggested she had not been the aggressor in the ax attack. Montgomery was acquitted by a nine woman, three man jury on October 29, 1980. She left the courtroom amid jeers and shouts of "murderer." Unpopular in the area, the Montgomerys moved to Atlanta, Georgia, in January 1981 where Candy volunteered for a time at a rape crisis center before quitting to return to college. Allan Gore married a divorcée he met through a church marriage encounter group less than six months after his wife's death.

438. Bloom, John, and Atkinson, Jim. *Evidence of Love.* Austin, Tex.: Texas Monthly Press, 1984. 359 pp.; 25 cm.

_____. [Same as 438.] Bantam ed. New York: Bantam Books, 1985. 360 pp.; 18 cm.; paperback.

Originally appeared as a two-part serialization entitled "Love and Death in Silicon Prairie" in *Texas Monthly* magazine, January/February 1984. Serialized in *Cosmopolitan*, May 1984.

"Moors Murders" *see* Brady, Ian Duncan (and) Hindley, Myra

"Mormon Blood-Atonement Killings" *see* Lundgren, Jeffrey Don

Morris, Raymond Leslie
(a.k.a. "The Cannock Chase Murderer," "The Monster of

Cannock Chase," "The A34 Child Murderer," "Uncle Len")

Born August 13, 1929, in Walsall, England. Foreman engineer. England; 1 murder (convicted, strongly suspected in 3 others); manual and ligature strangulation; September 1965–August 1967.

"I've never made a mistake in my life."—Statement made by Morris to his first wife

British child killer brought to justice by one of the largest manhunts ever conducted in England. In the mid–1960s, Cannock Chase, an open space encompassing nearly 85 square miles located 20 miles north of Birmingham, England, was a popular site for family picnickers and illicit lovers. From 1965 through 1967, however, a 29-year-old local resident named Raymond Leslie Morris transformed the area's idyllic splendor into a killing field and dumping ground for the raped and brutalized bodies of three of his child victims. Born in Walsall on August 13, 1929, Morris' childhood contained nothing to hint that he would become the object of a manhunt even larger than the search for the more infamous child killers, the Moors Murderers. Twice married, Morris' insatiable sex drive (seemingly fanned by the images of the actresses he saw on television) exhausted his first wife. Two days before Christmas in 1959 he informed her after eight years of marriage that she had one week to find another place to live. She moved out, but later told authorities that he frightened her into continuing to have sex with him twice a week on an irregular basis until they divorced on July 15, 1964, after almost 12 years of marriage and three sons. Slightly over a month later, Morris remarried a 21-year-old woman 14 years his junior. Boasting an IQ of 120, he went through a variety of jobs before becoming a foreman engineer in April 1967 in a precision instruments factory.

Six-year-old Margaret Reynolds was abducted from the Birmingham suburb of Aston on September 8, 1965. Months later on December 30, 1965, in nearby Bloxwich, five-and-a-half-year-old Diane Joy Tift was last seen in a launderette. The public, already traumatized by the October 1965 arrests of the Moors Murderers, Ian Brady and Myra Hindley, cooperated fully with police. In Bloxwich alone, 6,000 houses and outbuildings were systematically searched and thousands of posters and leaflets were distributed throughout Great Britain. Searchers scoured 25 square miles of open land in Birmingham and Walsall while divers checked streams, mine shafts, quarries and sewers. Over 50,000 people were interviewed with particular attention paid to mental patients and those previously convicted of indecent acts with children. On January 12, 1966, the bodies of two young girls were found dumped one on top of the other off the A34 trunk road in the muddy water of the Mansty Gulley on the Cannock Chase near a place called Pottal Pool. The top body was immediately identifiable as Diane Tift, but a medical examiner could only postulate that the skeletonized remains below her were those of Margaret Reynolds. Tift had been raped and her death caused by a mixture of strangulation and suffocation. Decomposition of Reynolds' body precluded establishing a cause of death though no one doubted she had met the same fate as Tift.

On August 14, 1966, 10-year-old Jane Elizabeth Taylor disappeared from the village of Mobberley. Despite an intensive search the child was never found and continues to this day to be technically classified as a missing person. Few detectives involved in the Cannock Chase investigation, however, doubt that the girl was killed by Morris. On August 19, 1967, seven-year-old Christine Ann Darby was picked out of a group of children in Walsall by a man driving a light-colored sedan. Darby entered the car to help the man with directions and was last seen by playmates driving away with him in the opposite direction she had told him to take. The next day, police found Darby's soiled underwear hanging on a tree branch in Cannock Chase near the A34 trunk road. Three hundred policemen searched the area, but it was a forestry worker who found Darby's plimsoll three miles away. The next day, 750 military and police personnel scoured the area looking for what they knew would be her corpse. On August 22, 1967, Darby was found covered with ferns at the foot of a tree on Cannock Chase. Naked from the waist down, she was splayed in the classic rape posture and her genital area had been severely torn from the molestation. A pathologist at the scene determined Darby had been asphyxiated by someone who held their hand across her nose and mouth. Tire tracks were found close to Darby's body and days later police uncovered a witness who said he saw a man backing a slate-gray Austin into the area where the body was found. Another witness independently verified the suspect's car as an Austin and offered a similar description of the driver. Based on these descriptions, an "Identikit" composite picture of the suspect was created and distributed on 40,000 posters throughout the British Isles. The same picture ran in color (a first in British history)

on the front page of the *Daily Express* on October 25, 1967. Two hundred police officers conducted a house-by-house inquiry of Walsall to request that every man between the ages of 21 and 50 complete a questionnaire explaining their whereabouts on the dates of the three murders. Concurrently, every Austin A.55 and A.60 in the Midlands (over 25,000 vehicles culled from 1,375,000 files) was checked to determine their owners' movements.

On November 4, 1968, a man in a green Ford Corsair with a light top attempted to force 10-year-old Margaret Aulton of Walsall into his car. When she resisted, he sped away but not before a witness took down a partial license plate number. Plates containing the partial numbers were cross-checked with a list of Ford Corsair owners. Only Raymond Leslie Morris of Flat 20, Regent House, Green Lane, Walsall owned a green Ford Corsair with a light top. During the subsequent police interview, Morris mentioned once owning a grey Austin A.55. Authorities had previously interviewed Morris four times in four years and had considered him a viable suspect in Darby's death until the unshakable alibi provided him by his wife, Carol, eliminated him. A further check, however, revealed that Morris was interviewed by police in October 1966 for picking up two girls (ages 10 and 11) and convincing them to let him photograph them in their underwear. He paid each girl two shillings to photograph him as he fondled the other's private parts over her clothing. Morris denied everything and although police found photographic equipment in his house, charges against him were dropped for lack of evidence. Interestingly, Morris' own brother had contacted the police in 1966 to denounce him as the murderer of Tift and Reynolds. In his statement, he described his brother as a cruel man of abnormal sexual appetite who was fully capable of murdering children.

Morris was arrested on November 15, 1968, and maintained his composure during interrogation until informed that his wife had recanted her alibi covering the time the Darby murder occurred. Morris then exclaimed, "Oh God! Oh God! She wouldn't! She wouldn't!" and refused to participate in a suspect line-up. Morris was charged with the murder of Darby the next day when a search of his flat uncovered photos of an eight or nine-year-old girl in various states of undress. In one photo a man's penis was near her vagina and in another, a wrist watch, identical to the one found hidden on Morris' ankle during booking, was clearly visible. The little girl was later identified as the five-year-old niece of Morris' wife. This revelation prompted Carol Morris to abandon her husband and agree to be the Crown's chief witness against him. Two charges of indecent assault against the niece and one for the attempted abduction of Aulton in Walsall were subsequently added to the murder charge against Morris.

Regina versus Morris began in the Staffordshire Court of Assizes on February 10, 1969, with the defendant pleading innocent to the murder of Darby and the attempted abduction of Aulton, but guilty to the molestation of the five-year-old depicted in the photographs. Seventy-eight witnesses testified for the prosecution. Despite a spirited defense, Morris' counsel could not shake the two eyewitnesses who put him at the murder scene. Carol Morris testified that she naïvely provided a false alibi for her husband because she did not believe him capable of murder. Courtroom drama reached a peak, however, when a female child in the audience pointed to Morris and shouted, "That's him!" Morris, posing as "Uncle Len," had allegedly abducted, raped, and then left the young girl for dead in a ditch in Bentley in January 1965. Testifying on his own behalf, Morris insisted that while in custody he was violently assaulted by police who never asked him to be in a line-up. A jury on January 14, 1969, needed only one hour and forty minutes to find Morris guilty on all counts. As a large crowd outside the court house chanted "Hang him! Hang him!" the judge imposed a sentence of life imprisonment on "the Monster of Cannock Chase." Morris was taken to Durham where he was housed in the top-security section reserved for child killers like fellow-prisoners Ian Brady and John T. Straffen. Investigators, unable to connect Morris with the murders of Margaret Reynolds or Diane Joy Tift, halted their investigations of these cases after his conviction for the Darby murder. A petition for appeal filed in Morris' behalf was denied. Morris' infamous Austin A.55 Cambridge was purchased at a Birmingham auction by a Worcestershire car dealer who publicly burned "the Car That Died of Shame" five weeks after the end of the trial on March 28, 1969. In 1983, prison medical officials classified Morris as a "dangerous psychopath" who would represent a continued danger to children should he ever be released.

439. Hawkes, Harry. *Murder on the A34.* Foreword by Arthur Rees. London: John Long, 1970. 191 pp., 8 plates : ill., map, ports.; 22 cm.

440. Molloy, Pat. *Not the Moors Murders: A Detective's Story of the Biggest Child-Killer Hunt in History.* Llandysfyl, Wales:

Gomer Press, 1988. 266 pp.: ill. (some col.), maps, facsims., ports.; 22 cm.

_____. [Same as 440, but paperback ed. retitled: *The Cannock Chase Murders.*] Sevenoaks: New English Library, 1990. [272] pp.: ill., maps, facsims., ports.; 18 cm.; paperback.

Firsthand account by one of the lead detectives on the case which primarily focuses on the massive police manhunt which resulted in Morris' capture. Excellent selection of photographs. Highly recommended.

Mossler, Candace Grace

(*acquitted;* a.k.a. "Candace Grace Weatherby" [maiden name], "Candace Grace Johnson" [first marriage], "Candace Grace Garrison" [third marriage], "The Swinging Granny")

Born February 20, 1920, in Buchanan, Georgia. Died October 26, 1976. Wife, heiress. Key Biscayne, Florida; 1 murder (acquitted); bludgeon, knife; June 30, 1964.

"I think tomorrow is another day. If a tragic situation is your fate, then that's your fate. We have our sorrows and our heartaches, but you have to put them behind you. I used to say to Judy Garland, 'You've got to be like a cat, Judy. You've got to learn to land on your feet in this world.'"—Mossler in a June 1976 *Esquire* article when asked if she had a philosophy of life

Unsolved murder thought to have revolved around the relationship between a related older woman and younger man. The brutal murder of 69-year-old Jacques Mossler in Key Biscayne, Florida, on June 30, 1964, generated all the elements necessary for great soap opera: a glamorous 44-year-old former model married to an alleged homosexual, but in love with the 24-year-old son of a younger sister. Authorities theorized that Candy Mossler and Melvin Lane Powers conspired to kill husband Jacques in order for the widow to collect an estate valued at $36 million. Their trial produced accusations of homosexuality, incest, and murder shocking enough to make readers of *Peyton Place* blush. Candace Weatherby, the fifth of ten children born to a Georgia farmer, dropped out of high school and married a civil engineer in 1939. The marriage dissolved two years later and Candy with her two children moved to New York to study fashion design and to model freelance. In 1947, she moved to New Orleans and opened the Candace Model Studios and Finishing School. While doing volunteer work Candy met wealthy Jacques Mossler, a 51-year-old divorced financier with four daughters. Marrying in 1948, the family grew in 1957 when they adopted the four children of Illinois murderer, Leonard Glenn, a former mental patient who killed his wife and stabbed an infant son.

At 6'4" and 220 pounds, Melvin Lane Powers, Candy's 24-year-old nephew, had been charitably compared to a young Burt Lancaster. Powers began working for Mossler in the spring of 1962 and, according to testimony, began a torrid affair with his aunt shortly thereafter. Moving into the Mossler mansion in Houston, Powers was evicted by the millionaire in the spring of 1963 after he learned of their affair. Their relationship remained tense up to the time of Mossler's murder. Jacques Mossler moved alone to Key Biscayne, Florida, and rented an apartment in the luxurious 32-unit Governor's Lodge. On the night of the murder, Candy and four of their children were visiting. Candy stayed up late to pay bills and left with the children to post them. Plagued by migraine headaches, she drove to a Miami hospital where she refused a pain injection from a nurse, preferring to wait a couple of hours for a doctor to arrive. While there, she received several phone calls the prosecution later insisted were from Powers tipping her that the murder had been committed. Released at 4:05 a.m., she returned to the apartment half an hour later to find the front door unlocked. Inside, she found Mossler dead from 39 stab wounds to the chest and multiple blunt object blows to the head. Clad only in an undershirt, Mossler's head had been covered with a blanket. A bloody palm print was found on a kitchen countertop. Neighbors reported to police hearing screams around 1:30–2:00 a.m. followed by sounds of a scuffle and running footsteps. A large man was observed moving in the shadows toward the parking lot and speeding away in a light colored car.

Suspicion settled on Powers when police established that he had flown from Houston to Miami on June 29, 1964, only to return to Houston on June 30, the day of the murder. A white Chevrolet licensed to one of Mossler's companies was found in a parking area at Miami International Airport with Powers' fingerprints in it. A bartender in a Miami lounge identified him as the customer who on June 29 had repeatedly asked for an empty king-sized bottle of Coke. The final bit of damning circumstantial evidence against Powers came when police identified the bloody palm print found at the murder scene as his. Powers was arrested at work on July 4, 1964, in a Houston trailer sales lot owned by the dead man. A search of Powers' trailer uncovered

photos of him with Candy along with amorous letters she had sent him. Candy Mossler was arrested in Miami over a year later on July 22, 1965, and also charged in the murder. She hired flamboyant Houston attorney Percy Foreman to defend Powers and separate counsel for herself.

The tabloid "Trial of the Decade" began on January 17, 1966, in Miami. Played to a standing room only crowd and covered by more than 50 newspapers, the star of the proceedings was Percy Foreman. A veteran of over 700 murder trials, he quickly demonstrated why his fee was $250,000 (he was ultimately paid $565,000). Portraying the dead man as a cruel homosexual who practiced all known forms of perversion except shoe fetishism, Foreman pointed the finger at two of the banker's business associates. No witnesses were produced to substantiate the validity of his attack on Mossler. Foreman similarly attacked some of the prosecution's witnesses who testified that the defendants had offered them money to kill Mossler. The witnesses were ex-cons and not credible. Neither did the police escape his verbal barrage. They had coerced witnesses to testify against the duo through threats of criminal prosecution. Lacking an eyewitness to the crime, Foreman asserted that the state's "evidence" was purely circumstantial. Seven weeks later on March 6, 1966, after deliberating three days, the all-male jury acquitted both defendants. The prosecution had only proved that aunt and nephew had been intimate. A tearful Candy kissed each juror and signed autographs. For years following the trial she received annual Christmas cards from some of them.

The strange saga of Candy Mossler did not end with her acquittal. In 1971 the 52-year-old heiress married

32-year-old electrical contractor Barnett Wade Garrison. On August 13, 1972, Garrison suffered massive brain damage in a fall from the roof of the 62-room Mossler mansion. Garrison, an unloaded pistol in his belt, had slipped while trying to enter Candy's locked third floor balcony window. Police ruled the fall accidental. The couple divorced in November 1972. Candy Mossler was found dead in the bed of her penthouse suite in Miami's posh Fountainebleau Hotel on October 26, 1976, the apparent victim of having smothered to death in her pillow during a heavily drugged sleep. Former lover Mel Powers subsequently became a high profile real estate developer in Houston who in May 1985 emerged from a Chapter 11 petition with a court-approved plan to repay $232 million in debts. The Mossler murder remains officially unsolved.

441. Holmes, Paul. *The Candy Murder Case.* Illustrated by Sanford Kossin. New York: Bantam Books, 1966. 218 pp.: ill.; 18 cm.; paperback.

Sensational paperback account which draws heavily from the trial transcript. Includes Sanford Kossin's trial sketches.

442. Honeycutt, Richard. *Candy Mossler: Her Life and Trial.* New York: Pocket Books, 1966. 154 pp.: ill.; 18 cm.; paperback.

Paperback original which loudly proclaims on its cover, "The story no newspaper dared tell! The shocking, provocative, intimate trial disclosures and the story of the passionate murder—the most scorching crime of the century." Appendices include the autopsy findings, Jacques Mossler's last will, and the prosecutor's opening statement to the jury.

Mothershed, William James (a.k.a. "Junior")

Born May 5, 1962, in Indianapolis, Indiana. University student. San Fernando, California; 1 murder; 9mm automatic; December 24, 1982.

Television: "Confessions: Two Faces of Evil" (1994), a two-hour, made-for-television movie, originally aired on NBC on January 17, 1994. Cast includes Jason Bateman (Bill Mothershed), James Wilder (Robert Berndt), and James Earl Jones (Charlie Lloyd).

"I honestly had no intentions of murdering that man, albeit I did."—From Mothershed's taped confession

Unusual case in which a suspect was arrested for murdering a police officer and later freed when the actual killer subsequently confessed. At 3:46 a.m. on Christmas Eve 1980, 30-year-old San Fernando, California, police officer Dennis Frank Webb radioed the dispatcher that he was stopping a pedestrian who matched a description of a man who had robbed two 7-Eleven convenience stores in the area, one only 90 minutes earlier. A fellow officer, arriving on the scene minutes later, found Webb critically wounded from six shots fired point blank from a 9mm automatic. The killer drove off in Webb's car and it was later found miles away at the remote Sepulveda Dam recreation area. Robert Paul Berndt, a 26-year-old former mental patient and security guard, was arrested on January 29, 1981, after he walked into a Clinton, Oklahoma, jail during a snowstorm for assistance and a computer check revealed that he was wanted on a fugitive burglary warrant in Texas. A search of Berndt's belongings uncovered an unmailed letter he had written to the FBI in which he implicated himself in the Webb killing. Clinton police alleged that Berndt confessed several times to the murder during questioning, but publicly the suspect maintained his innocence. The case against Berndt was severely weakened when a clerk at one of the 7-Eleven stores declared that he was absolutely sure that the suspect was not the robber.

On March 29, 1981, an 18-year-old former scholarship student at the New Mexico Institute of Mining and Technology, William James Mothershed, was arrested in Socorro, New Mexico, for Webb's murder and two counts of robbery. Mothershed evidently had told friends about the killing after returning from a Christmas vacation in Los Angeles. A New Mexico police dispatcher overheard the friends discussing the killing and turned Mothershed in. Another friend told police that he had sold Mothershed a 9mm Smith & Wesson Model 59 automatic and some ammunition prior to the suspect's vacation. Authorities matched shell casings found at the scene of the homicide with those previously fired from the gun. In a taped confession, Mothershed subsequently admitted killing Webb with the weapon, dismantling it, and then disposing of the pieces in various locations. Following a month long trial in which he pleaded not guilty, Mothershed was convicted on April 28, 1982, of first degree murder and two counts of robbery. Because he was 18 at the time of the killing and had no previous criminal record, Mothershed was spared the death penalty and sentenced on June 2, 1982, to life imprisonment without the possibility of parole. Charges were dropped against Ronald Paul Berndt after Mothershed's arrest, but the drifter was subsequently convicted on two counts of first degree murder

stemming from the fatal shootings of a bartender and a patron at the Tinhorn Bar in Phoenix, Arizona, on January 26, 1981. On October 24, 1983, the Arizona Supreme Court unanimously upheld Berndt's sentence of 737 years, ten months, and five days in the state penitentiary. He will be eligible for parole in 2006.

443. Rivele, Stephen J. *The Mothershed Case.* New York: Bantam Books, 1992. 310 pp.; 18 cm.; paperback.

Paperback original based upon transcripts and interviews by a professional writer better known for his books on the Mafia and the CIA.

Mullin, Herbert William

Born April 18, 1947, in Salinas, California. Maintenance worker, odd jobs. Santa Cruz, California, area; 13 murders (11 convictions, confessed to 2 others); baseball bat, hunting knife, .22 caliber revolver, rifle; October 1972–February 1973.

"I'm telling you to die. I'm telling you to kill yourself, or be killed so that my continent will not fall off into the ocean."—Mullin explaining to a psychiatrist his motive for having murdered 13 people

Diagnosed paranoid schizophrenic who believed he could prevent the "great earthquake" predicted for California by murdering victims who had telepathically communicated to him their willingness to be sacrificed. For a three-year period in the early 1970s the quiet California community of Santa Cruz became what one law enforcement official called "the murder capital" of the United States. From October 1970 through April 1973 three killers, two of them serial, accounted for 26 murders in the area. John Linley Frazier, a 24-year-old paranoid schizophrenic, slaughtered prominent eye surgeon Dr. Vincent Ohta, his wife, their two children, and his secretary on October 19, 1970. Serial sex murderer Edmund Emil Kemper, III, known as the "Co-ed Killer," killed, raped, and dismembered eight women (including his mother) around the University of California–Santa Cruz campus during the period from May 1972 through his arrest on April 23, 1973. Most prolific of all the Santa Cruz killers, however, was Herbert William Mullin, a 25-year-old former mental patient who murdered 13 people in an effort to prevent the earthquake predicted to destroy California.

Born in Salinas, California, on April 18, 1947, the same month and day as the great earthquake of 1906, Mullin was a seemingly normal child. His ex–Marine father and devoutly religious Roman Catholic mother raised him in an atmosphere of strict discipline. Mullin attended private Catholic schools for ten years and graduated in the top third of his class. A football standout despite being only 5'8", Mullin earned a scholarship to Cabrillo College and graduated two years later with an associate degree in highway engineering. His parents sensed a change in their son's behavior when, upon transferring to San Jose State College, Mullin switched his major to philosophy. He dropped out after only six weeks. The death of his best friend in an August 1965 car crash seemingly initiated the changes in Mullin which became full-blown in the fall of 1967. He became obsessed with Eastern religions, began experimenting with LSD and marijuana, broke off a marriage engagement claiming to be a homosexual, and announced to his father that he had become a conscientious objector. In March 1969, Mullin's odd behavior at a family dinner led to his voluntary commitment at the Mendocino State Hospital. Doctors there diagnosed him as suffering from schizophrenia aggravated by drug use. In early November 1969, Mullin was forcibly committed to the psychiatric ward at San Luis Obispo General Hospital. At the urging of "voices," he had shaved his head and burnt the end of his penis with a cigarette. Mullin was diagnosed as a paranoid schizophrenic whose prospects for recovery were "grave." Discharged, he traveled to Hawaii where he was hospitalized and given the mood-altering drugs Thorazine and Stelazine. Mullin returned to the mainland and for a year and a half drifted through San Francisco's sleazy Tenderloin District living in cheap hotels and engaging in homosexual affairs.

In September 1972, Mullin returned to the Santa Cruz area with a mission to save the continent from natural cataclysm. The voices had revealed a great truth to him: when the world's death rate was not high enough the chances for a natural disaster were greatly increased. To prevent the major earthquake predicted for California, Mullin's twisted logic demanded that he create a series of "minor disasters" to bring the death rate into balance. The first "minor disaster" occurred on October 13, 1972, as Mullin was driving his blue and white station wagon in the Henry Cowell State Park near Santa Cruz. He spotted 55-year-old transient Lawrence White and clubbed the man to death with a baseball bat. Eleven days later, Mullin picked up 24-year-old Cabrillo College coed Mary Margaret Guilfoyle as she was hitchhiking to a job interview. He drove her to a secluded area outside Santa Cruz, plunged a Finn Double-X hunting knife into her heart, removed most of her organs, and scattered them around the crime scene. Mullin later confessed that the butchery was inspired by accounts he read of the anatomical experiments conducted by Michelangelo and Leonardo da Vinci. Guilfoyle's skeletal remains were found by target shooters on February 12, 1973. Roman Catholic priest Father Henri Tomei was next to die. On November 2, 1972, All Souls' Day, Mullin entered Saint Mary's Catholic Church in the San Jose suburb of Los Gatos and stabbed Father Tomei in the heart, back, and head as the priest was leaving the confessional.

As Mullin's schizophrenia deepened he believed prospective victims were in telepathic communication with him and were begging him to kill them. He legally purchased a .22 caliber RG-14 six-shot revolver in December 1972 and on January 25, 1973, drove to the home of small-time drug dealer James Gianera. Though onetime friends in high school, Mullin blamed Gianera for introducing him to drugs as part of a broader plot to destroy his mind. Gianera had since moved and current resident, Kathy Francis (a.k.a. Kathleen Prentiss), directed Mullin to his new address. Confronting Gianera, he shot the man to death and killed his wife Joan with a hunting knife. Mullin drove back to the home of Kathy Francis and shot the woman and her two boys, David, 9, and Daemon, 4. He completed the carnage by stabbing Francis in the chest and her sons in the back. On February 10, 1973, Mullin returned to Henry Cowell State Park and confronted four young campers: Brian Scott Card, 19, Mark Johnson (a.k.a. Mark John Dreibelbeis), Robert Michael Spector,

18, and David Allan Oliker, 18. Threatening to inform park officials about their illegal campsite, Mullin pulled his revolver and killed the teenagers. Before leaving the scene he stole their .22 caliber rifle. Card's older brother Jeff found the bodies on February 17, 1973. Seventy-two-year-old Fred Perez was working in the driveway of his rental property in Santa Cruz on the morning of February 13, 1973, when Mullin pulled up in his station wagon, aimed his .22 caliber rifle, and shot the old man through the heart. A neighbor witnessed the shooting, described Mullin's car to police, and he was picked up minutes later.

When ballistics tied the revolver found on the front seat of his car to the murders of the Gianeras and three members of the Francis family, Mullins was charged on February 15, 1973, with six counts of first degree murder including that of Fred Perez. Four more murder counts were added on February 20, 1973, when ballistics determined that Mullin's .22 revolver had killed the four teenaged campers. He would not be prosecuted in the murders of White or Guilfoyle. Mullin confessed to all the murders explaining that his personal "sacrifice" was necessary to help avert the earthquake threatening to destroy California. His victims, Mullin asserted, had telepathically given him their okay to kill them so that a potentially more devastating catastrophe might be avoided. Opening arguments in the ten count first degree murder trial began in Santa Cruz on July 30, 1973, with Mullin pleading not guilty by reason of insanity. The prosecution conceded that Mullin was a sick man, but produced psychiatrists who testified that he was sane at the time of the killings. Following three days of deliberation, a jury on August 19, 1973, found Mullin guilty on two counts of first degree murder in the cases of James and Joan Gianera and of second degree murder in the remaining eight counts. On September 18, 1973, the former mental patient was sentenced to two life terms to run concurrently and eight sentences of five years to life to run consecutively. On December 11, 1973, Mullin was convicted in Santa Clara County on one count of second degree murder in the death of Father Henri Tomei. As of September 1991, Mullin has been turned down for parole seven times.

444. Lunde, Donald T., and Morgan, Jefferson. *The Die Song: A Journey into the Mind of a Mass Murderer*. 1st ed. New York: W. W. Norton, 1980. 315 pp.; 24 cm.

_____. [Same as 444 minus subtitle.] New York: Playboy Paperbacks, 1981. 287 pp.; 18 cm.; paperback.

Strong account by defense psychiatrist Lunde who maintains that then California governor Ronald Reagan's cutbacks in state mental health funds repeatedly kept Mullin, and other violent offenders, from receiving much needed treatment.

Nance, Wayne Nathan
(a.k.a. "Brutus," "Conan the Barbarian")

Born October 18, 1955, in Missoula, Montana. Died September 4, 1986. Furniture store delivery man and warehouseman, part-time bar bouncer. Montana; 6 murders (4 confirmed, strong suspect in 2 others); knife, .22 caliber pistol; 1974–September 4, 1986.

"Women are just an appliance. You put 'em on the bed and plug 'em in." —Nance expressing his view of women to a male coworker

Serial killer whose 12-year reign of terror in Montana ended when he was killed attempting to murder two additional victims. Considered "weird" by everyone who knew him, Nance's penchant for sadism emerged early. As an eight year old growing up in Missoula, Nance was observed by a neighbor dumping a box of kittens down an incinerator. His obsession with the occult began in his junior year in high school. To prove his allegiance to Satan, Nance twisted a coathanger into the shape of a pentagram, heated it, and branded the burning symbol into his arm. He confided to a friend that in order to join a coven he would have to commit a murder before he was 19. On April 11, 1974, the body of 39-year-old Donna Linebeck Pounds was found in the basement of her home in West Riverside, Montana. The wife of a minister, Pounds had been tied up, raped, forced to crouch under a basement stairwell, and shot five times in the head with a .22 caliber Ruger pistol taken from her bedroom. Police found the barrel of the gun shoved into her vagina. Nance, then an 18-year-old high school senior, was a school friend of the dead woman's son and a frequent visitor to their home. The teenager passed a lie detector test, but bragged to classmates that police considered him as their prime suspect. Returning to Missoula following a "general discharge by reason of misconduct" from the Navy, Nance flunked out of the University of Montana. In September 1981 he found employment in a Missoula furniture store as a delivery man and warehouseman.

In late January 1980 the desiccated body of a teenaged "Jane Doe" was found along I-90 in the mountains near Missoula. Death had resulted from a stab wound to the chest and examiners estimated the girl had been dead a year and a half. The body was later identified as 15-year-old runaway Devonna Nelson who disappeared from Seattle in July 1978. While investigators could not pin her murder on Nance, he was in Seattle visiting a friend during the time of her disappearance and to date remains the only suspect in the unsolved murder. Police continued from December 1984 through September 1985 to find the remains of murdered young "Jane Does" dumped in the mountains outside Missoula. The skeletonized remains of two victims dubbed by police "Debbie Deer Creek" and "Robin" were found on Christmas Eve 1984 and September 9, 1985, within three miles of one another. Each had been shot in the back of the head and temple with small caliber pistols.

On the night of December 13, 1985, Nance invaded the Hamilton, Montana, home of Michael and Teresa Shook and their three children. Nance shot Teresa in the leg with a .22 caliber Ruger pistol and bludgeoning her husband into submission, tied him up and repeatedly stabbed the man in the chest. Forcing her into her bedroom, Nance tied her to the bed and raped the woman next to the crib of her two-and-a-half-year-old daughter. Afterwards, police believe that Nance tried to remove the slug from her ankle with a hunting knife before smothering the woman with a pillow. To eliminate potential witnesses, Nance torched the house before leaving, but the fire failed to catch. The children survived narrowly escaping death from smoke inhalation.

Nance saved his most deadly obsession, however, for his boss, 33-year-old furniture store manager Kristen Zimmerman Wells. Happily married to Douglas Wells, a local gunsmith, she was unaware that Nance carried her photo in his wallet and placed others in an album devoted to her. On the night of September 4, 1986, Nance invaded their home in Missoula. He tied Kris Wells to an upstairs bed and forced her husband, dazed from a severe bludgeoning, into the basement where he lashed him to a post and stabbed him in the chest. Leaving the man for dead, Nance went upstairs to rape Kris. Despite his injury, Doug freed himself and found a Savage 250 rifle on a workbench. Hearing movement in the basement, Nance charged down the stairs where Wells shot him in the stomach at close range. In the ensuing battle, Nance crawled back into Kris' bedroom as Doug repeatedly struck him in the head with the stock of the rifle, ultimately breaking it. Though mortally wounded, Nance managed to pull a .22 caliber Ruger pistol and shoot his attacker in the leg. While attempting to fire another round, Nance's hand was deflected by Wells causing the killer to fatally shoot himself in the head. An autopsy on Nance's body revealed that Wells had struck him with the rifle butt at least 60 times. Though authorities disagree on Nance's final body count, local officials credit him with the murders of Donna Pounds, "Robin," and Michael and Teresa Shook. He continues to be the only suspect in the unsolved murders of Devonna Nelson and the "Jane Doe" found on September 9, 1985.

445. Coston, John. *To Kill and Kill Again.* Onyx True Crime; JE 323. New York: Onyx, 1992. 339 pp., [16]pp. of plates: ill.; 18 cm.; paperback.

Paperback original based on interviews (including Wells) and written with the cooperation of the Missoula County sheriff's office. "The terrifying true story of Montana's baby-faced serial sex murderer."—Cover.

Narciso, Filipina Bobadilla *see* Perez, Leonora M.

Neelley, Alvin Howard, Jr.
(a.k.a. "Nightrider")

Born July 15, 1953, in Trion, Georgia. Convenience store worker. Fort Payne, Alabama, and Rome, Georgia; 2 murders (once considered a suspect in 15 others); gun, caustic chemicals; September–October 1982.

"I've met hardened criminals in jail that I fear far less than her."—Neelley discussing his wife Judith in a 1984 prison interview; *see also* Neelley, Judith Ann.

Neelley, Judith Ann
(a.k.a. "Judith Adams" [maiden name], "Lady [of] Sundown" [c.b. handle], "Lady Goodyear" [c.b. handle], "Slopeski," "Bride of Frankenstein," "Casey")

Born June 7, 1964, in Murfreesboro, Tennessee. Convenience store worker. Fort Payne, Alabama, and Rome, Georgia; 2 murders (once considered a suspect in 15 others); gun, caustic chemicals; September–October 1982.

"I pray for strength. I don't ask God ... for me not to be electrocuted. I just ask that if I'm going to be electrocuted, to give me strength to go through it."—Neelley in a 1983 prison interview

The "brains" behind the cold-blooded murder of at least two persons

as authorities contend or, as her attorney argues, a wife battered to the point of mindless submission by a brutish husband who threatened to kill her if she refused to do his bidding. Judith Neelley first met future husband Alvin, a 27-year-old car thief, in Murfreesboro, Tennessee, in the summer of 1979. The 15-year-old high school student saw the older Neelley as a way to escape a miserable home life. Since her father's death when she was nine the family had known only hard times. Not long afterwards, Judith's mother was arrested and charged with contributing to the delinquency of a teenaged boy. By the time Judith was 15, her mother was openly entertaining a steady stream of men in their doublewide house trailer. The tenth grader dated Neelley for months before the older man admitted he was already married. He divorced, the two eloped, and married in Ringold, Georgia, on July 14, 1980. Constantly on the move in Georgia, Alabama, and Texas, the pair worked together in various convenience stores staying only long enough to pilfer money from their cash drawers before moving on. In 1980 "Boney and Claude," as police later dubbed them, robbed a woman at gunpoint in a mall parking lot in Rome, Georgia. Neelley was sentenced to five years in prison while his pregnant, underaged wife was first placed in the Rome Youth Development Center (where she gave birth to twins), then transferred to a YDC in Macon.

While waiting to be reunited, the pair exchanged torrid love letters in which Judith intimated that she hated the staff at the centers. She would later insist that she had been sexually abused by staff members. Released in November 1981, Judith moved in with Neelley's parents in Cleveland, Tennessee, to await her husband's release. She was arrested a week later for robbing an Exxon station. Neelley was released in April 1982 and the pair (with children in tow) hit the road together in separate cars. Neelley, the "Nightrider," and Judith, "Lady Sundown," kept in touch via c.b. radios as they wandered a three-state area breaking into post office boxes for checks and forging money orders. On the nights of September 10 and 11, 1982, Judith Neelley's hatred of some of the staff members at the Rome, Georgia, Youth Development Center exploded into violence. On September 10, she called the home of a male teacher at the YDC and taunted him with death threats before firing two bullets into his house from a speeding car. The next night, Judith threw a Molotov cocktail against the house of a female employee at the Floyd County juvenile detention home.

On September 25, 1982, the Neelley's lured 13-year-old Lisa Ann Millican away from the Riverbend Mall in Rome, Georgia, where she was on a day's outing from a home for neglected girls. The teenager was held captive in cheap hotels for three days and forced to have sex with the pair in front of their children. On September 29, 1982, authorities received three anonymous calls telling them where they could find Millican's body. Later that day Millican's corpse was found dashed on the rocks at the bottom of an 80-foot cliff in the Little River Canyon near Fort Payne in northern Alabama. She had been shot three times in the back with a .38 pistol and pushed over the edge of the canyon. Three plastic syringes were recovered from the scene. In her confession, Judith later admitted that under orders from her husband she had injected the girl six times in the neck

and back with Liquid Drano and Liquid Plumr over a 30-minute period. After Neelley complained that it was taking Millican too long to die, Judith finally shot the girl and dumped her over the cliff. According to Judith, Neelley then masturbated while looking down on the girl's battered corpse.

On October 4, 1982, Judith picked up 22-year-old Janice Kay Chatman and her common-law husband John William Hancock, 26, in Rome, Georgia. Judith called "Nightrider" on the car's c.b. radio and drove to the outskirts of town where she rendezvoused with Neelley and their two children. Judith marched Hancock into a woods at gunpoint and fired a .38 caliber slug into his shoulder. Hancock survived to flag down a truck driver hours later. Not so fortunate, Chatman was kidnapped, raped at a nearby motel, and later found shot to death near a small creek bed about two and a half miles inside Chattooga County. Seeking a connection between the murders of Millican and Chatman, authorities played Hancock the audiotape of the phone conversation between police and the unknown woman who tipped them where to find Millican's body. Hancock positively identified the voice on the tape as the woman who shot him. In a further bit of excellent police work, authorities tied Judith to the harassment of the juvenile detention workers in Rome, Georgia. On October 12, 1982, Hancock picked the Neelleys out of a photo lineup and warrants were issued for them on charges of aggravated assault. When finally identified as suspects in the case, the Neelleys had already been arrested three days earlier near Murfreesboro, Tennessee, for passing forged money orders.

In custody, both sought to minimize their involvement in the murders by blaming the other. Albert Neelley, professing fear of his wife, claimed that they had murdered at least 15 women in their roles as recruiters and enforcers in a two state prostitution ring. While authorities could never link the pair to any of the alleged killings, none doubted their ability to commit the crimes. Neelley drew and signed a map that led police to the site where Janice Chatman's body had been dumped. Judith confessed to the murders of Millican and Chatman and, as the "trigger man" in both cases, was extradited to Alabama to face charges in the Millican case of first degree murder and abduction with intent to harm, terrorize, and sexually violate. Alvin Neelley, never charged in the Millican case, remained in Tennessee after cutting a deal in which he pleaded guilty to the kidnapping-murder of Janice Chatman in exchange for two consecutive life sentences.

Facing possible death in Alabama for Millican's kidnap and gruesome murder, Judith's opening legal gambit was an attempt to be tried as a youthful offender which, if convicted, would carry only a $1000 fine and a three-year prison sentence. When this request was denied, Judith entered a plea of innocent by reason of insanity on December 17, 1982, and began mounting a classic "battered woman syndrome" defense. Ironically, she was again incarcerated when she gave birth to her third child on January 3, 1983. Jury selection began in the kidnapping-murder trial in Fort Payne, Alabama, on March 7, 1983. Unable to get her confession disallowed, Judith's entire defense rested upon making the jury believe that she was entirely under the influence of Alvin Neelley at the time she repeatedly injected Millican with caustic cleaning solutions, shot her,

then pushed her body off a cliff. On the stand, Judith spent three days claiming she had been turned into a mindless robot by Neelley's nightly beatings and demands for sex. Once when she refused him, he inserted a baseball bat up her vagina. According to Judith, Neelley had ordered her to kidnap Millican as a sex-mate for him, then forced her to kill the girl. In their closing argument, the defense likened Judith to the "Bride of Frankenstein," a mere extension of the will of Alvin Neelley. The jury received the case at 4:40 p.m. on March 21, 1983, and the next day at 10:45 a.m. found her guilty of kidnapping and murder. Rather than seeing her as a "victim," they believed an FBI agent's description of Judith as a woman who "enjoyed torturing people and killing them." On April 18, 1983, a judge set aside the jury's recommendation of life imprisonment and sentenced her to death. She subsequently pleaded guilty to kidnapping Janice Chatman and on December 13, 1983, was given a life sentence in Tennessee to run consecutively with the death sentence in Alabama. A week later she was sentenced to ten more years for shooting John Hancock.

On March 9, 1987, the United States Supreme Court rejected Judith Neelley's appeal for a new trial and on January 9, 1989, let stand her death sentence. The one-time youngest woman ever to be sentenced to die in the United States spends her days on death row quietly reading the Bible, painting, composing poetry, and writing between 30 to 60 letters a week to family and friends. On May 21, 1994, 26-year-old Alisa Dianne Wall was found dead in her home near Gadsden, Alabama, from a self-inflicted gunshot wound to her neck. Near the body, authorities recovered photographs of

Judith Neelley and a cassette tape in which Wall outlined their suicide pact. Officials at Tutwiler Prison for Women found Neelley in her cell bleeding from slashes to her wrist self-inflicted with a disposable razor. Days before, Neelley had called Wall's father and asked, "You don't mind if Alisa and I are in love with each other?" Neelley survived the suicide attempt.

446. Cook, Thomas H. *Early Graves: A Shocking True-Crime Story of the Youngest Woman Ever Sentenced to Death Row.* New York: Dutton, 1990. xiv, 303 pp.: ill.; 24 cm.

_____. [Same as 446.] New York: Onyx, 1992. xiv, 336 pp., [8]pp. of plates: ill.; 18 cm.; paperback.

_____. [Same as 446.] New York: Penguin Group, 1992. xiv, 336 pp., [8]pp. of plates: ill.; 18 cm.; paperback.

Good account of the crimes by a two-time Edgar Award nominee based on interviews (including Alvin Neelley), police records, and trial transcripts.

Neilson, Donald
(a.k.a. "The Black Panther," "Donald Nappey" [birth name], "John Moxon," "G. Tile," "John Ashe," "The Phantom," "Handy Andy")

Born August 1, 1936, in Morley, Leeds, England. Joiner. England; 5 murders (convicted of 4); shotgun, Hi Standard .22 caliber automatic pistol, ligature strangulation (wire); February 15, 1974–December 1975.

"From the beginning I was one man who put himself up against the lot of them."

Robber, murderer, and kidnapper dubbed the "Black Panther" on account of the signature black hood he wore during a string of nocturnal burglaries.

Beginning in early 1971, numerous sub–post office robberies were committed throughout England by a black-hooded man wearing dark camouflage and armed with a sawed-off shotgun. The Black Panther claimed his first victim, 54-year-old sub-postmaster Donald Lawson Skepper, on February 15, 1974, in the New Park suburb of Harrogate. The sub-postmaster was shot during a struggle with the armed intruder. Fellow sub-postmaster Derek Astin met an identical fate on September 6, 1974, at his station in Higher Baxenden, a village suburb of Accrington. The murder of yet another sub-postmaster, 56-year-old Sidney Grayland, and the bludgeoning of his wife Peggy in Langley on November 11, 1974, evoked a demand for protection from his 21,000 colleagues throughout Britain. Shortly after Grayland's murder, the Post Office and the National Federation of Sub-Postmasters offered a joint reward of £25,000 for information leading to the killer's arrest and conviction, the largest reward offered in Britain up to that time. In the meantime, police had launched a massive manhunt for the Black Panther after shell casings found at the various scenes tied him to each killing.

On January 14, 1975, 17-year-old Lesley Whittle was kidnapped from her home in Highley. A ransom note punched out on a Dymo-machine on long strips of red self-adhesive tape warned the family not to notify police and to deliver, according to instructions, £50,000 in ransom. The next night, Gerald Smith, a security guard at a transport depot in Dudley some 35 miles from the Whittle home, was shot six times after confronting a man loitering near the Dudley Zoo car park. Smith survived, but died on March 25, 1976, from complications suffered in the shooting 14 months earlier. In a stolen car found at the scene, police recovered more instructions on Dymo-tape and an audiotape made by the young girl outlining her kidnapper's ransom demands. Following a televised plea by Whittle's father, authorities were given a flashlight found near a spillway atop an underground drainage system in Bathpool Park. A Dymo-tape message affixed to the flashlight, "Drop suitcase into hole," prompted authorities to search the labyrinth of sewer tunnels beneath the park. On March 7, 1975, Whittle's nude body was found suspended from a wire loop clamped to a ladder in a drainage shaft some 60 feet below the surface of the park. A sleeping bag on a nearby ledge convinced authorities that the Black Panther had used the extensive network of sewer tunnels as a base of operation. Nine months later on December 11, 1975, the most wanted man in Britain was caught by accident when two policemen in Mansfield Woodhouse, Nottinghamshire, noticed a suspicious looking individual loitering near a post office. When confronted, the man whipped out a sawed-off shotgun and forced the officers into their car. Driving through the mining village of Rainworth a scuffle broke out between the gunman and the officer. The officer, who was next to him in the backseat, was wounded by a shotgun blast. The suspect was subsequently beaten into submission by some men waiting in line outside of a fish and chips shop.

Identified as Donald Neilson, a 39-year-old married joiner with a teenaged daughter, the suspect initially refused to cooperate with police, but confessed after a search of his home revealed weapons and black hoods. A physical fitness devotee with a fetish for the military, Neilson often took his family on pretend military maneuvers on the Yorkshire moors. At two separate trials in July 1976 (first for Whittle followed by another for the three sub-postmasters), Neilson argued that each death had been the result of a series of "mishaps." Contrary to the prosecution's claim that he eliminated Whittle because she could identify him, the Black Panther maintained that the teenager accidentally slipped from the platform and was hanged by the wire he used to tether her. The three post office killings occurred when the gun accidentally went off during his struggles with the men. On July 21, 1976, Neilson was sentenced to five life sentences for the four murders and for the infliction of grievous bodily harm on the wife of Grayland. In April 1994, Home Secretary Michael Howard recommended to Prime Minister John Major that Neilson and 19 other notorious murderers currently serving life sentences in Britain should never be released.

447. Hawkes, Harry. *The Capture of the Black Panther: Casebook of a Killer.* London: Harrap, 1978. 271 pp., [16]pp. of plates: ill., facsims., 2 forms, 1 map, ports., 23 cm.

An editor at *The Birmingham Post & Mail*, Hawkes focuses on the massive manhunt for the Black Panther which at the time was Britain's largest and, at an estimated cost of over £1 million, its costliest. Appendices include a "Chronological list of dates in text" and a "Table of charges and sentences." Includes index.

Nelson, Erle Leonard
(a.k.a. "The Gorilla Man [or] Murderer," "The Dark [or] Hobo [or] Mad Strangler,"

"The Dark Slayer," "Evan Louis Fuller," "Adrian Harris," "Williams," "Charles Harrison," "Woodcots," "Walter Woods," "Harry Harcourt," "Virgil Wilson," "Roger Wilson")

Born May 12, 1897, in San Francisco, California. Executed January 13, 1928. Itinerant laborer. Pennsylvania, California, Oregon, Washington, Iowa, Missouri, Michigan, Illinois, Canada; 26 murders (suspected of at least 3 others); manual and ligature strangulation; October 1925–June 1927.

"I am innocent in the sight of God and man and I forgive those who have wronged me and I beg forgiveness of those I have injured."—Nelson's last words

Serial sex killer of sub-average intelligence whose simian appearance led the press to dub him "the Gorilla Man." By the age of two, both of Erle Leonard Nelson's parents had died of syphilis. At ten, Nelson was struck by a streetcar while riding his bike and was carried home unconscious with a gaping hole in his temple where he stayed in a coma for a week. As a result of this brain injury, Nelson suffered severe headaches and memory lapses for the rest of his life. After serving prison sentences for robbery and petty theft, Nelson was institutionalized in California's Napa State Hospital for the Insane on May 21, 1918, following an unsuccessful sexual attack on a 12-year-old San Francisco girl. Doctors there diagnosed his condition as a "constitutional psychopathic state." Nelson escaped and married Mary Teresa Martin, a woman eight years his senior, on August 5, 1919. Insanely jealous of her, Nelson's erratic behavior

was further punctuated by severe headaches, visual and auditory hallucinations, and his unexplained absences from home for weeks at a time. Reconfined to the asylum, Nelson escaped again and remained at large until his arrest for murder.

The first of Nelson's 26 documented sex killings occurred in Philadelphia on October 18, 1925, and established a *modus operandi* used in most of his other murders. Mrs. Olla McCoy, a black landlady, was found strangled in her home. Raped after death, McCoy's hands were bound behind her with cloth tied with a peculiar sailor's knot. Like many of the subsequent victims, McCoy had a "Room for Rent" sign posted in a front window. Committing two other murders in Philadelphia in November 1925, neighbors of one of the victims provided police with a description of Nelson that would ultimately be used to peg him as "the Gorilla Man": a dark complexioned man of about 35, some 5'8" tall, weighing around 160 pounds with "black piercing eyes." Drifting to California in early 1926, Nelson committed three rape-slayings in San Francisco, and one each in Oakland and Stockton before traveling to Portland, Oregon, for a trio of killings during a three-day period in October 1926. In each instance, the victim was a landlady whose jewelry and money had been stolen. Between November 18, 1926, and June 2, 1927, Nelson hitchhiked across the country committing 12 additional murders in California (1), Washington (1), Oregon (1), Iowa (1), Missouri (3), Pennsylvania (1), New York (1), Michigan (2), and Illinois (1). Since his first murder in October 1925, Nelson had killed over 20 women, one eight-month-old baby, left fingerprints at many of the murder scenes, and had been seen and described by over 50 witnesses.

After strangling 37-year-old Mary Sietsma with an electrical cord in Chicago on June 2, 1927, Nelson (using the alias "Woodcots") hitchhiked to Winnipeg, Canada, where he secured a room in a boardinghouse. On June 9, 1927, 14-year-old schoolgirl Lola Cowan disappeared while selling artificial flowers. Her body was found days later beneath Nelson's bed in the rooming house. A day after Cowan's disappearance Nelson bludgeoned, strangled, and raped housewife Emily Patterson in her home, hiding the body beneath her bed. Nelson was arrested in Wakopa (five miles from the United States border) on June 16, 1927, after a motorist he hitchhiked with recognized a newspaper description of "the Gorilla Murderer." Transported to the Killarney Provincial Police Detachment, Nelson escaped the same day by picking the lock of his cell with a rusted nail file he found under his bunk. He was recaptured 12 hours later in the town attempting to hop a train. Tried in Winnipeg on November 1, 1927, for the murder of Emily Patterson, Nelson mounted an insanity defense supported by two witnesses (his wife and his aunt) who testified as to his well-documented history of mental instability. The prosecution argued that while Nelson was admittedly below average in intelligence, his attempt to elude capture by using aliases and constantly changing clothes while on the run demonstrated that he knew right from wrong. A jury needed only 48 minutes on November 4, 1927, to find Nelson guilty of Patterson's murder and the serial killer received the mandatory death sentence. Hanged at Winnipeg's Vaughn Street Jail on January 13, 1928, Nelson's body lay in state at a local funeral home where an estimated 4,000 people filed past the open casket before the body was shipped by rail to his wife in Palo Alto, California. Most authorities believe that in addition to his 26 known sex killings, Nelson was also responsible for a triple murder committed in Newark, New Jersey, in 1926.

448. Anderson, Frank W. *The Dark Strangler: A Study in Strange Behaviour.* Canadian Crime Classics. Calgary: Frontier, 1974. iv, 38 pp.: ill.; 27 cm.; pamphlet.

Concise, accurate retelling of the Nelson saga prefaced by the essay "A Psychiatric Viewpoint" by Gordon W. Russon, M.D., C.R.C.P.(C.)

449. Nash, Jay Robert. *The Dark Fountain: A Novel of Horror.* New York: A & W, 1982. 298 pp.; 22 cm.

_____. [Same as 449.] New York: New American Library, 1983. 241 pp.; 18 cm. ("A Signet book"); paperback.

Fictional account of the Nelson case by prolific true crime historian Jay Robert Nash, author of the ambitious, but highly flawed five volume *Encyclopedia of World Crime* (1989).

Newell, Hugh William Alexander

Born May 20, 1914, in Toronto, Canada. Executed February 12, 1942. Royal Canadian Air Force airman. Centre Island, Toronto, Canada; 1 murder; ligature strangulation (rope or silk stocking); September 29, 1940.

"Thank you—for nothing!"—Newell's reaction to the judge's unfavorable summing up in his second murder trial

Royal Canadian Air Force airman tried three times in 1941 for the ligature strangulation murder of his wife before finally being convicted and executed.

Twenty-six-year-old Hugh Newell and his Finnish wife, the former Aune Marie Paavola, had discussed divorce before he took her on a day trip to Centre Island, a resort area south of Toronto, on September 29, 1940. Newell, already seeing another Finnish woman named Elna Miriam Lehto, stood to lose half his service pay to his wife should they divorce. Luring Paavola to a secluded wooded area, Newell strangled her with a rope or a silk stocking and buried the body under some brush. The young woman's body was found a week later by an employee of the parks department. Evidence recovered at the scene included a length of tarred hempline, torn pieces of a YMCA envelope bearing an RCAF insignia, and bluish fibers caught on a willow branch near the body. When questioned about his wife's disappearance, Newell told authorities that he suspected Paavola had run off with another man. The airman was formally charged with murder on October 31, 1940, after witnesses on the island placed him there with Paavola on the day of the murder. Though forensic experts could not conclusively tie the fibers found at the scene to Newell's uniform, the location of a tear in the cuff of his trousers was the same distance from the ground as the fibers found on the willow branch. The first trial ended in a hung jury on March 15, 1941, when jurors voting 9–3 for conviction could not unanimously agree on a verdict. A second trial began on May 5, 1941, and throughout the 25 days it lasted Newell vigorously maintained that police had framed him by planting the fiber evidence on the island. Some jurors were swayed by Newell's claim as evidenced by the 7–5 vote for conviction, but in the absence of a unanimous verdict the proceedings

ended in yet another hung jury on June 4, 1941. On October 6, 1941, the first anniversary of the discovery of Paavola's body, Newell was tried for the third time. The trial, which dragged on for 42 days, was highlighted by the airman's inconsistent testimony and his lover Lehto's admission that the writing on the torn envelope found near the murder scene was Newell's. This time, the jury needed only a little over five hours to convict on November 22, 1941. Meticulous to the last, Newell momentarily delayed his execution on February 12, 1942, by demanding to be hanged in a new shirt and tie. The airman reportedly shouted, "I am innocent!" as the trap fell.

450. Guillet, Edwin C. *This Man Hanged Himself!: A Study of the Evidence in the King Versus Newell*. Famous Canadian Trials. Toronto: Ontario Publishing Company Limited, 1943. xvii, 210 pp., [10]pp. of plates: ill., ports., facsim.; 21 cm.

_____. [Same as 450, but paperback ed. retitled: *The Walk and the Kiss*.] A Pocket Book ed. Richmond Hill, Ont.: Simon & Schuster of Canada, 1973. 238 pp., 8 leaves of plates: ill., ports.; 18 cm. ("A Canadian pocket book"); paperback.

The author, who did not attend the trial, based this case study primarily upon some 4,000 pages of evidence and the 129 exhibits at Newell's third trial. The final chapter discusses the legal issues arising from the case and suggests some possible changes in Canadian law.

Nichols, Donald Boone

Born circa 1931. Survivalist. Big Sky, Montana; 1 murder; .22 caliber pistol; July 16, 1984.

Television: "The Abduction of

Kari Swenson" (1987), a two-hour, made-for-television movie, originally aired on NBC on March 8, 1987. Cast includes Tracy Pollan (Kari Swenson), Joe Don Baker (Sheriff John Onstad), M. Emmett Walsh (Don Nichols), and Michael Bowen (Dan Nichols). "The woman was for both of us, but was originally my idea."

Self-styled Montana mountain man who kidnapped a woman for his son, then killed one of her would-be rescuers. Kari Swenson, a 23-year-old member of the U.S. women's biathlon team, was jogging along a mountain trail near the Big Sky ski area south of Bozeman on July 15, 1984, when she was abducted by Donald Boone Nichols, 54, and his 20-year-old son, Dan. The elder Nichols, vehemently anti-Establishment, had spent the previous 12 summers with his devoted son in Montana's back country before moving there permanently in August 1983. Prior to Swenson's kidnapping, the pair discussed abducting a female to become the son's "mountain woman" and had purchased a dog chain and padlock. After the abduction, Swenson was taken to their crude camp, chained to a felled tree, but not molested. Early the next morning, James Schwalbe, 30, and Alan Goldstein attempted a rescue. During the encounter, Dan Nichols' .22 caliber pistol accidentally discharged shooting the woman in the chest. Goldstein, brandishing a pistol, was fatally shot in the head by Donald Boone Nichols. The duo fled into the wilderness leaving Swenson behind to be rescued several hours later. Father and son eluded a massive manhunt for five months before being captured by Madison County Sheriff Johnny France on a mountainside between Virginia City and Bozeman on December 15, 1984. Tried separately in Virginia City,

Dan Nichols was convicted of kidnapping and assault, but acquitted of the murder charge in May 1985 after his father confessed to shooting Goldstein. The 20 year old was sentenced to 20 years, but paroled in June 1991. On July 12, 1985, convictions for deliberate homicide, kidnapping, and aggravated assault netted Donald Boone Nichols an 85-year prison term. An appeal based on negative pre-trial publicity was rejected by the U.S. court of appeals on December 10, 1991.

451. France, Johnny, and McConnell, Malcolm. *Incident at Big Sky: The True Story of Sheriff Johnny France and the Capture of the Mountain Men.* 1st ed. New York: Norton, 1986. 285 pp., [11]pp. of plates: ill., map; 24 cm.

_____. [Same as 451.] New York: Pocket Books, 1987. viii, 312 pp.: ill., map; 17 cm.; paperback.

Firsthand account by the sheriff who single-handedly captured the mountain men. France subsequently hired a personal manager and a New York advertising agency to field movie offers.

"Night Stalker Killings" *see* **Ramirez, Richard Leyva**

Nilsen, Dennis Andrew (a.k.a. "Des")

Born November 23, 1945, in Fraserburgh, Scotland. Civil servant. North London, England; 15 murders; ligature strangulation (necktie, cord), drowning; December 1979–February 1983.

Film: Cold Light of Day (GB, 1990), a Creative Artists Inc. production directed by Fhiona Louise. Cast includes Bob Flag (Jordan March), Geoffrey Greenhill (Inspector Simmons), and Martin Byrne-Quinn (Joe). "I wished I could stop but I could not. I had no other thrill or happiness."—From Nilsen's prison journals

British homosexual serial killer who apparently murdered his victims so that they would never leave him. A solitary child largely neglected by his father, Nilsen developed a strong attachment to his grandfather. His sudden death profoundly affected the six year old who was told by his mother that the old man was merely "sleeping." Nilsen later credited the realization that his beloved grandfather would never again return with permanently blighting his personality. Enlisting in the army in 1961 at age 15, Nilsen served in various capacities until his discharge in late 1972. One post, a stint in the Army Catering Corps, taught Nilsen the rudiments of butchery, a skill he put to later use in his murderous career. Military service also solidified Nilsen's interest in men. He indulged in a series of anonymous, unfulfilling sexual encounters. In late 1972 Nilsen enrolled in the Metropolitan Police Training School in North London, but his effectiveness as a police officer was undermined by his nightly pub crawls through gay bars. After a year on the force, Nilsen resigned in December 1973 and landed a civil servant position at a job center for the unemployed. During this period, Nilsen's sense of isolation and stifling loneliness began to overwhelm him. Tired of the bar scene and with only his mongrel dog Bleep for company, he sat in his flat night after night listening to rock music on headphones while drinking himself into a stupor. The acrimonious end of a live-in relationship with a man during 1976–1977 left Nilsen totally alone.

In his brilliant book on the case, *Killing for Company*, Brian Masters writes that Nilsen's motivation for killing was never purely sexual, but rather born of a twisted, unfulfilled need to alleviate his utter loneliness by killing victims for their company. The first of Nilsen's 15 killings "for company" occurred on December 30, 1978. The civil servant picked up an anonymous Irish youth in a gay bar, took him to his flat in the Muswell Hill area of North London, and strangled him to death with a tie as the teen slept in a drunken stupor. Nilsen washed the body and kept it under his floorboards until August 1979 when he burned it in the garden of his flat. On December 3, 1979, Nilsen befriended Canadian tourist Kenneth Ockenden. After a night of heavy drinking at Nilsen's flat, Ockenden was strangled to death with a stereo cord as he listened to music on headphones. Nilsen kept the Canadian around for weeks, dressing him up, applying makeup to cover decomposition, and holding the corpse while watching television. Nilsen claimed 10 other victims while living at 195 Melrose Avenue. With repetition, Nilsen's murders took on an air of ritual. He either strangled or drowned the men, cleansed and cared for their corpses, used them as masturbatory aids, then discarded them after the smell of their rotting flesh could no longer be masked by disinfectant. As the number of bodies piled up under his floorboards, Nilsen was forced to find ever more creative ways to dispose of his victims. Using a kitchen knife, the former butcher removed their internal organs and dumped them through a hole in his garden wall where nocturnal animals consumed any incriminating evidence. Dismembered body parts were separately bagged and kept in cupboards throughout the apartment until they could be burned en masse in a bonfire.

In late 1981, Nilsen moved to an attic flat at 23 Cranley Gardens, North London. From November 25, 1981, through February 1, 1983, the reclusive civil servant garroted or drowned three more men. Lacking floorboards under which to store victims, Nilsen placed their bodies in the bathtub and wardrobe. After they had served their purpose, the bodies were dismembered, cut into small chunks, then flushed down the toilet. "Problem" body parts like heads were first defleshed by boiling in a soup pot after which they were crushed and discarded in the trash. Ironically, Nilsen's new method of disposal led directly to his arrest. On February 8, 1983, a plumber was called to Cranley Gardens by residents unable to flush their toilets. Ascertaining that the sewer was blocked, the plumber removed a manhole cover and was met by the nauseating stench of rotting flesh. After the plumber left for the night, Nilsen was able to remove several chunks of putrefied flesh, but in the morning the blocked sewer yielded human knuckles and bone slivers. Nilsen was subsequently questioned by police in his flat where he confessed and calmly showed them plastic bags of body parts stuffed in a wardrobe. Tried in October 1983, Nilsen's counsel maintained that the 37-year-old government worker was too deranged to be held accountable for his actions. The prosecution bolstered an airtight forensics case with testimony from three survivors of Nilsen's attacks. Convicted on November 4, 1983, of six murders and two attempted murders, Nilsen was sentenced to life imprisonment with a recommendation that he not be paroled for at least 25 years (until November 4, 2008).

452. McConnell, Brian, and Bence, Douglas. *The Nilsen File*. London: Futura, 1983. 191 pp.; 18 cm.; paperback.

453. Masters, Brian. *Killing for Company: The Case of Dennis Nilsen*. London: J. Cape, 1985. xvi, 336 pp., [16]pp. of plates: ill.; 23 cm.

_____. [Same as 453.] Postscript by Anthony Storr. New York: Stein and Day, 1986. xvi, 336 pp., [16]pp. of plates: ill.; 23 cm.

_____. [Same as 453.] Sevenoaks: Coronet, 1986. 352 pp.: ill., facsims, ports.; 18 cm.; paperback.

_____. [Same as 453 with variant subtitle: *The Story of a Man Addicted to Murder*.] 1st U.S. ed. New York: Random House, 1993. xviii, 324 pp.: ill.; 25 cm.

Classic study which ranks among the best books ever written on a killer's psyche. Masters enjoyed unique access to Nilsen and his study is based largely on the serial killer's voluminous prison journals. This documentation, almost unique in the annals of crime (see entry on Carl Panzram), reveals Nilsen to be an intelligent and curiously sensitive individual who has profound insights into the nature of his mental illness. Masters released the American edition of this seminal work in 1993 to invite comparison between the crimes of Nilsen and those of Milwaukee serial killer Jeffrey Lionel Dahmer. Includes facsimile pages from Nilsen's journals which describe in text and drawings the dismemberment of his victims. A masterpiece.

Nodder, Frederick
(a.k.a. "Frederick Hudson," "Uncle Fred")

Born circa 1897. Executed December 30, 1937. Motor-mechanic. Hayton, England; 1 murder; ligature strangulation; January 6, 1937.

"I shall go out of this court with a clear conscience, sir."—Nodder to Mr.

Justice Macnaghten after being found guilty of the murder of Mona Lilian Tinsley

A pedophile known as "Uncle Fred" to the children of the family he once lodged with under the alias "Frederick Hudson." He was serving time for the kidnapping of their young daughter when charged with her murder. On January 5, 1937, ten-year-old Mona Lilian Tinsley disappeared on her way home from school in Newark, Nottinghamshire, a manufacturing town of 20,000 in the English Midlands. Several witnesses, including a classmate of Tinsley's, reported seeing the child at a bus stop in the company of a man in his forties later identified as motor mechanic Frederick Nodder. Under the name "Frederick Hudson," Nodder had lodged with the Tinsleys for three weeks in October 1935 and was well liked by the family, especially the children who affectionately called him "Uncle Fred." Police questioned Nodder the next day at "Peacehaven," his house in nearby Hayton, and arrested him on an outstanding warrant of non-payment of child support while trying to build a murder case against him. A neighbor noticed a young girl staying with Nodder and a search of his home revealed papers filled with childish scrawls and writing later identified as that of the missing girl. When positively identified by a bus conductor as the man in the company of Mona Tinsley, Nodder admitted being with the child but only because she asked him to be. According to Nodder's story, he took her to his house because she wanted to visit her aunt in Sheffield. He sent her on alone the next day with a letter explaining her absence and was shocked when she never arrived. On January 10, 1937, Nodder was charged with kidnapping

and languished in jail while a massive search was undertaken to find the young girl's body. It still remained unrecovered on March 11, 1937, when following a two-day trial Nodder was found guilty of kidnapping and sentenced to nine years of penal servitude.

On June 6, 1937, exactly five months after her disappearance, Tinsley's body was found partially submerged in the River Idle three-quarters of a mile below Bawtry. Forensics confirmed the child was strangled before being placed in the water. Nodder was charged with her murder and pleaded not guilty as the trial opened at the Nottingham Assizes on November 22, 1937. World renowned pathologist Sir Bernard Spilsbury refuted the defense's contention that the mark found on Tinsley's neck could have been caused by the catching of her dress on a branch so that she slowly choked to death before falling into the water where she was found. Nor did the jury believe Nodder's account that he benevolently placed Tinsley on a bus to her aunt's house, instead subscribing to the prosecution's theory that after raping the child he strangled her to ensure her silence. The jury was out for less than an hour before returning with a verdict of guilty on November 23, 1937. Noting that "Justice has slowly but surely overtaken you," Mr. Justice Macnaghten sentenced the murderer to death. Nodder's appeal was subsequently dismissed and he was hanged at Lincoln Prison on December 30, 1937.

454. Duke, Winifred, ed. *The Trials of Frederick Nodder: The Mona Tinsley Case.* Notable British Trials. London: W. Hodge, 1950. xiii, 242 pp., [9] leaves of plates: ill.; 22 cm.

Transcripts from Nodder's trials for

kidnapping (March 9–11, 1937) and murder (November 22–23, 1937) are offered in this entry in the Notable British Trials Series. Includes a well written introduction by editor Duke and a chronology of leading dates in the Mona Tinsley case.

"Ogden Hi-Fi Shop Massacre"
see Pierre, Dale Selby (and) Andrews, William A.

Olson, Clifford Robert
(a.k.a. "The Beast of British Columbia")

Born January 1, 1940, in Vancouver, British Columbia. Construction worker. British Columbia; 11 murders; bludgeon, knife; November 1980–July 1981.

"I don't owe the people of Canada a goddamn thing." — Olson, in a July 7, 1991, Montreal *Gazette* interview, reacting to the controversy surrounding the $100,000 payment he was given in exchange for leading authorities to the bodies of his victims

Olson, a Canadian serial child killer once described by a journalist as "our very own Charles Manson," has achieved a sort of perverse celebrity in British Columbia as a national symbol of evil. Born in Vancouver in 1940, Olson spent 21 of the last 24 years in prison for fraud, armed robbery, and sexual assault before his final arrest for murder. Five months after his release from prison on July 6, 1980, Olson began what would become the largest killing spree in British Columbia history. First to die was 12-year-old Christine Weller, abducted from her home in the Vancouver suburb of Surrey in November 1980. Her nude and mutilated body was found in a heavily

wooded area south of town on Christmas Day. Between April and July 30, 1981, ten other children (three boys and seven girls) ranging in ages from 9 to 18 disappeared within a 150-mile radius of Vancouver. In most instances, the boys had been bludgeoned to death and the girls stabbed or strangled. In some cases the victims had been sexually abused. Olson, a 41-year-old self-employed construction worker and the married father of an infant son, was considered a suspect in the slayings and placed under police surveillance. He was arrested on Vancouver Island on August 12, 1981, after authorities observed him pick up two female hitchhikers. A search of Olson's van revealed an address book containing the name of Judy Kozma, a 14 year old whose mutilated body had been recovered from Lake Weaver near Agassiz on July 25, 1981. Olson pleaded not guilty to ten counts of first degree murder as his trial opened in Vancouver on January 11, 1982. Three days later, he changed his plea to guilty to the ten murders plus an additional murder count on another local teenage girl. In sentencing the convicted serial killer to 11 concurrent life terms, the judge told Olson that "there is no punishment in a civilized society that is adequate" and recommended that he never be released from prison. Political and public furor erupted after it was learned that the Royal Canadian Mounted Police and British Columbia officials had bargained with the killer over the bodies of his victims. Olson, in exchange for providing information to authorities on four known victims and leading them to the graves of seven others, earned $100,000 for his wife and child. In November 1982, Olson convinced law enforcement officials that he had committed three other unsolved murders and offered to clear them in exchange for being moved to a prison near Vancouver that was closer to his wife and child. Olson was flown from Kingston Penitentiary to Ontario, saw his wife, then reneged on the deal. Returned to Kingston, Olson has distinguished himself as one of the most litigious and hated prisoners in the Canadian corrections system. Since being incarcerated he has filed 30 unsuccessful court actions against prison officials based on complaints ranging from being stopped from joining the Book of the Month Club to being refused free Tylenol. Fed up with the constant stream of litigation, a federal court judge in October 1994 declared Olson a "vexatious litigant" and barred him from starting any more lawsuits without the court's permission. In Kingston Penitentiary, Olson occupies Cell 21 in Lower H-Block, a specially constructed cell made of stone and black-welded steel with a solid plexiglass floor to ceiling wall in front of the bars to prevent fellow-convicts from spitting or tossing hot liquids or urine at him. He spends most of the 23 hours a day he is incarcerated working on his manuscript, "Clifford Olson: Portrait of a Serial Killer." In 1996, on the 15th anniversary of his conviction, Olson will automatically receive a judicial review of his case that could grant him parole eligibility.

455. Ferry, Jon, and Inwood, Damian. *The Olson Murders.* Langley, B.C.: Cameo Books, 1982. 176 pp.; 18 cm.; paperback.

The authors contend that at least four and possibly ten of Olson's 11 victims might have been saved if the Royal Canadian Mounted Police had been quicker in linking the crimes to Olson's reputation as a violent sex offender. Not surprisingly, the RCMP refused to cooperate with Ferry and Inwood who based their research on newspaper accounts and interviews with friends and families of the victims.

456. Mulgrew, Ian. *Final Payoff: The True Price of Convicting Clifford Robert Olson.* Toronto: McClelland-Bantam, 1990. xiii, 221 pp.; 24 cm. ("Seal books.")

_____. [Same as 456.] Seal rack ed. Toronto: McClelland-Bantam, 1991. xiv, 250 pp.; 18 cm. ("Seal books"); paperback.

Mulgrew focuses on the legal and ethical questions of the unprecedented, and never since repeated, payoff to Olson and argues that despite the claims of British Columbia officials and the RCMP the serial killer *did* profit personally from the deal. Proof is provided that some of the money was spent on Olson's legal fees, postage stamps, a newspaper subscription, and a television set for his cell at Kingston Penitentiary. Appendices include text of the contract between the RCMP and Olson's solicitor.

Pan, Rui-Wen
(a.k.a. "Body-Parts Killer," "Li Ling," "Po")

Born August 11, 1954, in China. Businessman, publisher. Toronto, Ontario, Canada; 1 murder; knife; February 20, 1988.

"In my mind you are the most dirty, cheap and shameful woman in the world."—Pan in a letter written to Shen on February 20, 1988, shortly after the end of their relationship

Chinese publisher and political activist finally convicted after a third trial of the murder-dismemberment of his girlfriend in Canada. In March 1988 a motorist near the eastern Ontario town of Rockport found a neatly severed leg in the middle of the Thousand Island Parkway. Over the next few weeks more remains identified as belonging to the same body were found throughout the province wrapped in green plastic trash bags. The dismemberment, accomplished with surgical precision and the absence of blood in the remains, led to speculation that the victim (identified as a woman) might possibly have been alive, but unconscious, when her body was drained and dissected. Acting on a missing person's report filed in late February 1988 on 28-year-old Chinese violinist Selina Lian Shen, authorities searched her Scarborough, Ontario, house for any item which had her blood on it. A stained sanitary napkin found in her garbage matched the rare blood type of a sample taken from the bone marrow of one of the body parts. Investigators learned that Shen had lived with Chinese businessman and pro-democratic publisher Rui-Wen Pan from 1985 to 1988. Two weeks before her disappearance on February 20, 1988, Shen moved into her own place following an argument with Pan over the romantic interest shown her by another man. Placed under police surveillance, Pan was arrested shortly after he was observed throwing four knives and a cleaver off a dock in the Beaches area into Lake Ontario.

Two separate first degree murder trials in 1990 and March–May 1991 ended in a hung jury and a mistrial, respectively. At a third trial in Toronto in April 1992, the prosecution again maintained that Pan's "obsessive jealousy" over the possibility of losing Shen to another man provided the motive for the murder and dismemberment. A graduate of the Chinese Academy of Medical Science with a degree certifying him as an X-ray technician, Pan's medical training (it was argued) exposed him to anatomy classes featuring dissection (a claim he denied). Pan explained that a front

page article in the May 14, 1988, issue of the *Toronto Star* describing how the body had been "cut up cleanly ... as though professionally dissected" caused him to panic and throw the knives and cleaver into Lake Ontario out of fear he would be framed for Shen's murder. After nearly four days of deliberation, a six-man, six-woman jury found the 37-year-old businessman guilty on May 1, 1992, of Shen's murder and dismemberment. Immediately sentencing Pan to life in prison, Mr. Justice David Watt stated, "I'm fully satisfied the jury came to the correct conclusion. This was a despicable crime." Under Canadian law Pan can apply for parole when he is 60. As of October 1994 he was still appealing his conviction.

457. Clark, Doug. *Unkindest Cut: The Torso Murder of Selina Shen.* Toronto: McClelland & Stewart, 1992. 334 pp., [16]pp. of plates: ill.; 18 cm. ("An M&S paperback original"); paperback.

A carefully researched account that not only covers the crime in far more detail than Pron and Donovan's book, but also explores the complexities of Chinese-Canadian culture.

458. Pron, Nick, and Donovan, Kevin. *Crime Story: The True Account of the Reporters, Cops, and Lawyers on the Trail of the Body-Parts Killer.* Toronto: Seal Books, 1992. viii, 356 pp., [8]pp. of plates: ill.; 24 cm.

_____. [Same as 458.] Toronto: Seal Books, 1993. x, 356 pp., [8]pp. of plates: ill.; 18 cm. ("A Bantam-Seal book"); paperback.

Pron, a reporter for the *Toronto Star*, wrote the article Pan claims frightened him into disposing of the knives and cleaver.

Pancoast, Marvin
(a.k.a. "The Playgirl Killer")

Born November 13, 1949. Died December 4, 1991. Clerk/photocopier at a talent agency. North Hollywood, California; 1 murder; bludgeon (baseball bat); July 7, 1983.

"I just wanted her to be quiet and go to sleep. I was tired."—Pancoast's explanation to police for murdering Vicki Morgan

Mentally unbalanced homosexual convicted of bludgeoning to death the mistress of a wealthy man. Had Marvin Pancoast not met Victoria "Vicki" Lynn Morgan, the former mistress of multimillionaire Diner's Club founder and department store owner Alfred Bloomingdale, he probably would have remained a nondescript "gofer" on the fringe of Hollywood society. Pancoast's anonymity, however, ended at 3:20 a.m. on July 7, 1983, when he walked into a North Hollywood police station and confessed to bludgeoning Morgan, 30, to death with a baseball bat as she slept. Characterized by a psychiatrist as a "homosexual-schizophrenic-alcoholic," Pancoast's need, yet inability, to be a Hollywood insider compelled him to seek work in the entertainment industry where he could at least be near the objects of his desire. While employed as a clerk for producer Allan (Grease) Carr, Pancoast stole the Rolodex containing the firm's list of celebrity phone numbers. He added more phone numbers to his collection during an 18-month stint as a photocopier in the William Morris Talent Agency before quitting in January 1983. From 1970 through 1983 Pancoast's psychiatric records reveal a string of voluntary and involuntary mental hospital admissions in which he was diagnosed as suffering from a borderline personality disorder, and psychotic depression.

Pancoast met Vicki Morgan in October 1979 while both were patients at the Thalians Community Health Center in Los Angeles. The odd couple shared much in common: depression, alcoholism, drug dependency, and shattered sex lives. Morgan's stay at Thalians was paid for by her long-time benefactor and adviser to President Ronald Reagan, Alfred Bloomingdale. The two met at a Sunset Strip eatery during the summer of 1970 when the 53 year old, struck by Morgan's beauty, gave the 17 year old a check for $8,000. It was the beginning of hundreds of thousands of dollars that the millionaire would lavish on Morgan during her 12 years as his mistress. The financial aspect of the affair ended abruptly in June 1982 when Bloomingdale's wife discovered the relationship and canceled her husband's $18,000-a-month payments to Morgan. Morgan retaliated on July 8, 1982, by filing a $10 million palimony suit against Alfred Bloomingdale which graphically described his sadomasochistic penchant for whipping bound prostitutes. Bloomingdale died of cancer on August 20, 1982. A judge later dismissed the suit's palimony provisions, but left intact a portion of the suit involving two written contracts between Bloomingdale and Morgan. The suit was finally settled in Morgan's favor on December 21, 1984, more than two years after her death. Her surviving son was awarded $200,000 from the Bloomingdale estate.

During her five-month stay at Thalians, Morgan permitted Marvin Pancoast to feed his masochistic desire for submission to a celebrity by allowing him to massage her feet and perform other menial tasks. Doctors warned Morgan that Pancoast had an unresolved love/hate relationship with his mother and that there were risks involved in her assuming a dominant role. Morgan ignored their warnings and years later in June 1983, three weeks before her murder, allowed Pancoast to move into her North Hollywood condominium to help with the $1000-a-month rent. Pancoast resumed his slavish devotion to Morgan, even offering to marry her so that the unemployed woman and her son could be listed on his health insurance. She refused to marry Pancoast whose previous personal relationships had been confined to having sex with anonymous men in parked cars and public restrooms. Destitute and depressed, Morgan filled her time by allegedly writing a "tell-all" biography called *Alfred's Mistress*, drinking a fifth of vodka a day, and augmenting her Valium habit with Pancoast's prescription.

In his confession, Pancoast accused Morgan of treating him like a "slave boy and lackey" while she acted like the "Queen of Sheba." "She needled me and she wouldn't quit," he complained. "She would sleep all day and get up at four o'clock in the afternoon." For three weeks Pancoast absorbed the abuse while alternately paying the bills and searching alone for a cheaper apartment for them to share. None met the standards of the former mistress used to making $18,000 a month for dispensing rough sex. In the early hours of July 7, 1983, Pancoast lost his patience. He waited until Morgan was in bed, adjusted the lights so she could not see him, turned on the water to cover any sound, then clubbed the sleeping woman to death with her son's baseball bat. An hour and forty-five minutes later he confessed to police. They found Morgan in bed covered by $500 Pratesi sheets embroidered with her initials, among the last of Bloomingdale's gifts she had yet to

pawn. Pancoast later claimed he murdered his roommate to end her depression over mounting financial worries.

In a final irony, Pancoast was but a fringe character in his own murder trial. Police ineptitude and contentions that a videotape existed showing Bloomingdale and two members of President Reagan's administration cavorting with prostitutes stole the spotlight away from the man whose sole claim to celebrity was the fact that he had brutally killed the discarded mistress of a millionaire. In custody, Pancoast kept a scrapbook of articles about himself and bragged about being on the front page. The trial's opening arguments began on June 11, 1984, with Pancoast entering a dual plea of not guilty and not guilty by reason of insanity. The defense maintained that despite Pancoast's confessions, Morgan had been murdered by government agents to prevent her from using the sex videotapes to blackmail high ranking government officials. The existence of these alleged tapes has never been proven. Police failure to secure the crime scene and their mishandling of the baseball bat (which resulted in the destruction of any fingerprints on the weapon) was either due to sheer ineptness or a deliberate attempt to fix blame on Pancoast. At one point, the defense even argued that a former journalist-lover of Morgan's had hypnotized Pancoast over the phone to commit the murder. The jury rejected these claims and in less than four-and-a-half hours convicted Pancoast on July 5, 1984. In the subsequent sanity phase of the trial Pancoast was found to have been rational at the time of the killing and was sentenced on September 14, 1984, to 26 years to life in prison. Pancoast died of AIDS (contracted before his imprisonment) in the California

State Prison at Chino on December 4, 1991.

459. Basichis, Gordon. *Beautiful Bad Girl: The Vicki Morgan Story.* Santa Barbara, Calif.: Santa Barbara Press, 1985. 303 pp., [8]pp. of plates: ill., ports.; 24 cm.
Basichis became romantically involved with Morgan in the months preceding her death after her agent approached him to write the story of her relationship with Bloomingdale.

460. Milton, Joyce, and Bardach, Ann Louise. *Vicki.* 1st ed. New York: St. Martin's Press, 1986. 343 pp., [16]pp. of plates: ill., ports.; 24 cm.

_____. [Same as 460.] St. Martin's Press non-fiction. New York: St. Martin's Press, 1986. 401 pp., [16]pp. of plates: ill.; 17 cm.; paperback.

Panzram, Carl
(a.k.a. "Jeff Davis," "Jack Allen," "Jefferson Rhoades," "Jeff Baldwin," "John O'Leary," "Copper John II")

Born June 28, 1891, in Minnesota. Executed September 5, 1930. Muleskinner, carnival worker, railroad guard and strike breaker, soldier, seaman, watchman, caretaker, labor foreman. Panama, Belgian Congo, Massachusetts, Connecticut, Pennsylvania, Kansas; 1 murder (conviction, claims 20 others); gun, bludgeon (iron bar), ligature strangulation (belt); circa 1910–June 1929.

"The only thanks you or your kind will ever get from me for your efforts on my behalf is that I wish you all had one neck and that I had my hands on it."—Panzram in a letter dated May 23, 1930, to the Society for the Abolishment of Capital Punishment

The diary Carl Panzram secretly scribbled in the fall of 1928 while in the district jail of Washington, D.C., is perhaps the most lucid account ever written of the development of a career criminal and murderer who ultimately lost every human feeling except unconquerable defiance. At eight, Panzram's German immigrant parents divorced and he was put to work on the family farm. Overworked and maltreated, Panzram was arrested at 11 for breaking into a neighbor's house for money to leave home. Sentenced to the Minnesota State Training School at Red Wing in 1903, Panzram credited that institution with teaching him "man's inhumanity to man." Panzram grew mentally and physically toughened under the beatings he received there and rebelled by burning down the laundry. Released in 1905, the 14-year-old hobo resolved to commit mayhem wherever the trains he hopped would take him. Weeks later while riding the rails, Panzram was sodomized by four men in a box car. Of lessons learned in childhood he wrote, "If I was strong enough and clever enough to impose my will on others, I was right."

At 17, Panzram lied about his age and enlisted in the army. He was soon caught stealing, court-martialed, and sentenced on April 20, 1907, to three years in the U.S. prison at Fort Leavenworth, Kansas. Following an unsuccessful escape, Panzram burned down the prison shop and was sentenced to hard labor. Thirty-seven months later Panzram emerged from Leavenworth an awesome physical specimen self-described as six feet tall and "190 pounds of concentrated hell-fired, man-inspired meanness." He drifted for the next several years working as a union strike breaker and traveling to Mexico to enlist in their Foreign Legion.

He quickly deserted and returned to the States to ride the rails, rape boys and burn barns. Arrested for burglary in Astoria, Oregon in 1915, Panzram cut a deal with authorities on a reduced sentence, but was given the maximum seven years. In retaliation, he torched the jail and was transferred to the Oregon State Prison. There, his one man war against the warden led to that official's resignation. Ten years were added to Panzram's sentence for an escape attempt and an attempted murder. Panzram, now 27, finally escaped in May 1918 and shipped out to Panama where he allegedly murdered ten sailors. In the Belgian Congo, he hired six blacks to hunt crocodiles, shot them all, and fed them to the animals. The next four years found Panzram wandering in 30 countries where he committed hundreds of robberies, multiple homosexual rapes, and numerous murders. Back in the States, he raped and murdered 12-year-old Henry McMahon in Salem, Massachusetts, on July 18, 1922. In mid–1923 he raped and strangled a young black boy with a belt in New Haven, Connecticut.

A burglary arrest in Larchmont, New York, netted Panzram five years in one of the nation's worst penal institutions, Clinton Prison in Dannemora. Beaten almost daily, Panzram sustained severe breaks in his legs, ankles, and spine during an escape attempt. While waiting 14 months to receive medical attention, his bones knitted, leaving him with a permanent limp. Released, Panzram vowed to commit some apocalyptic act against society like lacing a city's water supply with arsenic. Thirty-six days and twelve burglaries later, Panzram was arrested in Baltimore for housebreaking and taken to Washington, D.C., on August 16, 1928. In custody, the 37-year-old criminal confessed to three murders committed around Boston, New Haven, and Philadelphia. At the November 12, 1928, trial for housebreaking Panzram threatened to kill the judge and jury if he was released. It took the jury one minute to find him guilty and Panzram, who had already spent 20 years behind bars, was sentenced to 25 more in his old alma mater, Leavenworth.

Upon his arrival at the prison on February 1, 1929, Panzram informed the deputy warden that he would kill any man who bothered him. He was assigned a job in the prison laundry under civilian foreman Robert "R.G." Warnke who was well known to write up inmates over minor infractions. Panzram soon ran afoul of Warnke who reported him for taking in other inmates' laundry for cigarettes and nickels. He was sent to solitary, lost privileges, and had his request for a job transfer denied. Returning to the laundry on June 20, 1929, Panzram picked up a ten-pound iron bar and struck Warnke five times in the head. Isolated in solitary, Panzram shared the same block which held Robert Stroud, the famous "Bird Man of Alcatraz." As several witnesses saw the murder and Panzram confessed committing it, the April 15, 1930, trial in Topeka, Kansas, was a formality. The jury was out only 45 minutes with Panzram sentenced to be hanged on September 5, 1929.

Panzram was satisfied with the sentence and looked forward to the hanging like "some folks do for their wedding night." He spent his time reading Schopenhauer, Nietzsche, and in deflecting the efforts of anti–capital punishment groups to spare his life. A delegation from one such group, the Society for the Abolition of Capital Punishment, visited him and asked that he sign an Appeal for Presidential

Clemency. Panzram cursed the group and fired off a letter to President Herbert Hoover asking him not to intercede. Fearful that he would, Panzram unsuccessfully attempted suicide on June 20, 1930. Shortly before 6:00 a.m. on September 5, 1929, Panzram hastened to the gallows, pausing only to spit in the direction of onlookers. Asked by the hangman if he had anything to say, Panzram snapped, "Yes, hurry it up, you Hoosier bastard! I could hang a dozen men while you're fooling around!" Pronounced dead at 6:18 a.m., Panzram was buried in the Leavenworth Cemetery under a concrete marker inscribed with his number, 31614.

461. Gaddis, Thomas E., and Long, James O. *Killer; A Journal of Murder.* New York: Macmillan, 1970. 388 pp.: ill., facsim., ports.; 21 cm.

_____. [Same as 461.] Greenwich, Conn.: Fawcett, 1973. 352 pp.: ill.; 18 cm.; paperback.

_____. [Same as 461.] Mattituck, N.Y.: Amereon House, 1987. 388 pp., [16]pp. of plates: ill., ports.; 23 cm.

Includes excerpts from Carl Panzram's autobiography. One of the best books ever written on the evolution of a cold-blooded killer. Essential reading.

Parker, Pauline Yvonne

Born May 26, 1938, in Christchurch, New Zealand. Student. Christchurch, New Zealand; 1 murder; bludgeon (brick); June 22, 1954.

"I feel very keyed up as though I were planning a surprise party. Mother has fallen in with everything beautifully and the happy event is to take place tomorrow afternoon. So next time I write in this diary Mother will be dead. How odd yet how pleasing."—

Entry in Parker's diary dated June 21, 1954; *see also* Hulme, Juliet.

"Peasenhall Mystery [or] Murder" *see* Gardiner, William George Last

Perez, Leonora M.
(charges dropped)

Born circa 1944 in the Philippines. Nurse. Ann Arbor, Michigan; 11 murders (charges dropped); drugs (Pavulon); July–August 1975.

"I don't know if my life will change because of it all."

Federal case against two Filipino nurses charged with poisoning their patients which contained elements of racism and overzealous investigation. In the hot weeks of July and August 1975 an epidemic of sudden breathing failures swept through the Veterans Administration Hospital in Ann Arbor, Michigan. During that period, 35 hospitalized veterans experienced more than 50 sudden breathing failures. On August 15, 1975, alone, five patients suddenly stopped breathing within a single hour. While most of the veterans responded to immediate resuscitation efforts, 11 patients during the period died. In the resultant federal investigation (conducted by the FBI because the alleged crimes occurred on government property), authorities determined that at least six of that number were murder victims. Two Filipino nurses who worked the afternoon shift at the hospital, Leonora M. Perez, 31, and Filipina B. Narciso, 30, were ultimately charged with two murders and poisoning seven other patients after the drug Pavulon, a muscle relaxant which paralyzes the diaphragm and other muscles involved in breathing, was found in the victims' embalmed tissues. A small dose of the drug was capable of causing instant suffocation if artificial respiration was not immediately administered. According to the government's case, both nurses injected Pavulon into the intravenous tubes that fed nutrients and medication into the men's veins. Both women pleaded innocent and, prompted by charges of racism, a defense fund was set up to cover their legal expenses. During three months of complex medical testimony, the government built a circumstantial, motiveless case against the Filipinos based largely on their access to the victims and Pavulon. Shortly before the case went to the jury, the murder charge against Perez was dropped for insufficient evidence. On July 13, 1977, Perez and Narciso were found guilty of poisoning five of their patients. Narciso was acquitted of murder. Citing the prosecution's "persistent misconduct," a U.S. district court judge overturned the nurses' convictions on December 19, 1977, and ordered a new trial. The government dropped all charges against Perez and Narciso on February 1, 1978, noting the unlikelihood of obtaining convictions against the pair in a case based entirely on circumstantial evidence and lacking an apparent motive.

462. Wilcox, Robert K. *The Mysterious Deaths at Ann Arbor.* New York: Popular Library, 1977. 253 pp.; 18 cm.; paperback.

Petiot, Marcel André Henri Félix

(a.k.a. "Captain Henri Valéri," "Tarzan," "The Second Landru," "The New Bluebeard,"

"The Vampire of the rue Le Sueur," "Dr. Eugène," "Dr. François Wetterwald")

Born January 17, 1897 in Auxerre, France. Executed May 25, 1946. Medical doctor. Paris, France; 27 murders (admitted killing 63); poison; 1941–1944.

Film: Docteur Petiot (FR, 1990). Directed by Christian de Chalonge. Cast includes Michel Serrault (Dr. Petiot), Berangere Bonvoisin (Georgette Petiot), and Pierre Romans (Drezner).

"None. I am a traveler who is taking all his baggage with him."—Petiot's reply when asked if he had any final remarks to make before being executed

French doctor and wartime "Resistance fighter" convicted of murdering 26 people who paid large sums to leave German-occupied France through his "escape network." On March 11, 1944, neighbors around 21 rue Le Sueur, a three-story private house in Paris owned by Dr. Marcel Petiot, complained to authorities of a greasy, noxious smoke which had poured from the building's chimney for a week. Inside the house, the dismembered and charred remains of 27 corpses were found scattered in a furnace and a limepit. The house, modified in September 1941, contained a specially designed triangular death chamber only visible from the outside by a hidden spy glass. The 49-year-old physician explained to police that he was a member of the Resistance and that the bodies were Nazis and collaborators executed by his group. Released, Petiot dropped out of sight and was not apprehended until October 31, 1944, when authorities arrested the doctor posing as "Henri Valéri" at a train station in Saint-Mande-Tourelles. During the interim, investigators had pieced together a detailed dossier on the serial killer which revealed a criminal history dating back to childhood. Despite being institutionalized at least twice with mental problems and serving prison sentences for theft, Petiot earned a medical degree in September 1921 and was elected mayor of Villeneuve-sur-Yonne in July 1926. After his arrest, Petiot freely admitted killing 63 people, but denied using an "escape network" scheme in order to murder and rob wealthy Jews and others willing to pay an estimated 50,000 francs each to leave occupied France. Petiot, the self-professed leader of a Resistance group, patriotically maintained that he had liquidated only the enemies of France.

While awaiting trial in the condemned section of the Prison de la Santé in Paris, Petiot produced a 300-page manuscript entitled *Le Hasard Vaincu* ("Beating Chance," or, "Chance Defeated") in which he described various methods for winning at gambling. Self-published at his own expense, Petiot signed the volume for those who attended his trial at the Palais de Justice which began on March 18, 1946. Contemptuous of the prosecution's claim that he injected deadly poison into 27 of his escapee victims under the guise of inoculating them against "foreign diseases," Petiot frequently argued with the state's attorney or passed the time drawing caricatures of his accusers. On the fifth day of the trial, the court convened at 21 rue Le Sueur where jurors walked among human bones in a firsthand inspection of Dr. Petiot's torture chamber where he would watch his victims' death throes through an elaborately constructed peep-hole. Confronted by the horror of the scene and the contents of the

victims' suitcases, the jury needed only three hours on April 4, 1946, to find "the Second New Landru" guilty of 26 of the 27 murders. A supremely calm Petiot was guillotined on May 25, 1946. To date, none of the estimated half million dollars he collected from his victims has been recovered.

463. Grombach, John V. *The Great Liquidator.* 1st ed. Garden City, N.Y.: Doubleday, 1980. xviii, 408 pp., [18] leaves of plates: ill.; 22 cm.

———. [Same as 463.] London: Sphere, 1982. xvi, 408 pp., [8]pp. of plates: ill., 1 plan, ports.; 18 cm.; paperback.

Definitive study by the director of the Secret Intelligence Branch of the U.S. War Department general staff (1942-1947) and later transferred to the foreign service of the State Department.

464. Maeder, Thomas. *The Unspeakable Crimes of Dr. Petiot.* 1st ed. Boston: Little, Brown, 1980. xiv, 302 pp., [8] leaves of plates: ill.; 22 cm. ("An Atlantic Monthly Press book.")

———. [Same as 464.] Penguin True Crime. London: Penguin, 1990. xx, 302 pp., [16]pp. of plates: ill., ports.; 20 cm.; paperback.

———. [Same as 464, but retitled: *Docteur Petiot.*] New York: Penguin Books, 1992. xii, 302 pp.: ill.; 19 cm.; paperback.

Well written and readable account of the Petiot case which lacks the comprehensiveness of Grombach's study. Includes a bibliography of English and French works.

465. Seth, Ronald. *Petiot: Victim of Chance.* London: Hutchinson, 1963. 207 pp.: ill.; 22 cm.

Seth, a self-described British secret agent operating in Paris in 1944, argues that Petiot was perhaps part of a Communist terrorist group given the special mission of raising funds to finance a Communist takeover of France.

Petrovich, Oliver

Born circa 1965. Mechanic. Great Neck, New York; 2 murders; 12 gauge shotgun; September 25, 1988.

"I wanted to strangle her because it would have been quiet and I didn't want my father around."—Excerpt from Petrovich's confession

Case of patricide committed because a father would not accept his son's black girlfriend. On September 25, 1988, police were called to the Svetozar Petrovich home in Great Neck, New York, by the Yugoslavian immigrant's son Oliver, a 23-year-old truck mechanic who still lived with his parents. According to Oliver Petrovich's statement, he returned home to find his mother Anna, 44, dead on the kitchen floor from a single shotgun wound to the head. His 59-year-old father was found in a first floor bedroom dead from two shotgun blasts in the chest. During police interrogation, Petrovich confessed to murdering his parents with a Browning .12 gauge shotgun following an argument over his 19-year-old black girlfriend Karlene Francis. Petrovich's father intensely disliked blacks and had told him not to bring the girl near his house. Since April 1988, however, the son had secretly lived with Francis in his second story bedroom. When his mother discovered the bizarre living arrangement she kept the news from her husband. However, on the day of the murder Anna Petrovich finally told him of the clandestine relationship. According to Petrovich, the family argued and after trying to strangle his mother he shot first her then his father. Accompanied by his lover, Petrovich tossed the murder weapon off the Throgs Neck Bridge into the East River where it was recovered the next day. In exchange for her cooperation, prosecutors did not file charges against Francis. Pleading not guilty to two counts of second degree murder, Petrovich's trial began in Mineola, New York, on September 28, 1989. The prosecution, bolstered by the confession, maintained that Petrovich had twice previously planned to kill his parents in order to inherit their property: a $400,000 house and a 20-unit apartment building in Flushing. If they were dead, he and the girl would be free to live in the house. Petrovich's counsel contended that the son was obsessed with the girl, terrified of his father, and was therefore unable to make a rational decision at the time he shot his parents. Shortly before closing arguments, Petrovich took a gamble by insisting to the judge that he not allow the jury to consider a lesser verdict of manslaughter as a compromise between murder and acquittal. If convicted, Petrovich could not inherit his parents' estate. Following nine hours of deliberation, a jury found Petrovich guilty of two counts of second degree murder on October 12, 1989. The convicted double killer was subsequently sentenced to the maximum prison term of 50 years to life.

466. Saslow, Linda. *For My Angel: A True Story of Forbidden Love, Obsession, and Murder.* Garden City, N.Y.: Guild America Books, 1991. 250 pp.: ill.; 22 cm. ("GuildAmerica books.")

"Phantom of the Opera Murder" *see* **Crimmins, Craig Stephen**

"Phoenix Trunk Murders" *see* **Judd, Winnie Ruth**

"Pied Piper Murders" *see* **Schmid, Charles Howard, Jr.**

Pierce, Darci Kayleen
(a.k.a. "Darci Kayleen Ricker" [maiden name])

Born circa 1967 in Toledo, Oregon. Department store clerk. Albuquerque, New Mexico; 1 murder; ligature strangulation, stabbing (car key); July 23, 1987.

"I feel like a real person for the first time in my life. This baby is going to live its entire life with me."

In a tragic instance of what one police official called a case of "maternal instinct run amok," a 19-year-old woman with a history of emotional problems murdered a pregnant woman for her unborn baby. Given away at the age of 11 days by her door-to-door salesman father to a family that he sold pots and pans to, Darci began having sex with a cousin at the age of six. The relationship lasted six years during which time a neighbor forced her to perform oral sex on him while she was still in the third grade. Darci dropped out of high school in 1985 and began living with future husband Ray Pierce. In the same year, Pierce experienced a molar pregnancy which produced a tumorlike growth not a fetus. After the "miscarriage" Pierce became obsessed with having a child. In the early summer of 1986 she lied about being pregnant, gained 50 pounds, and took maternity leave from her job as a department store clerk. When unable to produce the fictional baby, Pierce claimed to have suffered a miscarriage. In late 1986 Pierce again lied about being pregnant and announced her baby's due date as May 1987. Believing her to be pregnant, Ray Pierce married her that December before moving them to Albuquerque, New Mexico, for his basic training at Kirtland Air Force Base. As the child's delivery date grew nearer, Pierce moved the date back to July. Finally, on July 23, 1987, the child's birth could no longer be postponed and Pierce told her family that labor was to be induced that afternoon at 5:00 p.m.

Earlier that day, Pierce waited in her car outside the base clinic for a pregnant woman to emerge. Using a starter's pistol to force 23-year-old Cindy Lynn Giles Ray into the car, Pierce drove the 8½ month pregnant woman into the Manzano Mountains just east of Albuquerque. After striking Ray in the head with the butt of the gun, Pierce strangled her into unconsciousness with a belt, and using the key of her victim's Chevy Blazer, "took" the baby in a crude Caesarean section operation. Smearing blood on her own thighs and dress, Pierce drove to the University of New Mexico Medical Center, leaving Ray to bleed to death. At the base hospital, her refusal to let doctors examine her led them to suspect that the newborn girl (named "Amanda Michelle" by Pierce) was not actually hers. Pierce later told them that she had purchased the child on the black market for $10,000. She confessed to Ray's murder the next day after police confronted her with a missing person's report filed by the pregnant woman's husband. Pierce was formally charged with first degree murder, kidnapping, and child abuse on July 27, 1987, after leading authorities to Ray's body. Miraculously, the child survived and was named Amelia Monik.

Pierce pleaded innocent by reason of insanity at her trial in Albuquerque which began with jury selection on March 7, 1988. Amid conflicting psychological testimony, Pierce was found mentally ill, but guilty of murder and the other counts on March 29, 1988. As the prosecution had previously stated their intent not to seek the death penalty, Pierce was sentenced on April 28, 1988, to life imprisonment for murder, 18 years for kidnapping, and 18 months on the child abuse complaint with the sentences to run concurrently. Under New Mexico law, Pierce is eligible for parole after 30 years and theoretically could be released in 2017 at the age of 49.

467. Carrier, Jim. *Hush, Little Baby.* New York: Pinnacle Books, 1992. 279 pp., [8]pp. of plates: ill.; 18 cm.; paperback.

A detailed paperback account of the case which includes an excellent selection of photographs.

468. Hughes, D.T. *Lullaby and Goodnight.* New York: Pocket Books, 1992. 281 pp.; 18 cm.; paperback.

A paperback account based on interviews (most notably with the victim's husband), police documents, and trial records.

Pierre, Dale Selby
(a.k.a. "Hi-Fi Killer," "P. Dale Selby" [legal name change], "Clayton Leon Cassiram," "Philbert Hamilton Bailey," "Cody Jaye Cavalho," "Houston Lee Hoyt," "Del Ray Hoyt," "Del Ray Khanhai," "Curtis Alexander")

Born January 21, 1953, near Mason Hill, Tobago. Executed August 28, 1987. United States Air Force airman. Ogden, Utah; 3 murders; poison, .25 caliber pistol, .38 caliber pistol; April 22, 1974.

"As I look back on everything I believe everything that happened to me was supposed to happen. Maybe there is a lesson in it somewhere I am supposed to learn."

One of the so-called "Hi-Fi Killers" who, with fellow black airman William A. Andrews, committed the most heinous crime in Ogden, Utah, history. On April 22, 1974, Pierre, Andrews, and getaway driver Keith Roberts robbed the Ogden Hi-Fi Shop. As Roberts loaded the van with thousands of dollars in stereo equipment, Pierre and Andrews crowded five hostages at gunpoint into the store's basement and tied them up. Allegedly at Pierre's instigation, Andrews poured Liquid Drano into a cup, gave it to his partner, then left the scene. Pierre, assuring the hostages that the cup contained vodka mixed with a German drug designed to make them sleep, forced each to drink, threatening to shoot them if they refused. As the victims writhed on the floor in agony, Pierre methodically shot each in the back of the head except for a 19-year-old female store clerk he raped before shooting. Orren Walker, father of one of the victims, survived the gunshot, but was further tortured by Pierre who first tried unsuccessfully to strangle him manually and then with an electrical cord before finally placing a ballpoint pen in his ear and repeatedly kicking it. Of the five hostages, only Orren and 16-year-old store employee Cortney Naisbitt survived the ordeal albeit with serious lifelong injuries.

The next day, two boys rummaging through a dumpster behind a barracks at nearby Hill Air Force Base ran across credit cards and personal effects belonging to the victims. Dale Pierre, a 20-year-old Trinidadian-born airman who lived at the barracks, was known to police who had questioned him six months before in connection with the brutal murder of a fellow airman. A search of Pierre's room yielded a key to a storage unit found to contain $24,000 worth of stolen stereo equipment and a half-filled bottle of Liquid Drano. Pierre and accomplice Andrews, 19, were arrested on April 23, 1974. Roberts was picked up days later and charged with aggravated robbery.

Following a one month trial in Farmington, Utah, Pierre and Andrews were each found guilty on November 15, 1974, on three counts of first degree murder and two counts of aggravated robbery. The jury hung on the murder counts against Keith Roberts, but convicted him on two counts of aggravated robbery. Roberts was subsequently paroled in 1987 after serving 13 years. On November 20, 1974, Pierre and Andrews were sentenced to death. During the 13 years Pierre fought against execution he maintained before the Utah Board of Paroles that he was drunk and high on tranquilizers at the time of the murders. According to Pierre, the killings would never have occurred if one of the victims had not called him "a godless nigger." Survivor Orren Walker, two feet from the alleged name caller, testified that no racial slur was ever uttered. On August 28, 1987, at the Utah State Prison, Pierre achieved the distinction of becoming the first prisoner in the state to be executed by lethal injection. Pierre's execution was the first in Utah since Mark Gary Gilmore died by firing squad on January 17, 1977. William Andrews became a *cause célèbre* whose appeal for clemency was supported by the National Association for the Advancement of Colored People, the American Civil Liberties Union, Amnesty International, and the Vatican. They argued that Andrews' trial was inherently unfair due to the fact that he, a black man, was convicted by an all-white jury. After spending almost 18 years on death row, Andrews was executed by lethal injection on July 30, 1992.

469. Kinder, Gary. *Victim, the Other Side of Murder.* New York: Delacorte Press, 1982. 305 pp.; 24 cm.

_____. [Same as 469.] New York: Dell, 1983. 298 pp.; 18 cm.; paperback.

_____. [Same as 469.] London: Fontana, 1983. 305 pp.; 18 cm.; paperback.

_____. [Same as 469.] New York: Dell, 1984. 298 pp.; 18 cm. ("A Laurel book"— T.p. verso); paperback.

_____. [Same as 469.] [Rev. ed, with new epilogue.] New York: Dell, 1991. 315 pp.; 18 cm.; paperback.

Described by a *Newsweek* reviewer as "Truman Capote's *In Cold Blood* turned inside out," Kinder's first book focuses on the victims (particularly the agonizing recovery of 16-year-old survivor Cortney Naisbitt) rather than the two killers. Pierre originally cooperated with Kinder between 1974 and 1980, but terminated the relationship when the author refused him a share of the royalties. Commenting on the killer's August 28, 1987, execution, Kinder observed: "I'm sure Pierre would commit the same crime all over again if he was let out on the street." The new epilogue to the 1991 revised paperback edition describes Pierre's execution by lethal injection.

Pikul, Joseph John

Born December 3, 1934, in Ware, Massachusetts. Died June 2, 1989. Securities analyst. Amagansett, Long Island, New York; 1 murder; manual strangulation, bludgeon; October 24, 1987.

"She tried to kill me, not physically, but mentally. I just couldn't take it anymore."—Pikul in a confession to police hours after his arrest on October 29, 1987

Sandra Mae Jarvinen, the first wife of Joseph John Pikul (pronounced "Pie-kul"), best summed up their marriage when she said, "He had the right to live his life. I had the right to serve him." After enduring 15 years of soul-killing physical and verbal abuse, Jarvinen divorced Pikul in the summer of 1974. Pikul, the son of a physically abusive alcoholic textile mill worker, became a top securities expert at a prestigious Manhattan investment firm, earned a six figure income, and lived in a luxury apartment in Greenwich Village. Pikul, however, was also a compulsive overeater and an alcoholic who abused his wife, the former Diane Whitmore Schnackenberg, and his two children, Claudia and Blake Joseph. Unlike her predecessor, Diane Pikul resisted her husband's attempt to dominate her and fought back with the only two weapons in her arsenal: a sarcastic wit and a foul mouth. The Pikul home became an emotional battleground punctuated by daily vicious arguments in which the securities analyst threatened to take the children in a divorce and leave his wife penniless. In February 1986, Diane discovered a "weapon" that she could use against Pikul to equalize any potential divorce settlement. After finding a check for several hundred dollars Pikul wrote to a lingerie shop, Diane, suspecting her husband of an affair, searched the apartment and uncovered dozens of bras and panties hidden in suitcases. A search of their summer home in Amagansett, Long Island, yielded ten more suitcases filled with lingerie, falsies, anal vibrators, homosexual pornography, and nearly 60 Polaroid photos of Pikul dressed as a woman. A half-hour-long video found in the cache featured Pikul in drag mincing around the house masturbating. Diane placed the video and photographs in a safety deposit box and contacted famed matrimonial attorney Raoul Lionel Felder in August 1986. Fearful of being blackmailed,

Pikul decided to try to make the marriage work. Against Felder's advice, Diane remained in the relationship.

By 1987, Pikul's high standard of living was devastating his finances. In addition to owing his first wife $28,000 in back alimony, he secretly rented an apartment in Battery Park City where he videotaped himself in drag and fed his cocaine habit. On the hope of catching Diane in an incriminating situation which he could use in court, Pikul bugged their home and carried a microcassette tape recorder in his pocket to document their arguments. During a particularly vicious one in September 1987, Diane accused him of having AIDS, berated him as a cowardly "faggot," and threatened to kill him if she had to. On October 24, 1987, the Pikuls met in their weekend home in Amagansett to discuss a divorce and the division of property. While the exact details of Diane's murder remain contested, that night the pair argued about the divorce as the children slept in their rooms. Pikul struck his wife in the head at least ten times with a blunt object, manually strangled her to death, wrapped the dead woman in a car cover, and partially buried her body on the beach near the house. After preparing breakfast for the children, Pikul returned alone to the beach, dug up the body, and stowed it in the back of his station wagon. Later that morning he drove with his children to a local hardware store and purchased plastic lawn bags, cord, 12 bags of ice, gloves, a shovel, and a wheelbarrow. Depositing the children with a friend, Pikul drove to his first wife's house in Norwell, Massachusetts, where he admitted to Jarvinen that he had "eliminated" Diane. She refused Pikul's request to let him bury the body on her property, explaining, "I have a high water table." Pikul instead dumped the body in a drainage ditch near the Governor Thomas E. Dewey Thruway three miles south of the Newburgh, New York, exit and disposed of the woman's credit cards in a dumpster behind a car wash in that city. Diane Pikul's body was found by a highway worker on October 28, 1987.

The recovery of Diane's body and her credit cards led authorities directly to Pikul and he was arrested on October 29, 1987. Strip searched at police headquarters, Pikul was found to be wearing a bra and panties under his gray flannel suit. Pikul was charged with the killing, posted a $350,000 bond, and to the public's shock and outrage, was permitted to retain custody of his children. After several months of legal wrangling, a judge in September 1988 ordered the children to be placed with cousins of the murdered woman. Opening arguments in Pikul's second degree murder trial began in Goshen, New York, on January 30, 1989. Testifying in his own behalf, Pikul insisted that while he caused Diane's death he did not murder her. According to Pikul, a violent argument began when he confronted her with an unfamiliar brand of condom he found under the bed in their room. He accused her of having an affair and threatened to fight her in divorce court for custody of the children. Diane reacted by attacking and wounding him with a butcher's knife. Pikul choked her to death in self-defense and later panicked when trying to hide the body. Expert medical testimony concluded that the wound on Pikul's side and hand could not have been caused by a knife and were probably self-inflicted. The prosecution contended that Pikul murdered his wife to retain custody of his children

and to prevent her from disclosing his secret life as a crossdresser in a divorce court. Pikul was convicted on March 15, 1989, and faced a possible 25 years to life at a sentencing hearing scheduled for June 12, 1989. On May 30, 1989, Pikul asked the court for a new trial based upon the discovery of an audiotape in which Diane threatened to kill him. While awaiting the court's ruling, Pikul was transferred from the Orange County jail to Arden Hill Hospital where he died of AIDS-related diseases including cancer and multiple opportunistic infections on June 2, 1989. In accordance with New York State law, Pikul's conviction was vacated on December 5, 1989, because he died while an appeal was pending. Technically, he died an innocent man. After years of litigation, the appellate division of the state supreme court ruled in August 1993 that Diane Pikul's children, not Joseph Pikul's family or creditors, would inherit her estate.

470. Pienciak, Richard T. *Deadly Masquerade: A True Story of High Living, Depravity and Murder.* New York: Dutton, 1990. viii, 420 pp.: ill.; 24 cm.

471. Weller, Sheila. *Marrying the Hangman: A True Story of Privilege, Marriage and Murder.* 1st ed. New York: Random House, 1992. xiv, 319 pp., [8]pp. of plates: ill.; 24 cm.

_____. [Same as 471 minus subtitle.] New York: Onyx, 1993. xi, 400 pp., [8]pp. of plates: ill.; 18 cm.; paperback.

Weller's feminist perspective portrays Diane Pikul, the victim, as a woman desperately trying to assume some control over her life. A bitter indictment of a legal system which permits a confessed killer to retain custody of the children he orphaned. The book grew out of Weller's *Ms.* magazine article, "Middle-Class Murder," which appeared in its May 1988 issue.

"Playmate Murder" *see* Snider, Paul Leslie

Poddar, Prosenjit
(a.k.a. "Little Hindu")

Born circa 1946 in Balurghat, India. Graduate student. Berkeley, California; 1 murder; knife; October 27, 1969.

"I am having some difficulties with her, and I want to teach her a lesson."—Poddar to a friend some time before his murder of Tarasoff

Hindu graduate student whose obsession with a fellow student led to her brutal murder and a landmark legal ruling. Prosenjit Poddar, a brilliant 23-year-old Indian graduate student majoring in naval architecture and marine engineering at the University of California at Berkeley, met Tanya Tarasoff, a 19-year-old freshman at Oakland's Merrit Junior College, at a folk dance at Berkeley's International House in the fall of 1968. Poddar, one of the few Indian Untouchables ever permitted to study in the United States, became obsessed with Tarasoff to the point that in 1969 he sought outpatient therapy at the UC–Berkeley's Cowell Memorial Hospital. During a counseling session, Poddar told a therapist of the violent fantasies he had toward Tarasoff, the woman who had rejected him. The therapist discussed the case with his superior and the decision was made to try and hospitalize Poddar. The therapist contacted university officials who, after questioning Poddar, warned him to stay away from Tarasoff. Neither the therapist or the campus police notified the city police or the potential victim of Poddar's threat. Two months later, on October 27, 1969, Poddar forced his way into Tarasoff's Berkeley home and stabbed the woman eight times in the chest, abdomen, and back with a 13-inch knife. Poddar pleaded innocent by reason of insanity, but was convicted of second degree murder (without premeditation) on August 26, 1970. The California Supreme Court overturned the conviction on appeal in 1974, citing that the trial judge had failed to adequately instruct the jury on the meaning of diminished capacity. At a new trial, the judge arranged a compromise that allowed Poddar to be released in exchange for his deportation to India. Poddar returned to Calcutta in 1974, married, and in 1976 won a scholarship to study naval architecture at an institution in Hannover, Germany. In September 1970 Tarasoff's parents filed a $200,000 wrongful death suit against the regents of the University of California for failing to warn them that Poddar had threatened their daughter's life. They were awarded an undisclosed amount of money after the California Supreme Court ruled in 1976 that a psychotherapist had a legal duty to warn an intended victim if threats were made against them by a mentally ill patient during therapy.

472. Blum, Deborah. *Bad Karma: A True Story of Obsession and Madness.* 1st ed. New York: Atheneum, 1986. 311 pp., [8]pp. of plates: ill., ports.; 25 cm.

_____. [Same as 472.] New York: Jove, 1988. 304 pp.: ill.; 18 cm.; paperback.

Podmore, William Henry
(a.k.a. "William Frank Thomas," "Nicholls")

Born circa 1901. Executed April 22, 1930. Mechanic, driver. Southampton, England; 1 murder; bludgeon (hammer); October 30, 1928.

"I still repeat that I know nothing whatever about it."—Podmore's statement to the court before being sentenced to death

British petty criminal who graduated to murder when he bludgeoned to death an agent for the Wolf's Head Oil Company in a garage in Southampton. Posing under the alias "William Frank Thomas," Podmore was hired as a mechanic and driver by Vivian Messiter, a 58-year-old representative for the Southampton-based oil company. According to the official version of the subsequent murder, Messiter learned that Podmore was writing up bogus orders and pocketing the commissions. On October 30, 1928, he confronted Podmore in the company garage at 42 Grove Street and was beaten to death with a hammer. Messiter's body, badly gnawed by rats, was found hidden behind some boxes some ten weeks later on January 10, 1929. The blood-clotted hammer was recovered nearby. Based on correspondence from a "W.F. Thomas" found in the dead man's home Scotland Yard detectives established Podmore's identity. He was traced to London, questioned about the murder, and arrested for fraud on January 29, 1929, and imprisoned for six months while police worked feverishly to build a murder case against him. On July 17, 1929, Podmore was arrested and charged with theft as he was discharged from prison. After serving an additional six months, Podmore was arrested for Messiter's murder on December 17, 1929, some 13½ months after the crime.

Podmore's six day trial opened at the Winchester Assizes on March 3, 1930, and focused largely on an examination of an oil sales receipt book in which several pages had been torn out. Special photographic techniques determined that pencil indentations left on the pages beneath contained records of sales to fictitious customers signed by "W.F. Thomas." Podmore, the prosecution maintained, killed Messiter when confronted about the swindle. Bolstering the prosecution's case, several fellow-prisoners testified that Podmore had made incriminating statements to them about the murder. On March 9, 1930, Podmore was found guilty after a jury deliberated only one hour and eighteen minutes. Sentenced to death, Podmore was hanged at Winchester Gaol on April 22, 1930, following an unsuccessful appeal.

473. Moulton, H. Fletcher, and Woodland, W. Lloyd. *The Trial of William Henry Podmore.* Famous Trials Series. London: Geoffrey Bles, 1931. 286 pp.; ill.; 22 cm.

Transcript excerpts from Podmore's trial at the Winchester Assizes, March 1930, for the murder of Vivian Messiter.

Podola, Guenther Fritz Erwin
(a.k.a. "Phone-Box Killer," "R.M. Levine," "Mr. Fisher," "Mike Colato," "Paul Camay")

Born February 8, 1929, in Berlin, Germany. Executed November 5, 1959. Petty criminal. London, England; 1 murder; 9mm automatic; July 13, 1959.

"I was determined to make myself a big shot in crime. I bought an automatic pistol for £5 and toted myself as a gunman for hire."—Podola writing in prison while awaiting execution

Small time blackmailer turned cop killer who made British legal history by claiming he was unfit to plead because of hysterical amnesia. On July 3, 1959, 30-year-old Guenther Podola broke into the South Kensington flat of Mrs. Verne Schiffman, an English-born American model. In addition to stealing Schiffman's passport, the German-born thief took a mink stole and jewelry worth £1785. Days later, posing as private detective "R. M. Levine" Podola contacted Schiffman by letter and threatened to blackmail her with incriminating pictures and tape recordings unless she agreed to pay him $500. Schiffman notified police who were ready with a phone tap when Podola called from a phonebox in a South Kensington Underground Station on July 13, 1959. Podola was still on the line with Schiffman when detective-sergeants Raymond William Purdy and John Sandford arrested him. Podola broke free and after a short chase was reapprehended. When Sandford left to call for backup, Podola pulled a 9mm automatic and shot Purdy point blank in the body, killing the father of three instantly. Prints lifted from a notebook Purdy confiscated from the blackmailer combined with others found at the scene established Podola's identity. Acting on a tip from an anonymous informant, police traced Podola to a 35-shilling-a-week room in South Kensington's Claremont House Hotel. On July 16, 1959, as officers broke into Podola's room the door struck the suspect above the left eye sending him careening headfirst into a fireplace. Podola struggled with police for several minutes before going limp. Regaining consciousness at the hospital, he appeared dazed and later claimed to remember little of events that occurred before the day after his arrest. A lumbar puncture determined that Podola had indeed sustained a cerebral contusion during the arrest. Five days later detective-sergeant Purdy was buried at Surbiton, Surrey, as 1,000 London police officers lined the last half mile of the mile-long funeral procession.

Podola's trial began in the Old Bailey on September 10, 1959. After the murder charge had been read, counsel for the defense raised the issue of Podola's amnesia. The action represented the first time in the history of England that amnesia was introduced as a basis for a plea of unfitness. A special jury was impanelled to determine the issue and heard testimony from psychologists divided in their opinion over whether Podola was suffering from amnesia or merely malingering. Podola's testimony revealed that while in Brixton Prison he had written a letter to a friend in which he discussed incidents that occurred before the time of his alleged amnesia. The jury's finding that Podola was not suffering from a genuine loss of memory cleared the way for the murder trial. Lacking the amnesia defense, Podola's guilt was quickly established and the gunman was sentenced to death on September 24, 1959, after a jury deliberated only 37 minutes. Following a failed appeal and the refusal of the Home Office to grant a plea of clemency supported by the West German Embassy in London, Podola was executed by hanging at Wandsworth Prison on November 5, 1959.

474. Furneaux, Rupert. *Guenther Podola.* Crime Documentary no. 1. London: Stevens, 1960. xi, 319 pp.: ill., ports.; 21 cm.

Furneaux, who attended Podola's trial, offers an excellent account of a landmark legal case. An appendix lists policemen murdered in England and Wales since 1900 compiled from lists supplied by the Home Office and by the Metropolitan Police.

"Porthole Murder" *see* Camb, James

Powell, Bernadette

Born circa 1952. Lansing, New York; 1 murder; pistol; July 9, 1978.

Video: To Love, Honor and Obey (1985), a one-hour video directed by Christine Chow, released by Third World Newsreel (New York). A documentary featuring the domestic violence faced by women of various ages, racial groups, and cultural backgrounds in the United States. Includes a seven-minute segment "Update: Bernadette Powell."

"I depersonalize myself from being here, otherwise I become disoriented. I dream about the past."—Powell on serving time

Twenty-six-year-old black mother of one whose murder of her physically abusive ex-husband became a *cause célèbre* among feminists and those advocating stronger domestic violence laws. During her five-year marriage to Herman D. Smith, Jr., Powell was routinely beaten by her husband. The pattern of abuse became so common that when Powell's mother called her on the phone and there was no answer she immediately notified police. Powell seemingly did everything a battered wife is counseled to do in order to build a new life; she obtained orders of protection, divorced Smith in 1977, moved to another house, and got another job. On July 9, 1978, according to Powell, she went to pick up her six-year-old son at her ex-husband's home in Endicott, New York, when Smith insisted on driving them back to her place in Ithaca. Instead, Smith threatened her with a gun and drove the pair to a Holiday Inn in Lansing, New York. Prior to falling asleep, Smith argued with

and threatened his ex-wife. Shortly afterwards, he awakened while she was removing the gun from the front of his pants. Powell allegedly shot Smith in self-defense. Tried in Ithaca, New York, in March 1979, Powell's claim that the murder weapon belonged to her husband was refuted by a witness who testified that he had sold her the gun and bullets on June 26, 1978. A close friend of Powell's alleged that two months prior to the shooting the defendant had expressed her desire to cause harm to her ex-husband. Other evidence adduced at the trial similarly contradicted the sequence of events testified to by Powell. Convicted of second degree murder on March 22, 1979, Powell was subsequently sentenced to 15 years to life, the minimum term allowed under the law. On June 25, 1985, Powell graduated magna cum laude with a bachelor's degree in social science and psychology from Mercy College as part of its "college behind bars" program with the Bedford Hills Correctional Facility. According to Powell, 33, she earned the degree to set an example for her 13-year-old son and to "fulfill a contract with God." She is eligible for parole in 1995 (no further information available at the time of this printing).

475. Jones, Ann. *Everyday Death: The Case of Bernadette Powell.* 1st ed. New York: Holt, Rinehart, and Winston, 1985. xv, 202 pp.; 22 cm.

Jones, who briefly summarized the Powell case in her 1980 book *Women Who Kill,* demonstrates in great detail how in her opinion a black woman was judged and sentenced primarily on the basis of sexual and racial stereotypes.

Powers, Harry F.
(a.k.a. "America's Bluebeard," "Bluebeard of the New

World," "Love Mart Slayer," "Mail-Order Bluebeard," "Mad Slayer of West Virginia," "Lothario of the West Virginia Hills," "Hiram/Henry Drenth," "Cornelius O. Pierson," "D. P. Lowther," "Connie," "Joseph Gildow [or] Gildeau")

Born circa 1889 in West Virginia. Executed March 19, 1932. Salesman, store clerk. Quiet Dell, West Virginia; 5 murders; ligature strangulation, bludgeoning (hammer); June– July 1931.

"I believe I'm entitled to a good dinner."—Powers to a sheriff after being sentenced to hang for the murder of Dorothy Pressler Lemke

West Virginia "bluebeard" who placed ads in the publications of matrimonial agencies to lure victims to their deaths in his specially designed torture garage. Posing as wealthy widower "Cornelius O. Pierson," 42-year-old Harry F. Powers joined the American Friendship Society in January 1931. In his carefully written ad, the married Powers passed himself off as a civil engineer anxious to marry a woman that he promised "would have nothing to do but enjoy herself." From the scores of letters that flooded his post office box in Clarksburg, West Virginia, Powers selected 45-year-old Mrs. Asta Buick Eicher, a wealthy widow in Park Ridge, Illinois, with three children: Grethe, 14, Harry, 12, and 9-year-old Annabelle. Following a spirited correspondence in which he promised marriage, "Pierson" traveled to Eicher's home and convinced the widow and her children to accompany him back to his "beautiful ten-room brick house" in Clarksburg. Eicher was last seen on June 22, 1931. Weeks later,

50-year-old divorcée Mrs. Dorothy Pressler Lemke left her Northboro, Massachusetts, home on the heels of a lengthy correspondence with a pen pal suitor named "Cornelius O. Pierson." Park Ridge, Illinois, police investigating Eicher's disappearance uncovered 27 love letters in her home from "Pierson" postmarked from West Virginia. Clarksburg authorities were contacted and a stakeout of Pierson's post office box revealed that he was receiving mail from women all over the country. More importantly, the surveillance verified that "Pierson" and Powers were the same man. Questioned at his modest home in Clarksburg, Powers mentioned building a garage on a piece of property owned by his wife in nearby Quiet Dell. Investigators visiting the site were assailed by the stench of rotting flesh. They found letters, Eicher's effects, and boxes of children's clothes inside the garage. Large enough to house three cars, the garage was constructed with reinforced concrete walls and contained four soundproof cells dug into the basement floor covered by a heavy wooden trapdoor. A rope hanging from the rafters of the garage situated over the door when opened afforded a drop of six feet into the cells below. On August 28, 1931, the bodies of Eicher and her three children were found buried in burlap in a sewer trench leading from the garage to a creek. Autopsies determined the victims had been hanged five weeks before. They had been starved before their murders. Only young Harry Eicher escaped the rope. The boy, gagged with garage waste, had been emasculated prior to being beaten to death with a hammer found at the scene. Lemke's body was recovered the next day.

Powers confessed to the murders

after being severely beaten by police during an eight-hour interrogation session, but later recanted his confession. As an estimated crowd of 40,000 people visited the Quiet Dell site to view the torture garage, Powers sat under heavy guard in the Harrison County Jail in Clarksburg. On the night of September 20, 1931, a mob of 4,000 threatened to storm the jail and take Powers by force. Unknown to them, authorities hustled Powers out the back door of the jail and transported him to the more secure state prison in Moundsville. Powers' trial for the murder of Lemke opened to a capacity crowd of 1,200 at Moore's Opera House in Clarksville on December 31, 1931. As street hawkers sold songs, phonograph records, and books about the "West Virginia Bluebeard" outside the courtroom, Powers lamely testified that "two other fellows" named "Cecil Johnson" and "Charles Rogers" had committed the murders. Compelling evidence clearly showed that Powers' murder of Lemke netted him only $15,000 of her money and property. Based on the preponderance of physical evidence against him, a jury needed only 1 hour and 50 minutes to find Powers guilty on December 10, 1931. Still publicly maintaining his innocence, Powers was hanged at the state prison in Moundsville on March 19, 1932. After his execution, a prison doctor produced a document signed by Powers in which he admitted killing all five victims. The "Lothario of the West Virginia Hills" was buried in the prison's potter's field after his wife refused to claim his body.

476. Bartlett, Evan Allen. *Love Murders of Harry F. Powers: Beware Such Bluebeards.* New York: Sheftel Press, 1931. 221 pp.: ill.; 21 cm.

Contemporaneous account (not covering Powers' trial and execution) written by his former attorney who represented him during the time he was employed by the Eureka Vacuum Cleaner Company. Poorly written and marred by numerous printing errors, the book is nevertheless a fascinating history of one of the most intriguing cases in the annals of 20th century murder. In a foreword, Bartlett disingenuously states that the sensational reading to follow "is respectfully submitted with the assurance that its mission is intended to be of wholesome helpfulness to mankind, and not to engender morbid desire or taint human souls."

"Preppy Murder" *see* **Chambers, Robert E., Jr.**

Puente, Dorothea Helen
(a.k.a. "Dorothea Helen Gray" [maiden name], "Dorothea H. [or] Sharon Johansson" [married name], "Dorothea H. Montalvo" [married name], "Eleonora Anderson," "Donna Johanson," "Sherriale A. Riscile," "Teya Singoalla Neyaarda")

Born January 9, 1929, in Redlands, California. Landlady. Sacramento, California; 9 murders (convicted of 3); poison (Dalmane); 1982–1988.

Video: Evil Spirits (US, 1991), a Grand Am production of a film directed by Gary Graver, was released direct-to-video on October 3, 1991, but showed theatrically in Los Angeles at the New Beverly Cinema on December 1 and 2, 1993. Inspired by the Puente case, the film's cast includes Karen Black, Michael Berryman, and Arte Johnson.

"I used to be a very good person, at one time."—Puente's self-appraisal made shortly after being arrested and accused of murdering nine people

Elderly serial killer who murdered social security recipients for their checks then buried their remains in the yard of her Sacramento, California, roominghouse. By 1982 Puente had graduated from forging federal checks and drugging and robbing old men she picked up in bars to murder. In April of that year Puente invited 61-year-old Ruth Munroe, her partner in a lunchroom business, to live at her three-story Victorian roominghouse at 1426 F Street in downtown Sacramento. Munroe brought all her possessions and $6,100 in cash. Seventeen days later Munroe died, the victim of a massive overdose of Tylenol and codeine. Police investigated the death, but based largely on information supplied by Puente, declared it to be either a suicide or an accident. Charged in May 1982 with administering stupefying drugs to four elderly people between August 5, 1981, and May 16, 1982, Puente arranged a plea bargain and served only 37 months of a 52-month sentence before being paroled from the California Institution for Women at Frontera. While in prison, Puente began a correspondence with 77-year-old Everson T. Gillmouth, a pensioner from Oregon with an Airstream trailer. Anxious to marry Puente, Gillmouth moved to Sacramento, made her a signatory on his bank account, and was living in his trailer in the front of her boardinghouse when she was released in September 1985. In November, Puente hired a longtime friend to build a coffin-sized storage box and to help her dispose of it on the banks of the Sacramento River in Sutter County. Gillmouth's corpse, wrapped in plastic and

mothballs, was found on January 1, 1986.

After Gillmouth's death, Puente (against the terms of her parole) opened her roominghouse to down-and-outers and quickly established a reputation of excellence among Sacramento's social service agencies. She further cemented her positive public image by becoming active in Hispanic causes and contributing to the political candidates of both parties. From August 1986 through August 1988, seven elderly persons disappeared from Puente's roominghouse while she continued to cash their monthly social security checks. Police finally became suspicious of Puente on November 7, 1988, after a social worker filed a missing person's report on a 52-year-old mentally disabled man named Alvaro Montoya who had been referred to the boardinghouse in February. Four days later homicide detectives questioned Puente in her home while other officers investigated the yard. While digging in some freshly turned dirt at the southeast corner of the property a searcher turned up pieces of cloth, a leg bone, and a shoe filled with a skeletonized foot. Puente expressed surprise at the find and remarkably was given permission by police to visit a nearby relative while they continued the excavation of her yard. Not surprisingly, Puente bolted and was finally captured on November 16, 1988, in Los Angeles. During Puente's flight, authorities uncovered the bodies of seven of the landlady's missing tenants wrapped in plastic and covered in mothballs. The body of 80-year-old Betty Mae Palmer (last seen in January 1986) was found buried in a sitting position a few feet from the sidewalk in front of the house. The elderly woman's head, hands, and feet were missing. Another victim, 64-year-old Dorothy Miller, was found with her arm held in position across her chest with silver duct tape. Due to the advanced state of decomposition pathologists were initially unable to determine a cause of death for any of the seven recovered bodies.

Formally charged with nine murders, Puente denied killing anyone although she admitted to cashing the victims' social security checks. Following a lengthy change of venue hearing which moved the proceedings from Sacramento to Monterey, opening statements in Puente's trial began on February 9, 1993. Using a more sophisticated technology, toxicologists detected traces of the tranquilizer Dalmane in each of the seven bodies buried in the yard. The defense claimed that in all but one case (that of Ruth Munroe) the individuals had died of natural causes. Puente had failed to notify authorities of the deaths out of fear that she would be sent back to prison on a parole violation. Six months later after testimony from 156 witnesses, over 3,100 courtroom exhibits, and more than 22,000 transcript pages the case went to the jury on July 15, 1993. Following a record 24 days of deliberation, a jury convicted Puente on three counts of murder (two first degree, one second degree) while deadlocking on the six other counts on August 26, 1993. The jury deadlocked again during the penalty phase of the trial conducted to determine whether the 64-year-old landlady would be sentenced to death or life imprisonment. A mistrial declared on October 13, 1993, effectively meant that Puente would serve life imprisonment without the possibility of parole, a sentence formally imposed on December 10, 1993.

477. Blackburn, Daniel J. *Human Harvest: The Sacramento Murder Story.* 1st ed. New York: Knightsbridge, 1990. 306 pp.: ill.; 24 cm.

_____. [Same as 477.] 1st ed. New York: Knightsbridge, 1990. 286 pp., [16]pp. of plates: ill., ports.; 18 cm.; paperback.

Published prior to trial proceedings against Puente, Blackburn's account places the murders within the context of a failed social services program and America's neglect of the elderly and disabled. Extensive appendices include excerpts from Puente's California Department of Corrections probation report and a Sacramento detective's summary of his initial interview with the murderess.

478. Norton, Carla. *Disturbed Ground: The True Story of a Diabolical Female Serial Killer.* 1st ed. New York: W. Morrow and Co., 1994. 415 pp.: ill.; 25 cm.

A former writer for the *Los Angeles Times* and *The San Jose Mercury*, Norton's book is the best researched. Appendices include toxicology reports and prescriptions for Dalmane (flurazepam) available to Puente dating from October 29, 1985, through November 1, 1988. Excellent index.

479. Wood, William P. *The Bone Garden: The Sacramento Boardinghouse Murders.* New York: Pocket Books, 1994. 338 pp.: ill.; 17 cm.; paperback.

Paperback account by the former Sacramento deputy district attorney who coined the term "bone garden" to describe the yard in which seven of her alleged victims were found.

Putnam, Mark Steven

Born July 4, 1959, in Coventry, Connecticut. FBI agent. Pikeville, Kentucky; 1 murder; manual strangulation; June 7, 1989.

Television: "Betrayed by Love" (1994), a two-hour, made-for-television movie based on Aphrodite Jones' book

The FBI Killer, originally aired on ABC on January 17, 1994. Cast includes Steven Weber (Avery/Mark Steven Putnam), Patricia Arquette (Deanne/Susan Daniels Smith), and Mare Winningham (Dana).

"And in an act of extreme rage, I reached across the car and grabbed her by the throat with both hands."—Putnam, in his confession of June 4, 1990, describing the murder of Susan Daniels Smith

In a grim and tawdry tragedy played out against the backdrop of eastern Kentucky's coal country, FBI agent Mark Putnam murdered his pregnant informant-lover, Susan Daniels Smith, and destroyed a promising career in law enforcement which had been the dream of his life. The quintessential all–American boy, Putnam had everything going for him: a strong family background, good looks, personal discipline, and intelligence. In 1978 he entered the University of Tampa majoring in criminology and managed to maintain a 3.0 grade point average while captaining the school's soccer team to an undefeated season and NCAA Division II championship in 1982. Putnam married the daughter of a wealthy real estate developer in 1984, and fathered a daughter. On October 6, 1986, Putnam realized a lifelong dream by graduating from the FBI Academy and in February 1987, the special agent was assigned to a two-man field office in Pikeville, Kentucky, 120 miles southeast of Lexington.

Susan Daniels, the fifth of nine children born to a poor family in Freeburn in the heart of eastern Kentucky's coal belt, had no future. Dropping out of school in the 8th grade, the attractive and flirtatious 15 year old soon developed a sexual and business rela-tionship with future husband, Kenneth Darrell Smith, a 22-year-old gambler and drug seller. When her parents tossed her out of the house for selling drugs, she lived with various relatives before settling in with Smith. They married in February 1981 and Susan bore their first child the following year. The marriage deteriorated and, amid an atmosphere of drugs and domestic violence, the two divorced in March 1985. They continued to live together, however, and produced another child in order to draw welfare money from both Kentucky and West Virginia.

Putnam, determined to impress his superiors so as to merit a quick transfer to a better post, threw himself into the Pikeville assignment. His wife, now pregnant with their second child, hated the area which she characterized as a cultural "wasteland" and made no effort at assimilation. A rash of local bank robberies potentially afforded Putnam the opportunity he needed to distinguish himself. Authorities suspected a 32-year-old ex-convict who rented a room in the home of Kenneth and Susan Smith. The FBI already had the Smith house under surveillance when Putnam requested a local sheriff's deputy to set up a meeting with the couple to discuss their cooperation in the investigation. The attraction between Putnam and Susan Smith at their initial meeting was instant, mutual, and commented upon by her jealous "husband" Kenneth Smith. Susan accepted the FBI agent's offer of $5,000 to inform on their boarder. Later that day, she confided to a skeptical sister that she planned to make Putnam fall in love with her. Susan, well known in the community for fabricating stories about seducing important men, was seldom believed by anyone.

Weeks after the meeting, Putnam

(in direct violation of FBI regulations) began a torrid affair with his informant. Whatever Putnam's reasons for the liaison, lust or career advancement, Susan looked upon the FBI agent as a way out. They continued to see each other and Susan remained on the FBI payroll after her criminal tenant's conviction in January 1988. The affair lasted throughout 1988 with the two lovers meeting either in his car or in cheap motels. Although Smith bragged about the affair, most people in the town refused to believe that an FBI agent with a beautiful wife and two children would risk a career and marriage by having a relationship with an uneducated, cocaine-addicted divorcée. When Smith told Putnam's wife of the affair, she refused to believe her. Reasoning that Putnam would leave his wife for her if she got pregnant, Smith stopped using contraceptives around Christmas of 1988.

Professionally, Putnam's "star" was rising in the Bureau. On the strength of Smith's information, he had solved another bank robbery and broken up a car "chop shop." By early 1989, Putnam was already phasing Susan out as an informer and contriving to leave Pikeville by telling his superiors that there had been bomb threats made against his family. For their safety, he had already moved his wife and children out of the area. In late March he told Susan of his impending transfer to Miami and she confronted him with news of her pregnancy. Putnam denied the child was his, but vaguely promised to take care of her. Still believing in the fantasy that Putnam would ultimately leave his wife to marry her and help raise their child, Smith began making frequent calls to him in Miami in which she threatened to disclose her pregnancy to Bureau officials and his

wife. Putnam promised to discuss the matter when he returned to Pikeville on June 5, 1989, to testify in the chop shop case. According to Putnam, he met with Susan in Pikeville on June 7 and then left town. Nine days later, a sister filed a missing person's report on Susan Daniels Smith. She was declared officially missing on June 19, 1989.

Due almost entirely to the persistence of the missing woman's family, the case was not buried. Questioned in his ex-wife's disappearance, Kenneth Smith passed a polygraph test and was eliminated as a suspect. In February 1990, the Kentucky State Police (KSP) requested Special Agent Putnam take a polygraph test even though its results were inadmissible in Kentucky courts. Putnam was evasive. Under mounting public pressure, the FBI and the KSP began a joint investigation of Mark Putnam on May 1, 1990. During a six-and-a-half-hour interview conducted by the FBI in Sunrise, Florida, on May 16, 1990, Putnam denied any connection with Smith's disappearance. Reinterviewed two days later, Putnam agreed to take a polygraph test in Washington weeks later. Putnam failed the test. Admitting his infidelity and guilt to his wife, Putnam resigned from the FBI on May 22, 1990, and instructed his attorney to enter into plea bargain discussions with the Commonwealth of Kentucky.

Over a three week period, attorneys negotiated a deal in which Putnam agreed to confess to Smith's murder and lead authorities to her remains in exchange for a reduced charge of first degree manslaughter and a guaranteed 16-year prison sentence to be served in a federal facility. A state's attorney later admitted that had a charge of murder against Putnam been pursued without a body, he probably could not have been convicted. Putnam issued a sworn statement on June 4, 1990, in which he admitted to strangling the five months pregnant Smith on June 8, 1989, during a heated argument over her pregnancy. According to Putnam, Smith and he drove around the Pikeville area in his rented car before parking on a secluded mountain road to discuss their predicament. Smith began slapping Putnam in the face after he told her that, if the child was his, he and his wife would adopt and raise it after it was born. "In an act of extreme rage," Putnam strangled her and later "placed" her body down a ravine off a coal mine road nine miles outside of Pikeville. Searchers recovered Smith's skeletonized remains on the day of Putnam's confession. On June 12, 1990, Putnam received his prearranged 16-year sentence and achieved the dubious distinction of being the only agent in FBI history to have committed a criminal killing while still on the payroll. He will be eligible for parole in 1998.

480. Jones, Aphrodite. *The FBI Killer.* Pinnacle True Crime. New York: Pinnacle Books, 1992. 304 pp.: ill., ports.; 18 cm.; paperback.

481. Sharkey, Joe. *Above Suspicion.* New York: Simon & Schuster, 1993. 284 pp., [8]pp. of plates: ill.; 24 cm.

_____. [Same as 481.] St. Martin's Paperbacks ed. New York: St. Martin's Paperbacks, 1994. x, 310 pp., [8]pp. of plates: ill.; 18 cm.; paperback.

Ramirez, Richard Leyva
(a.k.a. "Night Stalker," "Valley Invader," "Walk-In Killer," "Jack the Knife," "Noah Jimenez," "Richard Moreno," "Richard Munoz," "Nicholas

Adame," "Richard Mena," "Ricardo," "Night Strangler")

Born February 28, 1960, in El Paso, Texas. Drifter, thief. Los Angeles area and San Francisco, California; 20 murders (13 convictions); pistol, bludgeon, knife; June 1984–August 1985.

Television: "Manhunt: Search for the Night Stalker" (1989), a two-hour, made-for-television movie, originally aired on NBC on November 12, 1989. Cast includes A. Martinez (Gil Carrillo), Lisa Eilbacher (Ann Clark), and Gregory Norman Cruz (Richard Ramirez). Note: "Manhunt: Search for the Night Stalker" was released on video by Academy Entertainment on September 19, 1991, in a 95-minute version retitled *Hunt for the Night Stalker.*

"Pieces of shit are killed every day."—Ramirez quoted in a November 1993 *Hustler* interview

Infamous southern California serial killer known as the "Night Stalker." For 15 months a man described by his surviving victims as six-foot-one, 155 pounds, with only "four or five teeth left" terrorized the Los Angeles area once ranging as far north as San Francisco to commit a murder and assault. Dubbed "the Night Stalker" by the press, the emaciated assailant killed at least 20 and raped 21 others. The killings were particularly gruesome even by L.A. standards, no mean feat for a city that had endured the carnage of Charles Manson, the "Hillside Strangler" (Kenneth Bianchi and Angelo Buono), and the "Sunset Strip Slayer" (Douglas Clark and Carol Bundy). Moreover, the killer struck without discrimination, raping women of all ages and nationalities, and molesting children. He used guns, knives, and bludgeons to dispatch his victims.

Seeming to prefer yellow and brown colored homes located close to freeway ramps, the "Night Stalker" often slipped into darkened homes through unlocked doors and windows after midnight, wounding or killing the victims as they slept. When he encountered a husband or a male companion, the killer immediately put them out of commission before attacking the woman. In one instance, he raped a woman beside the body of her dead husband, and in another, raped and sodomized a mother in front of her small son. The body of another victim was found with her eyes gouged out. After the initial stabbing death on June 27, 1984, of 79-year-old Jennie Vincow in her apartment in the Eagle Rock section of Los Angeles, the body count steadily rose between mid–March and early August of 1985. As fear gripped Greater Los Angeles and gun sales soared, police began to recognize the killer's distinctive signature; the slash wounds to the throat and body, his use of restraints (handcuffs, thumbcuffs), and the familiar language he used when demanding loot. Often, investigators found spray-painted satanic pentagrams on the inside walls of the victims' homes and one woman related that her attacker forced her to swear allegiance to Satan while she was being raped. Concurrent with the murders, mutilations, and rapes, were a series of sexual assaults directed against young children of both sexes. As the Night Strangler Task Force worked to tie the cases together, the object of their search, 25-year-old Richard Ramirez, was living in Skid Row hotels and parked cars in East Los Angeles.

Born into a large working class Catholic family in El Paso, Texas, on February 28, 1960, Ramirez was a loner from the start. Never joining the youth gangs in the barrio, the boy stayed in his room for hours listening to rock music on the radio, emerging at night to kill time in video game arcades. Avoiding his parents, Ramirez seldom took meals at home preferring instead to live off the junk food, chocolate, and Pepsi which rotted his teeth. By 17, Ramirez was breaking into homes and spent six months in a reform school. Released, the 17 year old dropped out of school after failing twice to pass the ninth grade and was soon arrested three times in El Paso for drug possession and reckless driving. After attending a "pre-trial intervention" counseling program stemming from a 1979 arrest for marijuana possession, Ramirez relocated to California where he supported his cocaine habit by burglary, car theft and pushing drugs. At 20, Ramirez became a confirmed satanist and later had a tattoo artist carve a devil's pentagram into the palm of his left hand. Fascinated by the 1979 album *Highway to Hell* by the Australian heavy metal band AC/DC, Ramirez adopted the cut "Night Prowler" as his own personal anthem. The group's name (mistakenly thought to be an acronym for "Anti-Christ/ Devil's Child") was found spray-painted on the walls at some of the murder sites. "Jack the Knife," a lyric from a song by heavy metal band Judas Priest, was found scrawled in lipstick on the wall of the San Francisco home of one of his last victims, 66-year-old Peter Pan. On August 17, 1985, Ramirez invaded Pan's home, shot and killed him in bed, then shot and beat his wife who survived the attack.

The case broke on August 30, 1985, when authorities publicly identified Ramirez as a "Night Stalker" suspect after they matched his partial fingerprint from a stolen car with prints left at the scene of a murder and rape in Mission Viejo five days before. Police issued an all points bulletin on Ramirez and his mug shot was featured on television and the front pages of newspapers. On August 31, 1985, the "Night Stalker" was chased down and badly beaten by angry citizens in East Los Angeles after he tried to steal a woman's car keys. After numerous defense-caused delays, Ramirez's trial opened in Los Angeles with jury selection on July 21, 1988. Ramirez, chained to the defense table, basked in the glow of attention often disrupting the proceedings by shouting "Hail Satan!" and flashing the pentagram on his palm at the gallery. Sixteen months and an estimated two million dollars later, Ramirez was found guilty on September 20, 1989, of 13 first degree murders and 30 related felonies. After deliberating 22 days during the penalty phase of the trial, the same jury recommended on October 4, 1989, that the "Night Stalker" be put to death under the "special circumstances" clause in California law. At his formal sentencing on November 7, 1989, Ramirez lashed out at the courtroom: "You maggots make me sick. You don't understand me. I am beyond Good and Evil. I will be avenged. Lucifer dwells in us all." As he left the scene, Ramirez flashed a two-finger "devil's horn" sign to his bevy of leather-clad female groupies and told reporters wanting his reaction to the death sentences, "Big deal. Death always went with the territory. I'll see you at Disneyland." Ramirez was subsequently transferred to the San Francisco county jail to await trial for the murder of Peter Pan and the attempted murder of his 67-year-old wife. The hundreds of women visiting the convicted serial killer during his three and one-half years of incarceration there so interrupted the jail's routine that a court ruled in September 1993 that he be sent to San Quentin Prison to await trial. While being processed into the maximum security prison on September 21, 1993, Ramirez set off a metal detector. X rays of the killer's rectum revealed the presence of a metal canister containing a key, a syringe, and a needle. In June 1995 the San Francisco prosecution was put on hold until after the State Supreme Court decides the appeal of the L.A. case sometime after the year 2000.

482. Linedecker, Clifford L. *Night Stalker: A Shocking Story of Satanism, Sex and Serial Murders.* St. Martin's Paperbacks ed. New York: St. Martin's Paperbacks, 1991. 302 pp., [8]pp. of plates: ill.; 18 cm.; paperback.

Paperback original by a veteran true crime writer.

Rattenbury, Alma Victoria (*acquitted;* a.k.a. "Alma Victoria Clarke" [maiden name], "Alma Victoria Dolling" [name taken from first marriage], "Alma Victoria Pakenham" [name taken from second marriage], "Lozanne")

Born circa 1895 or 1896 in Kamloops, British Columbia. Died April 3, 1935. Popular song lyricist. Bournemouth, England; 1 murder (acquitted); bludgeon (carpenter's mallet); March 24, 1935.

Theatre: Cause Célèbre: A Play in Two Acts (1977) by Terence Rattigan was first presented by John Gale at Her Majesty's Theatre, London, on Monday July 4, 1977. Directed by Robin Midgley, the cast includes Glynis Johns (Alma Rattenbury), Anthony Pedley (Francis Rattenbury), and Neil Daglish (George Wood/George Percy Stoner).

Television: "Cause Célèbre" (1988), a two-hour adaptation of Rattigan's play by Ken Taylor for Anglia Television, opened the 1988 season of the PBS series "Mystery" and aired on October 13 and 20, 1988. Cast includes Helen Mirren (Alma Rattenbury), Harry Andrews (Francis Rattenbury), and David Morrissey (George Bowman/George Percy Stoner).

"That is right—I did it deliberately, and I would do it again."—Rattenbury to police when charged

Tragic case in which an older woman/younger man affair resulted in the murder of the woman's aged husband. Alma Victoria Rattenbury, a Canadian-born lyricist of popular songs, married noted architect Francis Mawson Rattenbury in 1928. Married twice previously with a son from one of the unions, Mrs. Rattenbury bore her aged husband a son in 1929. The family moved from Canada to Bournemouth, England, and resided in a comfortable house on Manor Park Road called "Villa Madeira" where the 67-year-old architect lived in semi-retirement with his 38-year-old wife. Though a genuine affection seems to have existed between husband and wife, the pair had not shared physical intimacy since their child's birth. Alma Rattenbury, her son, and a devoted companion (Irene Riggs) lived upstairs in the house while Rattenbury spent his evenings drinking himself to unconsciousness in his ground floor room. On September 25, 1934, Alma Rattenbury placed the following ad in *The Bournemouth Daily Echo*: "Daily willing lad, 14–18, for housework. Scout-trained preferred." George Percy Stoner, a 17-year-old semi-illiterate, answered the ad and was hired as a chauffeur-handyman. Though twice his age, Alma Rattenbury took Stoner as her lover and

by November the teenager was living at Villa Madeira. On March 19, 1935, Alma informed her husband that she was going to London for an operation. Instead, she checked into the Kensington Palace Hotel with Stoner where they spent four days making love, eating in fine restaurants, and buying expensive clothes for the youth.

The affair reached its crisis shortly after Alma returned home. When she informed her lover that she planned to accompany her husband on a visit to a friend's home in Bridport on March 25, Stoner flew into a jealous rage. Angrily brandishing an air pistol in her face, Stoner accused her of having sex with Rattenbury and threatened to kill her. Alma reassured Stoner that she would not share a room with her husband and the youth sulked off to his grandparents' house where he borrowed a carpenter's mallet. Later that evening, March 24, 1935, Francis "Ratz" Rattenbury was bludgeoned three times from behind as he slept in his armchair in the downstairs drawing room. He died without regaining consciousness in a nearby nursing home on March 28, 1935. When authorities were summoned they found Alma Rattenbury in a highly excited and drunken state listening to loud music on the grammophone. As she continued to drink, she tried to kiss several police officers, and loudly admitted that she killed her husband. Sedated with a half a grain of morphia, Alma was put to bed and interviewed early the next morning. After again insisting that she killed Rattenbury, she was arrested. Stoner was arrested at Bournemouth station on March 28, 1935, after Alma's companion, Irene Riggs, informed police that the teenager had told her that he committed the murder.

The intensely sexual relationship between the older woman and younger man shocked the prevailing moral code, and public opinion ran high against the defendants as their joint trial opened at the Old Bailey on May 27, 1935. Unlike the usual scenario in dual defendant cases, neither Stoner or Rattenbury turned on one another. Alma did not recant her confession, though she insisted that due to the combination of alcohol and morphia she could not remember anything that happened after finding her husband's body. Three doctors testified that her memory loss was real and therefore her subsequent confessions were unreliable. Stoner took full responsibility for the murder although he maintained that he was under the influence of cocaine at the time. This "mitigating" factor was dismissed, however, when Stoner incorrectly described the drug as "brown with black specks in it." On May 31, 1935, a jury was out only 47 minutes before returning a verdict that freed Rattenbury and found Stoner guilty but with a recommendation to mercy. Rattenbury, damned in the press as a faithless wife and seductress of youth, committed suicide three days after her acquittal on April 3, 1935, by plunging a knife six times into her chest on the bank of a stream in Christchurch near Bournemouth. A suicide note written on the backs of envelopes and scraps of paper complained about the press' scathing attack on her character. Stoner's appeal was dismissed on June 24, 1935, but in a possible reaction to a petition calling for mercy signed by 350,000 people, he was reprieved the next day and his death sentence commuted to penal servitude. Stoner was released in 1942 after serving seven years. In September 1990 George

Stoner, age 73, admitted to sexually attacking a 12-year-old boy in a lavatory near his home in Bournemouth and was placed on probation for two years. Stoner was arrested after authorities found him nude in lavatories except for a hat, socks, and shoes.

483. Havers, Michael; Shankland, Peter; Barrett, Anthony. *Tragedy in Three Voices: The Rattenbury Murder.* London: Kimber, 1980. 249 pp., [6] leaves of plates: ill.; 24 cm.

_____. [Same as 483, but paperback ed. retitled: *The Rattenbury Case.*] Penguin True Crime. London: Penguin Books, 1989. 249 pp., [12]pp. of plates: ill., music, ports.; 20 cm.; paperback.

A well researched account which profits from the cooperation of Alma Rattenbury's two sons who provided the authors with their mother's correspondence. An excellent selection of photographs includes the page from the June 9, 1935, issue of the *Sunday Graphic and Sunday News* which reproduces the words and music of a song written by Rattenbury while in prison. Includes source notes and an index.

484. Jesse, F. Tennyson, ed. *Trial of Alma Victoria Rattenbury and George Percy Stoner.* Notable British Trials. London; Edinburgh: W. Hodge, 1935. 298 pp., [6] leaves of plates: ill., ports.; 22 cm.

_____. [Same as 484.] Notable British Trials. Toronto: Canada Law Book, 1935. 298 pp., [6] leaves of plates: ill., ports.; 22 cm.

_____. [Same as 484.] [New ed.] Notable British Trials. London; Edinburgh: W. Hodge, 1950. 298 pp., [6] leaves of plates: ill., ports.; 22 cm.

Transcript of the trial in the Central Criminal Court, London, May 1935, for the murder of Mrs. Rattenbury's husband, Francis Mawson Rattenbury. Appendixes include Stoner's appeal, the inquest on Alma Victoria Rattenbury, and a statement made by Mrs. Rattenbury to police on March 27 and 28, 1935.

485. Napley, David. *Murder at the Villa Madeira: The Rattenbury Case*. Great Murder Trials of the Twentieth Century. London: Weidenfeld and Nicolson, 1988. x, 226 pp., [8]pp. of plates: ill., 1 plan, ports.; 23 cm. (Also a 1990 paperback ed.)

Napley's excellent account analyzes the trial and concludes that it "did not meet those high standards which have come to be expected of British justice." He suggests that Rattenbury, not Stoner, delivered the fatal blows.

486. Rattigan, Terence. *Cause Célèbre: A Play in Two Acts*. London: H. Hamilton, 1978. 81 pp.; 23 cm.

_____. [Same as 486 with variant subtitle: *A Play*.] Acting ed. London; New York: S. French, 1978. 70 pp.: ill.; 22 cm.

Theatrical dramatization of the Rattenbury-Stoner case.

487. Reksten, Terry. *Rattenbury*. Victoria, B.C.: Sono Nis Press, 1978. xiv, 204 pp., [12] leaves of plates: ill., ports.; 24 cm.

Reksten's biography of Francis Mawson Rattenbury, the noted architect of British Columbia's parliament buildings and Victoria's Empress Hotel, devotes five chapters to his murder.

Rogers, Dayton Leroy
(a.k.a. "Molalla Forest Killer," "Steve Davis")

Born September 30, 1953, in Moscow, Idaho. Small engine mechanic. Portland, Oregon; 8 murders; knife, ligature strangulation (possible); January–August 1987.

"They didn't follow the rules."— Rogers commenting on the all-woman jury's recommendation that he be executed for the murders of six women

A serial killer who littered the forests around Portland, Oregon, with the bodies of dead prostitutes and topless dancers. Hookers working Portland, Oregon's infamous Union Avenue, referred to locally as "Prostitute Row," were familiar with the "john" known as "Steve, the gambler." Steve cruised the area nightly in search of prostitutes willing to indulge his eccentric tastes for bondage, foot fetishism, and masturbation. If his bites sometimes left a hooker's breasts and feet bleeding, he was after all paying them between $50 to $100 a "date." By the summer of 1987, though, Steve had developed a reputation among many of the Union Avenue prostitutes as "rough trade" and many refused his company at any price. Still, none made the connection between Steve and the disappearances of several of their co-workers between July 8 through August 2, 1987, until 33-year-old Dayton Leroy Rogers was arrested on August 7, 1987 for the torture/murder of a hooker. Rogers' arrest and the subsequent revelation that he was also the "Molalla Forest Murderer" of seven prostitutes brought unprecedented cooperation between authorities and the community of prostitutes from which he selected his victims. Due in large part to their testimony, Rogers would emerge in sharp relief as a sexual sadist whose fantasy life, like that of fellow Oregonian and serial murderer Jerome Henry Brudos, was fuelled by an all-consuming foot fetish that drove him to commit ritualistic acts of assault, torture, mutilation, and murder.

Raised by strict Seventh Day Adventist parents, Rogers grew up in a stultifying atmosphere of punishment and censorship. Characterized by a psychiatrist after his conviction as suffering from "frontal lobe syndrome," Rogers evidently sustained organic brain damage as a result of childhood beatings by his father. Preaching that women who engaged in premarital sex should be stoned, Rogers' father once drew skirts on a photograph of hula girls featured on a record album cover. In his early teens, Rogers began peeping at his sisters and using their shoes as masturbatory props. At 16, he moved to Eugene, Oregon, to paint houses and, over his parents' objections, married a 16-year-old girl. Less than 30 days later on August 25, 1972, Rogers stabbed a 15-year-old girl in the stomach with a hunting knife telling her, "I just couldn't trust you." Days before they had driven to the same secluded area on the outskirts of Eugene and had sex. Rogers plea-bargained the charge down to second degree assault, pleaded not guilty, and on February 13, 1973, was given four years' probation. Six months later, a drunken Rogers was arrested for attacking two girls with a beer bottle. A court-ordered psychiatric evaluation concluded that he was a "sexually dangerous ... sociopathic personality." Rogers was found not guilty by reason of insanity on assault charges and admitted to the Oregon State Hospital in Salem on March 6, 1974. While there, his wife divorced him. Placed in a sex offenders program, Rogers became a model prisoner, helping to organize Seventh Day Adventist services and learning small engine repair. Inwardly, his sexual fantasies teemed with scenes of violence inflicted against women in bondage. Pronounced "cured" by prison authorities, Rogers was released on December 12, 1974.

On October 25, 1975, Rogers' remarriage to a devout Christian proved no bar to his abducting and raping at least four women from December 1975 through February 1976. In each instance, he would drive the woman to a secluded area, pull a knife, threaten to mutilate or kill her, bind her hands with electrical wire, and then either rape her or masturbate while fixating on her feet. Though charged in the various rape cases, Rogers was always acquitted, but given five years on June 25, 1976, for violating the conditions of his 1973 parole. He picked up another five years for coercion in a case involving the abduction and rape of two young girls. Though theoretically facing ten years' imprisonment, Rogers was released over some official objection in January 1982. A year later his parole supervision was terminated.

On the night of August 7, 1987, Rogers left the small engine repair shop he owned in Canby, a Portland suburb, and cruised Union Avenue in his blue 1985 Nissan pickup. Long an alcoholic, Rogers had been drinking screwdrivers all evening made by pouring miniature bottles of Smirnoff vodka into a disposable orange juice bottle. Early on the morning of August 8, he picked up 25-year-old prostitute Jennifer Lisa Smith who recognized him as a regular customer. Rogers drove to the nearby suburb of Oak Grove and parked in a lot next to an all-night restaurant. Smith stripped and, using the laces from her tennis shoes, Rogers tied her feet and hands. Minutes later around 3:00 a.m., he began stabbing the helpless woman in the back, breasts, throat, and vagina with a Regency-Sheffield steak knife. Smith fell from the car, but Rogers continued his attack in the lot until her agonized screams drew people from the restaurant. Rogers fled on foot and recovered his truck minutes later. In the high speed chase that followed, the bystander pursuing Rogers wrote down the Nissan's license plate. Rogers was arrested later that day at his business where he insisted he had been working all night. Smith bled to death from 11 stab wounds soon after the attack.

Authorities began to suspect Rogers of more murders when blood found in the trunk of his pickup failed to match either his or Smith's. More tellingly, charred remains of five belt buckles, a number of bra hooks, and metal eyelets from at least five shoes, including the victim's, were found in a wood stove in his home. On August 31, 1987, a deer hunter in the Molalla Forest, about 30 miles southeast of Portland, discovered the nude and badly decomposed corpse of a young woman whose left foot had been severed above the ankle. In the following days, the site would yield the bodies of six more young women that investigators estimated had been dumped there between January and August 1987. While decomposition ruled out determining exact causes of death, all had received multiple stab wounds to their backs. In addition to other mutilations, the feet of three of the victims had been sawed off and placed near their bodies. Approximately 38 miniature Smirnoff bottles, knotted shoelaces, 34 plastic orange juice bottles, and a Regency-Sheffield steak knife were recovered at the scene. Officials identified six of the seven bodies as Union Avenue prostitutes Lisa Marie Mock, 23, Maureen Ann Hodges, 26, Reatha Marie Gyles, 16, Nondace Kae Cervantes, 26, Christine Lotus Adams, 35, and Cynthia Diane DeVore, 21. A seventh body, belonging to a woman in her late twenties of "either Indian or Asian descent," has to this date remained unidentified.

Though not immediately charged in the murders, Rogers was pinpointed by the Molalla Forest Task Force as the "focal suspect" in their investigation. Initial similarities between these murders and those attributed to the Washington state Green River Killer were quickly discounted. Rogers had been incarcerated during the time many of these earlier, out-of-state murders had been committed and autopsy reports on the Molalla Forest victims proved markedly dissimilar to those victims of the Green River Killer. The Task Force interviewed 50 Portland prostitutes, 26 of whom provided specific information on Rogers that could tie him to the Molalla Forest victims. One hooker related a July 7, 1987, incident in which Rogers had driven her to a wooded area only four miles from the Molalla Forest dumping ground. His behavior so frightened the woman that she suffered a concussion from diving from his speeding car onto a logging road. Others confirmed Rogers' practice of making screwdrivers by mixing airline bottles of vodka into plastic containers of orange juice.

On February 4, 1988, Rogers' trial for the aggravated murder of Jennifer Smith began in Oregon City. Rogers pleaded not guilty and further stunned the courtroom by contending that he had accidentally stabbed the Portland prostitute to death in a struggle after she tried to rob him following their sexual bondage encounter. Admitting to the jury that "you won't like my client," Rogers' attorney argued that the killing was done in self-defense. In compelling testimony, numerous prostitutes detailed their almost identical encounters with the sadistic Rogers. The defense dismissed them as a "silent conspiracy" designed to convict an innocent man. In four hours on the stand, Rogers stuck to his story that the 11 wounds found on Smith's naked body were not the result of sexual torture, but inflicted during a struggle to thwart her robbery attempt. The jury received the case on February 19, 1988, and deliberated 13 hours before finding him guilty the next day. Mistakenly believing that a life sentence meant Rogers could never be paroled, the jury recommended imprisonment over execution. Rogers was sentenced to life on March 1, 1988. Some jurors reported feeling "raped" when they learned that the man they had just convicted would be eligible for parole in 20 years.

On May 4, 1988, Rogers was indicted for six of the Molalla Forest murders. He was not charged in the death of the unidentified woman. Jury selection began on February 6, 1989, and lasted almost two months before, ironically, 12 women were impanelled. Despite facing a staggering amount of physical evidence recovered from the body site linking him to the killings, Rogers pleaded not guilty to six counts of aggravated murder at the trial's opening in Oregon City on March 30, 1989. Hairs recovered from his pickup were microscopically similar to those of three of the victims. The steak knife found near one of the bodies was identical to one Rogers admitted using to kill Jennifer Smith. The empty airline bottles of vodka and orange juice containers found among the dead constituted what the prosecution called Rogers' signature, his "mark of Zorro." Eleven prostitutes recounted vivid tales of Rogers' bizarre sexual appetites and told of his threats to mutilate them with a knife. Rogers was found guilty on all counts after a jury deliberated only six hours on May 4, 1989. Following more than 19 hours of deliberation, the same jury unanimously voted on June 7, 1989, that Rogers receive the death penalty. An appeal for a new trial was rejected in June 1989 and Rogers' conviction for the Molalla Forest murders was upheld on October 24, 1990. In 1992, the court determined that

Rogers was entitled to a new penalty-phase proceeding that could convert his death sentence to life imprisonment.

488. King, Gary. *Blood Lust: Portrait of a Serial Sex Killer.* New York: Onyx, 1992. 352 pp., [8]pp. of plates: ill.; 18 cm.; paperback.

A paperback original based on police files, psychological reports, trial transcripts, and personal interviews. King, to his credit, does not utilize fictional or composite characters. "Business-man. Family man. Savage murderer."—Cover.

Rossney, Damian *see* Gates, Wyley

Rouse, Alfred Arthur (a.k.a. "Blazing Car Murderer")

Born April 6, 1894, in Herne Hill, London, England. Executed March 10, 1931. Traveling salesman. Hardingstone, England; 1 murder; strangulation, fire; November 6, 1930.

"Very well; I am glad it is over. I was going to Scotland Yard about it. I am responsible. I am very glad it is over; I have had no sleep."—Rouse's statement to authorities when apprehended at the Hammersmith bus terminus on November 7, 1930

Commercial traveler executed for the murder of an unknown hitchhiker in the case popularly known as the "Blazing Car Mystery." The son of an actress and formerly a sacristan at St. Saviour's Church in Stoke Newington, Rouse's criminal career seems to have stemmed from a severe head injury sustained in World War I. On May 25, 1915, Rouse was struck in the head by shrapnel from a shellburst while fighting in Givenchy, France. The resulting operation on the left temporal lobe of his brain rendered Rouse unfit for military service and he was discharged in 1916 to the care of his wife. The change in Rouse's post-injury behavior was dramatic. Taking a job as a commercial traveler for a brace and garter firm, Rouse used his good looks and easy charm to seduce nearly 80 women drawn from the ranks of shopgirls and chambermaids. By November 1930, Rouse had bigamously married and fathered at least three children by two separate women for which he was paying child support. To add to his emotional and financial worries, Rouse's current mistress (Ivy Muriel Jenkins) was imminently expecting their child at her home in the Welsh town of Gelligaer.

At 2:00 a.m. on November 6, 1930, two cousins were walking down a country road to their homes in Hardingstone after attending a Bonfire Night dance at Northampton when they spotted a fire near a hedgerow some 50 yards away. A man they later identified as Rouse climbed out of a ditch on the opposite side of the lane and said, "It looks as if someone has had a bonfire," as he passed them in the opposite direction. Upon investigating the source of the blaze, the cousins found a Morris Minor car engulfed in flames leaping to the height of 15 feet. The local constabulary was alerted, put out the fire, and discovered a charred body burned beyond recognition splayed face down across the front seat of the gutted car. Only the license plate survived and police used it to trace the car's ownership to Rouse. Remarkably, in view of the official theory that Rouse substituted a murdered stranger for himself in the blaze in order to start a new debt-free life somewhere else, he

first hitchhiked to his home in London (where his wife heard, but did not see him) then traveled to Gelligaer to be with his pregnant mistress. There he saw a newspaper account of the blaze complete with a photo of the burned car and the cousins' description of the man they saw near the scene of the fire. Attempting to return to London by bus, Rouse was apprehended on November 7, 1930, in the Hammersmith bus terminal. While in custody at Angel Lane police station in Northampton, Rouse was overheard by a police inspector making indiscreet remarks about the numerous liaisons he engaged in with his "harem" and his plans to sell his house and divorce his wife. The statements were never introduced in court.

Rouse's trial for the murder of the unknown man opened on January 26, 1931, at the Northampton Winter Assizes. The defendant maintained that he had picked up a male hitchhiker and after driving some distance stopped on an isolated country road to relieve himself. Before he left, Rouse asked the man to fill the car up with the gas from the can in the backseat. According to Rouse, the man had mentioned something about smoking prior to filling up the car. While relieving himself in a field Rouse looked up to see the car engulfed in flames with the man inside. Unable to save him, he panicked and ran away. The prosecution countered Rouse's claim with expert testimony that suggested that the car's carburetor had been tampered with so that it would leak gas. Noted pathologist Sir Bernard Spilsbury testified that the facedown position of the body on the seat pointed to the fact that the victim was conscious before the fire started. Also, a surviving piece of cloth from the crotch of the victim's trousers was found to have been soaked with gasoline. On January 31, 1931, Rouse was found guilty and sentenced to death. Following Rouse's failed appeal, his confession was printed in the *Daily Sketch* on March 11, 1931—one day after he was hanged at Bedford Gaol. In it, he admitted attempting to fake his own death in order to start a new life by strangling the hitchhiker, dousing him with gas, tampering with the carburetor, then setting the car ablaze.

489. Cannell, J.C. *New Light on the Rouse Case.* London: J. Long, 1931. 215 pp., [6] leaves of plates: ill., ports.: 22 cm.

Cannell, a journalist on the staff of the *Daily Sketch*, offers new insights into the case he calls "the most remarkable of our century."

490. Normanton, Helena, ed. *Trial of Alfred Arthur Rouse.* Notable British Trials. Edinburgh: W. Hodge, 1931. xlviii, 316 pp.: ill.; 22 cm.

_____. [Same as 490.] [2nd ed.] Notable British Trials. Edinburgh; London: W. Hodge, 1952. xlviii, 316 pp.: ill.; 22 cm.

Trial at the Northampton Winter Assizes, January 26–31, 1931, for the murder of an unidentified man.

491. Tremayne, Sidney, ed. *The Trial of Alfred Arthur Rouse: The Blazing Car Murder.* Famous Trials Series. London: G. Bles, 1931. 358 pp., [9] leaves of plates: ill., ports.; 22 cm.

Day-by-day transcript of Rouse's trial introduced by Tremayne's short essay recapping the chronology of the case. Rouse's testimony, containing "interesting revelations of personality," is printed verbatim.

Rowland, Walter Graham

Born March 26, 1908, in New Mills, Derbyshire, England. Executed February 27, 1947. Laborer. Manches-ter, England; 2 murders; bludgeon (hammer), strangulation; October 20, 1946.

"I am an innocent man. This is the greatest injustice which has ever happened in an English court. Why did you have the man who confessed here and not hear him? I am not allowed justice because of my past."—Rowland's reaction to the dismissal of his appeal

Convicted killer executed for the murder of a prostitute despite the fact that another man confessed to committing the crime. On the morning of October 20, 1946, the body of 40-year-old Olive Balchin was found at the site of a bombed out building in Manchester. A 10 shilling prostitute known in the area for servicing clients among the rubble of bombed out sites, Balchin had been beaten to death with a leather dresser's hammer found near her body. Routine inquiries conducted in hotels in the vicinity of the murder scene led police to 38-year-old Walter Graham Rowland, a laborer with a long history of criminal activity. In 1934 Rowland was convicted of the strangulation murder of his two-year-old daughter, sentenced to death, but reprieved after a jury recommended mercy. He was released from prison in 1942. When questioned at his boarding house on October 26, 1946, Rowland allegedly told a detective, "You don't want me for murdering that fucking woman, do you?" Rowland later denied making the statement and professed his innocence. He was formally charged with Balchin's murder the next day.

Three witnesses (including the shopkeeper who sold him the hammer the day before the murder) picked Rowland out of an identity parade as the man last seen with Balchin. Rowland acknowledged knowing Balchin and admitted that if his suspicions were confirmed that the prostitute had given him a venereal disease he would have strangled her. Despite the lack of blood and fingerprints on the murder weapon, the case against Rowland was further bolstered by technical evidence. Material found in the cuffs of his trousers proved to be similar to that found on the bombed site. Bloodstains found on Rowland's shoe were of human origin but not of sufficient quantity to determine its group. Rowland was tried at the Manchester Autumn Assizes and found guilty on December 16, 1946, after a jury deliberated 1 hour and 50 minutes. In an eloquent pre-sentencing statement to Mr. Justice Sellers, Rowland reiterated his total innocence and insisted that the "worse crime" was that "someone with the knowledge of the crime is seeing me sentenced ... for a crime I did not commit." Rowland was sentenced to death.

Weeks before Rowland's appeal, a prisoner at Liverpool confessed to the murder of Olive Balchin. Thirty-eight-year-old David John Ware, a petty criminal suffering from lifelong bouts of manic depression, made three statements to police in which he described in varying detail the killing of the prostitute. Rowland based his appeal on Ware's confession, but the court of criminal appeal refused to consider the statement and his appeal was dismissed on February 17, 1947. A Home Office inquiry supported the court's decision and Ware subsequently recanted his confession. Rowland, still maintaining his innocence, was hanged at Strangeways Prison on February 27, 1947. Ironically, Ware was arrested in July 1951 for the attempted murder of a woman with a hammer he had purchased the same day. Found guilty of

attempted murder in November 1951, Ware was judged to be insane and sent to Broadmoor where he hanged himself on April 1, 1954.

492. Cecil, Henry, ed. *Trial of Walter Graham Rowland.* Celebrated Trials Series. General editor: Jonathan Goodman. Newton Abbot; North Pomfret, Vt.: David & Charles, 1975. 164 pp.: ill., ports.; 23 cm.

Cecil (a pseudonym) weighs the evidence, examines the controversial legal issues surrounding the case, and concludes Rowland, not Ware, was plainly guilty. Excerpts from the four-day trial are offered with Cecil's extensive commentary. Appendixes include a chronology and the report by Mr. John Catterall Jolly, KC to the Home Office concerning the inquiry into the confession of David John Ware.

Ruppert, James Urban
(a.k.a. "The Professor")

Born April 12, 1934, in Fairfield, Ohio. Unemployed draftsman. Hamilton, Ohio; 11 murders; guns; March 30, 1975.

"My name is James Ruppert. I am a suspect in a homicide."—Ruppert in a telephone call to police after murdering 11 family members

Mentally disturbed individual whose record for committing the largest mass murder of family members (11) was surpassed in 1987 by Ronald Eugene Simmons (14). On March 30, 1975, Easter Sunday, 41-year-old bachelor James Ruppert entered his mother's home in Hamilton, Ohio, armed with three pistols and a .22 caliber semiautomatic rifle. Within minutes the unemployed draftsman systematically opened fire murdering the 65-year-old widow, his brother, his sister-in-law, and their eight children ranging in age from 4 to 17. After showering, Ruppert called police to report the shooting. An autopsy revealed that 41 of the 44 bullets fired by Ruppert were sufficient to cause death. Found sane and competent to stand trial, Ruppert pleaded not guilty by reason of insanity to 11 counts of aggravated murder at his trial in Hamilton, Ohio, in June 1975. Under advice of counsel, Ruppert waived his right to a jury trial in favor of being tried by a panel of three judges. Psychiatric experts for the defense maintained that Ruppert had a ten-year history of mental illness aggravated by an overwhelming hatred for his mother and feelings of inferiority in relation to his brother. At the time of the shootings, Ruppert was a paranoid schizophrenic with a psychosis so pronounced that he blamed his brother for everything, including his car trouble. The massacre was evidently touched off when the man asked, "How's the Volkswagen running?" The prosecution countered that the killings were not committed in a fit of uncontrollable rage, but were planned so that Ruppert could inherit almost $300,000 from the combined estates of his mother and brother. On July 3, 1975, the three-judge panel found Ruppert guilty by a 2–1 split decision (one judge finding him innocent by reason of insanity) and he was sentenced to 11 consecutive life sentences. In August 1977 the 1st District Ohio Appeals Court overturned the conviction on the ground that the lead judge erred in telling Ruppert that the three-judge panel's ruling had to be unanimous in order to convict.

Jury selection in Ruppert's retrial commenced in Findlay, Ohio, on July 14, 1982. Ruppert again pleaded not guilty by reason of insanity and much of the six-week trial (postponed once due to

the death of a juror) was devoted to psychiatric testimony. Defense psychiatrists reiterated their findings that Ruppert was a paranoid schizophrenic who believed that his mother and brother were part of an FBI conspiracy to prove that he was a Communist and a homosexual. On July 23, 1982, Ruppert was convicted of murdering his mother and brother, but acquitted by reason of insanity of the other nine murders. He was immediately sentenced to two consecutive life terms. The conviction was upheld by the appeals court in March 1984. Two years later a court decision blocked the mass murderer from receiving any money from the estates of his victims.

493. Stozich, Nancy K. *When the Hating Stops.* Findlay, Ohio: N. Stozich, 1984. 117 pp.: ill.; 23 cm.; trade paperback.

Stozich, a high school English teacher in Findlay, Ohio, and wife of a state representative, attended Ruppert's second trial. This self-published volume records her impressions of the event and offers shorthand notes of the proceeding. Ruppert's fascinating case deserves a much better treatment than this thinly veiled Christian tract.

Ruxton, Buck
(a.k.a. "Bukhtyar Rustomji Ratanji Hakim," "Buck Hakim")

Born circa 1899 in Bombay, India. Executed May 12, 1936. Medical doctor. Lancaster, England; 2 murders; possible bludgeoning or manual strangulation; September 14–15, 1935.

"I killed Mrs. Ruxton in a fit of temper because I thought she had been with a man. I was mad at the time. Mary Rogerson was present at the time. I had to kill her." —Ruxton's confession published shortly after his execution

Historically important case in which a painstaking forensic investigation led to the conviction of a wife murderer. On September 29, 1935, four bundles of rotting human remains were found in a gully near a bridge over the Annan River in the Scottish town of Moffat. The bundles contained two heads, feet, partial torsos and pelvises, portions of 17 limbs, and 43 pieces of soft tissue including two sections of female external sex organs. A shredded piece of newspaper, the *Sunday Graphic* of September 15, 1935, was found wrapped around a body part and provided authorities with their first solid lead. This special edition was sold only in and around Morecambe and Lancaster where police subsequently concentrated their inquiries for persons reported missing. Two weeks earlier, the mother of 20-year-old Mary Jane Rogerson had reported her daughter missing from the Lancaster home of Doctor Buck Ruxton, a 37-year-old Parsee doctor and his common-law "wife" Isabella, 36. Rogerson, a nursemaid to the couple's three children, was last seen on September 14, 1935, the same day that Dr. Ruxton later insisted that his wife had embarked on a trip to visit her sisters in Blackpool. When she failed to arrive, Ruxton suggested she had perhaps run off with a man.

As forensic scientists worked to identify the two female bodies from their partial remains, authorities focused their investigation on Ruxton. A week before Mrs. Ruxton's disappearance, police responded to a domestic disturbance call at the couple's home at 2 Daulton Square. Dr. Ruxton, insanely jealous over Isabella's suspected marital infidelity, had threatened his wife with a gun and knife. When subse-

quently questioned concerning his wife's disappearance, police noticed a bandage on Ruxton's right hand which he explained covered a deep cut sustained while opening a can of pears with a tin opener. More ominously, Ruxton had recently had bloodstained carpets removed from the house, tore wallpaper down to redecorate, and initially gave one of his suits stained with blood to a housekeeper then later ordered her to burn it. Days after the pair's disappearance, the same housekeeper noted a foul smell emanating from the Ruxton's locked bedroom which the doctor then attempted to mask by spraying eau de cologne.

Ruxton was arrested on October 13, 1935, and charged with the murder of Rogerson. Charged on November 5, 1935, with the murder of Isabella Ruxton, the doctor was tried only for his wife's murder at his trial in Manchester Assizes beginning on March 2, 1936. Despite the physical evidence against Ruxton, a conviction could not be obtained unless forensic scientists from the universities of Glasgow and Edinburgh could confirm that one of the bodies was Isabella Ruxton. Complex medical testimony including a reconstruction of Isabella's face by an X ray overlay inexorably led to the establishment of the victim's identity. Expert testimony further established that distinguishing body parts which would have easily led to an identification (Mrs. Ruxton's pronounced teeth, eyes, a scar on her thumb) had been removed by the murderer. Dr. Ruxton's tearful testimony failed to sway a jury convinced by the overwhelming forensic evidence which supported the prosecution's contention that he had killed his wife in a jealous fit and also Rogerson when she tried to intercede. Ruxton was found guilty on March 13, 1936, and sentenced to death. Following a dismissed appeal, the doctor was hanged at Manchester's Strangeways Prison on May 12, 1936.

494. Blundell, R.H., and Wilson, G. Haswell, (eds.) *Trial of Buck Ruxton.* Notable British Trials. London: W. Hodge, 1937. lxxxvii, 457 pp.: ill.; 22 cm.

_____. [Same as 494.] Notable British Trials. Toronto: Canada Law Book, 1937. lxxxvii, 457 pp.: ill.; 22 cm.

_____. [Same as 494.] 2nd ed. Notable British Trials. London: W. Hodge, 1950. lxxxvii, 457 pp., [15] leaves of plates: ill., ports., facsim.; 22 cm.

An excellent case summary introduces relevant transcripts from the trial. Appendices include medical and forensic reports.

495. Glaister, John, and Brash, James Couper. *Medico-Legal Aspects of the Ruxton Case.* Edinburgh: Livingstone, 1937. xvi, 284 pp.: ill.; 26 cm.

_____. [Same as 495.] Baltimore: William Wood, 1937. xvi, 284 pp.: ill.; 26 cm.

Glaister, the regius professor of forensic medicine at the University of Glasgow, and Brash, professor of anatomy at the University of Edinburgh, were responsible for compiling the forensic evidence which convicted Ruxton. Their highly technical volume examines the dismembered remains of the bodies and demonstrates how Mrs. Ruxton's identity was established through a forensic reconstruction of her face starting from a skull in an advanced state of decomposition. Includes a detailed index and 172 illustrations.

496. Potter, T.F. *The Deadly Dr. Ruxton: How They Caught a Lancashire Double Killer.* Preston: Carnegie, 1984. iii, 44 pp.: ill., 1 map, ports.; 21 cm.; paperback.

497. Wilton, George W. *Fingerprints: Scotland Yard: Ruxton Trial Revelations.* North Berwick, Scot.: Tantallon Press, 1957. 29 pp.: ill.; 25 cm.; pamphlet.

While ostensibly an examination of the fingerprint evidence in the Ruxton case, barrister Wilton's pamphlet is more appropriately a broadside to advocate Dr. Henry Faulds, a medical missionary in Japan, "as the foremost of fingerprint pioneers."

Sangret, August (a.k.a. "The Wigwam Murderer")

Born August 28, 1913, in Battleford, Saskatchewan, Canada. Executed April 29, 1943. Private in Regina Rifles. Hankley Common near Godalming, England; 1 murder; knife, bludgeon (wooden stake); October 7, 1942 (discovery of body).

"I guess you have found her. Everything points to me. I guess I shall get the blame."—Sangret's initial statement to detectives on October 12, 1942

The case known in true crime literature as "The Wigwam Murder" began on October 7, 1942, with the discovery of a mummified arm and leg protruding from a mound of earth on Hankley Common near England's Surrey-Sussex border. The corpse's skull had been repeatedly stabbed with a knife with a hooklike blade and shattered by numerous blows from a wooden stake found nearby. Personal effects in the grave identified the body as that of 19-year-old Joan Pearl Wolfe, an indigent "camp-follower" known locally as the "wigwam girl" and the "squaw woman" because of her relationship with August Sangret, a 29-year-old illiterate Canadian soldier of mixed Cree Indian and French stock garrisoned nearby. A letter from Wolfe informing her lover that she was pregnant was also found. Sangret denied killing Wolfe, but was placed under military arrest when he admitted violating policy by keeping her in a "wigwam" he built outside of camp. While in detention, Sangret was further implicated when a blocked drain in the stockade yielded a knife with a blunt, hooklike blade identified by a fellow-soldier as one he found sticking in a tree behind Sangret's shack. Authorities suspected that Sangret was responsible for discarding the weapon in the drain. An impressive forensic reconstruction of Wolfe's battered skull combined with the prosecution's assertion that Sangret killed the woman during an argument, then buried her body under a mound of dirt in accordance with his Cree ancestry highlighted the February 1943 trial. A jury found the soldier guilty on March 1, 1943, but surprisingly recommended he be treated with mercy. The recommendation was disregarded and, following a dismissal of appeal, Sangret was hanged at Wandsworth Prison on April 29, 1943.

498. Critchley, Macdonald, ed. *The Trial of August Sangret.* Notable British Trials. London: William Hodge, 1959. xxxiv, 233 pp.: ill.; 23 cm.
Transcript of Sangret's trial for the murder of Joan Pearl Wolfe, held in the County Hall, Kingston-on-Thames, Surrey Winter Assizes, February 24–26, March 1–2, 1943.

Schmid, Charles Howard, Jr. (a.k.a. "Pied Piper of Tucson," "Smitty," "Angel Rodriguez," "Paul David Ashley")

Born July 8, 1942, in Tucson, Arizona. Died March 30, 1975. Unemployed at time of arrest. Tucson, Arizona; 3 murders; bludgeon (rock), ligature strangulation (guitar string); May 31, 1964, and August 16, 1965.

"I want to kill someone. I want to kill a girl."—Schmid to accomplice Mary Rae French

Charismatic triple murderer whose "cool" attitude made him an idol to certain segments of Tucson, Arizona's restless teenage population. Darkly handsome at 5'3", Schmid stuffed tin cans in his boots to appear taller, dyed his hair jet black to emulate Elvis Presley, and daubed a grease mark beauty spot on his cheek. The former high school star gymnast bragged to his coterie of teenage girls that he knew 100 ways to make love and threw wild parties at a house given him by his parents. On the morning of May 31, 1964, Schmid wondered aloud to sometime girlfriend Mary Rae French, 19, what it would be like to kill someone. That night, "Smitty," French, and friend John Saunders, 19, lured 15-year-old Alleen Rowe to the desert outside of Tucson where Schmid beat her to death with a rock and buried her in a shallow grave. Over a year later on August 16, 1965, Schmid's girlfriend Gretchen Fritz, 17, and her sister Wendy, 13, disappeared on the way to a drive-in. Schmid later confided to friend Richard Bruns that he strangled them both with a guitar string and dumped their bodies in the desert. Bruns became involved when he accompanied Schmid to rebury the sisters. Schmid was arrested on November 10, 1965, after Bruns confessed to police. He was found guilty of the Fritz murders on March 1, 1966, and sentenced to death (later commuted to life imprisonment when the U. S. Supreme Court outlawed the death penalty). He was subsequently set to be tried for the murder of Alleen Rowe, but on the advice of his famed attorney F. Lee Bailey, pleaded guilty to second degree murder receiving 50 years to life in lieu of another death penalty. Although a model inmate, Schmid briefly escaped from the Arizona State Prison on November 11, 1972, but was captured four days later in a Tucson train yard. On March 20, 1975, Schmid, who had legally changed his name to Paul David Ashley in 1974, was stabbed 20 times by two inmates. The removal of a lung and an eye failed to save him and the "Pied Piper of Tucson" died on March 30, 1975.

499. Gilmore, John. *The Tucson Murders.* New York: Dial Press, 1970. 274 pp., [8]pp. of plates: ill., ports.; 22 cm.

_____. [Same as 499, but updated and retitled: *Shallow Graves: A True Account of Multiple Murder.*] Rev. ed. Bernalillo, N.M.: Dangerous Concepts, 1993. (This title had not been published as of May 1996.)

Gilmore, a freelance journalist, enjoyed unprecedented access to Schmid during his first trial for the murders of Gretchen and Wendy Fritz. This detailed account reproduces Schmid's prison diaries and letters.

500. Moser, Don, and Cohen, Jerry. *The Pied Piper of Tucson.* New York: New American Library, 1967. 211 pp., [8]pp. of plates: ill., ports.; 22 cm.

Life news bureau chief Moser expands his March 4, 1966, *Life* magazine article of the same title to cover Schmid's trials and subsequent confession. The authors place Schmid's personal charisma into the context of Tucson, Arizona's disaffected youth.

Schreuder, Frances Bernice
(a.k.a. "Frances Bernice Bradshaw" [maiden name])

Born April 6, 1938, in Salt Lake City, Utah. Socialite. Salt Lake City, Utah; 1 murder (accomplice); .357 Magnum pistol; July 23, 1978.

Television: "At Mother's Request" (1987), a two-part, four-hour miniseries based on Coleman's book of the same title, originally aired on CBS on January 4 and 6, 1987. Cast includes Stefanie Powers (Frances Schreuder), Doug McKeon (Marc Schreuder), and Frances Sternhagen (Berenice Bradshaw). "Nutcracker: Money, Madness and Murder" (1987), a three-part, six-hour miniseries based on Alexander's book of the same title, originally aired on NBC on March 22–24, 1987. Cast includes Lee Remick (Frances Bradshaw Schreuder), Tate Donovan (Marc Schreuder), and John Glover (Richard Behrens).

"Oh! Thank God!"—Schreuder's reaction, according to son Marc, upon being told that he had murdered her father

A murder-for-inheritance scheme in which a domineering mother ordered her emotionally dependent son to kill his wealthy grandfather. On July 23, 1978, 76-year-old Mormon millionaire Franklin James Bradshaw was found shot to death in his auto parts warehouse in Salt Lake City, Utah. Legendary for his frugality, Bradshaw strongly disapproved of daughter Frances Bernice Schreuder's posh Manhattan lifestyle and threatened to cut her out of his will. Fearful of perhaps losing access to an estate estimated at $10.4 million, Schreuder, a twice divorced mother of three, unsuccessfully attempted to hire hitmen on two separate occasions before finally convincing her 17-year-old son Marc to kill the old man. Following years of police work aided by Schreuder's estranged sister, Marc Schreuder was arrested in October 1981. At trial, the son admitted killing his grandfather at his mother's request in order to please the woman. On July 6, 1982, Marc Schreuder was convicted of second degree murder and subsequently sentenced to five years to life in prison. When arrested at her fashionable Manhattan apartment on March 19, 1982, Frances Schreuder had become a patron of the arts, having bought her way onto the board of directors of the New York City Ballet by "anonymously" donating large sums of money. Tried in Salt Lake City, Schreuder's September 27, 1983, conviction for first degree murder was based largely on son Marc's testimony which offered a compelling psychological insight into their unhealthy mother-son relationship. Schreuder was sentenced to life imprisonment on October 3, 1983.

501. Alexander, Shana. *Nutcracker: Money, Madness, Murder: A Family Album.* Garden City, N.Y.: Doubleday, 1985. 444 pp.; 24 cm.

_____. [Same as 501.] New York: Dell, 1985. 448 pp.; 18 cm.; paperback.

_____. [Same as 501.] G.K. Hall Large Print Book Series. Boston: G.K. Hall, 1986. 652 pp. (large print): geneal. table; 24 cm.

502. Coleman, Jonathan. *At Mother's Request: A True Story of Money, Murder, and Betrayal.* 1st ed. New York: Atheneum, 1985. 624 pp.: ill., ports.; 25 cm.

_____. [Same as 502 minus subtitle.] New York: Pocket Books, 1986. 792 pp., [8] leaves of plates: ill.; 17 cm.; paperback.

_____. [Same as 502.] London: Hamilton, 1986. 624 pp.: ill., ports.; 25 cm.

Scott, Leonard Ewing
(a.k.a. "Robert Leonard Ewing Scott," "Charles Contreras, Ph.D.," "Robert McDonald," "H. Hunt," "Lewis Stuart")

Born September 27, 1896, in St. Louis, Missouri. Died August 17, 1987. Paint salesman. Los Angeles, California; 1 murder; bludgeon (rubber mallet); May 16, 1955.

"Well, I guess some people like Lincolns and some people like Fords."—Scott's cryptic comment upon being convicted of his wife's murder

Landmark California legal case which marked the first time a defendant in a murder case was convicted in the absence of a body. On May 16, 1955, millionaire socialite Evelyn Throsby Scott, 63, disappeared from her luxurious Bel Air home at 217 North Bentley Avenue. Her husband of nearly six years, 61-year-old paint salesman L. Ewing Scott, failed to notify police of her disappearance for nine months until pressure from the missing woman's family and friends led the district attorney's office to interview him on February 13, 1956. During a marathon interrogation session, Scott denied that he told Evelyn's friends that she was suffering from alcoholism and mental illness which necessitated her institutionalization in some unidentified sanatorium. According to Scott, on the night of Evelyn's disappearance he drove to Westwood Village to purchase a can of tooth powder at her request. She was gone when he returned. He did not report her missing because she had pulled similar stunts in the past. Investigators determined that shortly after Evelyn's disappearance Scott forged her name to documents giving him access to her sizable checking account. More ominously, friends reported Scott saying that he would never divorce the missing woman, but would wait seven years and have her declared legally dead. While waiting, Scott proposed marriage to another woman. On March 10,

1956, police searched Scott's home and found a partial dental plate, five false teeth, clothing hooks, and eyeglasses near a backyard incinerator. Dental and optometry records confirmed the teeth and glasses belonged to Evelyn Throsby Scott.

While attempting to build a murder case against Scott, authorities indicted the paint salesman on April 27, 1956, on multiple charges of fraud, grand theft, and forgery. When Scott failed to show up for a May 1956 court date an arrest warrant was issued. On April 15, 1957, the fugitive (using the alias "Lewis Stuart") was arrested at a customs checkpoint as he tried to enter Canada from Detroit driving a new car purchased with his wife's money. Two days later he was formally charged with murder. Opening arguments in the landmark trial began on October 14, 1957, with the prosecution facing the difficult task of attempting to win a conviction against Scott without a body. Successfully building the case on the concept of "corpus delicti," the prosecution proved by overwhelming circumstantial evidence that Evelyn Scott was dead, that death was caused by a "criminal agency," and that her husband was the perpetrator. Still insisting that Evelyn was alive, Scott was convicted on December 21, 1957, and sentenced to life imprisonment. Incarcerated at San Quentin, Scott rejected two separate parole opportunities in 1974 and 1976 because he felt accepting them would be tantamount to admitting guilt for a crime he refused to concede occurred. On March 26, 1978, the 81 year old was given an unconditional discharge.

After denying the murder for 30 years, the 89-year-old Scott admitted killing his wife to writer Diane Wagner during a taped interview conducted on August 6, 1984. According to Scott, they were in the bedroom of their Bel Air home when he struck Evelyn once in the head with a hard rubber mallet following an argument in which he accused her of trying to poison him. He wrapped her naked body in a gardener's tarpaulin, drove to Las Vegas, and buried the corpse in the desert six miles east of the Sands Hotel. Despite the confession, most law enforcement officials believed that Scott disposed of the body by burning it in the incinerator of his home. Destitute, Scott died in 1987 at the age of 91 at the Skyline Convalescent Hospital in Silverlake, California. More than a week after his death, Scott's body remained unclaimed at the Los Angeles County morgue.

503. Wagner, Diane. *Corpus Delicti.* 1st ed. New York: St. Martin's/Marek, 1986. 244 pp.; 22 cm.

_____. [Same as 503.] 1st St. Martin's Press Paperbacks ed. New York: St. Martin's Press, 1987. 290 pp.; 18 cm.; paperback.

Excellent account of the case based on interviews with the participating attorneys, family members of the dead woman, and L. Ewing Scott. Wagner, for five years a part-time reporter in the Los Angeles Bureau of *The New York Times*, concludes the book with Scott's startling confession. Asked by Wagner why he decided to confess 30 years after the murder, Scott replied, "Well, it makes a good story, doesn't it?"

Seddon, Frederick Henry

Born circa 1871 in England. Executed April 18, 1912. Insurance superintendent. London, England; 1 murder; poison (arsenic); September 14, 1911.

"That's done it!"—Seddon's resigned reaction to hearing that the auction of his furniture had fetched a small price

Money grubbing insurance agent accused with his wife of poisoning a tenant for profit and subsequently convicted more because of his superior demeanor on the witness stand than on the circumstantial evidence against him. Described as "cold and hard as a paving stone," 40-year-old insurance agent Frederick Henry Seddon's singleminded pursuit of money and hardheaded business practices had made him a success. Living with his wife, Margaret, their five children and his father in a 14-room house at No. 63 Tollington Park, North London, Seddon rented out the top floor to help pay his mortgage. On July 25, 1910, Eliza Mary Barrow, a parsimonious ill-tempered woman of 49, let rooms with Seddon. Distrustful of banks, Barrow often kept over £200 of gold sovereigns in her room. Sometime during the 14 months she lodged with Seddon, Barrow entered into a business relationship with the insurance agent. In return for an annuity paying ten pounds a month, she sold him £1600 of India stock and some real estate properties. On September 1, 1911, Barrow was struck down with acute diarrhea and after weeks of intense pain, severe cramping and vomiting, died on September 14, 1911. The death was officially ruled as due to epidemic diarrhea and exhaustion. Seddon hurriedly arranged a pauper's funeral accepting a commission on the deal. Relatives of Barrow, living a few streets away from Seddon, were not apprised of her death until after the funeral and then by accident. When Seddon was unable to supply them with a plausible explanation regarding the gold and bank notes they knew she had in her possession, the relatives contacted the authorities.

On November 15, 1911, Barrow's body was exhumed and found to contain a lethal level of arsenic. Seddon was arrested on December 4, 1911, and his wife Margaret on January 15, 1912. Their trial began at the Old Bailey on March 4, 1912, and was marked by the insurance agent's haughtily aloof demeanor which many observers felt prejudiced the jury against him. Evidence established that Seddon's young daughter Maggie had purchased fly papers containing arsenic shortly before Barrow died, but the chemist's identification of her was tainted by the fact that he had previously seen her photograph in the paper. Fellow Mason Mr. Justice Bucknill summed up against Seddon and in favor of his wife whose testimony showed that her husband had kept her in total ignorance of his business affairs. On March 14, 1912, a jury deliberated one hour before returning a guilty verdict against Seddon, but acquitting his wife. With his appeal dismissed and the home secretary refusing to be swayed by 300,000 signatures on a petition requesting his reprieve, Seddon was hanged at Pentonville Prison on April 18, 1912, as a crowd of 7,000 kept a death watch outside the gate. Mrs. Seddon, remarried and living in California, sold her story to the British newspaper *Weekly Dispatch* which printed her signed declaration on November 17, 1912. In it, Mrs. Seddon stated that she witnessed Seddon administer poison to Barrow and remained silent because of his threat to shoot her if she told anyone. She recanted the confession two weeks later citing her reasons for making it as a need for money and a desire to stop her neighbors from pointing her out as a murderess.

504. Young, Filson, ed. *Trial of the Seddons*. 1st ed. Notable English Trials.

Edinburgh; London: W. Hodge, 1914. xxx, 420 pp.: ill., facsim., ports.; 23 cm.

_____. [Same as 504.] Notable English Trials. Toronto: Canada Law Book, 1914. xxx, 420 pp., [8] leaves of plates: ill., facsim., ports.; 22 cm.

_____. [Same as 504.] Notable English Trials. Philadelphia: Cromarty, 1914. xxx, 420 pp.: ill., facsim., ports.; 23 cm.

_____. [Same as 504.] 1st ed. Notable British Trials. Edinburgh; London: W. Hodge, 1925. xxx, 420 pp., [5] leaves of plates: ill.; 22 cm.

_____. [Same as 504.] 2nd ed. Notable British Trials. Edinburgh; London: W. Hodge, 1952. xxx, 420 pp., [8] leaves of plates: ill., ports.; 22 cm.

Young, present at the Old Bailey during the trial of the Seddons, credits the insurance agent's superior demeanor with affecting the jury's negative verdict against him. Appendices to the trial transcript include Seddon's letter to his wife written on the eve of his execution.

Sellers, Sean Richard (a.k.a. "Ezurate," "Devil Child")

Born May 18, 1969, in Corcoran, California. Night club bouncer, restaurant worker. Oklahoma City, Oklahoma; 3 murders; .357 and .44 Magnum handguns; September 8, 1985, and March 5, 1986.

"I stood there and looked at them. And my mother ... there was blood running out of the side of her head. I stood there, and I laughed."—Sellers describing the murder of his parents in a television interview aired in August 1987

The arrest of 16-year-old Sean Sellers in March 1986 for the ritual murders of three people (including his parents), produced a firestorm of national headlines proclaiming the influ-

ence of satanism and questioning the morality underlying the execution of minors. To evangelical Christians, Sellers represented the innocent first seduced by the role-playing game Dungeons & Dragons and then ensnared in the occult web woven by rock music, drugs, and cult books like Anton Szandor LaVey's *The Satanic Bible*. Psychiatry, however, offers a more mundane explanation of how emotional deprivation can contribute to the transformation of a sensitive, intelligent boy into a psychopathic killer. Sellers' birth parents divorced when he was three and his mother, Vonda, remarried former Green Beret "Lee" Bellofatto in 1977. Though loving parents, their jobs as cross-country truckers kept them continually on the road during which time the boy lived with relatives. By age nine, Seller had lived with his parents a total of six months, by 15 he had been uprooted at least six times before the family finally settled in Oklahoma City, Oklahoma. Outwardly, Sellers seemed unaffected by years of parental neglect and an unstable homelife. He excelled at school and, though largely friendless, was self-reliant. Sellers, however, had turned to drugs and satanism.

By 12, he was obsessed with Dungeons & Dragons and a year later attended his first satanic service. In 1985, the 15 year old declared himself the high priest of his own coven and conducted black masses in which he slashed initiates with knives and drank their blood. Sellers hid vials of blood in a home refrigerator and consumed it daily to nurture "Ezurate," a personal demon he invoked in nocturnal rituals. An obsession with the Japanese assassination rites of Ninjitsu led Sellers and a friend to start a martial arts club, "The Elimination," in reality, a front to enlist satanic converts. Sellers' fight with a schoolmate over the virtues of satanism led to a teacher's discovery of his copy of *The Satanic Bible*. Called by school authorities, Sellers' parents found a satanic altar in their son's room. In the ugly argument that ensued, Lee shouted, "You do not exist" at the teen. Sellers spent the summer doing drugs, hanging out in occult bookstores, and attending midnight showings of *The Rocky Horror Picture Show*. Convinced his power would be enhanced by breaking all the Ten Commandments, Sellers and a friend, Richard Thomas Howard, 17, singled out Robert Paul Bower, a 36-year-old convenience store clerk in Oklahoma City who had once refused to sell them beer, for ritual slaughter. In the early morning hours of September 7, 1985, Sellers, accompanied by Howard, shot Bower to death with a .357 Magnum.

The murder of Bower opened an occult "portal" for Sellers and he threw himself into satanic worship with a renewed vigor chronicling his progress in a grimoire entitled "Book of Shadows." Remarkably, he confessed the murder to two friends who remained silent. While working as a bouncer in a local teen club, Sellers met and fell in love with a young girl ironically named Angel. His parents' disapproval of the girl widened the rift between them. In early 1986, Sellers began making a black hood and robe to wear in their ritual murder. On March 4, 1986, Sellers' parents were once again contacted by school officials after he wrote an English class essay praising satanism. In his room they uncovered his diary and satanic paraphernalia. The next night, after an elaborate ritual, Sellers, clad only in black underwear, crept into his parents' room and shot the sleeping pair with his stepfather's .44 Magnum

pistol. After clumsily staging a burglary, Sellers drove to Howard's home, confessed the crime, and returned to the scene the next morning to "discover" the double homicide.

Police arrested Sellers the same day after school officials informed them of the essay. Howard agreed to testify against Sellers in a plea bargain arrangement. Failing in a bid to have the 16 year old tried as a juvenile, Sellers' attorney filed an innocent plea based on the argument that being in the thrall of Satan constituted insanity. Prosecutors painted Sellers as a "thrill killer" who murdered to escape parental control. A jury deliberated less than three hours before returning a verdict of guilty on all counts on October 2, 1986. Sentenced to die by lethal injection, the 16 year old became the youngest death row inmate in "Big Mac," Oklahoma's McAlester Prison. In June 1989 a divided U.S. Supreme Court upheld a ruling allowing state execution of minors. The teenager has since experienced a religious conversion described in his book, *Web of Darkness*, and has used appearances on talk shows like *Geraldo* to warn others against the pitfalls of satanism and to argue against the death penalty. Sellers, 25, married the former Jeannine Suzanne Rochan, 22, in a death row ceremony conducted at McAlester on Valentine's Day, 1995. The pair were brought together after Rochan, a born-again Christian, saw Sellers on *Geraldo* and "could see Jesus in his eyes."

505. Dawkins, Vickie L., and Higgins, Nina Downey. *Devil Child*. 1st St. Martin's Press mass market ed. New York: St. Martin's Press, 1989. x, 278 pp., [8]pp. of plates: ill., ports.; 18 cm.; paperback.

506. Sellers, Sean. *Web of Darkness*. Tulsa, Okla.: Victory House, 1990. 173 pp.; 20 cm.; paperback.

Shawcross, Arthur John

(a.k.a. "The Genesee River Killer," "The Cannibal of the Genesee," "The Rochester Strangler," "The Rochester Nightstalker," "Monster of the Rivers," "Oddie," "Crazyboy," "Mitch")

Born June 6, 1945, in Kittery, Maine. Food service worker. Watertown and the Rochester area of New York; 13 murders (11 women in Rochester area, 2 children); manual strangulation, suffocation; 1972, 1988–1989.

Television: "Mind of a Serial Killer" (1992), broadcast as an installment in the PBS television series *Nova*. A one-hour production of Mercury Productions in association with WGBH Boston. Video of the program distributed by Films for the Humanities & Sciences (Princeton, N.J., 1992).

"Vietnam taught me how to kill." Paroled child killer convicted of the murders of 11 women (mostly prostitutes) in the vicinity of Rochester, New York. The son of a Marine decorated for bravery during World War II and a tenth grade dropout mother, Arthur Shawcross was bluntly described by one relative "as a weird little bastard from the time he learned to walk." As a child, Shawcross was dogged by nightmares. He was a chronic bedwetter up through his adolescence. At six he made the first of several attempts to run away from his Brownville, New York, home. Psychiatrists would later claim that Shawcross deeply resented the attention his parents paid his younger siblings (a brother and two sisters). The child withdrew into a world of fantasy playmates earning him the nicknames "Oddie" and "Crazyboy" at school where he was the butt of cruel jokes and beatings by older classmates. Shawcross reacted by venting his anger out on his siblings and took to carrying an iron bar to school. At nine, Shawcross' mother learned of an illegitimate child fathered by her husband in Australia during the war. Already the family's dominant personality, the woman became even more shrewish, cowing her husband and children with abusive language. Failing school and unable to win the affection of his beloved mother, Shawcross directed his violent impulses toward animals. The child snapped the necks of snared rabbits, hammered chipmunks into pulp, scraped the feathers off baby birds, and tossed darts at frogs nailed to his dart board. The violence in Shawcross became even more pronounced when he reached adolescence. At school, he bullied students and teachers before dropping out at 17 in his freshman year.

Drifting from job to job, Shawcross concentrated on thievery, arson, and sex. He fantasized about having sex with his sister, drilled holes in the walls of his parents' bedroom to watch them have sex, and by night peeped into neighborhood windows. In December 1963, the 18 year old was arrested in Watertown, New York, for burgling a Sears, Roebuck store and sentenced to 18 months' probation as a youthful offender. Following a failed 1964 marriage, Shawcross married again before being drafted into the Army in April 1967 and shipped to Vietnam. According to Shawcross' unsubstantiated claims, the violence he saw in Vietnam turned him into a serial killer. Upon his return to the United States, the soldier bragged about his wholesale slaughter of "gooks," later telling psychiatrists that while "in country" he had murdered several prostitutes, placed their decapitated heads on stakes, and ate parts of their bodies. Within seven months of being honorably discharged in the spring of 1969, Shawcross divorced his second wife and was sentenced to five years in Attica for a gas station burglary, three arsons, and other offenses. A psychiatric evaluation at the Auburn Correctional Facility where he was transferred six months later diagnosed Shawcross as a "schizoid arsonist" with latent homicidal tendencies. Nevertheless, he was paroled on October 18, 1971, after serving 22 months, settling in Watertown, New York. A third marriage did not prevent the ex-con from attacking a 16-year-old girl in an underground room in Watertown's old railroad station. The girl did not report the rape when Shawcross paid her $10.

Around May 7, 1972, 11-year-old Jack Owen Blake disappeared in Watertown, New York. Shawcross, known in the area for wrestling with kids and stuffing leaves down their pants, was considered a good suspect, but no evidence was found to tie him to the child's disappearance. On Labor Day weekend that same year, the body of eight-year-old Karen Ann Hill, reported missing by her mother hours before, was found hidden beneath some stones under the Pearl Street Bridge over the Black River in Rochester, New York. The girl had been beaten, strangled, raped, sodomized, and had mud and soot forced down her throat. Shawcross, recently fined for spanking a six-year-old boy and stuffing grass down the front of his pants, was taken in for questioning and

later confessed to the murders of Hill and Blake. Acting on information supplied by the confessed killer, Blake's decomposed body was found in a state of undress suggestive of sexual molestation. Faced with weak forensic evidence in the Blake case and no witnesses to Hill's rape, the Jefferson County prosecutor cut a deal with Shawcross on October 17, 1972. The violent pedophile pleaded guilty to one count of first degree manslaughter in Hill's death in exchange for an indeterminate prison sentence of up to 25 years with a chance for parole. Shawcross subsequently served almost 16 years in the maximum security Green Haven Correctional Facility before being paroled in March 1987 over the negative recommendations of prison psychiatrists who evaluated him as a dangerous psychotic with homicidal tendencies. The New York State parole board tried unsuccessfully to place Shawcross in Binghamton, Delhi, and Fleischman, but in each city police departments and concerned citizens forced him to relocate. Finally, in a move later universally criticized, the parole board placed the convicted child killer in Rochester without notifying the local police.

In Rochester, Shawcross lived with yet another wife, Rose Marie Walley, and took a mistress, Clara Neal, whose car he used to cruise Rochester's seedy red light district. On March 15, 1988, Dorothy "Dotsie" Blackburn, a 27-year-old prostitute and drug addict disappeared while working downtown. Her body was found nine days later in a culvert near Salmon Creek. An autopsy determined death was due to manual strangulation and that the killer had taken a bite out of her vagina. Next to die was Anna Marie Daly Steffen, a 28-year-old known prostitute reported missing in July 1988. Her strangled body was found September 11, 1988, in the Genesee River Gorge. In 1989, Shawcross strangled, raped, and dumped the bodies of nine young prostitutes in remote areas in and around Rochester only varying his pattern once. In early November 1989, Shawcross suffocated 30-year-old June Stotts, a mildly retarded friend of his wife's, in a secluded area near the Genesee River after she began screaming during sex. According to his later confused confessions, Shawcross revisited the scene a week afterwards and performed oral sex on the corpse. Often, Shawcross claimed, he killed the prostitutes when they attempted to rob him or mock his inability to sexually perform. One of his last known victims, 34-year-old prostitute June Cicero, was strangled in mid–December 1989 after she ridiculed Shawcross for failing to achieve an erection. Shawcross dumped her body off a bridge into a snowdrift covering Salmon Creek near Rochester's Northampton Park. Days later, he returned to the site, excised her vagina with a hacksaw, and ate it frozen. Authorities found Cicero's body and staked out the scene in the hope that the killer would return to the site. Their patience paid off on January 4, 1990, when a police helicopter notified ground units that a car had stopped on the bridge and a man had looked over the bridge into the frozen river in the direction of the corpse. Shawcross was arrested, and after talking with his wife, confessed to numerous murders. On December 14, 1990, a Rochester jury rejected his claim of insanity and convicted Shawcross on ten counts of second degree murder. The serial killer was sentenced to the maximum penalty, 250 years in prison, on February 1,

1991. He was later convicted and sentenced to 25 years to life for the murder of Elizabeth Gibson, 29, in 1989. Subsequent theories put forth to explain Shawcross' propensity for violence have included post-traumatic stress syndrome, brain damage stemming from a history of head injuries, and more likely, a chromosomal anomaly.

507. Norris, Joel. *Arthur Shawcross, the Genesee River Killer: The Grisly True Crime Account of the Rochester Prostitute Murders!* New York: Pinnacle Books, 1992. 308 pp., [12]pp. of plates: ill.; 18 cm.; paperback. (Includes sound cassette of Shawcross' confession.)

Paperback account based on newspaper accounts, source material provided by the public defender of Wayne County, New York, who represented Shawcross in the Gibson murder trial, and 24 hours of interviews conducted with the serial killer. Norris' conclusions: Shawcross suffers from post-traumatic stress syndrome and a chromosomal disorder.

508. Olsen, Jack. *The Misbegotten Son: A Serial Killer and His Victims: The True Story of Arthur J. Shawcross.* New York: Delacorte Press, 1993. 520 pp.; 24 cm.

_____. [Same as 508.] New York: Island Books, 1993. 581 pp.; 18 cm.; paperback.

_____. [Same as 508.] London: Headline, 1994. 520 pp., [8]pp. of plates: ill.; 23 cm.

Definitive account based on interviews with all the principals in the case. In the final chapter, Dr. Richard Theodore Kraus concludes that Shawcross suffers from an "XYY" chromosomal anomaly (an extra male chromosome) which predisposed him towards violence.

Sheppard, Samuel H.
(*acquitted;* a.k.a. "Dr. Sam")

400 SHEPPARD

Born circa 1924. Died April 6, 1970. Medical doctor. Bay Village, Ohio; 1 murder (acquitted); bludgeon; July 4, 1954.

Film: The Lawyer (US, 1970), a Furie Productions release directed by Sidney J. Furie, is loosely based on the Sheppard case. Cast includes Barry Newman (Tony Petrocelli), Robert Colbert (Jack Harrison/Sheppard character), and Diana Muldaur (Ruth Petrocelli). This film was the basis for the NBC television series "Petrocelli" (September 1974–March 1976).

"My point is that we must never let lies about us, or injustice toward us, turn us in the wrong way. We must never stoop so low as those who have lied and cheated their way in life. At times it is difficult to figure what is right when those who should be honest are not, but our only answer is the Christian one."—Sheppard in a June 1955, prison letter to his 10-year-old niece

The son of a respected Cleveland doctor, Sam Sheppard followed in his father's footsteps and studied osteopathy and neurosurgery. Upon graduation from medical school in California, Sheppard became partners with his two older brothers in the large osteopathic empire founded by their father. Though only 30, "Dr. Sam" became the head of neurosurgery at the family-controlled Bay Village Hospital named after the wealthy Cleveland suburb on the shore of Lake Erie. In the early evening of July 3, 1954, Sheppard returned from work to the two-story Bay Village home overlooking Lake Erie which he shared with his wife Marilyn Reese Sheppard, and their seven-year-old son, Sam, Jr., known as "Chip." The couple, former high school sweethearts, had been married nine years and Marilyn Sheppard was four months' pregnant. That night, the Sheppards entertained a neighborhood couple prior to preparing for a large Independence Day party at their home the next day. Sheppard was asleep on the couch when the neighbors left shortly after midnight and Marilyn, not wanting to disturb him, went upstairs to bed. According to Sheppard's account, he was awakened sometime later by his wife's screams and, running up the stairs into their bedroom, "saw a form grappling with something or someone." Seconds later, he was struck down from behind and lost consciousness. He awoke to find his wife dead on the bed and, hearing a noise downstairs, groggily went to investigate. The doctor saw a form leaving the house through a screen door and followed it down to the lake where he was again knocked unconscious. Sheppard awoke on the shore and later called a friend who notified authorities.

An autopsy determined that Marilyn Sheppard had been savagely bludgeoned at least 27 times with a heavy instrument believed to have been a surgical tool. While the ransacked bedroom suggested robbery as a possible motive, police were skeptical of the doctor's account of the incident, refusing to believe that the violence of the attack had not awakened the sleeping child in the next bedroom or the family dog. Nor could Sheppard produce the bloodstained shirt he allegedly wore during his pursuit of the intruder. As Sheppard recuperated in the family hospital from what his brother diagnosed as a "broken neck" (actually only superficial cuts and a black eye), public sentiment turned against the doctor due largely to a series of scathing editorials about the case published by the *Cleveland Press*. Headlines referring to him as "Getting Away with Murder" were common and the police were criticized for their "tragic mishandling of the Sheppard murder investigation." Rumors ran rampant that Sheppard was guilty and still at large only because of his family's money. The doctor maintained his innocence even offering a $10,000 reward for information about the case. Bowing to public and press pressure, the authorities arrested Sheppard at his father's home on July 30, 1954. Released on $50,000 bail, Sheppard was indicted by a grand jury on August 6, 1954, after it was learned he had lied about not being sexually involved with a former lab assistant at the hospital.

Court proceedings against Sheppard began in Cleveland on October 18, 1954, in what proved to be the longest murder trial in U.S. history up to that time. Thirty-one witnesses were called including the doctor's mistress who testified about their secretive 15 month affair, a relationship the prosecution offered as a possible motive for the murder. Although no murder weapon was found or forensic evidence produced which tied Sheppard to the killing, the doctor was convicted of second degree murder on October 18, 1954, after a seven-man, four-woman jury deliberated four days. Sheppard was sentenced to life in prison. Weeks later on January 7, 1955, Sheppard's mother, broken by the trial, shot herself in the head with a pistol. Eleven days later, Sheppard's ailing father died in the family hospital where his convicted son had once been head of neurology. Appeal after appeal was denied until F. Lee Bailey, a Boston attorney only six years out of law school, argued Sheppard's case before the U.S. Supreme Court in 1966. Ruling that "inherently prejudicial publicity" had prevented Sheppard from receiving a fair trial, the Court voided Sheppard's conviction on June 6, 1966. At Sheppard's retrial in Cleveland, Bailey cast doubt on the police handling of evidence, contemptuously dismissing the prosecution's case as "ten pounds of hogwash in a five pound bag." On November 16, 1966, 12 years after his wife's murder, Sheppard was acquitted of the crime and later relocated to Youngstown, Ohio, to practice medicine. Tragedy, however, continued to dog Sheppard. A marriage to a German woman divorcée who had become his pen pal while he was in prison ended in divorce in 1969. Plagued by malpractice suits filed in the wake of the death of two of his patients, Sheppard left medicine and became a professional wrestler. The former doctor had been married five months to the 20-year-old daughter of his wrestling manager when he died of natural causes in Columbus, Ohio, on April 6, 1970, at the age of 46.

509. Bailey, F. Lee, and Aronson, Harvey. *The Defense Never Rests.* New York: Stein and Day, 1971. 262 pp.; 25 cm.

_____. [Same as 509.] New York: New American Library, 1972. x, 316 pp.; 18 cm. ("A Signet book"); paperback.

510. Holmes, Paul. *Retrial: Murder and Dr. Sam Sheppard.* Illustrated by Sanford Kossin. New York: Bantam Books, 1966. 240 pp.: ill.; 18 cm.; paperback.

511. _____. *The Sheppard Murder Case.* 1st ed. New York: McKay, 1961. 332 pp.: ill.; 21 cm.

_____. [Same as 511.] London: Cassell, 1962. 332 pp.; 22 cm.

_____. [Same as 511.] New York: Bantam, 1962. vi, 247 pp.; 18 cm.; paperback.

_____. [Same as 511.] London: Cassell, 1962. vi, 247 pp.; 18 cm.; paperback.

512. Pollack, Jack Harrison. *Dr. Sam: An American Tragedy.* Chicago: H. Regnery, 1972. xiii, 247 pp.: ill.; 24 cm.

_____. [Same as 512.] Rev. ed. New York: Avon, 1975. xiii, 238 pp.; 18 cm.; paperback.

513. Sheppard, Sam. *Endure and Conquer.* 1st ed. Cleveland: World, 1966. x, 329 pp.; 24 cm.

514. Sheppard, Stephen, and Holmes, Paul. *My Brother's Keeper.* New York: D. McKay, 1964. xiii, 305 pp.; 21 cm.

Simmons, Ronald Gene
(a.k.a. "James Johnson")

Born July 15, 1940, in Chicago, Illinois. Executed July 25, 1990. Former Air Force master sergeant, truck driver, convenience store clerk. Arkansas; 16 murders; ligature strangulation, .22 caliber pistol; December 1987.

"Justice delayed, finally done, is justifiable homicide." — Simmons' last words

The largest family mass murderer in the history of American homicide. It took Ronald Gene Simmons only 24 minutes on the morning of December 28, 1987, to consummate a murderous rampage that left two people dead and four others wounded in the small Arkansas town of Russellville. On that morning, the 47-year-old father of seven methodically drove to four area businesses and used two .22 caliber pistols to exact a terrible revenge on those he felt had "hurt" him. Dead in his wake from four gunshot wounds to the head lay Kathy Kendrick, a 25-year-old divorcée and former beauty queen, with whom Simmons had become infatuated during his two-year tenure as a clerk at the truck line. Simmons was reprimanded in 1986 after Kendrick reported his unwanted sexual

advances to her supervisor, Joyce Butts. He quit shortly afterwards. Part-time Taylor Oil employee J.D. Chaffin, 33, was also fatally shot through the eye when he had the misfortune to walk into the middle of Simmons' attempted execution of company owner Rusty Taylor. Simmons had worked indirectly for Taylor for over one-and-a-half years as a weekend cashier at the Sinclair Mini-Mart owned by the man. Taylor sustained two gunshot wounds to the chest before Simmons drove to the mini-mart where he seriously wounded a cashier and the store's manager. The rampage ended at Woodline Motor Freight with the shooting of office manager Joyce Butts, the hated supporter of Kathy Kendrick. Butts would survive open heart surgery, but have no memory of the shooting. Moments after the attack, a calm Simmons surrendered to a female office worker and was taken into custody.

What authorities initially believed to be a straightforward case of revenge-driven workplace violence was but a prelude to the tableau of horror awaiting them at Simmons' secluded hilltop home in nearby Dover, Arkansas. A converted mobile home, the ramshackle house sat off Highway 7 atop a foothill in the shadow of the Ozark Mountains. A crudely handpainted sign announced to visitors that they were on "Mockingbird Hill," Simmons' private Xanadu. On the path up to the silent home, sheriffs encountered similar signs marking such imaginary landmarks as "Little Princess Lane" and "Lady Bug Drive." Cars littered the front yard and a barbed wire fence divided Simmons' property from a neighbor's. Plainly visible through an unlocked window were two bodies resting on the living room floor near a Christmas tree. In all, the house yielded the corpses of five Simmons family members who had obviously been visiting the homestead for the holidays. Dennis McNulty, husband of Simmons' daughter Sheila Marie, had been shot once in the face at close range as he entered the house. Near him, Sheila Marie had died from six shots to the face. The bullet-ridden bodies of William Simmons (Gene's son) and wife Renata (shot seven times in the head and neck) were found nearby in the dining room. In a small bedroom, seven-year-old Sylvia McNulty, Sheila Marie's daughter by her own father's incest, lay face down on a bed. She had been strangled with a nylon fish-stringer. An autopsy estimated the time of death for the victims in the house to be December 26, 1987.

The search for the remaining family members resumed the next morning at dawn. At 8:30 a.m. authorities discovered a three-foot-by-six-foot plot of loose dirt reeking of kerosene and covered with sheets of corrugated tin. Diggers unearthed strings of barbed wire ten inches below the ground's surface before uncovering the bodies of seven more members of Simmons' family. Three of his daughters ranging in age from 8 to 17 had been strangled to death as had his 14-year-old son, Eddie. Eldest son, Ronald Gene Simmons, Jr., 26, had died of four shots to the face. The strangled body of his three-year-old daughter, Barbara, lay on top of him. First to be dumped in the mass grave had been the elder son's wife, Becky, a victim of two gunshots to the face. The bodies had been doused in kerosene to mask the stench of rotting flesh and wrapped in barbed wire to discourage foraging animals. A more poignant discovery awaited stunned authorities 100 yards west of the Simmons' home

when they opened the trunks of two disabled cars. Each revealed a green plastic garbage bag containing the body of an infant. Twenty-month-old William "Trae" Simmons, III, Simmons' grandson by his son William, had been strangled as had his 21-month-old cousin, Michael McNulty, found in the other car. The infants' dripping wet bodies led investigators to believe that they had been submerged overnight in a barrel of water kept in the bathroom and then interred in the car trunks.

In custody, Simmons refused to discuss his motivations for the murders, screaming at his court-appointed attorneys, "I won't tell you bloodsucking bastards anything." Surviving relatives and a police background check, however, painted a stark portrait of the man who had become the nation's largest family mass murderer. A solitary child, Simmons threw tantrums for attention, failed to respond to discipline, and bullied other children. Enlisting in the Navy in 1957, Simmons began a 17-year military career that included meritorious non-combat service in Vietnam and in the United States Air Force's Office of Special Investigation. He met wife Rebecca at a USO dance in 1959 and they married in 1960. Their first child, Ronald Gene, Jr., was born the next year. Rebecca would continue to produce children at an almost yearly rate until she decided for health reasons (over Simmons' vocal objections) to have a tubal ligation in 1979. No longer in love with a wife unable to bear him children, Simmons transferred his sexual attention to his favorite child, teenaged daughter Sheila Marie. In July 1980, Simmons raped the girl and justified his repeated acts of incest on the grounds that it was his paternal duty to protect and prepare his daughter for the rigors of adulthood. By the end of 1980, Sheila was pregnant and Simmons informed the family that he was the father. Son Ronald Gene reported the incident to a Health and Social Services Division caseworker in Cloudcroft, New Mexico, and Air Force Master Sergeant Simmons was confronted with possible legal action. By the time the caseworker's request for a consent decree removing the three oldest girls from the home was filed on June 8, 1981, Simmons had left the military, relocated to Ward, Arkansas, and later to the town of Dover. Lacking manpower, New Mexico authorities dropped the case. On June 17, 1981, Sheila Marie gave birth to her father's daughter, Sylvia Gail.

Simmons turned the house on Mockingbird Hill into his own private citadel where he held sway and manipulated every aspect of his family's life. He assigned the children to work crews and they spent their after school hours and weekends digging outhouses and hauling concrete blocks for a wall to further shield Simmons from the outside world. Simmons discouraged their friendships with other children by forbidding any guest to invade his sacrosanct domain. He monitored all letters and refused to allow a phone in the house. The concentration camp–like atmosphere slowly took its psychic toll on the family. In a smuggled letter written to a secret friend months before her murder, his 17-year-old daughter Loretta wrote, "I just can't take it anymore," a sentiment echoed by Simmons' wife Becky who wrote to son William, "I want out…"

Simmons' absolute control over his family began to disintegrate in the early 1980s when he enrolled Sheila in a business school. While there, she began dating classmate Dennis McNulty, who, despite learning of her incestuous relationship with her father, often visited the house. Pregnant again with her father's child, Sheila had an abortion in December 1982. Many credit Sheila's marriage to McNulty in August 1984 as being the catalyst for Simmons' deadly rampage. When Sheila announced in early 1985 that she was pregnant by her husband, Simmons felt as though his daughter had betrayed him. Simmons turned his sexual attention to Woodline Motor Freight coworker Kathy Kendrick, but she rebuffed him. In a spring 1986 meeting, Simmons attempted to reconcile with his broken family, but was rejected. In the summer of 1987, Simmons told Dennis McNulty that he was no longer welcome at his house. A couple of months later, Becky wrote to her son that she planned on leaving Simmons. In November 1987, one month before the murders, Simmons informed a deliveryman at the Sinclair Mini-Mart where he worked that he would "get even" with all those who had maligned him.

On May 9, 1988, Simmons stood trial in Ozarka, Arkansas, for the murders of Kathy Kendrick and J.D. Chaffin. Still refusing to cooperate with his attorneys, Simmons insisted that he wanted a guilty verdict and his own execution. The jury obliged him on May 12, 1988, and recommended the death penalty plus 147 years. In an address to the court, Simmons asked that nothing delay "this very correct and proper sentence." The jury's sentence was affirmed at a subsequent hearing on May 16, 1988, and Simmons was scheduled to die on June 27, 1988. A series of petitions filed by a religious group and another Arkansas death row inmate blocked Simmons' execution up to the time he was tried for the murders of his 14 family members in Clarksville, Arkansas, on February 6, 1989. A disinterested, impassive Simmons listened to his lawyers construct a fantastic scenario that had him away from home when Dennis McNulty killed the entire family and then committed suicide. Simmons had merely disposed of the bodies after discovering the carnage. Attempting to ensure his own conviction, Simmons slugged the prosecutor in the jaw on February 10, 1989; hours later, the jury found him guilty. An execution date of March 16, 1989, was set, but again legal wrangling would result in another stay and a 13-month delay. At 9:02 p.m. on June 25, 1990, at Cummins Prison, Simmons became the first person in Arkansas to be executed by lethal injection. Though five family members attended services for him, none claimed his body and he was buried in a pauper's grave near Grady, Arkansas.

515. Marshall, Bryce, and Williams, Paul. *Zero at the Bone.* New York: Pocket Star Books, 1991. 302 pp.; 22 cm.

_____. [Same as 515.] New York: Pocket Books, 1991. 302 pp.: ill.; 18 cm. ("A Pocket Star book"); paperback.

The authors maintain that Simmons murdered his family when he realized that he was losing his absolute control over them.

516. Moore, Jim. *Rampage: America's Largest Family Mass Murder.* Fort Worth, Texas: Summit Group, 1992. xxvi, 213 pp., [8]pp. of plates: ill.; 24 cm.

Sims, Paula Marie
(a.k.a. "Paula Marie Blew" [maiden name])

Born May 21, 1959, in Missouri. Housewife. Brighton and Alton, Illi-

nois; 2 murders; drowning; June 17, 1986, and May 4, 1989.

Television: "Precious Victims" (1993), a two-hour, made-for-television movie based on the book of the same title by Don W. Weber and Charles Bosworth, Jr., originally aired on CBS on September 28, 1993. Cast includes Park Overall (Paula Sims) and Robby Benson (Robert Sims).

"I put her in the bathtub. And then I walked out. I didn't *decide* to walk out. I didn't decide anything. I just walked out."—Sims describing the murder of her infant daughter Loralei Marie to author Audrey Becker

Unusual case of a mother who drowned her two infant daughters during a three-year timespan ostensibly because she preferred male children. On June 17, 1986, Paula Sims notified Brighton, Illinois, police that a masked gunman had entered her home while her husband Robert was at work. The intruder forced her to lie on the basement floor while he kidnapped her 13-day-old daughter, Loralei Marie. Sims' 15-month-old son Randy was left untouched. One week later the infant's body was found in a wooded ravine near the house. Decomposition precluded determining a cause of death. Although both Paula and Robert Sims failed polygraph tests, police were unable to file charges against them due to a lack of physical evidence. Almost three years later on April 29, 1989, six-week-old Heather Sims was abducted under almost identical circumstances from her parents' new home in Alton, Illinois. Paula Sims reported being struck in the head by the same gunman who took Loralei Marie in 1986. When she regained consciousness, Heather was missing, but son Randy was undisturbed. As before, Robert Sims was at work, but resolutely stood by his wife's explanation of events. X-rays and blood tests failed to find any evidence that Sims had sustained a head injury. On May 4, 1989, the child's body was found in a trash can near a lock and dam on the Missouri side of the Mississippi River across from Alton, Illinois. Heather's body had been nearly frozen in a black plastic garbage bag before being dumped. Death was due to suffocation. Paula Sims was subsequently arrested when the FBI determined that trash bags found in her home were identical to the one wrapped around her dead child. Robert Sims was not charged although authorities strongly suspected his involvement. Sims pleaded innocent to the infant's first degree murder at her trial in Peoria, Illinois, on January 11, 1990. Several witnesses testified to her preference for male children and recalled instances in which she expressed disappointment over having given birth to two girls. Sims was found guilty on January 30, 1990, and subsequently sentenced to life imprisonment without possibility of parole. She lost an appeal to the appellate court of Illinois on May 4, 1993.

517. Becker, Audrey. *Dying Dreams: The Secrets of Paula Sims*. New York: Pocket Books, 1993. viii, 341 pp., [8]pp. of plates: ill.; 17 cm.; paperback.

Becker alleges that Sims confessed to her in 1992 that she let both children drown in a bathtub while overcome with postpartum depression.

518. Weber, Don W., and Bosworth, Charles. *Precious Victims*. New York: Signet, 1991. 431 pp., [8]pp. of plates: ill.; 23 cm.

_____. [Same as 518.] New York: Penguin Group, 1991. 431 pp., [8]pp. of plates: ill.; 18 cm. ("A Signet book"); paperback.

_____. [Same as 518.] London: Virgin Books, 1992. [400]pp.: ill.; 18 cm.; paperback.

_____. [Same as 518.] Newly updated. New York: Signet, 1993. 440 pp., [8]pp. of plates: ill.; 18 cm. ("A Signet book"); paperback.

Solid collaboration between Weber, the Madison County assistant state's attorney who prosecuted the case, and Bosworth, the lead reporter who covered the trial for the *St. Louis Post-Dispatch*. In May 1993, a three-judge appellate court panel rejected the contention of Sims' attorney that Weber had jeopardized his client's rights by writing about the case.

Slater, Oscar Joseph
(*reprieved*; a.k.a. "Oscar Joseph Leschziner" [birth name], "Anderson," "George," "Sando," "Great Suspect of 1909")

Born circa 1873 in Oppelin, Germany. Died February 3, 1948. Gambler. Glasgow, Scotland; 1 murder; bludgeon; December 21, 1908.

"I know nothing about the affair. You are convicting an innocent man."—Slater's contention of innocence

A German-Jew unjustly convicted of the murder of an elderly Glasgow woman later reprieved almost 20 years after his case became a *cause célèbre*. On December 21, 1908, 82-year-old Marion Gilchrist was savagely bludgeoned to death in the dining room of her opulent flat at 15 Queen's Terrace, Glasgow. Though no one witnessed the murder, Gilchrist's 21-year-old maid, Helen Lambie, returned to the flat from an errand in time to see a man run from a spare bedroom into the street. A witness in the street, 14-year-old Mary Bowman, was nearly knocked down by the passing man. Known for keeping large amounts of jewelry in her flat, Gilchrist had been robbed of a single diamond brooch. Inquiries at a Glasgow pawn shop revealed that Oscar Slater, a German-born Jew of dubious reputation, had pawned a diamond brooch before setting sail for New York on December 26, 1908, aboard the *Lusitania*. Slater was detained in the United States and the two witnesses brought to New York where they identified him as the murderer after first being shown his photograph by Glasgow authorities under great public pressure to quickly solve the case. More damning to the reputation of the police, however, was the fact that they had singlemindedly pursued Slater as their prime suspect after learning that not only was the brooch pawned by the professional gambler *not* the victim's, but that it had been pawned three weeks *before* the murder. Tried in Edinburgh in May 1909, Slater's questionable character became the central issue in the trial in which the "eyewitnesses" offered conflicting descriptions of the man they saw hurriedly leaving Gilchrist's flat. Slater was found guilty by majority verdict on May 6, 1909, and sentenced to hang on May 27, 1909. Two days before the execution, Slater's sentence was commuted to life imprisonment. Strong public sentiment against the conviction spearheaded by Sir Arthur Conan Doyle and other notables led to the reopening of Slater's case and he was vindicated on appeal on July 20, 1928, after spending almost 19 years in Petershead Prison. The government subsequently paid Slater £6000 in compensation. Slater died in Ayr, Scotland, on February 3, 1948, at the age of 75.

519. Conan Doyle, Arthur. *The Case of Oscar Slater*. New York: Hodder &

Stoughton, George H. Doran, 1912. 103 pp.; 19 cm.

520. Hunt, Peter. *Oscar Slater: The Great Suspect*. London: Carroll & Nicholson, 1951. 248 pp.: ill.; 23 cm.

_____. [Same as 520.] Foreword by Anthony Boucher. Rev. ed. Collier Mystery Classics. New York: Collier Books, 1963. 288 pp.; 18 cm.; paperback.

521. Park, William. *The Truth About Oscar Slater: With the Prisoner's Own Story*. With a statement by Sir Arthur Conan Doyle. London: Psychic Press, [1926?] 186 pp.: front.; 19 cm.

522. Roughead, William, ed. *Trial of Oscar Slater*. Notable Scottish Trials. Edinburgh; Glasgow: W. Hodge, 1910. lxxx, 321 pp.: front., plates, ports., 2 fold. plans; 23 cm.

_____. [Same as 522.] 2nd ed., rev. Notable Scottish Trials. Edinburgh: W. Hodge, 1915. lxxiv, 306 pp.: front., plates, ports., 2 fold. plans; 22 cm.

_____. [Same as 522.] 2nd ed. Notable Scottish Trials. Toronto: Canada Law Book, 1915. lxxiv, 306 pp.: ill.; 23 cm.

_____. [Same as 522.] 2nd ed. Notable British Trials. New York: J. Day, 1927. lxxiv, 306 pp.: front., plates, ports. 2 fold. plans; 23 cm.

_____. [Same as 522.] 3rd ed. Notable British Trials. Edinburgh: W. Hodge, 1929. lxiii, 338 pp., 16 leaves of plates: ill., ports., plans (fold); 22 cm.

_____. [Same as 522.] 4th ed. Notable British Trials. Edinburgh; London: W. Hodge, 1950. lxiii, 338 pp., [16] leaves of plates: ill.; 22 cm.

_____. [Same as 522.] Notable British Trials. Sydney, Aus.: Butterworth, 1988. 321 pp.: ill.; 26 cm.

523. Toughill, Thomas. *Oscar Slater: The Mystery Solved*. Foreword by Peter M. Hill. Edinburgh: Canongate, 1993. xiv, 242 pp., [24]pp. of plates: ill.; 24 cm.

Smart, Pamela Ann
(a.k.a. "Pamela Ann Wojas" [maiden name], "Ice Princess," "Maiden of Metal," "Pame," "Wojo," "Seka," "Giraffe")

Born August 16, 1967, in Miami, Florida. Media services director. Derry, New Hampshire; 1 murder (accomplice); gun; May 1, 1990.

Television: "Murder in New Hampshire: The Pamela Smart Story" (1991), a two-hour, made-for-television movie, originally aired on CBS on September 24, 1991. Cast includes Helen Hunt (Pamela Smart), Chad Allen (Billy Flynn), and Hank Stratton (Greg Smart).

"The people who actually murdered Greg will someday leave prison, and I'm sentenced to spend the rest of my natural life here, and that just doesn't seem fair."—Smart in a January 1995 interview

Taboo-breaking murder in which an attractive high school teacher seduced a teenager into killing her husband. The classic all–American girl, Pam combined intelligence with good looks to excel in high school where she was class president and a varsity cheerleader. A communications major at Florida State University in Tallahassee, the popular coed indulged her passion for rock music by hosting as the "Maiden of Metal" the "Metal Madness" program on the college radio station. Graduating with honors in 1989, she married Greg Smart on May 7 of that year. The two had met in 1983, seemingly sharing little more than an avid interest in heavy metal and similar upper middle class backgrounds. Upon graduation, the couple adopted a "yuppie" lifestyle and moved into a condominium in upscale Derry, New

Hampshire. Greg, following in his father's footsteps, became a hotshot insurance salesman at MetLife. Pam accepted the position of media center director for the area's high school district. Her office building in Hampton stood directly across the street from the Winnacunnett High School attended by her future lover and murder accomplice, 15-year-old William "Billy" Flynn.

Outwardly, the Smart marriage appeared solid. They were affectionate in public and shared a devotion to their shih tzu, Halen, named after Pam's favorite group, Van Halen. In reality, their marriage was slowly disintegrating. In December 1989 Greg admitted having a drunken affair and a few days before Christmas allegedly slapped Pam in the face and tried to strangle her. Things were brighter for her at work where she impressed students with her good looks, enthusiasm, and passion for heavy metal bands that extended to the customized HALEN license plate on her Honda CRX. Pam befriended troubled 15-year-old Cecelia Pierce, making the girl her student intern. Through Pierce, Pam met high school sophomore Billy Flynn and his tight circle of friends: Vance Lattime, Jr., 17, and Patrick (Pete) Randall, 18. Pam and Flynn were thrown together by their work on a school self-awareness program and the prosecution later argued that the older woman carefully orchestrated the teen's seduction in order to dupe the young virgin into murdering her husband Greg. Simple divorce would not do, Smart allegedly told Flynn and Pierce, because Greg would get "the dog, the furniture, the money and the condo."

In February 1990 she gave Flynn some cheesecake snapshots of herself provocatively attired in a bikini. Days later, she confided to Pierce that she was in love with the boy. On February 5, she told the stunned Flynn of her feelings, complaining bitterly about her "abusive" husband. Around Valentine's Day, with Greg out of town on a ski trip, she invited Pierce and Flynn over to her condo to watch videos. After viewing *9½ Weeks*, Pam led the boy to her bedroom where she slipped into turquoise lingerie and reenacted the scene in the film where Kim Basinger dances seductively for Mickey Rourke. After making love, Pam intimated to Flynn that there could only be a repeat session if Greg were dead. Fearful of losing his 23-year-old lover, Flynn finally agreed to enlist Lattime and Randall in the murder. When difficulties aborted an earlier attempt on Greg's life, Smart accused the youth of not "loving her" and threatened to end the relationship. Flynn tearfully promised to try harder next time.

According to her co-conspirators, Smart instructed the boys to make the murder appear as though Greg had interrupted a break-in. She agreed to their asking price of $1000 each to be paid on an "installment plan": $500 down for each with the balance to be paid in weekly increments of $50. Anything they stole from the apartment they could keep. Pam refused to buy them a gun, but did give Flynn $30 for hollow-point ammunition. Lattime supplied a .38 caliber snubnose revolver from his father's gun collection. On May 1, 1990, a week before their first wedding anniversary, Pam admonished the boys in killing Greg not to get blood on the sofa or traumatize Halen by letting the dog see the murder. She left the back door of the condo open and went to her alibi, a school board meeting. Flynn and Randall were waiting for Greg when he returned home around 9:00 p.m. As he

entered, they shoved him into the foyer on his knees. Randall held Greg down by his hair at knifepoint as Flynn pressed the gun inches away from the kneeling man's head. Uttering, "God, forgive me," Billy Flynn shot his lover's husband once in the head. The murderers, fleeing with items stuffed in a black pillowcase, were picked up in a car by Lattime and 20-year-old Raymond Fowler. When Pam returned later that night to Apt. 4E in the Summerhill Condominiums, she found Greg's body. Two days later, she stuffed Greg's personal belongings in plastic garbage bags and delivered them to his grieving parents.

Pam's lack of emotion over Greg's death, the $140,000 in insurance money she stood to collect, and her ceaseless comments to the media about the crime aroused police suspicion. An anonymous call received by authorities on May 14, 1990, linked Pam to Cecelia Pierce, the adult's affair with a minor, and the murder for insurance angle. Police contacted Pierce who, after initially refusing to incriminate Pam, agreed to wear a wire in four conversations with her. During one such meeting between the two in July 1990 Pam allegedly acknowledged to Pierce key details about her role in the murder. Flynn, Randall, and Lattime were picked up in June 1990 and cut a deal in early 1991 which let them plead guilty to a lesser second degree murder charge carrying a maximum sentence of 40 years, with 12 years deferred for good behavior. Raymond Fowler was subsequently arrested and charged as an accomplice to first degree murder. They would join 21 other witnesses in testifying against Pam. Smart was arrested in August 1990 and charged as an accomplice to first degree murder.

Opening arguments for the most

highly publicized trial in New Hampshire history began on March 5, 1991. In addition to international press coverage, the proceedings were televised locally. The defense, while acknowledging the affair between Flynn and Smart, called the conspiracy theory "the most vile concoction ever" presented in a New Hampshire courtroom. Pam Smart was being framed by teenage "thrill killers" trying to save themselves from life imprisonment. Smart took the stand and dismissed the incriminating tapes as her attempt to elicit more information about a police investigation from which she was excluded. She pretended to know details about the murder to prompt Pierce into giving her information. She withheld telling police of her affair with Flynn out of fear they would automatically conclude she was involved in the murder. Shortly after 1:00 p.m. on March 23, 1991, after listening to 12 days of testimony and deliberating more than 13 hours, the jury found Smart guilty. In accordance with state law, she was sentenced to life imprisonment with no chance of parole.

Steadfastly protesting her innocence, Smart maintains that she is a "victim of [a] brutal media blitz." She busies herself teaching high school courses to fellow-inmates for $1.50 a week and contributing to the "Friends of Pamela Smart Newsletter" published by her family. On August 7, 1991, more than 300 people paid $10 each to attend a fund-raising picnic on her behalf. The highlight of the evening was Pam's address to her supporters via a phone-loudspeaker hookup from her cellblock in which she decried the injustice of her sentence. On October 12, 1993, the U.S. Supreme Court refused to hear Smart's appeal.

524. Englade, Ken. *Deadly Lessons*. St. Martin's Paperbacks ed. New York: St. Martin's Paperbacks, 1991. 293 pp.: ill.; 18 cm.; paperback.

_____. [Same as 524.] London: Grafton, 1993. 293 pp., [8]pp. of plates: ill., ports.; 18 cm.; paperback.

Paperback original quickly written from newspaper accounts to cash in on the media frenzy surrounding the case. "The true story of the seductress, the student, and a cold-blooded murder in New England."—Cover

525. Maynard, Joyce. *To Die For*. New York: Dutton, 1992. 240 pp.; 23 cm.

_____. [Same as 525.] New York: Signet, 1993. 366 pp.; 18 cm.; paperback.

Fictional account based on the Smart case.

526. Sawicki, Stephen. *Teach Me to Kill*. New York: Avon Books, 1991. xi, 288 pp., [8]pp. of plates: ill.; 18 cm.; paperback.

Freelance magazine writer Sawicki's account is based on police reports, trial transcripts, and interviews with the principals including the murdered man's parents. The better of the two case histories written to date. "The shocking true story of Pamela Smart—the schoolteacher who gave lessons in love ... and murder!"—Cover

Smith, George Joseph
(a.k.a. "Brides in the Bath Murderer," "Bluebeard of the Bath," "George Baker," "John Lloyd," "Henry Williams," "George Oliver Love," "George Oliver Lodge," "George Rose," "Charles Oliver James")

Born January 11, 1872, at Bethnal Green, London, England. Executed August 13, 1915. Confidence man. England (Herne Bay, Blackpool, London); 3 murders; drowning; July 13, 1912–December 18, 1914.

"I may be a bit peculiar but I am certainly no murderer."—Smith's denial in court to the charge of murder

Infamous British "Bluebeard" who drowned three wives in their baths in order to profit from their wills and insurance. As a youth George Joseph Smith confined his criminal activities to petty theft and larcenies, but in 1899 he graduated to bigamy and began a series of "marriages" designed initially to defraud his "wives." On August 26, 1910, Smith (posing under the alias of "Henry Williams") married Beatrice ("Bessie") Constance Annie Mundy, 33. Within three weeks he absconded with her inheritance, leaving in his wake a vicious note accusing his bride of having given him a venereal disease. In a remarkable and tragic coincidence, Mundy ran across her missing husband nearly two years later on March 14, 1912, at the seaside town of Weston-super-Mare. Renewing their marriage, the pair settled in Herne Bay where on July 8, 1912, Smith had a solicitor draw up mutual wills. The next day, Smith visited an ironmonger, selected a £2 bathtub, and had it delivered to the house they rented. After establishing with a local doctor that his wife was subject to "epileptic seizures," Smith drowned Mundy as she bathed on the morning of July 13, 1912. A coroner's jury ruled she had suffered an epileptic seizure during her bath and drowned. As the sole beneficiary of Mundy's will, Smith received over £2000.

Resurfacing in the coastal town of Southsea in October 1913, Smith ingratiated himself to 25-year-old nurse Alice Burnham when he learned her father was holding £100 in trust for her. Over her family's objections, Burnham married Smith on November 4, 1913. One month later he insured his bride's life for £500. Moving to Blackpool,

Smith was adamant that the rooms they rent contain a bath. As with Mundy, he insisted his wife consult a doctor concerning her "severe headaches." On December 12, 1913, Burnham met the same fate as her predecessor. The coroner's verdict of accidental death cleared the way for Smith to collect her life insurance. Following a fraudulent marriage in September 1914, Smith, now posing as land agent "John Lloyd," looked for another victim in the seaside resort of Clifton. There he met 38-year-old spinster Margaret Elizabeth Lofty, insured her life for £700, and married her on December 17, 1914, in Bath. The next day Lofty was found dead in her bath in a London flat. Death was attributed to an attack of syncope.

Lofty's death, reported in the *News of the World*, was noticed by Alice Burnham's father who contacted police. Their investigations established Smith's identity and linked the three drowning deaths. Smith was arrested on February 1, 1915, and ultimately charged with the murder of Beatrice ("Bessie") Annie Constance Mundy. Tried in London's Old Bailey beginning on June 22, 1915, Smith contended that the deaths were only "phenomenal coincidences" and constantly interrupted the proceedings to angrily maintain that the numerous witnesses against him had been bribed by authorities. Noted pathologist Dr. Bernard Spilsbury explained that the murders were committed by grabbing the victims' ankles and lifting their feet into the air. The sudden intake of water into the submerged mouth and nostrils of the women caused almost instantaneous shock and unconsciousness. A jury needed only 25 minutes on July 1, 1915, to find the "Brides in the Bath Murderer" guilty and he was sentenced to death. An unrepentant Smith was hanged at Maidstone County Prison on August 13, 1915.

527. La Bern, Arthur J. *The Life and Death of a Ladykiller.* London: L. Frewin, 1967. 175 pp., [8]pp. of plates: ill., ports.; 22 cm.

A factually accurate novelization of the case which is rich in period flavor. Includes the text of Smith's infamous letter to wife and first victim "Bessie" Mundy in which he accuses her of giving him a venereal disease.

528. Lyons, Frederick J. *George Joseph Smith: The Brides in the Bath Case.* The Rogue's Gallery. London: Duckworth, 1935. 200 pp.; 19 cm.

Interesting (if overly florid) account of Smith's life and crimes that contends (perhaps erroneously) that the murderer was a "dual personality" as manifested by his ability to commit heinous crimes then vociferously deny them all the way to the gallows. Includes a detailed chronology.

529. Sims, George R. *The Bluebeard of the Bath: A Story of Marriage and Murder.* London: C. A. Pearson, 1915. 128 pp.

According to Arthur J. La Bern (*The Life and Death of a Ladykiller,* see 527) the only library copy of this account of the Smith case was in the British Museum and "was destroyed by enemy action during World War II."

530. Watson, Eric R., ed. *Trial of George Joseph Smith.* Notable British Trials. Edinburgh; London: W. Hodge, 1922. x, 329 pp., [12] leaves of plates: ill., ports.; facsims.; 22 cm.

———. [Same as 530.] Notable British Trials. Toronto: Canada Law Book, 1922. x, 329 pp., [12] leaves of plates: ill., ports., facsims.; 22 cm.

———. [Same as 530.] Notable British Trials. Calcutta: Butterworth, 1922. x, 329 pp., [12] leaves of plates: ill., ports., facsims.; 22 cm.

———. [Same as 530.] Notable British Trials. London: W. Hodge, 1949. x, 329

pp., [12] leaves of plates: ill., ports., facsims.; 22 cm. (Reprint of 1922 edition.)

Excellent entry in the Notable British Trial Series which fully documents the murder trial *Rex v. George Joseph Smith* which took place in the Central Criminal Court, London, June 22–July 1, 1915. A chronology of "Leading Dates in the G. J. Smith Case" is included.

Smith, Perry Edward
(a.k.a. "Perry O'Parsons," "Bob Turner")

Born October 27, 1928, in Huntington, Nevada. Executed April 14, 1965. Drifter. Holcomb, Kansas; 4 murders; shotgun, knife; November 15, 1959.

"I didn't want to harm the man. I thought he was a very nice gentleman. I thought so right up to the moment I cut his throat."—Smith, in an early confession, commenting on Herbert W. Clutter; *see also* Hickock, Richard Eugene.

Snider, Paul Leslie
(a.k.a. "The Jewish Pimp")

Born April 15, 1952. Died August 14, 1980. Promoter. Los Angeles, California; 1 murder; 12 gauge Mossberg pump shotgun; August 14, 1980.

Film: Star 80 (US, 1983), a Warner/Ladd production directed by Bob Fosse. Cast includes Mariel Hemingway (Dorothy Stratten), Eric Roberts (Paul Snider), and Cliff Robertson (Hugh Hefner).

Television: "Death of a Centerfold: The Dorothy Stratten Story" (1981), a two-hour, made-for-television movie, originally aired on NBC on November 1, 1981. Cast includes Jamie

Lee Curtis (Dorothy Stratten), Bruce Weitz (Paul Snider), and Mitchell Ryan (Hugh Hefner).

Video: Portrait of Dorothy Stratten (US, 1984), a 63-minute documentary released by Playboy Programs.

"That girl could make me a lot of money."

Case of murder-suicide in which an estranged husband killed his *Playboy* playmate wife. Dorothy Stratten (real name Dorothy Ruth Hoogstratten) was 17 years old when Paul Snider spotted her in late 1977 waitressing at a Dairy Queen in East Vancouver, Canada. Nine years older than the beautiful but unworldly Stratten, Snider (nicknamed the "Jewish Pimp") was known around town as a small time drug pusher and police informer who lived off women. Soon after their meeting Snider began a sexual relationship with the teenager with an eye towards turning her stunning good looks into big money. Though uncomfortable with Snider's request that she pose naked for photos he planned to submit to *Playboy* magazine's national hunt for its 25th Anniversary Playmate, Stratten relented after six months of steadily increasing pressure from her lover. Two weeks after receiving the photos, *Playboy* publisher Hugh Hefner had Stratten flown to Los Angeles for a professional photo shoot. Impressed by her natural beauty and innocence, Hefner featured Stratten as Playmate of the Month in August 1979 and eventually selected her as Playmate of the Year for 1980. Enamored of the Los Angeles lifestyle, Snider moved quickly to consolidate his hold over his rising star. On June 1, 1979, he married Stratten in Las Vegas, afterwards announcing that as her husband and manager he now deserved 50 percent of her earnings for life. As Stratten's career blossomed with roles in movies, Snider was relegated to promoting wet underwear and tee-shirt contests in local bars. After meeting and falling in love with film director Peter Bogdanovich, Stratten decided to end her marriage. On August 14, 1980, she agreed to meet Snider at their house in West Los Angeles to discuss a financial settlement. Hours later their naked bodies were found in the bedroom where Snider had shotgunned Stratten in the face before turning the weapon on himself. Either before or after her death Stratten had been savagely sodomized on a handmade bondage rack found near the bed. The 20-year-old beauty was cremated and her ashes buried near Marilyn Monroe's grave in Westwood Cemetery. Fittingly, Hugh Hefner later purchased the plot next to Monroe's. Stratten's younger sister, Louise Hoogstratten, married Peter Bogdanovich on December 30, 1988.

531. Bogdanovich, Peter. *The Killing of the Unicorn: Dorothy Stratten (1960-1980.)* 1st ed. New York: W. Morrow, 1984. xvii, 186 pp.: ill.; 25 cm.

_____. [Same as 531.] London: Macdonald, 1985. 178 pp.; 21 cm.

Snyder, Ruth May
(a.k.a. "Ruth May Brown" [maiden name], "Momie," "Momsie," "Granite Woman," "Marble Woman," "Long Island Messalina," "Blonde Sinner," "Bloody Blonde")

Born March 27, 1895, in New York, New York. Executed January 12, 1928. Telephone operator, bookkeeper. Long Island, New York; 1 murder; bludgeon (sash weight), manual strangulation; March 20, 1927.

"Father, forgive them, for they know not what they do."—Snyder's last words

A tawdry sexual affair culminating in the murder of the woman's older husband which has inspired countless *noir* books and films. Ruth May Brown, a one-time telephone operator and typist, married her former boss Albert Edward Snyder, the art editor of *Motor Boating* magazine, on July 24, 1915. Never really sexually excited by the man 13 years her senior, Mrs. Snyder later admitted that she only married him because she liked the solitaire diamond engagement ring he offered her. A female child was born in November 1917 and in 1923 the family moved into a stylish three story house at 9327 222nd Street in Queens Village, Long Island. Over the years the marriage slowly disintegrated, no doubt hastened by Mrs. Snyder's impulsively extravagant spending habits and her husband's insistence that a photograph of his deceased former fiancée be hung over their bed. In June 1925, Mrs. Snyder, 30, was on a clothes buying trip in New York with a friend when she was introduced to her companion's acquaintance, Henry Judd Gray, a 32-year-old traveling salesman with the Bien Jolie Corset Company. Gray, an unhappily married man with one child, became instantly enamored of the "flapper" with peroxided blonde hair, and soon the couple were making love on a regular basis in New York's Waldorf Astoria Hotel while Mrs. Snyder's daughter, unknowingly used to camouflage her mother's illicit activity, waited in the lobby. Gray referred to his married lover as a queen, masochistically fawned over her, and in moments of passion called her "Momsie" and "Momie." In a series of sophomoric love letters and clandestine meetings,

Mrs. Snyder called the diminutive Gray "Lover Boy" and spun vivid accounts of the abuse she allegedly suffered at the hands of her hated husband. According to statements later made by Gray, Mrs. Snyder attempted to murder her husband on at least three occasions in 1926 after taking out a $100,000 life insurance policy on him.

The affair had lasted nearly two years when Mrs. Snyder began to increase the pressure on Gray to help murder her husband by withholding sex and threatening to tell his wife of their relationship. Gray, who had inexorably degenerated into an alcoholic under the strain and guilt of the affair, reluctantly agreed to help his lover. At "Momsie's" direction, Gray purchased a vial of chloroform to render Albert Snyder senseless, and a five-pound, foot-long sash weight while on a business trip in Kingston, New York. The next day Gray bought a coil of picture wire and, fortified by a quart of rye, waited outside the Long Island house of his intended victim before losing his nerve and leaving. Given a final ultimatum by Mrs. Snyder, Gray arranged an alibi in Syracuse, New York, and traveled by train back to New York on March 19, 1927. Carrying a satchel containing the sash weight, picture frame wire, and the bottle of chloroform, Gray let himself into the Snyders' empty house, hid in his lover's room, and drank heavily while waiting for the couple to return from a party. Arriving shortly after 2:00 a.m., Albert Snyder retired to his bedroom while his wife conferred with Gray. Around 3:00 a.m., Gray entered the sleeping man's room and struck him a glancing blow with the sash weight. Snyder fought back and as Gray strangled him with a tie, Mrs. Snyder continued bludgeoning him with the sash weight. Afterwards, the killers stuck cloth saturated with choloroform into the dazed man's mouth and nostrils and bound his hands with wire and his feet with a neck tie. Still fearful that her husband was alive, his wife strangled him with the picture wire. The pair disarranged the room to make it appear like a robbery/murder and Gray tied up his lover before leaving the scene.

Detectives noted inconsistencies in Mrs. Snyder's account of the crime and Gray, picked up at his hotel in Syracuse, soon crumbled after police informed him that his lover had confessed to being involved in the murder though implicating him as the instigator and actual killer. The bloodstained sash was found in the basement of the Long Island home and Gray confessed to throwing the satchel containing the other weapons off the train into the Hudson River. Their petition to be tried separately denied, the pair's sensational trial began on April 18, 1927, in the Supreme Court at Long Island City, Queens County. Throughout the 18-day proceeding, each defendant tried to shift the majority of the blame onto the other as the tawdry drama was played out in a courtroom jammed with celebrities like Peggy Hopkins Joyce, the Marquis and Marquise of Queensbury, and Fannie Hurst. Counterfeit admission tickets to the courtroom were sold for $50 each and street hawkers offered miniature sash weights mounted on stickpins for ten cents a piece. On May 9, 1927, the jury found the pair guilty of first degree murder and they were subsequently sentenced to death in the electric chair. Moments after the verdict, Mrs. Snyder (who spent much of the trial dressed in widow's black fingering a crucifix) converted to Roman Catholicism in the slim hope that New York Governor

Alfred E. Smith would not allow a fellow Catholic to be executed. While at Sing Sing awaiting the outcome of their lengthy appeals process, both penned death house autobiographies. Mrs. Snyder's *My Own True Story—So Help Me God!* was syndicated in the Hearst papers and sold in pamphlet form on newsstands for a quarter. In it, the convicted murderess likened herself to Christ stating that "I, too have been betrayed by a Judas (only there were two *d*s in mine)." Gray's autobiography chronicling his moral disintegration into adultery, alcoholism, and murder was aptly entitled *Doomed Ship*. Their appeals denied, Mrs. Snyder was the first to be electrocuted at Sing Sing on January 12, 1928, with her submissive lover executed minutes later. Thomas Howard, an enterprising photographer on special assignment for the New York paper *Daily News*, posed as a reporter and gained admittance as a witness in the death chamber. Outfitted with an ankle camera secreted under his trouser leg and seated within 12 feet of Mrs. Snyder as she sat strapped into the electric chair, Thomas was able to surreptitiously snap one of the most famous pictures in the history of true crime as thousands of volts of electricity coursed through her body. For his effort and ingenuity, the reporter was given a $100 bonus and reassigned to the paper's prestigious bureau in Washington, D.C.

532. Cook, Fred J. *The Girl in the Death Cell.* New York: Fawcett, 1953. 176 pp.; 18 cm.; paperback.

533. Kobler, John, ed. *The Trial of Ruth Snyder and Judd Gray: Edited with a History of the Case.* 1st ed. Garden City, N.Y.: Doubleday, Doran, 1938. xiii, 377 pp.: ill., plates, ports.; 24 cm.

Kobler's excellent summary of the case and chronology serves as a preface to the trial transcript. In addition to several rare photos, an appendix reproduces some of the correspondence between Snyder and Gray discovered by police. The definitive study of the case.

Sobhraj, Charles
(a.k.a. "The Bikini Killer," "Damon Seaman," "Alain Gautier," "Henricus Bitanja," "Alain Gittienne")

Born April 6, 1944, in Saigon, South Vietnam. Confidence man, thief, smuggler. India, Thailand, Nepal; 10 murders (possibly 16); drugs, strangulation; September 1972–July 1976.

Theatre: Serpent Kills (1989), a play by Blake Brooker and Jim Millan, was presented as a co-production of the Canadian-based One Yellow Rabbit and Toronto's Crow's Theatre in 1989.

"What makes a man a murderer? Either they have too much feeling and cannot control themselves, or they have no feelings. It is one of the two."

International confidence man, smuggler, drug dealer, and serial killer responsible for at least 10 deaths in numerous Asian countries. The illegitimate son of a Vietnamese mother and an Indian father born in Saigon during the Japanese occupation, Sobhraj was well known to authorities even as a child. By the time he travelled to Marseilles, France, to be with his mother and stepfather, Sobhraj had become a chronic bedwetter whose career as a thief and confidence man was blossoming. Twice imprisoned in France for auto theft, Sobhraj married upon his release but soon tired of a life of dull respectability. With funds stolen from his sister, Sobhraj and his wife

established themselves in Bombay, India, in the early 1970s where he embarked upon a career of smuggling and stealing passports from American hippies. After escaping detention in Pakistan, Sobhraj committed his first murder in September 1972 while attempting to enter India. He drugged the driver of his hired car, placed the man in the trunk, and later finding him dead from suffocation, dumped the body in a river. Resurfacing in Istanbul in November 1973, Sobhraj enlisted the aid of his younger brother Guy to drug and rob rich tourists. Arrested in Athens, Greece, Sobhraj escaped and entered the heroin business in Delhi where he killed a local pusher. In Delhi, Sobhraj met a Canadian girl, Marie-Andree Leclerc, who would thereafter figure prominently in his life as a partner and lover.

Operating out of a flat in Delhi, Sobhraj enlisted several Western dropouts to run drugs while he also maintained a lucrative operation in stolen gems. On October 13, 1975, Sobhraj (with the aid of an Indian confederate) killed American Teresa Knowlton after he suspected her of shortchanging him in a drug deal. Soon afterwards, a Turkish competitor was beaten to extract information, his neck broken, and his body burned. The pair were waiting in Bangkok when the dealer's contact, Stephanie Parry, arrived. Sobhraj drugged the French woman then strangled her. On December 11, 1975, Dutch tourists Cornelia Hemker and Henricus Bitanja arrived at Sobhraj's apartment in Bangkok where he had invited them to stay weeks earlier after befriending them in Hong Kong. Sobhraj drugged the pair, and five days later he and the Indian strangled them to death and burned their bodies. Days before Christmas 1975, the burnt bodies of two tourists were found near Katmandu close to a hotel where Sobhraj was using the passport of his Dutch victim Henricus Bitanja. Questioned by police, Sobhraj slipped out of Nepal before followup investigations could be made. In early January 1976, Sobhraj murdered Israeli Allen Aren Jacobs in Goa for his passport. He later poisoned three Frenchmen (they survived), drugged a schoolteacher in Hong Kong for his letter of credit, and was arrested there with false passports. Sobhraj bribed his way out of detention and similarly escaped arrest in Penang for cashing stolen traveler's checks. After losing $200,000 gambling in a Rouen casino, Sobhraj returned to Bombay where he and his lover Leclerc planned to drug and rob more tourists. Not discouraged by accidentally killing French tourist Luke Solomon with a lethal drug overdose, Sobhraj befriended a group of 60 French students in Agra and proceeded to poison them all with pills he told them would "prevent dysentery." They survived and Sobhraj was arrested on July 5, 1976, bringing to an end an almost four-year career of murder which claimed an estimated 10 victims.

In August 1978, Sobhraj was sentenced to seven years in New Delhi's Tihar Prison for the murder of Luke Solomon. On May 3, 1982, Sobhraj and his mistress Leclerc were sentenced to life imprisonment at Varanasi for the 1976 murder of Israeli tourist Allen Jacobs; however, both were acquitted following a successful appeal in 1983. Leclerc, suffering from terminal ovarian cancer, was allowed by Indian authorities to return to Canada for treatment in July 1983. She died in Levis on April 20, 1984. Sobhraj, fighting extradition to Thailand where he would most certainly be executed,

escaped from Tihar on March 16, 1986, after giving guards pieces of a drugged birthday cake. The international serial killer was recaptured on April 6, 1986, as he celebrated his 42nd birthday at a restaurant in Goa. By pleading innocent to the 1986 escape, Sobhraj used India's elephantine court structure against itself. During eight years spent awaiting the start of his May 1994 trial, Sobhraj used his wealth to buy special privileges at Tihar where he is respectfully addressed by prisoners and staff alike as "Charles-sahib." According to Thailand law if Sobhraj is not brought to trial within 20 years of the murders in that country, the charges will be automatically dropped. Sobhraj estimates that the 107 witnesses he has lined up for his defense on the Indian prison break charge will easily take two years to question. If so, Sobhraj could be free in 1996 even if found guilty of escaping prison and sentenced to the maximum ten-year sentence which he has already served while awaiting trial.

534. Neville, Richard, and Clarke, Julie. *The Life and Crimes of Charles Sobhraj.* London: J. Cape, 1979. xiv, 351 pp., [8] leaves of plates: ill.; 23 cm.

_____. [Same as 534, but U.S. ed. retitled: *Charles Sobhraj.*] New York: Pocket Books, 1979. viii, 374 pp., [8] leaves of plates: ill.; 18 cm.; paperback.

_____. [Same as 534.] London: Pan Books, 1980. xii, 352 pp., [8]pp. of plates; 18 cm.; paperback. (Also a 1989 printing.)

_____. [Same as 534, but retitled: *Bad Blood: The Life and Crimes of Charles Sobhraj.*] London: Pan Books, 1980. xiii, 353 pp., [8]pp. of plates: ill., 1 facsim., ports., 1 plan; 18 cm.; paperback.

_____. [Same as 534, but retitled: *Shadow of the Cobra: The Life and Crimes of Charles Sobhraj.*] London: Penguin, 1989. xii, 362 pp.; 18 cm.; paperback.

Sobhraj confesses to the Thailand murders claiming he was well paid by a heroin king to eliminate rivals in the international drug trade. The authors conclude that Sobhraj is a "brilliant psychopath."

535. Thompson, Thomas. *Serpentine.* 1st ed. Garden City, N.Y.: Doubleday, 1979. xii, 563 pp.; 24 cm.

_____. [Same as 535.] London: Macdonald Futura, 1980. xii, 659 pp.; 24 cm.

_____. [Same as 535.] London: Macdonald Futura, 1980. xii, 659 pp.; 18 cm. ("A Futura/Jade book"); paperback.

_____. [Same as 535.] New York: Dell, 1981. 639 pp., [2] leaves of plates: ports.; 18 cm.; paperback.

Meticulously detailed account written by a former *Life* bureau chief posted in Paris. Definitive.

Sodeman, Arnold Karl

Born June 12, 1900, in Australia. Executed June 1, 1936. Laborer. Australia; 4 murders; strangulation; November 8, 1930–December 1, 1935.

"The only reason it is children is because adults would not go away with me. I am sure it would make no difference if it were an adult if I could lure them away."—Sodeman, explaining his choice of victims

Australian child killer with a history of mental illness whose execution sparked debate over the legal implications of insanity. On November 8, 1930, 12-year-old Mena Griffiths was last seen leaving Fawkner Park playground in the Melbourne suburb of South Yarra with an unknown man. The next day her strangled body was found on the bathroom floor of a vacant house, a gag made from part of her underwear tied across her mouth. Griffiths, unlike the killer's next three victims, had been sexually assaulted. A

check of sex offenders recently discharged from jail led to the arrest of Robert James McMahon. Released from Pentridge Gaol three weeks before after serving six years for an assault with intent to rape, McMahon maintained his innocence and witnesses failed to identify him in a line-up. McMahon appeared without counsel before the coroner's court in Melbourne on December 30, 1930, and despite giving a plausible alibi (that police never checked) was committed for trial. The case was dropped when an investigation produced eight witnesses that placed McMahon miles away at Leeton on the day of the murder. McMahon was released on February 18, 1931, after spending 76 days in jail. During his incarceration the killer struck again.

On January 10, 1931, the body of 16-year-old Adeline Hazel Wilson was found among grassy weeds in a vacant lot near her home in Ormond, exactly one mile from where Griffiths' body had been found nine weeks earlier. The similarities between the two killings were seemingly apparent yet police initially failed to make the connection. Strangled like Griffith, Wilson had a stocking thrust in her mouth held in place by a gag made from a torn strip of her underwear knotted tightly at the back of her neck. Placed face down in the grass with her hands tied behind her back and feet bound, the girl had not been raped. No arrests were made although police at one time considered Wilson's father as their prime suspect. The killer was silent for almost four years when he next struck on January 1, 1935, at the seaside resort of Inverloch. The body of 12-year-old Ethel Belshaw, strangled and bound in the exact manner of Wilson, was found lying face down in long grass near the beach. Authorities interviewed 18,000 people before focusing their investigation on the 18-year-old brother of one of the dead girl's friends. He was subsequently cleared at a coroner's court where Arnold Karl Sodeman, a man who took part in the search for Belshaw, testified that he had seen the girl on the day she disappeared.

Six-year-old Jane Rushmer disappeared on December 1, 1935, as she was leaving a playground in Leongatha. She was found the next day one half mile from her home face down under a ti-tree bush strangled and bound like previous victims Wilson and Belshaw. Witnesses reported seeing a man riding a bicycle with a little girl on the handlebars in the area where the body was found. Sixteen miles away in a construction camp in North Dumbalk, a coworker of Arnold Sodeman jokingly told him that a man fitting his description was seen riding a bike like the one he owned in the area where Rushmer was killed. The usually docile Sodeman reacted so angrily that his colleague contacted police. Sodeman, the married father of an eight-year-old daughter, was questioned on December 5, 1935, and subsequently confessed to murdering all four girls. Prior to being tried for Rushmer's murder at Melbourne's criminal court on February 17–18, 1936, Sodeman was examined by psychiatrists to determine his competency to stand trial. Their interviews with the self-confessed killer revealed multiple cases of familial insanity on Sodeman's paternal side (his grandfather, father, and brother had all died in mental institutions). Sodeman spoke of struggling to control his "mania" to kill which was unleashed when he drank. At trial, Sodeman pleaded insanity and three doctors (two of them government

medical officers) agreed that the killer was mentally ill and insane at the time of the murders. Nevertheless, Sodeman was found guilty on February 18, 1936, and following failed appeals was hanged at Pentridge Gaol on June 1, 1936. A postmortem examination of Sodeman's brain revealed the early stages of leptomeningitis, a brain disease.

536. Bourke, J.P., and Sonenberg, D.S. *Insanity and Injustice*. Milton, Q.: Jacaranda Press, 1969. 135 pp., [4]pp. of plates: ill.; 21 cm.

Bourke, Sodeman's counsel during his trial for the murder of June Rushmer, examines the legal issue of insanity (defined by the McNaghten Rules) as applied to his client's case. Includes the essay "Sodeman and Medicine" by Dr. L. Howard Whittaker, visiting senior specialist (psychiatry) repatriation department of social studies at the University of Melbourne and lecturer in criminology at the University of Melbourne, Victoria. Crime scene photographs of Sodeman's four victims illustrate the remarkable similarities between the murders.

Sorrentino, Paul

Born circa 1964. High school student. Miami County, Kansas; 1 murder; shotgun; April 17, 1980.

"Boy, that was easy."—Statement attributed to Sorrentino by accomplice James Crumm, Jr. after the former helped murder Christen Hobson; *see also* Hobson, Sueanne Sallee.

"Son of Sam Murders [or] Killings" *see* Berkowitz, David

Speck, Richard Franklin (a.k.a. "Richard Benjamin Speck" [birth name], "Ebb

Dangler," "Johnson," "David
Stayton," "Richard Franklin
Lindbergh," "B. Brian,"
"Spike," "Prisoner CO1065")

Born December 6, 1941, in Kirkwood, Illinois. Died December 5, 1991.
Merchant seaman (deckhand), carpenter. Chicago, Illinois; 8 murders; ligature, and manual strangulation; knife;
July 14, 1966.

"I hit those girls so fast that they
never knew what happened."—Statement allegedly made by Speck to a
jailer in Peoria during his April 1967
murder trial

Described at the scene by Cook
County coroner Andrew Toman as "the
crime of the century," Richard Speck's
systematic slaughter of eight student
nurses on the southeast side of Chicago
on July 14, 1966, is credited with having brought the concept of mass murder to the forefront of America's
national consciousness. On August 1,
1966, slightly more than two weeks
after the carnage in Chicago, 25-year-
old Charles Joseph Whitman climbed
to the top of the Texas Tower on the
University of Texas–Austin campus
and for 80 minutes sprayed the surrounding streets with gunfire. Whitman managed to wound 31 and kill 16
before police shot him to death. Considered together, these sensational one
event multi-victim crimes marked the
beginning of the public's fascination
with mass murder and presaged the
even more frightening phenomenon of
serial murder.

One of eight children, Speck was
born in Kirkwood, Illinois, on December 6, 1941. The death of his father in
1947 initiated the process by which the
six-year-old Speck would be transformed from a normal child into a psychopathic rapist and murderer. With

the remarriage of his mother on May
10, 1950, the family moved to Dallas,
Texas. Speck's real father, the only close
relationship he would ever have, was
replaced by an alcoholic stepfather who
physically and psychologically abused
the youngster. Speck developed into a
sulky loner who began drinking heavily at 13, the age of his first arrest for
burning rags in a lot. At 16, the acne-
scarred teenager flunked out of technical school, began running and drinking
with a crowd of older men, and was
constantly in trouble for fighting in
bars. By 19, Speck had already been
treated five separate times for gonor-
rhea. When he finally left Dallas in
March 1966, his rap sheet totalled 41
arrests for charges ranging from being
drunk and disorderly, to break-ins and
committing violence against women.
Speck married 15-year-old high school
freshman Shirley Annette Malone on
January 19, 1962, and when not spending half of the four years they remained
married in jail or prison, either beat his
wife up or forced her to have sex with
him four to five times a day. He was
serving time in a McKinney, Texas, jail
for disturbing the peace on July 5,
1962, when his daughter was born.
Speck refused to pay either his wife's
hospital bills or donate blood to defray
costs. The pair divorced in March 1966.

Speck was on parole from a Texas
penitentiary after serving 16 months
for forgery and burglary when he
accosted a woman at knifepoint in
Dallas on January 4, 1965. Apprehended, Speck was sentenced to 490
days for aggravated assault, but an
administrative error released him early
on July 2, 1965. On March 8, 1966, he
botched a break-in attempt at a Dallas
grocery store and fled to his sister's
house in Illinois to escape arrest.
Weeks later on April 2, 1966, Speck

raped a 66-year-old woman at knife-point in her Monmouth, Illinois, home. Mary Kay Pierce, a 32-year-old bar maid in Monmouth, disappeared after work on April 9, 1966. Four days later her body was discovered in a hog house behind the tavern. A heavy blow to the stomach had ruptured her liver. Interviewed once by police, Speck fled to Chicago before he could be reinterviewed. Items recovered from his room conclusively identified him as the rapist of the elderly woman.

Speck surfaced in the skid row section of Chicago's southeast side where he spent his days drinking heavily and half-heartedly looking for work as a deckhand at the National Maritime Union Hiring Hall. Standing 6'1" and weighing 160 pounds, Speck's pronounced Southern drawl, pockmarked face, and heavily tattooed body clearly distinguished him from the other residents of the squalid Shipyard Inn. A tattoo on his left forearm prophetically read "Born to Raise Hell" and later proved instrumental in identifying him to police. Directly across from the hiring hall near South Chicago Community Hospital stood a block of three townhouses in the Jeffery Manor section of East 100th Street which the hospital rented to accommodate some senior nursing students and a few Filipino exchange students. Speck noted the daily routine of the women as he waited to be assigned to an ore ship on Lake Michigan.

On July 13, 1966, Speck took a .22 caliber Rohm pistol from a 53-year-old mother of 10 he had forced at knifepoint to have sex with him in his room at the Shipyard Inn. After spending the remainder of the day drinking and popping amphetamines in the downstairs bar, Speck returned to his room, dressed in black and, armed with the stolen pistol and a three-inch switchblade knife, walked to the nurses' residence at 2319 East 100th Street around 10:30 p.m. Gaining entrance to the two-story townhouse by prying open the back window with the knife and sliding the screen to unlock the door, Speck climbed the stairs and knocked on the door of the bedroom shared by two 23-year-old Filipino exchange students, Corazon Amurao and Merlita Gargullo. Speck pushed past Amurao as she opened the door and, brandishing the gun at the frightened women, forced the pair at gunpoint to lead him down the hall to where Filipino exchange student Valentina Pasion, 23, and senior nursing students Pamela Wilkening, 20, Nina Jo Schmale, 24, and Patricia Matusek, 20, shared a bedroom. Assuring the women that he would not harm them, Speck was demanding money from them to finance a trip to New Orleans when he heard a noise downstairs. He was waiting at the front door when 22-year-old Gloria Jean Davey returned from her date around 11:30 p.m. She too was forced to join the others in the upstairs bedroom. Using his knife to slice a bedsheet into strips, Speck tied the seven students' hands and feet as they sat on the bedroom floor. At 12:45 a.m., he led Pamela Wilkening out of the room and raped her in another bedroom. Twenty minutes later Suzanne Farris, 21, and Mary Ann Jordan, 20, returning from a night out, entered the bedroom containing the bound nurses. Speck confronted the pair and herded them into the bedroom containing the trussed-up Wilkening. At 3:30 a.m., four-and-a-half hours after breaking into the apartment, Speck left through the front door leaving it open. On his leisurely stroll back to his room at the Shipyard

Inn he tossed the knife into the Calumet River.

Chicago learned of the "crime of the century" around 5:30 a.m. when Corazon Amurao cautiously emerged from under the bed where she hid to escape the fate of her friends. Stepping around some bodies, she crawled out of a window onto an outside ledge and for 20 minutes screamed, "They are all dead! They are all dead! My friends are all dead! Oh, God, I'm the only one alive" before anyone took notice. Based on Amurao's description of the event and the position of the eight bodies in the apartment, police were able to reconstruct Speck's methodical carnage. Farris and Jordan, the last to arrive, were the first to die when they reacted to finding Wilkening tied spreadeagled on the floor of the bedroom. Speck, stabbing Farris 18 times in the chest and back, strangled her to death with a white nurse's stocking which was found tightly wound around her neck and knotted in the back. On the floor near her, Jordan had been stabbed once in the left eye, 3 times in the chest, and once in the neck. Wilkening died from a single stab wound through the heart.

Before returning to the bedroom where the six others were bound, Speck washed the blood off his hands and changed into a clean tee-shirt so as not to alarm the young women. He led Nina Schmale out of the room while the others tried to hide. The process continued in 20- to 30-minute intervals until around 3:30 a.m. when Speck, unaware that Amurao had hidden herself beneath a double bunk bed, left the apartment. Three rooms filled with bodies confronted investigators entering the townhouse. In the living room, Gloria Jean Davey lay face down on a sofa with her hands tied behind her, a strip of cloth cut from her blouse knotted around her neck. She had been sodomized and police later found one of Speck's tee-shirts wrapped in Davy's underwear. Patricia Matusek, still bleeding from a kick to her stomach, was found in the bathroom. A bedsheet was knotted around her neck. A bedroom down the hall from the room housing the bodies of the first three nurses to die, contained three more bodies. Valentina Pasion, dead from a six inch gash to the throat, lay on the floor covered by Merlita Gargullo's body. Stabbed four times in the neck, she had been strangled with a piece of bedsheet. Schmale, her face covered by a pillow, was bound and spreadeagled on the bed. She too had been strangled with a piece of bedsheet, but Speck had pricked her three times in the neck with a knife before she died.

Based on Amurao's detailed description of the murderer, police canvassed the area around the crime scene and came up with Speck's name at the union hiring hall. On July 16, 1966, police matched prints left at the murder scene with a set of Speck's obtained from the Coast Guard. That same day, every newspaper in Chicago ran a front page photo of the tattooed drifter identifying him as the murderer. Speck spent the day after the murder barhopping and making plans to jump a freight train out of Chicago. He moved to Chicago's northside skid row district and checked into room number 584 of the Starr Hotel on West Madison under the alias "B. Brian." Drinking heavily in his room at the flophouse on the night of July 16, Speck slashed his right wrist and the inside of his left elbow with a broken wine bottle. Taken by ambulance to Cook County Hospital, an emergency room physician recognized Speck from the newspaper photos and notified police. He was placed under arrest early on the morning of July 17 following surgery to stop his bleeding. Two days later, Corazan Amurao identified Speck as the murderer in his room at Cermak Memorial Hospital.

Before a trial date was set, a court-appointed panel of six psychiatrists determined that although Speck was a sociopathic alcoholic, he was sane at the time of the murders and competent to stand trial. Cook County Jail psychiatrist Marvin Ziporyn disagreed. Dr. Ziporyn, who spent over 100 hours interviewing Speck, maintained that a history of childhood head injury combined with severe alcohol and amphetamine abuse had rendered the 24 year old mentally ill at the time he committed the murders. Opening arguments in *The People of the State of Illinois versus Richard Franklin Speck* were heard in a Peoria courtroom on April 3, 1967. A court-appointed public defender argued Speck's innocence, produced two unimpressive alibi witnesses, and attacked the State's fingerprint evidence. Nothing, however, could overcome sole survivor Corazon Amurao's dramatic identification of Speck and her re-enactment of the crime. When the case went to the jury on April 15, 1967, they needed only 49 minutes to find Speck guilty of eight murders and to recommend the death penalty. On June 5, 1967, Speck was sentenced to death by electrocution, a sentence voided by the U.S. Supreme Court's June 1972 ruling declaring the death penalty unconstitutional. The new sentence imposed on Speck guaranteed that unless granted parole, which he was subsequently denied seven times, the mass murderer could not be released before the year 2564.

Incarcerated in Joliet's Stateville Prison, Inmate CO1065 kept to himself and, according to the warden, passed his time smoking, painting walls, and sleeping. Like fellow–Illinois murderer John Wayne Gacy, Speck took up oil painting in prison, but inexplicably quit around 1980. Perhaps in a bid to distance himself from the notoriety of his case, Speck burned the "Born to Raise Hell" tattoo off his forearm with a cigarette. On December 5th, 1991, one day before his fiftieth birthday, America's most famous mass murderer suffered a massive heart attack and died at the Silver Cross Hospital in Joliet. In May 1996, a video secretly recorded in Stateville Prison in 1988 surfaced which showed Speck taking drugs and having sex with a black inmate. In it, Speck admitted the murders and joked, "If they knew how much fun I was having in here, they would turn me loose."

537. Altman, Jack, and Ziporyn, Marvin. *Born to Raise Hell: The Untold Story of Richard Speck*. New York: Grove Press, 1967. 255 pp.: ill., facsims., ports.; 24 cm.

_____. [Same as 537, but paperback ed. retitled: *Speck: The Untold Story of a Mass Murderer*.] Introduction by Thomas M. Gannon. Delavan, Wis.: Hallberg, 1984. 271 pp.: ill., facsims.; 22 cm.; trade paperback.

Cook County Jail psychiatrist Ziporyn conducted numerous interviews with Speck before and during his trial. Speck gave the psychiatrist written authorization to tell his story which Ziporyn failed to mention to his superiors, the State, or the killer's defense attorneys.

538. Breo, Dennis L., and Martin, William J. *The Crime of the Century: Richard Speck and the Murder of Eight Student Nurses*. New York: Bantam Books, 1993. xiii, 462 pp., [16]pp. of plates: ill.; 18 cm.; paperback.

The authors expand their 1986 *Chicago Tribune Magazine* cover story documenting the twentieth anniversary of the murders into a paperback original based on interviews with the principals in the case (including survivor Corazon Amurao) and court records. The best book to date on the Speck murders.

539. Carpozi, George. *The Chicago Nurse Murders*. New York: A Banner Book, 1967. 240 pp. ; 18 cm.; paperback.

Starkweather, Charles Raymond
(a.k.a. "Little Red")

Born November 24, 1938, in Lincoln, Nebraska. Executed June 25, 1959. Warehouseman, garbage man. Lincoln and Bennet, Nebraska, and Douglas, Wyoming; 11 murders; 12 gauge shotgun, .410 shotgun, .22 caliber rifle, knife; December 1957–February 1958.

Film: Badlands (US, 1973), a Consolidated Color production produced, directed, and written by Terrence Malick. Cast includes Martin Sheen (Kit/Charles Starkweather) and Sissy Spacek (Holly). *The Boys Next Door* (US, 1985), a New World Pictures release directed by Penelope Spheeris. Cast includes Maxwell Caulfield (Roy Alston), Charlie Sheen (Bo Richards), and Patti D'Arbanville (Angie).

Television: "Murder in the Heartland" (1993), a two-part, four-hour miniseries, originally aired on ABC on May 3 and 4, 1993. Cast includes Tim Roth (Charlie Starkweather), Fairuza Balk (Caril Ann Fugate), and Brian Dennehy (John McArthur).

"If you pull the chain on a toilet, you can't blame it for flushing, can you?"—Starkweather, in a conversation with a psychiatrist, blaming society for his 11 murders

To the average Nebraskan of the late 1950s 19-year-old Charles Starkweather and his 14-year-old girlfriend Caril Ann Fugate represented teenage rebellion in its most terrifying aspect. Their eight-day, two-state murder spree resulted in the deaths of ten persons and virtually compelled the frightened residents of Lincoln to buy guns in record numbers and barricade their homes. At the height of the hysteria following the discovery of the bodies of millionaire C. Lauer Ward, his wife, and their maid, Nebraska Governor Anderson called out 200 members of the National Guard and had them patrol the streets of Lincoln in jeeps mounted with machine guns. Tensions in the area eased with the killers' arrest in Douglas, Wyoming, on February 1, 1958, but many unanswered questions still remained—chiefly, Starkweather's motivations for the murders and the true extent of Fugate's participation, if any, in them. Basking in his newfound notoriety, the former garbage man admitted that the murders were a way for him to "be somebody," an astute observation coming from a socially maladjusted teenager who affected the posture and mannerisms of his idol, actor James Dean, to escape the realities of his own life.

The third of eight children born into a poor, but happy, family in Lincoln, Nebraska, Charles Starkweather became an object of derision the first day he attended school. Classmates mercilessly jeered the undersized red-haired boy with the bowlegs and speech impediment. As he grew older, however, they did so at their own risk. To compensate for his size (5'5", 150 pounds), Starkweather became an accomplished street fighter who provoked altercations with larger boys in the hope of winning their respect when he beat them. Although his IQ was tested at 110, he was a poor student who always sat in the back of the class. An eye examination at 15 revealed Starkweather to be severely myopic and incapable of seeing objects over 20 feet away. The 16 year old dropped out of school in the ninth grade and, when not working as a garbage man for $42 a week, was either getting into fights or racing his car. Fascinated by James Dean, Starkweather aped the teen idol's troubled persona which seemed to dovetail perfectly with his own bouts of deep depression and violent outbursts. Caril Ann Fugate, 13 years old in 1956, was attracted to the moody teenager and began dating him over the objections of her parents. Starkweather showered the girl with gifts and threatened to kill anyone else who tried to date her. He later acknowledged to a psychiatrist that caring for Fugate almost made him stop hating himself.

Starkweather committed his first "non-spree" murder in the early morning of December 1, 1957. Needing cash to buy gifts for Fugate, he pulled into the Crest gas station outside Lincoln and entered the office carrying a .12 gauge shotgun. Twenty-one-year-old Robert Colvert was on duty and handed over $108 to the gun-wielding masked man who threatened to kill him. Starkweather then forced Colvert to drive down a little used dirt road on the outskirts of Lincoln and, ordering him out of the car, shot him first in the chest, reloaded, then pumped a round execution-style into the back of his head. Starkweather later confessed that murdering Colvert cemented his relationship with Fugate and made him feel as though he was beyond the laws of man.

Accounts vary widely as to what actually occurred on January 21, 1958, at the Lincoln home Fugate shared with her stepfather Marion Bartlett, mother Velda Bartlett, and her two-and-a-half-year-old half-sister Betty Jean. Soon after Starkweather arrived at 924 Belmont Street, a violent argument erupted between him and Velda Bartlett in which she ordered him to discontinue seeing Fugate. As the shouting match escalated to blows Starkweather shot the woman in the face and her husband Marion in the head. According to Starkweather, Fugate was present as he began striking Betty Jean Bartlett with the butt of the .22 rifle. He stopped the child's annoying cries of pain by repeatedly stabbing her in the throat with a foot-long kitchen knife. Afterwards, he used the knife on both Velda and Marion to make sure they were dead. Starkweather disposed of Velda in an outhouse and after packing the child's body in a cardboard box placed it on top of the toilet seat near her mother's body. He threw Marion Bartlett into a chicken coop. Starkweather maintained that he and Fugate spent the next six days in the house watching television, making love, and turning back all inquiries with a hastily scrawled, misspelled sign placed in the door warning "Stay away Every Body is sick with the Flue." Fugate, in possibly the most intensely debated issue in the history of 20th century murder, maintained that she was at school at the time of the murders. Upon returning home, Starkweather informed her that her family was being held hostage elsewhere and would be safe as long as she cooperated with him.

Armed with a .32 caliber pistol, a sawed off shotgun, and a hunting knife, the pair left Fugate's home on January 28, 1958. Two miles east of the small

Nebraska town of Bennet, Starkweather's car became stuck in snow on a dirt road near the farm of 70-year-old August Meyer. Starkweather and Fugate walked to the farm where they were greeted by Meyer who often let the teenager hunt on his land. A violent argument ensued in which Starkweather later said he was forced to shoot the old man point blank in the head with a sawed-off .410 shotgun in "self defense." He dragged Meyer's body into a nearby wash house and shot the old man's dog when it refused to stop barking. After eating and robbing the house of cash and guns, the pair walked to the nearby highway where they were picked up hitchhiking by 17-year-old Robert Jensen, Jr., and his fiancée Carol King, 16. Starkweather forced Jensen to drive to a storm cellar, the only remains of an abandoned school, near Meyer's farm. He herded the pair into the cellar and pumped six shots into Jensen's head and one into King's. Someone slashed King's genitals with a stiletto-type weapon (never recovered by police) and Starkweather later told authorities that Fugate had committed the atrocity out of "jealousy."

The pair escaped in Jensen's car eventually driving to an upper class Lincoln neighborhood in search of a better one when it developed engine problems. Starkweather had worked as a garbage man in the area and was familiar with the home of millionaire industrialist C. Lauer Ward, the 47-year-old president of both the Capital Bridge Company and the Capital Steel Company. Ward had just left for work on the morning of January 30, 1958, when Starkweather forced his way into the man's home past live-in maid Lillian Fencl, 51. Wife Clara Ward, 47, heard the commotion and was taken

prisoner by Starkweather when she came downstairs to investigate. He bound the pair, and placing them in separate upstairs bedrooms, proceeded first to stab Ward in the back, neck, and chest before walking down the hall to butcher Fencl. No friend to barking dogs, Starkweather broke the neck of Ward's miniature poodle with the butt of a .22 rifle. The teen killer was waiting behind the door when C. Lauer Ward returned home from work. Ward was barely over the threshold when Starkweather shot him in the head.

Intent on escaping to Washington State, the fugitives loaded up Mrs. Ward's black 1956 Packard with canned goods and headed down Highway 34 miraculously avoiding the hundreds of National Guardsmen and local police patrolling the streets of Lincoln. The FBI entered the case after the discovery of the bodies in the Ward home and initiated a block-by-block search of the town. With descriptions of the pair and the car they were driving announced on the radio every few minutes, Starkweather was anxious to dump the ostentatious Packard. On February 1, 1958, 37-year-old Merle Collison, a traveling shoe salesman from Montana, was sleeping in the front seat of his car on a dirt road off a highway near Douglas, Wyoming, when Starkweather tapped on the window and demanded to exchange cars with him. When Collison refused, Starkweather shot him nine times with a .22 caliber pump gun. As the multiple killer was trying to drag the body out of the car, a passing motorist stopped and was struggling with Starkweather when Wyoming deputy sheriff William Romer happened on the scene. Fugate ran to his car shouting, "He's killed a man," her only documented attempt to escape during the eight-day murder spree. Starkweather jumped into the Packard and at speeds topping 120 miles per hour drove towards Douglas with Romer in hot pursuit. Responding to the deputy sheriff's radio call for help, other officers joined the chase which ended when one of them shot out the back window of Starkweather's car, injuring the fugitive with flying glass. At the time of his arrest, Starkweather initially told officials that Fugate had nothing to do with the murders, but later changed his story to make her a willing and active participant.

Starkweather was extradited back to Nebraska where he and self-professed helpless hostage Fugate faced first degree murder charges in the death of Robert Jensen, Jr. He tried to block his court-appointed attorney's plea of not guilty by reason of insanity by refusing to submit to an electroencephalograph, preferring to die rather than be judged insane because, as he told his counsel, "Nobody remembers a crazy man." *The State v. Charles Raymond Starkweather* began amid tight security in a packed courtroom in Lincoln on May 5, 1958. During the 18-day trial the prosecution agreed with a defense psychiatrist who asserted that Starkweather suffered from a personality disorder, but drew the differing conclusion that he was sane at the time he killed Jensen. None believed Starkweather's testimony that he shot Jensen six times in the head in self-defense and after deliberating nearly 24 hours the jury found him guilty and specified the death penalty. In a separate trial in October 1958, a jury similarly refused to believe Fugate's story that she was Starkweather's unwilling hostage and sentenced her to life imprisonment for the first degree murder of Jensen committed in the perpetration of a robbery.

Awaiting death in his private eight-and-a-half by eleven foot cell in the hospital of the Nebraska State Penitentiary, the James Dean clone turned to religion. He wrote to his parents professing his newfound belief that though "Man may take my life ... my soul belongs to Him." The teen killer warned other teenagers to go to school, obey their parents, and to love God adding, "If I had followed these simple rules as I was advised to many times, I would not be where I am today." Starkweather's father attempted to defray mounting legal fees by obtaining permission from the prison's deputy warden to sell locks of his son's hair, but was told it was not appropriate. The failure of state and federal appeals cleared the way for Starkweather's execution. When asked on the eve of the event to donate his eyes to an eyebank, Starkweather refused saying, "Why should I? Nobody ever gave me anything." The 11-time killer was executed shortly after midnight on June 25, 1959, and was pronounced dead minutes after three separate 2200-volt shocks of electricity were passed through his body.

Fugate continued to adamantly maintain her innocence and on October 30, 1973, her life sentence was commuted to a prison term of 30 to 50 years. The Nebraska parole board, citing her exemplary behavior as a part-time dietician in a local nursing home, paroled Fugate on June 20, 1976, after she had spent 18 of her 32 years in prison. Fugate resettled in Lansing, Michigan, where she took employment as a nurse's aide in an area hospital. The controversy over whether Fugate was an active participant in the killings or Starkweather's hostage hit the national news again on February 21, 1983. In an attempt to finally clear her name, Fugate agreed to submit to a polygraph test on the nationally syndicated television program "Lie Detector" hosted by noted criminal attorney F. Lee Bailey. According to the results, Fugate was answering truthfully when she said she was not Starkweather's willing accomplice. Nebraska Attorney General Paul Douglas, an assistant prosecutor in the pair's 1958 trials, remained unconvinced noting that the questions submitted to her in the test may have been too superficial to find the truth. In the program's aftermath, a survey of 604 adults in Lincoln, Nebraska, by SRI Research Center, Inc., revealed that 51 percent did not believe Fugate opposed to 22 percent who did. The remaining 27 percent said they were not sure. Fugate has since maintained her innocence on the syndicated television program "A Current Affair" (November 6, 1989) and through the mail. In September 1990 she sent 200 copies of testimony from her murder trial to randomly selected residents in Lincoln, Nebraska. Much of the testimony indicated that she was not present at the time of her family's murder. With the Starkweather case firmly entrenched in popular culture by two movies and a song by Bruce Springsteen, it seems unlikely that Caril Ann Fugate will ever realize the dream she professed upon winning her parole: "I just want to be an ordinary little dumpy housewife—wash the socks, burn the toast."

540. Allen, William. *Starkweather: The Story of a Mass Murderer.* Boston: Houghton Mifflin, 1976. viii, 195 pp., [6] leaves of plates: ill.; 22 cm.

_____. [Same as 540.] New York: Avon Books, 1977. 205 pp., [8] leaves of plates: ill.; 18 cm.; paperback.

541. Beaver, Ninette; Ripley, B.K.; Trese, Patrick. *Caril.* 1st ed. Philadelphia: Lippincott, 1974. 320 pp.: ill.; 25 cm.

_____. [Same as 541.] New York: Bantam Books, 1976. xii, 398 pp.; 18 cm.; paperback.

542. Desmond, Glenn D. *Charles and Caril: An Orgy of Blood: The True Story of One of the Greatest Mass Murder Rampages in American History.* New York: Vantage Press, 1980. 171 pp.: port.; 21 cm.

Desmond was a reporter for KFAB, an Omaha radio station, when Starkweather and Fugate began their rampage.

543. Dyer, Earl. *Headline: Starkweather: From Behind the News Desk.* 1st ed. Lincoln, Neb.: Journal-Star, 1993. 186 pp.: ill.; 23 cm.

Portions first printed in *Parade* magazine.

544. O'Donnell, Jeff. *Starkweather: A Story of Mass Murder on the Great Plains.* Lincoln, Neb.: J & L Lee, 1993. viii, 191 pp.: ill., maps; 22 cm.; paperback.

Well researched trade paperback account which features extensive appendices, one of which charts the major conflicts in Starkweather's seven confessions to the murders. According to the author, "this book of 'faction' is based primarily upon testimony given at Charlie's and Caril's trials during the spring of 1958." Worth reading.

545. Reinhardt, James M. *The Murderous Trail of Charles Starkweather.* Police Science Series. Springfield, Ill.: Thomas, 1960. 151 pp.: ill.; 24 cm.

Reinhardt, a professor of criminology at the University of Nebraska, spent nearly 30 hours interviewing Starkweather before and after his trial and concludes that the "young chain-killer" was delusional, paranoiac, and ultimately, mad. Essential.

"Starved Rock Murders" *see*
Weger, Chester Otto

Steinberg, Joel Barnet

Born May 25, 1941, in Bronx, New York. Attorney. New York City, New York; 1 murder; bludgeon (fists); November 1 or 2, 1987.

"What you are saying is that she's not going to be an Olympic athlete, but she'll survive."—Steinberg's alleged reply to a doctor's prognosis that his daughter, if she lived, would suffer permanent brain damage

A case in which the beating death of an adopted child by her father generated national debate on child abuse, adoption rights, and the effects of long-term maltreatment on the human psyche. In the early morning of November 2, 1987, police were called to the Greenwich Village townhouse of 46-year-old attorney Joel Barnet Steinberg by his unmarried companion of 17 years Hedda Nussbaum, a 45-year-old former children's book editor. In the 911 call, Nussbaum reported that her 6-year-old adopted daughter Lisa had stopped breathing after choking on food. When authorities arrived at the filthy apartment at 14 West 10th Street they found the unkempt young girl barely breathing. Her adopted 16-month-old brother Mitchell was tied in his playpen with twine and covered in urine. Both parents refused to cooperate with police, but after Nussbaum (covered in cuts and bruises) stated that she had waited 10 hours before reporting Lisa's condition, authorities began to suspect child abuse. Later that day, Steinberg and Nussbaum were arrested and charged with attempted murder after a doctor examining Lisa's massive head injuries determined that they could not have resulted from a fall as they had reported. Lisa, pronounced brain dead on November 4, 1987, died the next day after being taken off a life

support system. Charges against the parents were upgraded to second degree murder.

As the case unfolded, authorities learned that the couple had illegally adopted Lisa in 1981 and Mitchell in 1986. Grand jury testimony revealed that Steinberg, a lawyer of shady reputation, was addicted to cocaine and at one time conspired to manufacture a pharmaceutical form of the drug. Charges were dropped against Nussbaum when it became clear that her years of drug addiction and physical abuse at the hands of Steinberg had rendered her emotionally incapable of intervening in her daughter's protection. Examined at the same time as Lisa, Nussbaum had nine broken ribs in addition to a broken jaw and nose. Moreover, Nussbaum's medical history over the last 12 years (which included over 40 broken bones and a ruptured spleen) bespoke of an escalating pattern of violence and domination by Steinberg. Medical testimony presented at Steinberg's October 1988 trial established that Lisa had died from a brain hemorrhage inflicted by repeated blows from a clenched fist the force of which was the equivalent of a fall from a three-story building. Steinberg's knuckles were bruised on the day of his arrest. Nussbaum's testimony against her companion of 17 years was devastating. Her face still disfigured from past beatings, Nussbaum told of letting her unconscious daughter lie on the bathroom floor for over 10 hours before calling an ambulance because she believed that Steinberg possessed special powers which could heal the child. The defense countered by accusing Nussbaum of killing Lisa out of a jealous rivalry over Steinberg's affections. After deliberating eight days, a jury convicted Steinberg of manslaughter in the first degree (with intent) on January 30, 1989. The disbarred attorney was subsequently sentenced to 8⅓ to 25 years in prison. In October 1994, Nussbaum filed a $3.6 million suit against her former companion for what she called the "physical and emotional devastation" of 12 years of repeated beatings. A decision is pending as of 1996.

546. Brownmiller, Susan. *Waverly Place.* 1st ed. New York: Grove Press, 1989. viii, 294 pp.; 24 cm.

_____. [Same as 546.] New York: New American Library, 1989. 351 pp.; 18 cm. ("A Signet book"); paperback.

Fictionalized account of the case.

547. Ehrlich, Sam. *Lisa, Hedda & Joel: The Steinberg Murder Case.* 1st St. Martin's mass market ed. New York: St. Martin's Press, 1989. 278 pp., [8]pp. of plates: ill.; 18 cm.; paperback.

548. Johnson, Joyce. *What Lisa Knew: The Truths and Lies of the Steinberg Case.* New York: Putnam, 1990. 302 pp.; 24 cm.

_____. [Same as 548.] New York: Kensington Pub. Corp., 1991. 414 pp.; 18 cm. ("A Zebra book"); paperback.

Stoner, George Percy

Born circa 1916 in Bournemouth, England. Chauffeur and handyman. Bournemouth, England; 1 murder; bludgeon (carpenter's mallet); March 24, 1935.

"When I did the job I believed he was asleep. I hit him and then came upstairs and told Mrs. Rattenbury"; *see also* Rattenbury, Alma Victoria.

Straffen, John Thomas

Born February 27, 1930, in Borden Camp, Hampshire, England. Machinist, gardener's laborer. Bath and Farley Hill, England; 3 murders; manual strangulation, bludgeon (rock); July 1951–April 1952.

"She had her back to me when I squeezed her neck. She went limp. I did not feel sorry. I forgot about it. I went back over the wall. I had no feeling about it. I forgot about it."—Straffen describing Brenda Goddard's murder to authorities

An insane child killer whose escape from Broadmoor and subsequent murder of a young girl generated an emotional and national debate in Britain over the incarceration or execution of mentally defective offenders. Although an older sister was mentally defective, Straffen was apparently normal until contracting encephalitis at six in India where his father was stationed in the military. Encephalograms later revealed severe damage to his cerebral cortex. Upon the family's return to Bath, England, in 1938, Straffen began exhibiting behavior problems. A chronic truant and pilferer by eight, Straffen appeared in juvenile court in June 1939 for stealing a little girl's purse. He received two years' probation, but a court officer, sensing the boy was unable to differentiate between right and wrong, referred him to a psychiatrist who classed Straffen as a "mental defective." His score of 58 on an IQ test taken in 1940 set his mental age at six. Straffen was placed in a residential school for mental defectives in June 1940 and moved to another facility at 12.

Timid and docile, Straffen was a solitary child who was generally friendly towards the staff of Besford Court, except when he sulked over being disciplined. The only negative incident occurred when the 14 year old was suspected of strangling an employee's two prize geese. Nothing was proven. Discharged at 16, Straffen returned home to work as a machinist, but quit after ten months. In early 1947 he began stealing small articles from unoccupied houses. On July 27, 1947, Straffen committed an act which hinted at the murderous violence within him. He placed his hand over a 13-year-old girl's mouth and asked, "What would you do if I killed you? I have done it before." Six weeks later, he strangled five chickens belonging to a father of a girl he had quarreled with. Arrested by police on charges of housebreaking, Straffen boastfully confessed to 13 other break-ins in which he was not even a suspect. In October 1947 he was institutionalized under Britain's Mental Deficiency Act of 1913. The committal papers noted he was "not of violent or dangerous propensities" and after 20 uneventful months Straffen was transferred to an agricultural hostel for defectives at Winchester. In February 1950 he was returned to his former institution in Bristol for stealing a bag of walnuts. One year later Straffen was licensed to the care of his mother in Bath.

Secretly, he resented the idea that his future discharge depended upon impressing authorities with his hard work and honesty. Since being arrested for assault in 1947 and then bragging to police about other alleged sexual offenses, Straffen was routinely questioned by police any time an assault occurred. In turn, he held them responsible for all his life's troubles. On July 10, 1951, police discovered the strangled body of seven-year-old Christine Butcher in Windsor. Though not responsible for the killing, it gave Straffen the avenue by which to "annoy" and "spite" his hated enemy. While on his way to the movies on July 15, 1951, Straffen passed by a field in Bath where five-year-old Brenda Constance God-

dard was picking wild flowers. On the pretext of showing her a better place to look, he lifted the child over a fence where he strangled and bashed her head against a rock. Goddard was not sexually assaulted and no attempt had been made to conceal her body. Straffen spent the rest of the day at the movies. Police checked with Straffen's employer and this combined with an erratic work record led to the 21 year old's firing on July 31, 1951. Outwardly calm and cooperative during police questioning, Straffen blamed them for the loss of his job and planned revenge.

On August 8, 1951, Straffen befriended nine-year-old Cicely Dorothy Batstone at the Forum cinema. He persuaded her to go with him to another movie house and then to a meadow on the outskirts of Bath. There, Straffen strangled the child and placed her body in the side of a hedge. Batstone was not violated. In the wake of the Goddard murder the public noticed any man alone with a young girl and several witnesses were able to identify Straffen as the man last seen with Batstone. He was picked up by detectives the next day and initially told conflicting stories of his encounter with the child before demonstrating how he had strangled her from behind. The befuddled Straffen mistakenly believed he could not be punished for the crime if someone had not actually seen him do it. Charged with the murders of Goddard and Batstone, Straffen was found insane and unfit to plead on October 17, 1952, at the Taunton Assizes. Declaring, "You might just as well try a baby in arms," the judge ordered Straffen to be detained in a mental institution "until His Majesty's pleasure be known."

Straffen, hiding his resentment of Broadmoor and those who put him there, seemingly adjusted well to the mental hospital. Six months passed before he escaped from the institution on April 29, 1952, by scaling a low place in the wall. Dressed in civilian clothes under his work jeans, Straffen blended in with the bucolic surroundings. While Broadmoor officials immediately noted the murderer's absence, in deference to the calm of the surrounding neighborhood the institution had never installed escape sirens. By 4:30 p.m. Straffen had reached the small village of Farley Hill some seven miles from Broadmoor. Moments later he spotted five-year-old Linda Bowyer riding her bike outside of a store. Roughly an hour later, Straffen strangled the child in a woods. When Broadmoor authorities recaptured him later in the day after a brief chase and a violent struggle, Straffen was surrounded by children. Though free only four hours and five minutes, he had taken another child's life and set into motion a national political debate over the security procedures employed by Broadmoor which ultimately resulted in more stringent rules for that institution. Straffen was subsequently convicted of Bowyer's death on July 25, 1952, and an execution date was set for September 6. Bowing to public pressure, the home secretary on August 29, 1952, recommended Straffen be reprieved and committed to Wandsworth Prison for life It was rumored in 1994 that Home Secretary Michael Howard had placed Straffen, 64, on a list with some 20 other incarcerated British killers who will never be paroled.

549. Fairfield, Letitia, and Fullbrook, Eric P., eds. *The Trial of John Thomas Straffen*. Notable British Trials. London: W. Hodge, 1954. xiii, 298 pp.: ill.; 22 cm.

Trials held at the Southampton Summer Assizes, Winchester: 1st trial, July 21–22, 1952; 2nd trial, July 22–25, 1952. Appeal to court of criminal justice, August 20, 1952.

Stuart, Charles M., Jr.

Born December 18, 1959, in Revere, Massachusetts. Died January 4, 1990. Fur store manager. Boston, Massachusetts; 2 murders; .38 caliber revolver; October 23, 1989.

Television: "Good Night, Sweet Wife: A Murder in Boston" (1990), a two-hour, made-for-television movie, originally aired on CBS on September 25, 1990. Cast includes Ken Olin (Charles Stuart), Annabella Price (Carol Stuart), and Margaret Colin (Michelle Caruso).

Audio: Murder in Boston, a two-sound cassette abridgement of Ken Englade's book of the same title, was published in 1990 by Audio Renaissance Tapes (Los Angeles, California).

"Good night, sweet wife, my love. I will never again know the feeling of your hand in mine, but I will always feel you. I miss you and I love you."—Eulogy written by Stuart from his hospital bed and read at his wife's funeral

A cunning wife murderer who managed to conceal his heinous crime by manipulating the racial fears and biases shared by many whites against blacks in urban settings. At around 8:30 p.m. on October 23, 1989, a Boston, Massachusetts, police dispatcher received an emergency call placed from a car phone by a severely wounded man who identified himself as Charles Stuart, a 29-year-old white fur store manager. Over the next ten minutes, Stuart managed to cling to consciousness long enough to direct police to the car containing him and his critically wounded wife, 30-year-old tax attorney Carol DiMaiti Stuart. What police found in the car supplemented by Stuart's description of their attack not only ignited a firestorm of public outcry in racially divided Boston, but became a top news story throughout the nation. According to Stuart, he and his wife (seven months pregnant with their first child) had just left a childbirthing class when a black man forced his way into their car at gunpoint. The assailant ordered Stuart to drive to the city's predominantly black Mission Hill district in Roxbury where he robbed them and shot Carol point blank in the head and Stuart in the abdomen. Carol was rushed to a hospital where hours before she died, a Caesarean section was performed to deliver the seven-month-old fetus. The baby, named Christopher, died 17 days later. Based on Stuart's description of their assailant, police conducted an intensive manhunt in the district. Cries of racism by Mission Hill residents were amplified by the arrest of a black suspect named Willie Bennett, a man with a 25-year criminal history. Stuart subsequently picked Bennett out of a police lineup as the man "most like" the one who attacked them. Bennett was held on other unrelated charges while authorities worked to firm up a murder case against him.

Upon his release from the hospital on December 5, 1989, Stuart immediately filed an insurance claim on his dead wife for $82,000. Days later he applied to collect another $100,000 on a separate policy. On January 3, 1990, he used some of the money to buy a new Nissan Maxima. Later that day, the man dubbed by the press as the "ultimate victim" was transformed into the "ultimate villain" when his younger brother Matthew stepped forward to discuss his knowledge of and involvement in the case. According to Matthew Stuart, he had agreed to help his brother commit insurance fraud, not murder. On the day of the killing, they met by pre-arrangement at the street intersection where the murder is believed to have occurred. Charles Stuart tossed his wife's Gucci bag containing the gun through the open window of his car into the window of Matthew's car with instructions to dispose of it. Matthew Stuart subsequently insisted to the prosecutor that he was unaware that Charles had possibly already shot his wife. Matthew drove to the nearby town of Revere and gave the items to a friend, John McMahon, who tossed them into a river. One day after his younger brother's startling revelation (January 4), Stuart committed suicide by jumping off Boston's Tobin Bridge into the Mystic River. A note found on the front seat of his new Nissan Maxima stated that he could not stand the pressure of being considered a suspect in his wife's death. Stuart's body was recovered hours later. Insurance checks totalling $480,000, more than enough to open up the restaurant which police believe he killed for, were waiting for his signature on the day he died. Days later in an act of community healing, the DiMaiti family began a foundation in their daughter's memory to grant scholarships to college-bound students from the Mission Hill district. In November 1992, Matthew Stuart pleaded guilty to committing life insurance fraud and received a 3–5 year sentence in the state prison at Walpole. Later that month, John McMahon pleaded guilty to being an accessory after the fact of murder and other charges and was sentenced to a one-year prison sentence. On April 18, 1994, Matthew

Stuart's first application for parole was denied.

550. Englade, Ken. *Murder in Boston.* St. Martin's Paperback ed. New York: St. Martin's Press, 1990. 268 pp., [8]pp. of plates: ill., ports.; 18 cm.; paperback.

———. [Same as 550.] London: Angus & Robertson, 1990. [288] pp.: ill., ports.; 19 cm.; paperback.

Englade concedes that this rush paperback "will not be the definitive book" on the Stuart case, but rather an "interim report designed to offer food for thought...." Drawing largely on newspaper accounts, Englade concludes that based upon the evidence to date (pre-Matthew Stuart and John McMahon convictions) Charles Stuart could not conclusively be proven guilty of the double murder. Includes a useful chronology.

551. Sharkey, Joe. *Deadly Greed: The Riveting True Story of the Stuart Murder Case That Rocked Boston and Shocked the Nation.* 1st ed. New York: Prentice Hall Press, 1991. 243 pp., [8]pp. of plates: ill.; 25 cm.

A former journalist and veteran true crime writer's account of the tragedy which he feels is a metaphor for the 1980s. The best book to date on the case.

Stuart, Rupert Max
(a.k.a. "Max Stuart," "Ropert Stuart," "Massey Khan," "Rex [or] Ron [or] Robert Sullivan," "Robert Hughes")

Born circa 1932 at Undoolya Station, Hermannsburg, Australia. Laborer. Ceduna, Australia; 1 murder; bludgeon (rock); December 20, 1958.

"That's what the bloody plonk does for you. I'd had nearly a flagon of wine or I wouldn't have grabbed her."— Statement allegedly made by Stuart immediately after his conviction

Controversial Australian case in which an aborigine was convicted of the rape-murder of a young white girl. On December 20, 1958, nine-year-old Mary Olive Hattam was playing with two friends on the beach near her home in Ceduna on the West Coast of South Australia. The children left Hattam alone to fetch a tub and returned to find her missing. Police later located the child's naked body in a small cave near the beach. Dead less than ten hours, Hattam had been violently raped before her head had been smashed with a stone found near the corpse. Police employed two aboriginal trackers to trace footprints found at the scene which they identified as having been made by an aborigine. Inquiries led authorities to Rupert Max Stuart, an illiterate 27-year-old aborigine recently fired from his job at a local traveling carnival for drinking. Stuart, who had a history of arrests for assaults on young girls, confessed to drunkenly raping Hattam, then killing her so she would not tell. At his trial in April 1959, a statement prepared by Stuart was read to the court in which he asserted his innocence and maintained that police had beaten a false confession from him. He was subsequently found guilty and sentenced to hang. A series of appeals followed based primarily upon Stuart's inability to understand English and therefore to have produced a confession an expert in the Aranda language called "well beyond the mental linguistic capacity of Stuart." Each appeal was denied, but public interest in the case generated largely by efforts on Stuart's behalf by Father Thomas Dixon, a missionary among aborigines, led to the convening of a Royal Commission in Adelaide on August 10, 1959. The commission deliberated for 77 days before upholding

Stuart's original conviction on October 26, 1959. Three weeks earlier Stuart's death sentence had been commuted to life imprisonment ostensibly to counteract newspaper claims that the Commonwealth Government was racist. Stuart was granted parole on August 14, 1973. Since that time, he has violated at least four paroles on charges of drinking and disorderly conduct.

552. Chamberlain, Roderic. *The Stuart Affair*. Adelaide: Rigby, 1973. 312 pp.: ill.; 22 cm.

_____. [Same as 552.] London: Hale, 1973. [9], 312 pp., [12]pp. of plates: ill., ports.; 22 cm.
   Chamberlain, the crown solicitor of South Australia and prosecutor in the case, reviews the evidence from his retirement, and remains convinced of Stuart's guilt. Certain segments of the Australian press are taken to task for generating undue controversy in a case Chamberlain felt was fairly straightforward.

553. Dixon, Thomas Sidney. *The Wizard of Alice: Father Dixon and the Stuart Case*. Morwell, Vic.: Alella Books, 1987. vi, 416 pp.: ill., ports.; 27 cm.
   The crusading Catholic priest's account of his successful efforts to save Stuart from execution. Contains large sections of the trial transcript and rebuttals to Chamberlain's conclusions.

554. Inglis, Kenneth Stanley. *The Stuart Case*. Parkville, Australia: Melbourne University Press, 1962. 321 pp.: ill.; 23 cm.
   Meticulously detailed account which effectively chronicles media reaction to the case. Inglis, a senior lecturer in history at Adelaide University, concludes that Stuart was "probably guilty."

Stutzman, Eli E., Jr.
(a.k.a. "Junior," "Eli Ali")

Born September 28, 1950. Hospital orderly, horse trainer, carpenter. Austin, Texas; 1 murder (convicted, suspected in 4 others); .22 caliber rifle; April 1985.
   "I wanted to leave Danny where God could find him."—Stutzman explaining to authorities why he placed his nine-year-old son's possibly lifeless body in a Chester, Nebraska, cornfield
   On Christmas Eve 1985, a motorist on U.S. 81 near the small south-central Nebraska town of Chester discovered the body of a young boy dressed in a blue one-piece blanket sleeper carefully placed in a roadside drainage ditch next to a frozen cornfield. An autopsy determined that the blond, freckled boy whose age was estimated at 10 had not been raped, strangled, beaten, or poisoned. Though the cause of death could not be officially ascribed, the time of death was fixed at approximately 36 hours before the discovery of the body. Melted snow around the boy's corpse suggested the possibility that he was still alive when left in the field to freeze to death. A retouched morgue photo supplying the child's missing facial features ravaged by hungry field mice was circulated to police departments nationwide in the hopes of identifying the boy. Deeply moved by the death of the unknown child, the people of Chester and the nearby town of Hebron named him Matthew, meaning "Gift of God," and buried him on March 21, 1986, in the Chester cemetery. Nearly 300 people attended the ceremony and laid toys and flowers around the gravestone upon which was etched "Little Boy Abandoned Found Near Chester, Neb. December 24, 1985..." A blank place was left on the marker for the child's name to one day be added. Two years passed before an article in the December

1987 issue of *Reader's Digest* entitled, "The Death of an Unknown Boy," dubbed the abandoned child "Little Boy Blue" and set into motion the machinery that ultimately led to his identification and the arrest of his father, Eli E. Stutzman, Jr.

The fourth of 13 children born to a minister in an ultra-conservative Amish sect forbidding all modern conveniences, Stutzman was well-known as a troublemaker in the Amish enclaves of Wayne and Holme counties in Ohio. A bright child with a slight stutter, Stutzman's early rebellion against the harsh rules of the Order was met with frequent whippings administered by his father. Unable to cope, he left his father's house at 21 to room with a neighboring family. Less than a year later in February 1972, Stutzman suffered a nervous breakdown. Afterwards, he complained of having constant erections and scribbled notes filled with cryptic references to Hell and Satan. In mid–May 1972, Stutzman's father had him committed to a mental institution and after his release he was banned from the Order in the summer of 1972 for disobedience and expressing a wish to leave the faith.

Stutzman drifted around Ohio for the next couple of years working as a handyman for various New Order Amish families. In November 1974 he agreed to cooperate in a drug sting set up by the Wayne County sheriff's office, but when officers arrived at the barn where Stutzman planned to meet the dealers they found him lying near death in a pool of blood. The place had been ransacked and blood dripped from the walls. Between bouts of consciousness, Stutzman managed to explain that the drug dealers had beat him so he would not testify against them. A closer examination of the scene uncovered razor blades and an IV needle filled with blood. Convinced that Stutzman had faked his own injuries and lied about the assault, investigators searched his room and recovered threatening notes written to himself in his own hand. Homosexual sex magazines and vibrators were found hidden beneath his bed. Stutzman immediately confessed the ruse and the drug case was dropped.

In 1975, Stutzman announced his intention to return to the Amish to marry Ida Gingerich, a girl he had known for over four years. The marriage was postponed to December 25, 1975, when a pre-nuptial blood test revealed that he had syphilis. Less than a month after the marriage, Stutzman offered a male cab driver $60 for oral sex. Daniel E. Stutzman, fated to become the unidentified corpse known as "Little Boy Blue," was born on September 7, 1976. With another child on the way in 1977, Stutzman moved his family onto a 95-acre farm near Dalton, Ohio. On the night of July 11, 1977, the barn was struck by lightning and set ablaze. According to Stutzman, his 26-year-old wife (who suffered from a previously undiagnosed "weak heart") collapsed and died while trying to save some milking equipment from the burning structure. A pathologist at the time expressed doubt over Stutzman's story, but unwilling to interfere with the Amish burial ritual, did not insist on an autopsy. Earlier on the day of the fatal fire, Stutzman had signed a will making him the sole beneficiary of all his wife's assets. He incurred the wrath of the Amish community by using the insurance money to modernize the farmhouse with electricity and convert from farming to raising horses. Exactly one year after the fire, Stutzman suffered another nervous breakdown and spent a week in a psychiatric unit. By early 1979, Stutzman no longer even attempted to maintain the charade of Amish religiosity and left the faith again.

Whether or not Eli Stutzman physically abused his son has never been fully established. There can be no doubt, however, that the unrestrained lifestyle he now dedicated himself to inflicted obvious emotional harm on the young boy. In early 1979 Stutzman began placing sex ads in the personals columns of gay magazines and tabloids. He converted the barn that the Amish community had raised for him after the death of his wife into a gay party house where the handsome, muscular former Amishman held sway among Wayne County's homosexual underground. No attempt was made to shield Danny from homosexual activity, but rather Stutzman confided to a friend that he wanted to "train him so he'll never have to deal with women." By mid–1982 when Stutzman sold his farm in Ohio to buy a ranch in Durango, Colorado, with a man he met through a sex ad, Danny's "education" had taken a sinister turn. Stutzman took the five-year-old to gay sex orgies and instructed the child to grab the participants' crotches. Not surprisingly, the boy developed some classic symptoms of child abuse: stuttering and emotional withdrawal combined with episodes of uncontrollable behavior.

Stutzman moved to Austin, Texas, in 1984 and opened up E.S. Construction, a small remodelling outfit that primarily employed gay men. He sold pot to supplement his income. In late 1984, 24-year-old Glen Albert Pritchett began working for Stutzman and soon afterwards moved in with him and Danny as a paying roommate. Pritchett's decomposing body was found in a roadside ditch south of Austin on May 12, 1985. Shot through the left eye with a .22 caliber bullet, Pritchett had been dead at least a month. By the time a fingerprint check identified Pritchett's connection to his employer, Stutzman and Danny were driving to Lyman, Wyoming, where he left the nine-year-old boy with his foster parents. Stutzman explained to the incredulous couple that he was off to find Pritchett's real murderer. Drifting through Ohio, Arizona, New Mexico, Kansas, and Indiana, Stutzman stayed with men he met through personal ads before returning to collect Danny on December 14, 1985. The pair drove off to visit relatives in Ohio for Christmas, but Stutzman arrived there alone. Danny, he told them, had chosen to remain in Wyoming to ski. Six months later, Stutzman notified the relatives that Danny had been killed in a car accident in Utah.

In December 1987, Danny was identified through a palm print found on a third grade report card supplied by a relative who had seen the *Reader's Digest* article. On December 14, 1987, Stutzman was arrested in a trailer park in Azle, Texas, 15 miles northwest of Fort Worth on a charge of felony child abuse. Extradited to Nebraska, a tearful Stutzman explained that Danny was suffering from a respiratory ailment when he picked him up in Wyoming. He dressed the boy in a blue sleeper, wrapped him in a blanket, and placed him atop the luggage in the car's backseat to sleep. Sometime during the drive, Danny slid off the luggage and became pinned between the bags and the side of the car. To Stutzman's horror, he found the child's head wrapped in the blanket. After trying to resuscitate him, he placed the child's body in a place "where God could find him," a drainage ditch in Chester, Nebraska. Authorities remained convinced, however, that Stutzman either suffocated or let the child freeze to death to remove him as a witness to Pritchett's murder or else just to be rid of him as an impediment to his gay lifestyle. Lacking any concrete evidence to support their suspicions, authorities were forced to cut a deal with Stutzman. In exchange for dropping the felony child abuse charge, Stutzman agreed to plead guilty to two misdemeanors. On January 11, 1988, Stutzman was sentenced to a year for abandoning a body and six months for concealing a death.

While serving time in Nebraska's Lincoln Regional Center Stutzman was indicted in Austin on July 19, 1988, for the 1985 slaying of Glen Pritchett. An unlikely alliance of Mennonite supporters and former gay lovers paid for his defense which was unable to convince an Austin jury that Stutzman had not murdered Pritchett during an argument. Stutzman was found guilty on July 21, 1989, and sentenced to 40 years. On December 19, 1990, a Texas court of appeals upheld the conviction. Stutzman has since emerged as a key suspect in the November 1985 murders of two Texas men, David Tyler and Dennis Slaeter. Diagnosed as HIV positive, Stutzman has re-embraced his religious faith in prison and is taking algebra and drafting classes in the hope of one day earning a college degree.

555. Olsen, Gregg. *Abandoned Prayers.* Popular Library ed. New York: Popular Library, 1990. viii, 373 pp., [8]pp. of plates: ill.; 18 cm.; paperback.

Paperback account based on police reports, grand jury testimony, court transcripts, trial evidence, and more than 300 interviews conducted over a two-year period.

"Sunset Murders" *see* **Clark, Douglas Daniel (and) Bundy, Carol Mary**

Sutcliffe, Peter William (a.k.a. "The Yorkshire Ripper," "Jack the Ripper," "Peter Williams")

Born June 2, 1946, in Bingley, England. Truck driver. Northern England (Leeds, Manchester, Bradford, Halifax, Huddersfield, Pudsey); 13 murders (7 attempted murders); bludgeon (hammer, chisel), knife, screwdriver, ligature strangulation; October 30, 1975–January 2, 1981.

"In this truck is a man whose latent genius if unleashed would rock the nation, whose dynamic energy would overpower those around him. Better let him sleep?"—A handwritten note found by police in Sutcliffe's truck

Murderer of 13 women (some of them prostitutes) over a five-year period in England's northern counties. He was media-tagged the "Yorkshire Ripper" because of the similarity of the sadistic attacks with those of the 19th century murderer "Jack the Ripper." On October 30, 1975, the Yorkshire Ripper claimed his first victim in the grimy industrial town of Leeds. Twenty-eight-year-old prostitute Wilma McCann was found dead on a playing field near the city's red-light district. In what police would come to recognize as the killer's *modus operandi*, McCann's skull had been crushed by hammer blows and her breasts, throat, and genitals repeatedly mutilated with a knife or sharpened screwdriver. The killings continued sporadically throughout England for the next five years claiming the lives of six more prostitutes and six "non-working" women. Seven other women, including two accosted before McCann's murder, survived disfiguring attacks. In what became the largest manhunt ever conducted in British police history, 300 investigators conducted over a quarter of a million interviews throughout England at a total cost of $8.8 million. On June 26, 1979, police received a three-minute audiotape from "Jack the Ripper" in which he taunted police over their inability to catch him. This tape ultimately proved a hoax and diverted countless thousands of manhours away from tracking the real killer.

Sheffield police were conducting routine spot checks on cars parked in the city's red light district on January 2, 1981, when they noticed one with false plates. Peter Sutcliffe, a married 35-year-old truck driver from Bradford, was taken into custody and later confessed to being the Ripper. At his Old Bailey trial in April 1981, Sutcliffe admitted to 13 killings and attempts at seven others, but pleaded "Not guilty to murder, but guilty of manslaughter on grounds of diminished responsibility." Although both the prosecution and defense agreed that he was a mentally unstable paranoid schizophrenic, the Crown maintained that he was sane at the time of the killings. The former gravedigger told the court of first hearing "the voice of God" while digging a grave in a northern England cemetery in 1967. After being cheated out of $22 by a prostitute in 1969, Sutcliffe said the voice prompted him to embark on a "divine mission" of killing prostitutes. A prison officer's testimony, however, disputed the killer's claim to being a divine emissary. He reported hearing Sutcliffe confide to his wife during a visit that he would be doing a lot of time in prison "unless I can convince people in here I am mad and [get]

maybe ten years in the loony bin." On May 22, 1981, the Yorkshire Ripper was found guilty of murder and sentenced to life with a recommendation that he not be released for at least 30 years. An appeal was rejected on May 24, 1982.

In the aftermath of the conviction, a government report issued in January 1982 roundly criticized the police's handling of the investigation as "guilty of inefficiency," "bad judgment," and of placing too much credence on the bogus audiotape. Authorities had sighted the killer 50 times and questioned him on nine occasions. Sutcliffe, an unpopular prisoner who allegedly told other inmates that their wives were "next on [his] list," was slashed in the face with a glass jar wielded by a fellow-prisoner in Parkhurst Prison in January 1983. In November 1983 the British tabloid *News of the World* reported that inmate leaders in Parkhurst had placed Sutcliffe under a death sentence declaring that "whoever kills [him] will be the criminal world's biggest hero." The Ripper was moved to Broadmoor, a top-security mental hospital, in March 1984. Officials there reported finding a hacksaw blade in his room on May 17, 1992. Later that month, Sutcliffe announced he had been "born again" and requested permission to become a Jehovah's Witness. On February 23, 1996, fellow Broadmoor patient and convicted robber Paul Wilson tried to garrote Sutcliffe with the wires from stereo headphones. Kenneth Erskine, the "Stockwell Strangler" of seven pensioners in 1986, saved his life.

556. Beattie, John. *The Yorkshire Ripper Story*. [London]: Quartet/Daily Star Publication, 1981. 160 pp., [16]pp. of plates: ill.; 20 cm.; paperback.

Daily Star reporter Beattie's factual

retelling of the case based on that paper's coverage of the murders. Contains startling reminiscences made by Sutcliffe's coworkers at the Bingley Cemetery where the former gravedigger allegedly desecrated corpses.

557. Burn, Gordon. *Somebody's Husband, Somebody's Son: The Story of Peter Sutcliffe.* London: Heinemann, 1984. 275 pp.; 25 cm.

_____. [Same as 557 with variant subtitle: *The Story of the Yorkshire Ripper.*] 1st American ed. New York: Viking, 1985. 274 pp.; 24 cm.

_____. [Same as 557.] London: Pan in association with Heinemann, 1985. 368 pp.; 18 cm.; paperback.

_____. [Same as 557 with variant subtitle: *The Story of the Yorkshire Ripper.*] New York: Penguin Books, 1986. 368 pp.; 18 cm.; paperback.

_____. [Same as 557 with variant subtitle: *The Story of the Yorkshire Ripper.*] New ed. London: Pan in association with Heinemann, 1990. 375 pp.; 18 cm.; paperback.

_____. [Same as 557 with variant subtitle: *The Story of the Yorkshire Ripper.*] New ed. London: Mandarin, 1993. 375 pp.; 18 cm.; paperback. (Originally published in London by Pan in association with Heinemann, 1990.)

Superior account of the crimes especially rich in details of the Yorkshire Ripper's early childhood and adolescence. Burn covered the trial for the *Sunday Times* and profited from the cooperation of Sutcliffe's family except for wife Sonia who sought an injunction against the book's publication. Burn's informative followup article on Sonia Sutcliffe, "The Woman at Number Six," appeared in the November 10, 1990, issue of *The Independent.*

558. Cross, Roger. *The Yorkshire Ripper.* London: Granada, 1981. 250 pp., [16]pp. of plates: ill., 1 facsim., ports.; 18 cm.; paperback.

_____. [Same as 558.] New York: Dell, 1981. 250 pp., [8]pp. of plates: ill.; 18 cm.;

paperback. (First published in Great Britain by Granada.)

Well written paperback original. Includes detailed index.

559. Nicholson, Michael. *The Yorkshire Ripper.* London: Star Books, 1979. 175 pp., [8]pp. of plates: ill., 1 facsim., 1 map, ports.; 19 cm.; paperback.

Nicholson's paperback account, written prior to Sutcliffe's arrest, offers a summary of the crimes to date and examines the psychological make-up of other serial murderers like Peter Kürten, Neville Heath, etc. Includes "Chronology of Murdered Women" (ending with the twelfth victim on September 2, 1979) and a "Chronology of Injured Women."

560. Ward Jouve, Nicole. *"The Streetcleaner": The Yorkshire Ripper Case on Trial.* London; New York: M. Boyars; New York: Distributed in the U. S. and Canada by Kampmann, 1986. 231 pp.: ill.; 23 cm.; trade paperback.

_____. [Same as 560.] London: Boyars, 1988. 231 pp.: ill., 1 facsim.; 22 cm.; trade paperback.

Thought-provoking feminist/psychological study of Sutcliffe. Liner notes dauntingly proclaim that the book "focuses on the brutalized culture of machismo that spawned him."

561. Yallop, David A. *Deliver Us from Evil.* London: Macdonald Futura, 1981. 355 pp., [16]pp. of plates: ill.; 24 cm.

_____. [Same as 561.] London: Macdonald Futura, 1981. 374 pp., [32]pp. of plates: ill.; 19 cm.; paperback.

_____. [Same as 561.] New York: Coward, McCann & Geoghegan, 1982. 355 pp., [16]pp. of plates: ill.; 24 cm.

_____. [Same as 561.] New ed. London: Corgi, 1993. 403 pp., [32]pp. of plates: ill., facsims., 1 map, ports.; 18 cm.; paperback.

Yallop takes the police to task for their handling of the case which he insists could have been solved more quickly. He believes that some of the murders attributed to Sutcliffe were committed by a copycat killer who in 1981 remained at large.

Swartz, Lawrence J.

Born circa 1966 in New Orleans, Louisiana. High school student. Cape St. Claire, Maryland; 2 murders; knife, maul; January 16, 1984.

Television: "A Family Torn Apart" (1993), a two-hour, made-for-television movie based on Leslie Walker's book *Sudden Fury,* originally aired on NBC on November 21, 1993. Cast includes Neil Patrick Harris (Brian Hannigan/ Lawrence J. Swartz), John M. Jackson (Joe Hannigan/Robert Swartz), and Linda Kelsey (Maureen Hannigan/Kay Swartz).

"I picked up the steak knife, stabbed her and got her around the neck. When I saw her blood, I felt, like, good in a sense, because I finally did something about them yelling at me." — Swartz to a state psychiatrist

An emotionally and perhaps physically abused teenager who brutally murdered his adoptive parents in a fit of rage. On January 17, 1984, Robert Swartz, a 51-year-old computer technician, and his wife Kay, a 43-year-old high school English teacher, were found stabbed to death at their home in the Chesapeake Bay community of Cape St. Claire, Maryland, by their 17-year-old adopted son Larry. Robert Swartz, stabbed 17 times, died in a downstairs clubroom. Wife Kay had been repeatedly stabbed in the same room, but managed to run outdoors where the killer caught her and split her head open with a sharp object. She was found naked near the backyard swimming pool next to a bloody shoe print in the snow later identified as belonging to Larry Swartz. A bloody handprint on the sliding door leading from the clubroom to the backyard was also found to be the teenager's. As police conducted interviews with friends of the victims, a disturbing history of continuing emotional abuse inflicted by the couple on their adopted children came to light. Devout Catholics, the Swartzes adopted three children from disadvantaged backgrounds. Strict disciplinarians who placed a high premium on academic achievement, the Swartzes punished their rebellious oldest son, Michael, by locking him out of the house all day and threatening to commit him to a mental institution. Three years before their murder, the couple turned custody of Michael over to the state, effectively ending their parental responsibilities.

Larry Swartz, the child of a New Orleans prostitute and a pimp, was abandoned by his mother when he was 20 months old. Shuttled between numerous foster homes, the child was returned by several prospective parents because of untreated emotional problems manifested by his eating of food from garbage cans. The Swartzes adopted Larry when he was six, stating on the official paperwork that they preferred a child with above average intelligence because of their emphasis on higher education. Unknown to them, the child had tested in the "dull normal range" on intelligence tests and, with an IQ of 78, was unable to make the high grades they expected of him. Their response to poor grades was to exert ever more rigorous discipline on the boy, at first suspending privileges, verbally abusing him, then as he grew older, refusing to let him drive or leave the house. Although police initially suspected the violent son Michael of the double homicide, the forensic evidence tying the quiet Larry to the crime became compelling.

Authorities arrested the teenager on January 24, 1984, and charged him with two counts of first degree murder. On April 18, 1985, just before the start of the trial, opposing counsel reached an agreement whereby Swartz pleaded guilty to two counts of second degree murder in exchange for a 12-year sentence at the Patuxent Institution, a penal facility specializing in the treatment of emotionally and mentally disturbed prisoners. The sentence, considered overly lenient by some members of the victims' family, was an acknowledgment by the state that Swartz had suffered years of untreated psychological abuse. In his confession, Swartz said the murders were prompted by a "sarcastic" comment made by his mother when he told her he may have failed a test. The teen "exploded," struck the woman in the head with a wood-splitting maul and repeatedly stabbed her in the neck with a steak knife. Robert Swartz was stabbed 17 times when he came to investigate her screams. During the attack, Kay Swartz managed to get outside where the boy ran her down near the pool and struck her in the head with the maul. To complete the family tragedy, Larry's brother Michael was found guilty (with another individual) on June 28, 1991, of stabbing a man 47 times over a jar of quarters worth less than $50 during a robbery in July 1990. In November 1991 Michael Swartz was sentenced to life without parole.

562. Walker, Leslie. *Sudden Fury: A True Story of Adoption and Murder.* 1st ed. New York: St. Martin's Press, 1989. 384 pp., [8]pp. of plates: ill.; 24 cm.

_____. [Same as 562 minus subtitle.] St. Martin's Paperbacks ed. New York: St. Martin's Paperbacks, 1990. viii, 385 pp., [8]pp. of plates: ill.; 18 cm.; paperback.

Walker, a reporter who covered the Swartz murders for the *Baltimore Sun*, delivers an excellent account of the tragic case which delves into the psychology of emotional abuse underlying the murders.

Tait, Robert Peter

Born December 14, 1924, in Glasgow, Scotland. Died February 19, 1985. Petty thief, former sailor in the Australian Royal Navy. Melbourne, Australia; 1 murder; bludgeon (fists); August 8, 1961.

Years before committing the murder which created a firestorm of controversy over the death penalty in Australia, Robert Tait had been diagnosed as an "aggressive psychopath" who became violent under the influence of alcohol. He was also known to police as an alcoholic sexual sadist who enjoyed wearing women's panties during the commission of petty thefts. On August 8, 1961, a drunken Tait broke into the vicarage of the All Saints Church of England in Melbourne. Theft turned to murder when 82-year-old housekeeper Ada Ethel Hall confronted Tait who savagely beat her to death with his fists. Though forensic specialists could find no evidence of intercourse, Hall's vagina had been savaged with a flashlight. Arrested nine days later in Adelaide on an unrelated breaking and entering charge, Tait confessed to Hall's murder on August 17, 1961. Extradited to Melbourne to face the charge, police discovered Tait was already on parole for a robbery with violence. Months before, he had severely beaten a 70-year-old woman in a Christian Science Reading Room during a botched robbery attempt. Tait pleaded "not guilty by reason of insanity" and the highly publicized trial began on December 4, 1961. He was quickly found guilty and sentenced to death by hanging. Two subsequent 1962 appeals were denied and an execution date was set for August 22. Heated political and public debate over Tait's sanity was fuelled by psychiatric reports contending that a fall through a glass skylight sustained by Tait as an eight-year-old left him with a lifelong learning disability. The government, bowing to public pressure, commuted Tait's sentence to life imprisonment with no chance of release. On November 16, 1962, he was committed to the Ararat Mental Home. Tait died of a heart attack in Melbourne's St. Vincent's Hospital on February 19, 1985.

563. Burns, Creighton. *The Tait Case.* Parkville, Victoria: Melbourne University Press, 1962. vi, 182 pp.; 22 cm.
    Burns, a reader in political science at the University of Melbourne, examines the wider political and social questions raised by the Tait case. An appendix includes "Transcript of Proceedings in the High Court of Australia—Tait and the Queen" dated October 31, 1962.

Taylor, Kenneth Z.

Born circa 1949 in Oak Hills, Ohio. Dentist. Manalpan Township, New York; 1 murder; bludgeon; November 11 or 12, 1984.
    Television: "In a Child's Name" (1991), a two-part, four-hour made-for-television movie based on Peter Maas' book of the same title, originally aired on CBS on November 17 and 19, 1991. Cast includes Michael Ontkean (Kenneth Taylor) and Karla Tamburrelli (Taylor's wife).
    Audio: In a Child's Name, a two-sound cassette abridgement of Maas'

book of the same title read by John Heard, was published in 1990 by Simon & Schuster Audio (New York).
    "I always looked forward to being a jolly grandfather with a house full of rowdy grandsons and cute little tomboyish or dainty granddaughters."
    Manalapan Township, New York, dentist who bludgeoned his wife to death and then (many believe) orchestrated his parents' campaign to adopt his infant son. On the night of November 11 or the early morning November 12, 1984, Kenneth Taylor smashed in the back of his wife's head at least nine times with a 20-pound barbell then dumped the body in a central Pennsylvania bird sanctuary. In custody, Taylor stated that he found his wife Teresa performing fellatio on their 15-month-old son and when he tried to stop her the cocaine crazed woman attacked him with a barbell. Taylor disarmed his wife and "gave it to her." Found guilty of murder, the dentist was sentenced October 4, 1985, to a minimum of 30 years in prison without parole. A lengthy child custody battle has since ensued between the child's paternal grandparents in Indiana and his maternal aunt and uncle in New York City.

564. Maas, Peter. *In a Child's Name: The Legacy of a Mother's Murder.* New York: Simon and Schuster, 1990. 378 pp., [4]pp. of plates: ill.; 25 cm.
    _____. [Same as 564 minus subtitle.] New York: Pocket Books, 1991. 430 pp.: ill.; 18 cm.; paperback.

"Ted Killings" *see* Bundy, Theodore Robert

Thatcher, Wilbert Colin (a.k.a. "The J.R. Ewing of Saskatchewan")

Born August 25, 1938, in Toronto, Ontario, Canada. Former politician and rancher. Regina, Saskatchewan, Canada; 1 murder; bludgeon, .357 Magnum pistol; January 21, 1983.

Television: "Love and Hate: A Marriage Made in Hell" (1989), a two-part, four-hour made-for-television movie adapted from Maggie Siggin's book *A Canadian Tragedy* and produced by the Canadian Broadcasting Corporation, originally aired on U.S. television on NBC on July 15 and 16, 1990. Cast includes Kenneth Welsh (Colin Thatcher) and Kate Nelligan (JoAnn Thatcher).

"The best way to survive in here is to see nothing and say nothing."— Thatcher describing prison life

A millionaire rancher-politician called the "J.R. Ewing of Saskatche-wan" is convicted of the bludgeoning and shooting death of his former wife. The marriage of Colin Thatcher, a 45-year-old former Tory cabinet minister in Saskatchewan, and his wife of 17 years, JoAnn, 43, ended in a bitter divorce and custody battle in 1980. Amid allegations of physical abuse and adultery, JoAnn Thatcher (after her remarriage, Wilson) was awarded a large financial settlement and custody of the two youngest of their three children. JoAnn Wilson narrowly missed being killed on May 17, 1981, after an unknown gunman shot her in the shoulder. Shortly afterwards, she relinquished custody of one of her children to Thatcher saying she feared for her life. On January 21, 1983, Wilson's body was found in the blood-spattered garage of her posh home in Regina. Bludgeoned at least 20 times in the head with a heavy curved blade, Wilson had been shot once above the right ear with a .357 Magnum. A gasoline credit card receipt signed by Thatcher was found at the scene. A joint investigation between Canadian and U.S. authorities culminated in Thatcher's arrest over a year later on May 7, 1984. Tried in Saskatoon in October 1984, Thatcher pleaded innocent and offered an alibi supported by his children. His former mistress, however, testified that Thatcher not only admitted that he tried to kill Wilson in 1981, but later told her how "strange" it felt "to blow your wife away." An ex-convict, granted immunity from prosecution, testified that Thatcher had offered him $50,000 to kill Wilson. He refused, but put Thatcher in touch with two hitmen who reneged on the contract after the former politician paid them $19,000. On November 5, 1984, Thatcher was convicted of either murdering or causing the death of his ex-wife and received a mandatory sentence of life without parole eligibility for 25 years. Thatcher exhausted his final appeal option in April 1994 after the minister of justice of Canada refused to ask an appeal court to review his conviction. On July 20, 1994, Thatcher married Bev Shaw, a widow with four children who began corresponding with him after seeing a television miniseries based on the case. The couple exchanged vows in a small chapel at the maximum security Edmonton Institution.

565. Bird, Heather. *Not Above the Law: The Tragic Story of JoAnn Wilson and Colin Thatcher*. Toronto: Key Porter Books, 1985. 240 pp.: ill.; 18 cm.; paperback.

566. Siggins, Maggie. *A Canadian Tragedy: JoAnn and Colin Thatcher: A Story of*

Love and Hate. Toronto: Macmillan of Canada, 1985. 497 pp.; 24 cm.

_____. [Same as 566.] Toronto: McClelland and Stewart-Bantam, 1986. 519 pp.; 18 cm. ("Seal books"); paperback.

567. Thatcher, Colin. *Backrooms: A Story of Politics.* Saskatoon, Sask.: Western Producer Prairie Books, 1985. 241 pp.; 24 cm.

568. Wilson, Garrett, and Wilson, Lesley. *Deny, Deny, Deny: The Rise and Fall of Colin Thatcher.* Toronto: J. Lorimer, 1985. x, 340 pp., [16]pp. of plates: ill.; 24 cm.

_____. [Same as 568.] Canadian Lives no. 47. Halifax, N.S.: Goodread Biographies, 1986. x, 341 pp., [16]pp. of plates: ill.; 18 cm.; paperback.

Thomas, Arthur Allan
(pardoned)

Born circa 1938 in New Zealand. Farmer. Pukekawa, New Zealand; 2 murders (pardoned); .22 caliber rifle; June 17, 1970.

Film: Beyond Reasonable Doubt (NZ, 1983), a Satori Entertainment release directed by John Laing. Screenplay by David A. Yallop based on his book of the same title. Cast includes John Hargreaves (Allan Thomas), David Hemmings (Bruce Hutton), and Tony Barry (John Hughes).

Convicted New Zealand double murderer who spent nine years in prison until a Royal Commission Inquiry in 1980 pardoned him based on a finding that police had planted incriminating evidence against him. On the night of June 17, 1970, David Harvey Crewe and his wife, Jeanette, were shot to death with a .22 caliber rifle in their home in Pukekawa, a small farming community 25 miles south of Auckland. Their bodies, weighted with scrap metal and a car axle, were tossed into the Waikato River. The Crewes's 18-month-old daughter was later found unhurt in the farmhouse. A roundup and ballistics check of all the .22 rifles in the area led police to 32-year-old Arthur Allan Thomas, a married resident of Pukekawa who at one time courted Jeanette Crewe. At trial, authorities produced a .22 caliber shell casing they claimed was found at the murder scene after *four months* of previously fruitless searching. Other circumstantial evidence, similar wire used to truss the bodies and matching features of the axle used to weight one, further tied Thomas to the murders. Thomas was found guilty of both killings in 1971 and sentenced to life imprisonment. A second trial, ordered by the court of appeal, ended in a similar verdict on April 16, 1973. When Thomas was pardoned in 1980, the New Zealand government subsequently awarded him over $1 million in compensation.

569. Bell, Terry. *Bitter Hill: Arthur Thomas, the Case for a Retrial.* Manurewa, N.Z.: Avant-Garde, 1972. 88 pp.: ill.; 22 cm.

570. New Zealand. Royal Commission to Inquire into the Circumstances of the Convictions of Arthur Allan Thomas for the Murders of David Harvey Crewe and Jeanette Lenore Crewe. *Report of the Royal Commission to Inquire into the Circumstances of the Convictions of Arthur Allan Thomas for the Murders of David Harvey Crewe and Jeanette Lenore Crewe.* Wellington, N.Z.: P.D. Hasselberg, Govt. Printer, 1980. 124 pp.: ill.; 24 cm.

"Presented to the House of Representatives by command of His Excellency the Governor-General."

571. Yallop, David A. *Beyond Reasonable Doubt?* Auckland: Hodder and Stoughton, 1978. xii, 363 pp., [12] leaves of plates: ill.; 22 cm.

Thompson, Tilmer Eugene (a.k.a. "Cotton")

Born circa 1928 in Elmore, Minnesota. Attorney. St. Paul, Minnesota; 1 murder; bludgeon, knife; March 6, 1963.

"Oh, God help you."—Thompson's reaction upon hearing hitman Dick W. C. Anderson graphically describe in court the murder-for-hire slaying of his wife

Murder-for-hire case in which an attorney had his wife killed in order to collect over $1 million in insurance. On March 6, 1963, an armed intruder hid in the basement of attorney T. Eugene Thompson's luxurious home at 1720 Hillcrest Avenue in St. Paul, Minnesota, while Thompson and his four children left for work and school. Alone in the house, Thompson's 34-year-old wife Carol rested in an upstairs bedroom. The intruder confronted her there, struck her in the back of the head with a rubber hose, and after disrobing her tried to drown the stunned woman in a bathtub filled with standing water. Carol revived and, hastily donning a robe, fled down the stairs to the front door. The intruder caught her there as she fumbled with the chain lock and proceeded to strike her so many times in the head with the butt of a gun that the plastic hand grip shattered. As she lay on the floor, the man found a paring knife in the kitchen and plunged it into her throat 25 times until the blade broke off. While washing the blood off his hands in an upstairs bathroom, Carol Thompson miraculously managed to open the door and stumble into a neighbor's yard. Panicked, the intruder fled. Carol died later that day of skull fractures and a massive brain hemorrhage.

Investigators were initially baffled by the murder of the popular woman who in addition to being a leader of a Brownie troop was also active in the Presbyterian Church as a Sunday school teacher. Robbery as a motive was ruled out when $4,400 was found untouched in the house. Carol's husband since March 27, 1948, 35-year-old T. Eugene Thompson, was a respected attorney, devoted family man, and church trustee and elder who had no known enemies. However, an in-depth background check on Thompson revealed the upstanding attorney drank and gambled heavily, had a mistress, and at the time of his wife's death had her life insured for over $1 million. Speculation on Thompson's possible involvement in the murder became so widespread that the attorney issued a public statement on March 26, 1963, in which he discussed the policies and why they had been purchased.

Police, who had recovered the gun's distinctive black-and-white plastic grip at the scene, now ran a photo of it in the local paper. A Minneapolis salesman stepped forward to report that a gun with a similar homemade grip had been stolen from his apartment three weeks before the murder. The case began to lead inexorably back to Thompson when two suspects picked up for robbery and assault admitted to burglarizing the salesman's apartment then selling the stolen 7.65mm Luger to a 39-year-old ex-boxer named Norman Mastrian. Thompson had once represented Mastrian and the two had gone to college together. One of the suspects further admitted that he was present at a meeting between Mastrian and roofing and siding salesman Dick W. C. Anderson when the latter was given the gun for a "hit" on a St. Paul housewife. Mastrian and Anderson were both arrested on April 19, 1963. Thompson was arrested on June 21, 1963, after Anderson's confession implicated the attorney with "effecting" the premeditated murder of his wife.

Following a change of venue from Ramsey to Hennepin County, Thompson's trial began in Minneapolis on October 28, 1963. In gory detail, Anderson described repeatedly bludgeoning and stabbing Carol Thompson after he was unable to make her death look like an accidental drowning. He was paid $3,000 for the job. After six weeks of testimony, the case went to the jury on December 5, 1963. The next day, Thompson was found guilty of first degree murder and sentenced to life in prison at hard labor. On April 11, 1964, Norman Mastrian was found guilty of the same charge and sentenced to life. Anderson, the hitman, pleaded guilty on June 22, 1964, and was also given life. After serving 19 years, he was recommended for a work release program on February 8, 1983. Thompson was paroled, but placed on lifelong probation, on March 15, 1983. Norman Mastrian, the go-between, was granted a full parole on April 1, 1983, after serving 20 years.

572. Giese, Donald John. *The Carol Thompson Murder Case.* New York: Scope Reports, 1969. xi, 274 pp.: ill., ports.; 22 cm.

Giese, the reporter who covered the Thompson case for the St. Paul *Pioneer Press,* also published an article ("Why Was Carol Killed?") in the September 14, 1963, issue of *The Saturday Evening Post.* Six years after the trial that convicted Thompson, Giese was cited for criminal contempt when he refused to reveal sources of information for news articles he wrote about the case. The contempt citation was overturned by the U.S. Supreme Court on August 1, 1969.

Thorne, John Norman Holmes
(a.k.a. "The Crowborough Chicken Farm Murderer")

Born circa 1900. Executed April 22, 1925. Chicken farmer. Crowborough, Sussex, England; 1 murder; bludgeon; December 5, 1924.

"It isn't fair. I didn't do it!"—Thorne's reaction to the denial of his appeal

Sussex chicken farmer convicted of the murder and dismemberment of his "fiancée" based largely on the testimony of famed pathologist Sir Bernard Spilsbury. Norman Thorne, a 24-year-old chicken farmer who barely eked out an existence on a two-and-a-half acre farm near Crowborough, agreed to marry Elsie Emily Cameron, 26, if she was, as the ex–shorthand typist insisted, pregnant with his child. On December 5, 1924, Cameron arrived at Thorne's farm to press her marriage demand and was informed by him that he was involved with another woman. They quarreled and according to Thorne's post-arrest testimony, he left Cameron alone in his squalid hut to meet the other woman. Cameron was not seen again. Questioned by police days after her disappearance, however, Thorne told them that Cameron had never arrived at the farm. When authorities revisited the farm on January 15, 1925, they dug up a suitcase containing body parts buried in a potato patch. Thorne directed them to various other buried sacks stuffed with parts of Cameron's body. A tin box containing her head was unearthed in a chicken run.

Tried in Lewes in March 1925, Thorne maintained that he had returned from visiting the other woman to find that Cameron had committed suicide by hanging herself with a clothesline from a crossbeam in his hut. Fearful that he would be considered a murderer, Thorne dismembered Cameron's corpse with a hacksaw and buried it on his property. Testimony confirmed that Cameron was a logical suicide risk. Feeble-minded and unable to hold a job, the ex–shorthand typist suffered from neurasthenia and recurring bouts of deep depression. Sir Bernard Spilsbury, a respected doctor and honorary pathologist to the Home Office, determined Cameron's death to have been caused by head blows, not asphyxia, and declared the marks found on her neck to be natural rather than caused by hanging. Ironically, the autopsy further revealed that Cameron was not pregnant. A final blow to Thorne's "suicide defense" was the absence of rope marks on the crossbeam of the hut. A jury needed only 28 minutes on March 16, 1925, to find Thorne guilty and he was sentenced to death. Following an unsuccessful appeal, the one-time Sunday school teacher was hanged at Wandsworth Prison on April 22, 1925.

573. Normanton, Helena, ed. *The Trial of Norman Thorne: The Crowborough Chicken Farm Murder.* Famous Trials Series. London: G. Bles, 1929. 367 pp.: ill.; 22 cm.
     An entry in the Famous Trials Series which reproduces relevant portions of the transcript from Thorne's trial at the Sussex Winter Assizes, March 11–16, 1925. Normanton's introductory essay is sympathetic to Thorne and suggests that the Crown's case against him was dubious as was his guilt.

"Times Square Torso Murders"
see **Cottingham, Richard Francis**

Tinning, Marybeth Roe
(a.k.a. "Back Seat Mary")

Born circa 1945. School bus driver, ambulance driver, waitress, nurse's aide. Schenectady, New York; 8 murders (confessed to 3, suspected of 5 others); suffocation (pillow); January 1972–December 1985.
     "I did not do anything to Jennifer, Joseph, Barbara, Michael, Mary Frances ... Just these three, Timothy, Nathan, Tami. I smothered them because I'm not a good mother."—Excerpt from Tinning's confession.
     In the 13-year period between January 1972 and December 1985 Marybeth Tinning of Schenectady, New York, lost nine of her children (eight natural, one adopted) to causes listed variously as natural or undetermined or Sudden Infant Death Syndrome (SIDS). Though nurses, neighbors, and family members suspected her involvement in the deaths, Tinning was able to continue her sinister cycle of infanticide due to blind spots within the medical, law enforcement, and social services systems. While the odds against one family losing nine infants to SIDS or other illnesses are statistically improbable, autopsies performed on six of the children showed no signs of abuse. Similarly, follow-up visits to the Tinning home by the child protective unit of Schenectady's Department of Social Services failed to reveal anything suspicious about Marybeth or her husband of nearly 20 years, Joseph. Marybeth seemingly reveled in the attention and sympathy she received from hospital staff each time she brought a dead or dying child into the emergency room and showed appropriate concern as they vainly tried to resuscitate the infant. Not one of her nine children lived to the age of five.

The cycle of Marybeth's pregnancies, the birth and inexplicable deaths of her children, followed by funerals where she rarely shed a tear became so commonplace that one relative just quit attending the functions.

An only child until age five, Marybeth Roe's suspicions that she was unwanted were confirmed by an aunt who told the youngster that she was "unplanned." Her father, a strict disciplinarian, cited her as the bad example to avoid when talking to his beloved younger son. Anxious to win her father's love, Marybeth succeeded only in annoying the man with her frequent crying spells. As punishment, he beat her with a flyswatter and once locked her in a closet for an entire day. Deprived of attention at home, Marybeth sought it at school where she screamed at and bullied the younger children. In high school, the plain young woman had few friends and although elected president of the Future Homemakers of America during her junior year, failed to make any significant impression on her classmates save one. In the 1961 Duanesburg, New York, Central High School yearbook a committee of students assigning a "Mark of Distinction" for each graduating senior summed up Marybeth in one word, "temper."

A blind date with General Electric worker Joseph Tinning resulted in marriage. Honest and hard-working, Tinning was the polar opposite of his dominant, emotionally supercharged wife. Showing little emotion or interest in anything other than work, he was described by one investigator as being so "emotionally passive" that not only did he show no curiosity over the deaths of his children, he also had difficulty in remembering all their names. On January 3, 1972, eight-day-

old Jennifer Lewis, the youngest of the Tinnings' three children, died in St. Clare's Hospital in Schenectady of acute meningitis. According to all accounts, the child's death (the only one not considered suspicious by authorities) irrevocably changed Marybeth Tinning. She took the child's body to her hospital bed, held it close to her, and pulled a sheet over them. Psychiatrists, attempting to fathom Tinning's subsequent murderous behavior, offered two explanations as to how Jennifer's death affected her. Some viewed the murders as Marybeth's attempt to work through her grief by re-creating the experience of her first baby's death and continually punishing herself. A more cynical explanation branded Tinning a "sympathy junkie" who enjoyed the attention that her children's deaths focused on her, a mental disease known as Munchausen syndrome.

Seventeen days after losing Jennifer, two-year-old Joseph, Jr., was brought dead to Schenectady's Ellis Hospital on January 20, 1972. Due to a lapse of procedure, no autopsy was performed and doctors pronounced the cause of death as cardiorespiratory arrest, a non-diagnosis that meant only that the child had stopped breathing. On March 2, 1972, Tinning's four-year-old daughter Barbara Ann died at the same hospital after allegedly telling her mother that she would soon see her dead brother in heaven. An autopsy was performed, but its results were never communicated to the medical examiner. Death was attributed to Reye's syndrome, at the time a little understood degeneration of the brain and liver marked by seizures. The case was reported to police, but dropped after investigators checked with doctors. Four months after her daughter's death, Tinning applied to the Department of Social Services to be a foster mother. About three weeks after he was born, Timothy Tinning died at Ellis Hospital on December 10, 1973. Admitting in retrospect that the entire incident was a "snafu," the medical examiner reported the death, but no autopsy was ever ordered. For lack of a better diagnosis, death was attributed to SIDS. Tinning later confessed to suffocating Timothy with a pillow to stop his crying.

Tinning's "temper" surfaced in spring 1974 when, after several arguments with husband Joseph over money, she poisoned his food with phenobarbital. Although nearly dying, the man refused to press charges preferring to let people think he had attempted suicide. Nor did he listen to his brother's advice to get a vasectomy to prevent Marybeth's nearly annual pregnancies. On September 2, 1975, Marybeth's five-month-old son Nathan stopped breathing. Instead of rushing him to a nearby hospital, Tinning drove the boy across town to the restaurant where she waitressed and begged for help. Nathan was ambulanced to St. Clare's emergency room, but died without regaining consciousness. Death was attributed to acute coronary edema although Tinning later confessed to suffocating him in the car with a sofa pillow. On February 20, 1979, three-and-a-half-month-old Mary Frances was rushed to St. Clare's in full cardiac arrest. A month before, the child had been revived in the hospital's emergency room in a case diagnosed as "aborted SIDS." Outfitted with an apnea monitor, the child was found unconscious in her crib by Tinning after it sounded. Mary Frances was resuscitated, but sustained irreversible brain damage. She died two days later

after being removed from a life support system. Death was attributed to SIDS.

An almost identical scenario unfolded in early 1980. Like his dead sister, three-year-old Jonathan was rushed unconscious to St. Clare's emergency room where he responded to resuscitation. Genetic tests were run on the child and he was sent home with an apnea monitor. Three days later Tinning returned with a barely breathing Jonathan who was already brain damaged. Kept alive on machines for four weeks, Jonathan died on March 24, 1980. An autopsy performed by an Albany, New York, pathologist without access to the reports on the earlier Tinning autopsies performed in Schenectady attributed the cause of death as "etiology undetermined." Suspicious investigators were unable to gather enough information to warrant opening a formal inquiry. The theory that the Tinning children died as a result of a recessive "death gene" was weakened with the death on March 2, 1981, of three-year-old Michael Raymond. The Tinnings were in the process of adopting the black child when he was brought dead to St. Clare's on March 2, 1981. Death was attributed to bronchial pneumonia despite the sinister coincidence that a month earlier the child had suffered a head injury in an allegedly accidental fall.

The death of three-month-old Tami Lynne (her only surviving child) on December 20, 1985, marked the end of Tinning's infanticide. According to Tinning, she found the child unconscious in her crib and unresponsive to CPR. Tami Lynne was pronounced dead at the hospital. Despite having lost eight children, Tinning had refused a doctor's suggestion to place an apnea monitor on the infant and then placed Tami's crib out of earshot of her room. Armed with the medical histories and autopsy reports on some of the other victims, pathologists looked into their certified causes of death and determined that except in the case of Jennifer, each death could have been due to suffocation. By January 1986 the Tinning Task Force concluded that suffocation alone explained the deaths of the Tinning children. On February 4, 1986, Marybeth was questioned by authorities at the state police barracks in Loudonville, New York. With her husband present during much of the seven-hour interrogation, Tinning confessed to smothering Tami Lynne with a pillow to stop her crying. She admitted that Timothy in 1973 and Nathan in 1975 had met similar fates. Tinning subsequently wrote and signed the confession.

Charged with second-degree murder in the death of Tami Lynne, Tinning maintained that police had coerced her confession during a marathon interrogation session in which she was denied food. A pre-trial hearing ruled the confession admissible in court, but prevented the prosecution from mentioning the deaths of the other Tinning children. Opening arguments in the case were heard in Schenectady on June 23, 1987. The defense maintained through a forensic scientist that Tami Lynne and the other Tinning children suffered from Werdnig-Hoffmann syndrome, a hereditary infantile disorder similar to Lou Gehrig's disease. An SIDS expert for the defense testified that the child had been smothered. After deliberating 23 hours over three days, the jury of seven men and five women found Tinning guilty on one count of second-degree murder by "depraved indifference to human life." Interviewed afterwards, jurors cited Tinning's confession as the primary consideration in their decision to convict. While awaiting sentencing, Tinning's lawyer claimed that among other acts of kindness his client was making a baby blanket for a pregnant inmate. On October 1, 1987, she was sentenced to 21 years to life, five years less than the harshest penalty for the crime. A 1988 appeal was unanimously turned down in the New York State Supreme Court's appellate division. Citing errors made by the prosecution, a Schenectady County judge in March 1990 dropped charges pending against Tinning in her confessed murders of Timothy and Nathan. Tinning will not be eligible for parole until she is 65.

574. Eggington, Joyce. *From Cradle to Grave: The Short Lives and Strange Deaths of Marybeth Tinning's Nine Children.* 1st ed. New York: Morrow, 1989. 363 pp., [8]pp. of plates: ill.; 24 cm.

_____. [Same as 574.] London: W.H. Allen, 1989. 379 pp., [8]pp. of plates: ill., ports.; 22 cm. (Paperback ed. also available.)

_____. [Same as 574.] Jove ed. New York: Berkley, 1990. viii, 373 pp., [8]pp. of plates: ill.; 18 cm. ("A Jove book"); paperback.

_____. [Same as 574.] London: True Crime, 1992. 379 pp., [8]pp. of plates: ill.; 18 cm.; paperback.

Well written and documented case study which offers real psychological insights into the murders. Includes index.

Toole, Ottis Elwood

Born March 5, 1947, in Jacksonville, Florida. Drifter. Florida and at least 25 other states; 5 murder convictions (confessed to 360, authorities estimate at least 110); knife, gun, bludgeon, strangulation, axe, fire; 1961–1982.

"Remember one time I said I wanted me some ribs? Did that make me a cannibal?"—Toole in a November 1983 conversation with Henry Lee Lucas taped by the Texas Rangers; *see also* Lucas, Henry Lee.

"Trailside Killings" *see* Carpenter, David Joseph

True, Ronald
(a.k.a. "Major True")

Born June 17, 1891, in Manchester, England. Died 1951. Flight instructor, assistant manager of mining company. London, England; 1 murder; bludgeon (rolling pin), ligature strangulation; March 5, 1922.

"Here's another for our Murderer's Club. We only accept those who kill them outright."—True speaking to another prisoner charged with murder

Drug-addicted killer of a West End prostitute whose death sentence was commuted to life imprisonment when government-appointed psychiatrists diagnosed him as insane. Born out of wedlock to a 16-year-old girl who married into wealth when he was 11, Ronald True enjoyed a healthy childhood filled with parental affection and privilege. By age six, however, the seeds of True's later insanity were already beginning to emerge. A chronic liar and a poor student, the boy inflicted cruelties on his pets and was seemingly unable to demonstrate any love for his devoted mother. When told at 14 that she was seriously ill, True casually remarked, "Oh well, if she dies all her property will be mine...." Painfully aware that her son would never succeed in England, True's mother sent the 17 year old to New Zealand in 1908 to learn farming. True

failed in less than a year and returned to England. From 1911 through 1914 he wandered the world looking for his niche, traveling first to Argentina, then to Canada where he served for a short while in the Northwest Mounted Police, on to Mexico, and finally to Shanghai in mid-1914 where it is believed he acquired a severe morphia habit.

At the outbreak of World War I True returned to England and joined the Royal Flying Corps. As a cadet at the Gosport Flying School he failed most of his written tests and suffered a severe brain concussion in February 1916 when the plane he was flying crashed at Farnborough. True emerged from a coma two days later and his behavior, always eccentric, became even more outlandish. Awarded "wings," True modified their design to make them three times larger than regulation. Complaining that his cap hurt his head, he wore it only when saluting a superior officer. After a second crash, the would-be pilot was invalided out of the service in March 1916 and sent to recuperate at the Alexandria Military Hospital in Cosham. He was later sent to a private home in Southsea when his behavior turned violent. True's morphia addiction was discovered there when doctors learned that normal dosages of the drug did little to ease the pain of his injuries. Undaunted, True tapped into an underground network to supplement his habit.

In 1917 True managed to find a job as a test pilot at the Yeovil Government Control Works, but was fired after a few months for incompetency. Posing as an invalided fighter pilot, True traveled to New York, married actress Frances Roberts, and persuaded the U.S. War Department to hire him as a flight instructor at their school in

Mineola. Once again he was dismissed for incompetency. True returned to England with his pregnant wife to find that his family had secured him a job on West Africa's Gold Coast as an assistant manager in the Taquah Mining Company. His strange behavior in the native compound alarmed company officials who terminated him after less than six months' employment. Back in England in August 1919, True's total dependency on morphia prompted his family to abandon the notion of finding him work. Instead, they placed him on an allowance sufficient to support his wife and child. By 1920, however, True's mental deterioration had reached such an advanced state that his mother and wife shuttled him between various nursing homes. Their attempts to wean True from morphia were met with violent outbursts and undermined by his illegal purchase of the drug. In September 1921 True was convicted of forging prescriptions for morphia.

He abandoned his family in mid-February 1922 and wandered in London's West End posing as "Major True." Over the next two months True sank even deeper into morphia-induced madness. Never without a gun in his pocket, True told acquaintances that Scotland Yard had given him permission to carry the weapon so that he could protect himself against another "Ronald True" who intended to kill him. He bragged of his intention to murder the man and anyone else who got in his way. On February 17, 1922, True met 25-year-old prostitute Gertrude Yates (known on the street as "Olive Young") at a lounge in the West End. Yates disliked the 31 year old and made every attempt to avoid him. True was persistent. On March 5, 1922, he showed up late at her basement flat at 13a Finborough Road, Fulham, and persuaded her to let him spend the night. The next morning as Yates dozed in bed, True was preparing tea in the kitchen when he noticed a rolling pin. As Yates sat up in bed drinking tea, True bashed her in the head five times with the rolling pen. He dragged the stunned woman into the bathroom, stuffed a towel down her throat, and used the belt from her robe to strangle the prostitute to death. True rummaged through the apartment and found £8 and some jewelry he could pawn. He informed the day servant who arrived an hour later not to disturb the sleeping woman. Moments after he left, the servant discovered Yates' body and called Scotland Yard.

True went immediately to buy a new suit, explaining to the salesman that the fresh bloodstains on his clothes were from a recent flying accident. Freshly attired, he had a haircut and shave at a barber shop where he left the package containing his bloodstained suit. Yates' jewelry fetched £25 at a pawn shop and True used the money to attend the Hammersmith Palace of Varieties with a friend on March 6, 1922, the night after the murder. Detectives traced True through his chauffeur service and arrested him in the theatre without incident as he sat in a box seat enjoying the show. True insisted that he knew nothing of the crime. Prior to his trial at London's Central Criminal Court on May 1, 1922, True underwent extensive psychological examinations by four independent psychiatrists. They were unanimous in diagnosing True as suffering from a congenital mental disorder aggravated by his long-term addiction to morphia and classified him as certifiably insane. Despite the strength and unanimity of medical opinion, however, True was convicted of murder on May 5, 1922, and sentenced to death. Following the dismissal of True's appeal, the home secretary appointed a board composed of three medical men to review the case. Based on their finding that the killer was hopelessly insane, the official respited the execution order and committed True to life imprisonment in Broadmoor, a penal hospital. The home secretary, amid a storm of public outcry calling for True's execution, eloquently defended his action before the House of Commons. Ronald True, aged 60, died in Broadmoor in 1951.

575. Carswell, Donald, ed. *Trial of Ronald True*. Notable British Trials. Edinburgh; London: W. Hodge, 1925. x, 295 pp.: ill.; 22 cm.
_____. [Same as 575.] Notable British Trials. Toronto: Canada Lawbook, 1925. x, 295 pp.: ill.; 22 cm.
_____. [Same as 575.] [New ed.] Notable British Trials. Edinburgh; London: W. Hodge, 1950. x, 295 pp., [4] leaves of plates: ill.; 22 cm.
Transcript of True's trial held at Central Criminal Court, Old Bailey, London, May 1922, for the murder of Gertrude Yates.

"Truro Murders" *see* Miller, James William

Tucker, Karla Faye
(a.k.a. "Karla Faye Griffith" [married name])

Born November 18, 1959, in Houston, Texas. Prostitute. Houston, Texas; 2 murders; bludgeon (hammer, pickax); June 13, 1983.
    "I got a nut with every stroke."— Tucker recorded on a police informant's wire referring to the orgasms she experienced while repeatedly striking Jerry Lynn Dean with a pickax

Convicted pickax murderess whose death penalty has mobilized support against the sentence from many including the family of her victims. Karla Faye Tucker started smoking marijuana at eight, shot heroin at ten, was a groupie with the Allman Brothers rock band at 13, and had known only two drug-free weeks in the 14 years prior to helping her lover, Daniel Ryan Garrett, 37, commit two of the most shocking murders in the history of Houston, Texas. On the night of June 13, 1983, Tucker, 23, Garrett, and a friend, Jimmy Leibrant, drove to the apartment of Jerry Lynn Dean, a 26-year-old sometime biker and cable television company installer, to steal his Harley-Davidson motorcycle and rough him up. Tucker hated Dean ever since she found him working on his motorcycle in the living room of the apartment she shared with a woman he was dating. Likewise, Dean kept the prized cycle he was rebuilding in the living room of his apartment. Tucker and Garrett entered the apartment while Leibrant waited outside. Inside, they found Dean asleep on a mattress piled on the bedroom floor, a pickax he used in his work nearby. Both Tucker and Garrett took turns battering Dean with the weapon until he died from 28 separate wounds. Deborah Ruth Thornton, a 32-year-old woman whom Dean had picked up at a beer party earlier in the day, was found crouching under the covers. She was struck 26 times with the pickax left buried in her chest. In the weeks following the double homicide, the pair bragged so much about the killings to Garrett's family that his brother, fearful that they would eliminate him as a witness, contacted police. He agreed to wear a wire and tape-recorded Tucker and Garrett confessing to the murders. On the tape,

Tucker admitted experiencing an orgasm every time she struck Dean with the pickax. At her trial, Tucker's attorney openly admitted his client's guilt in a ploy to avoid the death penalty. It failed and Tucker was sentenced to death in April 1984. Garrett was convicted and sentenced to death in a separate trial, but the conviction was overturned on January 13, 1993, on grounds of improper jury selection. While awaiting a new trial, Garrett died on June 14, 1993, of cirrhosis of the liver one day after the tenth anniversary of the double homicide. Tucker experienced a religious conversion in prison and has since taken college correspondence courses, taught herself sign language, and enjoys the strong support of many (including the former prosecutor and several prison guards) who argue that her sentence should be commuted to life without the possibility of parole. Appeals have failed and execution dates have been set and then stayed. If executed, Tucker will be the first woman put to death in Texas since 1863 when Chipita Rodriguez was hanged for the murder of a horse trader. On November 9, 1993, the Texas court of appeals granted Tucker an indefinite stay of execution.

576. Lowry, Beverly. *Crossed Over: A Murder, a Memoir.* 1st ed. New York: Knopf, 1992. 245 pp.; 22 cm.

_____. [Same as 576.] 1st ed. New York: Warner Books, 1994. 291 pp.; 17 cm.; paperback.

Novelist Lowry (who lost her 18-year-old son in an unsolved hit-and-run) became obsessed with Tucker's case and writes compassionately about the young murderess' crime and rehabilitation. The book is dedicated "For Karla: long life."

Umstadter, Travis

Born October 30, 1966. Carpenter. Seeleyville, Pennsylvania; 1 murder; .22 caliber Excam revolver; August 15, 1986.

"I see him die every day, and I feel myself die more every day."—Umstadter testifying about his victim at trial

Revenge killing of an alcohol-impaired driver by the brother of the young woman killed in the car he was operating. On the night of August 15, 1986, Kristen Marie Umstadter, a popular 17-year-old high school student, and two girlfriends were cruising on Route 652 near Seeleyville, Pennsylvania, in a car driven by 20-year-old Glenn Evans. Driving the car erratically at speeds reaching 85 miles per hour, Evans attempted to pass a slower car in a no passing zone, lost control, and crossed the center line into the path of an oncoming station wagon. The crash severed Umstadter's aorta, and her two friends suffered head injuries, but Evans emerged from the car nearly unscathed. Reeking of beer, Evans admitted to state troopers that he had been drinking that night. Unaware that Umstadter had died at the scene, Evans maintained that she had caused the accident by grabbing the steering wheel to avoid hitting the oncoming car. A blood check performed two hours and ten minutes after the accident established Evans' blood alcohol level to be .09, just below the .10 standard establishing intoxication under Pennsylvania law. Evans pleaded not guilty to a charge of homicide by motor vehicle while under the influence of alcohol and other offenses and was released on $5,000 bail. Travis Umstadter, the dead girl's 20-year-old brother, was particularly devastated by her death and like his parents refused to believe that Kristen, founder of the local chapter of Students Against Drunk Driving, might have been drinking on the night of her death as Evans maintained. Evans was tried on January 19, 1987, and witnesses at the scene of the crash testified that he emerged from the wreckage shouting, "She fucked with the wheel." As the blood/alcohol test revealed Evans was barely within the legal limit for sobriety, technically he could not be called a drunk driver. On January 21, 1987, Evans was found not guilty of the more serious charge of vehicular homicide while under the influence of alcohol, but convicted of involuntary manslaughter, homicide by motor vehicle, and five lesser charges. The two named charges each carried possible 5-year sentences and $10,000 fines. He remained free on $5,000 bond pending a pre-sentencing report.

The Umstadter family refused to accept the verdict and Travis told a drinking buddy days after the trial, "Glenn won't live until spring." After drinking heavily the night before, Umstadter arrived at Evans' apartment in Seeleyville in the early morning of January 28, 1987. According to Umstadter's later confession, the men spoke amicably for nearly two hours until Umstadter pressed Evans for more detailed information about the fatal accident. Evans responded angrily, "If that dumb bitch sister of yours hadn't grabbed the steering wheel, she would be living today," and then brandished a pair of scissors in Umstadter's face. Umstadter pulled a .22 caliber pistol from the waistband of his trousers and shot Evans four times in the head and neck. By pre-arrangement with the district attorney, Umstadter surrendered to authorities on February 19, 1987. Free on $50,000

bond, Umstadter married in June 1987 months before jury selection began in his first degree murder trial on August 3, 1987. Determined to have been drunk at the time of the killing, Umstadter was acquitted of first degree murder a week later, but found guilty of murder in the third degree. At a September 17, 1987, sentencing hearing, Umstadter was given the maximum sentence of not less than 10 years nor more than 20 years. Subsequent superior court and state supreme court appeals have been denied.

577. Dorman, Michael. *Blood and Revenge: A True Story of Small-Town Murder and Justice.* New York: Dell, 1991. 212 pp.; 17 cm.; paperback.

Van Houten, Leslie Sue (a.k.a. "LuLu," "Leslie Marie Sankston," "Louella Alexandria," "Leslie Owens")

Born August 23, 1949, in Altadena, California. Cult member. Los Angeles, California; 2 murders (2 convictions); knife, bludgeon; August 10, 1969.

"Sorry is only a five-letter word."— Van Houten when asked at the time of her first trial if she felt sorry for her victims; *see also* Manson, Charles Milles.

Vaquier, Jean Pierre (a.k.a. "J. Wanker")

Born circa 1879 in Niort, Aude, France. Executed August 12, 1924. Wireless operator, inventor. Byfleet, Surrey, England; 1 murder; poison (strychnine); March 29, 1924.

"I can only say that I am innocent. I swear on my mother's and my father's graves, still fresh, that I am quite innocent of the crime of which I have been accused."—Vaquier to Mr. Justice Avory after being found guilty of the murder of Alfred Poynter Jones

French poisoner executed in 1924 for the murder of his mistress' husband. On January 9, 1924 Mrs. Mabel Theresa Jones of Byfleet, Surrey, was vacationing alone at the Hotel Victoria in Biarritz, France, when she met the brilliantined dandy Jean Pierre Vaquier, a wireless operator employed by the hotel. Despite the language barrier (Vaquier frequently referred to his French-English dictionary), the pair began a torrid affair. Mrs. Jones left France on February 8, 1924, returning to her husband Alfred Poynter Jones, the owner of the Blue Anchor Hotel in Byfleet. The next day the Frenchman followed her to England hoping to sell the patent rights to a sausage machine he invented. During his six-week stay at the Blue Anchor Hotel, Vaquier lived off Mrs. Jones while continuing to make love with her on a regular basis. On March 29, 1924, Alfred Jones fell into convulsions and died after drinking some bromo salts later found to contain strychnine. Press photographs taken of Vaquier led to his arrest on April 19, 1924, after a chemist in London recognized him as the customer "J. Wanker" who had purchased strychnine weeks before. Tried at Guildford, Vaquier failed to convince the jury that found him guilty on July 5, 1924, that he had purchased the strychnine for use in his wireless experiments. The elegant Frenchman was hanged at Wandsworth Prison on August 12, 1924.

578. Blundell, R.H., and Seaton, R.E., eds. *Trial of Jean Pierre Vaquier*. Notable British Trials. Edinburgh; London: W. Hodge, 1929. xxiv, 208 pp., [10] leaves of plates: ill., ports.; 22 cm.

_____. [Same as 578.] Notable British Trials. Toronto: Canada Law Book, 1929. xxiv, 208 pp., [10] leaves of plates: ill., ports.; 22 cm.

Transcript of Vaquier's trial at the Surrey Summer Assizes, July 1924, for the murder of Alfred Jones.

Walker, Buck Duane
(a.k.a. "Wesley Walker," "Roy Allen")

Born circa 1938. Drug dealer, felon. Palmyra Atoll (Line Islands); 2 murders (1 conviction, suspected of 1 other); .22 caliber pistol; August 30, 1974.

Television: "And the Sea Will Tell" (1991), a two-part, four-hour, made-for-television movie based on Bugliosi and Henderson's book of the same title, originally aired on CBS on February 24 and 26, 1991. Cast includes Richard Crenna (Vincent Bugliosi), Hart Bochner (Buck Walker), Rachel Ward (Jennifer), Deidre Hall ("Muff" Graham), and James Brolin ("Mac" Graham).

Audio: And the Sea Will Tell, a two-sound cassette, three-hour abridgement of the Bugliosi and Henderson book of the same title narrated by Richard Crenna, was published in 1992 by Simon & Schuster (New York).

"I'm not sticking my neck in no chopping block."—Walker's alleged reply to Stearns' request that he face trial before her on the charge of murdering "Muff" Graham

On June 1, 1974, career criminal Buck Walker, 36, and his lover Stephanie Stearns, 28, fled the Hawaiian island of Kauai on their sailboat the *Iola* to escape federal drug charges. After four weeks sailing in the dangerously leaking under-provisioned vessel, the novice sailors landed on remote

Palmyra Island, a coral atoll 1,000 miles southwest of Hawaii. Days later, experienced seaman Malcolm "Mac" Graham, III, 43, and his 42-year-old wife Eleanor ("Muff") sailed into the Palmyra lagoon on their well provisioned 38-foot, two-masted ketch *Sea Wind*. Tempers flared over the two months the couples shared the island and friends of the Grahams were concerned when the last radio communication they received from them was August 28, 1974. Two months later, Walker and Stearns (posing as the "Allens") turned up in Honolulu in the *Sea Wind*, partially disguised, renamed, and repainted. The pair were subsequently convicted in separate trials on federal charges of boat theft and the transport of stolen goods. Stearns received two years with Walker sentenced to 10 years plus an additional three for the drug conviction he fled from. After serving 42 months, Walker escaped from the McNeil Island Federal Penitentiary in Washington State on July 10, 1979, was recaptured and sentenced to five more years.

In January 1981, the mystery of what happened to the Grahams was at least partially solved when a trunk-sized aluminum box containing charred human bones and a skull was found on the beach at Palmyra. Forensics confirmed the skull was that of "Muff" Graham and the hole in its temple suggested that she had died violently, perhaps of a gunshot wound. Walker and Stearns were charged with her murder and their trials severed. At his federal trial in May 1985, Walker maintained that on August 30, 1974, he and Stearns visited the Grahams for drinks at their invitation. They arrived to find the couple absent, but a search revealed their dinghy capsized in the lagoon. As he had won the *Sea Wind* in chess games with Graham, Walker took the newer boat and left the island. The prosecution argued that Walker murdered the couple to get their boat because his was leaking and short of provisions. Their case was bolstered by a prison witness who testified that Walker had bragged about forcing "Mac" Graham to "walk the plank." Walker was found guilty on June 11, 1985, and subsequently sentenced to life imprisonment to be served consecutively after his 18-year sentences on drug, escape, and stolen property charges. Stearns retained Vincent Bugliosi, the famed Los Angeles district attorney's prosecutor who won convictions against Charles Manson, et al. Bugliosi and co-counsel Leonard Weinglass, a well-known lawyer for the political left, successfully raised doubt in the jury's mind as to Stearns' involvement in the murder and she was acquitted on February 28, 1986. A three-judge panel of the Ninth U. S. Circuit Court of Appeals unanimously upheld Walker's conviction on February 20, 1987. He will be eligible to apply for parole in 2006 when he is 68 years old.

579. Bugliosi, Vincent, and Henderson, Bruce B. *And the Sea Will Tell*. 1st ed. New York: Norton, 1991. 574 pp.: ill.; 24 cm.

_____. [Same as 579.] 1st Ballantine ed. New York: Ballantine, 1992. 657 pp.: ill.; 18 cm.; paperback.

Remarkably detailed, but overlong account of the case cowritten by Bugliosi, Stephanie Stearns' defense attorney. Required reading for anyone interested in how a murder defense is prepared then won against seemingly impossible odds. The authors, without explanation, rename Stephanie Stearns "Jennifer Jenkins."

Wallace, William Herbert
(reprieved)

Born circa 1878. Died February 26, 1933. Insurance agent. Liverpool, England; 1 murder (reprieved); bludgeon (poker or iron bar); January 20, 1931.

"What can I say in answer to a charge of which I am absolutely innocent?"—Wallace's response to being placed under arrest for the murder of his wife

Mild-mannered Prudential Assurance Company agent convicted, but later reprieved, of bludgeoning his wife to death. On January 19, 1931, a telephone message from "R. M. Qualtrough" was left for William Herbert Wallace, a member of the Liverpool Central Chess Club, at Cottle's City Pub where the group conducted its meetings. Qualtrough requested that Wallace meet him the next night at 7:30 p.m. on an insurance matter at 25 Menlove Gardens East in Mossley Hill. When given the message, Wallace stated that he did not know a Mr. Qualtrough and was unfamiliar with the address supplied by the prospective client. The next evening around 7:00 p.m., the 52-year-old insurance agent took a tram to the Menlove Garden area of Liverpool and spent an hour wandering the district asking several people the location of the fictitious address. Returning to his home at 29 Wolverton Street around 8:45 p.m., Wallace was surprised to find the doors locked against him. He summoned his neighbors and surprisingly opened the back door without much effort. The neighbors entered the house with Wallace to find the body of 50-year-old Julia Wallace, his wife of 16 years, on the floor of the front sitting room before the fire. Her head had been smashed in with a blunt object (the fireplace poker was missing) and the walls and furniture in the room were spattered with blood. Beneath her, a partially burned mackintosh belonging to Wallace was found giving rise to speculation that she fell into the fire during the brutal attack. Wallace, seemingly unconcerned about his dead wife, calmly surveyed the house and reported that £4 belonging to his company had been stolen from a cash box. Investigators, suspicious of Wallace's stoic demeanor, quickly determined the house had not been broken into and dismissed the Qualtrough character as the suspect's clever attempt to shift suspicion away from himself. Wallace was arrested on February 2, 1931, and charged with the willful murder of his wife.

The Wallace trial opened before Mr. Justice Wright at the Liverpool Spring Assizes on April 22, 1931. Lacking a murder weapon or an apparent motive to explain the murder, the prosecution based its case on purely circumstantial evidence. The absence of blood on Wallace's clothing, it was argued, was explained by his donning of the mackintosh found under the body to shield himself against blood splatters. Another theory, that Wallace was naked during the attack and bathed afterwards, was refuted by the absence of damp towels in the house. Despite a highly favorable summing up by Mr. Justice Wright who stopped just short of stating that the prosecution had failed to prove its case, Wallace was convicted and sentenced to death on April 25, 1931. The verdict was quashed by the Lord Chief Justice on May 19, 1931, and Wallace was freed. He returned to work, but unable to endure the cruel taunts of those who once supported him, left the next month to take up residence at "The Summer House," a small bungalow in Meadowside Road, Bromborough, on the Cheshire side of the Mersey. Wallace, however, had only moved five miles from Liverpool, not far enough to escape local gossip and vicious poison pen letters. Broken in health and spirit, Wallace died of a chronic kidney complaint in Clatterbridge Hospital on February 26, 1933. His last words, spoken to a visiting nephew, were "Do good with your life." On March 1, 1933, Wallace was buried next to his wife in Liverpool's Anfield Cemetery. Recent scholarship (Goodman, Wilkes) points to Richard Gordon Parry, a 22-year-old insurance agent, as the murderer of Julia Wallace.

580. Goodman, Jonathan. *The Killing of Julia Wallace.* Foreword by Edgar Lustgarten. London: Harrap, 1969. 323 pp., [17]pp. of plates: ill., facsims., ports.; 23 cm.

_____. [Same as 580.] Foreword by Edgar Lustgarten. New York: Scribner, 1969. 323 pp., [17] plates: ill., facsims., maps, plans, ports.; 23 cm.

_____. [Same as 580.] Foreword by Edgar Lustgarten. Rev. ed. London: Severn House, 1976. 323 pp., [16]pp. of plates: ill., facsims., ports.; 23 cm.

_____. [Same as 580.] Foreword by Edgar Lustgarten. New York: Scribner, 1977. 323 pp., [8] leaves of plates: ill., facsims., ports.; 23 cm.

Excellent study in which Goodman in the chapter "A Different Verdict," presents evidence he maintains "conclusively" proves Wallace's innocence. Goodman's "Mr. X," (whom he maintains possibly committed the murder) is Richard Gordon Parry although he never names him. Appendix includes Wallace's statement volunteered to Detective-Inspector Gold at about midnight on Tuesday, January 20, 1931. Includes bibliography and index.

581. Hussey, Robert F. *Murderer Scot-Free: England's Only 'Non-Proven' Murder Judgment; A Solution to the Wallace Puzzle.* Newton Abbot, Eng.: David & Charles, 1972. 200 pp.: ill.; 22 cm.

_____. [Same as 581.] 1st American ed. South Brunswick: Great Albion Books, 1972. 200 pp.: ill.; 23 cm.

582. Rowland, John. *The Wallace Case.* London: Carroll & Nicholson, 1949. 185 pp.: ill., ports.; 23 cm.

583. Wilkes, Roger. *Wallace, the Final Verdict.* London: Bodley Head, 1984. 269 pp., [16]pp. of plates: ill.; 23 cm.

_____. [Same as 583.] True Crime Series. London: Triad, 1985. 301 pp., [16]pp. of plates: ill., facsims., plans, ports.; 18 cm.; paperback.

Wilkes, who calls the Wallace case the "greatest British murder mystery since Jack the Ripper," firmly believes in the insurance agent's innocence and posits Richard Gordon Parry as the murderer. This book grew out of a program that the author appeared on with Jonathan Goodman, et al. for Radio City, Merseyside's independent radio station, on the fiftieth anniversary of the murder. Appendices include Wallace's first statement to the police, excerpts from Wallace's diaries, and comments by Raymond Chandler. Includes bibliography and index. Consult the bibliography for numerous fictional works based on the case.

584. Wyndham-Brown, W.F., ed. *The Trial of William Herbert Wallace.* London: V. Gollancz, 1933. 320 pp.: ill., ports., facsim.; 22 cm.

Watson, Charles Denton (a.k.a. "Tex," "Charles Montgomery," "Texas Charlie")

Born December 2, 1945, in McKinney, Texas. Cult member. Los Angeles, California; 7 murders (7 convictions); gun, knife, bludgeon; August 9–10, 1969.

"I am the Devil and I'm here to do the Devil's business."—Watson to Voytek Frykowski shortly before he killed him; see also Manson, Charles Milles.

Weger, Chester Otto
(a.k.a. "Madman of Starved Rock," "Rocky")

Born March 3, 1939, in Derby, Iowa. Dishwasher, house painter. Starved Rock State Park near Utica, Illinois; 3 murders, bludgeon (tree branch); March 14, 1960.

In what still ranks as one of the most shocking crimes in Illinois history, the bodies of three prominent Riverside socialites were found by a search team bound and bludgeoned to death in a cave at Starved Rock State Park near Utica, Illinois, on March 16, 1960. The victims, Frances Murphy, 47, Mildred Lindquist, 50, and Lillian Oetting, 50, were each married to successful Chicago executives, active in community work, and members of the Riverside Presbyterian Church. Police estimate that within hours of arriving at the popular state park on March 14, 1960, for a shared vacation of hiking and photography, the women encountered Chester Weger near the frozen waterfall in St. Louis Canyon. Employed as a dishwasher in the park's lodge, the 21 year old was but one of several suspects questioned by authorities during an eight-month investigation which demonstrated the police's ineffectiveness and the inadequacies of the state's crime lab. Though now nationally recognized as among the best crime labs in the country, critics at the time charged that the facility was less equipped than many high school chemistry labs. Weger initially passed

30 hours of lie detector tests administered by state experts, but failed a subsequent reexamination months later conducted by local authorities that focused on the twine found binding the wrists of the victims and the scratches on Weger's face at the time of the murder. The twine at the murder scene proved identical to that used in the kitchen of the lodge. When police showed Weger's mug shot, among others, to a woman raped on September 13, 1959, in Matthiessen State Park near Oglesby, Illinois, she positively identified him as her assailant. Arrested on November 16, 1960, on the rape charge, Weger confessed to the triple homicide under intense questioning. Weger produced a written confession the next day and was transported by police to Starved Rock State Park where he re-enacted the crime.

According to Weger, what began as a simple robbery escalated into murder when Frances Murphy worked free of her twine bindings and struck him in the head with a pair of binoculars as he was leaving the scene. Weger beat her to death with a frozen tree limb. He panicked, killed the other two bound women, placed their bodies in the cave, and disarranged their clothing to make it appear that the murders were sexually motivated. Indicted on three counts of murder, Weger was tried for the Oetting killing in a LaSalle County Courthouse in Ottawa, Illinois, on January 30, 1961. On March 3, 1961, his 21st birthday, Weger was convicted and sentenced to life imprisonment. He was not prosecuted for the other murders. Afterwards, jurors were shocked to learn that under Illinois law the convicted killer would be eligible for parole in 20 years. Weger continues to profess his innocence claiming that he was beaten into a confession by police anxious to escape the negative press surrounding their inability to rapidly solve the crime. A model prisoner, he is currently serving his life term in the Stateville Correctional Center near Joliet. As of 1996, his annual request for parole has been denied over 20 times.

585. Stout, Steve. *The Starved Rock Murders.* Utica, Ill.: Utica House, 1982. 210 pp.: ill.; 22 cm.; trade paperback.

Wigginton, Tracey
(a.k.a. "The Vampire Killer")

Born circa 1964. Factory worker. Brisbane, Australia; 1 murder; knife; October 1989.

Lesbian vampire killer with "mind control powers" who savagely slaughtered a man then drank his blood. In October 1989 Tracey Wigginton, a 25-year-old factory worker and self professed vampire, was drinking champagne with her lover of one week, Lisa Ptaschinski, 25, and two other women at a lesbian nightclub in Brisbane, Australia, when she decided to indulge her thirst for blood. Shortly after midnight, they picked up 47-year-old city council worker, Edward Baldock, and drove him to a riverbank in a Brisbane suburb. As Ptaschinski watched, Wigginton stabbed Baldock 15 times almost severing his head in the frenzied attack. According to Ptaschinski, Wigginton went into a feeding frenzy and afterwards looked as though she had had a three-course meal. Wigginton was arrested within 24 hours and the other three surrendered the next day. She pleaded guilty to the murder and was sentenced to life imprisonment. Ptaschinksi and the others pleaded not guilty and at their trial

before Brisbane's Supreme Court in January and February 1991 offered compelling testimony concerning Wigginton. Her lover testified that in addition to worshipping Satan, Wigginton believed herself to be a vampire and avoided sunlight and mirrors. Ptaschinski permitted the vampire to tie a tourniquet around her wrist, pump up the vein, make a small incision, and suck the blood as it came out. "She could make people disappear except for their eyes [and] could read my mind," said Ptaschinski. Unable to satisfy her blood hunger through her lover, Wigginton was able to persuade the lesbians to kill. Ptaschinski was sentenced to life imprisonment on February 15, 1991.

586. Hicks, Ron. *The Vampire Killer: A Journey into the Mind of Tracey Wigginton.* Sydney: Bantam Books, 1992. vii, 343 pp.: ill.; 18 cm. ("A Bantam book"); paperback.

"Wigwam Murder" *see* Sangret, August

Wilder, Christopher Bernard
(a.k.a. "Beauty Queen Killer," "Lynn Thomas Bishop," "L. K. Kimbriell, Jr.," "L. K. Kimbrell," "Bernard Christopher Wilder," "Chris B. Wilder," "Christopher Wilder," "Lynn Ivory," "David Pierce," "David Pugh")

Born March 13, 1945, in Sydney, Australia. Died April 13, 1984. Electrical and building contractor. Florida, Texas, Oklahoma, Kansas, Colorado, Utah, Nevada, California, New York; 8 murders (possibly 17); .357 Magnum, filet knife; February–April 1984.

"I'd like to social date more. I have what I call a need to meet and socialize on a more wider basis than I have been doing. I want to date, I want to meet and enjoy the company of a number of women."—Excerpt from a 1981 videotape interview made by Wilder for a Florida video dating service

Australian-born serial killer whose multi-state reign of terror prompted the FBI to place him on its "Ten Most Wanted List." The oldest of four sons born to a United States Navy career man and his Australian wife, Christopher Bernard Wilder spent much of his early life shuttling back and forth between the two continents. Authorities first became aware of his criminal nature in 1962 when the 17 year old helped some friends gang rape a girl on a beach in Australia. Ordered to undergo psychiatric therapy which included electroshock, Wilder ultimately incorporated the treatment into his sadistic sex life by using electrical torture on his victims. Following an abortive eight-day marriage, Wilder moved to Florida in 1969 and spent the seventies working as a carpenter and managing a topless bar in Miami. During those years he was repeatedly arrested for sexual offenses against teenaged girls. In 1979 Wilder entered into partnership with a local contractor to start the Boynton Beach–based companies Sawtel Electric and Sawtel Construction. The businesses, combined with Wilder's speculation in Florida real estate, made the 39-year-old bachelor a millionaire. Rich, handsome, and well-mannered, Wilder moved into a luxurious home in Boynton Beach and adopted a swinging bachelor lifestyle replete with sports car racing and beautiful women.

On June 21, 1980, Wilder, posing as a photographer looking for young women to model in a pizza ad, picked up a young woman in West Palm Beach. At a local pizza parlor, Wilder laced the girl's food with LSD and raped the drugged teenager in the front of his pickup. Arrested for rape, Wilder pleaded down to a lesser charge of attempted sexual battery and was placed on five years probation with mandatory counseling with a sex therapist. Wilder's sex crimes continued during a vacation in Australia in December 1982 where he kidnapped two 15-year-old girls off a beach in New South Wales and forced them to pose for pornographic pictures. Arrested the next day, Wilder was charged with kidnapping and assault. He was allowed to leave the country only after his parents posted a $350,000 bail and he agreed to return for the trial, eventually set for April 3, 1984. On June 15, 1983, Wilder used a gun at Boynton Beach City Park to force two girls, ages ten and twelve, to perform oral sex on him. Afterwards, he returned them to the park and told them not to tell anyone.

On February 26, 1984, former Miss Florida pageant contestant Rosario Gonzalez, 20, was last seen leaving her job at the Miami Grand Prix with a man fitting Wilder's description. Her body has never been found. On March 5, 1984, school teacher Elizabeth Kenyon, 23, was last seen with Wilder at a Coral Gables gas station. A one-time Miss Florida contestant and Orange Bowl Princess, Kenyon met Wilder in 1982. The FBI unofficially entered the Kenyon case on March 14, 1984, and based on Wilder's past history of sex offenses they considered him to be their prime suspect. Sensing imminent arrest, Wilder purchased a non-descript 1973 Chrysler New Yorker two days before Kenyon's disappearance. Armed with a 357 Magnum pistol, ammunition, handcuffs, a roll of duct tape, rope, a sleeping bag, and a 15-foot electric cord connected to a switch, Wilder fled the Boynton Beach area on a 46-day odyssey of rape, torture, and murder stretching thousands of miles from Florida to California to New England. On the seat beside him lay a copy of John Fowles' book *The Collector*, the story of an obsessed young man who kidnaps and imprisons the girl of his dreams.

On March 18, 1984, aspiring model Theresa Ferguson, 21, was last seen leaving a mall in Indian Harbour, Florida, with a man later identified as Wilder. Her body was found four days later in a Polk County canal 70 miles from the point of her abduction. Two days afterwards Wilder passed himself off as a fashion photographer in a Tallahassee, Florida, shopping mall to entice a 19-year-old Florida State University coed to leave with him. In a motel room in Bainbridge, Georgia, Wilder repeatedly raped and tortured the woman with an electrical device then applied Superglue to her eyelids. Wilder fled the scene when the coed managed to lock herself in the bathroom and scream for help. Driving to Beaumont, Texas, he abducted 24-year-old Lamar University nursing student and mother of two, Terry Diane Walden, on March 23, 1984. Walden's body, savaged by multiple knife wounds and bound by three types of rope, was found in an irrigation ditch near the city three days later. Wilder ditched his Chrysler and drove off in Walden's Mercury Cougar.

On March 25, 1984, Wilder, using his *modus operandi* as a fashion photographer, abducted newlywed Wendy Sue Logan, 21, from a mall in Oklahoma City, Oklahoma. The next day

her body was found under a tree in the Milford Reservoir near Milford Lake, Kansas. Dead less than an hour, the victim had been raped and stabbed in the chest, and her hair cut short. A survivor of Wilder's later explained that the serial killer's obsession with actress Jennifer Beals in the film *Flashdance* prompted him to cut his victims' hair to look like her. On March 29, 1984, Wilder surfaced in Grand Junction, Colorado, where he abducted 18-year-old Sheryl Lynn Bonaventura from the Mesa Mall. Dead from multiple stab wounds and a gunshot, the victim's nude body was found on May 3, 1984, under a tree at a rest stop near Kanab, Utah. On April 1, 1984, 17-year-old Michelle Korfman disappeared from a mall in Las Vegas, Nevada, where she was a contestant in the *Seventeen* magazine beauty contest. Wilder, posing as a photographer, approached eight women before Korfman agreed to leave the shopping center with him to be photographed. A photograph taken at the pageant showed Wilder in the crowd. The victim's decomposed body was found May 11, 1984, in the Valley Forge Canyon of Angeles National Forest in California.

Wilder next struck on April 4, 1984, in Torrance, California. Posing again as a photographer, he abducted 16-year-old Tina Marie Risico at gunpoint from a shopping center. Over the next few days, Wilder raped, tortured, and threatened Risico with death unless she agreed to help him obtain other victims. On April 5, 1984, the FBI placed Wilder on their "Ten Most Wanted List." Often only hours behind the killer, the FBI traced Wilder's cross country murder spree via his use of his business partner's stolen credit card. Over 500 agents now worked full-time on apprehending Wilder who, with his captive, was moving eastwards. On April 10, 1984, Risico identified herself as "Tina Marie Wilder" and lured 16-year-old Dawnette Sue Wilt out of the Southlake Mall in Merrillville, Indiana. In the parking lot, Wilder forced Wilt into the backseat of the car and raped her as Risico drove. Over the next two days the trio stayed in motels in Akron, Ohio, and Syracuse, New York, where Wilder subjected the teenager to a nightly ritual of rape and electroshock torture. On April 12, 1984, Wilder, accompanied by Risico, drove Wilt to a wooded area near Penn Yan, New York. After trying unsuccessfully to suffocate the teenager, Wilder stabbed her three times in the back with a filet knife and left her for dead. Wilt survived and was picked up walking along a roadside.

Hours later in Victor, New York, 33-year-old Sunday school teacher Elizabeth Dodge was in the wrong place at the wrong time. Anxious to ditch murder victim Terry Walden's Mercury Cougar, Wilder staked out a mall near Victor. He selected Dodge's 1982 Pontiac Trans-Am and abducted the woman as she was stepping out of the car. With Risico following behind in the Trans-Am, Wilder drove Dodge to a gravel pit on the outskirts of town where he unceremoniously shot her once in the back of the head. On April 13, 1984, Wilder demonstrated uncharacteristic compassion by driving Risico to Boston's Logan Airport and placing her on a plane bound for Los Angeles. Shortly afterwards, he attempted to abduct a 19-year-old woman near Beverly, Massachusetts, but she managed to jump out of his car and notify police. Authorities issued an all points bulletin covering an area from New Jersey to the Canadian border. That afternoon, Wilder pulled into a service station in

Colebrook, New Hampshire, just 12 miles from the Canadian border. As he was talking to the attendant, two state troopers drove by and recognized the stolen car from an FBI description. Wilder reacted to their approach by diving into the front seat of his car for the pistol. One trooper dove in on top of the killer and the gun discharged twice during the struggle. The first shot passed through Wilder and lodged under the officer's right rib. The second .357 Magnum round, according to the autopsy, penetrated Wilder's heart causing instantaneous death due to "cardiac obliteration." Both troopers were subsequently awarded the Medal of Valor, the highest award granted by state police. Wilder's brain was removed for study prior to his cremation in Boynton Beach. The ashes were given to his family.

In July 1984, the families of 10 young women murdered by Wilder filed claims in excess of $50 million against his estate. The largest claim, $25 million, was filed by the family of Elizabeth Dodge. On April 26, 1986, Wilder's estate (estimated at $300,000) was ordered to pay $3 million to the husband of murder victim Terry Diane Walden. Inconclusive evidence has subsequently linked Wilder to the 1965 murders of two young women in Sydney, Australia, and to the murders of seven women throughout Florida.

587. Gibney, Bruce. *The Beauty Queen Killer*. Pinnacle Books ed. New York: Pinnacle Books, 1984. 212 pp., [8]pp. of plates: ill.; 18 cm. ("A Pinnacle book"); paperback.

Highly flawed paperback original quickly written from news accounts to cash in on the case's notoriety. Useful for its inclusion of a psychiatric report on Wilder dated January 7, 1977, which erroneously concludes "he is not dangerous to others because of a propensity for sex offenses...."

Williams, Wayne Bertram
(a.k.a. "Atlanta Child Killer")

Born May 27, 1958, in Atlanta, Georgia. Freelance photographer, record producer. Atlanta, Georgia; 28 murders (2 convictions); asphyxiation, strangulation; July 1979–May 1981.

Television: "The Atlanta Child Murders" (1985), a two-part, five-hour, made-for-television miniseries, originally aired on CBS on February 10 and 12, 1985. Cast includes Calvin Levels (Wayne Williams), Jason Robards (Alvin Binder), and James Earl Jones (Major Walker).

"I maintained all along through this trial my innocence and still do so today. I hold no malice against the jury, the prosecutors or the court. I hope the person or persons who committed these crimes can be brought to justice. I wanted to see this terror ended. I did not do it."—Williams to the judge after being sentenced to two life terms in prison

So-called "Atlanta Child Killer" convicted on circumstantial evidence of strangling or asphyxiating 28 young blacks during a nearly two-year period. The terror in Atlanta began in July 1979 with the discovery of the bodies of two black teenagers in an isolated section on that city's southwest side. As the months passed, the bodies of other black children and teenagers were found openly discarded in parks. The predominantly male victims ranged in age from 7 to 27 and had been strangled or suffocated. The absence of signs of sexual assault led investigators to consider the murders as racially motivated, a potentially dan-

gerous situation in an already deeply divided city. By mid-1980 the bodies of black children were being discovered at a rate of one every 3½ weeks and Atlanta residents were numbed with fear and distrust. Bowing to mounting public protest, Atlanta authorities established a special task force comprised of 100 local, state, and federal lawmen which ultimately would spend $6 million before a suspect was arrested. Still the killings continued with bodies now turning up in the Chattahoochee River. On May 22, 1981, the body count had climbed to 26 when police officers on a pre-dawn stakeout around the Jackson Parkway Bridge heard a loud splash in the waters of the Chattahoochee. Unable to see anything, they radioed a nearby chase car manned by FBI agents. Moments later, the agents spotted a white Chevy station wagon crossing the bridge and followed it for more than a mile before pulling it over at an entrance ramp to Interstate 35. The driver, Wayne B. Williams, a 23-year-old black freelance photographer and would-be record producer, denied tossing anything into the water and was released two hours later.

Three days later, the nude body of Nathaniel Cater, a 27-year-old black day care worker, was found washed up on the banks of the Chattahoochee River 1.2 miles downstream from where officers heard the splash. Cater had been strangled. Weeks later, the Chattahoochee yielded victim 28 when frogmen discovered the body of Jimmy Ray Payne, a 21-year-old black man strangled at about the same time as Cater. Police focused their investigation on Williams and twice searched the house he shared with his retired schoolteacher parents in a middle class black neighborhood in northwest

Atlanta. Williams was placed under open surveillance for four weeks during which time a team of forensic specialists worked to tie him to the murders. On June 21, 1981, Williams was arrested after fibers from a bedspread and carpet in his home and car as well as hair from his dog were linked with those recovered from the hair of Nathaniel Cater. Williams was later charged with Payne's murder after similar hair and fiber evidence linked him to the homicide.

As testimony began in his trial in Atlanta on January 6, 1982, Williams continued to steadfastly maintain his innocence. Although only charged with two killings, the prosecution introduced testimony tying Williams to 10 other victims and produced witnesses who allegedly saw him with Cater and Payne before their murders. Williams denied ever meeting the men and refuted claims that he had offered male teenagers money for sex. In the absence of any eyewitnesses to the killings, however, the prosecution's case ultimately hinged on the fiber and hair evidence. Prosecutor Gordon Miller noted that the state had found 28 different types of fibers on the bodies which matched 18 different items taken from Williams' home and car. The odds against such a combination, he argued, were 1 in 150 million and were "so significant as to amount to a signature, just as if the defendant had signed his name on the death warrants" of the victims. Though not legally obligated to provide a motive for the murders, the prosecution maintained that Williams despised his own race and was driven to kill by his failure to make it as a photographer or record producer. After a 35-day trial which featured 197 witnesses and 728 pieces of evidence, a jury of eight blacks and four whites

needed less than 12 hours to convict Williams on February 27, 1982. As the state had not sought the death penalty, Williams was automatically given to two consecutive life sentences.

Williams has continued to maintain his innocence amid growing speculation that he was perhaps a timely and convenient scapegoat for the crimes and there can be little argument that the arrest and conviction of a black man for the Atlanta Child Killings averted a potentially violent racial conflict in that troubled city. At a hearing for a new trial conducted in October 1991, Williams' claim of innocence was bolstered by the testimony of a senior Georgia Bureau of Investigation agent who revealed the existence of secretly recorded conversations between Ku Klux Klansmen who bragged about killing up to 20 of Atlanta's murdered black youths. In other recordings, destroyed by the FBI after the case was ruled closed, a Klansman was heard making the statement: "Let's go out and kill another black kid tonight." An informant with Klan connections at the time of the murders told authorities that the group's plan was to kill one black child a month until the city erupted into a race riot. Despite passing a lie detector test, his claim was discounted. A GBI agent testifying at the hearing stated, "Because of the explosive situation and our worries of severe racial problems, it was decided that all this should remain absolutely secret." Superior Court Judge Harold Craig refused to allow the wiretap material into evidence "at this time."

588. Baldwin, James. *The Evidence of Things Not Seen*. 1st ed. New York: Holt, Rinehart and Winston, 1985. xiv, 125 pp.; 22 cm.

_____. [Same as 588.] New York: Henry Holt, 1986. xiv, 125 pp.; 21 cm. ("An Owl book.")

_____. [Same as 588.] London: M. Joseph, 1986. xiv, 125 pp.; 23 cm.

_____. [Same as 588.] Foreword by Derrick Bell with Janet Dewart Bell. 10th Anniversary Owl book ed. New York: H. Holt, 1995. xvi, 125 pp.; 21 cm. ("An Owl Book.")

Noted black author James Baldwin expands his 1981 *Playboy* magazine essay on the case and suggests that Williams was prejudged a murderer in the media before the trial even started. Scant on facts about the case, Baldwin primarily uses this slim volume as a platform from which to launch a stinging diatribe against white society.

589. Dettlinger, Chet, and Prugh, Jeff. *The List.* 1st ed. Atlanta: Philmay Enterprises, 1983. 516 pp., [4]pp. of plates: ill.; 24 cm.

Wood, Catherine May
(a.k.a. "Catherine Carpenter," "Rasputin of Alpine Manor," "Rat Woman," "Cookie." Known in conjunction with Gwendolyn Gail Graham as "The Dykes of Death")

Born March 7, 1962, in Soap Lake, Washington. Nurse's aide. Warren, Michigan; 6 murders (suspected of 8); suffocation (wash cloth/towel); January–April 1987.

"As long as Gwen can't hurt anybody else, I'm good with anything else that happens."—Wood circa October 24, 1990

The revelation that two female nurse's aides had murdered six women residents of a Michigan nursing home stunned the conservative city of Grand Rapids and raised questions nationwide over the quality of institutionalized care given the elderly. The further revelation that the murders were at least partially motivated by what papers labelled a "lesbian love bond," made the "Alpine Manor Murder Case" one of the most sensational serial murder cases in the criminal history of Michigan. Physically at least, the two principals, Catherine May Wood, 26, and Gwendolyn Gail Graham, 25, were a study in contrast. Nearly six feet tall and weighing close to 300 pounds, Wood towered over the sturdily built Graham who at 5'2" weighed 140 pounds. Belying the physical mismatch, the prosecution's theory of the case (based on Wood's plea-bargained testimony) held that Gwen Graham was the dominant personality of the pair. She masterminded the killings and controlled the emotionally dependent Wood, who out of fear of losing her, only reluctantly took part in the killings. Following her conviction, Graham was evaluated by an independent forensic psychologist who disagreed with the prosecution's understanding of the Wood-Graham relationship. The evaluation determined that while Graham was capable of committing murder, she lacked the ability to plot the crimes. Several of the pair's Alpine Manor coworkers had also testified at trial that Cathy Wood, not Graham, controlled the relationship even telling Graham how to dress and wear her hair.

The early lives of both women were marred by familial abuse and emotional deprivation. Wood, battered by a drunken father and ignored by an unloving mother, sought comfort in food. As an unhappy teenager her weight ballooned to nearly 400 pounds and the reclusive girl spent hours alone reading. At 14 Wood began seeing a teenager named David, but after dating

him for a year-and-a-half she discovered that "David" was actually a girl
named Debbie who enjoyed imperson-
ating boys. The 15-year-old had sex
with "David," but learned never to trust
anyone again. In 1979 she married Ken
Wood, a General Motors worker, and
gave birth to a daughter. Six years later
she walked out on the marriage and in
August 1985 began working as a nurse's
aide on the midnight shift at Alpine
Manor, a full care nursing home in the
Grand Rapids suburb of Warren.
Shedding nearly 100 pounds, Wood
dyed her hair blond to look like Marilyn Monroe, started drinking heavily
at a local gay bar, and began the first of
many lesbian relationships. Fascinated
with the sex lives of Alpine Manor's
numerous gay employees, the charismatic Wood quickly asserted her personality over the group by playing
matchmaker and hosting parties at her
home. Through Wood and her friends,
the influx of gay employees into the
nursing home soon caused it to be
nicknamed "Gay Manor."

Born in Santa Maria, California,
Gwen Graham suffered at the hands of
a sadistic father who, when not raping
her, punished his daughter by plunging
her head into a toilet. Acting on a
twisted logic, Graham used a lighted
cigarette to burn herself 31 times on
both arms reasoning that the scars
would never let her father forget the
shame of his abuse. In a similarly motivated act, Graham once reacted to a
lesbian lover's threat to leave her by
repeatedly slashing herself on the arm
with a razor. Shortly after moving with
a lover to Grand Rapids from Tyler,
Texas, Graham began working as a
nurse's aide in Alpine Manor on June
23, 1986. By late September, Graham
and Wood had each left their lovers
and set up house together in Wood's

home. Integrating physical restraint
apparatus pilfered from the nursing
home into their bondage games, the
pair enjoyed an active sex life that left
Graham's back scarred with fingernail
scratches and both women's necks
marked with hickeys. At work, the
infatuated lovers passed one another
saccharine love notes signed with
acronyms like OGINYK ("Oh Gwen I
Need Your Kisses").

According to Wood's later testimony, by October 1986 the relationship had begun to take on a sinister
undertone. In that month, Wood alleged that Graham expressed her desire
to kill someone in the nursing home.
The murders would "relieve" Graham's
tension and bind the two lovers together forever. They would take turns
killing patients and as an inside joke
choose victims whose initials would
spell out the acronym M-U-R-D-E-R.
The plan was later abandoned when it
proved too difficult to find defenseless
patients with the proper initials. Alpine
Manor afforded the pair the ideal
killing ground. The facility averaged
five to ten deaths a month and autopsies were seldom performed. More importantly, since the clientele was largely
composed of the infirm and senile,
potential victims were plentiful, easily
subdued, and if able to survive an
attack, seldom believed by anyone
should they complain. For weeks prior
to the first murder, the pair stalked the
nursing home weeding out potential
victims by pinching their noses shut.
Those who struggled lived. Some
terrified residents mentioned the incidents to staff and family, but were tragically discounted.

Sixty-year-old Alzheimer's patient
Marguerite Chambers was the first to
die. Around 8:00 p.m. on January 18,
1987, Graham entered room number

614, and as Wood stood guard at the door, suffocated the incapacitated woman by placing a rolled up wash cloth under her chin and another over her nose. The method left no tell-tale fingerprints or facial trauma and Chambers' death was declared "natural" due to myocardial infarction. As in every subsequent murder, the lovers took the next day off from work. On February 10, 1987, the pair suffocated 95-year-old Myrtle Luce, but left a clue when they notated her chart with the initials of an aide who had called in sick. Six days later Mae Mason, 79, was found dead in her bed from "cardiac arrest." She was cremated on February 17, 1986. On February 26, 1987, the pair committed a double murder: 98-year-old Ruth Van Dyke and Belle Burkhard. As a souvenir, Graham took one of Burkhard's socks and later used it in a bondage game to "suffocate" Wood during sex. Ironically, 11 days earlier bruises had been noted on Burkhard's nose, cheek, and temples, but were dismissed as routine seizure-type injuries. She too was cremated. The only murder not done for "fun," "emotional relief," or "love" was committed on April 7, 1987. To end 97-year-old Edith Cook's suffering, the pair suffocated her. Cook's false teeth were taken as a souvenir that Graham later tossed in the trash.

Since coming to Alpine Manor Graham had bedded at least four women and one man. An affair with coworker Heather Barager turned serious and Graham left Wood in July 1987, but returned after a week when Wood threatened to expose the murders. Ultimately, Graham disentangled herself and moved with Barager to Tyler, Texas. Remarkably, both killers had on various occasions confided the murders to coworkers, but their con-

fessions had been dismissed as bids for attention. In early August 1987 Wood admitted the murders to her ex-husband who listened in horror as she explained how much "fun" it was to kill people. Fourteen months after hearing her confession, Ken Wood entered a Walker, Michigan, police station on October 6, 1988, and unburdened himself to detectives. Cathy Wood was picked up the next day and though initially accusing her husband of playing a practical joke, admitted that she had walked in on Graham suffocating Marguerite Chambers. In subsequent interviews and in two polygraph tests, Wood stated that Graham had concocted the murders as a way to bind them together forever. Afraid of losing her, Wood supported the plan, but supposedly balked when it was her turn to commit a murder. Thereafter, she reluctantly stood guard while Graham smothered the patients with rolled up wash cloths. To keep Wood in check, Graham supposedly left rolled up wash cloths as "calling cards" in conspicuous places in patient's rooms and in the house they shared.

On December 4, 1988, Graham was arrested in Tyler, Texas, for the murders of Chambers and Cook. Wood was arrested hours later in Grand Rapids. As part of a plea bargain arrangement, Wood agreed to testify against Graham in exchange for being allowed to plead guilty to a second degree murder and conspiracy charge. Graham pleaded not guilty to five counts of first degree murder in the deaths of Marguerite Chambers, Edith Cook, Mae Mason, Myrtle Luce, and Belle Burkhard. Jury selection began in Grand Rapids on September 11, 1989. Two days later in his opening statement, the prosecutor characterized the murders as "a bizarre case committed by bizarre people." Already assured of serving several years in prison, Wood testified against her former lover, painting Graham as the dominating force in their relationship. The lover who supplanted Wood, Heather Barager, testified that Graham had told her of killing six people. Pointing to the lack of physical evidence supporting Wood's claims, the defense characterized the woman as a pathological liar out to gain revenge on Graham for leaving her. The forensic report conducted on the exhumed body of Marguerite Chambers proved inconclusive and some of the victims (Mason, Burkhard) had been cremated. Testifying on her own behalf, Graham denied killing anyone and insisted that the so-called tales of murder she told were jokes between her and Wood. A jury needed only six hours on September 19, 1989, to find Graham guilty on five counts of murder and on one count of conspiracy. Under the terms of her plea arrangement, Wood was sentenced on October 11, 1989, to 20–40 years for the second degree murder of Chambers. Also stipulated in the agreement was the assurance that she and Graham be kept in separate institutions. Wood will be eligible for parole in 16 years. Twenty-one days later on November 1, 1989, Graham received the mandatory sentence of life imprisonment without the possibility of parole for each of the five murders and one other "natural life" sentence for conspiracy.

590. Cauffiel, Lowell. *Forever and Five Days.* New York: Kensington, 1992. xi, 467 pp., [16]pp. of plates: ill.; 24 cm. ("Zebra books.")

_____. [Same as 590.] New York: Kensington, 1993. 527 pp., [16]pp. of plates: ill.; 18 cm. ("Zebra books"); paperback.

Excellent case study based on police and court transcripts and interviews with the principals including Wood and Graham. Recommended.

Wood, Robert William Thomas George Cavers
(*acquitted*; a.k.a. "The Camden Town Murder")

Born circa 1879 in Edinburgh, Scotland. Camden Town, London, England; 1 murder (acquitted); knife; September 12, 1907.

"If England wants me, she must have me."—Wood to his girlfriend as he was being taken to police headquarters for questioning

First instance in which an accused murderer was acquitted after exercising the right afforded a defendant under the Criminal Evidence Act of 1898 to give evidence on his own behalf. On September 12, 1907, the nude body of 23-year-old prostitute Emily Elizabeth Dimmock (known as "Phyllis") was found by the man she lived with at No. 29 St. Paul's Road, Camden Town (a squalid district of London often referred to as "the poor man's West End"). Face down in bed, Dimmock's throat had been slashed nearly to the point of decapitation. The room had been ransacked and an album containing Dimmock's postcard collection was found on the floor. Police traced Dimmock's movements to the "Rising Sun" tavern in Camden Town where she often met her clients. One of them told authorities that days before her murder, Dimmock had shown him a postcard signed "Alice" and a letter signed "Bert" which appeared to be written by the same hand. Dimmock's live-in companion subsequently found the postcard in question whose writing matched three other cards in the dead prostitute's collection. The "Rising Sun" postcard was printed in several newspapers along with a police request for information leading to the writer's identity. Ruby Young, a part-time prostitute and artist's model, recognized the writing as that of her boyfriend Robert Wood, a talented 28-year-old pattern designer for the London Sand Blast and Glass Works on Grays Inn Road. Confronted by Young, Wood persuaded her not to go to the police with a convincing story which explained his passing association with Dimmock. Wood was arrested on October 4, 1907, after Young confided the incident to a journalist friend who notified the authorities.

Evidence of Wood's double life came to light as his trial opened before Mr. Justice Grantham at the Old Bailey on December 12, 1907. Actors, dramatists, and social leaders flooded the courtroom to hear intimate details about the likable young man's involvement with the dead prostitute. By some accounts, Wood had known Dimmock for 15 months prior to her death. An eyewitness who allegedly saw Wood leaving Dimmock's house early in the morning on the day of the murder was discredited under skillful cross examination. In the absence of physical evidence and a demonstrable motive for the murder, the Crown's case against Wood broke down. Appearing in his own defense, Wood made an excellent impression in stark contrast to many of the witnesses against him who were drawn from the ranks of prostitutes and alcoholics. By the end of the trial public opinion had shifted squarely behind Wood and the judge's favorable summing up was repeatedly interrupted by cheers from many observers in the courtroom. On December 18,

1907, the jury needed only 17 minutes to find Wood not guilty. Spontaneous public celebrations ensued and some West End theatrical performances were interrupted to announce the news of Wood's acquittal. Wood subsequently changed his name and lived a quiet life.

591. Hogarth, Basil, ed. *The Trial of Robert Wood (The Camden Town Case).* Notable British Trials. London: W. Hodge, 1936. vi, 268 pp.: ill., front., ports., facsim.; 22 cm.

_____. [Same as 591.] Notable British Trials. Toronto: Canada Law Book, 1936. vi, 268 pp.: ill.; 22 cm.

Transcript of the Wood's trial in the Central Criminal Court, London, December, 1907, for the murder of Emily Dimmock. Appendix includes the essay, "The Law and the Man: A Psychological Study of the Great Trial," by Sir Hall Caine.

592. Napley, David. *The Camden Town Murder.* Great Murder Trials of the Twentieth Century. London: Weidenfeld and Nicolson, 1987. viii, 149 pp., [1] leaf of plates: ill., port.; 23 cm.

_____. [Same as 592.] 1st U.S. ed. Great Murder Trials of the Twentieth Century. New York: St. Martin's Press, 1987. viii, 149 pp.: ill.; 22 cm.

Sir Napley, a well-known British solicitor often appearing on radio and television, presents in story form the facts of the "Camden Town Murder."

"Wood Chipper Murder" *see* **Crafts, Richard Bunel**

Woodfield, Randall Brent
(a.k.a. "The I-5 Bandit," "The I-5 Killer," "Squirrely," "Michael," "Just Me")

Born December 26, 1950, in Salem, Oregon. Bartender. Washington, Oregon,

California; 1 murder (conviction, strongly suspected of 11 others); .32 and .38 caliber pistols; January 1981–March 1981.

"Everyone is equal—everyone has problems and will stand before God for Judging others…"—Woodfield writing from prison to an unidentified correspondent

From December 1980 through March 1981 the I-5 highway, an 800 mile stretch of freeway running along the Pacific coast from British Columbia to Mexico, was terrorized by a serial rapist, robber, and murderer who wandered the corridor committing at least 26 known crimes in Washington, Oregon, and California. Described by victims as a tall, good looking man with an athletic build, the "I-5 Bandit" rarely varied his *modus operandi*. Targeting fast food restaurants and convenience stores staffed by young women, he struck late at night using a silver .32 caliber pistol to intimidate the counter help. After robbing the cash drawer, he herded the employees into a backroom, used surgical tape to bind their hands, and forced them at gunpoint to fellate him. Some he shot, others he inexplicably left alive to describe him to police. Their description of the assailant rarely varied: he wore a piece of surgical tape over the bridge of his nose, sported a fake beard, and was acne-scarred. A psychological profile of the offender suggested a macho-type loner caught in the grip of a sexual frenzy. Another observation proved chillingly accurate: when apprehended, the killer would prove to be just like "the guy next door."

Randall Brent Woodfield seemed like the all–American boy. Raised by well-educated upper middle class parents, he was handsome, popular, and a good student who excelled in athletics.

Physically, Woodfield blossomed in high school and lifted weights to develop his 6'2", 170-pound frame into a coach's dream. As a junior, he made All-State in football as a wide receiver and dreamed of a professional career with the Green Bay Packers. As an adolescent, however, his darker side emerged. While in junior high in Newport, Oregon, the one-time Rotary Club "Boy of the Month" began exposing himself to young girls. School and police authorities did not want to ruin the star athlete's career, so Woodfield was never punished or referred to treatment. Woodfield's exhibitionism accelerated during his years as a student in a junior college in Ontario, Oregon. In 1969 a spate of exposing incidents led to his transfer to Mount Hood Community College for a single semester. In the hopes of attracting the eye of a pro football scout, Woodfield enrolled as a physical education and health education major at Portland State University in 1971.

At the same time, he turned to religion and became a member of the Campus Crusade for Christ and the Fellowship of Christian Athletes. His conversion failed to curb his exhibitionism and Woodfield was arrested in Vancouver, Washington, on August 7, 1972, for indecent exposure. Convicted, the sentence was suspended. An arrest in Portland on June 22, 1973, for indecent exposure and resisting an officer followed and netted him an almost six-month jail sentence which he never served. Woodfield was again arrested for public indecency on February 22, 1974, and was put on probation for five years with mandatory counseling. He never attended a session. Two days before his arrest, the Green Bay Packers selected Woodfield as their seventeenth round draft pick. By mid–1974 the would-be wide receiver was cut from the Packers' travelling squad. Perhaps as a result of failing to realize his dream, Woodfield's criminal activity became more frequent and violent. During the first months of 1975 several Portland women were accosted at knifepoint and forced to fellate their attacker. Woodfield was arrested in a Portland park in April 1975 after accosting and threatening an undercover police woman with a paring knife. He pleaded guilty to second degree robbery, but was not charged with a sex offense which might have later marked him as a suspect in the I-5 killings. On June 10, 1975, Woodfield received a 10-year sentence in the Oregon State Penitentiary. He was paroled in July 1979 after serving less than four years.

The series of robberies, rapes, and murders attributed to the "I-5 Bandit" began on December 9, 1980, in Vancouver, Washington, where a 22-year-old female gas station cashier was robbed by a man wearing a false beard and brandishing a silver gun. Over the next five days, a man wearing a strip of surgical tape over the bridge of his nose robbed fast food places in Eugene and Albany, Oregon. Robbery was paired with sexual assault when he next struck at a restaurant in Lake Forest Park, Washington, north of Seattle on December 21, 1980. The robber forced a 25-year-old waitress into a restroom where he held a gun against her head while she masturbated him. On January 18, 1981, following weeks of robberies and sexual assaults in Oregon and Washington, the "I-5 Bandit" became the "I-5 Killer" by claiming his first victim in Salem, Oregon. Lisa Garcia, 21, and Shari Hull, 20, were cleaning an office building north of Salem around 10:00 p.m. when a gun-

man with a Band-Aid over his nose entered the building, forced the pair into a backroom, and ordered them to strip and then fellate him. After satisfying himself, he forced them to lie face down on the floor and then methodically pumped three rounds at pointblank range into Hull's head and two into Garcia's. Hull died without regaining consciousness, but Garcia was able to notify police and later testify against Woodfield.

On February 3, 1981, the killer travelled down I-5 to Mountain Gate, California, near Redding to claim two more victims. Donna Lee Eckard, 37, and her 14-year-old stepdaughter Janell Charlotte Jarvis were found side-by-side in Eckard's bed. Each had been secured with white surgical tape, orally sodomized, then repeatedly shot in the head with a .32 caliber pistol. Jarvis, dead from seven shots to her head, had been anally sodomized after death. Eckard had not been raped. The next day in Yreka, California, a 21-year-old woman was snatched off the street at gunpoint and forced to fellate a man wearing a piece of surgical tape over his nose. He released the naked woman hours later. Later on February 15, 1981, the rape-murder of 18-year-old Julie Reitz, a one-time girlfriend of Randy Woodfield, in her Beaverton, Oregon, home presaged a ten-day spree of robberies and sexual assaults in the state.

Police matched the tape and bullets in the Hull killing with those used in the Eckard-Jarvis murders and realized the crimes were related. Woodfield emerged as a suspect in the Reitz killing when friends of the dead woman informed police that he had recently phoned her and was seen in Beaverton the day before the killing. On March 3, 1981, authorities interviewed Woodfield at his Eugene,

Oregon, home and found a roll of white adhesive tape. A subsequent search of his phone records corresponded so closely to locations, dates, and times where crimes attributed to the "I-5 Killer" had been committed that one detective likened the evidence to a "road map" to mayhem. Woodfield was arrested on a parole violation on March 5, 1981, while police frantically scoured his home looking for clues to support a murder charge. An unusual .32 caliber bullet similar to those used in the shootings of Garcia, Hull, Jarvis, and Eckard was found in his gym bag. The 30 year old was charged with murder, attempted murder, and two counts of sodomy on March 9, 1981, after Lisa Garcia had picked him out of a lineup the day before.

With a variety of other charges pending against him in various Oregon jurisdictions as well as in California and Washington, Woodfield heard opening arguments begin in the Garcia-Hull case in Salem, Oregon, on June 11, 1981. Woodfield's protestation of innocence and fingerpointing at other suspects, however, were no match for the overwhelming physical evidence against him and he was convicted of Hull's murder, the attempted murder of Garcia, and on two counts of sodomy. While awaiting sentencing, Woodfield was charged in Redding, California, with the murders of Donna Lee Eckard and Janell Jarvis. Noting that Woodfield's trial could cost the state of California over $2 million and confident that Oregon would never release him, the district attorney of Shasta County decided in September 1983 not to prosecute in the double homicide. On October 12, 1981, Woodfield was sentenced to life imprisonment plus 90 years to run consecutively for the Garcia-Hull convictions. Jury selection began in Corvallis, Oregon, on November 2, 1981, for sodomy and illegal gun possession charges filed against Woodfield as a result of his alleged attack on a 19-year-old waitress in a restroom of a fast food restaurant in Corvallis on February 25, 1981. Found guilty on November 6, 1981, Woodfield was subsequently sentenced to 35 years. Combined with his other convictions, the "I-5 Killer" will be eligible for parole in 2031 when he is 81.

Woodfield's time in the Oregon State Penitentiary has been anything but uneventful. In October 1983 the convicted killer was struck in the left thigh by a bullet fragment fired by a corrections officer trying to break up an inmate disturbance in which he was not involved. He made the news again in mid–1984 when he allegedly proposed marriage to convicted murderess Diane Downs. In May 1987, Woodfield filed a $12 million lawsuit against true crime writer Ann Rule (writing as "Andy Stack") alleging that her 1984 book on his case, *The I-5 Killer*, libelled him, invaded his privacy, and irreparably harmed his reputation. The suit was dismissed in January 1988 when it was ruled that the statute of limitations for the claim had expired. In June 1987 both Downs and Woodfield earned their two-year associate degrees in general education. Woodfield continues to lift weights and to correspond with several women who are convinced of his innocence.

593. Rule, Ann [Stack, Andy]. *The I-5 Killer*. Andy Stack's True Crime Annals; vol. 3. New York: New American Library, 1984. 222 pp.; 18 cm. ("A Signet book"); paperback.

_____. [Same as 593.] Newly updated. Andy Stack's True Crime Annals; vol. 3. New York: New American Library, 1988.

240 pp., [8]pp. of plates: ill.; 18 cm. ("A Signet book"); paperback.

Ann Rule originally wrote this book in 1984 under her pseudonym "Andy Stack." Updated edition (1988) notes "Ann Rule writing as Andy Stack."

Wuornos, Aileen Carol (a.k.a. "Lori Kristine Grody," "Susan Lynn Blahovec," "Cammie Marsh Greene," "Sandra B. Kretsch")

Born February 29, 1956, in Troy, Michigan. Prostitute. Central Florida; 7 murders (6 convictions); .22 caliber pistol; November 1989–November 1990.

Film: Aileen Wuornos: The Selling of a Serial Killer (GB, 1992), a documentary by Nick Broomfield coproduced by Lafayette Films and Channel 4. Cast includes Aileen Wuornos (herself), Steven Glazer (Himself/ Wuornos' attorney), and Arlene Pralle (herself/Wuornos' adoptive mother).

Television: "Overkill: The Aileen Wuornos Story" (1992), a two-hour, made-for-television movie, originally aired on CBS on November 17, 1992. Cast includes Jean Smart (Aileen Wuornos) and Park Overall (Tyria Moore).

"On a killing day those guys always wanted to go way, way back in the woods. Now I know why they did it: they were gonna hurt me." —Alleged statement made by Wuornos in August 1991 to a female Volusia County corrections officer

Twenty-four-year-old prostitute incorrectly identified by authorities as "America's first female serial killer" (see Belle Gunness) who murdered then robbed seven victims in Central Florida. According to the Daytona lawyer who represented her in a 1981 armed robbery case, Aileen "Lee" Wuornos "had the most hellish life I've ever known." Born in 1956 to a 16 year old, Wuornos was abandoned by her mother six months after her birth to be raised by her alcoholic grandparents. By 12, she was drinking heavily and engaging in promiscuous sex for beer and cigarettes. Pregnant at 14, allegedly the result of a rape which occurred while hitchhiking, Wuornos was placed in a home for unwed mothers. The boy she gave birth to was immediately put up for adoption. Wuornos subsequently learned that her biological father, serving time at Kansas State Penitentiary for molesting a seven year old, had hanged himself with a bed sheet in his cell. Shortly afterwards, her grandmother died of cirrhosis of the liver followed quickly by the death of a beloved brother from cancer. A tenth grade dropout, Wuornos began using more powerful drugs and supporting herself through prostitution. A May 1976 marriage "for security" to a man in his seventies ended a month later when Wuornos could no longer stand him beating her with his cane. Following a 1978 breakup with a boyfriend in Daytona Beach, Florida, she attempted suicide by shooting herself in the abdomen with a shotgun. Drunk and high on Librium, Wuornos robbed a Majik Mart in Edgewater, Florida, at gunpoint in 1981, following a quarrel with her live-in boyfriend. The $61 robbery netted her three years in prison.

Wuornos was turning eight to ten tricks a night when she met 28-year-old Tyria Jolene Moore in June 1986 at the Zodiac, a gay bar in Daytona. The pair quickly became lovers and lived in a number of cheap hotel rooms and apartments in the area while Moore worked as a motel maid and Wuornos continued to prostitute throughout Central Florida. Wuornos was hitch-hiking on I-4 near I-75 outside of Tampa, her standard method of picking up customers, when Richard Charles Mallory, a 51-year-old electronics repair shop owner from Clearwater, picked her up on November 30, 1989. Mallory's decomposed body was later found on December 13, 1989, beneath a scrap of carpet in a remote woods near Daytona. He had been shot four times in the chest at close range with a .22 caliber pistol. Wuornos drove Mallory's car from the scene and, posing as "Cammie Greene," pawned the man's camera and the car's radar detector. Afterwards, she told her frightened lover about the killing. The pattern continued throughout 1990. Six white middle class men between the ages of 40 and 65 who stopped along major highways in Central Florida to give Wuornos a ride (for whatever reason) were later found shot to death and dumped in woods in Pasco, Citrus, Marion and Volusia counties. In fear of her lover, Moore left Wuornos in late November 1990.

Largely on tips received after a segment on the Florida killings aired on the television program "America's Most Wanted," Wuornos was arrested without incident on January 9, 1991, after sleeping all night on the porch of "The Last Resort," a biker bar in Harbor Oaks, Florida. A key found on the prostitute led authorities to a mini-warehouse in Daytona containing evidence (watches, clothes) tying her to six of the seven victims. Tyria Moore was located in Pennsylvania and told investigators (who believed she was not involved in the killings) that Wuornos had told her of the murders. At Moore's direction, the .22 caliber pistol used to shoot Mallory was recovered from a stagnant waterway in Rose Bay south of Daytona. Moore further cooperated with authorities by getting Wuornos to implicate herself in the killings during a telephone call to her former lover. On January 16, 1991, Wuornos confessed at the Volusia county jail. In the videotaped statement, she maintained that she killed the men in self-defense after they physically or verbally abused her. While awaiting trial, Wuornos was legally adopted in November 1991 by Arlene Pralle, a 44-year-old evangelical Christian horse breeder from Williston, Florida. Tried for Mallory's murder in January 1992, Wuornos testified to killing the electronics repairman after he anally raped then attempted to strangle her. After a jury took just 91 minutes on January 27, 1992, to find her guilty of first degree murder, Wuornos raged, "Sons of bitches! I was raped! I hope you get raped! Scumbags of America!" Sentenced to death in Mallory's murder, Wuornos received an additional three death sentences after pleading no contest in March 1992 to three murders in Marion and Citrus counties. In June 1992 she pleaded guilty to and received her fifth death sentence for the murder of Charles E. Carksaddon, a 40-year-old Missouri native whose naked and bullet-riddled body was found in a woods off I-75 in central Pasco. Wuornos subsequently pleaded guilty to another murder and was given her sixth death sentence on February 5, 1993. As of May 1996, the State Supreme Court has upheld all six of her convictions.

594. Kennedy, Dolores, and Nolin, Robert. *On a Killing Day.* Chicago: Bonus Books, 1992. 283 pp.: ill.; 24 cm.

Kennedy, best known for her

unquestioning support of convicted killer William Heirens (see 277), befriended Arlene Pralle, the woman who adopted Wuornos, and this book chronicles that relationship. Pralle has since been pilloried by some in the press as an opportunist. Appendix includes excerpts from Wuornos' three hour confession given at the Volusia County branch jail on January 16, 1992. Includes bibliography and index.

595. Reynolds, Michael. *Dead Ends.* Warner Books ed. New York: Warner, 1992. 292 pp., [8]pp. of plates: ill.; 18 cm.; paperback.

A paperback original by the reporter who covered the story for Reuters. Reynolds conducted interviews with investigators, principal attorneys, and crime lab technicians, but failed in his attempt to discuss the case with Wuornos.

596. Russell, Sue. *Damsel of Death.* London: True Crime, 1992. 481 pp., [8]pp. of plates: ill., ports.; 18 cm.; paperback.

A British journalist's well-documented study of the case. Instructive.

"Yarmouth Beach Murder" *see* Bennett, Herbert John

"Yorkshire Ripper Murders" *see* Sutcliffe, Peter William

Young, Graham Frederick (a.k.a. "M.E. Evans," "The St. Albans Poisoner," "The Mad Professor")

Born September 7, 1947, in North London, England. Died August 1, 1990. Assistant storeman. North London and Bovingdon, Hertfordshire, England; 3 murders; poison (antimony, thallium); April 1962–November 1971.

"When I get out, I'm going to kill one person for every year I've spent in this place."—Young to a nurse in Broadmoor

Poisoner released from Broadmoor who later claimed two more victims with thallium. At an age when most boys dream of becoming sports heroes, 12-year-old Graham Young's ambition was to become a famous poisoner. Three people would die and several others suffer agonizing pain before he would realize his twisted dream. The death of Young's mother three months after his birth forced his father Frederick to separate the family for two-and-a-half years. Daughter Winifred was sent to a grandmother, and Graham was sent to live with his father's sister, Aunt Winnie. Frederick Young's 1950 marriage to Molly reunited the family. From the first, Young disliked his stepmother. A shy, secretive child, Young eschewed friendships to spend time reading in the local library. At nine he was already obsessed with poisons and rummaged through the trash cans of a local pharmacy to find discarded vials. By 12, Young was a minor expert in toxicology and possessed an extensive library on the subject. He read voraciously on crime, revelling in the exploits of poisoners like Dr. Edward William Pritchard, the 19th century Glasgow physician who used antimony to murder his wife and mother. As a teenager, Young dabbled in black magic and began a lifelong obsession with Hitler, papering the walls of his room with photos of the leaders of the Third Reich. Clandestinely, Young combined his research in chemistry with an interest in the occult and bragged to his friends that he was a member of a Willesden coven. And, in the name of science, he ritually sacrificed neighborhood cats. With the gift of a chemistry set from his father, Young refined his toxicological experiments on mice. Dubbed "the Mad Professor" by classmates, Young poisoned the rodents, recorded their death throes in a notebook, and performed autopsies on their bodies. When only 13½, Young found that by lying about his age and flaunting his knowledge of chemicals he could impress chemists into selling him poisons legally restricted to those 17 or older. He signed the chemist's poison register as "M.E. Evans." In April 1961, he began stockpiling antimony, a slow-working poison which caused vomiting, cramping, and intense stomach pain in its victim. Never without a vial of it on his person, he referred to it as "my little friend."

Young began experimenting with the drug on school chum, Chris Williams. For over a year, the boy experienced severe stomach pain following every meeting with Young. In 1960, Young's parents found the poison in his room and punished him. Beginning early in the winter of 1961, Molly and the rest of the family suffered persistent stomach attacks which often required hospitalization. Only the 13-year-old Young and his pet bird were spared. Young's desire to poison his family became an obsession. He supplemented his stock of antimony with arsenic, digitalis, and thallium, a deadly poison used industrially in the manufacture of optical lenses. By age 14, Young had secreted enough poison in his bedroom to kill 300 people. In early 1962, Molly began to waste away and baffled doctors watched her die on Easter Sunday, April 21, 1962. Death was attributed to complications she suffered in a bus crash the previous summer. A concerned Young badgered the family into cremating the body of the 38-year-old woman. The evidence destroyed, he was never charged with her murder.

His father soon fell ill and required frequent hospitalization. Doctors diagnosed the illness as either antimony or arsenic poisoning, but when confronted, Young denied poisoning his father.

A science master, alarmed over the boy's poison experiments in the school lab, searched Young's desk. Along with numerous vials of poison, the search yielded a notebook filled with scientific findings and odes to poisons illustrated with sketches of dying men. Remembering the sick Williams boy, the teacher arranged for a psychiatrist posing as a career counselor to speak with Young. During the interview, Young's obsession with toxicology became apparent. The psychiatrist notified police and, when a search of his room uncovered numerous poisons, Young was arrested on May 23, 1962, for the malicious administration of poison to Williams, Young's father, and his sister. Young confessed, explaining that as a "self-educating scientist," he wanted only to observe the effects of poison on his subjects. Even though he knew it was wrong, he could not control his obsession to poison. A psychiatric evaluation revealed that the teenager was a classic psychopath totally devoid of a moral sense.

On July 5, 1962, he pleaded guilty to all three counts. A psychiatrist warned that the 15 year old could poison again at any time. In July 1962, he was committed to the medical institution Broadmoor with the added order that he not be released for a period of 15 years without the express authority of the home secretary. An unpopular patient, Young was looked upon with suspicion by staff and fellow patients. Early in his incarceration Young tried to escape, failed, and then was unsuccessful in an attempt to poison staff members by putting a caustic cleaning compound in a tea urn. Anxious to regain his freedom, Young became a model patient from his fifth year on with the result that a June 1970 report to the Home Office gave him a clean bill of health. The nursing staff knew better. Once during an unguarded moment Young remarked to a nurse, "When I get out, I'm going to kill one person for every year I've spent in this place." On the advice of doctors, the Home Office released the "cured" Young on February 4, 1971, six years before their original order.

As part of the terms of his parole, Young took vocational instruction at the Slough Training Centre. Days after arriving he befriended fellow-trainee Trevor Sparks who soon began suffering abdominal pains following his nightly drinking bouts with Young. In April 1971, Young applied to the firm of John Hadlands Ltd. in the Hertfordshire village of Bovingdon for a position as an assistant storeroom clerk. Manufacturers of specialist high speed optical and photographic instruments, the company used thallium to produce optical lenses, but none was on-site during Young's employment. Instead, Young went to a London pharmacy and used the name "M.E. Evans" to purchase thallium and other poisons. Young was hired by Hadlands on May 10, 1971, after receiving a glowing recommendation from the Centre. Hadlands employees befriended the quiet 23 year old who daily fetched them tea in their individually marked mugs. Less than a month after Young started, his boss in the storeroom, 59-year-old Robert Egle, took ill. The next day, a driver fell sick after Young brought him tea. Egle worsened and died on July 7, 1971, after suffering eight agonizing days. Throughout the

illness of the man who had often loaned him bus fare, Young constantly asked for medical updates on Egle and even attended funeral services in the company of the firm's owner. When an autopsy suggested that Egle had died of broncho-pneumonia, the man was cremated without an inquest. Two months later, 60-year-old Fred Biggs suffered debilitating stomach pains and numbness in his limbs. Soon, three other employees developed similar symptoms after drinking tea with Young. Amazingly, he confided to a coworker that it was easy to poison someone and make it look like natural causes. The man told no one and fell sick himself days later. After 20 days of intense pain, Biggs died on November 19, 1971.

Terrified Hadlands employees spoke of the plague or evil spirits as responsible for the illnesses and deaths, discounting the official explanation that the "Bovingdon bug," a severe viral infection, was the cause. At a group morale talk given to the employees by a local medical officer, Young aroused suspicion by demonstrating his knowledge of poisons. Police were called and Young was arrested on November 20, 1971, after it was learned that he had spent nine years in Broadmoor. A search of his room revealed vials of poisons, pictures of Nazis, and a coded diary labelled "A Student's and Officer's Case Book" which minutely recorded his poisoning activities. Young boasted to detectives of killing his stepmother, Egle, and Biggs and deciphered the initials in the diary identifying his victims. Young pleaded not guilty to two counts of murder, two counts of attempted murder, four counts of poisoning, and two alternative charges at his July 19, 1972, trial. During his two days on the stand, he calmly described the "Diary of Death" as a work of fiction, blamed the deaths on the "Bovingdon bug," and claimed his "confession" was made only to get police to give him food and access to an attorney. He was confident the forensic evidence would not support his confession. It took the jury only an hour to return guilty verdicts on all murder and attempted murder charges. Young was sentenced to four life terms in prison. The newspaper *Daily Mail* spoke for many British citizens when it called Young's release from Broadmoor "an indictment of the Home Secretary, who signed the release papers...." On August 1, 1990, Young, 42, suffered a fatal heart attack in his single cell at Parkhurst Prison.

597. Holden, Anthony. *The St. Albans Poisoner: The Life and Crimes of Graham Young.* London: Hodder and Stoughton, 1974. 159 pp., [8] leaves of plates: ill.; 23 cm.

598. Young, Winifred. *Obsessive Poisoner: The Strange Story of Graham Young.* London: Hale, 1973. 175 pp., [8]pp. of plates: ill., ports., facsim.; 22 cm.

A portrait of Young by a sister who survived his attempts to poison her.

Yukl, Charles William, Jr.
(a.k.a. "Yogi Freitag," "Fred Williamson")

Born February 14, 1935, in Baltimore, Maryland. Died August 22, 1982. Music and voice teacher, office manager. New York, New York; 2 murders; ligature strangulation; October 24, 1966, and August 19, 1974.

"The woman I killed had no talent.... And I saw that woman as a symbol. In destroying her I wanted to destroy the kind of woman I hated."—Yukl explaining to a psychiatrist why he killed his first victim

A psychotic double murderer often cited as an illustrative example of the problems of plea bargaining, prison sentences, rehabilitation, and parole procedures. Charles Yukl (pronounced Yookle), the son of accomplished musicians, was a 31-year-old voice teacher living in Greenwich Village when Suzanne Reynolds, a 25-year-old receptionist with dreams of becoming an actress, answered his ad for lessons in a community newspaper. On October 24, 1966, while his wife was away from their apartment, Yukl strangled Reynolds with a tie and dragged her corpse to a vacant apartment where, after having sex with it, he mutilated the body with a razor. Yukl, the manager of the apartment building, explained to his wife that he found the body while making rounds. During a marathon interrogation session, police noticed bloodstains on his shoes, trousers, and underwear. In a plea bargain arrangement, Yukl agreed to first degree manslaughter and was sentenced to not less than seven years, six months, or more than 15 years. A model prisoner at New York's Wallkill Correctional Facility, Yukl was released over the objections of the prosecuting attorney after serving only five years, four months.

Yukl returned to Greenwich Village and placed a bogus ad in a weekly New York theatrical newspaper soliciting actresses to be in a "movie." Karin Schlegel, a student at the Lee Strasberg Theatrical Institute, was one of several young women who responded. On August 19, 1974, Yukl enticed Schlegel to his apartment to "pose" for a Lifebuoy soap ad. Like his first victim, Yukl strangled Schlegel with a tie, but barely had time to hide the body inside a bed frame before his wife returned to the apartment. Husband

and wife slept on top of Schlegel's corpse until the next morning when Yukl dragged the body to the roof of the apartment building after his wife left for work. The body was found almost immediately. Yukl was arrested after it was learned that he had called Schlegel the night before and a trail of blood was found leading from his apartment to the roof. While awaiting his April 20, 1976, trial, Yukl attempted suicide four times. Though initially pleading not guilty by reason of insanity, he changed his plea to guilty on the first day of the trial and was later sentenced on June 3, 1976, to 15 years to life with the judge's recommendation that he never be paroled. Like his stint in Wallkill, Yukl was again judged to be a model prisoner. A bureaucratic error reduced his sentence by five years making the double murderer eligible for parole in June 1984. However, on August 22, 1982, Yukl used a piece of mattress cover as a rope to hang himself in his cell.

599. Tannenbaum, Robert K., and Greenberg, Peter S. *The Piano Teacher: The True Story of a Psychotic Killer.* New York: New American Library, 1987. 277 pp.; 24 cm.

Surprisingly sympathetic account of Yukl cowritten by Tannenbaum, the assistant district attorney who prosecuted him in the Schlegel murder. Based on court documents, police records, interviews, psychiatric reports, and letters and essays written by Yukl.

Zeigler, William Thomas, Jr. (a.k.a. "Tommy")

Born circa 1940. Furniture store owner. Winter Garden, Florida; 4 murders; pistols, bludgeon (metal linoleum crank); December 24, 1975.

"I am not afraid to die. I know where I'll be going.... I know I am innocent of these crimes, and God knows it, too."—Zeigler, in 1992, commenting on the likely eventuality that the Florida Supreme Court will reject his appeal for a new trial

What authorities called among "the bloodiest and most bizarre" killings in the history of Central Florida occurred in the small town of Winter Garden on the night of Christmas Eve 1975. Police, responding to William T. Zeigler, Jr.'s, emergency call for help, arrived at his family-owned retail furniture store to witness the 35 year old attempting to unlock the front door from the inside. He had been shot once in the abdomen at close range. Inside the 10,600 square foot building, authorities found Zeigler's 31-year-old wife, Eunice, in the store's kitchen near the customer service area dead from a gunshot wound to the back of the head. Her mother, Virginia Edwards, lay amid a living room display near the front of the store. She too had been shot in the head and once in the arm. Most of the violence, however, had exploded in the back of the store near a showroom. Eunice's father, Perry Edwards, had struggled before succumbing to 17 blows to the head and 5 gunshots, 2 in the head. A .357 Magnum pistol lay on the floor within inches of his left hand. The body of Charlie Mays, a 35-year-old black man who often shopped at the store, was found 15 yards away. Mays' brain pan had been cracked by a savage beating administered with a metal linoleum crank found near his body. The man had also been shot once in the back and abdomen. Four pistols lay scattered around his body and money was stuffed into his trousers. Police estimated that within a two hour period 28 shots had been fired in the store.

At the hospital, a barely coherent Zeigler reported that he was shot in the store as he scuffled with at least two robbers. At one point, he stated that he had surprised Charlie Mays in the store and each man had shot the other in the ensuing struggle. By early Christmas morning Orange County sheriff's officers had discounted Zeigler's story and made him their prime suspect. According to their theory, Zeigler first shot his wife, then his in-laws, and finally Mays when the man arrived at the store to pick up a television set. Zeigler planted money and store receipts on Mays' body to fake a robbery, then shot himself in the abdomen, before calling authorities to report the murders. Prosecutors would later argue that Zeigler's army reserve training in the medical corps enabled him to self inflict a non–life threatening gunshot wound. Testimony from two witnesses supported this official version of events.

Edward Williams, a 47-year-old black man, told of waiting in his pickup in the driveway of Zeigler's home around 7:30 p.m. on Christmas Eve. There to help Zeigler deliver some large gift items, his employer drove up 15 minutes later accompanied by two men. Zeigler entered the house and moments later emerged to tell Williams he would return in ten minutes. He drove off with the men. Twenty minutes later, Zeigler returned alone, parked the car in the garage, and exited holding a small bag. He wet a cloth and appeared to wipe around the car. Together they drove to the store in Williams' pickup. Zeigler entered the building alone and called for Williams to follow. According to his sworn statement, Williams entered the darkened store and as he was groping to find his way saw Zeigler outlined in a doorway pointing what he believed to be a gun at him. The gun misfired three times and Williams, followed closely by Zeigler, fled into the store's fenced back parking lot. Williams refused to believe Zeigler's claim not to have recognized him and would not re-enter the building despite Zeigler's excited pleas that not to do so would "frame" him. To placate Williams, Zeigler handed him the .38 pistol. It was then Williams noticed blood on Zeigler and fled over the fence. Hearing of the trouble at the store the next day, Williams turned the pistol into police. Tests later identified the gun as the weapon that fired the fatal shots found in the bodies of Perry and Virginia Edwards.

According to the statement of Felton Thomas, a 27-year-old black itinerant fruit picker, he drove with Charlie Mays to the Zeigler furniture store around 7:30 p.m. on Christmas Eve to pick up a television set. Zeigler was not there, but drove up five minutes later in his Cadillac. Zeigler drove the pair out of town, produced three pistols, and had the men test fire the guns by shooting at orange groves. When they returned to the store ten minutes later, Zeigler realized that he had forgotten his keys and broke a back window to gain entry. When Thomas refused to enter the darkened building, Zeigler drove home with the men to get a key. According to Thomas, Zeigler went into the garage and returned with a key and a box of bullets. As they drove back to the store, Mays reloaded the guns at Zeigler's request. Thomas again refused to enter the store until Zeigler turned on the lights, something he seemed reluctant to do. The last Thomas saw of Mays and Zeigler the men were entering the building together. Thomas walked to a nearby discount center where he met a friend who took him to a nearby city. The testimony of Williams and Thomas bolstered the state's theory that Zeigler's purpose in luring the black men into the store was to murder them, fake a robbery, and then pin the killings on them. Zeigler's motive remained unclear until it was learned that some months before his wife's murder he had significantly increased her life insurance premium. A more lurid motive for the murders was provided by a friend of Zeigler's dead wife. According to her statement, Eunice Zeigler had caught her husband having homosexual sex with a prominent local man. Zeigler, fearful that disclosure would ruin him in conservative Winter Garden, threatened to kill her if she told anyone. Eunice reportedly confided the incident to her parents who had promised that they would take her away from Zeigler when they visited at Christmas. For police, the homosexual angle explained why the fly on Charlie Mays' pants had been unzipped and his pants pulled down to his knees. The absence of blood spots on Mays' underwear suggested that the killer had straddled him during the bludgeoning. Significantly, Zeigler's alleged homosexuality was never corroborated and was not introduced at his trial.

In special proceedings conducted at his bedside in West Orange Memorial Hospital, Zeigler was arrested on December 29, 1975. On June 4, 1976, a change of venue request moved the trial to Jacksonville, Florida, where opening statements commenced four days later. The defense portrayed Zeigler as an innocent victim of a robbery in which Charlie Mays and others had played a murderous role. Zeigler loved his wife, got along well with his in-laws, and had no financial worries.

While the FBI's footprint expert noted similarities between Zeigler's shoes and a footprint left in Mays' blood, it was not enough for a positive match. Tests conducted for the state by another forensic expert showed greater similarities between Zeigler's shoes and the bloody footprint. Unable to discredit Edward Williams' damning testimony, the defense gambled that by placing Zeigler on the stand the jury would see that of the two, the successful white businessman was the more credible witness. On July 2, 1976, Zeigler was found guilty on two counts of first degree murder (Eunice Zeigler, Charlie Mays) and on two counts of second degree murder (Perry and Virginia Edwards). Earlier that day, the U.S. Supreme Court had cleared the way for executions in Florida by declaring the state's death penalty to be constitutionally acceptable. At a later sentencing hearing, a judge overruled the jury's recommendation for life imprisonment and imposed the death penalty on Zeigler. To date, Zeigler has received two stays of execution, but remains unsuccessful in obtaining another trial based upon new evidence and what many of his supporters feel to have been gross procedural errors in his trial.

600. Finch, Phillip. *Fatal Flaw: A True Story of Malice and Murder in a Small Southern Town.* 1st ed. New York: Villard Books, 1992. viii, 327 pp.: ill.; 25 cm.

Finch, a former newspaper editor in California, maintains that Zeigler is innocent and that the case against him was botched from the beginning by sloppy police work and by a prosecutor who discounted any piece of evidence that did not fit in with the state's theory of the case.

"Zodiac"

Unknown. California; 6 murders (37 by his own estimation); gun; October 30, 1966—October 11, 1969.
"The S.F. police could have caught me last night if they had searched the park properly instead of holding road races with their motorcicles [*sic*] seeing who could make the most noise."— Zodiac in a letter received by a San Francisco newspaper on October 12, 1969, the day after the unknown killer's last "official" murder

An unknown California serial killer of at least 6, and possibly as many as 37 by his own count, who taunted police with letters and phone calls. From October 30, 1966, with the stabbing murder of his first known victim in Riverside through the shooting death of his last official victim, a San Francisco cab driver on October 11, 1969, the "Zodiac" waged a one-man war against the citizens of California. Like "Son of Sam" killer David Berkowitz, the Zodiac often attacked men and women on dates. In three separate attacks on couples in Vallejo, California, on December 20, 1968, and July 4, and September 27, 1969, the Zodiac murdered all three women, one man, while two other men survived with massive injuries. Hours after the July 4, 1969, attack, the Zodiac telephoned Vallejo police to claim credit for the murders. Later, the Zodiac posted three coded letters to Bay Area newspapers that when decoded explained his motivation for the killings; an effort to "collect slaves" to serve him in the afterlife. In the months to come, the Zodiac's "logo," a circle bisected by a Zodiacal cross, would become a familiar and terrifying calling card. The day after the shooting murder of San Francisco cab driver Paul Stine on Octo-

ber 11, 1969, the Zodiac mailed patches of the dead man's bloodstained shirt to the *San Francisco Chronicle* along with a letter deriding the incompetence of the local police. In closing, he wrote "School children make nice targets, I think I shall wipe out a school bus some morning. Just shoot out the front tire & then pick off the kiddies as they come bouncing out." Ten days after Stine's murder, the killer telephoned the Oakland police and offered to give himself up if he could be represented either by F. Lee Bailey or Melvin Belli. Time was reserved on a local early morning talk show in the Bay Area the next day and for 15 minutes Melvin Belli spoke with the Zodiac about the murders. A meeting between the two was set up, but the Zodiac failed to appear. Since that time, the Zodiac Killer has resurfaced three times in letters to the police in 1971, 1974, and 1978. In the last letter dated April 24, 1978, the killer announced, "I am back with you" although no traceable killings were committed. The case remains officially unsolved.

601. Graysmith, Robert. *Zodiac.* 1st ed. New York: St. Martin's/Marek, 1986. xii, 337 pp., [30]pp. of plates: ill.; 22 cm.

_____. [Same as 601.] Berkley Non-Fiction. New York: Berkley Books, 1987. 337 pp., [32]pp. of plates: ill.; 18 cm.; paperback.

Graysmith identifies the killer as "Robert Hall Starr," a Vallejo resident known to police, and credits the Zodiac with 49 "possible" victims taken between October 1966 and May 1981. Several detectives have roundly rejected Graysmith's theorizing.

602. Penn, Gareth. *Times 17: The Amazing Story of the Zodiac Murders in California and Massachusetts, 1966–1981.* San Rafael, Calif.: Foxglove Press, 1987. 378 pp.: ill., maps; 28 cm.; paperback.

Appendix:
A Classification
of the Cases

References are to page numbers

Acid: De Kaplany, Geza 115–17; Haigh, John George 195–98
Acquittal: Adams, John Bodkin 2–3; Andre, Carl 6–7; Barney, Elvira Dolores 13–14; Daniel, Vicki Loretha 109–10; Gardiner, William George Last 169–71; Gates, Wyley 172–73; Greenwood, Harold 186–88; Griggs, Ronald Geeves 190–91; Knowles, Benjamin 270–71; Light, Ronald Vivian 292–93; Montgomery, Candace Lynn 325; Mossler, Candace Grace 329–31; Rattenbury, Alma Victoria 377–80; Sheppard, Samuel H. 399–402; Wood, Robert William Thomas George Cavers 471–72
Asphyxiation: Berdella, Robert Andrew, Jr. 20–23; Bianchi, Kenneth Alessio 26–29; Bulloch, Dennis Neal 48–52; Buono, Angelo, Jr. 58; Chambers, Robert E., Jr. 70–71; Donald, Jeannie 124–26; Fox, Sidney Harry 150–51; Hall, Archibald Thomson

198–201; Hatcher, Charles Ray 206–9; "Jack the Stripper" 242–43; Legere, Allan Joseph 285–86; Morris, Raymond Leslie 325–29; Thorne, John Norman Holmes 447–48; Williams, Wayne Bertram 466–68
Axe: Brady, Ian Duncan 33–38; Gunness, Belle 192–95; Hindley, Myra 229; Legere, Allan Joseph 285–86; Lucas, Henry Lee 298–302; Mackay, Patrick David 307–10; Montgomery, Candace Lynn (acquitted) 325; Toole, Ottis Elwood 451–52; Tucker, Karla Faye 454–55

Bludgeon: Allaway, Thomas Henry 4–5; Allen, Peter Anthony 5; Atkins, Susan Denise 9; Baniszewski, Gertrude 9; Beck, Martha Jule (Seabrook) 15; Bundy, Carol Mary 52; Bundy, Theodore Robert 52–58; Busacca, Thomas F. 58–60; Carignan, Harvey

Louis 62–64; Crafts, Richard Bunel 94–95; Demeter, Peter 117–19; Douglas, William Henry James, Jr. 126–28; Einhorn, Ira Samuel 132–34; Evans, Gwynne Owen 138–40; Fernandez, Raymond Martinez 141–46; Franklin, George Thomas, Sr. (conviction overturned) 151–54; Fry, John Carl 156–58; Gallego, Gerald Armand 167–69; Garrow, Robert F. 171–72; Gillette, Chester Ellsworth 177–79; Gillies, Jesse James 179–81; Graham, Lewis Texada, Jr. 183–84; Gray, Henry Judd 185; Griffiths, Peter 189–90; Gunness, Belle 192–95; Haigh, John George 195–98; Hall, Archibald Thomson 198–201; Herrin, Richard James 223–24; Hulme, Juliet 236–38; Kitto, Michael Anthony 266; Krenwinkel, Patricia Dianne 276; Kürten, Peter 276–80; Legere, Allan Joseph 285–86; Leopold, Nathan Freudenthal, Jr. 289–92;

Sex Killings: Allaway, Thomas Henry 4–5; Berdella, Robert Andrew, Jr. 20–23; Bianchi, Kenneth Alessio 26–29; Brady, Ian Duncan 33–38; Brudos, Jerome Henry 42–45; Bulloch, Dennis Neal 48–52; Bundy, Carol Mary 52; Bundy, Theodore Robert 52–58; Buono, Angelo, Jr. 58; Camb, James 60–61; Carignan, Harvey Louis 62–64; Carpenter, David Joseph 64–68; Chambers, Robert E., Jr. 70–71; Chikatilo, Andrei Romanovich 75–78; Christie, John Reginald Halliday 78–81; Clark, Douglas Daniel 81–84; Collins, John Norman 86–88; Corll, Dean Arnold 89–90; Cottingham, Richard Francis 93–94; Crimmins, Craig Stephen 95–98; Dahmer, Jeffrey Lionel 102–7; DeSalvo, Albert Henry 119–22; Eyler, Larry W. 140–41; Fish, "Albert" Hamilton Howard 146–49; Gacy, John Wayne 161–67; Gallego, Gerald Armand 167–69; Garrow, Robert F. 171–72; Gein, Edward Theodore 173–76; Gillies, Jesse James 179–81; "Green River Killer" 185–86; Griffiths, Peter 189–90; Hansen, Robert C. 201–4; Hatcher, Charles Ray 206–9; Heath, Neville George Clevely 214–17; Heidnik, Gary Michael 217–20; Heirens, William George 220–23; Henley, Elmer Wayne 223; Hindley, Myra 229; Hoolhouse, Robert William 233–34; "Jack the Stripper" 242–43; Joubert, John J. 254–56; Judy, Steven Timothy 258; Kallinger, Joseph

Michael 258–61; Kemper, Edmund Emil, III 261–65; Knowles, Paul John 271–74; Kraft, Randy Steven 274–75; Kürten, Peter 276–80; Legere, Allan Joseph 285–86; LeGeros, Bernard John 286–87; Logan, Michael David 295; Lucas, Henry Lee 298–302; Manuel, Peter Thomas Anthony 320–22; Miller, James William 323–24; Morris, Raymond Leslie 325–29; Nance, Wayne Nathan 335–37; Neelley, Alvin Howard, Jr. 337; Neelley, Judith Ann 337–40; Nelson, Erle Leonard 341–43; Nilsen, Dennis Andrew 345–47; Nodder, Frederick 347–49; Olson, Clifford Robert 349–50; Panzram, Carl 354–56; Ramirez, Richard Leyva 375–77; Rogers, Dayton Leroy 380–83; Shawcross, Arthur John 397–99; Sodeman, Arnold Karl 418–19; Speck, Richard Franklin 419–24; Straffen, John Thomas 430–32; Stuart, Rupert Max 434–35; Sutcliffe, Peter William 438–41; Tait, Robert Peter 442–43; Toole, Ottis Elwood 451–52; Wilder, Christopher Bernard 462–66; Woodfield, Randall Brent 472–76; Yukl, Charles William, Jr. 481–82

Strangulation: Beck, Martha Jule (Seabrook) 15; Bennett, Herbert John 17–18; Bianchi, Kenneth Alessio 26–29; "Bible John" 29–30; Brady, Ian Duncan 33–38; Bundy, Theodore Robert 52–58; Buono, Angelo, Jr. 58; Camb, James 60–61; Christie, John Reginald Halliday

78–81; Coleman, Dennis, Jr. 85–86; Collins, John Norman 86–88; Corll, Dean Arnold 89–90; Cottingham, Richard Francis 93–94; Dahmer, Jeffrey Lionel 102–7; DeSalvo, Albert Henry 119–22; Dobkin, Harry 123–24; Donald, Jeannie 124–26; Evans, Timothy John 140; Fish, "Albert" Hamilton Howard 146–49; Fox, Sidney Harry 150–51; Gacy, John Wayne 161–67; Gallego, Gerald Armand 167–69; Gray, Henry Judd 185; "Green River Killer" 185–86; Hatcher, Charles Ray 206–9; Heirens, William George 220–23; Henley, Elmer Wayne 223; Herrin, Richard James 223–24; Hindley, Myra 229; "Jack the Stripper" 242–43; Joubert, John J. 254–56; Judy, Steven Timothy 258; Kemper, Edmund Emil, III 261–65; Knowles, Paul John 271–74; Kraft, Randy Steven 274–75; Kürten, Peter 276–80; Landru, Henri Désiré 280–81; Legere, Allan Joseph 285–86; Leonski, Edward Joseph 287–89; Lonergan, Wayne Thomas 295–96; Lucas, Henry Lee 298–302; Mahon, Patrick Herbert 312–13; Manuel, Peter Thomas Anthony 320–22; Merrett, John Donald 322–23; Morris, Raymond Leslie 325–29; Neilson, Donald 340–41; Nelson, Erle Leonard 341–43; Newell, Hugh William Alexander 343–44; Nilsen, Dennis Andrew 345–47; Nodder, Frederick 347–49; Panzram, Carl 354–56; Pierce, Darci Kayleen

Author and Title Index to the Bibliographic Entries

References are to bibliographic entry numbers

General Index

References are to page numbers